Dictionary of
Naval Abbreviations

THIRD EDITION

DICTIONARY OF NAVAL ABBREVIATIONS

Compiled and edited by Bill Wedertz

Naval Institute Press
Annapolis, Maryland

Library of Congress Cataloging in Publication Data

Wedertz, Bill.
    Dictionary of naval abbreviations.

    Bibliography: p.
    1. Naval art and science—Abbreviations.   2. Naval
art and science—Acronyms.   3. United States.   Navy—
Abbreviations.   4. United States.   Navy—Acronyms.
I. Title.
V23.W43   1984   359'.001'48   84-14792
ISBN 0-87021-155-2

Printed in the United States of America

To Peg,
for her patience,
understanding, and support
in preparing the third edition.
And to my children:
Mandy, B.J., and Harper.

Foreword

My fascination with the strange language of abbreviations and acronyms began nearly a quarter of a century ago—on 21 December 1959—when I first read a cryptic message that directed:

WEDERTZ, B. (NMN), AR, USN, 540 26 86, TO RPT RTC SDIEGO FOR 12 WKS CRUIT TRA . . . and my career (not the fascination) ended with another message that directed:

WEDERTZ, B. (NMN), JOCS, USN, 299 36 1370, TO TRF FLTRES EFF 29 FEB 1984.

For the first several years, I acquired such terms and their definitions sporadically. However, as word spread throughout the Navy of my growing list, I began receiving calls and letters—some with questions about definitions, others with contributions to the list.

After nearly eight years of sifting through both official and unofficial publications, I had developed from a handful of 3×5 cards a full-blown, 150-page manuscript. Someone suggested that the collection might be worth publishing, since there was no such comprehensive source available within the naval establishment.

It took several more years, but after studying the marketability of such a publication, the U.S. Naval Institute published the first *Dictionary of Naval Abbreviations (DICNAVAB)* in 1969. The second edition was published in 1976 and this, the third edition, in 1984.

The first edition manuscript, I thought at the time, was overwhelming—nearly 500 pages. The third edition manuscript ran 1,286 pages, with nearly three times the number of terms in the first edition. Interestingly, many of the terms in the first edition were outdated World War II terminology. In this edition, as with the second, I have attempted to purge all such obsolete abbreviations with the goal of making the book as up-to-date as possible.

As you'll soon discover—if this is your first time using this book—there is no exacting science about the creation and application of naval abbreviations and acronyms. The rule is simple: there is no rule. This is because there is often more than one definition for an abbreviation or acronym. It is imperative, therefore, that you have at least a general idea of the area, program, project, or office to which the term is referring. For instance, take the very first abbreviation in this edition: A. If the term relates to a naval aviation observer code the answer is "Aerology." However, if it refers to the frequency of a report, the answer is "Annual." An air mass is "Arctic/Antarctic," and a type of ship is "Auxiliary." There are thousands of such examples throughout this book.

For typographic reasons, all abbreviations are in capital letters. In most cases, the upper and lower case combinations occur in naval commands and units. The rule is:

initial caps for the first letter of each word. Examples would be: COMNAVSYSCOM and COMFAIRKEF which can also be written as ComNavSysCom and ComFAir-Kef. A similar rule is used in the creation of "true" acronyms, such as COMET, meaning "Computer-Operated Management Evaluation Technique." The other COMET listed in this book, defined as "CONUS Meteorological Teletype," is not a true acronym since the word is formed from the CO in CONUS and the ME in Meteorological.

When *DICNAVAB* was begun 25 years ago, computers were in their infancy. Today, they are used widely in a variety of ways and have had a dramatic impact on this volume's terminology. Nearly all computers and their cousins, the word processors, use abbreviated forms of English. As our use of computers and word processors increases, the world of abbreviated language will swell accordingly. One of the benefits of the computer age should be the elimination of much of the duplication of terms.

However, until computers can be made to communicate with one another more effectively and a regular system of trading basic information is established, it will still take a lot of people to help compile the data for *DICNAVAB*. Although there have been many contributors, including those who offered a single term or a correction, there are several who stand out. CAPT R.E. Teis, commanding officer of the Navy Recruiting District in Pittsburgh, sent along nearly 4,000 terms collected during a fifteen-year period for inclusion in this edition. Norman Polmar, a well-known U.S. Naval Institute author of *Ships and Aircraft of the U.S. Fleet, Guide to the Soviet Navy*, and others, has made regular contributions for more than a year. Another significant contribution came from CAPT Channing M. Zucker, the director of the Defense Mapping Agency's Office of Distribution Services. Personnelman First Class Daniel Gordon, of the Personnel Support Detachment, Keflavik, Iceland, also assisted with the information on rates and ratings appearing in this edition.

Dictionary of
Naval Abbreviations

A

A
Aerology (NAO code)
Annually (report frequency)
Arctic/Antarctic (air mass)
Auxiliary

A, ANS
Answer

AA
Absolute Altitude
Acting Appointment
Airman Apprentice
All After
Anti-Aircraft
Arithmetrical Average (surface finish)

AA, ARLAN, ARLEX
Arlington Annex

A/A
Analysis of Accounts
Angle of Attack

AAA
Anti-Aircraft Artillery
Authorized Accounting Activity
Awaiting Aircraft Availability

AA&A
Armor, Armament and Ammunition

AAB
Aircraft Accident Board
Aviation Armament Bulletin

AABCP
Advanced Airborne Command Post

AABNCP
Advanced Airborne National Command Post

AAC
Alaskan Air Command
Anti-Aircraft Common (projectile)
Area Control
Aviation Armament Change

A/AC
Aft Across the Hatch (stowage)

AADC
Advanced Avionic Digital Computer

AADD, A²D²
Auxiliary Active Digital Display (sonar)

AAE
Ancillary Armament Equipment

AAF
Atlantic Amphibious Force

AAFSS
Advanced Aerial Fire Support System

AAH
Advanced Attack Helicopter

AAHA
Awaiting Action and Higher Authority

AAHM
Anesthetics and Certain Other Harmful
  Materials

AA(HS)
High School Airman Apprentice

AAI
Aircraft Accident Investigation
Angle of Approach Indicator

AAL
Aircraft Approach Limitations
Aircraft Assignment Letter

AALC
Amphibious Assault Landing Craft

AALS
Acoustic Artillery Location System

AAM
Air-to-Air Missile

AAMG
Anti-Aircraft Machine Gun

AAMREP
Air-to-Air Missile Weapons System Flight
  Report

AAO
Artillery Air Observer
AUTOVON Assistance Operator

AAOC
Anti-Air Operations Center

AAP
Affirmative Action Plan
Allied Administrative Publication
Allowance Appendix Package
Analyst Assistance Program

AAPP
Affirmative Action Program Plan

AAR
Aircraft Accident Report

AASR
Airport and Airways Surveillance Radar

AATB
Advanced Amphibious Training Base

AATC
Advanced Air Training Command

AATC, AATRACEN
Anti-Aircraft Training Center

AATRACEN, AATC
Anti-Aircraft Training Center

AATS
Armament Auxiliaries Test Set
Automatic Altitude Trim System (for helos)

AAV
Airborne Assault Vehicle

AAW
Anti-Air Warfare

AAWC
Anti-Air Warfare Center

AAWEX
Anti-Air Warfare Exercise

AAWS
Automatic Attack Warning Systems

AB
Able-Bodied (seaman)
Aerial Burst (bombs)
Air Base
All Before
Crane Ship
Harbor Launch (USCG)

AB, A/B
Afterburner
Air Blast
AB, ABBR
Abbreviation
ABAND
Abandoned
ABAR
Advanced Battery Acquisition Radar
ABBR, AB
Abbreviation
ABC
Accounting and Budgetary Control
Advanced Base Components
Advanced Biomedical Capsule
American-British-Canadian
Argentina, Brazil and Chile
Atomic, Biological and Chemical (warfare or
defense)
ABCAIRSTD
American-British-Canadian Air
Standardization Agreement
ABCCTC
Advanced Base Combat Communications
Training Center
ABCD
Advanced Base Construction Depot
ABCM
Master Chief Aviation Boatswain's Mate
ABCS
Senior Chief Aviation Boatswain's Mate
ABD
Abbreviated Dial
Aboard
Advanced Base Dock
Airborne Division (or Direct)
ABDACOM
Advanced Base Depot Area Command
ABE1
Aviation Boatswain's Mate E (Launching and
Recovery Equipment) First Class
ABE2
Aviation Boatswain's Mate E (Launching and
Recovery Equipment) Second Class
ABE3
Aviation Boatswain's Mate E (Launching and
Recovery Equipment) Third Class
ABEAA
Aviation Boatswain's Mate E (Launching and
Recovery Equipment) Airman Apprentice
ABEAN
Aviation Boatswain's Mate E (Launching and
Recovery Equipment) Airman
ABEC
Chief Aviation Boatswain's Mate E
(Launching and Recovery Equipment)
ABF1
Aviation Boatswain's Mate F (Fuels) First
Class

ABF2
Aviation Boatswain's Mate F (Fuels) Second
Class
ABF3
Aviation Boatswain's Mate F (Fuels) Third
Class
ABFAA
Aviation Boatswain's Mate F (Fuels) Airman
Apprentice
ABFAN
Aviation Boatswain's Mate F (Fuels) Airman
ABFC
Advanced Base Functional Components
(system)
Chief Aviation Boatswain's Mate F (Fuels)
ABH
Above Burst Height
ABH1
Aviation Boatswain's Mate H (Aircraft
Handling) First Class
ABH2
Aviation Boatswain's Mate H (Aircraft
Handling) Second Class
ABH3
Aviation Boatswain's Mate H (Aircraft
Handling) Third Class
ABHAA
Aviation Boatswain's Mate H (Aircraft
Handling) Airman Apprentice
ABHAN
Aviation Boatswain's Mate H (Aircraft
Handling) Airman
ABHC
Chief Aviation Boatswain's Mate H (Aircraft
Handling)
ABI
Aviation Billet Indicator
ABIOL
Advanced Base Initial Outfitting List
ABISL
Advanced Base Initial Support List
ABL
Above Base Line
Allocated Base Line
Automated Biological Laboratory
ABM
Anti-Ballistic Missile
ABN
Aerodrome Beacon
Airborne
VA/VAH Bombardier/Navigator (code)
ABOOW
Assistant Battalion Officer-of-the-Watch
ABPA
Advanced Base Personnel Administration
ABPG
Advanced Base Proving Ground
ABPO
Advanced Base Personnel Officer
ABPU
Advanced Base Personnel Unit

ABR
Additional Billet Requirements
Amphibian Boat Reconnaissance (aircraft)
ABRACADABRA
Abbreviations and Related Acronyms
Associated with Defense, Business and
Radio-electronics
ABRB
Advanced Base Receiving Barracks
ABRD
Advanced Base Receiving (or Reshipment)
Depot
ABRES
Advanced Ballistics Reentry System
ABRS
Angle Rate Bombing System
ABS
Absolute
Acrylonitrile Butadiene Styrene (plastic)
ABSAP
Airborne Search and Attack Plotter
ABSD
Advanced Base Sectional Dock
Advanced Base Supply Depot
ABSLA
Approved Basic Stock Level of Ammunition
ABSTEE
Absentee
ABT
About
ABTF
Airborne Task Force
ABTU
Advanced Base Training Unit
ABUT
Abutment
ABV
Above
AC
Adopted Child(ren)
Aircraft Commander
Airframe Change
Alternating Current
Altocumulus (cloud formation)
Amphibious Corps
Atlas Centaur (rocket)
(AC)
Qualified as an Aircrewman
A/C
Air Conditioning
A/C, ACCT
Account
A/C, ACFT
Aircraft
AC1
Air Controlman First Class
AC2
Air Controlman Second Class
AC3
Air Controlman Third Class

ACA
Airlift Clearance Authority
Awaiting Combat Assignment
ACAA
Air Controlman Airman Apprentice
ACAD
Academy
ACAD CL YR
Academy Class Year
ACAL
Aircraft Configuration Allowance List
ACAN
Air Controlman Airman
ACAPS
Automated Costing and Planning System
ACAS
Aircraft Collision Avoidance System
ACAT
Acquisition Category
ACB, PHIBCB
Amphibious Construction Battalion
ACBD
Active Commission Base Date
ACBWS
Automatic Chemical-Biological Warning
System
ACC
Accounting Category Code
Accumulation (lines)
Air Center Commander
Alternate Command Center
Altocumulus Castellanus (cloud formation)
Antarctic Circumpolar Current
Area Control Center
Aural Comprehension Course
Automatic Chroma Control (color)
Automatic Combustion Control
Chief Air Controlman
ACCB
Airframe Change Control Board
ACCCIT
Aircraft Carrier Climate Control Investigation
Team
ACCEL
Accelerate
Acceleration
ACCESS
Afloat Cost Consumption Effectiveness
Surveillance System
Automatic Computer-Controlled Electronic
Scanning System
ACCF
Area Communications Control Function
(DCS)
ACC/FWC
Automatic Combustion Control and
Feedwater Control
ACCGAT
Accumulator Gating (NSSS)
ACCHAN
Allied Command Channel

ACCM
Master Chief Air Controlman
ACCOM
Accommodate
Accommodation
ACCOMP
Accomplish(ment)
ACCS
Senior Chief Air Controlman
ACCT, A/C
Account
ACCTG
Accounting
ACCY
Accessory
ACD
Administrative Commitment Document
Advanced Copies Delivered
Aviation Commission Date
ACDA
Aviation Combat Development Agency
ACDIFDEN
Active duty in a flying status not involving
flying
ACDIFDENIS
Active duty under instruction in a flying status
not involving flying
ACDIFINOPS
Active duty under instruction in a flying status
involving operational or training flights
ACDIFINSPRO
Active duty under instruction in a flying status
involving proficiency flying
ACDIFOPS
Active duty in a flying status involving
operational or training flights
ACDIFOTCREW
Active duty in a flying status involving
operational or training flights as a
crewmember
ACDIFOTINSCREW
Active duty under instruction in a flying status
involving operational or training flights as a
crewmember
ACDIFOTINSNONCREW
Active duty under instruction in a flying status
involving operational or training flights as a
non-crewmember
ACDIFOTNONCREW
Active duty in a flying status involving
operational or training flights as a
non-crewmember
ACDIFPRO
Active duty in a flying status involving
proficiency flying
ACDIV
Assault Craft Division
ACDT
Accident

ACDU, ACTDU, AD
Active Duty
ACDUINS
Active duty under instruction
ACDUOBLI
Active duty obligation
ACDUTRA, ACTDUTRA
Active duty training
ACE
Activity Civil Engineer
Aircraft Condition Evaluation
Atmospheric Control Experimentation
Automatic Checkout Equipment
ACE, ACEUR
Allied Command, Europe
ACEL
Aerospace Crew Equipment Laboratory
ACEORP
Automotive and Construction Equipment
Overhaul and Repair Plant
ACEPD
Automotive and Construction Equipment
Parts Depot
ACFAT
Aircraft Carrier Firefighting Assistance Team
ACFEL
Arctic Construction and Frost Effects
Laboratory
ACFT, A/C
Aircraft
ACG
Airborne Coordinating Group
ACGM
Aircraft Carrier General Memorandum
ACI
Allocated Confirmation Identification
AC&I
Acquisition, Construction and Improvement
ACIM
Axis Crossing Interval Meter
ACINT
Acoustic Intelligence
ACIP
Aviation Career Incentive Pay
ACIS
Aeronautical Chart and Information Squadron
Automated Claims Information System
ACK
Acknowledge
ACL
Aeronautical Computer Laboratory
Aircraft Circular Letter
Automatic Carrier Landing
ACLANT
Allied Command, Atlantic
ACLS
Air Cushion Landing System
All-Weather (or Automatic) Carrier Landing
System

ACM
Accumulator
Additional Crewmembers (on aircraft)
Air Combat Maneuvering
Drill Minelaying and Recovery Vessel
ACMI
Air Combat Maneuvering Instrumentation
ACMR
Air Combat Maneuvering Range
ACMS
Automated Career Management System
ACN
Activity Control Number
Advance Change Notice
ACNO
Assistant Chief of Naval Operations
ACNO(COMM)/DNC
Assistant Chief of Naval Operations
(Communications)/Director, Naval
Communications
ACO
Administrative Contracting Officer
Attack Cut-Out
ACOB
Actual Current on Board (status)
ACOC
Area Communications Operations Center
(DCS)
Automatic Control Operations Center
ACOCC, LANTCOMOPCONCEN
Atlantic Commander Operational Control
Center
ACOFS, ACS
Assistant Chief of Staff
ACOG
Aircraft on Ground
ACOM
Area Cutover Manager
ACP
Airlift Command Post
Allied Communications Publication
Area Coordinating Paper
ACPT
Accept
ACPY
Accompany
ACR
Advanced Capabilities Radar
Aircraft Control Room
Airlift Control Radar
Allowance Change Request
Anti-Circular Run
Approach Control Radar
ACRE
Automatic Checkout and Readiness
Equipment
ACRN
Acounting Classification Reference Number
ACRS
Across
Advisory Committee on Reactor Safeguards

ACS
Air Capable Ship
ACS, ACOFS
Assistant Chief of Staff
ACSAP
Automated Cross-Section Analysis Program
ACS/FOR
Assistant Chief of Staff/Force Development
ACSI
Assistant Chief of Staff for Intelligence
ACSR
Aluminum Conductors, Steel-Reinforced
ACSS
Antilles Consolidated School System
ACT
Acting
Action
Active
Aircraft Commander Time
American College Test
Aviation Classification Test
ACT, ACTY
Activity
ACT/CONV
Activation/Conversion
ACTDIAREC
CO of activity at which separated directed to
perform following functions connection with
separations processing: Make loss entry in
Officer Personnel Diary; make Gain and
Loss entries in Enlisted Personnel Diary;
close out entries service record, health
record and pay accounts, and forward
these reports to proper commands or
systems in the Navy Department.
ACTDU, ACDU, AD
Active duty
ACTDUTRA, ACDUTRA
Active duty for training
ACTG
Advanced Carrier Training Group
ACTH
Arbitrary Correction to Hit
ACT/IC
Active/In Commission (vessel status)
ACT/IS
Active/In Service (vessel status)
ACT/OC
Active/Out of Commission (vessel status)
ACT/OS
Active/Out of Service (vessel status)
ACTRANSFLEETRES
CO of activity at which separated directed to
effect transfer to Fleet Reserve in
accordance with instructions contained in
enclosure forwarded with confirmation copy
of this message, concurrent with
termination of temporary appointment.
Make appropriate entries on officer and
enlisted personnel diaries in accordance
with NMIS NAVPERS 15642 Part I.

ACTREP
Activities Reporting (shipping)
ACTVISE
CO of activity at which separated directed to
advise COMNAVMILPERSCOM ____
effective date of discharge and address for
mailing purposes
ACTY, ACT
Activity
ACTYS
Activities
ACU
Academic Credit Unit
Armament Control Unit
Assault Craft Unit
ACV
Air Cushion Vehicle
ACW
Automated Keyed Continuous Wave
AC&W
Air Communications and Weather
AD
Acoustic Decoupler
Air Defense (or Depot)
Aircraft Depth (bomb)
Air-Start Diesel Engine
Destroyer Tender
AD, A/D
Aerodrome
A/D
Acceptance and Delivery
Analog-to-Digital (conversion)
AD, ACDU, ACTDU
Active duty
A²D², AADD
Auxiliary Active Digital Display (sonar)
ADA
Active Duty Agreement
Actual Arrival Date
Advisory Area
Airborne Data Automation
Automatic Data Analyzer
ADAC
Acoustic Data Analysis Center
ADAKSARCOORD
Coast Guard Search and Rescue
Coordinator, Adak (AK)
ADAL
Authorized Dental Allowance List
ADALCON
Advise All Concerned
ADAP
Active Duty Assistance Program (team)
Analog-Digital Automatic Program (tester)
ADAPTS
Air Deliverable Anti-Pollution Transfer System
ADAR
Adanced Design Array Radar
ADARCO
Advise date of reporting in compliance with
these orders

ADAS
Automatic Data Acquisition System
Auxiliary Data Annotation Set
ADATS
Automated Data and Telecommunications
Service (GSA)
ADAWS
Action Data Automation Weapon System
A-DAY
Announcement Day
ADBD
Active Duty Base Date
ADC
Air Data Computer
Air Defense Command (or Capable)
Assistant Defense Counsel
Automated Data Collection
Chief Aviation Machinist's Mate
AD&C
Ammunition Distribution and Control
ADCAD
Airways Data Collection and Dissemination
ADCASHAL
Advance cash allowance authorized
ADCC
Air Defense Control Center
ADCEP
Advanced Structural Concept and Evaluation
Program
ADCNO
Assistant Deputy Chief of Naval Operations
ADCNO(CP/EEO)
Assistant Deputy Chief of Naval Operations
(Civilian Personnel/Equal Employment
Opportunity)
ADCOM
Administrative Command
Advanced Communications (program)
ADCON
Advise All Concerned
ADCONSEN
With the Advice and Consent of the Senate
ADCOP
Associate Degree Completion Program
ADCS
Advanced Defense Communications System
Senior Chief Aviation Machinist's Mate
ADCSP
Advanced Defense Communications Satellite
Program
ADD, ADDN
Addition(al)
ADDAS
Automatic Digital Data Assembly System
ADDC
Air Defense Direction Center
ADDELREP
Provided no excess leave involved,
authorized ____ days additional delay in
reporting, to count as leave

ADDL
Aircraft Dummy Deck Landing
ADDN, ADD
Addition(al)
ADDPLA
(And) to such additional places as may be
necessary
ADDS
Advanced Data Display System
Air Development Delivery System
ADDU
Additional duty
ADD UNIF ALW
Additional Uniform Allowance
ADE
Aircraft Data Entry
ADEE
Addressee
ADF
Automatic Direction Finder (equipment)
Auxiliary Detonating Fuze
ADG
Degaussing Ship
ADI
Area of Dominant Influence
Altitude-Direction Indicator
ADIS
A Data Interchange System
Automatic Data Interchange System
ADIU
Airborne Data Insertion Unit
ADJ
Adjusted
ADJ, ADJT
Adjutant
ADJ1
Aviation Machinist's Mate J (Jet Engine
Mechanic) First Class
ADJ2
Aviation Machinist's Mate J (Jet Engine
Mechanic) Second Class
ADJ3
Aviation Machinist's Mate J (Jet Engine
Mechanic) Third Class
ADJAA
Aviation Machinist's Mate J (Jet Engine
Mechanic) Airman Apprentice
ADJAN
Aviation Machinist's Mate J (Jet Engine
Mechanic) Airman
ADJC
Chief Aviation Machinist's Mate J (Jet Engine
Mechanic)
ADJG
Adjutant General
ADJ/PPR
Adjusted Permanent Pay Record
ADJ/RCT
Adjusted, Reviewed Copy of Temporary Pay
Record

ADJT, ADJ
Adjutant
ADJ/TDA
Adjusted, Transcript Deserter's Account
ADL
Armament (or Authorized) Data List
Armament Datum Line
ADLS
Air Dispatch Letter Service
ADM
Admiral
Atomic Demolition Munition
ADMAT
Administrative-Material (inspection)
ADMIN
Administration
Administrative
ADMINO
Administrative Officer
ADMINSUPPU
Administrative Support Unit
ADMIRE
Automated Diagnostic Maintenance
Informtion Retrieval
ADMIT
Aeronautical Depot Maintenance Industrial
Technology
ADMRL
Applications Data for Material Readiness List
ADMS
Automatic Digital Message-Switching
ADMSC
Automatic Digital Message-Switching Center
ADMSG
Advise by Electrically-Transmitted Message
ADNOMOVPEN
Advised not to move dependents until
suitable quarters located
ADO
Advanced Development Objective
Associated Disbursing Officer
ADP
Acceptance Data Package
Air Defense Position
Air Delivery Platoon
Alternative Defense Posture
Automatic Data Processing
Automatic Deletion Procedure
ADPBUD
Automatic Data Processing Budget
ADPESO
Automatic Data Processing Equipment
Selection Office
ADPM
Automatic Data Processing Machine
ADP/MIS
Automatic Data Processing/Management
Information System
ADPPRS, ADPRES
Automatic Data Processing Program
Reporting System (DOD)

ADPRES, ADPPRS
Automatic Data Processing Program
Reporting System (DOD)
ADPS
Automatic Data Processing System
ADPSO
Automatic Data Processing Selection Office
ADPTOS
Automatic Data Processing Tactical
Operation System
ADR
Advisory Route
Aircraft Direction Room
Aircraft (or Aeronautical) Directive
Requirements
Aircraft (or Arrival) Discrepancy Report
Applied Data Research
ADR1
Aviation Machinist's Mate R (Reciprocating
Engine Mechanic) First Class
ADR2
Aviation Machinist's Mate R (Reciprocating
Engine Mechanic) Second Class
ADR3
Aviation Machinist's Mate R (Reciprocating
Engine Mechanic) Third Class
ADRAA
Aviation Machinist's Mate R (Reciprocating
Engine Mechanic) Airman Apprentice
ADRAN
Aviation Machinist's Mate R (Reciprocating
Engine Mechanic) Airman
ADRC
Chief Aviation Machinist's Mate R
(Reciprocating Engine Mechanic)
ADRNBN
Aerodrome Beacon
ADS
Advance Diving System
Advance (or Accelerated) Declassification
Schedule
Aegis Display System
Air Defense Section
Assault Data System
Audio Distribution System
ADSC
Automatic Data Service Center
ADSD
Active Duty Service Date
ADSHIPDA
Advise Shipping Data
ADSHIPDAT
Advise Shipping Date
ADSOC
Administrative Support Operations Center
ADSPO
Automatic Data Processing Selection Office
ADSTADIS, ASTADIS
Advise status and/or disposition

ADSTAP
Advancement, Strength and Training
Planning
ADSUP
Automated Data Systems Uniform Practices
ADT
Amphibious Training Demonstrator
Automatic Detection and Tracking
ADTAKE
Advise what action taken
ADTU
Auxiliary Data Translator Unit
ADU
Accumulation Distribution Unit
Aircraft Delivery Unit
ADV
Advance
ADVAILTRANS
Advise appropriate command having
cognizance of transportation when
available for transportation
ADVAILTRANSCONUS
Advise appropriate command having
cognizance of transportation when
available for transportation to Continental
Limits of the United States
ADVAILTRANSPOE
Advise (command designated) date available
for transportation from port of embarkation
ADVAL
Advise availability
ADV-BR
Advanced Branch (training)
ADVCHG
Advance Change
ADVHED
Advance Headquarters
ADV/L
Advance Leave
ADVN
Advanced
ADV/P
Advanced Pay
ADVS
Advises
ADVSCOL
Advanced School
ADVSY, ADVY
Advisory
ADVY, ADVSY
Advisory
ADWS
Automated Digital Weather Switch
AE
Ammunition Ship
Availability of Equipment
A&E
Analysis and Evaluation
AE1
Aviation Electrician's Mate First Class

AE2
Aviation Electrician's Mate Second Class
AE3
Aviation Electrician's Mate Third Class
AEAA
Aviation Electrician's Mate Airman Apprentice
AEAN
Aviation Electrician's Mate Airman
AEB
Air, Emergency Breathing (system)
AEC
Atomic Energy Commission
Chief Aviation Electrician's Mate
AECC
Aeromedical Evacuation Control Center
AECL
Aircraft and Equipment Configuration List
AECS
Senior Chief Aviation Electrician's Mate
AED
Assurance Engineering (or Effectiveness)
Division
AEDA
Ammunition, Explosives and Other
Dangerous Articles
AEEL
Aeronautical and Electronic Engineering
Laboratory
AEF
Advanced Electronics Field (training program)
AEFF
Assurance Engineering Field Facility
AEG
Active Element Group
Aeromedical Evaluation Group
AEI
Aerial Exposure Index
AEL
Allowance Equippage List
Small Ammunition Ship
AELW
Airborne Electronics Warfare (course)
AEM
Missile Support Ship
AEN
Advance Evaluation Notice
AEO
Air Electronics (or Engineering) Officer
AEOB
Advanced Engine Overhaul Base
AEOS
Aft Engineering Operating Station
AEP
Average-Evoked Potentials
AEPS
Aircraft Escape Propulsion System
AER
Aeronautics
Alteration Equivalent to Repair
AERC
Aircraft Engine Record Card

AERO
Aerographer
Aeronautic(al)
AEROF
Aerological Officer
AEROG
Aerologist
AEROMED
Aeromedical
Aeromedicine
AERO R BN
Aeronautical Radio Beacon
AERO R RGE
Aeronautical Radio Range
AERP
Advanced Equipment Repair Program
AERREFRON
Aerial Refueling Squadron
AERS
Aircraft Equipment Requirement Schedule
AESC
Automatic Electronic Switching Center
AESR
Aeronautical Equipment Service Record
AEW
Airborne Early-Warning
Airborne Electronic Warfare
AEW/C
Airborne Early-Warning and Control
AEWRON, VW
Fleet Air Reconnaissance Squadron
AEWS
Advanced Electronic Warfare System
AEX
Agreement to Extend Enlistment
AF
Anti-Fouling (paint)
Audio Frequency
Automatic Following (radar)
Stores Ship
AFAADS
Advanced Forward Area Air Defense System
AFAITC
Armed Forces Air Intelligence Training Center
AFAVC
Atlantic Fleet Audio-Visual Center
AF/B
After Bulkhead in Hatch (stowage)
AFC
Airframes Change
Automatic Frequency (of Flow) Control
AFCE
Automatic Flight Control Equipment
AFCM
Master Chief Aircraft Maintenanceman
AFCS
Adaptive (or Automatic) Flight-Control System
AFDB
Large Auxiliary Floating Drydock
(Non-Self-Propelled)

AFDCB
Armed Forces Disciplinary Control Board
AFDK
After Dark
AFDL(C)
Small Auxiliary Floating Drydock (Concrete)
AFDM
Medium Auxiliary Floating Drydock (Non-Self-Propelled)
AFDO
Assistant Fighter Direction Office
AFDS
Amphibious Force Data System
Auxiliary Fighter Director Ship
AF/E
After End of the Hatch (stowage)
AFEB
Armed Forces Epidemiological Board
AFEM
Armed Forces Expeditionary Medal
AFES
Armed Forces Exchange Service
AFFD
Affirmed
AFFF
Aqueous Film-Forming Foam
AFGU
Aerial Free Gunnery Unit
AFHPSP
Armed Forces Health Professional Scholarship Program
AFI
Africian-Indian (Ocean regional area)
Auxiliary Functional Unit
AFIL
AMVER File
AFINSPATH, AFIP
Armed Forces Institute of Pathology
AFIO
Agreement for Fighter Interceptor Operations
AFIP
Armed Forces Information Program
AFIP, AFINSPATH
Armed Forces Institute of Pathology
AFJ
Armed Forces Journal (publication)
AFO
Artillery Forward Observer
AFP
Armed Forces Police
AFPCB
Armed Forces Pest Control Board
AFPD
Armed Forces Police Detachment (or Department)
AFPDS
Armed Forces Production Distribution Service
AFPR
Armed Forces Procurement Regulations
AFQT
Armed Forces Qualification Test

AFR
Aircraft Flight Record
AFRADBIORSCHINST, AFRRI
Armed Forces Radiobiology Research Institute
AFRBA
Armed Forces Relief and Benefit Association
AFRRI, AFRADBIORSCHINST
Armed Forces Radiobiology Research Institute
AFRS
Automatic Flight Reference System
AFRSF
Atlantic Fleet Range Support Facility
AFS
Combat Stores Ship
AF&S
Administrative and Finance Services
AFSA
American Flagship Available
AFSC, AFSTAFFCOL
Armed Forces Staff College
AFSSC
Armed Forces Supply Support Center
AFSTAFFCOL, AFSC
Armed Forces Staff College
AFSU
Auxiliary Ferry Service Unit
AFSWP
Armed Forces Special Weapons Project
AFT
After
AFTA
Advanced First-Term Avionics
AFTI
Advanced Fighter Technology Integrator
AFTN
Aeronautical Fixed Telecommunications Network
Afternoon
AFW
Auxiliary Fresh Water (system)
AFWL
Armed Forces Writers' League
AFWR
Atlantic Fleet Weapons Range
AFWST
Armed Forces Women's Selection Test
AFWTF, LANTFLTWPNTRAFAC
Atlantic Fleet Weapons Training Facility
AFY, AIRFAC
Air Facility
AG
Air Group
Miscellaneous Ship
AG, ARMGRD
Armed Guard
A/G
Air/Ground (communications)
A-G, A-GEAR
Arresting Gear

AG1
Aerographer's Mate First Class
AG2
Aerographer's Mate Second Class
AG3
Aerographer's Mate Third Class
A/G/A
Air/Ground/Air
AGAA
Aerographer's Mate Airman Apprentice
AGACS
Automatic Ground-to-Air Communications
System
AGAFBO
Atlantic and Gulf American Flag Berthing
Operations
AGAN
Aerographer's Mate Airman
AGB
Icebreaker
AGBT
Airborne Expendable Bathythermograph
Sonobuoy
AGC
Automatic Gain Control
Chief Aerographer's Mate
AGC, ARMGRDCEN
Armed Guard Center
AGCA
Automatic Ground-Controlled Approach
AGCL
Small Communications Ship
AGCM
Master Chief Aerographer's Mate
AGCS
Senior Chief Aerographer's Mate
AGCY, AGY
Agency
AGD
Attack Geometry Display
Axial Gear Differential
Seagoing Dredge
AGD/CSD
Axial Gear Differential/Constant-Speed Drive
AGDE
Escort Research Ship
AGDS
Deep Submergence Support Ship
AGE
Automatic (or Aerospace) Ground Equipment
A-GEAR, A/G
Arresting Gear
AGEH
Hydrofoil Research Ship
AGER
Environmental Research Ship
AGF
Miscellaneous Command Ship
AGFCS
Automatic Gunfire Control System

AGFF
Frigate Research Ship
AGFSRS
Aircraft Ground Fire Suppression and Rescue
Systems (project)
AGHS
Hydrofoil Research Ship
AGI
Adjutant General Inspection
Intelligence Collector (ship)
AGIC
Automatically-Generated Integrated Circuit
AGIO
Armed Guard Inspection Officer
AGIS
Armed Guard Inspection Service
AGL
Above Ground-Level
Lighthouse Tender
AGM
Air-to-Ground Missile
Alternative Generator Model
Missile Range Instrumentation Ship
AGMR
Major Communications Relay Ship
AGN
Again
AGO
Air Gunnery Officer
AGOE
Advisory Group for Ocean Engineering
(SNAME)
AGOR
Oceanographic Research Ship
AGOS
Air-Ground Operations School
Air Gunnery Officers School
Ocean Surveillance Ship
AGP
Patrol Craft Tender
AGR
Air-to-Ground Ranging
AGS
Alternating Gradient Synchrontron
Armed Guard School
Surveying Ship
AGSS
Auxiliary Research Submarine
AGT
Adage Graphics Terminal
Agent
Target Service Ship
AGTR
Technical Research Ship
AGY, AGCY
Agency
AH
Attack Heavy (pilot code)
Hospital Ship
A/H
Alter Heading

AHD
Advanced Helicopter Development
AHP
Air, High Pressure
Evacuation Hospital Ship
AHRRN
Automatic Hydrologic Radio Reporting
Network
AHRS
Altitude-Heading-Reference System
AHT
Acoustic Homing Torpedo
AI
Airborne Interceptor
Air Intelligence
Automated Instruction
Automatic Input
Awaiting Instruction
A&I
Alteration and Improvement (program)
AIA
Action Item Assignment
AIB
Aircraft Instrument Bulletin
AIC
Advanced Intelligence Center
Air (or Airborne) Intercept Control
AICEM
Anti-Intercontinental Ballistic Missile
AICO
Action Information Control Officer
AICS
Advanced Interior Communications System
Air Intercept Control School
AICUZ
Air Installations Compatible-Use Zones
(program)
AID
Air Inspection Directorate
Air Intake Ducting
Assembly Instruction Device
Automatic Initial Distribution
AIDE
Adapted Identification Decision Equipment
AIDJEX
Arctic Ice Dynamics Joint Experiment
AIDO
Air Intelligence Duty Officer
AIDS
Airborne Integrated Data Systems
AIE
Authorized in Excess
AIETA
Airborne Infrared Equipment for Target
Analysis
AIF
Air Intelligence Force
AIFI
Automatic In-Flight Insertion
AIG
Address Indicating Group

AIG(A)
Assistant Inspector General for Auditing
AIL
Airborne Instrument Laboratory
Artificial Intelligence Laboratory (MIT)
AILAS
Automatic Instrument Landing Approach
System
AILSS
Advanced Integrated Life-Support System
AIMACO
Air Material Command
AIMD
Aircraft Intermediate Maintenance
Department
AIMS
Air Traffic Control, Radar Beacon System,
IFF, Military Secure System
American Institute of Merchant Shipping
AIMSO
Aircraft Intermediate Maintenance Support
Office
AINO
Assistant Inspector of Naval Ordnance
AIO
Action Information Organization
Air Intelligence Officer
AIP
Aeronautical Information Publication
Avition Indoctrination Program
AIR
Aircraft Inventory Record
Aviation Item Report
AIRACLIS
Air Activities Logistic Information Center
AIRAD
Airman Advisory
AIRANTISUBRON, VS
Air Antisubmarine Squadron
AIRANTISUBRONDET
Air Antisubmarine Squadron Detachment
AIRARMUNIT
Aircraft Armament Unit
AIRASRON
Aircraft Antisubmarine Squadron
AIRASUPPU
Air Antisubmarine Support Unit
AIRCON
Automatic Information and Reservations
Computer-Oriented Network
AIRDEFCOM
Air Defense Commander
AIRDEVRON, VX
Air Development Squadron
AIRELO
Air Electrical Officer
AIERO
Air Engineering Officer
AIREP
Air Reports (Metro) in Plain Language

AIREVACWING
Air Evacuation Wing
AIRFAC, AFY
Air Facility
AIRFAM
Aircraft Familiarization (course or phase)
AIRFERRON, VRF
Aircraft Ferry Squadron
AIRIS
Air-Stores-Issuing Ship
AIRLANT
Air Forces, Altantic Fleet
AIRLMAINT
Airline-Like Maintenance
AIRMET
Airmen's Meteorological (condition)
AIRMG, AMG
Aircraft Machine Gunner
AIROPS
Air Operations
AIRPAC
Air Forces, Pacific Fleet
AIRSUPPTRAU, ASTU
Air Support Training Unit
AIRTEVRON
Air Test and Evaluation Squadron
AIRTEVRONDET
Air Test and Evaluation Squadron
Detachment
AIRTRANSRON, VR, VRC
Air Transport Squadron
AIRTRARON
Air Training Squadron
AIS
Accelerated Inspection System
Advanced Information System
Aeronautical Information Service
Airbone Instrumentation System
Air Intelligence Service
Automated Information System
AISV
Amphibious Infantry-Support Vehicle
AIT
Autogenous Ignition Temperature
AITC
Action Information Training Center
AJ
Anti-Jam(ming)
Applied Journalism (DINFOS department)
Attack Jet (pilot code)
AJA
Adjacent
AJCC
Alternate Joint Communication Center
AJTWC
Alternate Joint Typhoon Warning Center
AK
Cargo Ship
AK1
Aviation Storekeeper First Class

AK2
Aviation Storekeeper Second Class
AK3
Aviation Storekeeper Third Class
AKAA
Aviation Storekeeper Airman Apprentice
AKAN
Aviation Storekeeper Airman
AKC
Chief Aviation Storekeeper
AKCM
Master Chief Aviation Storekeeper
AKCS
Senior Chief Aviation Storekeeper
AKD
Cargo Ship, Dock
AKF
Refrigerated Cargo Ship
AK-FBM
Polaris Cargo Resupply Ship
AKL
Light Cargo Ship
AKN
Net Cargo Ship
AKR
Vehicle Cargo Ship
AKS
Stores-Issue Ship
AKSS
Cargo Submarine
AKV
Cargo Ship and Aircraft Ferry
AL
Acquisition Logistician
Approach and Landing (charts)
Arrival Locator
Lightship
AL, A/L
Air Liaison
ALAIRC
Alaskan Air Command
ALARM
Alerting Long-Range Airborne Radar for
Moving Targets
ALARR
Air-Launched Acoustical Reconnaissance
ALBI
Air-Launched Ballistic (or Boost) Intercept
ALBM
Air-Launched Ballistic Missile
ALC
American Language Course
Automatic Level Control
ALCAPP
Automatic List Classification and Profile
Production
ALCC
Airborne Launch Control Center
ALCEP
AUTOSERVCOM Life Cycle Extension
Program

ALCOM
Algebraic Compiler
All Commands
ALCOMLANT
All Commands, Atlantic
ALCOMPAC
All Commands, Pacific
ALCOR
ARPA/Lincoln Labs C-band Observable
Radar
ALCPT
American Language College Placement Test
ALCS
Automatic Launch Control System
ALDPS
Automated Logistic Data Processing System
ALERTS
Airborne Laser Electronic Real-Time
Surveillance
ALF
Aloft
Auxiliary Landing Field
ALG
Along
ALL/LL QTY
Allowance or Load List Quality
ALLOW, ALW
Allowance
ALLSTAT
All-Purpose Statistical Package
ALMB
Air-Launched Missile Ballistics
ALMC
Air-Launched Missile Changes
ALMILACT
All Military Activities
ALN
Ammunition Lot Number
ALMAR
All Marine (activities)
ALNAV
All Navy (activities)
ALNAVSTA
All Naval Stations
ALNN
Air-Launched Non-Nuclear (ordnance)
ALNOT
Alert Notice
ALNW
Air-Launched Nuclear Weapon
ALO
Air Liaison Officer
ALOC
Allocate
ALOFT
Airborne Light Optical Fiber Technology
ALOT, ALOTMT
Allotment
ALOTMT, ALOT
Allotment

ALOTS
Airborne Lightweight Optical Tracking System
ALP
Air Liaison Party
Air, Low-Pressure
Automated Learning Process
ALPA
Airline Pilots Association
ALPEC
Ammunition Loading Production Engineering
Center
ALPS
Automated Leave and Pay System
Automated Library Processing Services
Automated Linear Programming System
ALPURCOMS
All-Purpose Communication System
ALREP
Air-Launched Report
Analysis and Evaluation Report
ALRI
Airborne Long-Range Input
ALRT
Time-Ordered Alerts (NNSS)
ALS
Advanced Logistics System
Approach Lighting System
Automatic Landing System
Auxiliary Lighter Ship
ALSAM
Air-Launched Ship-Attack Missile
ALSD
Ames Life-Sciences Directorate
ALSEAFRON
Alaskan Sea Frontier
ALSEC
Alaskan Sector
ALSTACON
All Stations Continental (United States)
ALSTG
Altimeter Setting
ALT
Administrative Lead Time
Alteration/Improvement Proposal
Alterations
Alterate
Alternating
Altimeter
Altitude
ALTAC
Algebraic Translator-Compiler
ALTAIR
ARPA Long-Range Tracking and
Instrumentation Radar
ALTCOMLANT
Alternate Commander, Atlantic
ALTCOMLANTFLT
Alternate Commander, Atlantic Fleet
ALTFFL
Alternating Fixed and Flashing (light)

ALTFGFL
Alternating Fixed and Group-Flashing (light)
ALTFL
Alternating Flashing (light)
ALTGPOCC
Alternating Group-Occulting (light)
ALTN
Alternate
ALT PROG
Alternate Program
ALTRAN
Algebraic Translator
ALTREV, ALTRV
Altitude Reservation
ALTRV, ALTREV
Altitude Reservation
ALU
Arithmetic Logic Unit
ALUSLO
American Litigation, United States Naval
Liaison Officer
ALUSNA
American Ligitation, United States Naval
Attaché
ALUSNOB
American Litigation, United States Naval
Observer
ALW, ALLOW
Allowance
ALWT
Advanced Lightweight Torpedo
AM
Acquisition Manager
Air Medal
Amplitude Modulation
Ampoule (U/I)
AM, AMER
America(n)
A-M
Active Mariner (program)
AMA
Air Material Area
ASROC Missile Assembly
AMAC
Aircraft Monitor and Control
AMAD
Aircraft Mounted Accessory Drive
AMAL
Authorized Medical Allowance List
AMAL/ADAL
Authorized Medical Allowance List/Authorized
Dental Allowance List
AMAS
Advanced Mid-Course Active System
AMASCP
Air Material Area Stock Control Point
AMB
Aircraft Mishap Board
Ambulance
Armament Material Bulletin

AMC
Activity Mission Code
Air Mail Center
Armament Material Change
Atlantic Marine Center (NOAA)
Automatic Maneuvering Control
Automatic Mixture Control
Aviation Maintenance Costs
Chief Aviation Structural Mechanic
AMCM
Airborne Mine Countermeasures
AMCS
Airborne Missile Control System
Senior Chief Aviation Structural Mechanic
AMD
Air Movement Directive (or Designator)
Aircraft (or Aviation) Maintenance Department
AMDO
Aeronautical Maintenance Duty Officer
AMDP
Aircraft Maintenance Delayed for Parts
AME
Angle-Measuring Equipment
Aviation Medical Examiner
AME1
Aviation Structural Mechanic E (Safety
Equipment) First Class
AME2
Aviation Structural Mechanic E (Safety
Equipment) Second Class
AME3
Aviation Structural Mechanic E (Safety
Equipment) Third Class
AMEAA
Aviation Structural Mechanic E (Safety
Equipment) Airman Apprentice
AMEAN
Aviation Structural Mechanic E (Safety
Equipment) Airman
AMEB
American Embassy
AMEC
Chief Aviation Structural Mechanic E (Safety
Equipment)
AMER, AM
America(n)
AMFAR
A Multifunction S-band Array Radar
AMFINFOS
American Forces Information Service
AMFSV
Auxiliary Mobile Fuel-Storage Vessel
AMFUR, AMPFUR
Amplified Failure and Unsatisfactory Report
AMG
Acquisition Management Guide
AMG, AIRMG
Aircraft Machine Gunner
AMGA
Award of Merit for Group Achievement

AMH1
Aviation Structural Mechanic H (Hydraulics)
First Class
AMH2
Aviation Structural Mechanic H (Hydraulics)
Second Class
AMH3
Aviation Structural Mechanic H (Hydraulics)
Third Class
AMHAA
Aviation Structural Mechanic H (Hydraulics)
Airman Apprentice
AMHAN
Aviation Structural Mechanic H (Hydraulics)
Airman
AMHAZ
Ammunition and Hazardous Materials
AMHC
Chief Aviation Structural Mechanic H
(Hydraulics)
AMHD
Average Man-Hours per Day
AMHS
Automated Materials-Handling System
AMI
Airspeed Mach Indicator
Amalgamated Military and Technical
Improvement Plan
Annual Military Inspection
AMIL
A Microprogramming Language (NRL)
AMIS
Advanced (or Audit) Management Information
System
AML
Advance Material List
Aeronautical Materials Laboratory
Applied Mathematics Laboratory
AMM
Anti-Missile Missile
AMMRL
Aircraft Maintenance Material Readiness List
AMO
Air Material Office
Area Monitoring Office
Aviation Medical Officer
AMP
Analytical Maintenance Program
AMPE
Automated Message Processing Equipment
AMPFUR, AMFUR
Amplified Failure or Unsatifactory Report
AMPH, AMPHIB
Amphibious
AMPHIB, AMPH
Amphibious
AMPHIBEX, PHIBEX
Amphibious Exercise
AMPI
Annual Military Personnel Inspection

AMPLE
Analytical Mode for Performing Logistic
Evaluation
AMPS
Automatic Message-Processing System
AMR
Advanced Material Requirement
Auxiliary Machinery Room
AMRAAM
Advanced Medium-Range Air-to-Air Missile
AMRAD
Advanced Research Projects Agency
Measurements Radar
AMS
Aeronautical Material Specification
Air Mass
Auxiliary Machinery Space
Minesweeper, High Speed
AMS1
Aviation Structural Mechanic S (Structures)
First Class
AMS2
Aviation Structural Mechanic S (Structures)
Second Class
AMS3
Aviation Structural Mechanic S (Structures)
Third Class
AMSA
Advanced Manned Strategic Aircraft
AMSAA
Aviation Structural Mechanic S (Structures)
Airman Apprentice
AMSAN
Aviation Structural Mechanic S (Structures)
Airman
AMSC
Acquisition Management Systems Control
Chief Aviation Structural Mechanic S
(Structures)
AMSD
Anti-Ship Missile Defense
AMSE
Aeronautical Material Support Equipment
AMSI
Atlantic Merchant Shipping Instructions
AMSL
Above Mean Sea Level
AMSO
Aeromedical Safety Officer
AMSP
Advanced Magnetic Silencing Project
Asbestos Medical Surveillance Program
AMST
Advanced Medium STOL Transport
AMSU
Aeronautical Material Screening Unit
AMSU, PHIBMAINTSUPPU
Amphibious Maintenance Support Unit
AMSULANT
Amphibious Maintenance Support Unit,
Atlantic

AMSUPAC
Amphibious Maintenance Support Unit,
Pacific
AMT
Amalgamated Military Technical
Amount
AMTA
Audio-Monitored Talk Amplifier
AMTI
Airborne Moving-Target Indicator
AMTRACBN
Amphibious Tractor Battalion
AMU
Atomic Mass Unit
AMVER
Automated Mutual-Assistance Vessel Rescue
(system)
AN
Airman
Alphanumeric
Army-Navy (ordnance)
AN, A/N
Aids to Navigation (USCG)
A/N
Alphanumeric
ANA
Air Force-Navy Aeronautical (bulletin)
ANAL
Analog
ANAL, ANLYS
Analysis
ANAPROP, AP
Anomalous Propagation (radar)
ANCA
Allied Naval Communications Agent
ANCH
Anchorage
ANCH PROHIB
Anchorage Prohibited
AND
Air Force-Navy Design
ANDB
Air Navigation Development Board
ANDVT
Advanced Narrowband Digital Voice Terminal
ANEW
A New Antisubmarine Warfare System
ANF
Anti-nuclear Force
ANFE
Aircraft Not Fully Equipped
ANGLICO
Air and Naval Gunfire Liaison Company
AN(HS)
High School Airman
ANIP
Army-Navy Instrumentation Program
AN(JC)
Junior College Airman
ANJSB
Army-Navy Joint Specifications Board

ANL
Annealed
Automatic Noise-Landing
Net Laying Ship
ANLYS, ANAL
Analysis
ANMB
Army-Navy Munitions Board
ANMCC
Alternate National Military Command Center
ANMI
Allied Naval Maneuvering Instructions
ANMPO
Army-Navy Medical Procurement Office
ANNA
Army, Navy, National Aeronautics (and Space
Administration)
ANNADIV
Annapolis (MD) Division
ANNFLYQUIRE
Annual Flying Requirement
ANN NO
Announcement Number
ANNREPT
Annual Report
ANO
Air Navigation Order
ANON
Anonymous
ANORS
Anticipated Not Operationally Ready (Supply)
ANP
Aircraft Nuclear Propulsion (development
proposition)
Air Navigation Plan
ANS, A
Answer
ANSI
Assistant Naval Science Instructor
ANSIA
Army-Navy Shipping Information Agency
ANSO
Assistant Naval Stores Officer
ANT
Antenna
Antenna Height Entry (NNSS)
ANTARCTICDEVRON
Antarctic Development Squadron
ANTARCTICDEVRONDET
Antarctic Development Squadron Detachment
ANTARCTICSUPPACT, ASA
Antarctic Support Activities
ANTDEFCOM
Antilles Defense Command
ANTI-C
Anti-Contamination (clothing)
ANTILOG
Antilogarithm
ANTISUB
Antisubmarine

ANTISUBFITRON, VSF
Antisubmarine Fighter Squadron
ANTS
Advanced Naval Training School
ANTU
Air Navigation Training Unit
ANX
Annex
ANZUK
Australia, New Zealand and United Kingdom
ANZUS
Australia, New Zealand and the United States
AO
Acousto-Optic
Administrative Office(r)
Aerodrome Officer
Air Observer
Appointing Order
Area of Operations
Audit Organization
Oiler
AO1
Aviation Ordnanceman First Class
AO2
Aviation Ordnanceman Second Class
AO3
Aviation Ordnanceman Third Class
A/O
All Over the Hatch or Hold (stowage)
AOA
Amphibious Objective Area
Angle of Attack
Atlantic Operating Area
AOAA
Aviation Ordnanceman Airman Apprentice
AOAN
Aviation Ordnanceman Airman
AOB
Advanced Operational Base
AOBS
Annual Officer Billet Summary
AOC
Agreed Operational Characteristics
Aircraft Operational Capability
Association of Old Crows
Aviation Officer Candidate
Chief Aviation Ordnanceman
AOCAN
Aviation Officer Candidate Airman
AOCM
Aircraft Out-of-Commission for Maintenance
Master Chief Aviation Ordnanceman
AOCP
Aircraft Out-of-Commission for Parts
Aviation Officer Continuation Pay
AOCR
Aircraft Operating-Cost Report
AOCS
Aviation Officer Candidate School
Senior Chief Aviation Ordnanceman

AOD
Aerodrome Officer-of-the-Day
AODC
Allowance Officer Desk Code
AOE
Aerodrome of Entry
Fast Combat Support Ship
AOES
Air-Ocean Environmental Specialist
AOG
Aircraft on Ground
Gasoline Tanker
AOH
Accepted on Hire
Aircraft Requiring Overhaul
Awaiting Overhaul
AOI
And-or-Invert (gate)
AOIL
Aviation Oil
AO(J)
Jumbo Oiler
AOL
Absent Over Liberty
Small Oiler
AOM
All Officers Meeting
AOML
Atlantic Oceanographic and Meteorological
Laboratory
AOO
Aviation Ordnance Officer
AOP
Air Observation Post
Atomic Ordnance Platoon
AOQ
Average Outgoing Quality
Aviation Officers' Quarters
AOQL
Average Outgoing Quality Limit
AOR
Air Operations Room
Allowance Override Requirement
Argon Oxygen Refining
Replacement Oiler
AOS
Amphibious Objective Study
AOSO
Advanced Orbiting Solar Observatory
AOSS
Airborne Oil Surveillance System
Submarine Oiler
AOT
Transport Oiler
AOTU, PHIBOPTRAU
Amphibious Operational Training Unit
AOV
APA items for Overseas Shipment
AOWS
Aircraft Overhaul Work-Stoppage

AP
  After Peak
  Aft Perpendiculars
  Air Patrol (or Plot, or Position, or Publication)
  Armor-Piercing (projectile)
  Assumed Position
  Attack Prop (pilot code)
  Aviation Pilot
  Transport (ship)
A/P
  Airplane
  Auto Pilot
AP, APR
  April
APA
  Appropriation Purchases Account
  Automatic Pulse-Analyzer
AP, ANAPROP
  Anomalous Propagation (radar)
APACHE
  Analog Programming and Checking
AP/AM
  Anti-Personnel/Anti-Material (cluster bomb)
APAR
  Automatic Programming and Recording
APATS
  Automatic Programmer and Test System
APB
  Auxiliary Barracks Ship (Self-Propelled)
APBI
  Advanced Planning Briefings for Industry
APC
  Academic Potential Coding (file)
  Academic Profile Code
  Activity Processing Code
  Air Project Coordinator
  Approach Power Compensator (or Control)
  Area of Position (or Positive) Control
  Armored Personnel Carrier
  Automatic Phase Control
  Small Coastal Transport
APCH, APP
  Approach
APCHE
  Automatic Programmed Checkout Equipment
APCON, APPCON
  Approach Control
APCS
  Approach Power Compensator System
APD
  Advanced Planning Document
  Air Procurement District
  High-Speed Transport
APDM
  Amended Program Decision Memorandum
APDP
  Automatic Payroll Deposit Plan
APDSMS
  Advanced Point Defense Surface Missile
    System

APE
  Air Forces Element (Iceland)
APEL
  Aeronautical Photographic Experimentation
    Laboratory
APERS
  Anti-Personnel
APEXER
  Approach Indexer
APG
  Advanced Pay Grade
APGC
  Air Proving-Ground Center (or Command)
APH
  Hospital Transport
API
  Area of Possible Incompatibility
  Armor-Piercing Incendiary
APIX
  Automated Personnel Information Exchange
APL
  Allowance Parts List
  Applied Physics Laboratory
  Barracks Craft (Non-Self-Propelled)
  High-Speed Transport (Non-Self-Propelled)
APLO
  Aerial Port Liaison Officer
APM
  All Pilots Meeting
  Assistant Project Manager
  Mechanized Artillery Transport
APMS
  Automated Publications Maintenance System
APN
  Aircraft Procurement, Navy
  Non-Mechanized Artillery Transport
APO
  Annual Program Objectives
  Asymptotically Pointwise Optimal
APOB
  Actual Projected on Board (allowance)
APOE
  Aerial Port of Embarkation
APOTA
  Automatic Positioning Telemetering Antenna
APP
  Adjusted Performance Percentile
  Advanced Procurement Plan
  Appendix
  Auxiliary Power Plant
APP, APCH
  Approach
APPAC
  Aviation Petroleum Products Allocation
    Committee
APPAC-L
  Aviation Petroleum Products Allocation
    Committee-London
APPCON, APCON
  Approach Control

APP/DEP
 Approach/Departure (controller)
APPL
 Applicable
 Applicant
 Application
APPN, APPROP
 Appropriation
APPR
 Approve
APPRES
 Applied Research
APPROP, APPN
 Appropriately
APPS
 Advanced Planning Procurement System
 Automated Photogrammeric Positioning
  System
APPT
 Appointment
APR
 Alterations and Project Reports
 Rescue Transport
APR, AP
 April
APREQ
 Approval Request
APRX
 Approximate
APS
 Automatic Program System
 Automatic Propulsion Control System
 Auxiliary Power Supply
APSA
 Ammunition Procurement and Supply System
APSET
 Aviation Personnel and Survival Equipment
APT
 Armor-Piercing Tracer
 Automatic Picture Transmission
 Troop Barge, Class B
APTE
 Automatic Production Test Equipment
APTES
 Administrative Professional and Technical
  Evaluation System
APTS
 Activity Providing Telephone Service
APU
 Auxiliary Power (or Propulsion) Unit
APV
 Transport and Aircraft Ferry
APWO
 Assistant Public Works Officer
AQ
 Aircraft (or Allowance) Quality
AQ1
 Aviation Fire Control Technician First Class
AQ2
 Aviation Fire Control Technician Second
  Class

AQ3
 Aviation Fire Control Technician Third Class
AQAA
 Aviation Fire Control Technician Airman
  Apprentice
AQAN
 Aviation Fire Control Technician Airman
AQCS
 Senior Chief Aviation Fire Control Technician
AQD
 Additional Qualification Designation
AQD/U
 Additional Qualification Designation/Utilization
AQL
 Acceptable Quality Level
AQT
 Applicant (or Aviation) Qualification Test
AQTY
 Allowance Quality
AR
 Aeronautical (or Aircraft) Requirement
 Air Refueling (or Rescue, or Reserve)
 Airman Recruit
 Amphibian Reconnaissance
 As Required (report frequency)
 Armor Reconnaissance
 Repair Ship
A&R
 Assembly and Repair
ARA
 Accelerated Readiness Analysis
 Airborne Radar Approach
 Aircraft Replaceable Assembly
 Assigned Responsible Agency
 Avionics Repairable Assemblies
ARAA
 Aerodrome Radar Approach Aid
ARAC
 Airborne Radar Approach Control (facility)
ARAPS
 Area Requirements and Product Status
ARB
 Air Registration Board
 Air Reserve Base
 Battle Damage Repair Ship
 RVAH Bombardier/Navigator (code)
ARBS
 Angular Rate Bombing System
ARC
 Accessory Record Card
 Acoustic Research Center
 Acquisition Review Committee
 Activity Readiness Code
 Alcohol Recovery (or Rehabilitation) Center
 Area of Responsibility Center
 Cable-Repairing Ship
ARCO
 Airborne Remote-Control Operator
 Auxiliary Resources Control Office
ARCP
 Air Refueling Control Point

ARCTICSARCOORD
Coast Guard Search and Rescue
Coordinator, Arctic
ARD
Alcohol Recovery (or Rehabilitation) Drydock
Auxiliary Repair Drydock (Non-Self-Propelled)
ARDA
Analog Recording Dynamic Analyzer
ARDF
Applications Research and Defense Fund
ARDL
Small Auxiliary Floating Drydock
(Non-Self-Propelled)
ARDM
Medium Auxiliary Repair Drydock
(Non-Self-Propelled)
AREACORD
For the purpose of area coordination or to
such other command designated by him in
appropriate instructions
AREAPETOFF
Area Petroleum Office
ARF
Automatic Return Fire
ARFCOS
Armed Forces Courier Service
ARFCOSTA
Armed Forces Courier Station
ARFOR
Area Forecast
AR/FOR
Active Records/Fiche-Oriented Retrieval
ARG
Amphibious Ready Group
Internal Combustion Engine Repair Ship
ARG-SLF
Amphibious Ready Group-Special Landing
Force (concept)
ARGUS
Analytical Reports Gathering and Updating
System
Automatic Routine Generation and Updating
System
ARH
Anti-Radiation Homing
Heavy-Hull Repair Ship
ARHAWS
Anti-Radiation Homing and Warning System
AR(HS)
High School Airman Recruit
ARI
Arithmetic (test)
ARIP
Air Refueling Initial Point
Automatic Rocket Impact Predictor
ARIS
Advanced Range Instrumentation Ship
Altitude and Rate Indicating System

ARL
Acceptable Reliability Level
Aeromedical (or Aeronautical) Research
Laboratory
Arctic Research Laboratory
Small Repair Ship
ARLAN, ARLEX, AA
Arlington Annex
ARLEX, AA, ARLAN
Arlington Annex
ARLIS
Arctic Research Laboratory Ice Station
ARLS
Automatic Resupply System
ARM
Anti-Radar (or -Radiation) Missile
Applied Research Motor
Armament
Heavy Machinery Repair Ship
ARMACS
Aviation Plans/Aviation Resources
Management and Control System
ARMD
Armored
ARMGD, AG
Armed Guard
ARMGRDCEN, AGC
Armed Guard Center
ARMM
Automatic Reliability Mathematical Model
ARMMS
Automated Reliability Maintenance
Measurement System
ARMS
Automatic Remote Manned System
ARN
Around
ARNG
Arrange(ment)
ARO
Air Radio Officer
Auxiliary Readout
ARODS
Airborne Radar Orbital Determination System
AROICC
Area Resident Officer-in-Charge of
Construction
AROU
Aviation Repair and Overhaul Unit
ARP
Aircraft Recommended Practice
Air Raid Precaution
Analytical Rework Program
Armament Release Panel
ARPA
Advanced Research Projects Agency
ARPARSCHCEN
Advanced Research Projects Agency
Research Center

ARPAT
Advanced Research Projects Agency
Terminal
ARPN
Aircraft and Related Procurement, Navy
ARPROIMREP
Arrival further proceed immediately and report
ARPROPORICH
Arrival further proceed to port in which
ARPROREP
Arrival further proceed and report
ARR
Arrival
ARREC
Armed Reconnaissance
ARREP
Arrival report
ARREPCOVES
Arrival reporting commanding officer of that
vessel (duty indicated)
ARREPISIC
Arrival report to superior in command, if
present, otherwise by message (duty
indicated)
ARRL
Aeronautical Radio and Radar Laboratory
ARRV, ARR
Arrive
ARS
Advanced Reconnaissance Satellite
Advanced Record System
Air Rescue Service
Alcohol Recovery Service
Automatic Routing System
Salvage Ship
ARSD
Aviation Repair Supply Depot
Salvage Lifting Ship
ARSR
Air Surveillance Radar
ARSSS
Automated Ready-Supply Stores System
ARST
Salvage-Craft Tender
ARSV
Armored Reconnaissance Scout Vehicle
ART
Academic Remedial Training (school)
Active Repair Time
Airborne Radiation Thermometer
Article
ARTC
Air Route Traffic Control
Alcohol Recovery Training Center
ARTCC
Air Route Traffic Control Center
ARTL
Awaiting Results of Trial

ARTRAC
Advanced Range Testing, Reporting and
Control
Advanced Real-Time Range Control
ARTRON
Artificial Neuron
ARTS
Automated Radar Terminal System
ARTY
Artillery
ARTYLO
Artillery Liaison Office(r)
ARU
Alcohol Rehabilitation Unit
ARV
Aircraft Repair Ship
ARVA
Aircraft Repair Ship (Aircraft)
ARVE
Aircraft Repair Ship (Engines)
ARVH
Aircraft Repair Ship (Helicopter)
AS
Aiming Symbol
Altostratus (cloud formation)
Ammonia Service
Analytical Stereoplotter
Annual Survey
Auxiliary Steam (system)
Submarine Tender
AS, ANTISUB
Antisubmarine
A/S
Airspeed
AS1
Aviation Support Equipment Technician First
Class
ASA
Aviation Supply Annex
ASAC
Altostratus and Altocumulus (cloud formation)
Antisubmarine Air Controller
ASAMP
AUTODIN Subscriber Activation Management
Plan
ASAMP-PAC
AUTODIN Subscriber Activation Management
Plan-Pacific
ASAP
Alcohol Safety Action Program (or Project)
Antisubmarine Attack Plotter
As Soon As Possible
ASAR
Air Search Acquisition Radar
ASAT
Air Search Attack Team
Anti-Satellite
Antisubmarine Attack Teacher
Automated Statistical Analysis Technique
ASATTU
Antisubmarine Attack Teacher Training Unit

ASB
Air Safety Board
Arctic Survey Boat (USCG)
ASBCA
Armed Services Board of Contract Appeals
ASBD
Active Service Base Date
Advanced Sea-Based Deterrent
ASC
Advanced Ship Concept
Air Support Control
Asset Status Card
AUTODIN Switching Center
Automated Service Center
Automatic Steering Control (computer)
Chief Aviation Support Equipment Technician
ASCA
Aircraft Stability Control Analyzer
Automatic Subject Citation Alert (ISI)
ASCAC
Antisubmarine Classification and Analysis
Center
Antisubmarine Combat Activity Center
ASCAC/TSC
Antisubmarine Classification and Analysis
Center/Tactical Support Center
ASCAT
Antisubmarine Classification Analysis Test
ASCB
Aviation Command Screening Board
ASCC
Aviation Supply Control Center
ASCII
Automatic Synchronous Control of
Intelligence Information
ASCM
Anti-Ship Cruise Missile
Master Chief Aviation Support Equipment
Technician
ASCO
Air Service Coordination Office
ASCOMED
Air Service Coordination Office,
Mediterranean
ASCOMM
Antisubmarine Warfare Communications
ASCOMMDET
Antisubmarine Warfare Communications
Detachment
ASCOP
Advanced Submarine Control Program
ASCS
Altitude Stabilization and Control System
Automatic Stabilization Control System
Senior Chief Aviation Support Equipment
Technician
ASCSR
Armed Services Commissary Store
Regulations

ASCU
Air Support Control Unit
Armament Station Control Unit
ASD
Activity Support Date
Aircraft Statistical Data
Aviation Supply Depot
ASD, ASSTSECDEF
Assistant Secretary of Defense
ASDARP
Aviation Supply Development and Readiness
(program)
ASD(C), ASSTSECDEF(COMPT)
Assistant Secretary of Defense (Comptroller)
ASDE
Airport (or Air) Surface Detection Equipment
ASDEC
Applied Systems Development and
Evaluation Center
ASDEFORLANT
Antisubmarine Defense Forces, Atlantic
ASDEFORPAC
Antisubmarine Defense Forces, Pacific
ASDEVDET
Anitsubmarine Development Detachment
ASD(HA), ASSTSECDEF(HELAFF)
Assistant Secretary of Defense (Health
Affairs)
ASD(I), ASSTSECDEF(INTEL)
Assistant Secretary of Defense (Intelligence)
ASDIC
Antisubmarine Detection Investigation
Committee
Armed Services Documents Intelligence
Center
ASD(ISA), ASSTSECDEF(INTSECAFF)
Assistant Secretary of Defense (International
Security Affairs)
ASDIV
Advanced Systems Division
**ASD(MRAL),
ASSTSECDEF(MPRRESAFFLOG)**
Assistant Secretary of Defense (Manpower,
Reserve Affairs and Logistics)
ASDO
Assistant Squadron Duty Officer
ASD(PA), ASSTSECDEF(PUBAFF)
Assistant Secretary of Defense (Public
Affairs)
ASD(R&D), ASSTSECDEF(RSCHDEV)
Assistant Secretary of Defense (Research
and Development)
ASDV
Swimmer Delivery Vehicle Support Craft
ASE
Allowable Setting Error
Automatic Stabilization Equipment
ASE2
Aviation Support Equipment Technician E
(Electrical) Second Class

ASE3
Aviation Support Equipment Technician E (Electrical) Third Class
ASEAA
Aviation Support Equipment Technician E (Electrical) Airman Apprentice
ASEAN
Aviation Support Equipment Technician E (Electrical) Airman
ASED
Aviation and Surface Effects Department
Aviation Service Entry Date
A/SEE
Antisubmarine Experimental Establishment
ASEG
All Services Evaluation Group
ASER
Armed Services Exchange Regulations
ASESB
Armed Services Explosive Safety Board
ASF
Activity Support File
Aeromedical Staging Facility
Aeronautical Staging Flight
AS(FBM)
Submarine Tender (Fleet Ballistic Missile)
A/SFDO
Antisubmarine Fixed Defenses Officer
ASFIR
Active Swept Frequency Interferometer Radar
ASG
Auxiliary Service Force
ASG, ASGN
Assign
ASGD
Assigned
ASGN, ASG
Assign
ASH
Assault Support Helicopter
ASH2
Aviation Support Equipment Technician H (Hydraulics and Structures) Second Class
ASH3
Aviation Support Equipment Technician H (Hydraulics and Structures) Third Class
ASHAA
Aviation Support Equipment Technician H (Hydraulics and Structures) Airman Apprentice
ASHAN
Aviation Support Equipment Technician H (Hydraulics and Structures) Airman
ASHE
Aircraft Salvage Handling Equipment
ASHMS
Automatic Ship's Heading Measurement System

ASI
Airspeed Indicator
Annual Supply Inspection
Automatic Start Interrupt (NNSS)
Aviation Status Indicator
ASIF
Airlift Services Industrial Fund
ASIS
Ammunition Stores Issuing Ship
Amphibious Support Information System
ASL
Above Sea Level
Aeronautical Structures Laboratory
Approved Suppliers' List
Atmospheric Sciences Laboratory (ESIG)
Salvage Tug
ASLADS
Automatic Shipboard Launch Aircraft Data System
ASLBM
Anti-Sea-Launched Ballistic Missile
ASLT
Assault
ASLTPHIBBN
Assault Amphibious Battalion
ASM
Administrative Support Manual
Air-to-Surface Missile
ASM2
Aviation Support Equipment Technician M (Mechanical) Second Class
ASM3
Aviation Support Equipment Technician M (Mechanical) Third Class
ASMAA
Aviation Support Equipment Technician M (Mechanical) Airman Apprentice
ASMAN
Aviation Support Equipment Technician M (Mechanical) Airman
ASMD
Anti-Ship Missile Defense
ASMIS
Automated Ships Management Information System
ASMS
Advanced Surface Missile System
ASN
Average Sample Number
ASN, ASSTSECNAV
Assistant Secretary of the Navy
ASNE
American Society of Naval Engineers
ASN(FM), ASSTSECNAVFINMGMT
Assistant Secretary of the Navy (Financial Management)
ASN(I&L), ASSTSECNAVINSTLOG
Assistant Secretary of the Navy (Installation and Logistics)

ASN(MRA), ASSTSECNAVMPRESAFF
Assistant Secretary of the Navy (Manpower and Reserve Affairs)
ASN(RES), ASSTSECNAVRES
Assistant Secretary of the Navy (Research and Development)
ASN(RE&S), ASSTSECNAVRESENGSYS
Assistant Secretary of the Navy (Research, Engineering and Systems)
ASN(SL), ASSTSECNAVSHIPLOG
Assistant Secretary of the Navy (Shipbuilding and Logistics)
ASO
Air Signal (or Staff, or Surveillance) Officer
Area (or Aviation) Safety Officer
Assistant Secretary's Office
Aviation Supply Office(r)
ASO/ICP
Aviation Supply Office/Inventory Control Point
ASOP
Automatic Operating and Scheduling Program
ASOS
Assistant Supervisor of Shipbuilding
Automatic Storm Observation Service
ASP
Advanced Signal Processing (or Processor)
Advanced Study Project
Air Superiority Program
Ammunition Supply Point
Antisubmarine Patrol
Assault Support Patrol (boat)
Atmospheric Sounding Projectile
ASPAN
ASP and Nike
ASPB
Assault Support Patrol Boat
ASPCB
Armed Services Pest Control Board
ASPO
Avionics System Project Officer
ASPPO
Armed Services Procurement Planning Office
ASPR
Armed Services Procurement Regulations
ASR
Airborne Search Radar
Airport (or Air) Surveillance Radar
Automatic Send-and-Receive (teletype)
Submarine Rescue Ship
ASR, A/SR
Air-Sea Rescue
ASRAP
Acoustic Sensor Range Prediction (system)
ASRGN
Altimeter Setting Region
ASROC
Antisubmarine Rocket
ASROC(ERA)
Extended-Range Antisubmarine Rocket
ASRS
Automatic Storage Retrieval System

ASRT
Air Support Radar Team
ASS
Airborne Surveillance System
ASS, APSS
Transport Submarine
ASSA
Cargo Submarine
ASSC
Advanced Shipboard Satellite Communications
Airborne Systems Support Center
ASSES
Analytical Studies of Surface Effects of Submerged Submarines
ASSET
Advanced Solar Turbo-Electric Conversion
Aerothermodynamic Elastic Structural Systems Environmental Tests
ASSIST
Afloat Supply Systems Improvement and Support Team
AS&SL
All Ships and Stations Letters
ASSOTW
Airfield and Seaplane Stations of the World
ASSP
Area Supply Support Plan
Transport Submarine
ASST, AST
Assistant
ASSTCOMNAVSECGRU
Assistant Commander Naval Security Group
ASSTNAVSEATECHREP
Assistant Sea Systems Command Technical Representative
ASSTSECDEF, ASD
Assistant Secretary of Defense
ASSTSECDEF(COMPT), ASD(C)
Assistant Secretary of Defense (Comptroller)
ASSTSECDEF(HELAFF), ASD(HA)
Assistant Secretary of Defense (Health Affairs)
ASSTSECDEF(INTEL), ASD(I)
Assistant Secretary of Defense (Intelligence)
ASSTSECDEF(INTSECAFF), ASD(ISA)
Assistant Secretary of Defense (International Security Affairs)
ASSTSECDEF(MPRRESAFFLOG), ASD(MRAL)
Assistant Secretary of Defense (Manpower, Reserve Affairs and Logistics)
ASSTSECDEF(PUBAFF), ASD(PA)
Assistant Secretary of Defense (Public Affairs)
ASSTSECNAV, ASN
Assistant Secretary of the Navy
ASSTSECNAVFINMGMT, ASN(FM)
Assistant Secretary of the Navy (Financial Management)

ASSTSECNAVINSTLOG, ASN(I&L)
Assistant Secretary of the Navy (Installation and Logistics)

ASSTSECNAVMPRESAFF, ASN(MRA)
Assistant Secretary of the Navy (Manpower and Reserve Affairs)

ASSTSECNAVRES, ASN(RES)
Assistant Secretary of the Navy (Research and Development)

ASSTSECNAVRESENGSYS, ASN(RE&S)
Assistant Secretary of the Navy (Research, Engineering and Systems)

ASSTSECNAVSHIPLOG, ASN(SL)
Assistant Secretary of the Navy (Shipbuilding and Logistics)

ASSY
Assembly

AST
Air Service Training
APA items only for Stateside Shipment

AST, ASST
Assistant

ASTAB
Automated Status Board

ASTADIS, ADSTADIS
Advise status and/or disposition

ASTAP
Accoustic Sensor Training Aids Program

ASTAPA
Armed Services Textile and Apparel Procurement Agency

ASTDS
Antisubmarine Tactical Data System

ASTER
Antisubmarine Terrier (missile)

ASTIA
Armed Services Technical Information Agency

ASTIAB
Armed Services Technical Information Agency Bulletin

ASTOR
Antisubmarine Torpedo (rocket)

ASTRO
Artificial Satellite, Time and Radio Orbit
Astronomical

ASTU, AIRSUPPTRAU
Air Support Training Unit

ASU
Administrative Screening Unit
Aircraft Scheduling (or Starting) Unit
Approval of Systems and Equipments for Service Use

ASUPT
Advanced Simulation in Undergraduate Pilot Training

ASV
Aerothermodynamic Structure Vehicle
Anti-Surface Missile

ASVAB
Armed Services Vocational Aptitude Battery

ASW
Antisubmarine (or Anti-Surface) Warfare
Auxiliary Sea-Water (system)

ASWCCS
Antisubmarine Warfare Centers Command and Control System

ASWCR
Airborne Surveillance Warning and Control Radar

ASWEPS
Antisubmarine Warfare Environmental Prediction System

ASWEX
Antisubmarine Warfare Exercise

ASWFITRON
Antisubmarine Warfare Fighter Squadron

ASWGRU
Antisubmarine Warfare Group

ASWO
(Naval) Air Stations Weekly Orders

ASWOC
Antisubmarine Warfare Operational Center

ASWICS
Antisubmarine Warfare Integrated Combat System

ASWORG
Antisubmarine Warfare Operations Research Group

ASWR
Antisubmarine Warfare Radar

ASWRC
Antisubmarine Warfare Research Center

ASWS
Antisubmarine Warfare Systems

ASWSAG
Antisubmarine Warfare Systems Analysis Group

ASWSC&CS
Antisubmarine Warfare Ship-Command and Control System

ASWSP
Antisubmarine Warfare Systems Project

ASWSPO, ASWSYSPROJOFC
Antisubmarine Warfare Systems Project Office

ASWSYSPROJOFC, ASWSPO
Antisubmarine Warfare Systems Project Office

ASWTACSCOL
Antisubmarine Warfare Tactical School

ASWTC, ASWTRACEN
Antisubmarine Warfare Training Center

ASWTNS
Antisubmarine Warfare Tactical Navigation System

ASWTRACEN, ASWTC
Antisubmarine Warfare Training Center

ASWTRO
Antisubmarine Warfare Test Requirements Outline

ASWTV
Antisubmarine Warfare Target Vehicle
AT
Acceptance Trials
Air-Tight
Air Transmit
Allowance Type
Assortment (U/I)
Awaiting Transfer
A/T
Action Taken (or Time)
Air Tracker
Anti-Torpedo (nets)
Attack Teacher
A&T
Acceptance and Transfer
AT1
Aviation Electronics Technician First Class
AT2
Aviation Electronics Technician Second Class
AT3
Aviation Electronics Technician Third Class
ATA
Actual Time of Arrival
Administration, Training and Advisor
(courses)
Airport Traffic Area
Auxiliary Ocean Tug
Aviation Training Aids
ATAA
Aviation Electronics Technician Airman
Apprentice
ATAB
Aviation Training Aids Branch
ATAC
Air Transport Advisory Council
ATAD
Absent on Temporary Additional Duty
Air Technical Analysis Division
ATAK, ATK
Attack
ATAN
Aviation Electronics Technician Airman
ATAP
Anti-Tank Armor-Piercing
Anti-Tank Personnel (bomb)
ATB
Aircraft Technical Bulletin
All Trunks Busy
Amphibious Training Base
ATBM
Advanced Tactical Ballistic Missile
ATC
Action Taken Code
Advanced Training Command
Air Training (or Transport) Command
Air Traffic Control
Assistant Trial Counsel
Chief Aviation Electronics Technician
(Mini)-Armored Troop Carrier

ATCA
Altitude Translation and Control Assembly
ATCC
Aircraft Traffic Control Center
ATCE
Ablative Thrust Chamber Engine
ATCH
Armored Troop Carrier (Helicopter)
Attach
ATCLO
Amphibious Training Command Liaison
Officer
ATCO
Aircraft Traffic Control Officer
Air Traffic Coordinating Office
ATCOR
Air Traffic Coordinator
ATCOREU
Air Traffic Coordinator, Europe
ATCORUS
Air Traffic Coordinator, United States
ATCRBS
Air Traffic Control Radar Beacon System
ATCS
Senior Chief Aviation Electronics Technician
ATCSS
Air Traffic Control Signaling System
ATCU
Air Transportable Communications Unit
ATD
Academic Training Division
Actual Time of Departure
Air Turbine Drive
ATDA
Augmented Target Docking Adapter
ATDR
Aeronautical Technical Directive Requirement
ATDS
Airborne (or Air, or Aviation) Tactical Data
System
ATE
Altitude Transmitting Equipment
Automatic Test Equipment
ATEP
Aegis Tactical Executive Program
ATF
Accession Transcription Form
Actual Time of Fall
Air Torpedo-Firing
Amphibious Task Force
Automatic Target Following
Aviation Training Form
Fleet Ocean Tug
ATFOS
Alignment and Test Facility for Optical
Systems
ATG
Amphibious Task Force
ATG/MAB
Amphibious Task Group/Marine Amphibious
Brigade

ATGSB
Admission Test for Graduate Study in
Business
ATHODYD
Aero-Thermo-Dynamic-Duct
ATI
Average Total Inspection
ATIC
Aerospace Technical Intelligence Center
ATIS
Automatic Terminal Information Service
ATJ
Aviation Training Jacket
ATJS
Advanced Tactical Jamming System
ATK, ATAK
Attack
ATKCARAIRWING, CVW
Attack Carrier Air Wing
ATKRON, VA
Attack Squadron
ATKRONDET
Attack Squadron Detachment
ATL
Aeronautical Turbine Laboratory
Awaiting Trial
(Ocean-Going) Tank Landing Craft
ATL, LANT, L
Atlantic
ATLAS
Automatic Tape Load Audit System
ATLD
Air-Transportable Loading Dock
AT/LR
Air Tracker/Long-Range
ATM
Air Turbine Motor
Altimeter Transmitter Multiplier
Atmosphere
Atmospheric Analyzer (system)
ATMP
Air Target Materials Program
ATMU
Aircraft Torpedo Maintenance Unit
ATN
Augmented Transition Network
AT NO
Atomic Number
ATO
Aircraft Transfer Order
Assisted Take-Off
Auxiliary Ocean Tug, Old
ATOLL
Acceptance or Launch Language
ATOM
Astronomical Telescope Orientation Mount
ATOP
Assisted Take-Off System
Automated Traffic Overload Protection

ATP
Acceptance Test Procedure
Allied Tactical Publication
Authority to Proceed
Authorized Test Procedure
ATR
Advanced Tactical Readout
Aircraft Trouble Report
Airline Transport Rating
Attenuated Total Reflectance
Automatic Tape Reader
Aviation Training Record
Rescue Ocean Tug
ATRS
Assembly Test-Recording System
ATS
Administrative Terminal System
Air-to-Ship
Air Traffic Services
Air Transportable Sonar
Air Turbine Starter
Salvage and Rescue Ship
AT/SR
Air Tracker/Short-Range
ATSS
Auxiliary Training Submarine
ATSU
Air Travel Security Unit
ATT
Advanced Technicians Test
ATTC
Aviation Technical Training Center
ATTD
Attitude
Aviation Technical Training Division
ATTN
Attention
ATTNDIR
Attention directed
ATTNINV
Attention invited
ATTNINVRETGUIDE
Attention invited NAVPERS 15891 series,
Navy Guide for Retired Personnel and
Their Families
ATTR
Average Time to Repair
ATTRS
Automatic Tracking Telemetry Receiving
System
ATU
Advanced Training Unit
Amphibious Task Unit
ATV
All-Terrain Vehicle
AT VOL
Atomic Volume
AT WT
Atomic Weight

AU
Air University
Auditor
AU, AUG
August
AUASM
Automatic Aimpoint Selection and
Maintenance
AUDGENNAV
Auditor General of the Navy
AUDIT
Automated Unattended Detection Inspection
Transmitter
AUG
Augment (indicator)
AUG, AU
August
AUGU
Augmenting Unit
AUM
Air-to-Underwater Missile
AUTEC
Atlantic Undersea Test and Evaluation Center
AUTH
Authority
Authorized
AUTHAB
Authorized Abbreviation
AUTHDELPHYSTRANS
If date of arriving port of embarkation as
specified by cognizant transportation office
and reporting date for physical examination
do not agree, authorized to delay in
reporting for physical until such time as will
enable him to arrive at port of embarkation
by specified date.
AUTHEXANDO
Authority granted to execute acceptance and
oath of office for_____.
AUTHGR
Authority granted
AUTHPROBOUT
Authorized to proceed on or about _____.
AUTHTRAV
Authorized to perform such travel via
commercial and/or government
transportation as may be necessary in
proper performance of duties. While
traveling via government air outside
CONUS, Class Three priority is certified.
Cost of this travel chargeable
(appropriation designated).
AUTO
Automatic
AUTODIN
Automatic Digital Network
AUTODIN EMOD
Automatic Digital Network-Evolutionary
Modernization

AUTODIN ICCDP
Automatic Digital Network-Integrated Circuits
Communications Data Processor
AUTOMAD
Automatic Adaption Data
AUTOMET
Automatic Correction of Meteorological
(errors)
AUTOPIC
Automatic Personal Identification Code
AUTOPROPS
Automatic Programming for Positioning
System
AUTOSERVOCOM
Automatic Secure Voice Communications
Network (DCS)
AUTOVON
Automatic Voice Network
AUTOWEAP
Automatic Weapon
AUW
Advanced Underseas Weapon
All Up Weight (gross)
AUWC
Advanced Underseas Weapons Circuitry
AUX
Auxiliary
AV
Seaplane Tender
AV, A/V
Audio-Visual
AV 115/145
Aviation Gas—for Navy/Air Force aircraft
AVAL, AVAIL
Available
AVB
Advance Aviation Base Ship
AVBLTY
Availability
AVC
Automatic Volume Control
Avionics Change
AVCAD
Aviation Cadet
AVCAL
Aviation Consolidated Allowance List
AVCM
Master Chief Avionics Technician
AVCS
Advanced Vidicon Camera System
AVD
Avoirdupois
AVE
Air Vehicle Equipment
AVELECTECH, AV
Aviation Electronics Technician
AVERDISROP
Avert Disruption of Operations
AVF
All-Volunteer Force

AVF PAR
ALL-Volunteer Force Program/Action Request
AVG
Average
AVGAS
Aviation Gasoline
AVH
Aircraft Rescue Boat
AVLB
Armored Vehicle Launched Bridge
AVLD
Acoustic Valve Leak Detector
AVM
Airborne Vibration Monitor
Guided Missile Ship
AVMAINTECH
Aviation Maintenance Technician
AVN
Aviation
AVN(CM)
Aviation Pay (Crewmember)
AVNL
Automatic Video Noise Limiting
AVNMATOLANT
Aviation Material Office, Atlantic
AVNMATORES
Aviation Material Office, Reserve
AVN(NCM)
Aviation Pay (Non-Crewmember)
AVO
Avoid Verbal Orders
AVOIL, AOIL
Aviation Oil
AVOPTECH
Aviation Operations Technician
AVORDTECH
Aviation Ordnance Technician
AVR
Aircraft (or Aviation) Rescue Vessel
AVR, AVTR
Aviator
AVROC
Aviation Reserve Officer Candidate (program)
AVS
Aviation Supply Ship
AVSAT
Aviation Satellite
AVT
Auxiliary Aircraft Landing Training Ship
AVTR, AVR
Aviator
AVVI
Attitude-Vertical Velocity Indicator
AW
Above Water
Airspace Warning (area)
All-Weather
Arc Weld
Armature Winding (wiring)
Automatic Weapons
Distilling Ship

AW1
Aviation Antisubmarine Warfare Operator
First Class
AW2
Aviation Antisubmarine Warfare Operator
Second Class
AW3
Aviation Antisubmarine Warfare Operator
Third Class
AWAA
Aviation Antisubmarine Warfare Operator
Airman Apprentice
AWACS
Airborne Warning and Control System
AWADS
Adverse Weather Aerial Delivery System
AWAN
Aviation Antisubmarine Warfare Operator
Airman
AWARS
Airborne Weather and Reconnaissance
System
AWB
Amphibious Warfare Branch
AWBER
Awaiting Berth(ing)
AWC
Chief Aviation Antisubmarine Warfare
Operator
VAW Airborne Intercept Controller (code)
AWCLS
All-Weather Carrier Landing System
AWCM
Master Chief Aviation Antisubmarine Warfare
Operator
AWCO
Area Wage and Classification Office
AWCREW
Awaiting Crew
AWCS
Automatic Weapons Control System
Senior Chief Aviation Antisubmarine Warfare
Operator
AWDISCH
Awaiting Discharge
AWDO
Air Wing Duty Officer
AWE
Accepted Weight Estimate
VAQ ECM/ESM Evaluator (code)
AWEA
Awaiting Weather
A&WI
Atlantic and West Indies
AWK
Water Tanker
AWL
Absent With Leave
AWLAR
All-Weather Low-Altitude Route

AWLOAD
Awaiting Load(ing)
AWM
Awaiting Maintenance (time)
AWMCS
Aviation Weapons Movement Control System
AWN
Automated Weather Network
AWO
Administrative Watch Officer
AWOC
All-Weather Operations Committee
AWOL
Absent Without Leave
AWORD
Awaiting Orders
AWP
Awaiting Parts
AWRS
Automatic Weapons Release System
AWS
Air Weather Service
Amphibious Warfare School
Aviation Warfare Specialist
AWSAIL
Awaiting Sailing (orders)
AWSD
Air Warfare Systems Development
AWSM
Air Weather Service Manual
AWST
Atomic Weapons Special Transport
AWSTA
All-Weather Station
AWT
Awaiting Trial (by court-martial)
AWTOW
Awaiting Tow
AWY
Airway
AX
Planned Auxiliary, New Construction
AX1
Aviation Antisubmarine Warfare Technician
First Class
AX2
Aviation Antisubmarine Warfare Technician
Second Class
AX3
Aviation Antisubmarine Warfare Technician
Third Class
AXAA
Aviation Antisubmarine Warfare Technician
Airman Apprentice
AXAN
Aviation Antisubmarine Warfare Technician
Airman
AXBT
Airborne Expendable Bathythermograph

AXC
Chief Aviation Antisubmarine Warfare
Technician
AXCS
Senior Chief Aviation Antisubmarine Warfare
Technician
AY
Assembly (U/I)
"Ahoy" (slang)
AZ
Azimuth
AZ1
Aviation Maintenance Administrationman First
Class
AZ2
Aviation Maintenance Administrationman
Second Class
AZ3
Aviation Maintenance Administrationman
Third Class
AZAA
Aviation Maintenance Administrationman
Airman Apprentice
AZAN
Aviation Maintenance Administrationman
Airman
AZC
Chief Aviation Maintenance
Administrationman
AZCM
Master Chief Aviation Maintenance
Administrationman
AZCS
Senior Chief Aviation Maintenance
Administrationman

B

B
Biennial (report frequency)
Boiler
Bombardier-Navigator (NAO code)
BA
Ball (U/I)
Breaks Above
Budget Activity
B&A
Bond and Allotment (system)
B/A
Breaking Action
BAAM
Basic Administration and Management
(program)
BABS
Beam Approach Beacon System (radar)
BACE
Basic Automatic Check Equipment
BADC
Binary Asymmetric Dependent Channel

BADG
Battle Group Anti-Air Warfare Display
BADGE
Base Air Defense Ground Environment
BAGAIR
(number of pounds indicated) baggage to accompany authorized for air travel outside CONUS
BAI
Bearing-Range Indicator
BAIC
Binary Asymmetric Independent Channel
BAKS, BKS
Barracks
BAL
Balance
Ballistics
Boats and Landing Craft
BALDNY
Ballistic Density
BALLUTES
Balloon-Parachutes
BALWND
Ballistic Wind
BAMBI
Ballistic Missile Boost Intercept
BAMP
Basic Analysis and Mapping Program
BANAVAVNOFFSCOL, BANO
Basic Naval Aviation Officers School
BAQ
Basic Allowance for Quarters
BAQ(AC)
Basic Allowance for Quarters for Adopted Child(ren)
BAQ(DISRET)
Basic Allowance for Quarters Pending Disability Retirement
BAQ(F)
Basic Allowance for Quarters for Father
BAQ(H)
Basic Allowance for Quarters for Husband
BAQ(LC)
Basic Allowance for Quarters for Legitimate Child(ren)
BAQ(M)
Basic Allowance for Quarters for Mother
BAQ(SC)
Basic Allowance for Quarters for Stepchild(ren)
BAQ(W)
Basic Allowance for Quarters for Wife
BAR
Browning Automatic Rifle
BARCAP
Barrier Combat Air Patrol
BARO, BRM
Barometer
BARSTUR
Barking Sands Tactical Underwater Range

BAS
Basic Airspeed
Basic Allowance for Subsistence
Bleed Air System
Bomb Assembly Spares
BAS-BR
Basic Branch Training (course)
BASEOPS
Base Operations
BASIC
Battle Area Surveillance and Integrated Communications
Beginners All-Purpose Symbolic Instruction Code
BASICPAC
Basic Processor and Computer
BAT
Basic Air Temperature
BAT, BB
Battleship
BAT, BN
Battalion
BATDIV
Battleship Division
BATFOR
Battleship Force
BATS
Ballistic Aerial Target System
BATT EFF PRIZE
Battle Efficiency Prize
BAYONGRP
Bayonne (NJ) Group
BB
Back-to-Back
Bottom Bounce
Breaks Below
BB, BAT
Battleship
B/B
Baby Incendiary Bomb
BBB
Basic Boxed Base
BBC
Boiler Blower Control
BBC, BC
Bareboat Charter
BBG
Guided Missile Capital Ship
BBH
Battalion Beachhead
BBL, BL, BRL
Barrel
BC
Back Course (approach)
Bathyconductograph
Battery Commander
Blind Copy
Block (U/I)
Body Count
Bolt Circle
Bottom Contour

BC, BBC
Bareboat Charter
BCC
Basic Cryptanalysis Course
BCD
Binary Coded Decimal
BCD, DISCH(BCD)
Bad Conduct Discharge
BCDD
Base Construction Depot Detachment
BCH
Beach
BCM
Become
Beyond Capability of Maintenance
BCN
Beacon
Bureau Control Number
BCP
Ballast Control Panel
Basic Control Program
BCST
Broadcast
BCU
Ballistics Computer Unit
BD
Blowing Dust (weather symbol)
Board
Bomb Disposal
Bundle (U/I)
BD, BDL
Bundle
BDA
Battle (or Bomb) Damage Assessment
BDC
Bottom Dead Center
BDCNR
Board of Correction for Naval Records
BDE, BRIG
Brigade
BDGC
Bad Conduct Discharge, General
Court-Martial after Confinement in Prison
BDGI
Bad Conduct Discharge, General
Court-Martial Immediate
BDGP
Bad Conduct Discharge, General
Court-Martial after Violation of Probation
BDHI
Bearing-Distance-Heading Indicator
BDI
Bearing Deviation Indicator
BDL
Baseline Demonstration Laser
Beach Discharge Lighter
BDL, BD
Bundle
BDM
Bomber Defense Missile

BDP
Base Development Planning
BDRY
Boundary
BDSI
Bad Conduct Discharge, Sentence of
Summary Court-Martial, Immediate
BDSP
Bad Conduct Discharge, Summary
Court-Martial after Violation of Probation
BDU
Bomb Dummy Unit
BE
Bale (U/I)
Base-Emitter
Beginning Event
Bombing Encyclopedia
BECO
Booster Engine Cut-Off
BED
Boat Engineering Department
BE/E
Basic Electricity and Electronics (course)
BE/E INLS
Basic Electricity and Electronics
Individualized Learning System
BEER
Battery Exhaust Emergency Recirculation
BEES
Basic Electricity and Electronics School
BEF
Blunt End Forward
BEGR
Bore Erosion Gauge Reading
BEHSTU
Behavioral Skill Training Unit
BEIP
Boiler Efficiency Improvement Program
BEL
Bureau Equipment List
BEM
Back Emergency (speed)
BEMAR
Backlog of Essential Maintenance and Repair
BEMO
Bare Equipment Modernization Officers
BENEF
Beneficiary
BENG
Basic Engineering
BENNY SUGG, BEN SUG, BENNY SUGGS
Beneficial Suggestion (program)
BEOG
Basic Educational Opportunity Grant
BEQ
Bachelor Enlisted Quarters
BERSEAPAT
Bering Sea Patrol
BERSL
Behavioral Sciences Research Laboratory

BESS
Bottom Environmental Sensing System
BEST
Basic Electronics Training (program)
Behavioral Skill Training
BETS
Bullseye Engineering and Technical Services
BF
Back Full (speed)
Board Foot (U/I)
Boat Foreman
Brazed Joint-Face Fed
Brought Forward
BFD
"Big Fatal Disease" (slang)
BFDK
Before Dark
BFE
Battlefield Exercise
BFL
Bill of Lading
Bomb Fall Line
BFR
Before
Briefer
BFRL
Basic Facilities Requirements List
BFWTT
Boilerwater/Feedwater Test and Treatment
BG
Bag (U/I)
Battle Group
BGM
Basegram
BGN
Begin
BGPP
Beneficiary Government Production Program
BGRV
Boost Glide Reentry Vehicle
BH
Bunch (U/I)
BHD
Bulkhead
BHN
Brinell Hardness Number (for metals)
BHND
Behind
BHP
Brake Horsepower
BHQ
Brigade Headquarters
BI
Background Investigation
Biographical (or Biological) Inventory
Block-In
Brick (U/I)
BIFF
Battlefield Identification-Friend or Foe

BIM
Basic Industrial Materials (program)
Beacon Identification Methods
Blade Inspection Method
BINOVC
Breaks in Overcast
BIO
Branch Intelligence Officer
BIOPAC
Biological Packs
BIPAD
Binary Pattern Detector
BIPP
Briefings/Issues/Projects/Programs
BIRDCAP
Rescue Aircraft Combat Air Patrol
BIRDIE
Battery Integration and Radar Display
Equipment
BIRO
Base Industrial Relations Office(r)
BIS
Bibliographic Information Sheet
Board of Inspection and Survey
BIST
Built-In Self-Test
BISTEP
Binary System
BIT
Binary Digit
Built-In Test
BITE
Built-In Test Equipment
BJM
Bluejackets' Manual, The (USNI book)
BJN
Basic Jet Navigation
BJU
Beach Jumper Unit
BK
Book (U/I)
Yardarm Blinker
BKS, BAKS
Barracks
BKT
Blinker Tube
BKW
Breakwater
BL
Base Line
Blank
Bomb Line
BL, BBL, BRL
Barrel (U/I)
B/L, BLADING
Bill of Lading
BLADING, B/L
Bill of Lading
BLC
Boundary Layer Control

BLD
  Build
BLEU
  Blind Landing Experimental Unit
BLIN
  BIT Light Inspection
BLIS
  Base Level Inquiry System
BLKD
  Blocked
BLO
  Below
  Bombardment Liaison Officer
BLP
  Bombing Landplane
BL&P
  Blind-Loaded and Plugged (projectile)
BLS
  Base Loading System
BLT
  Battalion Landing Team
BL&T
  Blind-Loaded and Traced (projectile)
BLU
  Bomb, Live Unit
BLUE
  Best Linear Unbiased Estimation
BM
  Back Marker
  Battle Manning
  Bench Mark
BM1
  Boatswain's Mate First Class
BM2
  Boatswain's Mate Second Class
BM3
  Boatswain's Mate Third Class
B/M, BMAT
  Bill of Material
BMA
  Basic Maintenance Allowance (for clothing)
BMAA
  Barracks Master-at-Arms
BMAC
  Computerized Automatic Test Bench
BMC
  Chief Boatswain's Mate
BMCM
  Master Chief Boatswain's Mate
BMCS
  Senior Chief Boatswain's Mate
BMD
  Ballistic Missile Defense
  Base Maintenance Division
BMEP
  Brake Mean Effective Pressure
BMEWS
  Ballistic Missile Early Warning System
BMG
  Browning Machine Gun

BMJ
  Basic Military Journalist (DINFOS course)
BMNT
  Beginning of Morning Nautical Twilight
BMOW
  Boatswain's Mate-of-the-Watch
BMR
  Basic Military Requirements
  Beachmaster
  Bomber
  River Monitor
BMRL
  Small River Monitor
BMS
  Ballistic Missile Ship
BMSA
  Boatswain's Mate Seaman Apprentice
BMSN
  Boatswain's Mate Seaman
BMU
  Beachmaster Unit
BN
  Bombardier Navigator
  Bombing/Navigator
BN, BAT
  Battalion
BNAO, BANAVAVNOFFSCOL
  Basic Naval Aviation Officers School
BN-CP
  Battalion Command Post
BNDRY, BNDY
  Boundary
BNDY, BNDRY
  Boundary
BNEP
  Basic Naval Establishment Plan
BNTH
  Beneath
BO
  Back Order(ed)
  Base Order
  Black-Out
  Block-Out
  Buyer's Option
BOA
  Basic Ordering Agreement
  Break-Off Altitude
BOA-MILS
  Broad Ocean Area Missile Impact Locating
    System
BOATSUPPU
  Boat Support Unit
BOB
  Barge on Board
  Branch Office, Boston (ONR)
  Bureau of the Budget
BOC
  Billet Occupational Code
  Branch Office, Chicago (ONR)

BOD
Basic Operational Data
Beneficiary Occupancy Date
B OF R
Board of Review
BOH
Break-Off Height
BOI
Boiler
BOL
Branch Office, London (ONR)
BOM
Bill of Material
Bomb
By Other Means
BOMEX
Barbados Oceanographic and Meteorological
Experiment
BOMID
Branch Office, Military Intelligence Division
BOOST
Broadened Opportunity for Officer Selection
and Training
BOOW
Battalion Officer-of-the-Watch
BOP
Blow-Out Preventer
Branch Office, Pasadena (ONR)
BOQ
Bachelor Officers Quarters
BO REL
Back Order Release
BORU
Boat Operating and Repair Unit
BOS
Base Operating Support
Basic Operating System
BOSN
Boatswain
BOSS-WEDGE
Bomb Orbital Strategic System-Weapon
Development Glide Entry
BOSTONSARCOORD
Coast Guard Search and Rescue
Coordinator, Boston (MA)
BOT
Beginning of Tape
Bottom
BP
Base (or Basic) Pay
Bolt (U/I)
Brazed Joint-Preinserted Ring
Budget Project(s)
B&P
Bidding and Proposal (effort)
BPA
Basic Pressure Altitude
Blanket Purchase Agreement (or Authority)
Blocked Precedence Announcement
BPB
Base Planning Board

BPD
Barrels per Day
BPDLS
Base Point Defense Launching System
BPDSMS
Base Point Defense Surface Missile System
BPED
Base Pay Entry Date—also PEBD
BPN
Bureau (or Budget) Project Number
BPO
Barracks Petty Officer
Base Post Office
Blood Program Office
Budget Project Officer
BPPG
Bureau Planned Procurement Guide
BPR
Bridge Plotting Room
BPS
Bits per Second (computer printout)
B&Q
Barracks and Quarters
BQC
Basic Qualification Course
BR
Back Reflection
Bar (U/I)
Bomber Reconnaissance (aircraft)
Breeder Reactor
Briefing Room
BR1
Boilermaker First Class
BRA
Bench Replaceable Assembly
BRAS
Ballistic Rocket Air Suppression
BRASO
Branch Aviation Supply Office
BRASS
Ballistic Range for Aircraft Survivability
Studies
BRC
Base Recovery Course
Chief Boilermaker
BR&CL
Branch and Class
BRCM
Master Chief Boilermaker
BRCS
Senior Chief Boilermaker
BRD
Underwater Mobile Submarine Radio
Detection Finder
BRF
Brief
BRFA
Boilermaker Fireman Apprentice
BRFN
Boilermaker Fireman

BRG
  Bearing
  Bridge
BRIG, BDGE
  Brigade
BRINSMAT
  Branch Officer, Inspector of Naval Material
BRIT
  Britain
  British
BRITE
  Bright Radar Indicator Tower Equipment
BRK, BT
  Break
BRKN
  Broken
BRL
  Ballistic Research Laboratory
  Bomb Release Line
  Boresight Reference Line
BRL, BBL, BL
  Barrel
BRL/EEP
  Bomb Release Line/End Exercise Point
BRM, BARO
  Barometer
BRNAVCOMMSTO
  Branch Navy Commissary Store
BRR
  Brigade Receiving Room
BR/RL
  Bomb Rack/Rocket Launcher
BRT
  Bright
BRU
  Boat Repair Unit
BRUSA
  British-United States Agreement
BS
  Backsight
  Blowing Sand (weather symbol)
  Bound Seam
  Broadcast Station
BSA
  Base Structure Annex
BSC
  Billet Sequence Code
  Broadcast Specialist Course (DINFOS)
BSD
  Biological Sciences Division (ONR)
BSDC
  Binary Symmetric Dependent Channel
BSIC
  Binary Symmetric Independent Channel
BSO
  Base Supply Officer
  Bomb Safety Office
BSP
  Billet Selection Program
BSQ
  Bachelor Staff Quarters

BST
  Bonded Spoon Type
BSU
  Base Service Unit
  Beach Support Unit
  Boat Support Unit
BT
  Ballistic Trajectory
  Bathythermograph
  Beam-riding Terrier (missile)
  Begin Tape
  Berth Term
  Bottle (U/I)
BT, BRK
  Break
BT1
  Boilerman Technician First Class
BT2
  Boilerman Technician Second Class
BT3
  Boilerman Technician Third Class
BTB
  Basic Test Battery
  Bomb Thermal Battery
BTC
  Chief Boilerman Technician
BTCM
  Master Chief Boilerman Technician
BTCS
  Senior Chief Boilerman Technician
BTDCPF
  Bathythermograph Data Collecting and
    Processing Facility
BTDPAF
  Bathythermograph Data Processing and
    Analysis Facility
BTE
  Battery Terminal Equipment
BTFA
  Boilerman Technician Fireman Apprentice
BTFN
  Boilerman Technician Fireman
BTL
  Beginning of Tape Level
BTM
  Bench, Missile Test
  Blast Test Missile
BTN, BTWN
  Between
BTR
  Better
BTRY, BTY
  Battery
BTU
  British Thermal Unit
BTU/HR
  British Thermal Unit per Hour
BTV
  Blast Test Vehicle
BTWN, BTN
  Between

BTY, BTRY
Battery
BU
Buoy Boat (USCG)
Bushel (U/I)
BU, BUR
Bureau
BU, B/U
Back-Up
BU1
Builder First Class
BU2
Builder Second Class
BU3
Builder Third Class
BUC
Chief Builder
BUCA
Builder Construction Apprentice
BUCN
Builder Constructionman
BUCS
Senior Chief Builder
BUD
Budget
BUD/S
Basic UDT/SEAL (training)
BUIC
Back-Up Intercept Control
BUL
Bulletin
BUMED, BUM&S, M&S
Bureau of Medicine and Surgery
BUM&S, BUMED, M&S
Bureau of Medicine and Surgery
BUNO
Bureau Number
BUPS
Beacon, Ultra-Portable "S" (band)
BUR, BU
Bureau
BUSH
Buy U.S. Here (contracts)
BUSL
Buoy Boat, Stern-Loading (USCG)
BUWC
Basic Underseas Weapons Circuit
BVE
Binocular Visual Efficiency
BVP
Beacon Video Processor
BVPS
Beacon Video Processing System
BW
Below Water
Biological Warfare
Butt Weld
B&W
Black and White
Bread and Water

BWAR
Budget Workload Analysis Report
B/WCC
Bomb to Warhead Conversion Components
BW/CW
Biological Warfare/Chemical Warfare
BW/FWT&TT
Boiler Water/Feedwater Test and Treatment
Training
B&WHB
Black and White Horizontal Bands (buoy
markings)
BWO
Backward Wave Oscillator
BWPA
Backward Wave Power Amplifier
BWR
Boiler Water Reactor
BWVB
Black and White Vertical Bands (buoy
markings)
BX
Box (U/I)
BY
Budget Year
BZI
Beam Zero Indication

C

C
Can (or Cylinder) (buoy)
Circling
Clear (weather symbol)
Controlled
Controller (NAO code)
C, CON, CONF
Confidential
C³
Command and Control Communications
CA
Civil Authorities
Closest Approach (NNSS)
Commercial Activity
Commercially Available
Compartment and Access (plan)
Construction Apprentice
Container Agreement
Contract Administration
Convening Authority
Cumulative Amount
Current Address
Heavy Cruiser
CA, CART
Cartridge (U/I)
C/A
Civic Action
Contract Administration

CAAC
Counseling and Assistance Center
CAAD
Counseling and Assistance Director
CAAR
Compressed Air Accumulator Rocket
CAB
Captured Air Bubble (boat)
Centralized Accounting and Billeting
CAC
Climate-Altitude Chamber
Combat Air Crew
Combined Action Company
Commander Air Center
Contact Area Commander
Contract Administration Control
Cost Account(ing) Code
CAC/FHS
Casualty Assistance Calls and Funeral
Honors Support (program)
CACHE
Computer-Controlled Automated Cargo
Handling Envelope
CACO
Casualty Assistance Calls Officer
CACP
Casualty Assistance Calls Program
CASS
Core Auxiliary Cooling System (reactors)
CAC&W
Continental Aircraft Control and Warning
CAD
Cartridge-Actuated Device
Central Accounts Division
Central Aircraft Dispatch
Civic Action Detachment
Civil Affairs Division
Computer Address Decoder (NNSS)
Computer-Aided Design(ing)
Contract Award Date
CADC
Central Air Data Computer
Combined Administrative Committee
Computer-Aided Design Council
CADD
Combat Zone, Additional Withholding Tax
Current Active Duty Date
CADFISS
Computation and Data Flow Integrated
Subsystem
CADIZ
Canadian Air Defense Identification Zone
CADM
Configuration and Data Management
CADNC
Computer-Aided Design and Numerical
Control
CADPO
Communications and Data Processing
Operation

CADRC
Combined Air Documents Research Center
CADRE
Completed Active Duty Requirements,
Enlisted
CAE
Computer-Assisted Enrollment
CAF
Clerical, Administrative and Fiscal
Combined Action Forces
Completed Assembly for Ferry
Contract Administration Functions
CAFAF
Commander Amphibious Forces, Atlantic
Fleet
CAFPF
Commander Amphibious Forces, Pacific Fleet
CAFSU
Carrier and Field Service Unit
CAFT
Consolidated Advance Field Team
CAG
Carrier Air Group
Catapult and Arresting Gear
Civil Affairs Group
Combined Action Group
CAGO
Cargo Apparent Good Order
CAI
Computer-Assisted Instruction
CAIC
Computer-Assisted Instruction Center
CAIG
Cost Analysis Improvement Group
CAIMS
Conventional Ammunition Integrated
Management System
CAINS
Carrier Aircraft Inertial Navigation System
CAIRC
Caribbean Air Command
CAL
Caliber
Confined Area Loading
CALIBR
Calibration
CALS
Communications Area Local Station
Computer Lesson Service
CAM
Channel Access Module
Computer-Aided Manufacturing
Content Addressable Memory
Contract Audit Manual (DCAA)
Cybernetic Anthropomorphous Machine
CAMAL
Continuous Airborne Missile-Launched and
Low-Level (system)
CAMAS
Computer-Assisted Manpower Analyses
System

CAMEL
Critical Aeronautical Material/Equipment List
CAMI
Continuing Action Maintenance Instructions
CAMP
Computer-Aided Mask Preparation
Computer Applications of Military Problems
CAMS
Commissioning Assession Management
System
Communications Area Master Station
CAMSI
Canadian, American Merchant Shipping
Instructions
Carrier Aircraft Maintenance Support
Improvement (program)
CAN
Canister
CANDR, C&R
Convoy and Routing
CANEL
Connecticut Advanced Nuclear Engineering
Laboratory (NEC)
CANTRAC
Catalog of Naval Training Courses
CAN-UK-US
Canadian-United Kingdom-United States
CAO
Change of Administrative Office
Civil Affairs Officer
Collateral Action Office(r)
Contract Administration Office
CAOC
Counter Air Operations Center
CAORF
Computer-Aided Operations Research Facility
CAOS
Completely Automatic Operational System
CAP
Capsule
Civil (or Combat) Air Patrol
Combined Action Platoon (or Program)
Command Action (or Advancement) Program
Communications Afloat Program
Contract Administration Office
Contractor Assessment Program
Coriolis Acceleration Platform
Corrective Action Program
Current Assessment Plan
CAP, CPTR
Capture
CAPCHE
Component Automatic Programmed Checkout
Equipment
CAPCP
Civil Air Patrol Coastal Patrol
CAPDET
Commercial Activities Program Detachment
CAPDETREGOFF
Commerical Activities Program Detachment
Regional Office

CAPE
Capability and Proficiency Evaluation
Communications Automatic Processing
Equipment
CAPPI
Constant-Altitude Plan-Position Indicator
CAPRI
Compact All-Purpose Range Instrumentation
Computerized Advance Personnel
Requirements Information (system)
CAPSQ-N
Capital Area Personnel Services Office-Navy
CAPT
Captain
CAPTOR
Encapsulated Torpedo (mine)
CAPUC
Coordinating Area Production Urgency
Committee
CAPWSK
Collision Avoidance, Proximity Warning,
Station-Keeping (equipment)
CAR
Caribbean (regional area)
Carrier
Cloudtop Altitude Radiometer
Combat Action Ribbon
Configuration Audit Review
CARAEWRON
Carrier Airborne Early Warning Squadron
CARAEWTRARON
Carrier Airborne Early Warning Training
Squadron
CARAIRSUPPDET, CASD
Carrier Air Support Detachment
CARAM
Content Addressable Random Access
Memory
**CARANTISUBAIRGRU, CARASWAIRGRU,
CVSG**
Carrier Antisubmarine Warfare Air Group
CARANTISUBGRU
Carrier Antisubmarine Warfare Group
CARASGRURES
Reserve Carrier Antisubmarine Group
**CARASWAIRGRU, CVSG,
CARANTISUBAIRGRU**
Carrier Antisubmarine Warfare Air Group
CARB
Carburetor
CARBAGAIR
Baggage for air cargo
CARBASORD
Carry out remainder of basic orders
CARBSEAFRON, CSF, CARIBSEAFRON
Caribbean Sea Frontier
CARDIV
Carrier Division
CARE
Cause and Removal Error

CAREPAY
Centralized Automated Reserve Pay (system)
CARF
Central Altitude Reservation Facility
CARGO
Consolidated Afloat Requisitioning Guide
CARIB
Caribbean (Sea)
CARIBDIV
Caribbean Division
CARIBSEAFRON, CSF, CARBSEAFRON
Caribbean Sea Frontier
CARINFRO
Career Information
CARINFOCEN
Career Information Center
CARP
Carpenter
Computer Air-Release Point
CARQUALS
Carrier Qualifications
CARS
Country, Area or Regional Specialist
CARSO
Country, Area or Regional Staff Officer
CART
Central Automated Replenish Technique
Central Automatic Reliability Tester
Combat-Ready Training
CART, CT
Cartridge
CARTASKFOR, CTF
Carrier Task Force
CARTU
Combat Aircrew Refresher Training
CAS
Calculated Airspeed
Carrier (or Close) Air Support
Casualty
Civil Affairs Section
Collision Avoidance System
Combined Antenna System
Completely Assembled for Strike
Contract Administration Services
Controlled American Source
Cost Accounting Standards
CASA, COMANTARCTICSUPPACT
Commander Antarctic Support Activities
CASB
Cost Accounting Standards Board
CASCAN
Casualty Cancelled
CASCON
Casualty Control Station
CASCOR
Casualty Correction Report
CASCP
Caribbean Area Small Craft Project
CASCU
Commander Aircraft Support Control Unit

CASD, CARAIRSUPPDET
Carrier Aircraft Support Detachment
CASD, CASDIV
Carrier Aircraft Services Division
CASDAC, CASDEC
Computer-Aided Ship Design and
Construction (procedure)
CASDIV, CASD
Carrier Aircraft Services Division
CASDO
Computer Application Support and
Development Office
CASDS
Computer-Aided Ship Design of Ships
Computer-Aided Structural Detailing of Ships
CASE
Commission on the Accreditation of Service
Experience
Computer-Aided System Evaluation
Counter-Agency for Sabotage and Espionage
CASEVAC
Casualty-Evacuee
CASEX
Casualty Exercise
CASINFOSUPPSYS, CISS
Casualty Information Support System
CASOFF
Control and Surveillance of Friendly Forces
CASP
Computer-Assisted Search Planning
CASPER
Contact Area Summary Position Report
CASREP
Casualty Summary Report
CASS
Carrier Aircraft Support Study
Central Automated Support System
Command Active Sonobuoy System
CAST
Computerized Automatic Systems Tester
CASU
Carrier Aircraft Service Unit
CASU(F)
Combat Aircraft Service Unit (Fleet)
CASUM
Civil Affairs Summary
CASWO
Confidential and Secret Weekly Orders
CAT
Carburetor Air Temperature
Cartridge Assembly Test
Catapult
Category
Civic (or Crisis) Action Team
Clear Air Turbulence
Collect and Transmit
Combined Acceptance Trials
Compute of Average Transients
CATCC
Carrier Air Traffic Control Center

CATCO
Carrier Air Traffic Control Officer
CATF
Commander Amphibious Task Force
CATG
Commander Amphibious Task Group
CATO
Computer for Automatic Teaching Operations
Cycloidal Activities in Two Oceans
CATOCOMP
Computer for Automatic Teaching
Operations-Compiler
CATORES
Computer for Automatic Teaching
Operations-Resident (program)
CATS
Centralized Automatic Test System
Civil Affairs Training School
Communications and Tracking System
CATT
Controlled Avalance Transit Time
CATU
Combat Aircrew Training Unit
CAVCO
Consolidated Audio-Visual Coordinating
Office
CAVE
Consolidated Aquanaut Vital Equipment
CAVT
Constant Absolute Vorticity Trajectories
CAVU
Ceiling and Visibility Unlimited
CAX
Cheltenham Annex
CAW
Carrier Air Wing
Computer-Assisted War (slang)
CAWEX
Conventional Air Warfare Exercise
CB
Carbuoy (U/I)
Center of Buoyancy
Citizen's Band (radio)
Circuit Breaker
Collector-Base
Common Battery
Crash Boat
Crew Boat (USCG)
Cumulonimbus (cloud formation)
CB, SEABEE, CBN
Construction Battalion
CBA
Classified by Association
CBALS
Carrier-Borne Air Liaison Section
CBC
Construction Battalion Center
Contraband Control
Large Tactical Command Ship

CBCMIS
Construction Battalion Center Management
Information System
CBD, CBNDET
Construction Battalion Detachment
CBL
Cable Length
Central Bidder's List
CBL, CMBL
Commercial Bill of Lading
CBLO
Chief Bombardment Liaison Officer
CBLS
Carrier-Borne Air Liaison Officer
CBMU
Construction Battalion Maintenance Unit
CBMUDET
Construction Battalion Maintenance Unit
Detachment
CBN
Cabin
Carbine
CBN, CB, SEABEE
Construction Battalion
CBNDET, CBD
Construction Battalion Detachment
CBO
Coding Board Officer
CBR
Chemical-Bacteriological- (or Biological-)
Radiological
CBRD
Construction Battalion Replacement Depot
CBRP
Chemical, Biological and Radiological
Protection
CBT
Clinical Laboratory Technician
Combat
CBTENGRBN
Combat Engineer Battalion
CBU
Cluster-Bomb Unit
Contact Back-Up
CC
Caption Code
Card Column
Cirrocumulus (cloud formation)
Combat Command
Command Ship
Communications Controls
Company Commander
Computer Communications
Condition Code
Construction Corps
Control Center (or Console)
Correspondence Course
Cost Center
Cubic Centimeter
Cushion Craft
Sea Sea (undersea craft)

C/C
Change of Course
C&C
Command and Control
Communications and Control
CCA
Carrier-Controlled Approach
Circuit Court of Appeals
Configuration Change Actions
CCAC
Combined Civil Affairs Committee
CCAC/L
Combined Civil Affairs Committee-London
CCAC/S
Combined Civil Affairs Committee-Supply
(subcommittee)
CCAEP
Computer-Controlled Action Entry Panel
CCAM
Computer Communications Access Method
CCAO
Chief Civil Affairs Officer (U.S.-Britain)
CCAP
Conventional Circuit Analysis Program
CCB
Change (or Configuration) Control Board
Combined Communications Board
Command and Control Boat
Contraband Control Base
Contract Change Board
CCBD
Configuration Control Board Directive
CCBP
Combined Communications Board
Publications
CCD
Central Commissioning Detail
Charge-Coupled Device
Commander Cruiser-Destroyer (Force)
Contract Change Directive
CCDB
Contractor's Control Data Bank
CCDR
Contractor Cost Data Reporting
CCEM
Component Control Expeditor Unit
CCF
Combined Cadet Force
Component Characteristic File
Configuration Control File (or Form)
CCGD
Commander Coast Guard District
CCGI
Commodity Coordinated Group Items
CCI
Carrier-Controlled Intercept
CCIS
Command Control Information System
CCIU
Component Control Issue Unit

CCL
Communications Circular Letter
Communications Control Link
Compartment Check-off List
Convective Condensation Level
CCM
Combined Cipher (or Coding) Machine
Constant Current Modulation
Controlled Carrier Modulation
Counter-Countermeasures
CCMA
Civilian Clothing Maintenance Allowance
CCMC
(Navy) Civilian Career Management Center
CCMU
Commander's Control and Monitoring Unit
CCN
Contract Change Notice (or Notification)
CCO
Combat Cargo Officer
Commercial Contracting Officer
Contract Change Order
CCOPS
Coordination and Control of Personnel
Surveys (system)
CCP
Cross-Check Procedure
CCPO
Consolidated (or Centralized) Civilian
Personnel Office
CCPOFD
Consolidated Civilian Personnel Office Field
Division
CCR
Capital Commitment Request
Closed-Circuit Radio
Coastal Confluence Region
Current Control Relay
CCRS
Computer-Controlled Receiving System
CCS
Combined Chiefs of Staff
Component Control Section
Contract Change System
C&CS
Communications and Control Subsystem
CCSB
Change Control Sub-Board
CCSC
Civil Affairs Staff Center
CCSD
Command Communications Service
Designator
CCSF, COMCARIBSEAFRON
Commander Caribbean Sea Frontier
CCSP
Contractor Claims Settlement Program
CCSS
Command and Control Shore Station

CCT
Coated Cargo Tanks (tankers)
Combined Cortical Thickness
Communications Control Team
Comprehensive College Test
CCTS
Combat Crew Training Squadron
CCTV
Closed-Circuit Television
CCU
Component Control Unit
CD
Camouflage Detection (film)
Card Distribution
Certification Data (sheets)
Classification of Defects
Code
Cold Drawn (steel)
Confidential Document
Conning Director
CD, CONDEF
Contract Definition
C/D
Correction/Discrepancy
C&D
Cover and Deception
C²D², CCDD
Command and Control Development Division
CDA
Command and Data Acquisition (station)
CDAS
Catapult Data Acquisition System
CDC
Caribbean Defense Command
Classification Document Control
Command and Data-Handling Console
Common Distributable Changes
Contract Definition Concept
Control Data Center
Credit Code
CDCE
Command Disaster Control Element
CDCF
Command Disaster Control Force
CDCG
Command Disaster Control Group
CDD
Certification of Disability for Discharge
CDDL, COMCRUDESLANT
Commander Cruiser-Destroyer Force, Atlantic
CDDMAN
Cruiser-Destroyerman (publication)
CDDP, COMCRUDESPAC
Command Cruiser-Destroyer Force, Pacific
CDE
Disaster Control Element
CDF
Class Determinations and Findings
Controlled Detonating Fuze

CDI
Classification Document Index (system)
Collateral Duty Inspector
Course Deviation Indicator
CDIS
Commandant, Defense Intelligence School
CDO
Central Disbursing Officer
Command Duty Officer
CDOG
Combat Development Objective Guide
CDONSA
Coordinator, Department of the Navy Studies and Analyses
CDOVHL
Crash Damage Overhead
CDP
Career Development Program
Communications Data Processor
Compressor Discharge Pressure
Configuration Data Package
Contract Definition Phase
Cost Data Plan
Customer Dividend Program
CDPG
Commander Disaster Preparedness Group
CDPI
Customer Dividend Program Indentification
CDPS
Communications Data Processing System
CDQCP
Civil Defense Quality Check Program
CDR
Complete Design Release
Configuration Data Requirements
Critical Design Review
CDR, COM, COMDR
Commander
CDRC
Computation and Data Reduction Center
CDRE, COMO, COMMO
Commodore
CDRJPAA
Commander Joint Military Postal Activity, Atlantic
CDRJPAALANT
Commander Joint Military Postal Activity, Atlantic
CDRJTE
Commander Joint Task Element
CDRL
Contractor Data Requirement List
CDS
Central (or Control) Distribution System (publications)
Construction Differential Subsidies
CDS, COMDESRON
Commander Destroyer Squadron
CDTC
Computer Detector Test Console

CDT&E
Contractor Development Test and Evaluation
CD/TPP
Contract Definition/Total Package
Procurement
CDW
Collision Damage Waiver (adjustment)
CDX
Central Differential Transmitter
CE
Center of Effort
Chief Engineer
Civilian (or Commercial) Enterprise
(publication)
Collector-Emitter
Common Era
Cone (U/I)
Cost-Effectiveness
CE1
Construction Electrician First Class
CE2
Construction Electrician Second Class
CE3
Construction Electrician Third Class
C&E
Communications and Electronics
C/E
Components/Equipment
CEARP
Continuing Education Approval and
Recognition Program
CEB
CNO Executive Board
CEC
Centralized Electronic Control
Chief Construction Electrician
Civil Engineer Corps
CECA
Construction Electrician Construction
Apprentice
CEC EIT
Civil Engineer Corps, Engineer-in-Training
CECN
Construction Electrician Constructionman
CECOFFSCOL, CECOS
Civil Engineer Corps Officer's School
CECOS, CECOFFSCOL
Civil Engineer Corps Officers' School
CECP
College Extension Course Program
CEC PE
Civil Engineer Corps, Professional Engineer
CEC RA
Civil Engineer Corps, Registered Architect
CECS
Senior Chief Construction Electrician
CED
Communications Engineering Department
Current Enlistment Date
CEE
Combat Emplacement Excavator

CEF
Captain, Escort Forces
CEGARS
Combined Entry Guidance and Attitude
Reference System
CEI
Communications-Electronics Instructions
Curriculum Evaluation and Improvement
CEIL, CIG
Ceiling
CEIP
Communications-Electronics Implementation
Plan
CEIS
Candidate Environmental Impact Statement
Cost and Economic Information System
CELSCOPE
Celestial Telescope
CEMB
Civilian Executive Management Board
CEN
Cultural Expression in the Navy (workshop)
CEN, CENTRL
Central
CEN, CTR, CNTR
Center
CENDRAFTO
Central Drafting Officer
CENOMISO
Central Naval Ordnance Management
Information System Office
CENPACSARCOORD
Coast Guard Search and Rescue
Coordinator, Central Pacific
CENRIVSARCOORD
Coast Guard Search and Rescue
Coordinator, Central Rivers
CENTCOM
Central Pacific Communications Instructions
CENTRA
Centralized Training Material Management
CEO
Casualty Evacuation Officer
CEOINC
Civil Engineer Officer-in-Charge
CEP
CNO Executive Panel
Common Electronic Parts
CEP, CIREP
Circular Error Probable (or Probability)
CEP1
Construction Electrician P (Power) First Class
CEP2
Construction Electrician P (Power) Second
Class
CEP3
Construction Electrician P (Power) Third
Class
CEPCA
Construction Electrician P (Power)
Construction Apprentice

CEPCN
Construction Electrician P (Power)
Constructionman

CEQC
COMNAVMAR Environmental Quality Control

CER
Complete Engine Repair
Complete Engineering Release

CERAP
Centerer and Radar Approach (control)

CERC
Centralized Engine Room Control

CERF
Commander Emergency Recovery Force

CERG
Commander Emergency Recovery Group

CERMET
Ceramic-to-Metal

CERPS
Centralized Expenditure and Reimbursement
Processing System

CERRC
Complete Engine Repair Requirement Card

CERS
Civilian Engineering Squadron
Commander Emergency Recovery Section

CERT
Certified
Certificate

CERTQUAR
Obtain certification of non-availability of
government quarters and government mess
or officers mess open in accordance with
Joint Travel Regulations, par. M 4551

CERU
Commander Emergency Recovery Unit

CES
Commission on Epidemiological Survey
(AFEB)

CES1
Construction Electrician S (Shop) First Class

CES2
Construction Electrician S (Shop) Second
Class

CES3
Construction Electrician S (Shop) Third Class

CESCA
Construction Electrician S (Shop)
Construction Apprentice

CESCN
Construction Electrician S (Shop)
Constructionman

CESE
Civil Engineering Support Equipment

CESF, COMEASTSEAFRON
Commander Eastern Sea Frontier

CESMIS
Civil Engineer Support Management
Information System

CESP
Civil Engineer Support Program

CET
Combat Engineer Tractor

CET1
Construction Electrician T (Telephone) First
Class

CET2
Construction Electrician T (Telephone)
Second Class

CET3
Construction Electrician T (Telephone) Third
Class

CETCA
Construction Electrician T (Telephone)
Construction Apprentice

CETCN
Construction Electrician T (Telephone)
Constructionman

CETS, CE&TS
Contractor Engineering and Technical
Services

CEU
Continuing Education Unit

CEV
Combat Engineer Vehicle
Convoy Escort Vehicle

CEW1
Construction Electrician W (Wiring) First
Class

CEW2
Construction Electrician W (Wiring) Second
Class

CEW3
Construction Electrician W (Wiring) Third
Class

CEWCA
Construction Electrician W (Wiring)
Construction Apprentice

CEWCN
Construction Electrician W (Wiring)
Constructionman

CEWRC
Civilian Employee Welfare and Recreation
Committee

CF
Cable-Firing (or -Fuzing)
Carry Forward
Centrifugal Force
Complement Fixation
Confer
Cumulus Fractus (cloud formation)

CF, CONFORM
Concept Formulation

CFA
Cognizant Field Activity
Contractor-Furnished Accessories

CFAD
Commander Fleet Air Detachment

CFAE
Contractor-Furnished Aeronautical Equipment

CFAR
Constant False Alarm Rate

CFAW
  Commander Fleet Air Wing
CFAWL
  Commander Fleet Air Wings, Atlantic
CFAWP
  Commander Fleet Air Wings, Pacific
CFC
  Controlled Force Circulation (boilers)
CF/CD
  Concept Formulation/Contract Definition
    (procurement procedure)
CFDB
  Concept Formulation Data Bank
CFE
  Contractor-Furnished Equipment
CFF
  Control Flip-Flop (NNSS)
  Critical Flicker Fusion
CF/HP
  Constant-Flow/High-Pressure (oxygen
    system)
CFI
  Certificate Flight Instructor
CFM
  Confirm
  Contractor-Furnished Materials
  Cubic Feet per Minute
CFN
  Confirmation of Numbers
CFO
  Commissioning and Fitting Out
  Connection Fitting Out
CFOC
  Contractor Fin Opener Crank
C-F/PCM
  Course-Fine/Pulse Code Modulator
CFRD
  Confidential and Formerly Restricted Data
CFS
  Contract Field Services
  Cubic Feet per Second
CFSR
  Contract Funds Status Report
CFU
  Control Functional Unit (data link)
CFWS
  Coordinated Federal Wage System
CG
  Centerless Ground
  Center of Gravity
  Centigram (U/I)
  Communications Group
  Compressed Gas
  Cost Growth
  (Depth) Capacity Gauge
  Guided Missile Cruiser
CGC, USCGC
  (United States) Coast Guard Cutter
CGE
  Cockpit Geometry Evaluation

CGE, COL
  College
CGFMF
  Commanding General, Fleet Marine Force
CGMAW
  Commanding General, Marine Air Wing
CGN
  Nuclear-Powered Guided Missile Cruiser
CGOS
  Combat Gunnery Officers School
CGRS
  Central Gyro Reference System
C&GS
  Command and General Staff
CGSE
  Common Ground Support Equipment
CGSEL
  Common Ground Support Equipment List
CH
  Chester (U/I)
  Chief of the _____
  Children (AFRT music code)
CH, CHAN
  Channel
C-H
  Candle-Hour
CHACOM, CNC
  Chief of Naval Communications
CHAF(F)ROC
  Chaff Rocket
CHAMPION
  Compatible Hardware and Milestone Program
    for Integrating Organizational Needs
CHAMPUS
  Civilian Health and Medical Program of the
    Uniformed Services
CHAN, CH
  Channel
CHANSY
  Charleston Naval Shipyard
CHAP
  Chaplain
CHARM
  Civil Aeronautics Agency High-Altitude
    Remote Monitoring
CHAR-TRAN
  Character Translation (DCI)
CHASGRP
  Charleston (SC) Group
CHAVMAINTECH
  Chief Aviation Maintenance Technician
CHB
  Cargo Handling Battalion
CHBOSN
  Chief Boatswain
CHC
  Chaplain Corps
CHCIVENG
  Chief of Civil Engineers
CHDLG
  Chief, Defense Liaison Group

CHDLG-INDO
Chief, Defense Liaison Group-Indonesia
CHEC
Checkered (buoy)
CHELECTECH
Chief Electronics Technician
CHEMBOMB
Chemical Bomb
CHESBAYGRU
Chesapeake Bay Group
CHESDIVNAVFACENGCOM
Chesapeake Division, Naval Facilities
Engineering Command
CHESDIVSEACON
Chesapeake Division, Ocean Construction
Platform
CHESDIVSUPPFAC
Chesapeake Division Support Facility
CHG
Change
Charge
CHIL
Consolidated Hazardous Item List
CHINFO
Chief of Information
CHK/DEBT-LIST
Back Checks and Indebtedness List
CHL
Confinement at Hard Labor
CHMDO
Chief, Mutual Defense Assistance Team
CHMEDT
Chief, Military Equipment Delivery Team
CHMILTAG
Chief, Military Technical Aid Group
CHNAVADVGRU
Chief, Naval Advisory Group
CHNAVDEV, CND
Chief of Naval Development
CHNAVMARCORMARS
Chief, Navy-Marine Corps Military Affiliate
Radio Station
CHNAVMAT, CNM
Chief of Naval Material
CHNAVMAT ERS
Chief of Naval Material Emergency
Relocation Site Commander
CHNAVMIS
Chief, U.S. Naval Mission to _____ (country)
CHNAVRSCH, CNR
Chief of Naval Research
CHNAVSECJUSMAGTHAI
Chief, Navy Section, Joint United States
Military Advisory Group, Thailand
CHNAVSECMAAG
Chief, Navy Section, Military Assistance
Advisory Group
CHNAVSECMTM
Chief, Navy Section, Military Training Mission

CHNAVSECUSMILGP
Chief, Navy Section, United States Military
Group
CHNOMISO
Chief, Naval Ordnance Management
Information System Office
CHOP
Change of Operational Control
CHORI
Chief of Office of Research and Inventions
CH/RM
Chill Room (stowage)
CHSAMS
Chief, Security Assistance Management and
Staff
CHT
Chemist
Collection, Holding and Transfer (system)
CHU
Centigrade Heat Units (calories)
CHUSDLG
Chief, United States Defense Liaison Group
CHUSNAVMIS
Chief, United States Naval Mission
CHUM
Chart Updating Manual
CI
Cirrus (cloud formation)
Configuration Inspection (or Item)
Control Indicator
Cost Inspector
Counterinsurgency
Critical Item
Cubic Inch (U/I)
C/I
Commercial/Industrial (program or activities)
CIA
Central Intelligence Agency
CIAC
Career Information and Counseling
CIACT
CNO Industry (or Civilian Industrial) Advisory
Committee for Telecommunications
CIB
COBOL Information Bulletin (publication)
Combat (or Command) Information Bureau
Communication Information Bulletin
Current Intelligence Brief
CIC
Clinical Investigation Center
Combat Information Center
Combat Intercept Control
Combined Intelligence Committee
Content Indication Code (AUTODIN)
Counter-Intelligence Corps (G-2)
Customer Identification Code (MAC)
CICC
Clinical Investigation Control Center
CICO
Combat Information Control Officer

CICWO
Combat Information Center Watch Officer
CID
Change in Design
Command Information Division
Component Identification Description
(number)
CIDNO
Contractor's Identification Number
CIDS
Consolidated Information on Data Schedule
Coordination of Direct Support (program)
CIF
Central Information File
C²IF
Command and Control Information Flow
CIG
Central Intelligence Group
CIG, CEIL
Ceiling
CIGTF
Central Inertial Guidance Test Facility
CII
Component (or Configuration) Identification
Index
CIL
Critical Item List
CIM
Communications Improvement Memorandum
CIMMS
Civilian Information Manpower Management
CIMS
Civilian Information Management System
Communications Instructions for Merchant
Ships
CINC
Commander-in-Chief
CINCAL
Commander-in-Chief, Alaska
CINCARIB
Commander-in-Chief, Caribbean
CINCEASTLANT
Commander-in-Chief, Eastern Atlantic Fleet
CINCENT
Commander-in-Chief, Allied Forces Central
Europe
CINCEUR
Commander-in-Chief, Europe
CINCLANT
Commander-in-Chief, Atlantic
CINCLANT ABNCP
Commander-in-Chief, Atlantic Airborne
Command Post (team)
CINCLANT CAO
Commander-in-Chief, Atlantic Coordination of
Atomic Operations
CINCLANTFLT
Commander-in-Chief, Atlantic Fleet
CINCLANTFLTRESAFFAIRS
Commander-in-Chief, Reserve Affairs Officer

CINCLANTREP
Commander-in-Chief, Atlantic Representative
CINCMEDAFSA
Commander-in-Chief, Middle East/South Asia
and Africa South of the Sahara
CINCNORAD
Commander-in-Chief, North American Air
Defense Command
CINCPAC
Commander-in-Chief, Pacific
CINCPACFLT
Commander-in-Chief, Pacific Fleet
CINCPACFLT ACE
Commander-in-Chief, Pacific Fleet, Alternate
Command Element Commander
CINCPACFLT ECC
Commander-in-Chief, Pacific Fleet,
Emergency Command Center Commander
CINCPACFLT ERS
Commander-in-Chief, Pacific Fleet,
Emergency Relocation Site Commander
CINCPACFLT OAC
Commander-in-Chief, Pacific Fleet, Oceanic
Airspace Coordinator
CINCPACFLTREP
Commander-in-Chief, Pacific Fleet
Representative
CINCPACFLTREPPACMISTESTCEN
Commander-in-Chief, Pacific Fleet
Representative, Pacific Missile Test Center
CINCPACHEDPEARL
Commander-in-Chief, U.S. Pacific Fleet
Headquarters, Pearl Harbor (HI)
CINCPACREP
Commander-in-Chief, Pacific Representative
CINCSOUTH
Commander-in-Chief, Allied Forces Southern
Europe
CINCSTRIKE
Commander-in-Chief, U.S. Strike Command
CINCUNC
Commander-in-Chief, United Nations
Command
CINCUNCKOREA
Commander-in-Chief, United Nations
Command, Korea
CINCUSNAVEUR
Commander-in-Chief, United States Naval
Forces, Europe
CINCUSNAVEURALT
Commander-in-Chief, United States Naval
Forces, Europe, Alternate Commander
CINCUSNAVEUR ERS
Commander-in-Chief, United States Naval
Forces, Europe, Emergency Relocation
Site Commander
CINCUSNAVEUR IDHS
Commander-in-Chief, United States Naval
Forces, Europe, Intelligence Data Handling
System

CINCWESTLANT
Commander-in-Chief, Western Atlantic Area
CINOS
Centralized Input/Output System
CIO
Combat Intelligence Officer
Conference on the Inhabitants of the Ocean
CIOR
Interallied Confederation of Reserve Officers
CIOS
Combined Intelligence Objectives
Subcommittee
Combined Intelligence Operations Section
CIP
Class Improvement Plan
Clinical Investigation Program
Coast-In Point
Combined Instrument Panel (for submarines)
Computer Image-Processing
CIPC
Combined Intelligence Priorities Committee
(U.S.-Britain)
CIR
Circulator
Cost Information Reports
CIRCLTR, C/L
Circular Letter
CIRCUITROUTE
Circuitous Route
CIREP, CEP
Circular Error Probable
CIRO
Consolidated Industrial Relations Office
CIRVIS
Communications Instructions, Reporting Vital
Intelligence Sightings
CIS
Cost Inspection Service
Curriculum and Instructional Standards
CI/SERE
Counterinsurgency/Survival, Evasion,
Resistance and Escape
CISP
Cast-Iron Soil Pipe
CISS, CASINFOSUPPSYS
Casualty Information Support System
CIT
Catalog Input Transmittal
Citation
Citizen
Compressor Inlet Temperature
CITC
Computer Indicator Test Console
CITE
Compression Ignition and Turbine Engine
(fuel)
Contractor Independent Technical Effort
CIU
Central Interpretation Unit (BAM)
CIV
Civil(ian)

CIVAFFAIRSGRU
Civil Affairs Group
CIVCLO
Civilian Clothing
CIV CONF
Civilian Confinement
CIV DEF
Civil Defendent
CIVEMP
Civilian Employee
CIVEMPAF
(Record System for) Civilian Employees of
Non-Appropriated Fund Activities
CIVENGLAB
Civil Engineering Laboratory
CIV-M-MARP
Civilian-Mobilization-Manpower
Allocation/Requirements Plan
CIVPERSADMSYS
Civilian Personnel Administration Services
Record System
CIVPERS/EEODIRSYS
Civilian Personnel/Equal Employment
Opportunity Directives System
CIVSUB
Civilian Substitution (program)
CIWS
Close-In Weapons System
CJTF
Commander Joint Task Force
CJTG
Commander Joint Task Group
CK
Cake (U/I)
Check(age) (ed)
CL
Centerline
Clearance
Coil (U/I)
Light Cruiser
CL, CLAS
Class
C/L, CIRCLTR
Circular Letter
C/L, CVL
Carrier Landing(s)
CLA
Certified Laboratory Assistant (ASCP)
Crew Loading Analysis
CLAC
Combined Liberated Areas Committee
CLAIMS
Conventional Ammunition Integrated
Management System
CLAM
Chemical Low-Altitude Missile (ramjet)
Classification Management
CLAMP
Closed Loop Aeronautical Management
Program

CLAS
Classification
Classified
Classify
CLAS, CL
Class
CLASP
Classification and Assignments Within Pride
Program
CLASSMATE
Computer Language to Aid and Stimulate
Scientific, Mathematical and Technical
Education
CLC
Communications Line Controller
Tactical Command Ship
CLCVN
Class Convening
CLDAS
Clinical Laboratory Data Acquisition System
CLEP
College-Level Examination Program
CLER
Clerical (aptitude test)
CLF
Civilian Labor Force
CLG
Light Guided Missile Cruiser
CLIFS
Costs, Life, Interchangeability, Function and
Safety
CLIP
Compiler and Language for Information
Processing
CLL
Consolidated Load List
CLNC
Clearance
CLO
Campus (or Command) Liaison Officer
CLOSENLJACKRET
Activity performing final separation
procedures directed to close out enlisted
jacket and forward it to NMPC (Code 38).
In "Remarks" section of page 14 show
effective date of retirement, grade in which
retired, and provisions of law under which
retired by reason of completion of more
than ____ years service.
CLP
Command Language Program
CLR
Center of Lateral Resistance
Clear
CLSA
Cooperative Logistic Support Agreement
CLSD
Closed
CLSSA
Cooperative Logistics Supply Support
Arrangement

CLTE
Commissioned Loss to Enlisted Status
(revocation of appointment)
CLUDACTDAT
Include accounting data on orders,
transportation requests, and meal tickets
covering such travel
CLUSA, CONUS
Continental Limits, United States of America
CM
Celestial Mechanics
Centimeters
Chemical Milling
Circular Mil (wire measure)
Configuration Management
Contract Modification
Contractural Milestone
Controlled Minefield
Corrective Maintenance
Countermeasures
Courts-Martial
Cumulonimbus Mammatus (cloud formation)
CM, C&M
Construction and Machinery
CM1
Construction Mechanic First Class
CM2
Construction Mechanic Second Class
CM3
Construction Mechanic Third Class
CMA
Civil-Military Affairs
Clothing Maintenance Allowance
Court of Military Appeals
CMAA
Chief Master-at-Arms
CMB
Code Matrix Block
CMBD
Combined
CMBL, CBL
Commercial Bill of Lading
CMC
Chief Construction Mechanic
Commandant of the Marine Corps
Communication Multiplexor Channel
CMCA
Construction Mechanic Construction
Apprentice
CMCN
Construction Mechanic Constructionman
CMCO
Confidential Material Control Officer
CMCRL
Consolidated Master Cross Reference List
CMCS
Communications Monitoring and Control
System
Senior Chief Construction Mechanic
CMD
Capital Military District

CMD, COMD
Command
CM&D
Countermeasures and Deception
CMDN
Catalogue Management Data Notification
CMF
Coherent Memory Filter
CMG
Chief Marine Gunner
CMH
Congressional Medal of Honor—also see MOH
C/MH
Cost per Manhour
CMI
Computer-Managed Instruction
CMIO
Communications Material Issuing Office
CMIS
Court-Martial Index and Summary
CML
Current Mode Logic
CML, COML
Commercial
CMM
Configuration Management Manual
CMMG
Civilian Manpower Management Guides
CMMI
Civilian Manpower Management Instructions—pronounced "Simmies"
CMML
Civilian Manpower Management Letters
CMN
Commission
CMO
Configuration Management Office
Controlled Materials Officer
Court-Martial Officer (or Orders)
CMOOW
Company Midshipman Officer-of-the-Watch
C-MOS
Complementary-Metal Oxide Semiconductor
CMP
Camp
Contract Maintenance Plan
Corps of Military Police
CMPCTR
Computer Center
CMPI
Civilian Marine Personnel Instructions
CMR
Common Mode Rejection
Contract Management Region
Court-Martial Reports
CMRF
Capital Maintenance and Rental Funds
CMRR
Common Mode Rejection Rate

C/MRS
Calibration/Measurement Requirements Summary
CMSS
Communications Security Material System
Compiler Monitor System
Construction Management System
CMT
Commissary Technician, Medical
Corrected Mean Temperature
Crewmember Trainee
CMTC
Civilian Military Training Camp
CMV
Common Mode Voltage
CN
Can (U/I)
Constructionman
Controller
CNA
Canadian Northwest Atlantic (area)
Center for Naval Analyses
CNA, CNAVAIR
Chief of Naval Air
CNAADTRA, CNAVAADTRA
Chief of Naval Air Advanced Training
CNAB
Commander Naval Air Bases
CNABTRA
Chief, Naval Air Basic Training
CNAG
Chief, Naval Advisory Group
CNAL, COMNAVAIRLANT
Commander Naval Air Forces, Atlantic
CNAP, COMNAVAIRPAC
Commander Naval Air Forces, Pacific
CNARESTRA
Chief of Naval Reserve Training
CNARF, COMNAVAIRESFOR
Commander Naval Air Reserve Force
CNAT, CNATRA
Chief of Naval Air Training
CNATECHTRA, CNATT
Chief of Naval Air Technical Training
CNATRA, CNAT
Chief of Naval Air Training
CNATT, CNATECHTRA
Chief of Naval Air Technical Training
CNAVADTRA, CNAADTRA, CNAVANTRA
Chief of Naval Air Advanced Training
CNAVANTRA, CNAVADTRA, CNAADTRA
Chief of Naval Air Advanced Training
CNAVRES
Chief of Naval Reserve
CNAVRESAIRLANTREP
Chief of Naval Reserve, Representative for Naval Air Forces, Atlantic
CNAVRESAIRPACREP
Chief of Naval Reserve, Representative for Naval Air Forces, Pacific

CNB, COMNAVBASE
Commander Naval Base
CNC
Change Notice Card (or Code)
Central Navigation Computer
CNC, CHACOM
Chief of Naval Communications
CNCL, CNL
Cancel(lation)
CND, CHNAVDEV
Chief of Naval Development
CNDO
Chief Navy Disbursing Officer
CNET, COMNAVEDTRACOM
Commander Naval Education and Training
(Command)
CNETLANTREP
Commander Naval Education and Training
Command, Representative Coordinator for
Atlantic
CNETPACREP
Commander Naval Education and Training
Command, Representative Coordinator for
Pacific
CNF
Central NOTAMS Facility
CNF, COMNAVFOR
Commander Naval Forces
CNFJ, COMNAVFORJAP(AN)
Commander, U.S. Naval Forces, Japan
CNFSD
Confused
CNG
Commander Northern Group
CNI
Chief of Naval Intelligence
Communications-Navigation Identification
CNIC, COMNAVINTCOM
Commander Naval Intelligence Command
CNL, CNCL
Cancel(lation)
CNM, CHNAVMAT
Chief of Naval Material
CNM, COMNAVMAR
Commander Naval Forces, Marianas
CNMO
Canadian Naval Mission Overseas
CNO
Chief of Naval Operations
Constitutional Officers
CNOB
Commander Naval Operating Base
CNOBO
Chief of Naval Operations Budget Office
CNO/RAAB
Chief of Naval Operations Reserve Affairs
Advisory Board
CNP
Celestial North Pole

CNR
Carrier-to-Noise Ratio
Changes to Navy Regulations
CNR, CHNAVRSCH
Chief of Naval Research
CNRA, COMNAVCRUITAREA
Commander Navy Recruiting Area
CNRC, COMNAVCRUITCOM
Commander Navy Recruiting Command
CNSG
Consolidated Nuclear Steam Generator
CNSY, CNSYD
Charleston Naval Shipyard
CNSYD, CNSY
Charleston Naval Shipyard
CNT
Certified Navy Twill (cloth)
CNT, CNTNTN
Continuation Pay for Medical/Dental Officers
CNT, CHNAVTRA
Chief of Naval Training
CNTECHTRA
Chief of Naval Technical Training
CNTNTN, CTN
Continuation Pay for Medical/Dental Officers
CNTPS
Consolidated Naval Telecommunications
Program System
CNTR, CTN, CEN
Center
CNTRL, CEN
Central
CNTS, CHNAVTRASUPP
Chief of Naval Training Support
CNWDI
Critical Nuclear Weapons Design Information
CO
Central Office
Change Order
Coastal (route)
Combined Operations
Commanding Officer
Conscientious Objector
Container (U/I)
CO, COMO
Communications Officer
CO, COY
Company
CO, KO
Contracting Officer
C/O
Care of
Change Order
COAC
Chief Operating Area Coordinator
COB
Chief of the Boat
Committee of Combined Boards
Current on Board (status)

COC
Certificate of Competency (or Conformance)
Chief of Chaplains
Civilian Orientation Cruise
Combat Operations Center
Control Officer's Console
COCO
Coordinator of Chain Operations (USCG)
COD
Carrier Onboard Delivery
Close Order Drill
CODAC
Collateral Duty Alcoholism Counselor
CODAG
Combined Diesel and Gas (propulsion)
CODAN
Coded (Weather) Analysis
CODAP
Comprehensive Occupational Data Analysis
Program
Control Data Assembly Program
CODAR
Correlation Display Analyzing and Recording
CODASYL
Conference on Data Systems Languages
CODIPHASE
Coherent Digital Phased Array System
CODIS
Coded Discharge
Controlled Orbital Decay and Input System
CODIT
Computer Direct to Telegraph
CODIZ
Cable-Operated Zero Impedance
CODOG
Combined Diesel or Gas (propulsion)
COE
Certificate of Eligibility
COEA
Cost and Operational Effectiveness Analysis
COED
Char Oil Energy Development (process)
Composition and Editing Display
Computer-Operated Electronic Display
COEEOCA
Commanders Equal Employment Opportunity
Advisory Council
C OF A
Certificate of Airworthiness
COFC
Container on Flat Car (shipping)
COFG, COG
Convenience of Government
COFI
Court of Inquiry
COFS, C/S, COS
Chief of Staff
COFT
Chief of Transportation

COG
Center of Gravity
Cognizance
Course Grain
COG, COFG
Convenience of Government
COGAG
Combined Gas and Gas (propulsion)
COGAGE
Combined Gas and Gas Turbine Electric
(propulsion)
COGAP
Computer Graphics Arrangement Program
COGARD, CG, USCG
Coast Guard
COGARDACFTPROGOFF
Coast Guard Aircraft Program Office
COGARDADMINLAWJUDGE
Coast Guard Administrative Law Judge
COGARDAIRSTA
Coast Guard Air Station
COGARDANFAC
Coast Guard Aids to Navigation Facility
COGARDANT
Coast Guard Aids to Navigation Team
COGARDARSC
Coast Guard Aircraft Repair and Supply
Center
COGARDAVTC
Coast Guard Aviation Training Center
COGARDAVDET
Coast Guard Aviation Detachment
COGARDAVTECHTRACEN
Coast Guard Aviation Technical Training
Center
COGARDBASE
Coast Guard Base
COGARDBST
Coast Guard Boating Safety Team
COGARDCOMMSTA
Coast Guard Communications Station
COGARDCOSARFAC
Coast Guard Coastal Search and Rescue
Facility
COGARDCOTP
Coast Guard Captain of the Port Office
COGARDCRUITOFF
Coast Guard Recruiting Office
COGARDEP
Coast Guard Depot
COGARDETNDBO
Coast Guard National Data Buoy Office
Detachment
COGARDEECEN
Coast Guard Electronics Engineering Center
COGARDEGICP
Coast Guard Inventory Control Points
COGARDES
Coast Guard Electronic Shop
COGARDESM
Coast Guard Electronic Shop Minor

COGARDESMT
Coast Guard Electronics Shop Minor
Telephone and Teletype

COGARDEST
Coast Guard Electronics Shop Major
Telephone and Teletype

COGARDFOGSIGSTA
Coast Guard Fog Signal Station

COGARDFSTD
Coast Guard Fire and Safety Test
Detachment

COGARDISF
Coast Guard Icebreaker Facility

COGARDINST
Coast Guard Institute

COGARDLOEPIC
Coast Guard Liaison Officer Eastern Pacific
Intelligence Center

COGARDLOCOMFLETRAGRU
Coast Guard Liaison Officer, Commander
Fleet Training Group

COGARDLOFEASTRACENPAC
Coast Guard Liaison Officer, Fleet
Antisubmarine Warfare Training, Central
Pacific

COGARDLONNAVDAMCONTRACEN
Coast Guard Liaison Officer, Navy Damage
Control Training Center

COGARDLOREP
Coast Guard Liaison Officer Representative

COGARDLORMONSTA
Coast Guard LORAN Monitor Station

COGARDLORSTA
Coast Guard LORAN Station

COGARDLTSTA
Coast Guard Light Station

COGARDMID
Coast Guard Marine Inspection Detachment

COGARDMILPAYCEN
Coast Guard Military Pay Center

COGARDMIO
Coast Guard Marine Inspection Office

COGARDMRDET
Coast Guard Maintenance Repair
Detachment

COGARDMSD
Coast Guard Marine Safety Detachment

COGARDMSO
Coast Guard Marine Safety Office

COGARDNDBO
Coast Guard National Data Buoy Office

COGARDNMLBS
Coast Guard National Motor Lifeboat School

COGARDNSF
Coast Guard National Strike Force

COGARDNSFGULF
Coast Guard National Strike Force, Gulf

COGARDNSFLANT
Coast Guard National Strike Force, Atlantic

COGARDNSFPAC
Coast Guard National Strike Force, Pacific

COGARDOCC
Coast Guard Operations Computer Center

COGARDOCEANU
Coast Guard Oceanographic Unit

COGARDOMSTA
Coast Guard Omega Station

COGARDONSOD
Coast Guard Omega Navigation Systems
Office Detachment

COGARDOPDAC
Coast Guard Operations Data Analysis
Center

COGARDORDSUPPFAC
Coast Guard Ordnance Support Facility

COGARDPSDET
Coast Guard Port Safety Detachment

COGARDPSSTA
Coast Guard Port Safety Station

COGARDRADSTA
Coast Guard Radio Station

COGARDRANDDC
Coast Guard Research and Development
Center

COGARDRECDEP
Coast Guard Records Depot

COGARDREPNAVREGMEDCEN
Coast Guard Representative, Naval Regional
Medical Center

COGARDREPUSAFH
Coast Guard Representative, United States
Air Force Hospital

COGARDREPTAMC
Coast Guard Representative, Tripler Army
Medical Center

COGARDREPSTUDREC
Coast Guard Representative, Student
Records

COGARDREPUSPHS
Coast Guard Representative, United States
Public Health Service Hospital

COGARDRESCEN
Coast Guard Reserve Center

COGARDRESTRACEN
Coast Guard Reserve Training Center

COGARDRIO
Coast Guard Resident Inspecting Officer

COGARDSIU
Coast Guard Ship Introduction Unit

COGARDSHIPTRADET
Coast Guard Ship Training Detachment

COGARDSICP
Coast Guard Stock Inventory Control Point

COGARDSTA
Coast Guard Station

COGARDSUPCEN
Coast Guard Supply Center

COGARDSUPRTCEN
Coast Guard Support Center

COGARDTRACEN
Coast Guard Training Center

COGARDSUPRTFAC
Coast Guard Support Facility
COGARDTRATEAM
Coast Guard Training Team
COGARDVTS
Coast Guard Vessel Traffic System
COGAS
Combined Gas and Steam (propulsion)
COGB
Continuous Orbital Guidance System
COGOG
Combined Gas or Gas (propulsion)
COGP
Commission on Government Procurement
COGSA
"Carriage of Goods by Sea" Act
COH
Completion of (or Complex) Overhaul
COHO
Coherent Oscillator
COHQ
Combined Operations Headquarters
COI
Center of Influence
Communications Operation Instruction
Community-of-Interest
Course of Instruction
COIC
Combined Operational Intelligence Center
COIN
Counter-Insurgency
Counter-Insurgent (aircraft)
Counter-Intelligence
COINT
Commands Interested (have by mail)
COL
Collateral
Computer-Oriented Language
Cost-of-Living (allowance)
COL, CGE
College
COL, COLM
Column
COLA
Cost-of-Living Allowance
COLANFORASCU
Commanding Officer, Landing Force Air
Support Control Unit
COLIDAR
Coherent Light Detection and Ranging
COLL
Collect(ion)
Commanding Officer's Leave Listing
COLM, COL
Column
COLOD
Completed Loading
COM
Commissioned Officers' Mess
Common
Computer-Operated (or Output on) Microfilm

COM, COMD
Command
COM, COMDR, CDR
Commander
COMA
Court of Military Appeals
COMAAC
Commander Alaskan Air Command
COMAC
Continuous Multiple-Access Collator
COMADC
Commander Air Defense Command
COMAEWW, COMAEWWING
Commander Airborne Early-Warning Wing
COMAEWWING, COMAEWW
Commander Airborne Early-Warning Wing
COMAIRASWING
Commander Air Antisubmarine Wing
COMAIRCANLANT
Air Commander, Canadian Atlantic Sub-Area
COMAIRPATGRU
Commander Air Patrol Group
COMAIRRECONGRU
Commander Fleet Air Reconnaissance Group
COMAIRRECONPATGRU
Commander Air Reconnaissance Patrol
Group
COMALAIRC
Commander Alaskan Air Command
COMALSEAFRON
Commander Alaskan Sea Frontier
COMANTARCTICSUPPACT, CASA
Commander Antarctic Support Activities
COMANTDEFCOM
Commander Antilles Defense Command
COMAREASWFOR
Commander Area Antisubmarine Warfare
Forces
COMARSURVRECFOR
Commander Maritime Surveillance and
Reconnaissance Force
COMARSURVRECFORDET
Commander Maritime Surveillance and
Reconnaissance Force Detachment
COMARSURVRECFORPASRAP
Commander Maritime Surveillance and
Reconnaissance Force, Passive ASRAP
Data
COMASWFORLANT
Commander Antisubmarine Warfare Forces,
Atlantic
COMASWFORPAC
Commander Antisubmarine Warfare Forces,
Pacific
COMASWGRU
Commander Antisubmarine Warfare Group
COMASWSUPPTRADET
Commander Antisubmarine Warfare Support
Training Detachment

COMASWWINGPAC
Commander Antisubmarine Warfare Wing, Pacific

COMATKCARAIRWING
Commander Attack Carrier Air Wing

COMATKCARSTRIKEFOR
Commander Attack Carrier Strike Force

COMATKSUBFOR
Commander Attack Submarine Force

COMAZSECASWGRU
Commander Azores Sector Antisubmarine Warfare Group

COMB
Combination
Combine

COMBATFOR
Commander Battle Force

COMBATSYSENGDEVSITE
Combat System Engineering Development Site

COMBATSYSTECHSCOLCOM
Combat Systems Technical Schools Command

COMBSVCSUPPSCOLANT
Combined Services Support Program School, Atlantic

COMBSVCSUPPSCOLPAC
Combined Services Support Program School, Pacific

COMCARAIRWING
Commander Carrier Air Wing

COMCARAIRWINGDET
Commander Carrier Air Wing Detachment

COMCARAIRWINGRES
Commander Reserve Carrier Air Wing

COMCARANTISUBAIRGRU, COMCARASWAIRGRU
Commander Carrier Antisubmarine Air Group

COMCARGRU
Commander Carrier Group

COMCARIBSEAFRON, CCSF
Commander Caribbean Sea Frontier

COMCARIBSECASWGRU
Commander Caribbean Sector Antisubmarine Warfare Group

COMCARSTRIKEFOR
Commander Carrier Striking Force

COMCBLANT
Commander Naval Construction Battalions, Atlantic

COMCBLANTDET
Commander Naval Construction Battalions, Atlantic Detachment

COMCBLANT MLO
Commander Naval Construction Battalions, Atlantic, Material Liaison Office

COMCBPAC
Commander Naval Construction Battalions, Pacific

COMCENSECT/WESTSEAFRON
Commander Central Section/Western Sea Frontier

COMCMDCOORDFOR
Commander Command and Coordination Force

COMCN
Communications Countermeasures

COMCOGARDACTEUR
Commander Coast Guard Activities, Europe

COMCOGARDEUR
Commander Coast Guard Force, Europe

COMCOGARDLANT
Commander Coast Guard Force, Atlantic

COMCOGARDFESEC
Commander Coast Guard Section Office, Far East Section

COMCOGARDGANTSEC
Commander Coast Guard Section Office, Guantanamo Section

COMCOGARDMARSEC
Commander Coast Guard, Maritime Section

COMCOGARDGRU
Commander Coast Guard Group

COMCOGARDLANTWWMCCS
Commander Coast Guard World-Wide Military Command and Control System, Atlantic

COMCOGARDRON
Commander Coast Guard Squadron

COMCOGARDSERON
Commander Coast Guard Southeast Squadron

COMCORTDIV
Commander Escort Division

COMCORTRON
Commander Escort Squadron

COMCOSDIV
Commander Coastal Division

COMCOSRON
Commander Coastal Squadron

COMCOSURVFOR
Commander Coastal Surveillance Force

COMCRUDESGRU
Commander Cruiser-Destroyer Group

COMCRUDESLANT, CCDL
Commander Cruiser-Destroyer Force, Atlantic

COMCRUDESLANTSUPPGRU
Commander Cruiser-Destroyer Force, Atlantic Support Group

COMCRUDESLANTSUPPGRUCHAR
Commander Cruiser-Destroyer Force, Atlantic Support Group, Charleston (SC)

COMCRUDESLANTSUPPGRUMPT
Commander Cruiser-Destroyer Force, Atlantic Support Group, Mayport (FL)

COMCRUDESLANTSUPPGRUNORVA
Commander Cruiser-Destroyer Force, Atlantic Support Group, Norfolk, Virginia

COMCRUDESPAC, CCDP
Commander Cruiser-Destroyer Force, Pacific

COMD, CMD
Command
COMDESDEVGRU
Commander Destroyer Development Group
COMDESFLOT
Commander Destroyer Flotilla
COMDESGRU
Commander Destroyer Group
COMDESLANT
Commander Destroyers, Atlantic
COMDESLANTDET
Commander Destroyers, Atlantic Detachment
COMDESPAC
Commander Destroyers, Pacific
COMDESPACDET
Commander Destroyers, Pacific Detachment
COMDESRON
Commander Destroyer Squadron
COMDG
Commanding
COMDR, COM, CDR
Commander
COMDT
Commandant
COMDTAFSC
Commandant, Armed Forces Staff College
COMDTCOGARD
Commandant, Coast Guard
COMEASTCONRADREG
Commander Eastern Continental Air Defense
Region
COMEASTLANT
Commander Eastern Atlantic Force
COMEASTSEAFRON, CESF
Commander Eastern Sea Frontier
COMEDCENT
Commander Central Mediterranean
COMEODGRU
Commander Explosive Ordnance Disposal
Group
COMET
Computer-Operated Management Evaluation
Technique
CONUS Meteorological Teletype (system)
COMET II
CONUS Meteorological Teletype, Second Net
(system)
COMEXDIV
Commander Experimental Division
COMFAIR
Commander Fleet Air
COMFAIRCARIB
Commander Fleet Air, Caribbean
COMFAIRDET
Commander Fleet Air Detachment
COMFAIRKEF
Commander Fleet Air, Keflavik (IC)
COMFAIRMED
Commander Fleet Air, Mediterranean

COMFAIRMEDET
Commander Fleet Air, Mediterranean
Detachment
COMFAIRKWEST
Commander Fleet Air, Key West (FL)
COMFAIRWESTPAC
Commander Fleet Air, Western Pacific
COMFAIRWESTPACDET
Commander Fleet Air, Western Pacific
Detachment
COMFAIRWINGNORLANT
Commander Fleet Air Wing, Northern Atlantic
COMFAIRWINGSLANT
Commander Fleet Air Wings, Atlantic
COMFAIRWINGSPAC
Commander Fleet Air Wings, Pacific
COMFEWSG
Commander Fleet Electronic Warfare Support
Group
COMFEWSGDET
Commander Fleet Electronic Warfare Support
Group Detachment
COMFITAEWWINGPAC
Commander Fighter Airborne Early Warning
Wing, Pacific
COMFITWING
Commander Fighter Wing
COMFLEACT
Commander Fleet Activities
COMFLEACTDET
Commander Fleet Activities Detachment
COMFLETACSUPPWING,
COMTACSUPPWING
Commander Fleet Tactical Support Wing
COMFLETRAGRU
Commander Fleet Training Group
COMFLETRAGRULANT
Commander Fleet Training Group, Atlantic
COMFLETRAGRUPAC
Commander Fleet Training Group, Pacific
COMFLETRAGRUWESPAC
Commander Fleet Training Group, Western
Pacific
COMGREPAT
Commander Greenland Patrol
COMGTMOSECTASWU
Commander Guantanamo (Bay, Cuba)
Sector, Antisubmarine Warfare Unit
COMHAWSEAFRON
Commander Hawaiian Sea Frontier
COMHELSEACONWING
Commander Helicopter Sea Control Wing
COMHELWINGRES
Commander Reserve Helicopter Wing
COMHELWINGRESREPLANT
Commander Reserve Helicopter Wing,
Atlantic Representative
COMHASWING
Commander Helicopter Antisubmarine Wing

COMICEASWGRU
Commander Iceland Antisubmarine Warfare Group
COMICEDEFOR, COMIDF
Commander Iceland Defense Force
COMICEDEFOR/COMICEASWGRU
Commander Iceland Defense Force/Commander Iceland Antisubmarine Warfare Group
COMICPAC
Commander Intelligence Center, Pacific
COMIDEASTFOR
Commander Middle East Force
COMIDF, COMICEDEFOR
Commander Iceland Defense Force
COMIFSDIV
Commander Inshore Fire Support Division
COMILDEPT
Commanding Officer Military Departments (USNS)
COMINE
Commander Minecraft
COMINEDIV
Commander Minecraft Division
COMINEFLOT
Commander Mine Flotilla
COMINEGRP
Commander Mine Group
COMINEGRPOK
Commander Mine Group, Okinawa
COMINELANT
Commander Minecraft, Atlantic
COMINEPAC
Commander Minecraft, Pacific
COMINERON
Commander Mine Squadron
COMINEWARCOM
Commander Mine Warfare Command
COMINEWARINSGRU
Commander Mine Warfare Inspection Group
COMINST
Communications Instructions
COMINTICEPAT
Commander International Ice Patrol
COMISH
Commander Military Attaché
COMJUWTF
Commander Joint Unconventional Warfare Task Force
COMKWESTEVDET
Commander Key West Test and Evaluation Detachment
COMKWESTFOR
Commander Key West Force
COML, CML
Commercial
COMLAIRAUTH
Where government aircraft is not available, travel via commercial aircraft authorized where necessary

COMLAIRDIR
Where government aircraft is not available, travel via commercial aircraft is directed
COMLANSHIPFLOT
Commander Landing Ship Flotilla
COMLANSHIPRON
Commander Landing Ship Squadron
COMLANTAREACOGARD
Commander, Altantic Area Coast Guard
COMLANTCOMELINTCEN
Commander Atlantic Electronic Intelligence Center
COMLANTFLTWPNRAN
Commander Atlantic Fleet Weapons Range
COMLATWING
Commander Light Attack Wing
COMLATWINGPAC
Commander Light Attack Wing, Pacific
COMLF
Commercial Line Feed
COMLO
Combined Operations Material Liaison Officer
COMLOGNET
Combat Logistics Network
COMLOGSUPPFOR
Commander Logistics Support Force
COMLOPS
Commercial Operations
COMLSTDIV
Commander Landing Ship Tank Division
COMLTRANSAUTH
Where government transportation is not available, travel via commercial transportation is authorized
COMLTRANSAUTHEXPED
Where government transportation is not available, travel via commercial transportation authorized where necessary to expedite completion of duty
COMM
Communications
COMMATWING
Commander Medium Attack Wing
COMMATVAQWINGPAC
Commander Medium Attack Tactical Electronic Warfare Wings, Pacific
COMMBN
Communications Battalion
COMMCEN
Communications Center
COMMDET
Commissioning Detail
COMMO, COMO, CDRE
Commodore
COMMOBSUPPUDET
Commander Mobile Support Unit Detachment
COMM RI
Communications Routing Indicator
COMMSTA
Communication Station

COMMSYSTECH
Communication Systems Technician
COMMTECH
Communications Technician
COMNAB
Commander Naval Air Base
COMNATODEFCOL
Commandant, North Atlantic Treaty
Organization Defense College
COMNAVACT
Commander Naval Activities
COMNAVACTUK
Commander Naval Activities, United Kingdom
COMNAVAIRRES, CNAR
Commander Naval Air Reserve
COMNAVAIRESFOR, CNARF
Commander Naval Air Reserve Force
COMNAVAIRLANT, CNAL
Commander Naval Air Force, Atlantic
COMNAVAIRPAC, CNAP
Commander Naval Air Force, Pacific
COMNAVAIRPACMATREP
Commander Naval Air Force, Pacific Material
Representative
COMNAVAIRPACREP
Commander Naval Air Force, Pacific
Representative
COMNAVAIRSYSCOM
Commander Naval Air Systems Command
COMNAVAIRSYSCOM ERS
Commander Naval Air Systems Command,
Emergency Relocation Site Commander
COMNAVAIRSYSCOMHQ
Commander Naval Air Systems Command
Headquarters
COMNAVAIRTESTCEN
Commander Naval Air Test Center
COMNAVAIRTRANSWING
Commander Naval Air Transport Wing
COMNAVAIRTRANSWINGPAC
Commander Naval Air Transport Wing,
Pacific
COMNAVBASE, CNB
Commander Naval Base
COMNAVBASEREP
Commander Naval Base Representative
COMNAVBEACHGRU
Commander Naval Beach Group
COMNAVBEACHPHIBREFTRAGRU
Commander Naval Beach and Amphibious
Refresher Training Group
COMNAVCOMM
Commander Naval Communications
Command
COMNAVCRUITAREA, CNRA
Commander Navy Recruiting Area
COMNAVCRUITCOM, CNRC
Commander Navy Recruiting Command
COMNAVCRUITCOM QAT
Commander Navy Recruiting Command
Quality Assurance Team

COMNAVDAC
Commander Naval Data Automation Center
COMNAVDISTWASHDC, CNDW
Commandant, Naval District Washington,
District of Columbia
COMNAVELEXSYSCOM
Commander Naval Electronic Systems
Command
COMNAVELEXSYSCOM ALT
Commander Naval Electronic Systems
Command Alternate Commander
COMNAVELEXSYSCOM ERS
Commander Naval Electronic Systems
Command Emergency Relocation Site
Commander
COMNAVELEXSYSCOMHQ
Commander Naval Electronic Systems
Command Headquarters
COMNAVFACENGCOM
Commander Naval Facilities Engineering
Command
COMNAVFACENGCOM ALT
Commander Naval Facilities Engineering
Command Alternate Commander
COMNAVFACENGCOMDET
Commander Naval Facilities Engineering
Command Detachment
COMNAVFACENGCOM ERS
Commander Naval Facilities Engineering
Command Emergency Relocation Site
Commander
COMNAVFACENGCOMHQ
Commander Naval Facilities Engineering
Command Headquarters
COMNAVFORFE
Commander U.S. Naval Forces, Far East
COMNAVFORAZORES, CNFA
Commander U.S. Naval Forces, Azores
COMNAVFORCARIB
Commander U.S. Naval Forces, Caribbean
COMNAVFORCARIBDET
Commander U.S. Naval Forces, Caribbean
Detachment
COMNAVFORICE
Commander U.S. Naval Forces, Iceland
COMNAVFORJAPAN, CNFJ
Commander U.S. Naval Forces, Japan
COMNAVFORKOREA
Commander U.S. Naval Forces, Korea
COMNAVFORKOREADET
Commander U.S. Naval Forces, Marianas
COMNAVFORPHIL
Commander U.S. Naval Forces, Philippines
COMNAVINTCOM
Commander Naval Intelligence Command
COMNAVLEGSVCCOM
Commander Naval Legal Service Command
COMNAVLOGPAC
Commander Naval Logistics Command,
Pacific

COMNAVMAR, CNM, COMNAVMARIANAS
Commander U.S. Naval Forces, Marianas
COMNAVMARIANAS, COMNAVMAR, CNM
Commander U.S. Naval Forces, Marianas
COMNAVMILPERSCOM, CNMPC
Commander Naval Military Personnel
Command
COMNAVOCEANCOM
Commander Naval Oceanography Command
COMNAVOPSUPPGRU
Commander Naval Operations Support Group
COMNAVOPSUPPGRULANT
Commander Naval Operations Support
Group, Atlantic
COMNAVOPSUPPGRUPAC
Commander Naval Operations Support
Group, Pacific
COMNAVRESPERSCEN
Commander Naval Reserve Personnel Center
COMNAVRESSECGRU
Commander Naval Reserve Security Group
COMNAVSEASYSCOM
Commander Naval Sea Systems Command
COMNAVSEASYSCOM ALT
Commander Naval Sea Systems Command
Alternate Commander
COMNAVSEASYSCOM ERS
Commander Naval Sea Systems Command
Emergency Relocation Site Commander
COMNAVSEASYSCOMHQ
Commander Naval Sea Systems Command
Headquarters
COMNAVSECGRU
Commander Naval Security Group
COMNAVSPECWARGRU
Commander Naval Special Warfare Group
COMNAVSPECWARGRUDET
Commander Naval Special Warfare Group
Detachment
COMNAVSUPPFOR
Commander Naval Support Force
COMNAVSUPPFORANTARCTICA
Commander Naval Support Force, Antarctic
COMNAVSUPPFORANTARCTICREP
Commander Naval Support Force, Antarctic
Representative
COMNAVSUPSYSCOM
Commander Naval Supply Systems
Command
COMNAVSUPSYSCOM ERS
Commander Naval Supply Systems
Command Emergency Relocation Site
Commander
COMNAVSUPSYSCOMHQ
Commander Naval Supply Systems
Command Headquarters
COMNAVSURFGRUMED
Commander Naval Surface Group,
Mediterranean

COMNAVSURFGRUMIDPAC
Commander Naval Surface Group,
Mid-Pacific
COMNAVSURFGRUWESTPAC
Commander Naval Surface Group, Western
Pacific
COMNAVSURFGRUWESTPACDET
Commander Naval Surface Group, Western
Pacific Detachment
COMNAVSURFLANT
Commander Naval Surface Force, Atlantic
COMNAVSURFLANTDET
Commander Naval Surface Force, Atlantic
Detachment
COMNAVSURFLANTREP
Commander Naval Surface Force, Atlantic
Representative
COMNAVSURFPAC
Commander Naval Surface Force, Pacific
COMNAVSURFPAC ADP
Commander Naval Surface Force, Pacific
Automatic Data Processing
COMNAVSURFPAC DET
Commander Naval Surface Force, Pacific
Detachment
COMNAVSURFPAC DISCUS
Commander Naval Surface Force, Pacific
Distributed Information System for
CASREP/UNIT Status
COMNAVSURFPAC ERS
Commander Naval Surface Force, Pacific
Emergency Relocation Site Commander
COMNAVSURFPACREP
Commander Naval Surface Force, Pacific
Representative
COMNAVSURFRES
Commander Naval Surface Reserve Force
COMNAVTELCOM
Commander Naval Telecommunications
Command
COMNET
Command Net(work)
Computer Network
COMNLONTEVDET
Commander New London (CN) Test and
Evaluation Detachment
COMNORASDEFLANT
Commander North Atlantic Antisubmarine
Defense Force
COMNORSECT
Commander Northern Section
COMNORSECT/WESTSEAFRON
Commander Northern Section/Western Sea
Frontier
COMNORSTRIKFOR
Commander Northern Striking Force
COMNORVATEVDET
Commander Norfolk, Virginia Test and
Evaluation Detachment

COMNRCBPAC
Commander Naval Reserve Construction
Battalions, Pacific
COMNRCF
Commander Naval Reserve Construction
Force
COMNRCFREP
Commander Naval Reserve Construction
Force Representative
COMNRIUWGRU
Commander Naval Reserve Inshore
Undersea Warfare Group
COMNRPC
Commander Naval Reserve Personnel Center
COMNUPWRTRAGRULANT
Commander Nuclear Power Training Group,
Atlantic
COMNUPWRTRAGRUPAC
Commander Nuclear Power Training Group,
Pacific
COMNUWPNTRAGRULANT
Commander Nuclear Weapons Training
Group, Atlantic
COMNUWPNTRAGRUPAC
Commander Nuclear Weapons Training
Group, Pacific
COMO
Commissioned Officers' Mess (Open)
COMO, CO
Communications Officer
COMO, COMMO, CDRE
Commodore
COMOCEANLANT
Commander Atlantic Ocean Sub-Area
COMOCEANSYSLANT
Commander Oceanographic Systems,
Atlantic
COMOCEANSYSLANT OC
Commander Oceanographic Systems,
Atlantic Operations Center
COMOCEANSYSPAC
Commander Oceanographic Systems, Pacific
COMOCEANSYSPAC MEC
Commander Oceanographic Systems, Pacific
Main Evaluation Center
COMOMAG
Commander Mobile Mine Assembly Group
COMOPCONCEN
Commander Operational Control Center
COMOPDEVFOR
Commander Operational Development Force
COMOPTEVFOR
Commander Operational Test and Evaluation
Force
COMOPTEVFORLANT
Commander Operational Test and Evaluation
Force, Atlantic
COMOPTEVFORPAC
Commander Operational Test and Evaluation
Force, Pacific

COMORTEXGRP
Commander Orange, Texas Group, Inactive
Reserve Fleet, Atlantic
COMOT
Clerical, Office Machine Operation and
Technical (evaluation system)
COMP
Component
Composite
COMP, COMPT
Comptroller
COMPACAREACOGARD
Commander, Pacific Area Coast Guard
COMPACELINTCEN
Commander Pacific Electronic Intelligence
Center
COMPACMISTESTCEN
Commander Pacific Missile Test Center
COMPAD
Combined Office, Material Procurement and
Distribution
COMPASECT
Commander Panama Section
COMPASECTASWGRU
Commander Panama Section Antisubmarine
Warfare Group
COMPASECT/CARIBSEAFRON
Commander Panama Section/Caribbean Sea
Frontier
COMPASECT/WESTSEAFRON
Commander Panama Section/Western Sea
Frontier
COMPASS
Computer-Assisted Classification and
Selection of Navy Recruits
Compiler-Assembler
COMPATASWDEVGRU
Commander Patrol Antisubmarine Warfare
Development Group
COMPATFOR
Commander Patrol Forces
COMPATFORSIXTHFLTDET
Commander Patrol Forces, Sixth Fleet
Detachment
COMPATRECONFOR
Commander Patrol and Reconnaissance
Force
COMPATWINGSLANT
Commander Patrol Wings, Atlantic
COMPATWINGSPAC
Commander Patrol Wings, Pacific
COMPATWINGSPACREP
Commander Patrol Wings, Pacific
Representative
COMPCOURDET
Upon completion of instruction and when
directed, detached (duty indicated). (Date
on or about which these orders are
effective may be indicated.)
COMP DEC
Comptroller's Decisions

COMPDESFLTSURG
Upon completion of duty you are hereby
designated as a flight surgeon
COMPET
Competitive
COMPEX
Competitive Evaluation Exercise
COMPGEN
Comptroller General
COMPHIBFOR
Commander Amphibious Force
COMPHIBFORLANT
Commander Amphibious Force, Atlantic
COMPHIBFORPAC
Commander Amphibious Force, Pacific
COMPHIBGRU
Commander Amphibious Group
COMPHIBGRUDET
Commander Amphibious Group Detachment
COMPHIBGRUEASTPAC
Commander Amphibious Group, Eastern
Pacific
COMPHIBREADYGRU
Commander Amphibious Ready Group
COMPHIBRON
Commander Amphibious Squadron
COMPHMRON
Commander Patrol Combatant Missile
Hydrofoil Squadron
COMPL
Complete(d)
Upon completion thereof
COMPORON, COMPRON
Composite Squadron
COMPRET
Upon completion return to duty station and
resume regular duties
COMPRSECTASWU
Commander Puerto Rico Section
Antisubmarine Warfare Unit
COMPS
Consolidated Military Pay System
COMPT, COMP
Comptroller
COMPTEM
Upon completion of temporary duty
COMPTEMDET
Upon completion of temporary duty, detached
COMPTEMDIRDET
Upon completion of temporary duty and when
directed, detach
COMPTEMINS
Upon completion of temporary duty under
instruction
COMPTOUR
Completing Tour (orders)
COMPTRADIRDET
Upon completion training and when directed,
detached

COMPVANTRADET
Upon completion of advanced training,
detached
COMPUERTORICOSECT
Commander Puerto Rico Section
COMPUERTORICOSECT/CARIBSEAFRON
Commander Puerto Rico Section/Caribbean
Sea Frontier
COMRADE
Computer-Aided Design Environment
COMRATS
Commuted Rations
COMRATS PT
Commuted Rations, Proceed Time
COMRDNAVFOR
Commander Rapid Development Naval Force
COMRECONATKWING
Commander Reconnaissance Attack Wing
COMREDATKCARAIRWING
Commander Readiness Attack Carrier Air
Wing
COMREL
Community Relations
COMRESDESRON
Commander Reserve Destroyer Squadron
COMRESPATWINGLANT
Commander Reserve Patrol Wing, Atlantic
COMRESPATWINGPAC
Commander Reserve Patrol Wing, Pacific
COMRESPATWINGPACDET
Commander Reserve Patrol Wing, Pacific
Detachment
COMRESTACSUPPWING
Commander Reserve Tactical Support Wing
COMRESTACSUPPWINGDET
Commander Reserve Tactical Support Wing
Detachment
COMRNCBLANT
Commander Reserve Naval Construction
Battalions, Atlantic
COMRNCF
Commander Reserve Naval Construction
Force
COMRIVSUPPRON
Commander River Support Squadron
COMSAR
Commander Search and Rescue
COMSAT
Communications Satellite
COMSC
Commander Military Sealift Command
COMSCELM
Commander Military Sealift Command,
Eastern Atlantic and Mediterranean
COMSCEUR
Commander Military Sealift Command,
Europe
COMSCFE
Commander Military Sealift Command, Far
East

COMSCGULF
Commander Military Sealift Command, Gulf

COMSCLANT
Commander Military Sealift Command, Atlantic

COMSCMED
Commander Military Sealift Command, Mediterranean

COMSCPAC
Commander Military Sealift Command, Pacific

COMSCSEA
Commander Military Sealift Command, Southeast Asia

COMSEABASEDASWWINGSLANT
Commander Sea-Based Antisubmarine Warfare Wings, Atlantic

COMSEC
Communications Security (course)

COMSEC I
Communications Security, Phase I (course)

COMSER
Commission on Marine Sciences, Engineering and Resources

COMSERVFOR
Commander Service Force

COMSERVGRU
Commander Service Force Group

COMSERVGRUDET
Commander Service Force Group Detachment

COMSERVLANT, CSL, COMSERFORLANT
Commander Service Force, Atlantic

COMSERVPAC, CSP, COMSERVFORPAC
Commander Service Force, Pacific

COMSERVPACPETSCOL
Commander Service Force, Pacific Petroleum School

COMSERVRON
Commander Service Squadron

COMSN
Commission

COMSOLANT
Commander South Atlantic Force

COMSOSECT
Commander Southern Section

COMSOSECT/WESTSEAFRON
Commander Southern Section/Western Sea Frontier

COMSPECBOATRON
Commander Special Boat Squadron

COMSPECBOATU
Commander Special Boat Unit

COMSTRATSUBFOR
Commander Strategic Submarine Force

COMSTRIKEFLTLANT
Commander Strike Fleet, Atlantic

COMSUBDEVGRU
Commander Submarine Development Group

COMSUBDEVGRUDET
Commander Submarine Development Group Detachment

COMSUBDEVGRU UMV
Commander Submarine Development Group Unmanned Vehicles

COMSUBDEVRON
Commander Submarine Development Squadron

COMSUBDEVRONTRADET
Commander Submarine Development Squadron Training Detachment

COMSUBDIV
Commander Submarine Division

COMSUBEASTLANT
Commander Submarine Force, Eastern Atlantic

COMSUBFLOT
Commander Submarine Flotilla

COMSUBFRONDEF
Commander Sub-Frontier Defense

COMSUBFRONDEF/CHESBAYGRU
Commander Sub-Frontier Defense/Chesapeake Bay Group

COMSUBFRONDEF/DELGRU
Commander Sub-Frontier Defense/Delaware Group

COMSUBFRONDEF/GULFGRU
Commander Sub-Frontier Defense/Gulf Group

COMSUBFRONDEF/NEWENGRU
Commander Sub-Frontier Defense/New England Group

COMSUBFRONDEF/SOGRU
Commander Sub-Frontier Defense/Southern Group

COMSUBGRU
Commander Submarine Group

COMSUBGRUDET
Commander Submarine Group Detachment

COMSUBLANT
Commander Submarine Forces, Atlantic

COMSUBLANTREP
Commander Submarine Forces, Atlantic Representative

COMSUBPAC
Commander Submarine Forces, Pacific

COMSUBPAC CC
Commander Submarine Forces, Pacific Command Center

COMSUBPAC ECC
Commander Submarine Forces, Pacific Emergency Command Center

COMSUBPAC OTH
Commander Submarine Forces, Pacific, Over-the-Horizon Fleet Commander

COMSUBPACREP
Commander Submarine Forces, Pacific Representative

COMSUBREFITRAGRU
Commander Submarine Refit and Training Group

COMSUBRON
Commander Submarine Squadron

COMSUBTRAGRU
Commander Submarine Training Group
COMSUBTRAGRUHAWAREA
Commander Submarine Training Group,
Hawaiian Area
COMSUBTRAGRUNORWEST
Commander Submarine Training Group,
Northwest Area
COMSUBTRAGRUWESCO
Commander Submarine Training Group, West
Coast Area
COMSURFRON
Commander Surface Squadron
COMSURFWARDEVGRU
Commander Surface Warfare Development
Group
COMSYSTO
Commissary Store
COMSYSTOREG
Commissary Store Region
COMSYSTOREGDET
Commissary Store Region Detachment
COMTAC
Communication/Tactical (publications)
COMTACGRU
Commander Tactical Air Control Group
COMTACRON
Commander Tactical Air Control Squadron
COMTACSUPPWING,
    COMFLETACSUPPWING
Commander Fleet Tactical Support Wing
COMTACWINGSLANT
Commander Tactical Wings, Atlantic
COMTAIWANPATFOR
Commander Taiwan Patrol Force
COMTONGRU
Commander Tongue Point Group, Inactive
Fleet, Pacific Fleet
COMTRALANT
Commander Training Force, Atlantic
COMTRAN
Commercial Translator
COMTRAPAC
Commander Training Force, Pacific
COMTRAWING
Commander Training Air Wing
COMUSAFSO
Commander United States Air Forces,
Southern Command
COMUSFAC
Commander United States Facility
COMUSFORAZ
Commander United States Forces, Azores
COMUSFORCARIB
Commander United States Forces, Caribbean
COMUSFORCARIBREP
Commander United States Forces, Caribbean
Representative
COMUSFORICE
Commander United States Forces, Iceland

COMUSFORJAPAN
Commander United States Forces, Japan
COMUSFORKOREA
Commander United States Forces, Korea
COMUSFORMAR
Commander United States Forces, Marianas
COMUSMACTHAI
Commander United States Military Assistance
Command, Thailand
COMUSMILGRU
Commander United States Military Group
COMUSNAVFORCONAD
Commander United States Naval Forces,
Continental Air Defense Command
COMUSNAVPHIL
Commander United States Naval Forces,
Philippines
COMUSNAVSO
Commander United States Naval Forces,
Southern Command
COMUSTDC
Commander United States Taiwan Defense
Command
COMWESTSEAFRON, CWST
Commander Western Sea Frontier
COMZ, COMZONE
Communications Zone
COMZONE, COMZ
Communications Zone
CON
Concrete
Conical
Constant
Consul
Control
CON, CONF, C
Confidential
CONAC
Contractor Acceptance Records
CONACTD
Continuous Active Duty
CONAD
Continental Air Defense Command
CONAG
Combined Nuclear and Gas (propulsion)
CONALOG
Contact Analog (non-digital computer)
CONAS
Commanding Officer, Naval Air Station
CONASAERO
These orders constitute assignment to duty in
part of aeronautical organization of the
Navy
CONC
Concentrate
CONC, CON
Concrete
COND, CDN
Condition
CONDEF, CD
Contract Definition

CONDUCTVIEW
Command delivery orders directed to conduct interview required by current NAVMILPERSINST 1300.26 prior to delivery

CONELRAD
Control of Electromagnetic Radiation (civil defense)

CONESTAB
Connection establishment

CONEX
Container Express

CONF
Conference
Confinement

CONF, CON, C
Confidential

CONFBUL
Confidential Bulletin

CONFLAG
Conflagration Control

CONFORM, CF
Concept Formulation

CONF-MH
Confidential-Modified Handling

CONOPS
CONUS Operations

CONPLAN
Operations Plan in Concept Format

CONPRESDU
Continue present duties

CONREP
In Connection with replenishment

CONSHELF
Continental Shelf

CONSOL
Consolidate

CONSOLREC
Consolidated Recreation

CONSPIC
Conspicuous

CONST
Construction

CONSTELEC
Construction Electrician

CONSTRUCTS
Control Data Structural System

CONSUB
Continuous Submarine Duty Incentive Pay

CONT
Continue

CONT, CONTD
Continued

CONTAREX
Conventional Targeting Exercise

CONTD, CONT
Continued

CONTFLDSERV
Contract Field Service (file)

CONTN
Contain

CONTR, KR
Contractor

CONTR, KT
Contract

CONTREAT
Continue treatment at (naval hospital or medical facility indicated)

CONUBS
Compact Nuclear Brayton System

CONUS, CLUSA
Continental Limits, United States of America

CONV
Convict(ed), (-tion)

CONVATE
Connection reactivation

CONVERS
Connection conversion

CONVEX
Convoy Exercise

CONVL
Conventional

CONVN
Convenient

COOP
Cooperative Observations Program

COOP, COOPLAN
Contingency of Operations Planning

CO-OP
Cooperative

COOPLAN, COOP
Contingency of Operations Planning

COORD
Coordinate

COORS
Communications Outage Restoral Section

COP
Coast-Out Point
Commanding Officer's Punishment
Continuation of Pay
Control for Operational Programs
Co-Pilot

COPARS
Contractor-Operated Spare Parts Store

COPE
Computer Operating and Programming Environment
Continuous Officer Professional Education

COPI
Computer-Oriented Programmed Instruction

COPNORSA
A certified copy of these orders with all endorsements shall be forwarded to Naval Officer Record Support Activity, Omaha, NE 68111

COPP
Combined Operations Pilotage Party

COPRESTRA
Within 30 days after completion separation processing forward copy of these orders and intended new address to Commander Naval Air Reserve Training, Glenview, IL.

COR
Cargo Outturn Reporting
Change Order Request
Circular of Requirements
Communication Operating Requirements
Contracting Officer's Representative
Corner
COR, CPS
Corps
COR, CORR, CRTN
Correction
CORA
Conditioned-Response Analog
CORCONU
Corrosion Control Unit
CORCY
Corrected Copy
CORD
Cascade Orifice Resistor Device
Coordinate, (-tion)
Coordination of Research and Development
Coordinator
CORDIC
Coordinate Rotation Digital Computer
CORDPO
Correlated Data Printout
CORDS
Civil Operations Revolutionary Development
Support
COREP
Combined Overload and Repair Control
CORES
Cooperative Radiation Effects Simulation
(program)
CORPS
CASREP and Outstanding Repair Parts
CORR
Correspondence
CORR, COR, CRTN
Correction
CORSCHOPSDET
Commanding Officer, Research Operations
Detachment
CORT
Escort
CORTDIV
Escort Division
CORTRON
Escort Squadron
CORTS
Conversion of Range and Telemetry Systems
COS
Central Operations System
CO2 Removal System
COS, COFS, C/S
Chief of Staff
COSA
Combat Operational Support Aircraft
COSAG
Combined Steam and Gas (propulsion)

COSAL
Coordinated Shipboard/Shore-based
Allowance List
COSAR
Compression Scanning Array Radar
COSBAL
Coordinated Shore-Based Allowance List
COSD
Combined Operations Support Depot
COSDIV
Coastal Division
COSFLOT
Coastal Flotilla
COSMD
Combined Operations Signal Maintenance
Depot
COSMO
Combined Operations Signal Maintenance
Officer
COSO
Combined Operations Signal Officer
COSRIVDIV
Coastal River Division
COSRIVRON
Coastal River Squadron
COSRIVRON MST
Coastal River Squadron Mobile Support
Team
COSRON
Coastal Squadron
COSSAC
Chief of Staff, Supreme Allied Command
COSSACT
Command Systems Support Activity
COT
Cockpit Orientation Trainer
Consecutive Overseas Tour
Consolidated (or Coordinated) Operability
Test
COTA
Certification as Occupational Therapy
Assistant
Confirming Telephone or Message Authority
of _____
COTAR
Correlation Tracking and Ranging
COTAT
Correlation Tracking and Triangulation
COTC
Commander Fleet Operational Training
Command
COTCLANT
Commander Fleet Operational Training
Command, Atlantic
COTCPAC
Commander Fleet Operational Training
Command, Pacific
COTCPACSUBCOM
Commander Fleet Operational Training
Command, Pacific Subordinate Command

COTR
Contracting Officer's Technical Representative

COUSS
Commanding Officer, United States Ship (name of ship)

COV
Covered
Covers

COVE
Committee on Value and Evaluation

COW
"Commanding Officer's Wife" (slang)

COWS
Change Order Work Sheet

COY, CO
Company

COZI
Communications Zone Indicator

CP
Capsule (U/I)
Command (or Control) Post
Constant Pressure
Contact Preclude
Continental Polar (air mass)

CPA
Central Program Agent
Closest Point of Approach
Cost Planning and Appraisal
Critical Path Analysis

CP&AA
Components, Parts, Accessories and Attachments

CPAD
Central Pay Accounts Division

CPAF
Cost-Plus-Award Fee

CPAM
CNO Program Analysis Memorandum

CPC
Coastal Patrol Boat
Computer Program Components
Crafts, Protective and Custodial (series)

CPCU
Custody Pending Completion of Use

CPD
Constant Pressure Date

CPDF
Central Personnel Data File

CPE
Contractor Performance Evaluation
Cytopathic Effect

CPEB
Central Physical Evaluation Board

CPEG
Contractor Performance Evaluation Group

CPES
Contractor Performance Evaluation System

CPF
Central Program Facility

CPFF
Cost-Plus-Fixed Fee

CPFG
CNO Policy and Fiscal Guidance

CPG, COMPHIBGRU
Commander Amphibious Group

CPHC
Central Pacific Hurricane Center

CPI
Crash Position Indicator

CPIC
Coastal Patrol and Interdiction Craft
Combined Photographic Interpretation Center

CPIF
Cost-Plus-Incentive Fee

CPI/FDR
Crash Position Indicator/Flight Data Recorder

CPL
Corporal
Crash Position Locator

CPM
Cards (or Counts, or Cycles) per Minute
Critical Path Method

CPMS
Communications Procedures Management System
Computerized Performance Monitoring System

CPO
Chief Petty Officer
Component Pilot Overhaul

CPOA
Completion of Post Overhaul Availability

CPOC
Chief Petty Officer of the Command

CPOIC
Chief Petty Officer-in-Charge

CPOW
Chief Petty Officer-of-the-Watch

CPP, COMPHIBPAC
Commander Amphibious Force, Pacific

CPPC
Cost-Plus-Percentage-of-Cost

CPPG
CNO Policy and Planning Guidance

CPPS
Critical Path Planning and Scheduling

CPPSO
Consolidated Personal Property Shipping Office

CPR
Component Pilot Rework
Continuing Property Records
Cost-Performance Report

CPR, COMPHIBRON
Commander Amphibious Squadron

CPS
Certificate of Prior Submission
Collective Protection System
Consolidated Package Store
Contract Plant Services
Conversational Programming System
Cycles per Second

CPS, COR
Corps

CPSR
Contractor Procurement System Review

CPSS
Component Percentage Shipping Schedule

CPT
Co-Pilot Time
Critical Path Technique (PERT)

CPTR, CAP
Capture

CPU
Central Processing Unit

CPX
Command Post Exercise

CQ
Carrier Qualification
Change of Quarters
Commercial Quality
Constraint Qualification

C/Q
Certificate of Assignment to Quarters

CQAP
Component Quality Assurance Program

CQC
Contractor Quality Control

C/Q(NOT)
Certificate of Assignment to Quarters Not
Issued

CQS
Common Query System

C/Q(TERM DATE)
Termination of Assignment to Quarters (date)

CR
Cold-Rolled (steel)
Conference Room
Congenic Resistant
Construction Recruit
Continuous Rod
Control Relay (or Rocket)
Crate (U/I)
Creditable Record
Crypto Top Secret

C/R
Change of Rating
Change of Request

CRA
Composite Research Aircraft
Craft

CRAB
Caging, Retention and Airborne Boresight

CRACC
Communications and Radar Assignment
Coordinating Committee

CRAE
Combat-Readiness Assessment Exercise

CRAF
Civil Reserve Air Fleet

CRAFTY
Conscientious, Responsible, Aboveboard,
Faultless, Timely, Yeomanly

CRAG
Carrier Replacement Air Group
Combat Readiness Air Group

CRAM
Card Random Access Memory
Compression, Retrieval and Maintenance (of
data)
Contractual Requirements Recording Analysis
and Management

CRASP
COSAL Requisitioning and Status Procedures

CRAW
Combat Readiness Air Wing

CRB
Computer Resources Board
Control Review Board

CRBRP
Clinch River Breeder Reactor Plant

CRC
Central Requirements Committee
Core Removal Coding

CRCC
Cyclic Redundancy Check Code

CRD
Classified Restricted Data

CRDF
Cathode Ray Direction Finding (equipment)

CRDL
Collateral Recurring Document Listing (DIA)

CRDM
Control Rod Drive Mechanism (reactors)

CRDS
Component Repair Data Sheet

CREDIT
Cost-Reduction Early Decision Information
Techniques

CREO
Career Reenlistment Objectives

CRES
Corrosion Resistant Steel

CRF
Career Recruiter Force
Cryptographic Repair Facility

CRI
Cenn Response Index
Code Relationship Index

CRIL
Consolidated Repairable Item List

CRIO
Communications Security Regional Issuing
Office

CRITHOUS
Advised of critical housing shortage

CRITIC
Critical Intelligence
CRO
Cathode-Ray Oscilloscope
Cathode-Ray Tube Readout
Civilian Repair Organization
CRP
Civilian Requirements Plan
Controllable and Reversible Pitch (propeller)
Coordinated Reconnaissance Plan
Corrugated Ribbon Packing
Cost-Reduction Program
CRPI
Card Reader-Punch Interpreter (unit)
CRPL
Central Radio Propagation Laboratory
CRPM
Combined Registered Publications
Memoranda
Communications Registered Publications
Memorandum
CRS
Calibration Requirements Summary
CRS, CUS
Course
CRSD
Contractor Required Shipment Date
CRSE
Course Interval (NNSS)
CRT
Cathode-Ray Tube
Combat-Readiness Training
CRTN, COR, CORR
Correction
CRU
Complete Capability Response Unit
Composite Reserve Unit
Cruiser
CRUDESFLOT
Cruiser-Destroyer Flotilla
CRUDESLANT, CDDL
Cruiser-Destroyer Force, Atlantic
CRUDESPAC, CDDP
Cruiser-Destroyer Force, Pacific
CRUDIV
Cruiser Division
CRUIT
Recruit(ing)
CRUITSTA
Recruiting Station
CRWO
Coding Room Watch Officer
CRYPTO
Cryptographic

CS
Carrier Suitable
Cirrostratus (cloud formation)
Civil Service
Cloud Shadow
Continuous Strip (film)
Contractor Sensitization
Coolant Sampling
CS, COMMSTA
Communication Station
C/S
Call Sign
Certificate of Service
Change of Speed
C/S, COFS, COS
Chief of Staff
C&S
Charges and Specifications
Clean and Sober
CSA
Configuration Status Accounting
CSAB
Combined Shipping and Adjustment Board
(U.S.-Britain)
CSAC
Central Ships Alignment Console
CSAG
Combat Systems Advisory Group (NMC)
CSAR
Communication Satellite Advanced Research
Configuration Status Accounting Report
CSBL
Consolidated Site Base Loading
CSC
Central Security Control
Civil Service Commission
Combined Shipbuilding Committee
Continuous Service Certificate
CSCA
Control Surface Decontamination Area
C-SCAN
Carrier System for Controlled Approach of
Naval Aircraft
CSCL
Care of Ship Checkoff List
C/SCSC
Cost/Schedule Control Systems Criteria
CSD
Constant-Speed Drive
Crew Systems Department
CSDIC
Combined Services Detailed Interrogation
Center
CSDIC-NOI
Combined Services Detailed Interrogation
Center-Non-Operational Intelligence
CSDP
Coordinated Ship Development Plan
CSDPP
Combat Systems Data Processing Project

CSDRBL
Considerable
CSE
Common Support Equipment
Critical Specifications Elements
CSED
Consolidated Ships Electronic Design
Coordinated Ship Electronics Device
CSF, CARBSEAFRON, CARIBSEAFRON
Caribbean Sea Frontier
CSG
Close Support Gun
CSGMP
Cross-Scan Ground Map Pencil
CSI
CONUS Sustaining Increment
Customer Satisfaction Index
CSID
Combat Systems Integration Department
CSI-DET
CONUS Sustaining Increment Detachment
CSIGO
Chief Signal Officer
CSL
Complete Service Life
Component Save List
CSL, COMSERVFORLANT, COMSERVLANT
Commander Service Force, Atlantic
CSM
Calendar Maintenance Supervisor
Command Security Manager
Contractor Support Milestones
CSMP
Current Ship's Maintenance Project
CSMS
Computerized Specifications Management
System
CSN
Nuclear Strike Cruiser (concept)
CSO
Club Safety Officer
CSP
Coherent Signal Processor
Command Selector Panel
Concurrent Spare Parts
Contractor Standardization Plan
CSP, COMSERVFORPAC, COMSERVPAC
Commander Service Force, Pacific
CSPD
Central Still-Photo Depository
CSPM
Communication Security Publication
Memorandum
CSR
Continuous Sampling Run
Contract Status Report
Current Sensitive Relay
CSRA
Civil Service Reform Act
CSRF
Commissary Store Reserve Fund

CSRFG
Commissary Store Reserve Fund Grant
CSS
Combat Systems Support
Common Skills Shops
Consolidated Support System
Contractor Support Services
C&SS
Clothing and Small Stores
CSSM
Computer System Security Manager
CSSO
Common Support Services Office
Computer System Security Officer
CSSP
Combined Services Support Program
CSSQT
Combat Systems Ships Qualification Trials
CST
Coast
Coding Speed Test
CSTA
Cross-Scan Terrain Avoidance
CSTDD
Combat Systems Test Development Director
CSTEX
Combat Systems Training Exercise
C-STOL
Controlled Short Take-Off and Landing
CSTOM
Combat Systems Tactical Operations Manual
CSTV
Control System Test Vehicle
CSU
Circuit-Switching Unit
CSV
Command Selector Value
CSWC
Crew-Served Weapons Captured
CSWR
Conversation Specifications and Work
Requirements
CT
Card Type
Central Time
Circuit Theory
Combat Team
Combined Trials
Contact (approach)
Continental (or Control) Transformer
CT, CTN
Carton
CTA
Control Area
CTA1
Cryptologic Technician A (Administrative)
First Class
CTA2
Cryptologic Technician A (Administrative)
Second Class

CTA3
Cryptologic Technician A (Administrative) Third Class
CTAC
Chief Cryptologic Technician A (Administrative)
CTACM
Master Chief Cryptologic Technician A (Administrative)
CTACS
Senior Chief Cryptologic Technician A (Administrative)
C/TB
Cargo/Tanker Branch
CTC
Contract Task Change
CTDO
Central Technical Doctrine Officer
Central Training (or Technical) Documents Office
CTDS
Code Translation Data System
CTE
Chief Test Engineer
Contractor Technical Evaluation
CTFM
Continuous Transmission, Frequency Modulated
CTG
Commander Task Group
CTI
Contractor Training Instruction
CTI1
Cryptologic Technician I (Interpretive) First Class
CTI2
Cryptologic Technician I (Interpretive) Second Class
CTI3
Cryptologic Technician I (Interpretive) Third Class
CTIC
Chief Cryptologic Technician I (Interpretive)
CTICM
Master Chief Cryptologic Technician I (Interpretive)
CTICS
Senior Chief Cryptologic Technician I (Interpretive)
CTIM
Cooked Therapeutic In-flight Meals
CTIS
Carrier Terminal Information Services
CTM1
Cryptologic Technician M (Maintenance) First Class
CTM2
Cryptologic Technician M (Maintenance) Second Class

CTM3
Cryptologic Technician M (Maintenance) Third Class
CTMC
Chief Cryptologic Technician M (Maintenance)
CTMCM
Master Chief Cryptologic Technician M (Maintenance)
CTMCS
Senior Chief Cryptologic Technician M (Maintenance)
CTN, CEN, CNTR
Center
CTN, CT
Carton
CTO1
Cryptologic Technician O (Communications) First Class
CTO2
Cryptologic Technician O (Communications) Second Class
CTO3
Cryptologic Technician O (Communications) Third Class
CTOC
Chief Cryptologic Technician O (Communications)
CTOCM
Master Chief Cryptologic Technician O (Communications)
CTOCS
Senior Chief Cryptologic Technician O (Communications)
CTR1
Cryptologic Technician R (Collection) First Class
CTR2
Cryptologic Technician R (Collection) Second Class
CTR3
Cryptologic Technician R (Collection) Third Class
CTRC
Chief Cryptologic Technician R (Collection)
CTRCM
Master Chief Cryptologic Technician R (Collection)
CTRCS
Senior Chief Cryptologic Technician R (Collection)
CTS
Capistrano Test Site
Communications Test Set
Communication Terminals, Synchronous
Contractor Technical Services
CTSA
Cryptologic Technician Seaman Apprentice
CTSN
Cryptologic Technician Seaman

CTSPTEP
Central Test Site for Personnel and Training
Evaluation Program
CTSPTEPDET
Central Test Site for Personnel and Training
Evaluation Program Detachment
CTSS
Compatible Time-Sharing System
CTT
Command Training Team
CTT1
Cryptologic Technician T (Technical) First
Class
CTT2
Cryptologic Technician T (Technical) Second
Class
CTT3
Cryptologic Technician T (Technical) Third
Class
CTTC
Chief Cryptologic Technician T (Technical)
CTTCM
Master Chief Cryptologic Technician T
(Technical)
CTTCS
Senior Chief Cryptologic Technician T
(Technical)
CTU
Commander Task Unit
CTV
Control Test Vehicle
CTZ
Control Zone
CU
Common-Used (or User)
Constructionman
Cubic (or Cube)
Cumulus (cloud formation)
CUCB
Cumulus and Cumulonimbus (cloud
formation)
CUCM
Master Chief Constructionman
CUDIXS
Common User Digital Information Exchange
System
CUO
Credit Union Office
CURR
Currency
Current
CURTS
Common User Radio Transmission System
CURV
Cable-Controlled Underwater Recovery
Vehicle
CUS, CRS
Course
CUST
Custody

CUSTR
Customer
CUT
Cutter
CV
Multi-purpose Aircraft Carrier
Coefficient of Variation
CVAN
Nuclear-powered Multi-purpose Aircraft
Carrier
CVBG
Carrier Battle Group
CVC
Consecutive Voyage Charter
CVCC
Aircraft CV Crane
CVFR
Controlled Visual Flight Rules
CVIC
Carrier Intelligence Center
CVL, C/L
Carrier Landing(s)
CVLI
Commissioned Vessel Liaison Inquiry
CVM
Seaplane Control Medium Nuclear Carriers
(concept)
CVN
Convene
Ocean Control Carrier (concept)
CVP
Computer Validation Program
CVR
Combat Reconnaissance Vehicle
Controlled Visual Rules
CVR(T)
Combat Vehicle Reconnaissance (Tracked)
CVSD
Continuously-Variable Slope Delta
**CVSG, CARASWAIRGRU,
   CARANTISUBAIRGRU**
Carrier Antisubmarine Warfare Air Group
**CVSGR, RESCARANTISUBAIRGRU,
   RESCARASWAIRGRU**
Reserve Carrier Antisubmarine Warfare Air
Group
CVT
Training Aircraft Carrier
CVU
Utility Aircraft Carrier
CVW
Carrier Air Wing
CVWS
Combat Vehicle Weapons System
CW
Carrier (or Continuous) Wave
Chemical Warfare
Chilled Water
Compensating Winding (wiring)
Control Work

CWA
Canadian Western Approaches
CWAS
Contractor Weighted Average Share
CWBS
Contract Work Breakdown Structure
CWBW
Chemical Warfare-Bacteriological (or
Biological) Warfare
CWCS
Common Weapon Control System
CWI
Continuous Wave Illuminator
CWO
Chief (or Communications) Watch Officer
Commissioned Warrant Officer
CWPD
Class Work Planning Document
CWRA
Civilian Welfare and Recreation Association
CWS
Chemical Warfare Service
Control Wheel Steering
CWSF, COMWESTSEAFRON
Commander Western Sea Frontier
CWSO
Command Weapons Systems Orientation
CWT
Hundred Weight
CWTPI
Conventional Weapons Technical Proficiency
Inspection
CX
Canister (U/I)
Control Transmitter
CY
Calendar (or Current) Year
CYL, CL
Cylinder
CZ
(Panama) Canal Zone
Combat (or Convergence) Zone
CZMA
Coastal Zone Management Act
CZMP
Coastal Zone Management Program

D

D
Daily (report frequency)
Darkness
Development
Dust (weather symbol)
Duty
D, DEC
Deceased

DA
Deaerating
Defense Aid
Delayed Action
Denmark (message traffic)
Dental Apprentice
Design Agent
Direction Action (bomb fuze)
Discrete Address
Double-Acting (or Attack)
Drift Angle
D/A
Digital-to-Analog (converter)
DAA
Data Access Arrangement
Designated Approving Authority
DAAS
Defense Automatic Addressing System
DAASO
Defense Automatic Addressing System Office
DAB
Design Appraisal Board
Destroyer Advisory Board
Disbursing/Accounting Branch
DABES
Drug and Alcohol Abuse Education Specialist
DABLC
Director, Advanced Bases Logistic Control
DABOA
Director, Advanced Base Office, Atlantic
DABOP
Director, Advanced Base Office, Pacific
DABRK
Daybreak
DAC
Days After Contract
Design Augmented by Computers
Digital-to-Analog Converter (NNSS)
Duplicate Aperture Card
DACM
Defensive Air Combat Maneuvering
DACOWITS
Defense Advisory Committee on Women in
the Service
DADAC
Digital-to-Analog Deck Angle Converter
DADCAP
Dawn and Dusk Combat Air Patrol
DADMS
Defense Mapping Agency Automated
Distribution Management System
DADS
Deficiency Analysis Data System
DAE
Data Acquisition Equipment
DAES
Drug Abuse Education Specialist
DAF
Data Acquisition Facility
Document Acquisition File

DAGO
District Aviation Gas Office
DAIR
Direct Altitude Identification Readout
DAIS
Director of Automatic Information Service
DAISY
Double Precision Automatic Interpretive
System
DALGT
Daylight
DALS
Data Acquisition Logging System
Distress Alerting and Locating System
DALVP
Delay enroute authorized, chargeable as
ordinary leave, provided it does not
interfere with reporting on date specified
and provided individual has sufficient
accrued leave
DAM
Damage
DAMCONTRACEN
Damage Control Training Center
DAME
Distance, Azimuth Measuring Equipment
DA-MON-YR
Day-Month-Year
DAMP
Downrange Antimissile Measurement Project
DAMS
Defense Against Missiles System
DAN
Day Number Entry (NNSS)
Disciplinary Action Notice
DANC
Decontamination Agent, Non-Corrosive
DANTES
Defense Activity for Non-Traditional
Education Support
DAO
District Accounting (or Aviation) Office(r)
Division Ammunition Office
DAP
Domestic Action Program
DAPA
Drug and Alcohol Program Advisor
DAPF
Data Analysis and Processing Facility
DAPS
Direct Access Programming System
DAR
Defense Acquisition Regulation
Departure Approval Request
Developed Area Ratio (propellers)
DARO
Defense ADPE Reutilization Office
DARPA
Defense Advanced Research Projects
Agency

DART
Decentralized Advanced Replenishment
Technique
Deployable Automatic Relay Terminal
Detection, Action, Response, Technique
Development Advanced Rate Techniques
Directional Automatic Realignment of
Trajectory
Disappearing Automatic Retaliatory Target
Dual-Axis Rate Transducer
DAS
Data Acquisition System
Datatron Assembly System
Defense Audit(ing) Service
Digital Analog Simulation
DASA
Defense Atomic Support Agency
DASC
Direct Air Support Center
DASCO
Digital-to-Analog Synchro Converter
DASD, DEPASSTSECDEF
Deputy Assistant Secretary of Defense
DASD(CP)
Deputy Assistant Secretary of Defense
(Civilian Personnel)
DASD(EO)
Deputy Assistant Secretary of Defense (Equal
Opportunity)
DASD(MP)
Deputy Assistant Secretary of Defense
(Military Personnel Policy)
DASH
Drone Antisubmarine Helicopter—also called
"Destroyer Antisubmarine Helicopter"
DASO
Demonstration and Shakedown Operations
DASO CREW EVAL
Demonstration and Shakedown Operations
Crew Evaluation
DASPAC
Defense Auditing Service, Pacific
DASSO
Data Systems Support Office
DASSO/FMSO
Data Systems Support Office/Fleet Material
Support Office
DAST
Division for Advanced Systems Technology
DASTARD
Destroyer Antisubmarine Transportable Array
Detector
DAT
Dependents' Assistance Team
Design Approval Test
Development Assist Team
Distillate Assistance/Advisory Team
Drug Abuse Team
DATA
Defense Air Transportation Administration
Dual Aerosol Transport Apparatus

DATACOL
Data Collection
DATACORTS
Data Correlation and Transfer System
DATANET
Data Network (DCS)
DATC
Development and Training Center
DATE DOS
Date Dependents Arrived at Overseas Station
DATICO
Digital Automatic Tape Intelligence Checkout
DATO
Disbursing and Transportation Office
DATP
Drug Abuse Testing Program
DAU
Daughter
DAVA
Directorate for Audio-Visual Activities (DOD)
DAVC
Delayed Automatic Volume Control
DAWN
Digital Automated Weather Network
DB
Data Bank
Day Beacon
Decibels
Demand Base
DB, D/B
Dive Bomber
DBH
Developmental Big Hydrofoil
Diameter at Breast Height
Division Beachhead
DBI
Demand Base Item
DBL
Double Reduction Gears
DBMS
Data Base Management System
DBO
Data Buoy Office (NOAA)
DBP
Data Buoy Project (USN-USCG)
DBSO
District Base Services Office
DC
Damage Control
Decagram (U/I)
Deck Court
Defense Counsel
Dental Corps
Development Characteristics
Digital Computer
Direct Current
Discarded Clothing
DC, DCH
Depth Charge
DC1
Damage Controlman First Class

DC2
Damage Controlman Second Class
DC3
Damage Controlman Third Class
D/C
Drift Correction
DCA
Damage Control Assistant
Defense Communications Agency
Drift Correction Angle
DCAA
Defense Contract Audit Agency
DCAEUR
Defense Communications Agency, Europe
DCAFLDOFC
Defense Communications Agency Field Office
DCAOC
Defense Communications Agency Operations
Center
DCAP
Deficiency Corrective Action Program
DCAPAC
Defense Communications Agency, Pacific
DCAS
Defense Contract Administration Services
DCASA
Defense Contract Administration Service Area
DCASMA
Defense Contract Administration Service
Management Area
DCASD
Defense Contract Administration Services
District
DCASO
Defense Contract Administration Services
Office
DCASPO
Defense Contract Administration Services
Plant Office
DCASPRO
Defense Contract Administration Services
Plant Representative Office(r)
DCASR
Defense Contract Administration Services
Region
DC-AUTOMET
Directional Controlled-Automatic
Meteorological (compensation)
DCB
Damage Control Booklet
Data (or Design) Control Board
Defense Communications Board
DCC
Chief Damage Controlman
Data Control Center
Debarkation Control Center
Display Control Console
District Communications Center
Drill, Command and Ceremony
DCC, DC CENTRAL
Damage Control Central

DC CENTRAL, DCC
Damage Control Central
DCCI
Data Converter-Control Indicator
DCCM
Master Chief Damage Controlman
DCCS
Defense Case Control System
Digital Camera Control System
Senior Chief Damage Controlman
DCDCR
Definition of Control, Display and
Communications Requirements
DCDP
Defense Center Data Processor
D-CDR, DEPCOM
Deputy Commander
DCE
Directorate of Communications-Electronics
DCF
Dependency Certificate Filed
Disaster Control Force
Discounted Cash Flow
DCFA
Damage Controlman Fireman Apprentice
DCFEM
Dynamic Cross-Field Electron Multiplication
DCFN
Damage Controlman Fireman
DCG
Damage Control Group
DCH
Damage Control Hulk
Data Communications Handler
District Chaplain
DCH, DC
Depth Charge
DCI
Damage Control Instructor
DCII
Defense Central Index of Investigations
DCL
Data Check List
DCM
Defense Combat Maneuvering
Design Criteria Manual
Directorate for Classified Management
DCMAILSUB
Discharge certificate signed by Secretary of
the Navy being retained in
NAVMILPERSCOM and will be mailed to
member's home subsequent to separation
DCMS
Director, COMSEC Material System
DCN
Design (or Drawing) Change Notice
Digital Computer Newsletter (publication)
Document Control Number
DCNM
Deputy Chief of Naval Management

DCNM, DEPCHNAVMAT
Deputy Chief of Naval Material
DCNM(D)
Deputy Chief of Naval Management
(Development)
DCNM(M&F)
Deputy Chief of Naval Management (Material
and Facilities)
DCNM(M&O)
Deputy Chief of Naval Management
(Management and Organization)
DCNM(P&FM)
Deputy Chief of Naval Management
(Programs and Financial Management)
DCNO
Deputy Chief of Naval Operations
DCNO(AIR)
Deputy Chief of Naval Operations (Air)
DCNO(D)
Deputy Chief of Naval Operations
(Development)
DCNO(FO&R)
Deputy Chief of Naval Operations (Fleet
Operations and Readiness)
DCNO(L)
Deputy Chief of Naval Operations (Logistics)
DCNO(MPT)
Deputy Chief of Naval Operations
(Manpower, Personnel and Training)
DCNO(P&P)
Deputy Chief of Naval Operations (Plans and
Policies)
DCNO(P&R)
Deputy Chief of Naval Operations (Personnel
and Naval Reserve)
DCNO(SW)
Deputy Chief of Naval Operations (Submarine
Warfare)
DCNOTEMAILSUB
Discharge certificate signed by Secretary of
the Navy and notification concerning Naval
Reserve appointment being retained in
NAVMILPERSCOM and will be mailed to
member's home subsequent to separation
DCO
Depth Cut-Out
District Clothing (or Communications) Officer
DCOFS, DCS
Deputy Chief of Staff
DCP
Decision Coordinating Paper
Design Change Proposal
Development Concept Paper (or Plan)
Director of Civilian Personnel
DCPA
Defense Civil Preparedness Agency
DCPG
Defense Communications Planning Group

DCPO
Damage Control Petty Officer
District Civilian Personnel Office(r)
DSA Civil Preparedness Office
DCPR
Defense Contractor's Planning Report
DCR
Decrease
Design Certification Review
DCRESMAILSUB
Discharge certificate signed by Secretary of
the Navy together with Naval Reserve
appointment being retained in
NAVMILPERSCOM and will be mailed to
member's home subsequent to separation
DCRO
District Civilian Readjustment Office(r)
DCRP
Disaster Control Recovery Plan
DCS
Defense Communications System
DCS, DCOFS
Deputy Chief of Staff
DCSC, DEFCONSTSUPCEN
Defense Contruction Supply Center
DCSLOG
Deputy Chief of Staff, Logistics
DCSP
Defense Communications Satellite Program
DC/SR
Display and Control/Storage and Retrieval
DCSS
Defense Communications Satellite System
DCSTC
Defense Communications Station Technical
Control
DCT
Depth-Charge Throwers
Depth Control Tanks
DCT, DRCT
Direct
DCTL
Direct-Coupled Transistor Logic (circuit)
DCU
Device (or Document) Control Unit
DD
Defense Department
Departure Date
Determination of Dependency
Development Directive
Double Drift
Drydock
Duty Driver
DD, DISCH(DD)
Dishonorable Discharge
DD, DES
Destroyer
DD, DOD
Department of Defense
D&D
Drunk and Dirty

DD(A&HR)
Deputy Director of Attachés and Human
Resources (DIA)
DDALV
Days delay enroute authorized, chargeable
as leave
DDALVAHP
Days delay at home or leave address within
CONUS authorized, chargeable as leave
provided it does not interfere with reporting
date as specified. Advanced leave may be
granted where necessary.
DDAM
Dynamic Design Analysis Method
DDAS
Digital Data Acquisition System
D-DAY
Day of landing or commencement of
hostilities
DDC
Deck Decompression Chamber
Defense Documentation Center
Defensive Driving Course
Direct Digital Control
DD(C)
Deputy Director for Collection (DIA)
DDCFSO
Defense Documentation Center Field Office
DDCPO
Division Damage Control Petty Officer
DDCSTI
Defense Documentation Center for Scientific
and Technical Information
DDD
Deadline Delivery Date
Diesel Direct Drive
Digital Depth Detector
Drug Detection Dog
DDE
Escort Destroyer
DD(E)
Deputy Director of Estimates (DIA)
DDEP
Defense Development Exchange Program
DDESB
Department of Defense Explosives Safety
Board
DDF
Design Disclosure Format
DDG
Guided Missile Destroyer
DDGC
Dishonorable Discharge, General
Court-Martial after Confinement in Prison
DDGI
Dishonorable Discharge, General
Court-Martial, Immediate
DDGOS
Deep-Diving Submarines, General Overhaul
Specifications

DDGP
Dishonorable Discharge, General
   Court-Martial after Violation of Probation
DDI
Director of Defense Information
DD(I)
Deputy Director of Intelligence (DIA)
DDIC
Department of Defense Disease and Injury
   Codes
DD(IS)
Deputy Director for Information Systems
   (DIA)
DDL
Data Description Language (CODASYL)
Data Distribution List
DDO
Deputy Disbursing Officer
District Dental Office(r)
Dummy Delivery Order
DDOA
Deputy Director of Operations and
   Administration
DDP
Design Data Package
DD(PCD&T)
Deputy Director for Personnel, Career
   Development and Training (DIA)
DDR
Radar Picket Destroyer
DDRE, DDR&E
Director of Defense Research and
   Engineering
DDRR
Digital Data Regenerative Repeater
Directional Discountinuity Ring Radiator
DDS
Deep-Diving System
Design Data Sheet (or Standard)
Design Disclosure Standard
DD(S)
Deputy Director for Support (DIA)
DDSE
Design Disclosure for Systems and
   Equipment
DDST
Deputy Director for Science and Technology
DD(S&TI)
Deputy Director for Scientific and Technical
   Intelligence (DIA)
DDT&E
Design, Development, Test and Evaluation
DDTO
District Domestic Transportation Office(r)
DDU
Document Distribution Unit
DDV
Deep-Diving Vehicle

DE
Densimeter
Development Engineering
Dose Equivalent (radiation)
Double-Ended
Pending Detachment (NAPMIS)
DE, DEC
December
D/E
Declared Excess
DEA
Data Exchange Agreement
DEC
Control Escort Vessel
Decision
Declination
Decode (NNSS)
DEC, D
Deceased
DEC, DE
December
DECA
Descent Engine Control Assembly
DECC
Defense Commercial Communications Center
DECCO
Defense Commercial Communications Office
DECEO
Defense Communications Engineering Office
   (DCA)
DECL
Declared
DECM
Deception (or Deceptive, or Defense, or
   Defensive) Electronic Countermeasures
DECMSN, DECOM
Decommission
DECMSND, DECOMD
Decommissioned
DECOM, DECMSN
Decommission
DECOMD, DECMSND
Decommissioned
DED
Deduct
DEDAD
Data Element Dictionary and Directory
DEE
Digital Evaluation Equipment
DEEPSUBSYS, DDS
Deep Submergency Systems
DEEPSUBSYSPROJO, DSSPO
Deep Submergency Systems Project Office
DEEPSUBSYSPROJTECHO, DSSPTO
Deep Submergency Systems Project
   Technical Office
DEER
Directional Explosive Echo-Ranging
DEERS
Defense Enrollment Eligibility Reporting
   System

DEF
Defend
Defense
DEFCLOTH&TEXSUPCEN
Defense Clothing and Textile Supply Center
DEFCOM
Defense Command
DEFCOMMSYS
Defense Communications System
DEFCON
Defense Condition
DEFCONSTSUPCEN, DSCS
Defense Construction Supply Center
DEFELECSUPCEN, DESC
Defense Electronics Supply Center
DEFER
Deferred
DEFGENSUPCEN, DGSC
Defense General Supply Center
DEFINDPLANTEQUIPCEN, DIPEC
Defense Industrial Plant Equipment Center
DEFINDSUPCEN, DISC
Defense Industrial Supply Center
DEFINDSUPDEP, DISD
Defense Industrial Supply Depot
DEFINTELAGCY, DIA
Defense Intelligence Agency
DEFINTELSCOL
Defense Intelligence School
DEFPERSUPPCEN, DPSC
Defense Personnel Support Center
DEFREMANEDCEN
Defense Resources Management Education
Center
DEFSEC
Defense Section
DEFSUBSUPCEN, DSSC
Defense Subsistence and Supply Center
DEFWEAPSYSMGMTCEN
Defense Weapons Systems Management
Center
DEG
Degree
DEG&DEP
Degaussing and Deperming
DEG/RANGE
Degaussing Range
DEH
Deepwater Escort Hydrofoil
DEIMOS
Development and Investigation of Military
Orbital Systems
DEIS
Defense Energy Information System
Draft Environmental Impact Statement
DEL
Delivered

DELCOMBI
Command delivering orders initiate
background investigation immediately by
submitting forms required by OPNAVINST
5510.1D, as applicable, with ultimate duty
station designated as recipient of results.
DELCOMBI ALFA
Command delivering orders initiate
background investigation immediately by
submitting forms to NAVMILPERSCOM,
with ultimate duty station designated
recipient of results.
DELCOMBI BRAVO
Command delivering orders initiate
background investigation immediately by
submitting form to NAVMILPERSCOM
(Code F1B) under letter of transmittal.
DELCOMBI CHARLIE
Command delivering orders initiate
background investigation by submitting
forms to ONI (OP-922Y5) with ultimate duty
station designated as recipient of results.
DELCOMPLYINST
Delivered orders comply with current
NAVMILPERSCOMINST 5510.3.
DELGRU
Delaware Group
DELINUS
Provided no excess leave involved,
authorized to delay (number of days
specified) in reporting, to count as leave,
any portion of which may be taken in
CONUS.
DELPARTURE
Provided no excess leave involved,
authorized to delay (number of days or until
date specified), to count as leave, any
portion of which may be taken prior to or
after departure.
DELREP
Provided no excess leave involved,
authorized delay (number of days or until
date specified) in reporting, to count as
leave (MILPERSMAN 1810360). If member
reports before NLT date, may not be paid
per diem for period NET date unless
authorized IAW NAVMILPERSCOMINST
1320.9. Keep old and new duty station
advised of address (MILPERSMAN
1810380). Flag officers also forward
itinerary to NAVMILPERSCOM (Code Of).
For circuitous travel and leave visits to
foreign countries see NAVMILPERSMAN
1810280.6 and 3020420. For leave
authorized TEMADD orders, indicate on
original orders date and hour TEMADD
commenced and was completed.

DELREPANY
Provided no excess leave involved, authorized to delay (number of days specified) in reporting, to count as leave, any portion of which may be taken prior to or after reporting at temporary duty station(s). Keep duty station advised of address. If he avails himself of this leave, indicate on original orders date and hour TEMADD commenced and was completed.

DELREPARUS
Provided no excess leave involved, authorized to delay (number of days or until date specified) to count as leave, any portion of which may be taken prior to or after arrival CONUS.

DELREPGRAD
Authorized to delay (number of days or until date specified) in reporting, to count as graduation leave. (MILPERSMAN 3820050.6 and 18110360.) Total amount of graduation leave shall not exceed 30 days and must be taken within three months of date of graduation, otherwise delay counts as advance leave. If member reports before NLT date, may not be paid per diem for period prior to NET date unless authorized IAW NAVMILPERSCOMINST 1320.9. Keep old and new station advised of address (MILPERSMAN 1810280).

DELREPVAN
Authorized to delay (number of days or until date specified) in reporting, to count as advance leave. (MILPERSMAN 1810360). If member reports before NLT date, may not be paid per diem for period prior NET date unless authorized IAW NAVMILPERSCOMINST 1320.9. Keep new station advised of address (MILPERSMAN 1810380).

DELRIVPOE
Delay in arriving at port of embarkation

DELTA
Detailed Labor and Time Analysis

DELTIC
Delay Line Time Compression

DELURN
Provided no excess leave involved, authorized to delay (number of days or until date specified) in returning to duty station, to count as leave. Keep duty station advised of address. If he avails himself of this leave, indicate on original orders date and hour TEMADD commenced and was completed.

DEM
Demand
Demote
Disability Evaluation

DEMBOMB
Demolition Bomb

DEMC
Defense Electronics Management Center

DEMIZ
Dew East Military Identification Zone

DEMO
Demolition

DEMO, DEMON
Demonstration

DEMOB
Demobilization

DEMON, DEMO
Demonstration

DEN
Data Element Number

DENBN
Dental Battalion

DENCO
Dental Company

DENT
Dental
Dental Civic Action Program

DENYG
Denying

DEO(A)
Dependents' Education Office (Atlantic)

DEO(P)
Dependents' Education Office (Pacific)

DEP
Deflection Error Probable
Deployment
Depot
Deputy

DEP, DEPN
Dependent

DEPCHNAVMAT, DCNM
Deputy Chief of Naval Material

DEPCHNAVMAT(MAT&FAC)
Deputy Chief of Naval Material (Material and Facilities)

DEPCOM, D-CDR
Deputy Commander

DEPCOMFEWSG
Deputy Commander Fleet Electronic Warfare Support Group

DEPCOMLANTNAVFACENGCOM
Deputy Commander Atlantic Naval Facilities Engineering Command

DEPCOMOPTEVFORLANT
Deputy Commander Operational Test and Evaluation Force, Atlantic

DEPCOMOPTEVFORPAC
Deputy Commander Operational Test and Evaluation Force, Pacific

DEPCOMPACNAVFACENGCOM
Deputy Commander Pacific Naval Facilities Engineering Command

DEPCOMPT
Deputy Comptroller

DEPCON
Departure Control

DEPDIR
Deputy Director
DEPEVACPAY
Dependents' Evacuation Pay
DEPN, DEP
Dependent
DEPNAV, DON
Department of the Navy
DEPNOTAUTH
Dependents not authorized at overseas duty
station. For entitlements, transportation of
dependents, and shipment HHG see JTR,
par. M 7005 and M 8253-2, and NTI, par.
1055-1.
DEPSUM
Daily Estimated Position Summary
DEPT
Department
DEPTNAVINSTR
Department of Naval Instruction
DEPNAVSCI
Department of Naval Science
DERAST
Diesel Engineering Readiness Assistance
Team
DERI
Deep Electric Research Investigation
DEROS
Date of Estimated Rotation from Overseas
Station
Departing Roster
DERP
Deficient Equippage Reporting Procedures
DES
Desert(er), (-tion)
Desirable
DES, DD
Destroyer
DES ACCTS
Deserter's Accounts
DESC, DEFELECSUPCEN
Defense Electronics Supply Center
DESCHA
Destination Change
DESDEVDIV
Destroyer Development Division
DESDEVGRU
Destroyer Development Group
DESDEVRON
Destroyer Development Squadron
DESDIV
Destroyer Division
DESEFF
Deserter's Effects
DESFLOT
Destroyer Flotilla
DESFLTSURG
Designated student naval flight surgeon
DESIG, DSG
Designate

DESIG, DSGN
Designation
DESIGDISBAGENT
Designated special disbursing agent, to
remain in force from date assuming duty
until date detachment
DESNAVAV
Designated student naval aviator
DESO
District Education Office(r)
DESOIL
Diesel Oil
DESREP
Destroyer Repair (or Representative)
DESRON
Destroyer Squadron
DEST
Destroy
DESTIN
Destination
DET
Design Evaluation Test
Detachment
Detail
Detainee
DETD
Detached Duty
DETG
Defense Energy Task Group
DETM
Determine
DET PAY
Detained Pay
DETRELBY
When relieved by (officer indicated) detach
from duty
DEV
Deviation (request)
DEV, DVLP
Development
DEVNO
Deviation Request Number
DEW
Directed Energy Weapon
Distant Early Warning
DEWIZ
Distant Early Warning Identification Zone
DF
Delay(ed) Fuze (or Failure)
Distribution Factor (radiation)
DF, D/F
Direction Finding
D&F
Determination and Findings
DFA
Designated Field Activity
DFCO
Duty Flying Control Officer
DFD
Digital Flight Display

DFGO
"Damn Fool Ground Officer" (slang)
DFH
Developmental Fast Hydrofoil
DFHMA
Defense Family Housing Management
    Account
DF I
Direction Finding, Phase I (course)
DF II
Direction Finding, Phase II (course)
DFM
Diesel Fuel, Marine
DFQAR
Defense Fuel Quality Assurance Residency
DFR
Dropped from Rolls as Deserter
DFS
Defense Fuel Support
Departure from Specifications
Distance-Finding Station
Dynamic Flight Simulator
DFSB
Defense Force Section Base
DFSC, DEFUELSUPCEN
Defense Fuel Supply Center
DFSTN
Direction-Finding Station
DFT
Deaerating Feed Tank
Director, Fleet Training
DFU
Drainage Fixture Unit
DFUS
Diffuse
DFW
Diesel Fuel Waiver
DG
Decigram (U/I)
Defense Grouping
Degaussing
Diesel Generator
Direction Gyro
DGBC
(Polaris) Digital Geoballistic Computer
DGD
Diesel Geared Drive
DGM
Defense Guidance Memorandum
DG-MG
Diesel Geared-Motor Geared
DGO
Degaussing Officer
DGRO
Degaussing Range Officer
DGSC, DEFGENSUPCEN
Defense General Supply Center
DGSE
Developmental Ground Support Equipment
DGTO
Degaussing Technical Officer

DGU
Display Generator Unit
DGV
Digital Generator Video
DGWO
Degaussing Wiping Officer
DGZ
Desired (or Designated) Ground Zero
DH
Decision (or Desired) Height
Desired Heading
Half-Dozen (U–I)
DHE
Data Holding Equipment
DHF
Demand History File
DHO
District Historical Office(r)
DHQ
Division Headquarters
DHSS
Data Handling Sub-System
DI
Defense Information
Design Integration
Diatom
Digital Inputs
Direct
Direct Impulse
Direction Indicator
Dispenser (U/I)
District Inspector
Drill Instructor
D&I
Disassembly and Inspection
DIA
Diaphone
DIA, DEFINTELAGCY
Defense Intelligence Agency
DIAC
Defense Industrial Advisory Council
DIADC
Defense Intelligence Agency Dissemination
    Center
DIAG
Diagonal
Diagram
DIAL
Defense Intelligence Agency Liaison
Deficiency in Allowance List(ing)
DIALGOL
Dialect of Algorithmic Language
DIAN
Decca Integrated Airborne Navigation
    (system)
DIANE
Digital Integrated Attack and Navigation
    Equipment
Distance Indicating Automatic Navigation
    Equipment

DIBA
Digital Integral Ballistic Analyzer
DIC
Dependency and Indemnity Compensation
Detailed Interrogation Center
DIC, DICT
Dictionary
DICBM
Depressed Trajectory Intercontinental Ballistic Missile
DICNAVAB
Dictionary of Naval Abbreviations (USNI Press)
DICOSE
Digital Communications System Evaluator
DICT, DIC
Dictionary
DID
Data Item Description
Digital Information Display
DI/DES
(Vessel) Disposed of by Destruction
DIDS
Data Item Descriptions
Defense Integrated Data System
Digital Information Display System
DIDU
Defense Item Data Ultilization (program)
DIECO
Department of Defense Item Entry Control Office
DIER
Department Instrument Equipment Reserve
DIES
Diesel
DIF
Duty involving flying
DIF, DIFF
Difference
DIFAR
Direction Low-Frequency Analyzer and Ranging (system)
DIFDEN
Duty in a flying status not involving flying
DIFDENIS
Duty under instruction in a flying status not involving flying
DIFDENRELAS
Duty in a flying status not involving flying as his relief
DIFDENREPT
Detailed to duty in a flying status not involving flying effective upon reporting
DIFF, DIF
Difference
DIF/FLC
Disposition (of vessel by) Foreign Liquidation Corporation
DIFF PAY
Difference in Pay

DIFINSOPS
Duty under instruction in a flying status involving operational or training flights
DIFINSPRO
Duty under instruction in a flying status involving proficiency flying
DIFM
Due in From Maintenance
DIFOPS
Duty in a flying status involving operational or training flights
DIFOPSDORSE
Detailed to duty in a flying status involving operational or training flights effective such date as hereon endorsed
DIFOPSEXIST
Existing detail to duty in a flying status involving operational or training flights effective upon reporting
DIFOT
Duty in flying status involving operational or training flights
DIFOTCREW
Duty in flying status involving operational or training flights as a crewmember
DIFOTDORSE
Duty in flying status involving operational or training flights effective such date as endorsed
DIFOTEXIST
Existing detail to DIFOT continues in effect
DIFOTINSCREW
Duty under instruction in flying status involving operational or training flights as a crewmember.
DIFOTINSNONCREW
Duty under instruction in flying status involving operational or training flights as a non-crewmember.
DIFOTREPT
Duty in flying status involving operational or training flights upon reporting
DIFOT RVK
Duty in flying status involving operational or training flights revoked
DIFPRO
Duty in a flying status involving proficiency flying
DIFTECH
Duty as a technical observer in a flying status involving operational or training flights
DIGOPS
Digest of Operations
DIGS
Defense Information Guidance Series (publication)
DIHEST
Directly-Induced High-Explosive Simulation Technique
DIIC
Dielectrically Isolated Integrated Circuit

DI/INT
Disposition (of vessel by) Department of Interior
DIIO
District Industrial Incentive Office(r)
DIIP
Defense Inactive Item Program
DILS
Doppler Inertial LORAN System
DIM
District Industrial Manager
DIM, DMSH
Diminish
DIMATE
Depot Installation Maintenance Automatic Test Equipment
DIMES
Defense Integrated Management Engineering System
Development and Improved Management Engineering Systems
DIMUS
Digital Multi-Beam Steering
DIN
Dingy (USCG)
DINA
Direct Noise Amplifier (airborne radar)
DINFOS
(Department of) Defense Information School
DINO
Deputy Inspector of Naval Ordnance
DIO
District Intelligence Officer
DIP
Defense Information Procedure
Defense Investigative Program
Deserter Information Point
Display Information Processor
Driver Improvement Program
Dual Inline Package
DIPEC, DEFINDPLANTEQUIPCEN
Defence Industrial Plant Equipment Center
DIR
Director
Disassembly Inspection Report
DIR, DIREC
Direction
DIRAFIED
Director, Armed Forces Information and Education Division
DIRAPCG
Director, Joint Agate Punch Control Group
DIRARFCOS
Director, Armed Forces Courier Service
DIRBY
When directed by
DIRC
Defense Investigative Review Council
DIRDET
When directed, detached (duty indicated)

DIREC, DIR
Direction
DIRFLDSUPPACT
Director, Field Support Activity
DIR/GEN
Director General
DIRHSG
You are directed to report to the appropriate housing referral office prior to negotiating any agreement for off-base housing
DIRID
Directional Infrared Intrusion Detector
DIRJOAP
Director, Joint Oil Analysis Program
DIRJOAPTSC
Director, Joint Oil Analysis Program Technical Support Center
DIRLAUTH
Direct liaison authorized
Direct Line of Authority
DIRMOBSEARAN
Director, Mobile Sea Range
DIRNAVCURSERV
Director, Naval Courier Service
DIRNAVHIS
Director of Naval History
DIRNAVINVSERV
Director, Naval Investigative Service
DIRNAVMARCORMARS
Director, Navy-Marine Corps Military Affiliate Radio Service
DIRNAVPUBPRINTSERV, DNPPS
Director, Navy Publications and Printing Service
DIRNAVRESINTPRO
Director, Naval Reserve Intelligence Program
DIRNAVSECGRUEUR
Director, Naval Security Group, Europe
DIRNAVSECGRULANT
Director, Naval Security Group, Atlantic
DIRNAVSECGRUPAC
Director, Naval Security Group, Pacific
DIRNCPB
Director, Naval Council of Personnel Boards
DIRNCPBDET
Director, Naval Council of Personnel Boards Detachment
DIRNSA
Director, National Security Agency
DIRNSCPO
Director, Navy Secretariat Civilian Personnel Office
DIRPRO
When directed proceed
DIRS
Dental Information Retrieval Program
DIRSDIMA
Director, San Diego (CA) Intermediate Maintenance Activity

DIRSP/PROJMGRFBM
Director, Special Projects/Project Manager
Fleet Ballistic Missile
DIRSSP
Director, Strategic Systems Projects
DIS
Defense Intelligence School
Defense Investigative Service
Distance
DIS, DISCH
Discharge
DIS, DISP
Dispatch
DIS, DSNT
Distant
DISAL
Disposition (of vessel by) Sale
DISAP
Disapproved
DISB
Disbursing
DISBO
Disbursing Officer
DISBOFFCOP
Disbursing officer making payment on these
orders forward copy of orders with copy of
paid voucher to (command indicated)
DISBSUBREPT
Disbursing officer making payment submit
monthly letter reports by 10th of following
month to NAVMILPERSCOM (Code 33) of
pay and allowances earned (including
special/incentive pay) in detail. Submit two
certified copies of orders when member
reports to or is detached from assignment.
Also submit two copies of all travel and per
diem payment vouchers.
DISC
Discontinued
Discrepancy Identification and System
Checkout
DISC, DEFINDSUPCEN
Defense Industrial Supply Center
DISC, DISCON
Discontinue
DISCH, DIS
Discharge
DISCH(BCD), BCD
Bad Conduct Discharge
DISCH(DD), DD
Dishonorable Discharge
DISCH(HON)
Honorable Discharge
DISCO
Defense Industrial Security Clearance Office
DISCOL
Discolored
DISCON
Discrepancy in Shipment Confirmation
DISCON, DISC
Discontinue

DISCORS
Discrepancy in Shipment Cargo Outturn
Reporting System
DISCOS
Disturbance Compensation System
DI/SCP
Disposition (of vessel by) Scrapping
DISCREP
Discrepancy Report
DISD, DEFINDSUPDEP
Defense Industrial Supply Depot
DISDEP
Distant Deployment
DISEM
Disseminate
DISEMB
Disembark
DISESTAB
Disestablishment
Upon disestablishment
DISGOV
Foreign Government Effected Discharge
DISGRAT
Discharge Gratuity
DISI
Defense Industrial Security Institute
DISNAV
U.S. Navy or its Agency Effected Discharge
DISOP
Discharge by Operator
DISP
Defense Industry Studies Program
Disposal
DISP, DSP
Dispatch
DISREPS
(Transportation) Discrepancy in Shipment
Report
DIS RET
Disability Retirement
DISS
Dissolve
DIS SERV
Disability Severance
DIST, DST
District
DISTDENTALO, DDO
District Dental Officer
DISTEX
District Relief Exercise
DISTMEDO, DMO
District Medical Officer
DISTR, DISTRIB
Distribute
DISTREAT
Upon discharge treatment
DISTRIB, DISTR
Distribute
DISUB
Duty involving underway operations in
submarines

DIT
  Document Input Transmittal
  Dynamic Instrumentation Test
DI/TES
  Disposition (of vessel by using as target and)
    Tests
DI/TRN
  Disposition (of vessel by) Transfer to Other
    Government Agency
DIV
  Diversion
  Diving
  Division
DIVCOM
  Division Commander
DIVEDU
  Duty involving the performance of diving duty
DIVERTORD
  Diversion Order
DIVINFO
  Division of Information
DIVPAY
  Diving Pay
DK
  Deck
DK1
  Disbursing Clerk First Class
DK2
  Disbursing Clerk Second Class
DK3
  Disbursing Clerk Third Class
DKC
  Chief Disbursing Clerk
DKCM
  Master Chief Disbursing Clerk
DKCS
  Senior Chief Disbursing Clerk
DKSA
  Disbursing Clerk Seaman Apprentice
DKSN
  Disbursing Clerk Seaman
DL
  Day Letter
  Deciliter (U/I)
  Departure Locator
  Destroyer Leader
  Frigate
D/L
  Data Link
DLA
  Defense Logistic Agency
  Dislocation Allowance
  Dual Launching Adaptor
DLC
  Diagnostic Coed Laboratory
  Direct Lift Control (system)
  Dymo Laser Composer
DLCO
  Deck Landing Control Officer
DLCR
  Drawing List Change Report

DLG
  Defense Liaison Group
  Guided-Missile Frigate (or Destroyer Leader)
DLGN
  Nuclear-Powered Guided Missile Frigate (or
    Destroyer Leader)
DLH
  Direct Labor Hours
DLI
  Deck-Launched Interceptor
  Defense Language Institute
DLL
  Design Level Logic
DLM
  Depot Level Maintenance
DLMP
  Depot Level Maintenance Plan
DLMS
  Digital Landmass System
DLNC
  Deputy Local Naval Commander
DLO
  District Legal Office(r)
DLP
  Defense Language Program
  Director of Laboratory Programs
DLPT
  Defense Language Proficiency Test
DLR
  Daily Level Readiness (system)
  Depot Level Repairable
DLRO
  Director, Labor Relations Office
DLSC
  Defense Logistics Service (or Support, or
    Systems) Center
DLSIE
  Defense Logistics Studies Information
    Exchange
DLT
  Deck Landing Training
DLTS
  Deck Landing Training School
DLVR
  Delivery
DLY
  Daily
DM
  Data Management
  Depot Maintenance
  Design Manual
  Dram (U/I)
  Fast Minelayer
  Master Diver
DM1
  Illustrator Draftsman First Class
DM2
  Illustrator Draftsman Second Class
DM3
  Illustrator Draftsman Third Class

DMA
Defense Mapping Agency
Degraded Mission Assignment
Depot Maintenance Activity
Direct Memory Access (computers)
DMAAC
Defense Mapping Agency Aerospace Center
DMABO
Defense Mapping Agency Branch Office
DMABODET
Defense Mapping Agency Branch Office
Detachment
DMADISTRCEN
Defense Mapping Agency Distribution Center
DMAHTC
Defense Mapping Agency
Hydrographic/Topographic Center
DMALO
Defense Mapping Agency Liaison Office
DMAO
District Management Assistance Office
DMAODS
Defense Mapping Agency Office of
Distribution Services
DMC
Chief Illustrator Draftsman
Decision Module Compiler
Deck Motion Compensator
Defense Manpower Commission
Digital Manpower Commission
Digital Micro-Circuit
Direct Multiplex Control
DMCGS
Descriptive Macro-Code Generation System
DMCM
Master Chief Illustrator Draftsman
DMCS
Senior Chief Illustrator Draftsman
DMDC
Defense Manpower Data Center
DME
Design Margin Evaluation
Diagnostic Monitor Executive
Distance Measuring Equipment
DMEC
Defense Metals Equipment Center
DMED
Digital Message Entry Device
DMET
Defense Management Education and Training
Distance Measuring Equipment Touchdown
DMFT
Decayed, Missing and Filled Teeth
DMI
Direct Material Inventory
DMISA
Depot Maintenance Interservice Support
Agreement
DML
Data Manipulator Language (CODASYL)

DML DY
Demolition Duty
DMM
Domestic Mail Manual
DMMS
Depot Maintenance Management Subsystem
DMO
Data Management Office(r)
Dependent (or District) Meteorological Office
District Marine (or Material) Officer
DMO, DISTMEDO
District Medical Officer
DMR
Date Material Required
Defective Material Report
DMRI
Date Material Required Increasing (urgency)
DMRR
Defense Manpower Requirements Report
DMS
Defense Management Summary
Defense Mapping School
Defense Materials Service (or System)
Fast Minesweeper
D(M&S)
Director for Management and Plans (DIA)
DMSA
Illustrator Draftsman Seaman Apprentice
DMSH, DIM
Diminish
DMSMS
Diminishing Manufacturing Sources and
Material Shortages
DMSN
Illustrator Draftsman Seaman
DMSO
Directors of Major Staff Offices
DMSSB
Defense Material Specifications and
Standards Board
DMST, DEMON
Demonstrate
DMTS
Dynamic Multi-Tasking System
DM&TS
Departure of Mines and Technical Surveys
DMX
Data Multiplex Unit (TDDL)
DMZ
De-Militarized Zone
DN
Denied
Dentalman
Down
DNA
Defense Nuclear Agency
Designated National Agency
DNA-AEC
Defense Nuclear Agency-Atomic Energy
Commission

DNC
Department of the Navy Civilian
Direct Numerical Control
DNCCC
Defense National Communication Control
Center
DNDT
Department of the Navy Declassification
Team
DNEC
Distribution Navy Enlisted Classification
(codes)
DNET
Director, Naval Education and Training
DNFYP
Department of the Navy Five-Year Program
DNG
Distinguished Naval Graduate Program
DNI
Director of (or Division of) Naval Intelligence
DNIAS
Day-Night Indirect Attack Seeker
DNL
Director, Navy Laboratories
DNOP
Director of Naval Officer Procurement
DNP
(Reservists) Drill in Non-Pay Status
DNR
Does Not Run
DNS
Dense
Density
DNT
Director, Naval Telecommunications
DO
Defense (or Delivery, or Direct) Order
Dental (or Disbursing) Officer
Diesel Oil
Drop Out
DO, D/O
Duty Officer
DOA
Date of (Contract) Award
Day of Ammunition
Director for Operations and Administration
Dissolved Oxygen Analyzer
DOAL
Director of Airlift
DOB
Date of Birth
Defense Office Building (Pentagon)
DOC
Data Output Console
Department of Commerce
Direct Operating Costs
DOCC
Defense Operations Communications
Complex
DOCU
Document

DOD
Died of Disease
DOD, DD
Department of Defense
DODAAD
Department of Defense Activity Address
Directory
DODDSLANT
Department of Defense Dependents School,
Altantic
DOODSPAC
Department of Defense Dependents School,
Pacific
DODCI
Department of Defense Computer Institute
DODGE
Department of Defense Gravity Experiment
DODI
Department of Defense Instruction
DODIC
Department of Defense Identification Code
DOD-IR
Department of Defense Intelligence Reports
DODISS
Department of Defense Index of
Specifications and Standards
DODMERB
Department of Defense Medical Examination
Review Board
DODMUL
Department of Defense Master Urgency List
DO DOD
Diagnostic Output Data Additional
Development
DODPM
Department of Defense, Military Pay and
Allowances Entitlement Manual
DOES
Defense Organizational Entry Standards
DOFL
Diamond Ordnance Fuze Laboratory
DOFS(W)
Director of Stores (Washington)
DOG
Division Officer's Guide (USNI Press)
DOI
Departmental Operating Instructions
DOICC
Deputy Officer-in-Charge of Construction
DOL
Deep Ocean Laboratory (NCEL)
Dolphin
DOMIR
Definition of Operator/Maintainer Information
Requirements
DON
Dimensionality of Nations (project)
DON, DEPNAV
Department of the Navy

DONADPM
Department of the Navy Automatic Data
Processing Management
DONAL
Department of the Navy Occupational Level
DON FEORP
Department of the Navy Federal Equal
Opportunity Recruitment Program
DONPIC
Department of the Navy Program Information
Center
DONSTPP
Department of the Navy Study Program Plan
DOO
District Operations Officer
District Ordnance Office(r)
DOOLAR
Deep Ocean Object Location and Recovery
(system)
DOOW
Diving Officer-of-the-Watch
DOP
Designated Overhaul Point
DOPMA
Defense Officer Personnel Management Act
DOR
Daily Operational Report
Date of Rank
Dropout Rate
Dropped Own Request
DORA
Dynamic Operator Response Apparatus
DORAN
Doppler Ranging
DORIS
Direct Order Recording and Invoicing System
DOS
Day of Supply
Dependents Arrived at Overseas Station
DOSS
Disk-Oriented Supply System
DOSV
Deep Oceanographic Survey Vehicle
DOT
Deep Ocean Technology (project)
Department of Transportation
Directory of Occupational Titles
DOUCHE
Description of Underwater Contacts Hastily
and Exactly
DOV
Disbursing Officer's Voucher
DOVAP
Doppler Velocity and Position
DOW
Died of Wounds
DOWB
Deep Ocean Work Boat
DOZ, DZ
Dozen (U/I)

DP
Data Processing
Detention of Pay
Development Proposal
Dial Pulse
Differential Pressure
(By) Direction of the President
Displaced Person(s)
Dual-Purpose
DP1
Data Processing Technician First Class
DP2
Data Processing Technician Second Class
DP3
Data Processing Technician Third Class
D&P
Development and Production
DPB
Disaster Preparedness Bill
DPAO
District Public Affairs Officer
DPC
Chief Data Processing Technician
Defense Planning Committee
Defense Plants Corporation
Defense Procurement Circulars
Duty Preference Card
DPCA
Displayed Phase Center Antenna
DPCM
Master Chief Data Processing Technician
DPCS
Senior Chief Data Processing Technician
DPD
Data Processing Department
District Port Director
DPDMR
Defense Property Disposal Precious Metals
Recovery Office
DPDO
Defense Property Disposal Officer
DPDP
Defense Property Disposal Program
DPDREG
Defense Property Disposal Region
DPDRPACDET
Defense Property Disposal Region, Pacific
Detachment
DPDRPACSO
Defense Property Disposal Region, Pacific
Sales Office
DPDT
Double Pole, Double Throw (switch)
DPE
Data Processing Equipment
Director, Planning and Evaluation
DPI
Data Processing Installation
DPIR
Detailed Photo Interpretation Report

DPLO
District Postal Liaison Office(r)
DPM
Direct Procurement Method
Draft Presidential Memorandum
DPO
District Personnel (or Plans, or Postal) Officer
Duty Petty Officer
DPOB
Date and Place of Birth
DPP
Disaster-Preparedness Plan
DPPO
District Publications and Printing Office
Division Police Petty Officer
DPR
Double Pulse Rating
DPRT
Depart
DPS
Data Processing System
Decision Package Set
Defense Printing Service
DPSA
Data Processing Technician Seaman
Apprentice
DPSC, DEFPERSUPPCEN
Defense Personnel Support Center
DPSC
Data Processing Service Center
DPSCPAC
Data Processing Service Center, Pacific
DPSCWEST
Data Processing Service Center, West
DPSK
Differential Phase Shift Keying
DPSN
Data Processing Technician Seaman
DPSR
Data Processing Service Request
DPST
Deposit
DPT
Depart
Development Prototype
DPTNAVSCI
Department of Naval Science
DPTO
Director, Personnel (or Passenger)
Transportation Office
DPU
Differential Pressure Unit
DPV
Diver Propulsion Vehicle
DPWO
District Public Works Office(r)
DQ
Drawing Quality

DR
Debit
Debtor
Deficiency Report
Dental Recruit
Discrimination Radar
Drive
Drum (U/I)
DR, D/R
Dead Reckoning
D/R
Directional Radio
DRA
Dead Reckoning Analyzer
DRAI
Dead Reckoning Analyzer Indicator
DRAMS
DESC Requirements Allocation Manpower
System
DRANS
Data Reduction and Analysis Subsystem
DRAT
Data Reduction and Analysis Tape
DRB
Design (or Data) Review Board
DRC
Deputy Regional Commander
DRCCC
Defense Regional Communications Control
Center
DRCT, DCT
Direct
DR&CWG
Data Reduction and Computing Work Group
DRD
Data Requirement Description
DRDT&E
Director, Research, Development, Test and
Evaluation
DR&E
Defense Research and Engineering
DRET
Direct Reentry Telemetry
DRF
Disaster Response Force
DRFP
Design-Rated Full Power
DRFT
Drift
DRI
Dead Reckoning Indicator
DRIF
Defense Freight Railway Interchange Fleet
DRIFT
Diversity Receiving Instrumentation for
Telemetry
DRIS
Defense Retail Interservice Support (manual)
Digital Read-In System
DRJ
Data Requirements Justification

DRM
    Destructive Readout Memory
    Direction of Relative Motion (or Movement)
DRMO
    District Records Management Officer
DRN
    Data Release Notice
DRO
    Daily Report of Obligations
    Day-Room Orderly
    Direct Read-Out
DRP
    Dead Reckoning Plotter
    Direct Requisitioning Procedure
DRPR
    Drawing Practice
DRRA
    Direct-Reading Range Assessor
DRRB
    Data Requirements Review Board
DRRI
    Defense Race Relations Institute
DRS
    Digital Range Safety
    Doppler Radar Set
DRSC
    Direct Radar Scope Camera
DRSCPO
    District Reserve Supply Corps Program
      Officer
DRSCS
    Digital Range Safety Control System
DRSS
    Data Relay Satellite System
DRT
    Dead Reckoning Tracer
    Disaster Recovery Training
DRTD
    Disaster Recovery Training Department
DRU
    Demolition Research Unit
DS
    Diver, Salvage
    Double Slave (LORAN station)
    Double-Stranded
DS1
    Data Systems Technician First Class
DS2
    Data Systems Technician Second Class
DS3
    Data Systems Technician Third Class
D/S
    Dropped Shipped
DSA
    Defense Shipping Authority
    Defense Supply Agency
    Design Services Allocation
    Dial Service Assistance
DSAA
    Defense Security Assistance Agency

DSAD
    Director, Systems Analysis Division
DSAO
    Data Systems Automation Office
DSAP
    Defense Security Assistance Program
DSAR
    Defense Supply Agency Regulation
DSARC
    Defense Systems Acquisition Review Council
DSB
    Defense Science Board
    Duty Steam or Power Boat
DSBCO
    Defense Surplus Bidders Control Office
DSC
    Chief Data Systems Technician
    Defense Supply Center (or Corporation)
    Distinguished Service Cross
DSCA
    Data Systems Coordinating Activity (DOD)
DSC IL
    Defense Supply Center Indication List
DSCM
    Master Chief Data Systems Technician
DSCS
    Defense Satellite Communications System
    Digital Safety Control Switch
    Senior Chief Data Systems Technician
DSCS, DEFCONSTSUPCEN
    Defense Construction Supply Center
DSD
    Data Systems Design (or Division)
    Defense Systems Division
DSDS
    Dual-Source Dynamic Synchro
DSE
    Development (or Direct) Support Equipment
DSEB
    Defense Shipping Executive Board
DSFL
    Deleted and Superseded FIIN List
DSG
    Defense Suppression Group
DSG, DESIG
    Designate
DSGN, DESIG
    Designation
DSIATP
    Defense Sensor Interpretation and Training
      Program
DSIPT
    Dissipate
DSL
    Deep Scattering Layer
DSLE
    Directorate of Security and Law Enforcement
DSM
    Distinguished Service Medal
DSMG
    Designed Systems Management Group

DSMS
Defense Systems Management School
DSNT, DIS
Distant
DSO
DEERS Support Office
District Security (or Service, or Supply)
Office(r)
DSOT
Daily Systems Operability Test (SAM)
DSOTS
Demonstration Site Operational Test Series
DSP
Deep Submergence Program
Defense Standardization Program
Designated Stock Point
DSP, DISP
Dispensary
DSPA
Data Systems Participating Agency
DSPG
Defense Small Projects Group
Drill Service in Paygrade
D&S PIERS
Destroyer and Submarine Piers
DSPO
Duty Security Petty Officer
DSRPAC
Defense Subsistence Region, Pacific
DSRV
Deep Submergence Rescue Vehicle
DSS
Data Systems Specification
DSS, DEEPSUBSYS
Deep Submergence Systems
DSSA
Data Systems Technician Seaman Apprentice
DSSC, DEFSUBSUPCEN
Defense Subsistence and Supply Center
DSSCS
Defense Special Security Communications
System
DSSN
Data Systems Technician Seaman
Disbursing Station Symbol Number
DSSO
Defense Surplus Sales Office
District Ship's Service Office(r)
DSSP
Direct (or Defense) Support Point
DSSPO, DEEPSUBSYSPROJO
Deep Submergence System Project Office
DSSPTO, DEEPSUBSYSPROJTECHO
Deep Submergence Systems Project
Technical Office
DSSV
Deep Submergence Search Vehicle
DSSW
Defense Supply Service-Washington
Department of State Telecommunications
(facilities)

DST
Destructor
Director for Science and Technology
DST, DIST
District
DSU
Data Storage Unit
DSV
Deep Submergence Vehicle
DSVL
Doppler Sonar Velocity Log
DSVOPS
Duty as an operator or crewmember of an
operational self-propelled submersible
including underseas exploration and
research vehicles
DSW
Diesel Sea Water (cooling water)
Differential Shunt Winding (wiring)
DT
Deep Tank (stowage)
Diagnostic Time (computers)
Dynamic Tear
DT1
Dental Technician First Class
DT2
Dental Technician Second Class
DT3
Dental Technician Third Class
D/T
Detector/Tracker
DTA
Differential Thermal Analysis
DTACCS
Director, Telecommunications and Command
and Control Systems
DTAS
Data Transmission and Switching
DTB
Destroyer Tactical Bulletin
DTC
Chief Dental Technician
Desert Test Center
Design To Cost
DTCM
Master Chief Dental Technician
DTCS
Senior Chief Dental Technician
DTE
Dial Telephone Exchange
DT&E
Developmental Test and Evaluation
DTEAS
Detection, Track, Evaluation and Assignment
System
DTF
Data Transmission Facilities
Dental Treatment Facility
DTG
Date-Time-Group

DTI
Division of Technical Information (AEC)
DTIS
Drill Time in Service
DTL
Detail(ed)
Diode-Transistor-Logic (circuit)
DTM
Director, Telecommunications Management
DTMB
Defense Traffic Management Branch
DTMF
Dual-Tone Multi-Frequency
DTMS
Defense Traffic Management Service
DTN
Detain
DTNSRDC
David W. Taylor Naval Ship Research and
Development Center
DTNSRDCDET
David W. Taylor Naval Ship Research and
Development Center Detachment
DTNTN
Detention of Pay
DTO
Direct Turn-Over
District Training (or Transportation) Office(r)
DTOC
Division Tactical Operations Center
DTPEWS
Design-to-Price EW System
DTRA
Defense Technical Review Activity
DTRM
Dual-Thrust Rocket Motor
DTS
Daily Test Schedule
Data Terminal Simulator
Deep Tactical Support
Defense Telephone (or Transportation)
System
DTS-W
Defense Telephone System-Washington
DTV
Diving Training Vessel
DU, DUT, DY
Duty
DUCON
Duty connection
DUDAT
Due Date (or Deadline)
DUE AT DES
Due at Destination
DUFLY
Duty involving flying status
DUFLYTECH
Duty involving flying as a technical observer
DUFLYTECHNAV
Duty involving flying as a technical observer
non-pilot navigator

DUINS
Duty under instruction
DUINS/TEMDUINS STU
Duty under instruction or temporary duty
under instruction as a student
DUKW
Amphibious Truck, Duck, Troop
DUNC
Deep Underwater Nuclear Counter
DUNS
Deep Underground Support Center
DUP, DUPE
Duplicate
DUPE, DUP
Duplicate
DUR, DURG
During
DURELAS
Duty as his relief
DURG, DUR
During
DURS
Dockside Underway Replenishment Simulator
DUSD
Deputy Under Secretary of Defense
DUSD(AP)
Deputy Under Secretary of Defense
(Acquisition Policy)
DUSD(C³I)
Deputy Under Secretary of Defense
(Communications, Command, Control and
Intelligence)
DUSD(PR)
Deputy Under Secretary of Defense (Policy
Review)
DUSIGN
To duty assigned by
DUSN
Deputy Under Secretary of the Navy
DUSODA
For such other duty as (designated
command) may assign
DUSTA
Duty Station
DUT, DU, DY
Duty
DUV
Data Under Voice
DV
Distinguished Visitor
(DV)
Qualified as a Diver
D&V
Damage and Vulnerability
DVC
Direct View Console
DVFR
Defense Visual Flight Rules
DVLP, DEV
Development

DVNG DY
Diving Duty
D-VOF
Defense Mapping Agency Vertical
Obstruction File
DVM
Digital Voltmeter
D/W
Dependent Wife
DWA
Died of Wounds Resulting from Action with
Enemy
DWC
Damaged Weapons Control
Display and Weapon Control
DWEST
Deep-Water Environmental Survival Training
DWG
Drawing
DWICA
Deep-Water Isotopic Current Analyzer
DWL
Designer's Waterline
DWN
Down
DWP
Deep-Water Pier (complex)
DWPNT
Dew Point
DWS
Design Work Study
DWSMC
Defense Weapons Systems Management
Center
DWT
Deadweight Tons
DWV
Drain, Waste and Vent
DX
Data Extraction
Destroyer, New Construction
Duplex Operation
DX/DXG
New Construction Destroyer Program
DXG
New Construction, Guided Missile Destroyer
DXGN
New Construction, Nuclear-powered Guided
Missile Destroyer
DY
Dynamotors
DY, DU, DUT
Duty
DYDAT
Dynamic Data (allocator)
DYN
Dynamics
DYNAMO
Dynamic Action Management Operations
DZ
Drop Zone

DZ, DOZ
Dozen (U/I)

E

E
East(ern)
Efficiency (award)
Electrical
Electronic Countermeasures (NAO code)
Equatorial (air mass)
Excellence (award)
Experimental—although usually X
E^3
Electromagnetic Environmental Effects
EA
Each
Economic Analysis
Educational Advisor
Emergency Action
End Article
EA1
Engineering Aid First Class
EA2
Engineering Aid Second Class
EA3
Engineering Aid Third Class
E/A
Enemy Aircraft
EAB
Emergency Air Breathing (system)
EAC
Chief Engineering Aid
Emergency Action Console
Expect Approach Clearance (time)
EACA
Engineering Aid Construction Apprentice
EACN
Engineering Aid Constructionman
EACS
Senior Chief Engineering Aid
EAD
Effective Air Distance
Enlisted Assignment Document
Entered on Active Duty
Equipment Availability Date
EADEP
Emergency Animal Disease Education
Program
EAG
Experimental Auxiliary (or Firing Ship)
EAID
Electronic Anti-Intrusion Device
EAM
Electric Accounting Machine
Equipment Acquisition Manual
Emergency Action Message

EAM/EDPM
Electric Accounting Machine and Electronic
Data Processing Machine

EAMTMTS
Eastern Area, Military Traffic Management
and Terminal Service

EAMU
Electronic Accounting Machine Unit

EAN
Expenditure Account Number

EANS
Emergency Action Notification System

EAOS
Expiration (or End) of Active Obligated
Service

EAP
Effective Air Path

EAPS
Engine Air Particle Separator

EAPU
Electrical Auxiliary Power Unit

EAR
Electromagnetic Activity Receiver

EARLPRADATE
Earliest practical date

EAS
Electronic Altitude Sensor
Equivalent Airspeed

EASTCO
East Coast

EASTCONRADREG
Eastern Continental Air Defense Region

EASTLANTMED
Eastern Atlantic and Mediterranean

EASTOMP
East Ocean Meeting Point

EASTPAC
Eastern Pacific

EASTROPAC
Eastern Tropical Pacific (investigations)

EASY
Efficient Assembly System

EAT
Environmental Acceptance Testing
Evaporator Assist Team
Expected Approach Time

EATP
Educational Assistance Test Program

EB
Early Burst (bomb)
Enlistment Bonus

EBA
Emergency Breathing Apparatus

EBAP
External Burning Assisted Projectile

EBC
External Baggage Container

EBICON
Electron Bombardment-Induced Conductivity

EBR
Electron Beam Recorder
Experimental Breeder Reactor (AEC)

EBS
Emergency Broadcast System

EBWR
Experimental Boiling Water Reactor

EC
Electronic Calibration (or Component)
Electronic Coding (cipher)
Engagement Controller
Engineering Construction
Exhaust Close(d)

ECA
Engineering Change Analysis (or
Authorization)
Engineering Cognizance Agreement

ECAC
Electromagnetic Compatibility Analysis Center

ECC
Electronic-Courier Circuit
Engineering Control Center (or Console)
Enlisted Classification Code
Enlisted Correspondence Course

ECCB
Equipment to Computer Converter Buffer

ECCL
Equipment and Component Configuration
Listing

ECCM
Electronic Counter-Countermeasures

ECC-OCC
Enlisted/Officer Combined Correspondence
Course

ECD
Emergency Category Designation
Estimated Completion Date
Exploratory Career Development

ECDW
Electronic Cooling Distilled Water

ECH
Echelon

ECI
Equipment and Component Index
Error Cause Identification
Extension Course Institute

ECL
Emitter Coupled Logic
English Completion Test (DLI)
Equipment Component List

ECM
Electronic Cipher (or Coding) Machine
Electronic Countermeasures

ECMO
Electronic Countermeasures Officer

ECN
Engineering Change Notice
Equipment Component Number

ECN-APL
Equippage Category Numbered Allowance
Parts List

ECO
Engineering Change Order
ECP
Emergency Command Precedence
Engineering Change Proposal
Enlisted Commissioning Program
ECPS
Engineering Change Proposal System
ECR
Engineering Change Request
Error Cause Removal (form)
ECRC
Electronic Component Reliability Center
ECRS
Equippage Control Redistribution System
ECU
Environmental Control Unit
ECW
Electronic Cooling Water
ED
Eastern District
Electro-Dialysis
Electron Devices
Engineering Department (or Development, or
Draftsman, or Duty)
Existence Doubtful (contact)
Extra Duty
ED, EDUC
Education
EDA
Estimated Date of Arrival
EDAC
Equipment Distribution and Condition (report)
Error Detection and Correction
EDAI
Engineering Design Advance Information
EDATS
Executive Data System
EDAVR, EDVR
Enlisted Distribution and Verification Report
EDC
Electronic Digital Computer
Engine-Drive Compressor
Engineering Document Control
Enlisted Distribution Commander
EDCMR
Effective Date of Change of Morning Report
EDD
Estimated Date of Departure (or Detachment)
EDDC
East Coast Naval Publications Distribution
Center
EDED
Electronic and Display Equipment Division
EDF
Engineering Data File
EDG
Exploratory Development Goals
EDGE
Electronic Data-Gathering Equipment
Experimental Display Generation

EDIAC
Engineering Decision Integrator and
Communication
EDIS
Engineering Data Information System
EDITAR
Electronic Digital Tracking and Ranging
(system)
EDM
Electrical Discharge Machinery
EDMF
Extended Data Management Facility
EDMICS
Engineering Data Management Information
Control System
EDMS
Engineering Drawing Micro-Reproduction
System
EDO
Engineering Duty Officer
EDOM
Engineering Department Organizational
Manual
EDOSCOL
Engineering Duty Officer School
EDP
Electronic Data Processing
Emergency Defense Plan
EDPAC
Electronic Data Processing and Compiling
EDPC
Electronic Data Processing Center
EDPE
Electronic Data Processing Equipment
EDPM
Electronic Data Processing Machine
EDPS
Electronic Data Processing System
EDR
Electronic Decoy Rocket
Employee Data Record
Engineering Document Record
Equivalent Direct Radiation
Exploratory Development Requirement
Extended Duty Reserve
EDRF
Experienced Demand Replacement Factor
EDS
Electronic (or Engineering) Data Systems
Environmental Data Service (NOAA)
EDSAR
Engineering Drawing Status and Release
ED(SI)
Engineering Department (Ships Installation)
(NAEC)
EDSPEC
Education(al) Specialist
EDT
Engineering Design Test
Estimated Delivery (or Departure) Time

EDTR
Experimental Development Test and
Research
EDTRASUPPDET, ETSD
Education and Training Support Detachment
EDTRASUPPTRADEV FEO
Education and Training Support Training
Device Field Engineering Office
EDU, EXPDIVUNIT
Experimental Diving Unit
EDUC, ED
Education
EDVR, EDAVR
Enlisted Distribution and Verification Report
EE
End Event
Expiration of Enlistment
E&E
Escape and Evasion
EEAP
Enlisted Education Advancement Program
EEAT
Emergency Expected Approach Time
EEBD
Emergency Escape Breathing Device
EED
Electro-Explosive Device
EEFI
Essential Elements of Friendly Information
EE&H
Electricity, Electronics and Hydraulics
(school)
EEI
Essential Elements of Information
EELS
Electronic Emitter Location System
EENT
End of Evening Nautical Twilight
Ear, Eye, Nose and Throat (clinic)
EEO
Equal Employment Opportunity (program)
EEOAC
Equal Employment Opportunity Advisory
Council
EEOC
Equal Employment Opportunity Commission
(or Coordinator)
EEODIRSYS
Equal Employment Opportunity Directives
System
EEOO
Equal Employment Opportunity Officer
EEP
Engineering Experimental Phase
EER
Equipment Evaluation Report
Explosive Echo-Ranging
EERC
Explosive Echo-Ranging Change
EE&RM
Elementary Electrical and Radio Material
(school)

EES
European Exchange System
EET
Engineering Evaluation Test
EF
Edge Finishing
EFC
Expected Further Clearance (time)
EFD
Engineering Field Division
EFD(MIS)
Engineering Field Division (Management
Information System)
EFF
Effect(ed), (-ive)
EFFCY
Efficiency
EFICD
Electrical Fittings Inventory Control Division
EFM
Expeditionary Force Message
EFPROUT
Effecting promotion, procedure outlined in
_____ will be followed
EFR
Electronic Failure Report
Equipment Facility Requirement
EFTO
Elementary Flying Training School
Encoded for Transmission Only
Encrypted (or Encoded) for Transmission
Overseas
EFW
Effective Fallout Wind
EG
Electro Gas
Escort Group
EGADS
Electronic Ground Automatic Destruct
Sequencer
EGL
Equippage Guide List
EGS
Electronic Glide Slope
Exhaust Gas System
EGT
Exhaust Gas Temperature
EH
Exercise Head
E-HA
Enroute High Altitude
EHF
Extra (or Extremely) High Frequency
EHP
Effective Horsepower
EHSV
Electrohydraulic Servo Valve
EI
End Item
Engineering Investigation (program)

EIA
Environmental Impact Assessment
EIB
Electronics Information Bulletin (publication)
EIC
Environmental Information Center
Equipment Identification Code
Exercise Intelligence Center
EICAM
Electronic Installation Change and
    Maintenance
EICS
Equipment Identification Coded System
EID
End Item Description (PCI)
Estimated Issue Date
EIL
Equipment Identification List
Explosive Investigative Laboratory
EIMO
Engineering Interface Management Office
E INT
Equal Interval (light)
EIOD
Extra Instruction or Duty
EIP
Electronic Installation Plan (ERP)
EIR
Expanded Infrared (sensor)
EIS
Electronic Installation Squadron
Environmental Impact Statement
EISO
Engineering and Integrated Support Office
EIT
Engineer-in-Training
EJ
Eject
EL
Electrical
Electroluminescent
Exchange, Limited
E-LA
Enroute Low Altitude
ELAP
Expanded Legal Assistance Program
ELAT
English Language Aptitude Test
ELD
Engineering Laboratory Technician
ELDG
Electrical, Defective, Government (GFE)
ELE
Element
Engine-Life-Expectancy
ELEC
Electrician
ELEC, ELECT
Electric
ELECT, ELEC
Electric

ELECTECH
Electronics Technician
ELECTMAINTCO
Electronic Maintenance Company
ELEV
Elevation
Elevator
ELEX
Electronic
ELF
Expeditionary Logistics Facility
Explosive-Actuated Light Filter
ELFC
Electroluminescent Ferroelectric Cell
ELG, EL/G
Emergency Landing Ground
ELIG
Eligible
ELIG RET
Eligible for Retirement
ELIM
Eliminate
ELIN
Exhibit Line Item Number
ELINT
Electronic Intelligence
ELINT, ELMINT
Electromagnetic Intelligence
ELM
Eastern Atlantic and Mediterranean (element
    or area)
ELMG
Engine Life Management Group
ELMINT, ELINT
Electromagnetic Intelligence
ELOM
Electro-Optical Light Modulator
ELOX
Electrical Spark Erosion
ELP
Edge-Lit Panel
Emergency Loading Procedure
ELS
Emergency Lighting Supply (or System)
ELSB
Edge-Lighted Status Board
ELSBM
Exposed Location Single-Buoy Mooring
ELSEE
Electronic Sky Screen Equipment
ELSW
Elsewhere
ELT
Engineering Laboratory Technician
ELTC
Enlisted Loss to Commission Status
EL WICOMATIC
Electrologic Wiring and Connecting Devices,
    Semi-Automatic

EM
Education (or Engineering) Manual
Electromagnetic
Electronic Memories
Electron Microscopy
Emission
Energy Management
Engine Maintenance
Enlisted Man (or Men)
Estimated Manhours
E/M
Electro-Mechanical
EM1
Electrician's Mate First Class
EM2
Electrician's Mate Second Class
EM3
Electrician's Mate Third Class
EMAR
Experimental Memory Address Register
EMB
Electronic Material Bulletin (publication)
Embark(ation)
EMBO
Embarkation Officer
EMBT
Emergency Ballast Tank (system)
EMC
Chief Electrician's Mate
Electromagnetic Compatibility
Electronic Material Change
Electronics Maintenance Center
Engineering Military Circuit
EMCM
Master Chief Electrician's Mate
EMCON
Electromagnetic Radiation Control
Emission Control
EMCS
Senior Chief Electrician's Mate
EMDP
Executive and Management Development
Program (DMA)
EME
Environmental Measurement Equipment
EMEC
Electronics (or Emergency) Maintenance
Engineering Center
EMER
Electromagnetic Environment Recorder
EMERG
Emergency
EMF
Electromotive Force
EMI
Electromagnetic Interference
Extra Military Instruction
EML
Estimated Month of Loss
E&ML, E/ML, EML
Environmental and Morale Leave

EMMP
Equipment Maintenance Management
Program
EMO
Electronics Material Officer
Engineering Maintenance Officer
Equipment Management Office
EMP
Electromagnetic Propulsion (or Pulse)
EMPASS
Electromagnetic Performance of Aircraft and
Ship Systems
EMPL
Employ(ment)
EMPRESS
Electromagnetic Pulse Radiation Environment
Simulator for Ships
EMR
Electromagnetic Radiation
Estimated Manual Release
EMSA
Electrician's Mate Seaman Apprentice
EMSKED
Employment Schedule (-ling)
EMSN
Electrician's Mate Seaman
EMSUBS
Equipment Management Subsystem
EMT
Elapsed Maintenance Time
Emergency Medical Technician
EMW
Electromagnetic Wave
EN
Enemy
Engineering Notice
Envelope (U/I)
EN1
Engineman First Class
EN2
Engineman Second Class
EN3
Engineman Third Class
ENC
Chief Engineman
Enlistment Cancelled
ENC, ENCL
Enclosure
ENCL
Enclose
ENCL, ENC
Enclosure
ENCM
Master Chief Engineman
ENCS
Senior Chief Engineman
END
Endorse(ment)
ENDG
Ending

ENF
Employment of Naval Forces (course)
ENFA
Engineman Fireman Apprentice
ENFN
Engineman Fireman
ENG
Engine(ering)
Engraving
ENGR
Engineer
ENGRCEN
Engineering Center
ENGREQUIPMAINTRPRPLT
Engineer Equipment Maintenance Repair Platoon
ENGRFAC
Engineering Facility
ENGRMAINTCO
Engineer Maintenance Company
ENGRPLT
Engineer Platoon
ENGRSPTBN
Engineer Support Battalion
ENGSCOLSHIPTRATMLANT
Engineering Schoolship Training Team, Atlantic
ENL
Enlist(ment)
ENLDEVDISTSYS
Enlisted Development and Distribution Support System
ENLMAUSTSYS
Enlisted Master File Automated System
ENR
Enroute
ENS
Ensign
ENSYS
Electromagnetic Environmental Synthesizer
ENT
Enter
Entrance
ENTDISABSEVPAY
Entitled upon separation to disability severance pay computed on basis of two months' active duty pay (basic pay) for each year of active service, but not to exceed a total of two years' active duty pay (basic pay). It has been determined that for the purpose of computing disability severance pay you will have completed on (date indicated) _____ active service.

ENTERCOPTWO
Enter only on DD Form 214N Copy Two NAVMILPERSCOMINST 1900.2H. If separation processing not at your command, officer will carry copy of this message in sealed envelope addressed to separation activity. This message will not be retained by officer after completion of separation processing. Enter across bottom Block 27, Copy Two: (Authority and separation code indicated). (Reenlistment code if indicated.)
ENTLUMPAY
According Sec. 265, Armed Forces Reserve Act of 1952, as amended, entitled to receive lump-sum readjustment payment computed on basis of two months' basic pay in grade in which service at time of release from active duty for each year of active service, ending at close of eighteenth year, but not to exceed a total of more than two years' basic pay or $15,000, whichever is less. On _____ he completed a total of _____ active service creditable for payment under this Act.
ENTNAC
Entrance National Agency Check
ENTR
Entire
EO
Electro-Optical (sensor)
Engineering Order (or Officer)
EO, EXEC ORD
Executive Order
EO1
Equipment Operator First Class
EO2
Equipment Operator Second Class
EO3
Equipment Operator Third Class
EOA
End of Address
Equal Opportunity Assistant
EOB
Electronic Order of Battle
End of Block
Estimated on Berth
Expense Operating Budget
EOC
Chief Equipment Operator
Electronic Operations Center
ELINT Orientation Course
Emergency Operating (or Operations) Center
End of Construction
End-of-Course (exam)
Extended Operating Cycle
EOCA
Equipment Operator Construction Apprentice
EOCC
Electroptics Coordinating Committee

EOCN
Equipment Operator Constructionman
EOCS
Senior Chief Equipment Operator
EOD
End of Data
Entering Office Date
Explosive Ordnance Disposal (team)
EODB
Explosive Ordnance Disposal Bulletins
(publication)
EODGRU
Explosive Ordnance Disposal Group
EODGRUDET
Explosive Ordnance Disposal Group
Detachment
EODGRULANT
Explosive Ordnance Disposal Group, Atlantic
EODGRUPAC
Explosive Ordnance Disposal Group, Pacific
EODMU
Explosive Ordnance Disposal Mobile Unit
EODP
Earth and Ocean Dynamics Program
EODS
Explosive Ordnance Disposal School
EODTECHCEN
Explosive Ordnance Disposal Technical
Center
EODTEU
Explosive Ordnance Disposal Training and
Evaluation Unit
EODTIC
Explosive Ordnance Disposal Technical
Information Center
EODT&T
Explosive Ordnance Disposal Technology
and Training
EOF
End of File
EOG
Electrolytic Oxygen Generator
EOGB
Electro-Optical Guided Bomb
EOI
Electronic Operating Instructions
EOISS, EQOPPINFOSYS
Equal Opportunity Information and Support
System
EOJ
End of Job
EOLT
End of Logical Tape
EOM
End of Message (or Month)
EOOW
Engineering Officer-of-the-Watch
EOPS
Equal Opportunity Program Specialist
EOQ
End of Quarter (report)

EOQI
Equal Opportunity Quality Indicators
EOQT
Economic Order Quality Techniques (course)
EOR
End of Reel
Explosive Ordnance Reconnaissance
EO/RR
Equal Opportunity/Race Relations
EOS
Enclosed Operating Space
Engineering Operating Space (or Station)
EOS/MT
Extended Operating System for Magnetic
Tapes
EOSS
Engineering Operational Sequence System
EOT
Electric Overhead Travel (crane)
End of Tape
Engine Order Telegraph
Equal Opportunity and Treatment
EOU
Enemy Objective Unit
EOWT
Electronic Warfare Officer Training
EP
Enemy Position
Engineering Practice
Estimated Position
Explosion-Proof
Extreme Pressure (oil rating)
E/P
Effectiveness/Productivity (program)
EPA
Extended Planning Annex
EPABX
Electronic Private Automatic Branch
Exchange
EPB
Enlisted Performance Branch
EPC
Environmental Policy Center
Equipment Process Card
EPCB
Electric Plant Control Benchboard
EPCER
Experimental Patrol Craft, Escort and Rescue
EPCP
Electric Propulsion Control Panel
EPD
Earliest Practical Date
Eastern Procurement Division
Eastern Production District
Extra Police Duty
EPDB
Environmental Protection Data Base
EPDO
Enlisted Personnel Distribution Office
EPDOLANT
Enlisted Personnel Distribution Office, Atlantic

EPDOPAC
Enlisted Personnel Distribution Office, Pacific
E-PERS
Enlisted Personnel
EPF
Emergency Plant Facilities
EPHC
Eastern Pacific Hurricane Center
EPI
Engine Performance Indicator
Expanded Position Indicator
EPIC
Extended Performance and Increased
Capabilities
EPIRB
Emergency Position Indicating Radio Beacon
EPLA
Electronics Precedence List Agency
EPM
Electric/Emergency Propulsion Motor
Equivalents per Million
EPMAC, ENLPERSMGTCEN
Enlisted Personnel Management Center
EPMU
Environmental and Preventive Medicine Unit
EPO
Energy Program Office
Enlisted Programs Officer
EPOR
Electronics Performance and Operational
Report
EPP
Effective Program Projections
Emergency Power Package
Energy Policy Project
Environmental (Quality) Protection Program
EPPI
Electronic Programmed Procurement
Information
EPPP
Emergency Production Planning Program
EPR
Electronic Requirement Report
Engine Pressure Ratio
Equipment Performance Report
Evaporator Pressure Regulators
EPS
Engineered (or Engineering) Performance
Standards
EPSRG
Exhibit Planning and Study Review Group
EPTE
Existed Prior to Enlistment (medical
condition)
EPU
Electrical Power Unit
EPUT
Events per Unit Time

EQ
Equator
Equipmentman
EQCC
Entry Query Control Console
EQCM
Master Chief Equipmentman
EQOPPINFOSYS, EOISS
Equal Opportunity Information and Support
System
EQP, EQPT, EQPMT, EQUIP
Equipment
EQPFOR
Equipment Foreman
EQPMT, EQP, EQUIPT, EQPT
Equipment
ER
Engineroom
Enhanced Radiation
Equipment-Related
Error Release
Established Record
Extended Range
E&R
Engineering and Repair
ERA
Expense for Return of Absentee
Extended-Range ASROC
ERAD
Energy Research and Development
ERATE
Examination Rate
ERBM
Extended-Range Ballistic Missile
ERC
Electronics Research Center
E/R/C
Equippage/Repair List/Consumables (code)
ERCS
Emergency Rocket Communications System
ERD
Engineering Review Diagram
Expense for Return of Deserter
ERDA
Environmental Research and Development
Agency
ERDL
Engineering Research and Development
Laboratory
ERF
Emergency Recovery Force
ERFPI
Extended-Range Floating Point Interpretive
(code)
ERG
Emergency Recovery Group
ERGS
Enroute Guidance System
ERILCO
Exchange of Ready-for-Issue in Lieu of
Concurrent Overhaul

ERL
Environmental Research Laboratories (NOAA)
Equipment Requirements List
ERMA
Electronic Recording Machine Accounting
ERN
Electronic Radar Navigation
ERO
Emergency Repair Overseer
Equipment Repair Order
EROS
Earth Resources Observation System
Eliminate Range O System
Experimental Reflection Orbital Shot
ERP
Effective Radiate Power
Equipment (or Enlisted, or Electronic) Requirements Plan
ERPAL
Electronic Repair Parts Allowance List
ERR
Electronic Requirements Report
Engine Removal Report
Error
ERS
Eastern Range Ships
Emergency Recovery Station
Emergency Relocation Site
Engine Room Supervisor
Environmental Research Satellite
ERSA
Electronic Research Supply Agency
Extended-Range Strike Aircraft
ER&SD
Employee Relations and Services Division (IRD)
ERT
Estimated Repair Time
ERTS
Earth Resources Technology Satellite
ERU
Emergency Recovery Unit
ERW
Elastic Resist Weld
ERY
Early
ES
Echo Suppressor
Electro Slag
ES³
Environmental Satellite System for the Seventies
ESA
Engineering Support Activity
ESAR
Electronically-Steerable Array Radar
ESAS
Event Sensing and Analysis System
ESC
Echo Suppression Center

ESCAPE
Expansion Symbolic Compiling Assembly Program for Engineering
ESCAT
Emergency Security Control of Air Traffic
ESD
Earth Sciences Division (ONR)
Electronic System Division
Elemental Standards Data
Engineering Standardization Directive
Equipment Statistical Data
ESF, EASTSEAFRON
Eastern Sea Frontier
ESFC
Equivalent Specific Fuel Consumption
ESG
Electrostatic Gyroscope
ESHP
Equivalent Shaft Horsepower
ESHU
Emergency Ship Handling Unit
ESI
Extremely Sensitive Information
ESL
Electromagnetic Systems Laboratory
Equipment Status Log
ESM
Edible Structural Material
Elastometric Shield Material
Electronic Support (or Surveillance) Measures
ESO
Educational Services Office(r)
Electronic Supply Office(r)
ESOC
Emergency Supply Operations Center
ESP
Electromagnetic Subsurface Profiling (radar)
Expendable Stored Projected
E&SP
Equipment and Spare Parts
ESPAR
Electronically-Steerable Phased Array Radar
ESPC
Expendable Stored Project Contract
ESQ
Enlisted Separation Questionnaire
ESQD
Explosives Safety Quality Distance
ESR
Electron Spin Resonance
Engineering Service Request
Equivalent Service Rounds
ESS
Educational Services Section
Electronic Switching System
Emplaced Scientific Station
ESSC
End Sweep Support Carrier
ESSM
Emergency Ship Salvage Material

ESSNSS
Electronic Supply Segment of the Navy
Supply System
EST
Enlistment Screening Test
Epidemiology and Sanitation Technician
Established
Estimate
ESTAB
Establish(ment)
ESU
Electrostatic Unit
ESVR
Examination Status Verification Report
ESWS
Enlisted Surface Warfare Specialist
ET
Elapsed (or Emphemeria, or Estimated) Time
End of Tape
Equipment Test
ET1
Electronics Technician First Class
E&T
Education and Training
ETA
Estimated Time of Arrival
Exception Time Accounting
ETAB
Extrathoracic Assisted Breathing
ETABC
Extrathoracic Assisted Breathing and
Circulation
ETAS
Estimated True Airspeed
ETB
Enlisted Training Branch
Estimated Time of Blocks
ETC
Chief Electronics Technician
Estimated Time of Completion
ETCG
Elapsed-Time Code Generator
ETCM
Master Chief Electronics Technician
ETCR
Estimated Time of Crew's Return
ETCS
Senior Chief Electronics Technician
ETD
Estimated Time of Departure
ETE
Estimated (or Elapsed) Time Enroute
ETF
Eastern Task Force
Estimated Time of Flight
ETI
Elapsed Time Indicator
Estimated Time of Intercept(ion)
ETIC
Estimated Time in Commission

ETM
Elapsed-Time Meter
ETM, ENLTRANSMAN
Enlisted Transfer Manual
ETMH
Estimated Total Manhours
ETMWG
Electronic Trajectory Measurements Working
Group
ETN1
Electronics Technician N (Communications)
First Class
ETN2
Electronics Technician N (Communications)
Second Class
ETN3
Electronics Technician N (Communications)
Third Class
ETNSA
Electronics Technician N (Communications)
Seaman Apprentice
ETNSN
Electronics Technician N (Communications)
Seaman
ETP
Electron Transfer Particles
Elevated Training Platform
Equal-Time Point
ETR
Engine Transaction Report
Estimated Time of Return (or Repair)
ETR1
Electronics Technician R (Radar) First Class
ETR2
Electronics Technician R (Radar) Second
Class
ETR3
Electronics Technician R (Radar) Third Class
ETRA
Estimated Time to Reach Altitude
ETRIS
Eastern Test Range Instrumentation Ship
ETRSA
Electronics Technician R (Radar) Seaman
Apprentice
ETRSN
Electronics Technician R (Radar) Seaman
ETS
Educational Training Service
Electronic Test Set
Emergency Throttle System
Engineering and Technical Services
Engineering Time Standards
Enlisted Training Section
Expiration of Term of Service
ETS REQ
Engineering and Technical Services Request
ETST
Electronics Technician Selection Test
ETW
End of Tape Warning

EU
Exchange, Unlimited
EUCOM
European Command
EUM
European and Mediterranean (regional area)
EUR, EU
Europe
EUSC
Effective United States Control
EV
Electron Volt
Every
EVAC
Evacuate
Evacuation
EVAL
Evaluation
EVAP
Evaporate
Evaporation
Evaporator
EVC
Electronic Visual Communications
EVE
Evening
EVEA
Extra-Vehicular Engineering Activity
EVID
Evidence
EVSP
Employee Voluntary Support Program
EW
Early Warning
Electronic Warfare
EW1
Electronic Warfare Technician First Class
EW2
Electronic Warfare Technician Second Class
EW3
Electronic Warfare Technician Third Class
E/W
East/West
EWAS
Economic Warfare Analysis Section
EWC
Chief Electronic Warfare Technician
Electronic Warfare Center
EWD
Economic Warfare Division
EWO
Electronic Warfare Officer
Emergency War Orders
Engineering Work Order
EWP
Emergency War Plan
Exploding Wire Phenomena
EWP/E
Electronics, Weapons, Precision and Electric
(facility)

EWQ
Enlisted Women's Quarters
EWR
Early Warning Radar
EWS
Engineering Watch Supervisor
EWSA
Electronic Warfare Technician Seaman
Apprentice
EWSN
Electronic Warfare Technician Seaman
EX
Electronics
Excess
Export
EX, EXCH
Exchange
EX, EXCP
Except
EX, EXPER
Experience
Experiment
EXAMETNET
Experimental Inter-American Meteorological
Rocket Network
EXCL
Exclusive
EXCP, EX
Except
EXDIV
Experimental Division
EX/DP
Express/Direct Pack
EXEC
Executive
Executive Officer
EXECASST
Executive Assistant
EXECORD, EO
Executive Order
EXEP
Expense Order
EXLV
Excess Leave
EXOS
Executive Office of the Secretary of the Navy
EXP
Expend
Express
EXPC
Expect
EXPDIVUNIT, EDU
Experimental Diving Unit
EXPED
Expeditionary
EXPER, EX
Experience
Experiment
EXPERT
Expanded PERT (program)

EXPLO
Explosive
EXPLOS ANCH
Explosive Anchorage (buoy)
EXPR
Expire
EXREP
Expedious Repair
EXSTA
Experimental Station
EXT, EXTN
Extension
EXT, XTND
Extend
EXTENL
Extension of Enlistment
EXTING
Extinguishing (light)
EXTN, EXT
Extension
EXTR
Extruded
EXTRM
Extreme
EXTSV, EXTV
Extensive
EXTV, EXTSV
Extensive

F

F
Bombardier/Navigator (TO code)
Farad
Final (approach)
Fixed (light)
Flanged (joint)
Fog (weather symbol)
Fordable (body of water)
FA
Awaiting Further Assignment (MAPMIS)
Family Allowance
Field Activity
Fireman Apprentice
Flight Attendant
Forces Afloat
Frequency Agility
F/A
Fuel/Air (mixture)
FAA
Family Allowance, Class A
FAAARTCC
Federal Aviation Administration Area
Regional Traffic Control Center
FAAB
Family Allowance, Classes A and B
FAAD
Forward Area Air Defense

FAADBTY
Forward Area Air Defense Battery
FAADC
Fleet Accounting and Disbursing Center
FAADCLANT
Fleet Accounting and Disbursing Center,
Atlantic
FAADCLANT BRO
Fleet Accounting and Disbursing Center,
Atlantic Branch Office
FAADCPAC
Fleet Accounting and Disbursing Center,
Pacific
FAAO, FLEAVNACCTO
Fleet Aviation Accounting Office
FAAOL, FAAOLANT, FLEAVNACCTOLANT
Fleet Aviation Accounting Office, Atlantic
FAAOLANT, FAAOL, FLEAVNACCTOLANT
Fleet Aviation Accounting Office, Atlantic
FAAOP, FAAOPAC, FLEAVNACCTOPAC
Fleet Aviation Accounting Office, Pacific
FAAOPAC, FAAOP, FLEAVNACCTOPAC
Fleet Aviation Accounting Office, Pacific
FAAR
Forward Area Alerting Radar
FAARATCF
Federal Aviation Administration Radar Air
Traffic Control Facility
FAARP
Forces Afloat Accident Reporting Procedures
FAB
Fabricate
Fabrication
Family Allowance, Class B
Fleet Air Base
FABIS
Filmless Automatic Bond Inspection
FABU
Fleet Air Base Unit
FAC
Facility
Factory
Final Approach Course
Fleet Activities Command
Fleet Augmentation Component
Forward Air Control(ler)
Frequency Allocation Committee
Functional Area Code
F/AC
Forward Across the Hatch (stowage)
FACCON
Facilities Control
FACI
First Article Configuration Inspection
FACR
First Article Configuration Review
FACS
Fast Attack Class Submarine
Federal Automated Career System
Floating Decimal Abstract Coding System

FACSFAC
Fleet Air Control and Surveillance Facility
FACSO
Facilities System Office
FACT
Factory Acceptance Trials
Factual Compiler
Flexible Automatic Circuit Tester
Fully-Automatic Compiler-Translator
FAD
Fleet Air Detachment
Flexible Automatic Depot
Force/Activity Designator
FADC
Fighter Air Direction Center
FADM
Fleet Admiral
FAE
Fuel-Air-Explosive
FAETU
Fleet Airborne Electronics Training Unit
FAETUDET
Fleet Airborne Electronics Training Unit
Detachment
FAETULANT
Fleet Airborne Electronics Training Unit,
Atlantic
FAETUPAC
Fleet Airborne Electronics Training Unit,
Pacific
FAF
Final Approach Fix
FAG
Field Artillery Group
Fleet Assistance Group
Forward Air Controller, Ground
FAGAIRTRANS
First available government air transportation
FAGLANT
Fleet Assistance Group, Atlantic
FAGPAC
Fleet Assistance Group, Pacific
FAGT, FAGTRANS
First available government surface
transportation
FAGTRANS, FAGT
First available government surface
transportation
FAH
Degrees Fahrenheit
FAIR
Fair and Impartial Random (SSS
development)
Fleet Air (command)
FAIRDEX
Fleet Air Defense Exercise
FAIRECONRON, VQ
Fleet Air Reconnaissance Squadron
FAIRECONRONDET
Fleet Air Reconnaissance Squadron
Detachment

FAIRECONRONOPTEAM
Fleet Air Reconnaissance Squadron
Operational Team
FAIRINTAUGMU
Fleet Air Intelligence Augmenting Unit
FAIRINTSUPPCEN
Fleet Air Intelligence Support Center
FAIRSUPPU, FASU
Fleet Air Support Unit
FAIRTRANS
First available air transportation
FAIRWESTPAC
Fleet Air Wing, Western Pacific
FAIRWG, FAIRWING
Fleet Air Wing
FAIRWING, FAIRWG
Fleet Air Wing
FAK
Freight, All Kinds (shipping)
FAMFIRE
Familiarization Firing
FAMHSGASSIGNSY
Family Housing Assignment Application
System
FAMHSGRQMTSURVSYS
Family Housing Requirements Survey Record
System
FAMIS
Financial and Management Information
System
FAMOS
Fleet Air Meteorological Observation Satellite
FAMU
Fleet Aircraft Maintenance Unit
FANDT, F&T
Fuel and Transportation
FAO
Fleet Administration Office
FAP
Family Advocacy Program
Family Assistance Plan
Force Personnel Assistance Group
FAPG
Fleet Air Photographic Group
FAPL
Fleet Air Photographic Laboratory
FAPRON
Fleet Air Photographic Squadron
FAR
Federal Aviation Regulation
Fixed-Array Radar
Fleet Alteration Report
Flight Aptitude Rating (test)
FARADA, FARANDA
Failure Rate Data
FARANDA, FARADA
Failure Rate Data
FARP
Forces Afloat Repair Procedures

FAS
Free Alongside Ship
Fueling at Sea
FASC
Force Automated Services Center
FASDU
Further assignment to duty
FASE
Fundamentally Analyze Simplified English
(computer language)
FASO
Field Aviation Supply Office
FASOTRAGRULANT
Fleet Aviation Specialized Operational
Training Group, Atlantic
FASOTRAGRULANTDET
Fleet Aviation Specialized Operational
Training Group, Atlantic Detachment
FASOTRAGRUPAC
Fleet Aviation Specialized Operational
Training Group, Pacific
FASOTRAGRUPACDET
Fleet Aviation Specialized Operational
Training Group, Pacific Detachment
FASOR
Forward Air (or Area) Sonar Research
FASRON
Fleet Aircraft Services Squadron
FAST
Fast Automatic Shuttle Transfer
Fense Against Satellite Threats
Final Acceptance Facility
Fleet Attitude Status
Forward Area Support Team
FASTU
Fleet Ammunition Ship Training Unit
FASTULANT
Fleet Ammunition Ship Training Unit, Atlantic
FASTUPAC
Fleet Ammunition Ship Training Unit, Pacific
FASU, FAIRSUPPU
Fleet Air Support Unit
FAT
Fast Automatic Transfer
Final Acceptance Trials
FA-T
Flight Attendant in Training
FATCAT
Film and Television Correlation Assessement
Technique
FATE
Fuzing, Arming, Test and Evaluation
FATHOM
Foreign Affairs Theory, Operations and
Monitoring
FATRANS
First available transportation
FATSO
First Airborne Telescopic and Spectrographic
Observatory

FATU
Fleet Air Tactical Unit
FAU
Flag Administration Unit
FAV
Favorable
FAW
Fleet Air Wing
FAWPRA
Fleet Air Western Pacific Repair Facility
FAWS
Flight Advisory Weather Service
FAWTU
Fleet All-Weather Training Unit
FAX
Facsimile
FAY
Fleet Activities, Yokosuka
FBA
Fighter Bomber (Aircraft)
FBH
Force Beachhead
FBM
Fleet Ballistic Missile
FBMNAVTESTUNIT
Fleet Ballistic Missile Navigation Test Unit
FBMOPTESTSUPPU
Fleet Ballistic Missile Operation Test Support
Unit
FBMS
Fleet Ballistic Missile System
FBMTC, FLEBALMISTRACEN
Fleet Ballistic Missile Training Center
FBMTLL
Fleet Ballistic Missile Tender Load List
FBMWS
Fleet Ballistic Missile Weapons System
FBMWSS
Fleet Ballistic Missile Weapons Support
System
FBP
Fleet Boat Pool
FBR
Feedback Report
FBS
Forward-Based Systems
FBW
Fly-by-Wire
FC
Fire Control
Fleet Commander
Full Capacity
Fund Code
F/C
Facilities Control
FCA
Field Calibration Activity
Flight Control Assemblies
FCAD
Field Contract Administration Division (ONM)

FCB
Foreign Clearance Base
FCC
Fleet Command Center
FCDNA
Field Command Defense Nuclear Agency
FCDSSA
Fleet Combat Direction System Support
Activity
FCDSTCP, FCDSTCPAC,
FLECOMBDIRSYSTRACENPAC
Fleet Combat Direction Systems Training
Center, Pacific
FCDSTC, FLECOMBDIRSYSTRACEN
Fleet Combat Direction Systems Training
Center
FCDSTCLANT,
FLECOMBDIRSYSTRACENLANT
Fleet Combat Direction Systems Training
Center, Atlantic
FCDSTCPAC, FCDSTCP,
FLECOMBDIRSYSTRACENPAC
Fleet Combat Direction Systems Training
Center, Pacific
FCE
Field Civil Engineer
FCFS
First-Come, First-Served
FCG
Foreign Clearance Guide
FCI
Functional Configuration Identification
FCLP
Field Carrier Landing Practice
FCO
Field Change Order
Flag Communications Officer
Flight Communications Operator
Flying Control Officer
FCO-T
Flight Communications Operator in Training
FCPC
Flight Crew Plane Captain
FCPC, FLECOMPUTPROGCEN
Fleet Computer Programming Center
FCPCLANT, FLECOMPUTPROGCENLANT
Fleet Computer Programming Center, Atlantic
FCPCPAC, FLECOMPUTPROGCENPAC
Fleet Computer Programming Center, Pacific
FCRC
Federal Contract Research Center
FCS
Facility Checking Squadron
Fire Control System
FCSC
Fire Control System Coordinator
Fleet Command Support Center
FCST
Forecast

FCT
Final Contract Trials
Flight Circuit Tester
Functional Context Training
FCTG
Fast Carrier Task Group
FCU
Flight (or Fuel) Control Unit
FD
False Deck (stowage)
Fighter (or Fire) Direction
Frequency Diversity
Functional Description
FDA
Focal-Distance-to-Diameter Ratio
FDAI
Flight Direction and Altitude Indicator
FDB
Forced Draft Blower
FDC
Fire Direction Center
Formation Drone Control
FDCS
Fighter Direction Control School
FDD
Floating Drydock
FDDL
Frequency Division Data Link
FDHDB
Flight Deck Hazardous Duty Billet
FDHDP
Flight Deck Hazardous Duty Pay
FDL
Fast Deployment Logistics
FDLS
Fast Deployment Logistics Ship
FDM
Frequency Division Multiplex
FDNET
Fighter Direction Network
FDO
Fighter Direction Officer
Flight Deck Officer
FDPM
Final Draft, Presidential Memorandum
FDR
Facts, Discussion, Recommendations (letter
construction)
Flight Data Recorder
FDRB
Foreign Disclosure Review Board
FDS
Fighter Direction Ship
FDT
Fighter Direction Tender
FDW
Feedwater
FDX
Full Duplex (operation)

FE
Far East(ern)
Field (or Flight) Engineer
FE, FRDENL, FRAUD ENL
Fraudulent Enlistment
FE, FEB
February
FEA
Feather (aircraft engine)
FEB
Federal Executive Board
Functional Electronic Block
FEB, FE
February
FEBA
Forward Edge of the Battlefield
FEC
Facilities Engineering Command
FED
Federal
F&ED
Facilities and Equipment Department (NSC)
F&EDCD
Facilities and Equipment Department's
Control Division (NSC)
FEDSIM
Federal Computer Performance Evaluation
and Simulation Center
FEGS
Federation and Employment Guidance
Service
FEI
Firing Error Indicator
FEIS
Final Environmental Impact Statement
FEMF
Flating Electronics Maintenance Facility
FEO
Federal Energy Office
FEORP
Federal Equal Opportunity Recruitment
Program
FEOS
Forward Engineering Operating Station
FEPC
Fair Employment Practices Code
FER
Ferry
Field Engineering Representative
FERON
If transferred, forward this directive
immediately to his commanding officer for
compliance or further transmittal as
appropriate, notifying originator in each
case the activity to which transferred and
your action if forwarding.
FERRON
Ferry Squadron
FESO
Facilities Engineering Support Office

FESS
Flight Experiment Shielding Satellite
FET
Field-Effect Transistor
Fleet Evaluation Trial
FE-T
Flight Engineer-in-Training
FETS
Field-Effects Transistors
FEU
Fleet Expansion Unit
FEX
Field (or Fleet) Exercise
FF
Failure Factor
Force Flagship
Foreign Flag
Frigate
FFA, FURAS
For further assignment
FFAR
Folding-Fin (or Forward-Firing) Aircraft
Rocket
FFB
Fact-Finding Bodies
FFC
For Further Clearance
Fuze Function Control
FFDO
Force Fighter Director Officer
FFF
Flight Facilities Flight
FFG
Fiscal and Force Capability Guidance
Guided Missile Frigate
FFL
Fixed and Flashing (light)
FFLOP
Field Fresnel Lens Optical Platform—see
FLOPF
FFP
Firm Fixed Price
Fleet Frequency Plans
Radar Picket Frigate
FFT
Fast Fourier Transform
For further transfer
FFTF
Fast Flux Test Facility (AEC)
FFW
Failure-Free Warranty
FG
Fine Grain
Fundamentals Graduate
FGO
Flag Gunnery Officer
FGPFL
Fixed and Group Flashing (light)
FHE
Fast Hydrofoil Escort

FHP
Fractional Horsepower
Funded Housing Project
FHTNC
Fleet Hometown News Center
FI
Fabrication Instruction
Fault Isolation
Face Immersion
Field Item
Fiscal Intermediary
Flight Idle
FIANA
File Analyzer and Report Generator
FIAT
Field Information Agency, Technical
FIBI
Filed, But Impracticable to Transmit
FIC
Fault Isolation Checkout (system)
Fleet Intelligence Center
Fleet Issue Control
Flight Information Center
Force Indicator Code
Frequency Interference Control
FIC CATIS
Fleet Intelligence Center Computer-Aided
Tactical Information System
FICEURLANT
Fleet Intelligence Center, Europe and Atlantic
FICL
Financial Inventory Control Ledger
FICON
Flight Conveyer
FICPACFAC
Fleet Intelligence Center, Pacific Facility
FIDAC
Film Input to Digital Automatic Computer
FIDO
Flight-Dynamics Officer
Fog, Intensive Dispersal of
FIES
Federal Information Exchange System
FIFO
First-In, First-Out (inventory control)
FIFOR
Flight Forecast
FIGAT
Fiberglass Aerial Target
FIGHTRON, FITRON, VF
Fighter Squadron
FII
Federal Item Identification
FIIG
Federal Item Identification Guide
Flight Instructions Indoctrination Group
FIIN
Federal Item Identification Number
FILG
Filing

FILL
Fleet Issue Load List
FILS
Flarescan Instrument Landing System
Fleet Integrated Logistics Support (reports)
FIM
Facing Identification Marks
FIMATE
Field-Installed Maintenance Automatic Test
Equipment
FIN
Finance
Financial
FIO
Fleet In and Out
Fleet Intelligence Officer
FIP
Fault Isolation Plan
Fleet Improvement (or Introduction) Program
Flight Indoctrination Program
Flight Information Publication
Force Inspection Procedure
FIPAS
Flight Information Publication, Alaska
Supplement
FIPC
Financial Information Processing Center
FIR
Financial Inventory Report
Flight Information Report (or Region)
Full Indicator Reading
Functional Item Replacement (program)
FIRE
Feedback Information Request Evidence
FIRE PLAN
Fleet Improved Readiness by Expediting
Procurement, Logistics and Negotiations
FIRFLT
First Fleet
FIRL
Fleet Issue Requirements List
FIRM
Fleet Introduction Replacement Model
Fleet Intensified Repairables Management
FIRMA
Fire and Maneuver
FIRST
Fleet Input and Reserve Support Training
FIS
Fiscal
Fleet Introduction Site
Flight Information Service
Force Information System
FISH
Fully-Instrumented Submersible Housing
FISO
Force Informational Services Officer
FISSG
Fleet Issue Ship Shopping Guide
FIST
Flight Instruction Standardization and Training

FIT
  Fabrication, Integration, Testing (of space
    systems)
  Fleet Introduction Team
FIT, FTR
  Fighter
FITAEWWING
  Fighter Airborne Early Warning
FITATKRON
  Fighter Attack Squadron
FITC
  Fleet Intelligence Training Center
  Flight Instructor Training Course
FITCLANT
  Fleet Intelligence Training Center, Atlantic
FITCPAC
  Fleet Intelligence Training Center, Pacific
FITGO
  Floating Input-to-Ground-Output (system)
FITRON, FIGHTRON, VF
  Fighter Squadron
FITRONDET
  Fighter Squadron Detachment
FITS
  Functional Individual Training System
FITWING
  Fighter Wing
FIUL
  Fleet Issue Unit Load
FJ
  Fighter Jet (pilot code)
F&J
  Fact and Justification
FL
  Flash(ing) (light)
  Flight Level
  Full Load
  Small Signal Search Light
FLAGADMINU
  Flag Administrative Unit
FLAGADMINUCOMNAVAIRLANT
  Flag Administrative Unit, Commander Naval
    Air Forces, Atlantic
FLAGADMINUCOMNAVAIRPAC
  Flag Administrative Unit, Commander Naval
    Air Forces, Pacific
FLAM
  Flammable (materials)
FLAME
  Flame-Launched Advance Material
    Experiment
FLARE
  Florida Aquanaut Research Expedition
FLASH
  Factual Lines About Submarine Hazards
FLAT
  Foreign Language Aptitude Test
FLAW, FLOGWING
  Fleet Logistics Air Wing

FLC
  Field Logistics Center
  Fleet Loading Center
  Force Logistics Command
FLCC
  Forward Logistics Control Center (LSC)
FLCNAVJUSMAG
  Field Logistics Center, Navy Joint United
    States Military Assistance Group
FLD
  Field
FLDARTYGRU
  Field Artillery Group
FLDBR
  Field Branch
FLDBRBUMED
  Field Branch, Bureau of Medicine and
    Surgery
FLDINTO
  Field Intelligence Office
FLDMEDSERVSCOL
  Field Medical Service School
FLD RATS
  Field Rations
FLDSUPPACT
  Field Support Activity
FLE, FLT
  Fleet
FLEA
  Flux Logic Element Array (radar)
FLEACT, FLTACT
  Fleet Activities
FLEAIRPHOTOLAB, FAPL
  Fleet Air Photographic Laboratory
FLEASWSCOL
  Fleet Antisubmarine Warfare School
FLEASWTRACEN
  Fleet Antisubmarine Warfare Training Center
FLEASWTRACENLANT
  Fleet Antisubmarine Warfare Training Center,
    Atlantic
FLEASWTRACENPAC
  Fleet Antisubmarine Warfare Training Center,
    Pacific
FLEASWTRAGRU
  Fleet Antisubmarine Warfare Training Group
FLEAVNACCTO, FAAO
  Fleet Aviation Accounting Office
FLEAVNACCTOLANT, FAAOL, FAAOLANT
  Fleet Aviation Accounting Office, Atlantic
FLEAVNACCTOPAC, FAAOP, FAAOPAC
  Fleet Aviation Accounting Office, Pacific
FLEAVNMATOPAC
  Fleet Aviation Material Office, Pacific
FLEBALMISUBTRACEN, FBMSTC
  Fleet Ballistic Missile Submarine Training
    Center
FLEBALMISUBTRACENLANT, FBMSTCLANT
  Fleet Ballistic Missile Submarine Training
    Center, Atlantic

FLEBALMISUBTRACENPAC, FBMSTCPAC
  Fleet Ballistic Missile Submarine Training
  Center, Pacific
FLECOMBDIRSYSTRACEN, FDSTC
  Fleet Combat Direction Systems Training
  Center
FLECOMBDIRSYSTRACENLANT,
  FCDSTCLANT
  Fleet Combat Direction Systems Training
  Center, Atlantic
FLECOMBDIRSYSTRACENPAC,
  FCDSTCPAC
  Fleet Combat Direction Systems Training
  Center, Pacific
FLECOMPRON, VC
  Fleet Composite Squadron
FLECOMPRONDET
  Fleet Composite Squadron Detachment
FLECOMPUTPROGCEN, FCPC
  Fleet Computer Programming Center
FLECOMPUTPROGCENLANT, FCPCLANT
  Fleet Computer Programming Center, Atlantic
FLECOMPUTPROGCENPAC, FCPCPAC
  Fleet Computer Programming Center, Pacific
FLEHOSPSUPPOFF
  Fleet Hospital Support Office
FLEINTROTM
  Fleet Introduction Team
FLELO
  Fleet Liaison Officer
FLELOGSUPPRON
  Fleet Logistics Support Squadron
FLELOGSUPPRONDET
  Fleet Logistics Support Squadron
  Detachment
FLEMARFOR, FMF
  Fleet Marine Force
FLEMARFORLANT, FMFLANT
  Fleet Marine Force, Atlantic
FLEMARFORPAC, FLFPAC
  Fleet Marine Force, Pacific
FLEMATSUPPO, FMSO
  Fleet Material Support Office
FLEMATSUPPODET
  Fleet Material Support Office Detachment
FLEMINWARTRACEN, FMWTC
  Fleet Mine Warfare Training Center
FLENUMOCEANCEN
  Fleet Numerical Oceanography Center
FLEOPINTRACEN, FOPINTRACEN, FOITC
  Fleet Operational Intelligence Training Center
FLEOPONTRACENLANT,
  FOPINTRACENLANT, FOITCL
  Fleet Operational Intelligence Training
  Center, Atlantic
FLEOPINTRACENPAC, FOPINTRACENPAC,
  FOITCP
  Fleet Operational Intelligence Training
  Center, Pacific

FLESOAPTEAM
  Fleet Supply Operations Assistance Program
  Team
FLESONARSCOL
  Fleet Sonar School
FLESUBTRAFAC
  Fleet Submarine Training Facility
FLETAC
  Fleet Tactical Field Office
FLETACSUPPRON, VR
  Fleet Tactical Support Squadron
FLETRACEN, FTC
  Fleet Training Center
FLETRAGRU, FTG
  Fleet Training Group
FLETRAGRUDET
  Fleet Training Group Detachment
FLETRAGRUWESTPAC, FTGWP
  Fleet Training Group, Western Pacific
FLETRAU
  Fleet Training Unit
FLEWORKSTUDYGRU, FWSG
  Fleet Work Study Group
FLEWORKSTUDYGRULANT, FWSGLANT
  Fleet Work Study Group, Atlantic
FLEWORKSTUDYGRUPAC, FWSGPAC
  Fleet Work Study Group, Pacific
FLEMIS
  Flexible Management Information System
FLESCOP
  Flexible Signal Collection and Processing
FLEXOPS
  Flexible Operations
FLG
  Falling
FLICON
  Flight Control
FLIDEN
  Flight Data Entry
FLIGA
  Flight Incident or Ground Accident
FLIP
  Flight Information Publication
  Flight-Launched Infrared Probe
  Floating Instrument Platform
FLIR
  Forward-Looking Infrared (radar)
FLN
  Flown
FLO
  French Liaison Office
FLOG
  Fleet Logistics
FLOGWING
  Fleet Logistics Air Wing
FLOLS
  Fresnel Lens Optical Landing System
FLOOD
  Fleet Observation of Oceanographic Data
FLOP
  Fresnel Lens Optical Practice

FLOPF
Fresnel Lens Optical Practice, Fleet—also FFLOP

FLOT
Flotilla

FLOTRONCOM
Flotilla or Squadron Commander

FLOT STOR
Floating Storage

FLOX
Fluorine and Oxygen

FLP
Field Landing Practice
Fighting Landplane

FLPA
Flight Level Pressure Altitude

FLR
Field-Level Repairable
Forward-Looking Radar

FLRY
Flurry

FLSD
Fleet Logistics Support Detachment

FLSG
Force Logistics Support Group (GLC)

FLSIP
Fleet Logistics Support Improvement Program

FLSIP-COSAL
Fleet Logistics Support Improvement Program Consolidated Stock Allowance List

FLSU
Force Logistics Support Unit (FLC)

FLT
Flight

FLT, FLE
Fleet

FLTAC
Fleet Analysis Center

FLTACFO
Fleet Analysis Center Field Office

FLTACREP
Fleet Analysis Center Representative

FLTAVCEN, FAVC
Fleet Audio-Visual Center

FLTAVCENEUR
Fleet Audio-Visual Center, Europe

FLTAVCENLANT
Fleet Audio-Visual Center, Atlantic

FLTAVCENPAC
Fleet Audio-Visual Center, Pacific

FLTAVCOMLANT
Fleet Audio-Visual Command, Atlantic

FLTAVCOMLANTDET
Fleet Audio-Visual Command, Atlantic Detachment

FLTAVCOMPAC
Fleet Audio-Visual Command, Pacific

FLTAVCOMPACDET
Fleet Audio-Visual Command, Pacific Detachment

FLTAVFAC, FAVF
Fleet Audio-Visual Facility

FLTAVFACLANT
Fleet Audio-Visual Facility, Atlantic

FLTAVFACPAC
Fleet Audio-Visual Facility, Pacific

FLTCERT
Flight Certificate

FLTCINC
Fleet Commander-in-Chief

FLTCOMBATSYSTRAUPAC
Fleet Combat Systems Training Unit, Pacific

FLTCON
Fleet (or Flight) Control

FLTCOORDGRU
Fleet Coordinating Group

FLTCORGRU
Fleet Composite Operational Readiness Group

FLTGUNSCOL
Fleet Gunnery School

FLTINTSUPPCEN
Fleet Intelligence Support Center

FLTMOD
Fleet Modernization

FLTRELSUPPACT
Fleet Religious Support Activity

FLTRELSUPPACTLANT
Fleet Religious Support Activity, Atlantic

FLTRELSUPPACTPAC
Fleet Religious Support Activity, Pacific

FLTSATCOMSYS, FSCS
Fleet Satellite Communications Systems

FLTSERVSCOL
Fleet Service School

FLTSIP
Fleet Support Improvement Program

FLTSOUNDSCOL
Fleet Sound School

FLTRACKCEN
Fleet Tracking Center

FLTTRAGRU, FTG
Fleet Training Group

FLTRASUPPRON
Fleet Training Support Squadron

FLTSUPPO
Fleet Support Office

FLTWEPCEN, FWC
Fleet Weapons Center

FLW, FOL
Follow

FLY DY
Flying Duty

FM
Facilities Maintenance
Fan Marker (approach)
Fathom
Financial Management
Foreign Military
Frequency Modulation

FM, FR
From
FMA
Field Maintenance Agent
FMAG
Field Maintenance Assistance Group
FMAG CRUDESLANT CHAR
Fleet Maintenance Assistance Group for
Cruiser-Destroyer Force, Atlantic,
Charleston (SC)
FMAG CRUDESLANT MPT
Fleet Maintenance Assistance Group for
Cruiser-Destroyer Force, Atlantic, Mayport
(FL)
FMAG CRUDESLANT NORVA
Fleet Maintenance Assistance Group for
Cruiser-Destroyer Force, Atlantic, Norfolk,
Virginia
FMAG MINEFORSUPPGRU CHAR
Fleet Maintenance Assistance Group for Mine
Force Support Group, Charleston (SC)
FMAG SERVLANT NORVA
Fleet Maintenance Assistance Group for
Service Forces, Atlantic, Norfolk, Virginia
FMB
Federal Maritime Board
FMC
Federal Manufacturer's Code
Fleet Management Center
Forward Motion Compensation
Fuel Management Computer
FMCDET
Fleet Management Center Detachment
FMD
Ferry Movement Directive
FMDCS
Fleet Maintenance Data Collection System
FMEA
Failure Mode and Effects Analysis
FMF, FLEMARFOR
Fleet Marine Force
FMFLANT, FLEMARFORLANT
Fleet Marine Force, Atlantic
FMFPAC, FLEMARFORPAC
Fleet Marine Force, Pacific
FMIC
Flight Manual Interim Changes
FMICS
Financial Management Information and
Control System
FMIP
Financial Management Improvement Program
FMLP
Field Mirror Landing Practice
FMLS
Fleet Maintenance and Logistics Support
FMO
Fleet Maintenance (or Medical) Officer

FMP
Family Member Prefix
Field Marching Pack
Fleet Modernization Program
Foreign Material Program
FMR
Field Modification Request
FMS
Field Maintenance Squadron
Fleet Music School
Foreign Military Sales
Fuze Maintenance Spares
FMSAEG
Fleet Missile Systems Analysis and
Evaluation Group
FMSAEGANX
Fleet Missile Systems Analysis and
Evaluation Group Annex
FMSO, FLEMATSUPPO
Fleet Material Support Office
FMSS
Fleet Medical Service School
FMTS
Field Maintenance Test Station
FMWTC, FLEMINWARTRACEN
Fleet Mine Warfare Training Center
FN
Fireman
FNA
Final Approach
FNH
Flashless Nonhydroscopic
FNOIO
Fleet Naval Ordnance Inspecting Officer
FNT
Front
FO
Field (or Flight) Order
Flag Officer
Flight Orderly
Font (U/I)
Foreign Object
Forward Observer
Fuel Oil
FOB
Forward Observer Bombardment
Forward Operating Base
Free on Board
FOBS
Fractional Orbital Bombardment System
FOBSTU
Forward Observer Target Survey Unit
FOC
Flight Operating Costs
Free of Costs (or Charges)
FOCAL
Formula Calculator
FOCC
Fleet Operational Control Center
FOCCEUR
Fleet Operational Control Center, Europe

FOCCLANT
Fleet Operational Control Center, Atlantic
FOCCPAC
Fleet Operational Control Center, Pacific
FOCSL
Fleet-Oriented Consolidated Stock List
FOD
Foreign Object Damage
FOG DET LT
Fog Detector Light
FOG SIG
Fog Signal (station)
FOI
Fleet Operational Investigation
Freedom of Information
FOINTRACEN, FOITC, FLEOPINTRACEN
Fleet Operational Intelligence Training Center
**FOINTRACENLANT, FOITCL,
    FLEOPINTRACENLANT**
Fleet Operational Intelligence Training
Center, Atlantic
**FOINTRACENPAC, FOITCP,
    FLEOPINTRACENPAC**
Fleet Operational Intelligence Training
Center, Pacific
FOIR
Field of Interest Register
FOITC, FOINTRACEN, FLEOPINTRACEN
Fleet Operational Intelligence Training Center
**FOITCL, FOINTRACENLANT,
    FLEOPINTRACENLANT**
Fleet Operational Intelligence Training
Center, Atlantic
**FOITCP, FOINTRACENPAC,
    FLEOPINTRACENPAC**
Fleet Operational Intelligence Training
Center, Pacific
FOL
Following
Forward Operating Location
FOL, FLW
Follow
FOLUP
Follow-Up
FOMIS
Fitting-Out Management Information System
FONE, PHONE, TEL, TP
Telephone
FONECON, TELCON
Telephone Conversation
FONL
Flag Officer's Newsletter (publication)
FOO
Forward Observer Officer
FOP
Financial Operating Plan
Fitting-Out Period
FOR
Fuel Oil, Reclaimed
Force

FORAC
For Action
FORACS
Fleet Operational Readiness Accuracy Check
Site
FORAS
For Assignment
FORCOPEXOS
Forward copy of orders with endorsements to
Administrative Office, Executive Office of
the Secretary (of the Navy).
FORDAD
Foreign Disclosure Automated Data
(systems)
FORDU
Foreign Duty (pay)
FORECONCO
Force Reconnaissance Company
FORF
Forfeiture
FORFTR, FOR PAY, FP
Forfeiture of Pay
FORM
Food Operations Reference Manual
FORN DY
Foreign Duty
FORNN
Forenoon
FOR PAY, FP, FORFTR
Forfeiture of Pay
FORSERVSUPPGRU, FSSG
Force Service Support Group
FORSERVSUPPGRUDET, FSSGDET
Force Service Support Group Detachment
FORSTAT
Force Status
FORTRAN
Formula Translation
FORTRANSIT
FORTRAN and System for Internal Translator
FOS
Full Operational Status
FOSA
Fixed Orifice Sound Attenuator
FOSAT
Fitting-Out Supply Assistance Team
FOSATLANT
Fitting-Out Supply Assistance Team, Atlantic
FOSATPAC
Fitting-Out Supply Assistance Team, Pacific
FOSC
Federal On-Scene Commander
FOSCO
Foreign Officer Supply Corps
FOSDIC
Film Optical Sensing Device for Input to
Computers
FOSIC
Fleet Ocean Surveillance Information Center

FOSICPAC
Fleet Ocean Surveillance Information Center, Pacific
FOSIF
Fleet Ocean Surveillance Information Facility
FOSIFWESTPAC
Fleet Ocean Surveillance Information Facility, Western Pacific
FOSS
Fiber Optic Sensor System
FOST
Flag Officer Sea Training
FOT
Frequency, Optimum Traffic
FOT&E
Follow-On Operational Test and Evaluation
FOTP
Fleet Operational Telecommunications Program
FOUO
For Official Use Only
FP
Fighter Prop (pilot code)
Final Plan
Fixed Price
Flag Plot
Foreward Peak (or Perpendicular)
Front Panel (NNSS)
FP, FOR, PAY, FORFTR
Forfeiture of Pay
FPA
Flight Path Angle
FPAF
Fixed-Price-Award Fee
FPB
Fast Patrol Boat
FPC
Fixed-Price Contract
Flight Purpose Code
FPDS
Fleet Probe Data System
FPE
Fire Protection Engineering
Fixed-Price with Escalation (contract)
FPH
Fast Patrol Hovercraft
FPI
Fixed-Price-Incentive
FPIC
Fixed-Price-Incentive Contract
FPIF
Fixed-Price-Incentive Fee
FPIS
Forward Propogation Ionospheric Scatter
FPIST
Fixed-Price-Incentive-Successive Targets
FPJMT
Four-Party Joint Military Team
FPL
Final Protective Line

FPM
Federal Personnel Manual
Feet per Minute
Flight Path Marker
FPMR
Federal Property Management Regulations
FPO
Fleet Post Office
FPQ
Field Performance Questionnaires
FPR
Federal Procurement Regulations
Fixed-Price Redeterminations (contracts)
FPRC
Fixed-Price Providing for Redetermination of Price Contract
FPS
Feet (or Frames) per Second
FPSO
Forms and Publications Supply Office
FPSTU
Full-Pressure Suit Training Unit
FPT
Fleet Project Team
Full-Power Trial
FPTS
Forward Propagation Tropospheric Scatter
FPU
First Production Unit
FPV
Free Piston Vessel
FQN
Family Quarters, Navy
FQ&P
First Qualities and Performance (branch)
FQT, FREQ
Frequency
FR
Facilitating Reflex
Federal Register
Fighter Reconnaissance
Flexor Reflex
Fleet Reserve
Food Relief Punt (USCG)
FR, FM
From
FRA
Fleet Readiness Assistants
FRAA
Fleet Repairables Assistance Agent
FRAG BOMB
Fragmentation Bomb
FRAM
Fleet Rehabilitation and Modernization (program)
FRAMP
Fleet Readiness Aviation Maintenance Personnel
Fleet Rehabilitation and Modernization Program

FRAN
  Fleet Readiness Analysis (system)
FRAT
  Free Radical Assay Technique
FRAUD, EN, FE, FRDENL
  Fraudulent Enlistment
FRB
  Federal Reserve Bank
FRC
  Facilities Review Committee
  Federal Records Center
  Fleet Resources Office
  Flight Research Center
  Full Route Clearance (necessary)
  Functional Residual Capacity
FRCU
  Fractocumulus (cloud formation)
FRD
  Formerly Restricted Data
FRDENL, FE, FRAUD ENL
  Fraudulent Enlistment
FREDS
  Flight Readiness Evaluation Data System
FREM
  Fleet Readiness Enlisted Maintenance
  (trainees)
FREN
  French
FREQ
  Frequency
FREQ, FQT
  Frequent
FRESH
  Foil Research Hydrofoil
F REV
  Further Review
FRF
  Flight-Readiness Firings
FRGS
  Force Reports Generation System
FRINGE
  File and Report Information Processing
  Generator
FRISCO
  Fast Reaction Integrated Submarine Control
FRM
  Form
FRN
  Force Requisition Number
FRO
  Fleet Records Office
  Front
FROF
  Freight Office
FRON
  Frontier
FROPA
  Frontal Passage
FROSFC
  Frontal Surface

FRP
  Fiberglass-Reinforced Plastic
  Fleet Replacement Pilot
  Fragmentation Bomb, Parachute
FRR
  Flight Readiness Review
FRRS
  Frequency Resource Record System
FRS
  Federal Reserve System
  Fleet Readiness Squadron
  Fleet Repair Service
FRSSACS
  Free Reaction Sphere Satellite Attitude
  Control System
FRST
  Frost
FRT
  Freight
FRU
  Fleet Readiness Unit
FRZ
  Freeze
FRZER
  Freezer (stowage)
FRZN
  Frozen
FS
  Feasibility
  Final Settlement
  Firing Set
  Fixed Satellite
  Flat Seam
  Fleet Status (or Support)
  Flight Service
  Fractostratus (cloud formation)
  Freon Service
FSA
  Family Separation Allowance
  Federal Security Agency
  Fire Support Area
FSAP
  Fleet Ships Assistance Program
FSA-R
  Family Separation Allowance (Restricted
  Station)
FSA-S
  Family Separation Allowance (Shipboard
  Operations)
FSA-T
  Family Separation Allowance (Temporary
  Duty)
FSB
  Federal Specifications Board
  Fire Support Base

FSC
Family Services Center
Federal Stock (or Supply) Class/Code
Federal Supply Catalog (or Classification)
Fire Support Coordinator
Fixed Satellite Communications (terminal)
Full Systems Capability

FSCC
Fire Support Coordination Center

FSCEN
Flight Services Center

FSCIL
Federal Supply Catalog Identification List

FSCM
Federal Supply Code for Manufacturers

FSCS, FLTSATCOMSYS
Fleet Satellite Communications System

FSCR
First Ship Configuration Review

FSD
Federal Systems Division
First Ship Delivered
Foreign Sea Duty
Frequency Shift Demodulator

FSDO
Flight Standards District Office

FSE
Field Support Equipment

FSG
Federal Supply Group

FSI
Federal Stock Item

FSIF
Flight Suit with Integrated Flotation

FSK
Frequency Shift Keying

FSL
Full-Stop Landing

FSM
Frequency Shift Modulator

FSMAO
Field Supply and Maintenance Analysis Office

FSML
Fleet Support Material List

FSMS
Firing Set Maintenance Spares

FSMT
Fleet Service Mine Test

FSN
Federal Stock Number

FSO
Fleet (or Force) Supply Office(r)

FSP
Floating Stock Platform

FSPB
Fire Support Primary Base

FS-POWDER
Flashless, Smokeless Powder

FSR
Field Service Representative
Fin-Stabilized Rocket
Full Systems Ready

FSS
Federal Supply Service (GSA)
Federal Supply Schedule
Fire Support Station
Fleet Service School
Flight Service Station
Foreign Shore Service
Full-Scale Section

FSSB
Flight Status Selection Board

FSSD
Foreign Service Selection Date

FSSG, FORSERVSUPPGRU
Force Service Support Group

FSSGDET, FORSERVSUPPGRUDET
Force Service Support Group Detachment

FS SHIPS
Fire Support Ships

FST
Field Survey Team (NMVO)

FSU
Ferry Service Unit
Fleet Support Unit

FS/UEG
Fleet Staff/Unit Expansion Group

FT
Awaiting Further Transportation (MAPMIS)
Fixation and Transfer (text)
Flight Test (division)
Fume Tight

F&T, FANDT
Fuel and Transportation

FTAR
Field Training Assistance Representative

FTAS
Fast Time Analyzer System

FTB
Failure to Break

FTB1
Fire Control Technician B (Ballistic Missile Fire Control) First Class

FTB2
Fire Control Technician B (Ballistic Missile Fire Control) Second Class

FTB3
Fire Control Technician B (Ballistic Missile Fire Control) Third Class

FTBC
Chief Fire Control Technician B (Ballistic Missile Fire Control)

FT BM
Feet Board Measure

FTBSA
Fire Control Technician B (Ballistic Missile Fire Control) Seaman Apprentice

FTBSN
Fire Control Technician B (Ballistic Missile Fire Control) Seaman
FTC
Fast Time Constant
Fleet Type Commander
Flight Test Center
FTC, FLETRACEN
Fleet Training Center
FTCM
Master Chief Fire Control Technician
FTCP
Flight Test Change Proposal
FTCS
Senior Chief Fire Control Technician
FTD
Fails to Drive
Field Training Detachment
Force, Type, District (code)
Freight Terminal Department
FTG
Fitting
Footage
FTG, FLTTRAGRU
Fleet Training Group
FTG1
Fire Control Technician G (Gun Fire Control) First Class
FTG2
Fire Control Technician G (Gun Fire Control) Second Class
FTG3
Fire Control Technician G (Gun Fire Control) Third Class
FTGC
Chief Fire Control Technician G (Gun Fire Control)
FTG DIVES
Footage Dives
FTGS
Fittings
FTGSA
Fire Control Technician G (Gun Fire Control) Seaman Apprentice
FTGSN
Fire Control Technician G (Gun Fire Control) Seaman
FTGWP, FLETRAGRUWESTPAC
Fleet Training Group, Western Pacific
FTHR
Farther
Further
FTIC
Firm Time in Commission
FTIM
Frequency and Time Interval Meter
FTM1
Fire Control Technician M (Missile Fire Control) First Class

FTM2
Fire Control Technician M (Missile Fire Control) Second Class
FTM3
Fire Control Technician M (Missile Fire Control) Third Class
FTMC
Chief Fire Control Technician M (Missile Fire Control)
FTMSA
Fire Control Technician M (Missile Fire Control) Seaman Apprentice
FTMSN
Fire Control Technician M (Missile Fire Control) Seaman
FTOC
Fahrenheit to Celsius
FTP
Field Transport Pack
Fleet Training Publication
FTR
Fails to Respond
FTR, FIT
Fighter
FTS
Federal Telecommunications System
Flight Traffic Specialist
FTSC, FLETECHSUPPCEN
Fleet Technical Support Center
FTSCDET, FLETECHSUPPCENDET
Fleet Technical Support Center Detachment
FTT
Fever Therapy Technician
FTU
Field Torpedo Unit
Fixed Temperature Unit
FTV
Flight Test Vehicle
FU
Follow-Up
FUBAR
"Fouled Up Beyond All Recognition" (slang)
FUBB
"Fouled Up Beyond Belief" (slang)
FUMTU
"Fouled Up More Than Usual" (slang)
FUR
Failure and Unsatisfactory Report
FURAS, FFA
For Further Assignment
FURASPERS
For further assignment by the Commander Naval Military Personnel Command to (duty indicated).
FURASUB(S)
For further assignment to duty in submarine(s)
FUR/EFR
Failure and Unsatisfactory/Electronic Failure Report

FURN
Furnish
FURNASER
Furnish full names, rates and social security numbers of men transferred in accordance with this directive.
FURORDMOD
Orders further modified
FUT
Fleet Utility
FW
Field Winding (wiring)
Fresh Water
F/W
Fixed Wing (aircraft)
FW/B
Forward toward the Bow (stowage)
FWC
Feedwater Control
FWC, FLTWEPCEN
Fleet Weapons Center
FWD
Forward
FWDC
Fresh Water Drain Collecting (system)
FWED
Fleet Weapons Engineering Department
FWMAF
Free World Military Assistance Forces (program)
FWP
Final Weight Report
FWS
Fighter Weapons School
FWSG, FLTWORKSTUDYGRU
Fleet Work Study Group
FWSGLANT, FLTWORKSTUDYGRULANT
Fleet Work Study Group, Atlantic
FWSGPAC, FLTWORKSTUDYGRUPAC
Fleet Work Study Group, Pacific
FW/SIFR
Fixed-Wing Special Instrument Flight Rules
FW/SVFR
Fixed-Wing Special Visual Flight Rules
FXP
Fleet Exercise Publication
FXR
Foxer (gear)
FY
Fiscal Year
FYDO
Five-Year Design Objective
FYDP
Five-Year Defense Program
FYFS&FP, FYFSFP
Five-Year Force Structure and Financial Program
FYI
For Your Information
FYIG
For Your Information and Guidance

FYU
Harbor Utility Unit
FZ
Fire Zone (bulkhead)

G

G
Controller (TO code)
Gravel
Gravity
Guilty
G, GRP, GRU, GU
Group
G-1
General Staff, Personnel
G-2
General Staff, Intelligence Section
G-3
General Staff, Operations Section
G-4
General Staff, Supply Section
G-5
General Staff, Physiological Warfare Branch (SHAEF)
G-6
General Staff, Civil Affairs Division (SHAEF)
GA
General Average
Ground Attacker (aircraft)
G/A
Ground-to-Air
G&A
General and Administrative (expense rate)
GAA
General Account of Advance
General Agency Agreement
Grease, Automotive and Artillery
GACTFOSIF
Graphic Analysis Correlation Terminal Fleet Ocean Surveillance Information Facility
GAE
General Classification Test/Arithmetic Test/Electronics Technician Selection Test
GAI
General Accounting Instructions
GAIL
Glide Angle Indicator Light
GAINS
Graphic Administrative Information System
GAM
General Accounting (or Aeronautical) Material
Guided Air(craft) Missile
GAN
Gyrocompass Automatic Navigation
GAO
General Accounting Office
General Administrative Order

GAO NOTE
General Accounting Office Notice of
Execution
GAP
Get Ahead Program
Graduate Academic Program
GAPA
Ground-to-Air Pilotless Aircraft
GAPB
General Aptitude Test Battery
GAR
Guided Aircraft Rocket
GARD
General Address Reading Device
GARP
Global Atmospheric Research Program
(WMO/ICSM)
GAS
Gasoline—see MOGAS
GASES
Gravity Anchored Space Experiments
Satellite
GASSC
Group Aviation Supply Support Center
GAT
General Aviation Transponder (FAA)
Greenwich Apparent Time
GATE
Global Atmospheric Research Program
Atlantic Tropical Experiment
GATTC
General Aviation Technical Training
Conference
GB
General Board
Government Bunkers
Imperial Gallon (U/I)
GBI
Gained By Inventory
GBL, GBLADING
Government Bill of Lading
GBLADING, GBL
Government Bill of Lading
GBLOC
Government Bill of Lading Office Code
GBRP
General Bending Response Program
GBU
Ground Back-Up
GBX
Ground Branch Exchange
GC
General Cargo
Graphic(s) Center
Great Circle (route)
Gun Capital
G&C
Guidance and Control
GCA
Ground-Controlled Approach (or Acquisition)
Guidance and Control Assembly

GCBS
Ground Control Bombing System
GCC
Ground Control Center
Gun Control Console
GCD
General and Complete Disarmament
GCE
Gun Control Equipment
GCFU
Germinal Center-Forming Unit
GCG
Guidance Control Group
GCI
Ground-Controlled Intercept
GCI/ADC
Ground-Controlled Intercept/Air Defense
Center
GCM
General Court-Martial
GCM, GCMED
Good Conduct Medal
GCMED, GCM
Good Conduct Medal
GCMP
General Court-Martial Prisoner
GCO
Gunfire Control Officer
GCP
Generator Control Panel
Guidance Control Package
GCR
Gas-Cooled Graphite-Moderated Reactor
GCS
Ground Communications System
Guidance Control Section
GCSS
Global Communications Satellite System
Ground-Controlled Space Systems
GCT
General Classification Test
GD
Guard
GDC
Guidance Display Computer
GDF
Ground Defense Forces
GDH
Ground Data Handling
GDL
Gas Dynamic Laser
GDM
General Development Map
GDP
Gun Director Pointer
GDP(CL)
Gun Director Pointer (Cross Leveler)
GDP(L)
Gun Director Pointer (Leveler)
GDP(P)
Gun Director Pointer (Pointer)

GDP(SS)
Gun Director Pointer (Sight Setter)
GDP(T)
Gun Director Pointer (Trainer)
GDS
General Declassification Schedule
GDU
Garbage Disposal Unit (TDU)
GE
General Expenses
GEB
General Engine Bulletin
GECOM
General Compiler
GED
General Education and Development (test)
GE&D
General Engineering and Development
GEDU
Gun Elevation Displacement Unit
GEEIA
Ground Electronics Engineering Installation
Agency
GEFD
Geographical Engineering Field Division
GEISHA
Gun Electron Injection for Semiconductor or
Hybrid Amplification
GEK
Geomagnetic Electrokinetograph
GEM
General Effectiveness Model
Ground Effects Machine
Ground Electronics Maintenance
Guidance Evaluation Missile
GEMD
Ground Electronics Maintenance Division
GEN
General
GEND
General Expenses, Naval Department
GENDET
General Detail
GENOTES
General Notices
GENR
Generate
Generator
GENSPECS
General Specifications
GEO
Geographic
GEOL
Geology
GEON
Gyro-Erected Optical Navigation
GEOREF
Geographic Reference (system)
GEPOL
Generalized Processor for
Command-Oriented Languages

GETOL
Ground Effect Take-Off and Landing
GEX
Government Employees Exchange
GF, GNDFG
Ground Fog (weather symbol)
GFA
Government-Furnished Accessories
GFAE
Government-Furnished Aircraft Equipment
GFCC
Gunfire Control Center
GFCS
Gunfire Control System
GFCS-B
Gunfire Control System-Backup
GFCSS
Gunfire Control Sub-System
GFDL
Geophysical Fluid Dynamics Laboratory
GFE
Government-Furnished Equipment
GFEL
Government-Furnished Equipment List
GFI
Government-Furnished Information
GFM
Government-Furnished Material
GFP
Government-Furnished Property
GFR
Glomerular Filtration Rates
GFS
Government-Furnished Support
Gunfire Support
GG
Great Gross (U/I)
GGS
Gravity Gradient Stabilization
GGTS
Gravity Gradient Test Satellite
GH
Grid Heading
GHA
Greenwich Hour Angle
GHE
Ground Handling Equipment
GHR
Gross Heat Rate
GHQ
General Headquarters
GHZ
Giga-Hertz
GI
General Issue
Gill (U/I)
Government Issue
GIB
General Information Book
"Guy in Back" (slang)

GIDEP
　Government-Industry Data Exchange
　　Program
GIGO
　Garbage In, Garbage Out
GIMMIS
　G-1 Manpower Management Information
　　System
GIO
　Government Information Organization
GIOC
　General Input/Output Computer
GIP
　Ground Instructor Pilot
GIPS
　Ground Information Processing System
GIPSE
　Gravity Independent Photo-Synthetic Gas
　　Exchanger
GIRLS
　Generalized Information Retrieval and Listing
　　System
　Global Interrogation Recording and Location
　　Maps
GIU
　General Intelligence Unit
GIUK
　Greenland, Iceland, and the United Kingdom
　　(gap)
GLASS
　"Good Luck and Smooth Sailing" (slang)
GLC
　Gas Liquid Chromatography
GLDR, GLI
　Glider
GLI, GLDR
　Glider
GLIPAR
　Guideline Identification Program for
　　Anti-missile Research
GLO
　Gun(nery) Liaison Officer
GLOBECOM, GLOCOM
　Global Communications (system)
GLOCOM, GLOBECOM
　Global Communications (system)
GLOTRAC
　Global Tracking (system)
GLP
　Government-Lent Property
GLS
　General Line School
GM
　Geometric Mean
　Gram (U/I)
　Guard Mail
GM, G/M
　Guided Missile
GMA
　Gas Metal Arc

GMAT
　Greenwich Mean Astronomical Time
GMCM
　Guided Missile Countermeasures
　Master Chief Gunner's Mate
GMCS
　Guided Missile Control System
　Senior Chief Gunner's Mate
GMD
　Ground Meteorological Site
GMDEP
　Guided Missile Data Exchange Program
GMFCS
　Guided Missile Fire Control System
GMG1
　Gunner's Mate G (Guns) First Class
GMG2
　Gunner's Mate G (Guns) Second Class
GMG3
　Gunner's Mate G (Guns) Third Class
GMGC
　Chief Gunner's Mate G (Guns)
GMGSA
　Gunner's Mate G (Guns) Seaman Apprentice
GMGSN
　Gunner's Mate G (Guns) Seaman
GML
　Guided Missile Launcher
GMLS
　Guided Missile Launching System
GMM1
　Gunner's Mate M (Missiles) First Class
GMM2
　Gunner's Mate M (Missiles) Second Class
GMM3
　Gunner's Mate M (Missiles) Third Class
GMMC
　Chief Gunner's Mate M (Missiles)
GMMSA
　Gunner's Mate M (Missiles) Seaman
　　Apprentice
GMMSN
　Gunner's Mate M (Missiles) Seaman
GMO
　General Medical Officer
GMOCU
　Guided Missile Operation and Control Unit
GMP
　Ground Map Pencil
GMRMR
　General Mobilization Reserve Material
　　Requirements
GMS
　General Maintenance System
　General Military Subjects (course)
　Ground Map Spoiled
GM&S
　General, Medical and Surgical
GMSER
　Guided Missile Service Report

GMSR
Guided Missile Service Record
GMST
General Military Subjects Instructor
GMT
General Military Training
Greenwich Mean (or Meridian) Time
GMT1
Gunner's Mate T (Technician) First Class
GMT2
Gunner's Mate T (Technician) Second Class
GMT3
Gunner's Mate T (Technician) Third Class
GMTC
Chief Gunner's Mate T (Technician)
GMTI
Ground Moving-Target Indicator
GMTO
General Military Training Office
GMTS
Guided Missile Test Set
GMTSA
Gunner's Mate T (Technician) Seaman
Apprentice
GMTSN
Gunner's Mate T (Technician) Seaman
GMU
Guided Missile Unit
GMV
Government Motor Vehicle
GN
Grain (U/I)
G&N
Guidance and Navigation
GNATS
Guidance and Navigational Tracking Satellite
GNC
Global Navigation Chart
GND
Ground
GNDCON
Ground Control
GNDFG, GF
Ground Fog
GNE
Government Nomenclature Equipment
GNR, GUN
Gunnery
GNST
Glossary of Naval Ship Types
GO
General Order
GOAC
Geographic OPAREA Coordinates
GOAR
Ground Observer Aircraft Recognition
GOC
General Officer Commanding
GO/CO
Government-Owned/Contractor-Operated
(facility)

GOE
Government-Owned Equipment
GOES
Geostationary Operational Environmental
Satellite
GOES-A
Geostationary Operational Environmental
Satellite-A
GOFAR
Global Ocean-Floor Analysis and Research
GOMAC
Government Microcircuit Applications
Conference
GOP
General Operational Plot
GOR
General Operational Requirement
GOS
Geochemical Ocean Studies
Grade-of-Service
GOSS
General Overhaul Specifications, Submarines
Ground Operational Support Equipment
GOV, GOVT
Government
GOVAIR
Including government aircraft
GOVAIRAUTHOUT
Travel via government aircraft authorized
outside CONUS Class _____ priority is
certified.
GOVAIRAUTHVAIL
Travel via government aircraft authorized
outside CONUS where available. Class
_____ priority is certified.
GOVAIRDIR
Travel via government aircraft is directed
where necessary.
GOVAIRDIROUT
Travel via government aircraft is directed
outside CONUS.
GOVAIRDIRVAIL
Travel via government aircraft is directed
outside CONUS where available. Class
_____ priority is certified.
GOVAIRPRI
While travelling via government air outside
CONUS Class _____ priority is certified.
GOVCOMAIRAUTH
Travel via government and/or commercial
aircraft authorized where necessary to
expedite completion of the duty. Class
_____ priority is certified for travel via
government aircraft.
GOVCOMAIRDIR
Travel via government and/or commercial
aircraft as may be elected by him directed
where necessary to expedite completion of
this duty. Class _____ priority certified for
travel via government aircraft.

GOVCOMLTRANSAUTH
Travel via government and/or commercial
U.S. registry transportation authorized
outside CONUS. See JTR, Par. M 4159-5
for entitlement to reimbursement for
commercial transportation procured at
personal expense. Excess travel time will
be charged as leave. (1) 120 (2) 165
pounds baggage to accompany you
authorized for air travel outside CONUS.

GOVMERAIR
Including government or commercial aircraft

GOVMERAIRAUTH
Travel via government and/or commercial
aircraft is authorized where necessary

GOVMERAIRDIR
Travel via government and/or commercial
aircraft is directed where necessary

GOVT, GOV
Government

GOVT HO
Government House

GOVT QTRS, GQ
Government Quarters

GOVTRANSDIROUT
Travel via government transportation directed
outside CONUS

GOVTRANSDIRVAIL
Travel via government transportation directed
outside CONUS where available

GOX
Gaseous Oxygen

GP
General Principle (or Purpose)
Geographic Point (or Position)
Glide Path
Gun Pointer

GPA
Government Property Administrator
Grade-Point Average

GPAC
General Purpose Airborne Computer

GPATS
General Purpose Automatic Test Station

GP BOMB
General Purpose Bomb

GPD
Gallons per Day

GPE
General Purpose Equipment

GPETE
General Purpose Electronics Test Equipment

GPFL
Group Flashing (light)

GPG
Grains per Gallon

GPH
Gallons per Hour

GPI
Ground Point of Impact
Ground Position Indicator

GPM
Gallons per Minute

GPO
Government Printing Office

GPOCC
Group Occulting (light)

GPRS
Goal Progress Reporting System

GPS
Global Positioning System

GPSS
General Purpose Simulation Studies

GPV
General Purpose Vehicle

GQ
General Quarters

GQ, GOVT, QTRS
Government Quarters

GR
Grain
Granted
Greece (message traffic)
Gross (U/I)
Ground Range

GR, G, GRP, GRU
Group

GRA
Government Reports Announcement

GRAD
Gradient
Graduate
Graduate Accumulation and Resume
Distribution

GRADS
Ground Radar Aerial Delivery Systems

GRAN
Global Rescue Alarm Network

GRB
Government Reservation Bureau

GRD
Geophysical Research Directorate
Ground
Guard

GRDL
Gradual

GRE
Graduate Record Examination

GREB
Galactic Radiation Experiment Background
(satellite)
General Reciprocating Engine Bulletin
(publication)

GREEMAIN
Orders contingent upon agreement to remain
on active duty until (date specified).
Execution of these orders constitute
your agreement to serve until date
specified. Member should notify
COMNAVMILPERSCOM if he does not
desire to execute these orders.

GREETOUR
Tour of duty to which member ordered is
_____ months with dependents. Movement
of dependents to new duty station at
government expense constitutes your
agreement to serve prescribed
accompanied tour at new duty station.

GREETOUROBLISERV
Tour of duty to which member ordered is
_____ months with dependents. Movement
of dependents to new duty station at
government expense constitutes your
agreement to serve prescribed
accompanied tour at new duty station. You
have _____ months' obligated service.

GREEXTEND
Orders contingent upon your agreement to
extend active duty until (date specified).
Execution of these orders constitutes an
agreement to serve until date indicated.
Member must notify
COMNAVMILPERSCOM if he does not
desire to execute these orders.

GREN
Grenade

GREPAT
Greenland Patrol

GRIPS
Ground Reconnaissance Information
Processing System

GRL
Gross Reference List

GRNC
Groups Not Counted

GRP
Glass-Reinforced Plastic

GRP, G, GR, GRU
Group

GRSL
Guam Reference Standards Laboratory

GRTG
Granting

GRU, G, GR, GRP
Group

GRUCOM
Group Commander

GRWT
Gross Weight

GS
General Schedule (CBC)
Glass (U/I)
Glide Slope
Ground Speed
Guard Ship

G/S
General Support

GSA
General Services Administration

GSC
Ground Speed Continuing

GSCM
Master Chief Gas Turbine Systems
Technician

GSCS
Senior Chief Gas Turbine Systems
Technician

GSDA
Ground Speed Drift Angle

GSDF
Ground Self-Defense Force

GSE
Government-Specified Equipment
Ground Support Equipment

GSE1
Gas Turbine Systems Technician E
(Electrical) First Class

GSE2
Gas Turbine Systems Technician E
(Electrical) Second Class

GSE3
Gas Turbine Systems Technician E
(Electrical) Third Class

GSEC
Chief Gas Turbine Systems Technician E
(Electrical)

GSEFA
Gas Turbine Systems Technician E
(Electrical) Fireman Apprentice

GSEFN
Gas Turbine Systems Technician E
(Electrical) Fireman

GSESD
Ground Support Equipment Statistical Display

GSEREWORKFAC
Ground Support Equipment Rework Facility

GSF, GULFSEAFRON
Gulf Sea Frontier

GSFS
General Specifications for Ships

GSGT
Gunnery Sergeant

GSI
Glide Slope Indicator
Government Source Inspection

GSLL
General Stores Load List

GSM
General Stores Material

GSM1
Gas Turbine Systems Technician M
(Mechanical) First Class

GSM2
Gas Turbine Systems Technician M
(Mechanical) Second Class

GSM3
Gas Turbine Systems Technician M
(Mechanical) Third Class

GSMC
Chief Gas Turbine Systems Technician M
(Mechanical)

GSMFA
Gas Turbine Systems Technician M
(Mechanical) Fireman Apprentice

GSMFN
Gas Turbine Systems Technician M
(Mechanical) Fireman

GSR
General Service Recruit
Ground Speed Returning

GSS
General Specifications for Ships
General Supply Schedule
Geostationary Satellite
Global Surveillance System

GST
General Staff Target
Greenwich Sidereal (or Standard) Time

GSTOS
General Specifications for Training
Operations and Manuals

GSU
Geographically Separated Units

GT
Great

GTA
Gas Tungsten Arc

GTC
Gas Turbine Compressor

GTCP
Gas Turbine Compressor and Power Plant

GTESM
Gas Turbine Exhaust System Model

GTM
Gas Turbine Model

GTP
Gas Turbine Power (or Propulsion) (unit)

GTR
Government Transportation Request

GTS
Gas Turbine Ship

GTSS
Gas Turbine Self-Contained Starter

GU
Guam

GUARD
Guaranteed Assignment Retention Detailing

GUARD II
Expanded Guaranteed Assignment Retention
Detailing

GUCL
General Use Consumables List

GULFGRU
Gulf Group

GUN
Gunboat
Gunner

GUN, GNR
Gunnery

GUPPY
Greater Underwater Propulsion Power

GV
Grid Variation

GVR
Geocentric Vertical Reference

GVWR
Gross Vehicle Weight Rating

GW
General Warning

GWC
Gross Weight Category

GWOTH
Ground Wave Over-the-Horizon (radar)

GWS
Gun Weapons System

GWT
Gross Weight Ton

GY
Gyro(scope)

GZ
Ground Zero

GZN
Grid Azimuth

H

H
Electronic Countermeasures Evaluator (TO
code)
Haze (weather symbol)
Hull (valve)

H24
24-Hour (continuous operations)

HA
Headquarters Administration
Home Address
Hospitalman Apprentice
Housing Allowance (or Authority)

HA, HIALT
High Altitude

HAA
Height Above Aerodrome

HAAC
Heavy Attack Air Commander

HAACT
Heavy Attack Air Commander Training

HAAW
Heavy Antitank Assault Weapon

HAC
Heavy Antitank Convoy
Helicopter Aircraft Commander

HACS
Hazards Assessment Computer System

HAD
Heat-Actuated Device
High-Altitude Diagnostic

HADES
Hypersonic Air Data Entry System

HAF
Helicopter Assault Forces

HAFC
High-Altitude Forecast Center
HA(HS)
High School Hospitalman Apprentice
HAIIS
Headquarters Administrative Issuance Index
System
HAIR
High Accuracy Instrumentation Radar
HAL
Height Above Landing
Helicopter Attack Light Squadron
Highly Automated Logic
HALO
High-Altitude, Low-Opening (parachuting
technique)
HALS
Hydrographic Airborne Laser Sounder
HAM
Hamlet
HAMS
Headquarters and Maintenance Squadron
HAMSDET
Headquarters and Maintenance Squadron
Detachment
HAP
High-Altitude Platform
HAPDEC
Hard Point Decoy
HAR
Harbor Advisory Radar
HARDEX
Harbor Defense Exercise
HARM
High-Speed Anti-Radiation (or -Radar) Missile
HARP
Heater Above Reheat Point
High-Altitude Relay Point
HARP, HARPY
High-Altitude Research Project
HARPY, HARP
High-Altitude Research Project
HARRS
High-Altitude Radio Relay System
HART
High Acceleration Rocket, Tactical
HASC
House Armed Services Committee
HASP
High-Altitude Sounding Projectile
HAST
High-Altitude Supersonic Target
HAT
Height Above Touchdown
HAT/LANT
Habitability Assistance Team/Atlantic
HAT/PAC
Habitability Assistance Team/Pacific
HATRON, VAH
Heavy Attack Squadron

HATS
Helicopter Attack System
HATWING
Heavy Attack Wing
HAV
Heavily Armed Vehicle
HAW
Helicopter Assault Wave
HAWK
Homing-all-the-Way Killer
HAWKITS
Hazards Awareness Kits
HAWSEAFRON, HSF
Hawaiian Sea Frontier
HB
Heavy Bomber (aircraft)
Horizontal Bands (buoy)
Horizontal Bomber
HBC
Health Benefits Counselor (USHBP)
HBN
Hazard Beacon
H-BOMB
Hydrogen Bomb
HBP
Health Benefits Program
Hospital Benefit Payment
HBPIO
Health Benefits Program Information Officer
HBR
Harbor
HBS
Harbor Boat Service
HC
Health Category
Heavy Clouds
High Capacity
Hydrocarbons
**HC, HCRON, HELCOMBSUPPRON,
HELSUPPRON**
Helicopter Combat Support Squadron
HCA
Headquarters Commitment Authorization
Held by Civil Authorities
HCC
Hand Control Clutch
Helicopter Crash Crane
HCCG
(Discharge under) Honorable Conditions,
Convenience of the Government
HCCM
(Discharge under) Honorable Conditions,
Convenience of the Man
HCDP
(Discharge under) Honorable Conditions,
Dependency Existing Prior to Enlistment
HCDS
Health Care Delivery System
HCEE
(Discharge under) Honorable Conditions,
Expiration of Enlistment

HCF
Highest Common Factor
HCFF
High Capacity Fog Foam
HCFF/AFFF
High Capacity Fog Foam/Aqueous
Film-Forming Foam
HCMS
(Discharge under) Honorable Conditions,
Medical Survey
HCMU
(Discharge under) Honorable Conditions,
Minor Enlistment Without Consent
HCO
Hangar (or Helicopter) Control Officer
HCP
Hangar Control Position
HCPTR, HEL, HELI, HELO
Helicopter
**HCRON, HC, HELCOMBSUPPRON,
HELSUPPRON**
Helicopter Combat Support Squadron
HCU
Harbor (or Helicopter) Clearance Unit
HCUDET
Harbor Clearance Unit Detachment
HCUS
(Discharge under) Honorable Conditions,
Unsuitable
HD
Harbor Defense
Head (land)
Heat Dissipation (factor)
Helo Direction (nets)
High Drag
HDC
Hangar Deck Control
Harbor Defense Command
Helicopter Direction Center (or Control)
HDCG
Honorable Discharge, Convenience of the
Government
HDCM
Honorable Discharge, Convenience of the
Man
HDDP
Honorable Discharge, Dependency Existing
Prior to Enlistment
HDDR
High Digital Density Recording
HDDS
Honorable Discharge, Dependency Arising
Since Enlistment
HDEE
Honorable Discharge, Expiration of
Enlistment
HDF, HFDF, HUFFDUFF
High Frequency Direction Finder
HDG
Heading

HDGP
High-Drag General-Purpose
HDHVPS
High Density High Voltage Power Supply
HDI
Horizontal Display Indicator
HDMP
Horizon Definition Measurement Program
HDMS
Honorable Discharge, Medical Survey
HDMU
Honorable Discharge, Minor Under Age of
Authorized Consent
HDMW
Honorable Discharge, Minor Enlisted Without
Consent
HDQTRS, HQ, HED
Headquarters
HDR
Home Dockyard Regulations
HDRSS
High Data Rate Storage System
HDX
Half Duplex (operation)
HE
Head (U/I)
High Explosive
Human Engineering
HEAF
Human Error Analysis Record
HEAT
High Explosive Antitank
HEAVYPHOTORON
Heavy Photographic Squadron
HECP, HECPOST
Harbor Entrance Control Post
HECPOST, HECP
Harbor Entrance Control Post
HED, HDQTRS, HQ
Headquarters
HEDSUPPACT
Headquarters Support Activity
HEF
High Energy Fuel
HEFOE
Hydraulic, Engine, Fuel, Oxygen, Electrical
HEI
High Explosive Incendiary (bomb)
HEIT
High Explosive Incendiary Traced (bomb)
HEL
High Energy Laser
HEL, HCPTR, HELI, HELO
Helicopter
HELANTISUBRON, HELSRON, HS
Helicopter Antisubmarine Squadron
HELANTISUBRONDET
Helicopter Antisubmarine Squadron
Detachment
HELATKRON
Helicopter Attack Squadron

HELCOMBSUPPRON, HC, HCRON, HELSUPPRON
Helicopter Combat Support Squadron
HELI, HCPTR, HEL, HELO
Helicopter
HELMINERON
Helicopter Mine Countermeasures Squadron
HELMINERONDET
Helicopter Mine Countermeasures Squadron
Detachment
HELO, HCPTR, HEL, HELI
Helicopter
HELOPS
Helicopter Operations
HELOPSUPPFAC
Helicopter Operational Support Facility
HELREC
Health Record(s)
HELSRON, HELANTISUBRON, HS
Helicopter Antisubmarine Squadron
HELSUPPRON, HC, HCRON, HELCOMBSUPPRON
Helicopter Combat Support Squadron
HELSUPPRONDET
Helicopter Combat Support Squadron
Detachment
HELTRARON, HT
Helicopter Training Squadron
HEM
Hemisphere
HEOS
High Eccentric Orbiting Satellite
HEPDEX
High Energy Proton Detection Experiment
HEPS
Helicopter Personnel Escape Protection and
Survival
HERALDS
Harbor Echo-Ranging and Listening Devices
HERDESNAVAV
Hereby designated as a student naval aviator
HERDET, HEREDET
Hereby detached (duty indicated)
HERDUFLY
Hereby detailed to duty involving flying
HEREDET, HERDET
Hereby detached (duty indicated)
HERO
Hazards of Electromagnetic Radiation to
Ordnance
HEST
High Explosive Simulation Technique
HET
Heavy Equipment Transport
High Explosive Traced (bomb)
HETS
Hyper-Environmental Test Station
HEX
High Explosive
Hydraulics, External (system)

HF
High Frequency
Human Factor
Hundred Feet (U/I)
HFDF, HDF, HUFFDUFF
High Frequency Direction Finder
HFE
Human Factors Engineering
HFP
Hostile Fire Pay
HFPER
Human Factors Program Final Report
HFPR
Human Factors and Personnel Resources
HFSE
Human Factors and Safety Engineering
HFTE
Human Factors Test and Evaluation
HG
Half Gross (U/I)
HGR
Hangar
HH
Hedge Hogs
Hogshead (U/I)
HHE
Household Effects
HHFT
Heavy Helo Fire Team
HHG
Household Goods
HHGLIMIT
Shipment of HHG to overseas duty station
indicated is limited to 2000 net pounds or
25 percent of weight limitation authorized
by JTR, whichever is greater. This
limitation does not apply to hold baggage
and professional items.
HHGLIMITFROM
Any restriction on shipment of HHG in orders
to present overseas duty station is also
applicable in return shipment of HHG from
that station.
HHMU
Hand-Held Maneuvering Unit
H-HOUR
Time of landing first waterborne assault wave
H&HS, HHS
Headquarters and Headquarters Squadron
HHTR
Hand-Held Tactical Radar
HHV
Higher Heating Value (fuel oil)
HHW
Higher High Water
HI
Height of Instrument
Hide (U/I)
High
H&I
Harrassing and Interdiction (fire)

HIALT, HA
  High Altitude
HIBEX
  High Acceleration Experimental (missile
  booster)
  High Impulse Booster, Experimental
HICAPCOM
  High Capacity Afloat Communications
  (system)
HICOM
  High Command
HIDAD
  Helicopter Insecticide Dispersal Apparatus,
  Dry
HIDAL
  Helicopter Insecticide Dispersal Apparatus,
  Liquid
HIFI, HI-FI
  High Fidelity
HIFOR
  High Level Forecast
HIFR
  Helicopter In-Flight Refueling
HI-HOE
  Helium, Hydrogen and Oxygen (ion
  measurements project)
HIM
  Hill Interaction Matrix
HIMS
  Heavy Interdiction Missile System
HINT
  High-Intensity (lights)
HIPAR
  High-Power Acquisition Radar
HIPEG
  High-Performance Experimental Gun
HIPERNAS
  High-Performance Navigation System
HIPRI
  High Priority
HIR
  Handbook of Inspection Regulations (or
  Requirements)
HI-R
  High-Intensity Survey Meter
HIR CLDS VBS
  Higher Clouds Visible
HIRL
  High-Intensity Runway Lights
HIS
  Hood Inflation System
HI-STEP
  High-Speed Integrated Space Transportation
  Evaluation Program
HIT
  Hypervelocity Impulse Tuned
HIVAC
  High-Value Asset Control
  High-Value Transaction (report)
HK
  Hank (U/I)

HL
  Hard Labor
  Heavy Lift
  Hectoliter
  Hot Line (telephone)
H/L
  High/Low (limit)
HLF
  Half
HLH
  Heavy-Lift Helicopter
HLSTO
  Hailstones
HLTTL
  High-Level Transistor-Transistor Logic
  (circuits)
HLW
  Higher Low Water
HL W/O C
  Hard Labor without Confinement
HM
  Hazardous Materials
  Hectometer
HM, HELMINERON
  Helicopter Mine Countermeasures Squadron
HM1
  Hospital Corpsman First Class
HM2
  Hospital Corpsman Second Class
HM3
  Hospital Corpsman Third Class
HMA
  Marine Attack Helicopter Squadron
HMC
  Chief Hospital Corpsman
HMCM
  Master Chief Hospital Corpsman
HMCS
  Senior Chief Hospital Corpsman
HM&E
  Hull, Mechanical and Electrical (equipment)
HMH
  Marine Heavy Helicopter Squadron
HMI
  Handbook of Maintenance Instructions
HML
  Marine Light Helicopter Squadron
HMM
  Marine Medium Helicopter Squadron
HMO
  Health Maintenance Organization
HMR
  Headquarters/House Modification Request
H&MS
  Headquarters and Maintenance Squadron
HMT
  Marine Helicopter Training Squadron
HMV
  Hydraulic, Main and Vital (system)
HMX
  Advanced Marine Helicopter Squadron

HMW
Height of Maxwind
HN
Hospitalman
Training Helicopter
HND, HUN
Hundred
HN(HS)
High School Hospitalman
HN(JC)
Junior College Hospitalman
HO
Observation Helicopter
H/O
Hours of Operation
HOB
Height of Burst
HOBOS
Homing Bomb Systems
HOBS
High Orbital Bombardment System
HOGE
Hover Out of Ground Effect
HOI, HOVI
Handbook of Overhaul Instructions
HOJ
Home-On-Jam
HOMP
Halifax Ocean Meeting Point
HON
Honorable
HOOP
Handbook of Operating Procedures (on
    Public Works)
HOPM
Hydraulic Oil Power Module
HOR
Home of Record
Horizontal (lights)
HOR CL
Horizontal Clearance
HORIZ
Horizontal
HOS, HOSP
Hospital
HOSP, HOS
Hospital
HOSPCO
Hospital Company
HOSP RATS
Hospital Rations
HOST
Hot Spot Tracking
HOUS
Housing
HOV
Hovering (depth control system)
HOVI, HOI
Handbook of Overhaul Instructions
HOW
Hercules-Over-Water (C-130 aircraft)

HOWBTRY
Howitzer Battery
HP
High Performance (or Pressure)
Horsepower
Hundred Pounds (U/I)
HPA
Head of Procuring Activity
High-Power Amplifier
HP&A
Hull Propulsion and Auxiliaries
HPAC
High-Pressure Air Compressor
HP/A/C
Homeport/Area/City (code)
HPB
Harbor Patrol Boat
HPC
Helicopter Plane Commander
High-Pressure Constant
HPCBR
High-Pressure Chamber
HPD
Harbor Police Department
Hard-Point Defense
High-Pressure Drain
HP-HR
Horsepower-Hour
HPM
High-Power Multiplier
HPNS
High-Pressure Nervous Syndrome
HPOX
High-Pressure Oxygen
HPP
High-Pressure Pump
Hydraulic Power Plant
HPT
High-Pressure Test
HPU
Hydraulic Power Unit
HQ, HDQTRS, HED, HEDQTRS
Headquarters
HQBN
Headquarters Battalion
HQBTRY
Headquarters Battery
HQCO
Headquarters Company
HQMTMTS
Headquarters, Military Traffic Management
    Terminal Service
HQNAVMARCORMARSTA
Headquarters, Navy-Marine Corps Military
    Affiliate Radio System Station
HQNAVMATCOM
Headquarters, Naval Material Command
HQSQDN
Headquarters Support Squadron
HQSVCBN
Headquarters, Service Battalion

HQSVCCO
Headquarters, Service Company
HR
High-Resolution (film)
Hospital Recruit
Hourly Report
Human Reliability
Transporter Helicopter
HRA
Harness Release Actuator
High-Radiation Area
Human Resources Administration
HRAV
Human Resources Availability Period
HRC
Hydraulics-Resonance Changer
HRD
High Rate Discharge
Human Resources Division
HRDC
Human Resources Development Command
(or Center)
HRDPO
Human Resources Development Project
Office
HR(HS)
High School Hospital Recruit
HRIR
High-Resolution Infrared Radiation
HRM
Human Resources Management
HRMC
Human Resources Management Center
HRMC/D
Human Resources Management
Center/Detachment
HRMD
Human Resources Management Detachment
HRMI
Human Resources Management Instructor
HRMS
Human Resources Management Specialists
HRMS, HUMRESMANSCOL
Human Resources Management School
HRMST
Human Resources Management Support
Team
HR/MTI
High Resolution/Moving Target Indicator
HRO
Housing Referral Office(r)
HRR
High Resolution Radar
HRSCO
Housing Referral Service Coordination Office
HRMSS
Human Resources Management Support
System
HRZN
Horizon

HS
Hundred Square Feet (U/I)
HS, HELANTISUBRON, HELSRON
Helicopter Antisubmarine Squadron
HSA
Headquarters Support Activity
HSBR
High-Speed Bombing Radar
HSD
Hydraulic Steering and Diving (system)
Heat Sensing Device
HSETC
Naval Health Sciences Education and
Training Command
HSF, HAWSEAFRON
Hawaiian Sea Frontier
HSG
Housing
HSGREFSVCSYS
Housing Referral Services Record System
HSI
Handbook of Service Instructions
Helicopter Antisubmarine Squadron Light
Horizontal Situation Indicator
HS/JR
High School/Junior College (graduate training
program)
HSL
High-Speed Launch
Light Helicopter Antisubmarine Squadron
HSNS
High School News Service (FHTNC)
HSPS
Highway Safety Program Services
(Department, HSC)
HSS
Hydrologic Sensing Satellite
HS&SS
Headquarters and Service Squadron
HSSSM
Highly-Sensitive Ship Synthesis Model
HST
Helicopter Support Team
HSTEC
Health Sciences Education and Training
Command
HT
Heat
High Tensile
Histologic Technician (ASCP)
Homing Terrier (missile)
HT, HELTRARON
Helicopter Training Squadron
HT1
Hull Maintenance Technician First Class
HT2
Hull Maintenance Technician Second Class
HT3
Hull Maintenance Technician Third Class
HTA
Heavier-Than-Air

HTC
Chief Hull Maintenance Technician
HTCM
Master Chief Hull Maintenance Technician
HTCS
Senior Chief Hull Maintenance Technician
HTD
Hand Target Designator
HTEXCH
Heat Exchanger
HTFA
Hull Maintenance Technician Fireman
Apprentice
HTFN
Hull Maintenance Technician Fireman
HTL
High-Threshold Logic
HTLS
Higher Torque/Low-Speed
HTRE
Heat Transfer Reactor Experiments
HTS
High-Tensile Steel
HT/SZ
Height/Size
HTT
Hydraulics, Turbine Throttle (control system)
HTV
Homing Test Vehicle
HU
Hull
HUD
Heads-Up Display
HUDWAC
Head-Up Display and Weapon Aiming
Computer
HUFFDUFF, HDF, HFDF
High Frequency Direction Finder
HUK
Hunter-Killer (task force or unit)
HUKS
Hunter-Killer Submarine
HULL
High Usage Load List
HUMINT
Human Intelligence
HUMRESMANCEN, HRMD
Human Resources Management Center
HUMRESMANDET, HRMD
Human Resources Management Detachment
HUMRESMANSCOL, HRMS
Human Resources Management School
HUMRESMANSCOLDET
Human Resources Management School
Detachment
HUMS
Humanitarian Reasons
HUN, HND
Hundred
HURCN
Hurricane

HURR-EVAC
Hurricane Evacuation
HUTRON
Helicopter Utility Squadron
HV
High Voltage
HV, HVY
Heavy
HVAC
Heating, Ventilation and Air Conditioning
HVAP
High-Velocity Armor-Piercing (projectile)
HVAR
High-Velocity Aircraft Rocket
HVAR(HE)
High-Velocity Aricraft Rocket (High Explosive)
HVATKRON
Heavy Attack Squadron
HVD
Hydroviscous Drive
HVDC
High-Voltage Direct-Current
HVDF
Direction Finder, High and Very High
Frequency
HVPHOTORON, HEAVYPHOTORON
Heavy Photographic Squadron
HVPS
High-Voltage Power Supply
HVTB
High-Voltage Thermal Battery
HVY, HV
Heavy
HW
Herewith
High Water
Hundred Weight
HWOCR
Heavy Water-Moderated, Organic-Coded
Reactor
HWVR
However
HY
Hundred Yards (U/I)
HY, HYD, HYDR
Hydraulic
HYD, HY, HYDR
Hydraulic
HYDAT
Hydrodynamic Analysis Tool
HYRD, HY, HYD
Hydraulic
HYDROG
Hydrographer
Hydrographic
HYDROLANT
Hydrographic Information for the Atlantic
HYDROPAC
Hydrographic Information for the Pacific
HYDROX
Hydrogen-Oxygen (fuel)

HYFT
  High-Yield Fallout Trajectory
HYSAP
  Hydrographic Survey Assistance Program
HYSTU
  Hydrofoil Special Trials Unit

I

I
  Airborne Intercept (NAO code)
  Incendiary (bomb)
  Initial (approach)
(I)
  To be Inactivated
IA
  Identical Additional (position)
IAAB
  Interim Aviation Airframe Bulletin
IAAA
  Integrated Advanced Avionics for Aircraft
IAC
  Initial Approach Course
  Integration, Assembly and Check-Out
  International Analysis Code
IACS
  Integrated Acoustic Communication System
  Integrated Armament Control System
IAD
  Initiation Area Discriminator
IADC
  Inter-American Defense College
I/ADCSP
  Interim/Advanced Defense Communications
    Satellite Program
IADPC
  Inter-Agency Data Processing Center
IADT
  Integrated Automatic Direction System
IADWS
  Interim Air Defense Weapons System
IAF
  (Office of) Information of the Armed Forces
  Initial Approach Fix
IAFB
  Interim Airframe Bulletin
IAFC
  Interim Airframe Change
IAGC
  Instantaneous Automatic Gain Control
IAL
  International Algebraic Language
IANTN
  Inter-American Naval Telecommunications
    Network Secretariat
IAO
  Inter-Agency Committee on Oceanography
IAPG
  Inter-Agency Advanced Power Group

IAR
  Intersection of Air Routes
IAS
  Indicated Airspeed
  Integrated Avionics System
IAT
  Indicated Air Temperature
IATCB
  Interdepartmental Air Traffic Control Board
IATN
  Inter-American Naval Telecommunications
    Network
IAW
  In Accordance With
IAYB
  Interim Accessory Bulletin
IAZ
  Inner Artillery Zone
IB
  Incendiary Bomb
  Inner Bottom
IBN
  Identification Beacon
IBOP
  International Balance of Payments
IBPDSMS
  Improved Basic Point Defense Surface
    Missile System
IBS
  Interbomb Spacing
IC
  Ice Crystals (weather symbol)
  In Commission (vessel status)
  Index Correction
  Individual Counsel
  Information Center
  Intake Close
  Integrated Circuits
  Inter(ior) Communications
  Intermediate Course
  Inventory Control
IC, ICE
  Iceland
IC1
  Interior Communications Electrician First
    Class
IC2
  Interior Communications Electrician Second
    Class
IC3
  Interior Communications Electrician Third
    Class
I&C
  Installation and Checkout (spares)
ICA
  Isolated Code Announcement
ICAF
  Industrial College of the Armed Forces
ICAO
  International Civil Aviation Organization

ICAS
Interface Control Action Sheet
ICAT
In Commission, Active (vessel status)
ICB
Interior Control Board
International Competitive Bidding
ICBM
Intercontinental Ballistic Missile
ICC
Chief Interior Communications Electrician
Information Control Console
Intermediate Cryptanalysis Course
ICCA, INITCCA
Initial Cash Clothing Allowance
ICCCA, INITCCCA
Initial Civilian Cash Clothing Allowance
ICCM
Intercontinental Cruise Missile
Master Chief Interior Communications
    Electrician
ICCS
Integrated Carrier Catapult System
Integrated Catapult Control System
Interface Configuration Control System
Senior Chief Interior Communications
    Electrician
ICD
Industrial Cooperation Division
Interface Control Drawing
Inventory Control Department
ICE
Increased Combat Effectiveness
ICE, IC
Iceland
ICEDEFOR, IDF
Iceland Defense Force
ICEM
Inverted Coaxial Magnetron
ICES
Integrated Civil Engineering System
International Council for Exploration of the
    Seas
ICFA
Interior Communications Electrician Fireman
    Apprentice
ICFN
Interior Communications Electrician Fireman
ICG
Icing
Interviewer's Classification Guide
ICGIC
Icing in Clouds
ICGICIP
Icing in Clouds in Precipitation
ICGIP
Icing in Precipitation
ICIR
In Commission, In Reserve (vessel status)
ICM
Improved Capability Missile

ICMA
Initial Clothing Monetary Allowance
ICMS
Integrated Circuit and Message Switch
ICN
Internal Control Number
ICO
In Case of
Interagency Committee on Oceanography
ICOR
In Charge of Room
ICOS, INCOS
Integrated Control System
ICP
Instrument Calibration Procedures
Inventory Control Point
ICR
Intercultural Relations
Item Change Request
ICRC
Interagency Classification Review Committee
ICRL
Individual Component Repair List
ICRM
Intercontinental Reconnaissance Missile
IC&RR
Inventory Control and Requirements Review
    (Board, CNO)
ICS
Intercommunication System
Inverse Conical Scan
ICSB
Interim Command Switchboard
ICSC
Interior Communication Switching Center
ICSMP
Integrated Command System Management
    Plan
ICSP
In Commission, Special (vessel status)
ICT
Individual Combat Training
ICTEC
Identification of Critical Tasks and Equipment
    Items
ICV
Individual Cell Voltmeter
ICW
In Connection With
Interrupted Continuous Wave
ICWG
Interface Control Working Group
ID
Inside Diameter
Intelligence Duties
ID, IDENT
Identification
Identify
IDA
Ionospheric Dispersion Analysis
Integrated Disbursing and Accounting

IDAC
Interconnecting Digital-Analog Converter
IDAFMS
Integrated Disbursing and Accounting
Financial Management System
IDART
Individual Drill Attendance and Retirement
Transaction (card)
IDC
Individual Defense Counsel
Information Design Change
Inner Dead-Center
Intransmit Data Card
IDC, INDEC
Interdepartmental Committee
IDCCC
Interim Data Communication Collection
Center
IDCS
Integrated Data Coding System
IDCSP
Initial Defense Communications Satellite
Program
IDD
Inter-Director Designation
IDDS
Instrumentation Data Distribution System
IDEF, INDEF, INDFT
Indefinite
IDENT, ID
Identification
Identify
IDF
Integrated Data File
IDF, ICEDEFOR
Iceland Defense Force
IDG
Inspector of Degaussing
integrated Drive Generator
IDGIT
Integrated Data Generation Implementation
Technique
IDHS
Intelligence Data Handling System (DOD)
IDLOC
Idle, Waiting for Load
IDMI
Interface Document Master Index
IDNE
Inertial Doppler Navigation Equipment
ID NO
Identification Number
IDP
Individual Development Plan
Integrated Data Processing
IDPM
Initial Draft, Presidential Memorandum
IDQA
Individual Documented Quality Assurance
IDREA
Idle, Other Reasons

IDRL
Intradivision Requirements List
IDRN
Intradivisional Review Notice
IDS
Instrument Development Section
Intelligence Data System
IDSCS
Initial Defense Satellite Communications
System
IDSOT
Interim Daily System Operational Test
IDT
Inactive Duty Training
IE
In Excess
Initial Equipment
IECI
Industrial Electronics and Control
Instrumentation
IECMS
Inflight Engine Condition Monitoring System
IED
Improvised Explosive Device
Independent Exploratory Development
IEM
Inactive Equipment Maintenance
IEP
Information Exchange Project
IER
Individual Education Record
I&EW
Intelligence and Electronic Warfare
IF
Ice Fog (weather symbol)
Insular Force
Intermediate Fix
Intermediate (or Intermittent) Frequency
IF-ADD ICMA
Insular Force-Additional Initial Clothing
Monetary Allowance
IFARS
Individual Flight Activity Reporting System
IFB
Invitation for Bid
IFBH
Intermediate Force Beachhead
IFBM
Improved Fleet Ballistic Missile
IFCS
Improved Fire Control System
IFD
Inter-Fighter Director
IFF
Identification Friend or Foe (system)
IFI
In-Flight Insertion
IFIM
International Flight Information Manual

IFIS
Instrument Flight Instructor's School
Integrated Flight Instrument System
IFM
Instantaneous Frequency Measurement
IFMS
Integrated Financial Management System
IFPM
In-Flight Performance Monitor
IFR
In-Flight Refueling
Instrument Flight Rules (or Requirement)
IFREQ
Industrial Forecast Requirements
IFS
Increased Forward Stocking
Inshore Fire Support Ship
IF-SICMA
Insular Force-Special Initial Clothing
Monetary Allowance
IFSS
International Flight Service Station
IF TACCA
Intermediate Frequency Time Averaged
Clutter Coherent Airborne (radar)
IFTRS
Individual Flying Time Report System
IFU
Intelligence Field Unit
IFV
Instantaneous Field of View
IG
Ingot (U/I)
Interdepartmental Group
IG, INSGEN
Inspector General
IGASS
Integrated Ground-Air Avionics System
IGE
In-Ground Effect
IGFVP
Interservice Group for Flight Vehicle Power
IGL
Installation Group List
IGOS
Inward Grade of Service
IGOSS
Integrated Global Ocean Station System
(ICO-WMO)
IGSC
Inspector General, Supply Corps
IHA
Interim Housing Allowance
IHAS
Integrated Helicopter Avionics System
IHCA
In Hands of Civil(ian) Authorities
IHO
Inspection Hold Order

IHP
Indicated Horsepower
Intermediate High Pressure
IHQ
International Headquarters
IHS
Information Handling System
IHSBR
Improved High-Speed Bombing Radar
IHU
Interservice Hovercraft Unit
II
Item Identification
I-I
Inspector-Instructor
IIDD
Interface Identification Data Document
IIIC
Immediate Imagery Interpretation Center
IIP
Industrial Incentive Plan (NAVFAC)
IIPS
Instantaneous Impact Prediction System
IIR
Integrated Instrumentation Radar
IIS
Intelligence Information System
IKOR
Instant Knowledge of Results
IL
Intermediate Land
I&L
Installation and Logistics
ILA
Instrument Landing Aid (or Approach)
ILAAS
Integrated Light Attack Avionics System
I-LAB
Instrumentation Laboratory
ILD
Information Lead Distance
ILLUM
Illuminated
Illuminating
ILM
Integrated Logistic Management
ILMP
Integrated Logistic Management Program
ILMT
Integrated Logistic Management Team
ILO
Integrated Logistics Overhead
ILOSS
Integrated Laser/Optical Sight Set
ILP
International Logistics Program
ILS
Inertial Latching Switch
Instrument (or Integrated) Landing System
Integrated Logistics Support

ILSM
Integrated Logistics Support Management
ILSMT
Integrated Logistics Support Management
Team
ILSP
Integrated Logistics Support Plan(ning) (or
Program, or Procedure)
ILSS
Integrated Life-Support System
ILW
International Low Water
IM
Inner Marker
Intercept Missile
Intermediate Maintenance
Intramural
Inventory (or Item) Manager
IM1
Instrumentman First Class
IM2
Instrumentman Second Class
IM3
Instrumentman Third Class
IMA
Intermediate Maintenance Activity
IMAP
Interactive Manpower Alternatives Processor
IMBLM
Integrated Medical and Behavioral Laboratory
Management
IMC
Chief Instrumentman
Instructional Materials Center
Instrument Meteorological Conditions
Item Management Codes
IMCC
Integrated Mission Control Center
IMC-IFR
Instrument Meteorological
Conditions-Instrument Flight Rules
IMCS
Senior Chief Instrumentman
IMDT, IMMED, IMT
Immediate
IMEP
Indicated Mean Effective Pressure
IMHE
Industrial Materials Handling Equipment
IMI
Instructor-Managed Instruction
IMIC
Interval Modulation Information Coding
IMIP
Industrial Management Improvement Program
IMM
Integrated Maintenance Management
Integrated Material Manager
IMMDELREQ
Immediate Delivery Required

IMMED, IMDT, IMT
Immediate
IMMIRS
Integrated Maintenance Management
Information Retrieval System
IMMP
Integrated Maintenance and Modernization
Planning
Integrated Maintenance Management
Program
IMMS
Intermediate Maintenance Management
System
IMMT
Integrated Maintenance Management Team
IMMUN
Obtain appropriate immunization in
accordance with Art. 22-30 NAVMEDDEPT
and Current BUMEDINST 6230.1
IMN
Indicated Mach Number
IMO
"I Move Oil" (rotary oil pump)
IMP
Image Projection
Inflatable Micrometeoid Paraglider
Integrated Maintenance Program
Interplanetary Monitoring Platform
IMPACT
Implementation Planning and Control
Technique
IMPS
Integrated Master Programming and
Scheduling
Interagency Motor Pool System (GSA)
Interplanetary Probes
IMRAN
International Marine Radio Aids to Navigation
IMREP
Immediately report
IMRL
Individual Material Readiness List
IMS
Industrial Manpower Section
Inertial Measurement Set
In-Flight (or Information) Management
System
Integrated Military System (or Staff)
International Military Staff
Inventory Management System
IMSA
Instrumentman Seaman Apprentice
Integrated Military Survivor Annuity
IMSN
Instrumentman Seaman
IMSU
Intermediate Maintenance Support Unit
IMT, IMDT, IMMED
Immediate
IMU
Inertial Measurement Unit

IN
Inlet
Inspection Notice
Interpreter
INA
Inactivator
Initial Approach
INA, INSAIR
Inspector of Naval Aircraft
INACT
Upon inactivation of (ship or station indicated)
INACT, INACTV
Inactive
INACTFLTLANT
Inactive Fleet, Atlantic
INACTFLTPAC
Inactive Fleet, Pacific
INACTNOTERM
If serving under orders authorizing
participation in Naval Reserve Training
Program in pay or non-pay status, orders
to inactive duty are not terminated, but are
not effective during period of temporary
active duty. Orders to inactive duty training
are effective day following completion of
temporary active duty.
INACTSERVCRAFAC
Inactive Service Craft Facility
INACTSHIPDET
Inactive Ship Maintenance Detachment
INACTSHIPFAC
Inactive Ship Maintenance Facility
INACTSHIPSTORFAC
Inactive Ship Storage Facility
INACTV, INACT
Inactive
INAD
Inadequated
INA/IC
Inactive-In Commission, In Reserve (vessel
status)
INA/IS
Inactive-In Service, In Reserve (vessel status)
INA/OC
Inactive-Out of Commission, In Reserve
(vessel status)
INA/OS
Inactive-Out of Service, In Reserve (vessel
status)
INAS
Industrial Naval Air Station
Inertial Navigation and Attack System
INBD
Inbound
INCAIR
Including air (travel)
INC BOMB
Incendiary Bomb
INCEP
Interceptor

INCL
Inclose
Include
Inclusive
INCOM
Incomplete
INCOS, ICOS
Integrated Control System
INCR
Increase
Increment
INCSEA
Incidents on and Over the High Seas
IND
Improvised Nuclear Device
Independent
Index
Information Network Department
Interceptor Director
INDAIR
Identification of Aircraft
INDC
Indicated
INDEBT
Indebtedness
INDEC, IDC
Interdepartmental Committee
INDEF, IDEF, INDEFT
Indefinite
INDEFT, INDEF, IDEF
Indefinite
INDIV
Individual
INDMAN, INDMGR
Industrial Manager (or Management)
INDMGR, INDMAN
Industrial Manager (or Management)
INDOCNREGREPCEN
Indoctrination Naval Regional Reporting
Center
INDT
Induction
INFLAM
Inflammable
INFNT
Iroquois Night Fighter and Night Tracker
INFO
Information
INFOREQ
Information required as to _____
INID/NOD
Immediate Network-In-Dial/Network-Out-Dial
INIS
International Nuclear Information System
INIT
Initial
Initiate
INITCCA, ICCA
Initial Cash Clothing Allowance
INITCCCA, INITCCCA
Initial Civilian Cash Clothing Allowance

INIT UNIF ALW
Initial Uniform Allowance
INJ
Injured
INJFACS
Injection Facilities
IN-LB
Inch-Pound
INLS
Individualized Learning System
INM, INSMACH
Inspector of Naval Machinery
INM, INSMAT
Inspector of Naval Material
INOP, INOPV
Inoperative
INP
If Not Possible
INR
Intelligence and Research
INREQ
Information Request
INS
Inches
Inertial Navigation System
Insert
Institute of Naval Studies
Insure
Internation Simulation
INS, INSP
Inspect(ion), (-or)
INSAIR, INA
Inspector of Naval Aircraft
INSAV
Interim Shipboard Availability
INSCAIRS
Instrumentation Calibration Incident Repair
Service
INSENG
Inspector of Naval Engineering
INSEREC
Indicate by appropriate entry on pages 9–10
of service record, and in orders, rating for
which men have been trained, to insure
assignment to appropriate duty
INSERECAV
Indicate by appropriate entry on pages 9–10
of service record, and in orders, rating for
which non-rated men have been trained, to
insure assignment to aviation duty
INSERECSUB
Indicate by appropriate entry on pages 9–10
of service record, and in orders, rating for
which men have been trained, to insure
assignment to submarine duty
INSGEN, IG
Inspector General
INSHOREPAT, INSPAT
Inshore Patrol
INSHOREUNSEAWARDIV
Inshore Undersea Warfare Division

INSHOREUNSEAWARGRU
Inshore Undersea Warfare Group
INSHOREUNSEAWARSURVU
Inshore Undersea Warfare Surveillance Unit
INSMACH, INM
Inspector of Naval Machinery
INSMAT, INM
Inspector of Naval Material
INSMATPET
Inspector of Naval Material, Petroleum
Products
INSMATPETMIDEASTAREA
Inspector of Naval Material, Petroleum
Products, Middle East Area
INSNAVMAT
Inspector of Navigational Material
INSORD
Inspector of Naval Ordnance
INSP, INS
Inspect(ion), (or)
INSPAT, INSHOREPAT
Inshore Patrol
INSPETRES
Inspector of Petroleum Reserves
INSPINSTF
Inspector Instructor Staff
INST
Institute
Instrument
INST, INSTL
Installation
INST, INSTN
Instruction
INSTFURASPERS
For course of instruction and further
assignment by Commander Naval Military
Personnel Command
INSTL
Install
INSTL, INST
Installation
INSTN, INST
Instruction
INSTR
Instructor
INST RATE
Instrument Rating
INSUPGENCRUIT
In accordance with this assignment, duties
are to inspect, supervise and generally
superintend method of recruiting within
_____ recruiting district. Authority to
carry out above over all officers and
enlisted men detailed to recruiting in the
above district is hereby conferred.
INSURV, I&S
Inspection and Survey

INT
Individual Needs Test
Interest
Interrogatory
Interval (NNSS)
INT, INTXN
Intersection
INT, INTL
International
INTAC
Intercept Tracking and Control Group
INTAV
Interim Availability
INTCOMBATSYSTESTFAC
Integrated Combat Systems Test Facility
INTCP
Intercept
INTEL
Intelligence
INTELCEN
Intelligence Center
INTELO, INTO, IO
Intelligence Officer
INTERCOM
Internal Communications (program)
INTERM, INTMED
Intermediate
INTERMSTA
Intermediate Station
INTEROBS
International Observations
INTERP
Interpretation
INTERPRON
Interpretation Squadron
INTL, INT
International
INTMED, INTERM
Intermediate
INTMT, INTMED
Intermittent
INTO, INTELO, IO
Intelligence Officer
INT QK, I QK
Interrputed Quick
INTR
Interior
INTRAN
Input Translator
INTRD
Interned
INTREP
Intelligence Report
INTRO
Introduction
INTS
Intense
Intensify
INTSUM, ISUM
Intelligence Summary

INTSV
Intensive
INTSY
Intensify
INTXN, INT
Intersection
INUS
Inside Continental Limits of the United States
INV
Inventory
INVES, INVEST
Investigate, (-tion), (-tor)
INVEST, INVES
Investigate, (-tion), (-tor)
INVOL, INVOLEX
Involuntary Extension
INVOLEX, INVOL
Involuntary Extension
IO
Information (or Intercept, or Investigating) Officer
Issuing Office
IO, INTELO, INTO
Intelligence Officer
I/O
Input/Output
Instructor/Observer
IOA
Instrumentation Operating Areas
IOB
Information Officer Basic (DINFOS)
IOC
Initial Operational Capability
IOC, IOCS
Input/Output Controllers
Integrated Optical Circuits
IOH
Item on Hand
IOIC
Integrated Operational Intelligence Center
IOICS
Integrated Operational Intelligence Center System
IOIS
Integrated Operational Intelligence System
IOL
Initial Outfitting List
IOM
Inert Operational Missile
I/OM
Input/Output Multiplexor
IOMF
Inactive-Officer Master File
ION
Institute of Navigation
IOP
Inspection Operations Pictorials
Interim Operating Procedures
IOR
Issue on Request (or Requisition)

IOT&E
Initial Operational Test and Evaluation
IP
Ice Plow (USCG)
Impact Point
Implementation of Plan
Information Program
Initial Point
Instructor Pilot
Instrumentation Package
Intermediate Pressure
Issuing Point
Items Processed
IPA
Indicated Pressure Altitude
IPB
Illustrated Parts Breakdown (listing)
IPBM
Illustrated Parts Breakdown Manual
IPC
Iceland Prime Contractor
Illustrated Parts Catalog
IPD
Instructional Program Development
Issue Priority Designator
IPDSMS
Improved Point Defense Surface Missile
System
IPE
Industrial Plant (or Production) Equipment
IPER
Industrial Production Equipment Reserve
IP/HHCL
Initial Point/H-Hour Control Line
IPIR
Initial Photo Interpretation Report
IPL
Information Processing Language
Interim Parts List
IPM
Industry Preparedness Measures
IPMS
Integrated Program Management System
IPN
Integrated Priority Number
IPOSS
Interim Pacific Oceanographic Support
System
IPP
Industrial Preparedness Planning (program)
Initial Pipper Position
IPPB
Intermittent Positive Pressure Breathing
IPPP
Industrial Preparedness Planning Program
IPPV
Intermittent Positive Pressure Ventilation

IPR
Intelligence Production Requirements
In-Progress Reviews
Interdepartmental Procurement (or Purchase)
Request
IPS
Intercept Pilot Simulator
Interpretative Programming System
Iron Pipe Size
IPSC
Information Processing Standards for
Computers (program)
IPSR
Intelligence Priorities for Strategic Planning
IPU
Immediate Pick-Up
IPV
Improve
IPW
Interpole Winding (wiring)
IPY
Inches per Year (corrosion rate)
IQ
Intelligence Quotient
I QK, INT QK
Interrupted Quick
IQO
Initial Quantity Order
IR
Ice on Runway
Independent Research
Industrial Relations
Informal (or Information, or Inspection) Report
Infrared
Instruction Register (NNSS)
I&R
Instrumentation and Range
IRAA&A
Increase and Replacement of Armor,
Armament and Ammunition
IRAH
Infrared Alternate Head (type Sidewinder
missile)
IRAM
Improved Repairables Asset Management
IRAN
Inspect and Repair as Necessary
IRAS
Infrared Automatic System
IRASER
Infrared Amplification by Stimulated Emission
of Radiation
IRATE
Interim Remote Area Terminal Equipment
IRB
Industrial Relations Board
Inspection Requirements Branch
IRBM
Intermediate Range Ballistic Missile

IRC
Industrial Relations Counselors
Inspection Record Card
Interservice Recruiting Committees
IRCAT
Infrared Clear Air Turbulence
IRCCS
Intrusion Resistant Communications Cable
System
IRC&M
Increase and Replacement of Construction
and Machinery
IRCS
Intercomplex Radio Communications System
IRD
Industrial Relations Department
IR&D
Independent Research and Development
IR&D/B&P
Independent Research and
Development/Bidding and Proposal (effort)
IRE
International Relations Exercise
IREC
Increase and Replacement of Emergency
Construction (ships)
IRG
Interdepartmental Regional Group
IR&G
International Relations and Government
(DINFOS department)
IRH
Inspection Requirements Handbook
IRIA
Infrared Information and Analysis
IRIG
Inter-Range Instrumentation Graph
Inertial Guidance Integrating Gyro
IR/IOD
Independent Research/Independent
Objectives Document
IRIS
Increased Readiness Information System
Infrared Information Symposium
Infrared Interferometer Spectrometer
Internation Systems Information System
IRL
Information Retrieval Language
Intersection of Range Legs
IRLS
Interrogation, Recording and Locating System
IRNV
Increase and Replacement of Naval Vessels
IRO
Industrial Relations Office(r)
IROAN
Inspect and Repair Only as Needed
IRP
Improved Replenishment Program
Industrial Readiness Planning

IR-P
Ice on Runway-Patchy
IR-PERS-REC
Industrial Relations Personnel Records
IRPOD
Individual Repair Parts Ordering Data
IRR
Improved Rearming Rate
IRRA
International Routing and Reporting Activity
IRREG
Irregular
IRRP
Improved Rearming Rate Plan
IRSS
Instrumentation and Range Safety Program
IRST
Infrared Search and Track
IRT
Infrared Temperature (detector)
IRU
General Individual Reinforcement Unit
(USNR)
IRV
Item Rating Value
IS
Instrumentation-Ship's Project
Intelligence System
Invalidated from Service
Inventory Schedule
I&S, INSURV
Inspection and Survey
IS1
Intelligence Specialist First Class
IS2
Intelligence Specialist Second Class
IS3
Intelligence Specialist Third Class
I²S
Integrated Information System
ISA
Inductee Special Assignment
International Security Affairs (or Agency)
ISAC
In Service, Active (vessel status)
ISAL
Information Service Access Lines
ISAP
Information Sort and Predict
ISB
Independent Sideband
ISC
Chief Intelligence Specialist
Infiltration Surveillance Center
Interservice Support Coordinator
ISCAS
Integrated Submarine Communications
Antenna System
I&SCD
Indoctrination and Special Courses
Department

ISCM
Master Chief Intelligence Specialist
ISCS
Integrated Submarine Communication System
Interim Sea Control Ship
Senior Chief Intelligence Specialist
ISD
Industrial Survey Division
Initial Search Depth
Initial Ship Design
Instructional Systems Development
ISDS
Integrated Ship Design System
ISE
Independent Ship Exercise
ISED
Information Systems Equipment Division
ISIC, ISINC
Immediate Superior in Command
ISINC, ISIC
Immediate Superior in Command
ISIR
In Service, In Reserve (vessel status)
ISIS
Integral Spar Inspection System
IS/ISD
Instructional Systems/Instructional Systems
Division
ISJTA
Intensive Student Jet Training Area
ISL
Inactive Status List
Integrated (or Initial) Stock List
Item Survey List
ISLW
Indian Spring Low Water
ISM
Industrial Security Manual (DOD)
Interim Surface Missile
IS&MD
Instructional Standards and Materials Division
ISMF
Inactive Ship Maintenance Facility
ISNAC
Inactive Ships in Naval Custody
ISO
Informational Services Office(r)
Installation Supply Office
Isolate
ISOLD
Isolated
ISP
Integrated Support Plan
ISPO
Instrumentation Ships Project Office
ISR
In-Service Repair
ISRB
Individual Serve Review Board

ISS
Industry Sole Source
Inertial Sub System
Interservice Supply Support
Issued
ISSA
Intelligence Specialist Seaman Apprentice
Interservice (or Intraservice) Supply Source
Agreement
ISSBN
Improved Fleet Ballistic Missile Submarine
ISSG
Illustrated Shipboard Shopping Guide
ISSM
Interim Surface-to-Surface Missile
ISSN
Intelligence Specialist Seaman
ISSOP
Intra-Fleet Supply Support Operations
Program
ISSOT
Intra-Fleet Supply Support Operations Team
ISSP
Interservice Supply Source Program
ISSR
Information System Service Request
ISSST
Integrated Submarine Sonar Systems
Technician
IST
Interswitch Trunk
ISTAR
Image Storage Translation and Reproduction
ISTRS
Index of Submarine Technical Repair
Standards
ISUM, INTSUM
Intelligence Summary
IT
Installation Tests
Item Type
ITA
Instrument Time, Actual
ITAAS
Integrated Aircraft Armament System
ITAG
Intelligence Threat Analysis Group
ITAL
Initial Trial Allowance List
ITAWDS
Integrated Tactical Amphibious Warfare Data
Systems
ITC
Instructor-Training Course (DINFOS)
ITCS
Integrated Target Control System
ITCZ
Intertropical Convergence Zone
ITD
Interim Technical Directive

ITE
  Indicated Terminal Efficiency
ITF
  Intermediate Terminal Facility
ITIS
  Interactive Terminal Interface System
ITL
  Industrial Test Laboratory
  Integrate-Transfer-Launch
  Intent to Launch
ITLD
  Individual Tube Leak Detector
ITM
  Index of Technical Manuals
ITNS
  International Tactical Navigation System
ITO
  Inspecting Torpedo Officer
  Installation Transportation Officer
  Instrument Take-Off
  Invitational (or International) Travel Orders
ITOS
  Improved TIROS Operational System (NOAA)
ITP
  Index of Technical Publications
  Initial Trial(s) Phase
  Integrated Test Package
ITRO
  Integrated Test Requirements Outline
  Interservice Training Review Organization
ITRP
  Interservice Training Program
ITS
  Instrument Time, Simulated
ITT
  Interrogator-Translator Team
ITV
  Instructional Television
IU
  Instrument (or International) Unit
IUC
  Immediate Unit Commander
IUDS
  Independent Variable Depth Sonar
IUS
  Interim Upper State
IUWD, INSHOREUNSEAWARDIV
  Inshore Undersea Warfare Division
IUWG, INSHOREUNSEAWARGRU
  Inshore Undersea Warfare Group
IUWSU, INSHOREUNSEAWARSURV
  Inshore Undersea Warfare Surveillance Unit
IVALA
  Integrated Visual Approach and Landing Aids
IVS
  Intervoice Communication System
IVN
  Intercity Voice Network (FTS)
IVVS
  Instantaneous Vertical Velocity Indicator

IWC
  Individual Weapons Captured
IWCS
  Integrated Wideband Communications
  System
IWD
  Intermediate Water Depth
IWR
  Infrared Warning Receiver
IX
  Information Exchange
  Unclassified Miscellaneous Ship
IXES
  Information Exchange System
IXR
  Intersection of Runways
IXSS
  Unclassified Miscellaneous Submarine

J

J
  Junction
  Radar (TO code)
JA
  Judge Advocate
JA, JAN
  January
JAAF
  Joint Action Armed Forces
JAAP
  Joint Aviation Attrition Panel
JACC
  Joint Airborne Communications Center
JACC/CP
  Joint Airborne Communications
  Center/Command Post
JACCI
  Joint Allocation Committee Civil Intelligence
  (U.S.-Britain)
JAD
  Joint Resource Assessment Data Base
JADOR
  Joint Advertising Directors of Recruiting
JADREP
  Joint Resource Assessment Data Base
  Report
JAG
  Judge Advocate General
JAGMAN
  Judge Advocate General's Manual
JAIEG
  Joint Atomic Information Exchange Group
JAMAC
  Joint Aeronautical Materials Activity
JAMTO
  Joint Airline Military Ticket Office
JAN
  Joint Army-Navy (operation, exercise or
  publication)

JAN, JA
January
JANAIR
Joint Army-Navy Aircraft Instrumentation
Research
JANAP
Joint Army-Navy-Air Force Publication
JANAST
Joint Army-Navy-Air Force Sea
Transportation (message)
JANCOM
Joint Army-Navy Communications
JANET
Joint Army-Navy Experimental and Testing
Board
JANGO
Junior Army-Navy Guild Organization
JANGRID
Joint Army-Navy Grid
JANIC
Joint Army-Navy Information Center
JANIS
Joint Army-Navy Intelligence Studies
JANNAF
Joint Army, Navy, NASA, Air Force
JANOT
Joint Army-Navy Ocean Terminal
JANP
Joint Army-Navy Publication
JAPO
Joint Area Petroleum Office
JARCC
Joint Air Reconnaissance Coordination
Center
JASASA
Joint Air Surface Antisubmarine Action
JASCO
Joint Assault Signal Company
JASDA
Julie Automatic Sonic Data Analyzer
JAIEG
Joint Atomic Information Exchange Group
JASIG
Joint AUTOVON Subscriber Implementation
Group
JASIG-PAC
Joint AUTOVON Subscriber Implementation
Group-Pacific
JASMMM
Joint Aviation Supply and Maintenance
Material Management
JASU
Jet Aircraft Starting Unit
JATCCS
Joint Advanced Tactical Command and
Control Service
JATO
Jet-Assisted Take-Off
JAWPS
Joint Atomic Weapons Publication System

JAYGEE, JG
Junior Grade
JB
Jet Boat (USCG)
Jiffy Bag
Joint Army-Navy Board
"Junior Birdman" (slang)
JB, JBAR
Jet Barrier
JBAR, JB
Jet Barrier
JBD
Jet Blast Deflector
JBUSDA
Joint Brazil-United States Defense
Commission
JC
Junction
JCA
Joint Communications Activity
JCAC
Joint Civil Affairs Committee
JCB
Joint Communications Board
JCC
Joint Communications Center
JCMPO
Joint Cruise Missiles Program Office
JCN
Job Control Number
JCOC
Joint Civilian Orientation Conference (DOD)
Joint Command Operational Center
JCRC
Joint Casualty Resolution Center
JCS
Joint Chiefs of Staff
JCSAN
Joint Chiefs of Staff Alerting Network
JCSNMCC
Joint Chiefs of Staff National Military
Command Center
JCSO, JSTAFFOFC
Joint Chiefs of Staff Office
JCS(SASM)
Joint Chiefs of Staff (Special Assistant for
Strategic Mobility)
JD
Job Description
Joint Determination (or Dictionary)
Jointed
JDC
Job Description Cards
JDCS
Joint Deputy Chiefs of Staff
JE, JUN
June
JEST
Jungle Environmental Survival Training
JET
Jet Engine Trainer

JETCAL
Jet Calibration
JETDS
Joint Electronics Type Designation System
JFAI
Joint Formal Acceptance Inspection
JETMART
Jet Market
JETT
Jettison
JFM
Joint Force Memorandum
JFMO
Joint Frequency Management and Spectrum
Engineering Office
JFP
Joint Frequency Panel
JEPH
JUMPS Field Procedures Handbook
JFS
Jet Fuel Starter
JG
Jug (U/I)
JG, JAYGEE
Junior Grade
JHC
Joint High Command
JHHGSO
Joint Household Goods Shipping Office
JI
Joint Identification
JIC
Joint Intelligence Center (or Committee)
JIEP
Joint Intelligence Estimate for Planning
JIFDATS
Joint Services In-Flight Data Transmission
System
JIS
Joint Intelligence Staff
JISPB
Joint Intelligence Studies Publishing Board
JITF
Joint Interface Test Force
JL, JUL
July
JLAS
JUMPS Leave Accounting System
JLC
Joint Logistics Committee
JLPC
Joint Logistics Plans Committee
JLRB
Joint Logistics Review Board
JLRSS
Joint Long-Range Strategic Study
JMAC
Joint Munitions Allocation Committee
JMAHEP
Joint Military Aircraft Hurricane Evacuation
Plan

JMC
Joint Meterological Committee
Joint Military Commission
JMED
Jungle Message Encoder-Decoder
JMEM
Joint Munitions Effectiveness Manual
JMPAB
Joint Military Priorities and Allocation Board
JMPTC
Joint Military Packaging Test Center
JMRO
Joint Medical Regulating Office
JMTB
Joint Military Transportation Board
JMTC
Joint Military Transportation Committee
JMVB
Joint Military Vessels Board
JNACC
Joint Nuclear Accident Coordinating Center
JNC
Jet Navigation Chart
JNG
Jointing
JNROTC
Junior Naval Reserve Officers' Training Corps
JNW
Joint Committee on New Weapons and
Equipment
JNWPU
Joint Numerical Weather Prediction Unit
JO
Job Order
Junior Officer
JO1
Journalist First Class
JO2
Journalist Second Class
JO3
Journalist Third Class
JOA
Joint Operating Agreement
JOBS
Job-Oriented Basic Skills (program)
JOC
Chief Journalist
Joint Operational Center
JOCM
Master Chief Journalist
JOCS
Senior Chief Journalist
JOG
Joint Operations Graphic
JOIDES
Joint Oceanographic Instructions-Deep Earth
Sampling (DOL)
JON
Job Order Number
J-OO
Jet Route _____

JOOD
Junior Officer-of-the-Deck
JOOW
Junior Officer-of-the-Watch
JOPREP
Joint Operational Reporting (system)
JOPS
Joint Operational Planning System
JOSA
Journalist Seaman Apprentice
JOSN
Journalist Seaman
JOSPRO
Joint Ocean Shipping Procedures
JOSS
Joint Overseas Switchboard System
JP
Jet Penetration (or Propulsion)
JP-4
Jet Fuel—used mostly for USAF aircraft
JP-5
Jet Fuel—Navy aircraft
JPB
Joint Planning (or Purchasing) Board
JPC
Joint Planning Committee
JPO
Joint Petroleum Office
JPPL
Joint Personnel Priority List
JPPSO
Joint Personal Property Shipping Office
JPSSOWA
Joint Personal Property Shipping Office,
Washington (DC) Area
JPRS
Joint Publications Research Service
JPS
Joint Planning Staff
JR
Jar (U/I)
JRCC
Joint Rescue Coordination Center
JRDOD
Joint Research and Development Objectives
Document
JROTC
Junior Reserve Officer Training Corps
JRS
Jet Repair Service
Joint Reporting Structure
JS
Joint Staff
JSAR
Joint Search and Rescue
JSARC
Joint Search and Rescue Center
JSC
Joint Security Control
Joint Strategic Committee
Joint Support Command

JSCP
Joint Strategic Capabilities Plan
JSESPO
Joint Surface-Effects Ship Program Office
JSIA
Joint Service Induction Area
JSI
Joint Support Item
J-SIID
Joint Service Interior Intrusion Detection
(system)
JSL
Joint Support (or Stock) List
JSM
Jump Set Memory (NNSS)
JSN
Job Sequence Number
JSOC
Joint Ship Operations Committee
JSOP
Joint Strategic Objectives Plan
JSP
Joint Staff Planners (JCS)
JSR
Journal of Ship Research (SNAME
publication)
JSSC
Joint Strategic Survey Committee
JSSG
Joint Signal Support Group
JSTAFFOFC, JCSO
Joint Chiefs of Staff Offices
JSTP
Joint System Test Plan (IDCSP)
JSTPS
Joint Strategic Target Planning Staff
JTA
Job Task Analysis
JTARS
Joint Tactical Aerial
Reconnaissance/Surveillance
JTARS MISREP
Joint Tactical Aerial
Reconnaissance/Surveillance Mission
Report
JTB
Joint Transportation Board
JTCG
Joint Technical Coordinating Group
JTCG/ME
Joint Technical Coordinating Group for
Munitions Effectiveness
JTDARMVAL
Joint Test Directorate Advanced Antiarmor
Vehicle Evaluation
JT&E, JTE
Joint Test and Evaluation
JTF
Joint Task (or Test) Force
JTG
Joint Task (or Test) Group

JTOC
Joint Tactical Operations Center
JTR
Joint Travel Regulations
JTSA
Joint Technical Support Activity
JTSTR
Jet Stream
JTWC
Joint Typhoon Warning Center
JUL, JL
July
JUMP CERT
Jump Certificate(d)
JUMPS
Joint Uniform Military Pay System
JUMPS/MMS
Joint Uniform Military Pay System/Manpower
Management System
JUN, JE
June
JUNC
Junction
JUSMAG
Joint United States Military Assistance Group
JUSPAO
Joint United States Public Affairs Office
JUSSC
Joint United States Strategic Committee
JUTCPS
Joint Uniform Telephone Communications
Precedence System
JUWTFA
Joint Unconventional Warfare Task Force,
Atlantic

K

K
ASW Tactical Evaluator (TO code)
KBA
Killed by Aircraft
KCAS
Knots Calibrated Airspeed
KCE
Key Configuration Element
KCMX
Keyset Central Multiplexor
KCN
Kit Control Number
KD
Cord (U/I)
Knocked-Down
KE
Keg (U/I)
KEV
Kilo-Electron Volt
KIA
Killed in Action

KIAS
Knots Indicated Airspeed
KISS
"Keep It Simple, Stupid" (slang)
KIT
"Keeping in Touch" (slang)
KMU
Kit Munition Unit
KN, KT
Knot(s)
KNA
Killed, Not Enemy Action
KO
Knock-Out
KO, CO
Contracting Officer
KPA
Keypunch Activity
KPH
Kilometers per Hour
KR
Carat (U/I)
KR, CONTR
Contractor
KS
Cask (U/I)
KSR
Keyboard Send-Receive
KT
Kiloton
Kit
KT, KN
Knot(s)
KTAS
Knots True Airspeed
K/V
Keypunch/Verify
KW
Kilowatt
KWIT
Key Word in Title
KWOC
Key Word Out of Context

L

L
Drizzle (weather symbol)
Latin (ARFT music code)
Navigator (TO code)
L, ATL, LANT
Atlantic
L, LCTR
Locator Beacon

L/A
Leave Address
LA, LOALT
Low Altitude
LA, LTA
Lighter-Than-Air
LAA
Light Anti-Aircraft (weapon)
LAACP
Local Alcohol Abuse Control Program
LAAM
Light Antiaircraft Missile
LAAMBN
Light Antiaircraft Missile Battalion
LAAR
Liquid Air Accumulator Rocket
LAAV
Light Airborne Antisubmarine Vehicle
LABIS
Laboratory Information System
LABS
Low-Altitude Bombing System
LAC
Liberal-Academic Complex
LACE
Liquid Air Cycle Engine
LAD
Landing Assistance Device
Los Angeles Division (NAR)
LADAR
Laser Detection and Ranging
LADD
Low-Angle Drogued Delivery (of nuclear
weapons)
LADS
Lightweight Air Defense System
LAE NOTE
Licensed Aircraft Engineers' Notice
LAGS
Laser-Activated Geodetic Satellite
LAHS
Low-Altitude High-Speed
LAMP
Logical Analytical Management Program
LAMPS
Light Airborne Multi-Purpose System
(helicopter)
LAMPSOP
Light Airborne Multi-Purpose System
Standard Operating Procedures Manual
LAN
Local Apparent Noon
LANCRA, LC, L/C
Landing Craft
LANFORTRACOM, LFTC
Landing Craft Training Command
LANFORTRAU, LFTU
Landing Force Training Unit

LANG
Language
LANNET
Large Artificial Neuron Network
LANS
Linear Active Two-Part Network
LANSHIPRON
Landing Ship Squadron
LANT, L, ATL
Atlantic
LANTCOM
Atlantic Command
LANTCOMINSGEN
Atlantic Command Inspector General
LANTCOMMBPO
Atlantic Command Military Blood Program
Office
LANTCOMOPCONCEN, ACOCC
Atlantic Fleet Commander Operational
Control Center
LANTCOMOPSUPPFAC
Atlantic Command Operations Support
Facility
LANTFAST
Atlantic Forward Area Support Team
LANTFLEASWTACSCOL
Atlantic Fleet Antisubmarine Warfare Tactical
School
LANTFLT
Atlantic Fleet
LANTFLTHEDSUPPACT
Atlantic Fleet Headquarters Support Activity
LANTFLTMATCONOFF
Atlantic Fleet Material Control Office
LANTFLTPEB
Atlantic Fleet Propulsion Examining Board
LANTFLTSOAP
Atlantic Fleet Supply Operations Assistance
Team
LANTFLTWPNRAN
Atlantic Fleet Weapons Range
LANTFLTWPNTRAFAC, AFWTF
Atlantic Fleet Weapons Training Facility
LANTINTCEN, LIC
Atlantic Intelligence Center
LANTMET
Atlantic Mobile Environmental Team
LANTNAVFACENGCOM
Atlantic Naval Facilities Engineering
Command
LANTNAVFACENGCOMBRO
Atlantic Naval Facilities Engineering
Command Branch Office
LANTREPCNAVRES
Atlantic Fleet Chief of Naval Reserve
Representative
LANTREPCOMNAVSURFRES
Atlantic Representative for Commander Naval
Surface Reserve Force

LANTRESFLT
Atlantic Reserve Fleet
LANTSOC
Atlantic Fleet Signals Security Operations
Center
LANTWWMCCS
Atlantic Fleet Worldwide Military Command
Control System
LAO
Legal Assistance Office(r)
LAP
Local Audit Program
LAPES
Low-Altitude Parachute Extraction System
LAPIS
Local Automated Personnel Information
System
LAPL
Lead Allowance Parts List
LAPLS
Lead Allowance Parts List System
LAR
Launch Alert Receiver
Liaison Action Record (PNS-PERA)
Liaison Action Request (SFBNS-PERA)
Liquid (or Long-Range) Aircraft Rocket
LARA
Light Armed Reconnaissance Aircraft
Low-Altitude Radar Altimeter
LARC
Large Automatic Research Computer
LARC-V
Lighter, Amphibious, Resupply, Cargo-Five
Ton
LARP
Launch and Recovery Platform
LARS
Laser-Aided Rocket Systems
LAS
Low-Altitude Satellite
LASER
Light Amplification by Stimulated Emission of
Radiation
LASH
Laser Anti-tank Semi-active Homing
Lighter-Aboard-Ship
LASM
Laser Semi-Active Missile
LASRM
Low-Altitude Supersonic Research Missile
LASS
Language and Assembly Language
LASSO
Landing and Approach System,
Spiral-Oriented
LAST
Last Satellite Position (NNSS)
Low-Altitude Supersonic Target (missile)
LASV
Low-Altitude Supersonic Vehicle

LAT
Local Apparent Time
LATKWEPSCOLPAC
Light Attack Weapons School, Pacific
LATR
Lateral
LAU
Launcher Mechanism, Aircraft-Installed Unit
LAV
Light Armored Vehicle
LAW
Library, Amphibious Warfare
Light Anti-tank Weapon
Local Air Wing
LAWRS
Limited Airport Weather Recording Station
LB
Local Battery
LB, LITH BRO
Lithium Bromide (air conditioning chemical)
L/B
Length/Beam (ratio)
Light Bomber (aircraft)
LBA
Limits of the Basic Aircraft
LBH
Leased Bachelor Housing
LBI
Lost by Inventory
LBIR
Laser Beam Image Recorder
LBNS
Long Beach Naval Shipyard
LBP
Length Between Perpendiculars
LBR
Local Base Rescue
Lumber
LBTF
Land-Based Test Facility
LBTS
Land-Based Test Site
LC
Labor Code
Legitimate Child(ren)
Lines of Communication
LC, L/C, LANCRA
Landing Craft
L/C
Learning Curve
Letter Contract
LCA
Landing Craft, Assault
LCAC
Landing Craft, Air Cushion
LCB
Limited Capability Buoy (NOAA)

LCC
  Amphibious Command Ship
  Labor Class Code
  Landing Craft Central (or Control)
  Life-Cycle Cost
LCCO
  Leadership Career Counseling Officer
LCDR, LTCOM, LT COMDR
  Lieutenant Commander
LCEOF
  Landing Craft Engine Overhaul Parties
LCG
  Landing Craft, Gun
  Longitudinal Center of Gravity
LCGP
  Landing Craft Group
LCKR
  Locker (stowage)
LCL
  Large Core Memory
  Less than Carload Lot
  Local
  Lower Control Limit
LCM
  Landing Craft, Mechanized
  Laser Countermeasures
LCMSO
  Landing Craft Material Supply Officer
LCNT
  Link Celestial Navigation Trainer
LCO
  Launch Control Officer (or Operator)
LCOCU
  Landing Craft Obstruction Clearance Unit
LCOS
  Lead Computing Optical Sight
LCPL
  Landing Craft, Personnel, Large
LCP
  Local Calibration Procedures
  Logistics Capabilities Plan
LCP-FY
  Logistics Capabilities Plan-Fiscal Year _____
LCPL
  Lance Corporal
LCPO
  Leading Chief Petty Officer
LCPR
  Landing Craft, Personnel, Ramped
LCR
  Limit Control Register (NNSS)
LCS
  Large Capacity Storage
LCSR
  Landing Craft, Swimmer Reconnaissance
LCSS
  Land Combat Support System
LCTD
  Located
LCTR, L
  Locator Beacon

LCU
  Landing Craft, Utility
LCV
  Landing Craft, Vehicle
LCVASI
  Low-Cost Visual-Approach Slope Indicator
LCVP
  Landing Craft, Vehicle and Personnel
LCZR
  Localizer Beacon
LD
  Layered Depth
  Long Distance
  Low Drag
LD, LOD
  Line of Departure (or Duty)
  List of Drawings
LDA
  Localizer, Direction(al) Aid
  Lowest Designated Assembly
LDAPS
  Long-Duration Auxiliary Power System
LDC
  Labor Distribution Card
LDD
  Letter of Determination of Dependency
LDF
  Local Defense Forces
LDG
  Landing
LDG LT
  Leading Light
LDGP
  Low-Drag General-Purpose
LDGSPTBN
  Landing Support Battalion
LDIN
  Lead-In (light system)
LDME
  Laser Distance Measuring Equipment
LDMX
  Local Digital Message Exchange
LDO
  Limited Duty Officer
  Long Distance Operator
LDO(T)
  Limited Duty Officer (Temporary)
LDR
  Line Driver Receivers (NNSS)
LDS
  Line Drawing System
LDSHP
  Leadership
LDTTY
  Land Line Teletype
LDX
  Local Digital Message Exchange
  Long Distance Xerography
LE
  Low Explosive

LEAD
Light-Emitting Diode
LEAP
Limited Education Assistance Program
LEASAT
Leased Satellite (system)
LEG OFF
Legal Officer
LEI
Local Engineering Instruction
LEL
Lower Explosion Limit
LEM
Logistics Element Manager
LEMP
Logistics Element Manager Plan
LEPT
Long-Endurance Patrolling Torpedo
LERTCON
Alert Condition
LEROY
Less Errors Rest on You
LES
Leading-Edge Slots
Leave and Earnings Statement (JUMPS)
Local Engineering Specification
LESS
Least Cost Estimating and Scheduling
LEX
Land Exercise
LF
Linear Foot (U/I)
Line Feed
Low Frequency
LF, LANFOR
Landing Force
LFC
Landing Force Commander
Large Format Comparator
Level of Free Convection
LFDM
Low Flyer Detection Modification
LFE
Laboratory for Electronics
LFIC
Landing Force Intelligence Center
LFM
Landing Force Manual
LFOC
Landing Force Operations Center
LFR
Inshore Fire Support Ship
Low-Frequency Range
LFRD
Lot Fraction Reliability Deviation
LFS
Amphibious Fire Support Ship
Landing Force Staff
LFSD
Landing Force Support Weapon

LFSS
Landing Force Support Ship
LFT
Lift
LFTC, LANFORTRACOM
Landing Force Training Command
LFTCPAC
Landing Force Training Command, Pacific
LFTU, LANFORTRAU
Landing Force Training Unit
LG
Land Ground
Left Gun
Length (U/I)
LGB
Laser-Guided Bomb
LGCOMB
Large Combatant
LGCP
Lexical Graphical Composer Printer
LGT, LT
Light
LGTD
Lighted
LGW
Laser-Guided Weapon
L/H
Lower Hold (stowage)
LHA
Amphibious Assault Ship (General-Purpose)
LHD
Amphibious Assault Ship (Multi-Purpose)
LDHC
Lateral-Homing Depth Charge
LHFT
Light-Helo Fire Team
L-HOUR
Landing of first helicopter assault wave
LHOX
Low and High Pressure Oxygen
LHV
Lower Heating Value
LHW
Lower High Water
LI
Lifted Index
LI, L/I
Letter of Interest
LI1
Lithographer First Class
LI2
Lithographer Second Class
LI3
Lithographer Third Class
L/I
Line Item
LIBEC
Light Behind Camera (technique)

LIC
Chief Lithographer
License
List of Instruments and Controls
Logistics Indoctrination Course
LIC, LANTINTCEN
Atlantic Intelligence Center
LICM
Master Chief Lithographer
LICS
Senior Chief Lithographer
LIDAR
Laser Information Radar
LIFESTA
Lifeboat Station
LIF-MOP
Linerally Frequency-Moderated Pulse
LIFO
Last-In, First-Out (inventory)
LIGHTPHOTORON, LTPHOTORON, VFP
Light Photographic Squadron
LIM
(Compass) Locator at Inner Marker Site
Linear Induction Motor
LIM, LMT
Limit
LIM, LTD
Limited
LIMDAT
Limiting Date
LIMDU
Limited Duty
LINS
Lightweight Inertial Navigation System
LIO
Lesser Included Offenses
LIQ
Liquid
LIR
Limited Isolation Requirement (noise control)
LIRSH
Listing of Items Requiring Special Handling
LISA
Lithographer Seaman Apprentice
LISN
Lithographer Seaman
LIT
Light Intratheater Transport
Literacy
Literature
LITH BRO, LB
Lithium Bromide (air conditioning chemical)
LK
Link (U/I)
LKA
Amphibious Cargo Ship
LKLY
Likely
LKR
Locker

LL
Load (or Lower) Limit
Long Length
LLC
Line Load Control
Salvage Craft
LLI
Longitude and Latitude Indicator
LLL
Low-Level Logic
Low-Light Level
LLT
Long Lead Time
LLTM
Long Lead Time Material
LLTV
Low-Light Level Television
LLW
Lower Low Water
LM
Land Mine
List of Materials
LM, LOM
Legion of Merit
L&M
Logistics and Maintenance
LMDS
Logistics Methodologies Documentation
System
L/MF
Low/Medium Frequency
LMFBR
Liquid Metal Fast Breeder Reactor (AEC)
LMG
Light Machine Gun
LMI
Logistic Management Institute
LMM
(Compass) Locator at Middle Marker Site
LMO
Lens-Modulated Oscillator
LMP
Light Marching Pack
LMT
Leadership and Management Training
Local Mean Time
LMT, LIM
Limit
LMTD
Log Mean Temperature Difference
LN1
Legalman First Class
LN2
Legalman Second Class
LNB
Large Navigation Buoy
LNC
Chief Legalman
Local Naval Commander
LNCM
Master Chief Legalman

LNCS
Senior Chief Legalman
LNDSPTPLT
Landing Support Platoon
LNG
Liquified Natural Gas
Long
Longitude (NNSS)
LNI
Log Neutralization Index
LNO
Limited Nuclear Operations
LO
Law (or Legal) Officer
Level Off
Lot
Low
Lube Oil
LOA
Length Overall
Letter of Offer and Acceptance
Limit Operator Attempts
Local Obligation Authority
LOALT, LA
Low Altitude
LOB
Line of Balance
LOBAR
Long Baseline Radar
LOC
Line(s) of Communication
Liquid Organic Cleaner
Localizer
Locate
Location
LOCI
List of Cancelled Items
Logarithmic Computing Instruments
LOC LF
Local Line Feed
LOCO TAC
Low-Cost Tactical Radar
LODE
Large Optics Demonstration Experiment
LODI
List of Deleted Items
LODIG
Loading
LODOR
Loaded, Waiting Orders or Assignment
LOE
Level of Essentiality
LOEC
List of Effective Cards
LOEP
List of Effective Parts (PURS)
LOF
Line of Fine
LOFAR
Low-Frequency Acquisition and Ranging

LOFC
Line of Communications
LOFTI
Low-Frequency Trans-Ionospheric (satellite)
LOFTPS
Lube Oil Fill, Transfer and Purification
System
LOG
Logistics
Management Oriented File (for NARDIS)
LOGAIR
Logistics Aircraft
LOGALGOL
Logical Algorithmic Language
LOGBALNET
Logistical Ballistic Network
LOGEX
Logistics Exercise
LOGICOMP
Logical Compiler
LOGLAN
Logical Language
LOGO
Limitation of Government Obligation
LOGREP
Logistics Replenishment (or Representative)
LOGREQS
Logistics Requisitions
LOH
Light Observation Helicopter
LOI
Letter of Instruction (or Intent)
LO/LO
Lift-On/Lift-Off
LOM
(Compass) Locator at Outer Marker Site
LOM, LM
Legion of Merit
LOMMA
List of Mining Materials Available
LONG
Longevity
LOO
Letter of Offer
LOOK TR
Lookout Tower
LOP
Line of Position
Local Operating Position (or Plot)
LOPAR
Low-Power Acquisition Radar
LOPU
Logistics Organizational Planning Unit
LO-R
Low-Intensity Range Survey Meter
LORAC
Long-Range Accuracy
LORACTEAM
Long-Range Accuracy Support Team
LORAN
Long-Range Navigation

LORAN D
  Long-Range Navigation Doppler Inertial
LORAN DM
  Long-Range Navigation Double Master
LORAN DS
  Long-Range Navigation Double Slave
LORAN S
  Long-Range Navigation Slave
LORAPH
  Long-Range Passive Homing (system)
LORMONSTA
  LORAN Monitor Station
LORSTA
  LORAN Station
LOS
  Land on Ship
  Law of the Sea
  Length of Service
  Line of Sight (or Supply)
  Local Operating Station
LOSC
  Law of the Sea Conference
  Local On-Scene Commander
LOSE
  Line-of-Sight-Expendables
LOSS
  Large Object Salvage System
  Lube Oil Service System
LOST/A
  Vessel Lost by Accident
LOST/E
  Vessel Lost by Enemy Action
LOST/P
  Vessel Lost Due to Weather/Perils of the Sea
LOT
  Large Operational Telescope
  Live Operational Training (course)
LOTON, LT/TN
  Long Ton
LOTS
  Logistics-Over-the-Shore (vehicle)
  LORAN Operational Training School
LOU
  Letter(s) of Understanding
LOX
  Liquid Oxygen
LP
  Low Pressure
LPA
  Amphibious Transport
LPAC
  Low-Pressure Air Compressor
LPCBR
  Low-Pressure Chamber
LPD
  Amphibious Transport Dock
LPF
  Launch Pontoon Facility
LPG
  Liquified Petroleum Gas

LPH
  Amphibious Assault Ship (Helicopter)
LPI
  Low Probability of Intercept (communications)
LPM
  Lines per Minute
LPMES
  Logistics Performance Measurement and
    Evaluation System
LPR
  Amphibious Transport (Small)
  Liquid Propellant Rocket
LPS
  Linear Programming System
LPSS
  Amphibious Transport Submarine
LPT
  Low-Pressure Test
LPTV
  Large Payload Test Vehicle
LQRR
  Low-Quality Recruiting Report
LR
  Life Raft
  Liter (U/I)
  Long-Range
L/R
  Latest Revision (issue)
LRA
  Light Replaceable Assembly
LRF
  Laser Range Finder
LRIR
  Low-Resolution Infrared Radiometer
LRO
  Long-Range Objectives
LRP
  Long-Range Preparedness (or Preparation)
LRPS
  Long-Range Planning System
LRR
  Long-Range Radar (or Requirements)
LRRP
  Long-Range Reconnaissance Patrol
LR/RT
  Long-Range Radio Telephone
LRSTFF
  Long-Range Scientific-Technical Planning
    Program
LRT
  Launch and Recovery Transport
  Long-Range Typhon
LRU
  Less-Release-Unit
  Line (or Lone) Replaceable Unit
LS
  Lapped Seam
  Light Ship
  Logistics Support
L/S
  Large Screen

LSA
Labor Surplus Area
Logistics Support Analysis
Logistics Support Area
Low Specific Activity
LSAT
Law School Admission Test
LSB
Least Significant BIT
Logistics Support Base
Lower Side Band
LSC
Law of the Sea Conference
Linear Shaped Charge
Logistics Support Center
LSD
Landing Ship, Dock
Large-Screen Display (system)
Lesson Specification Document
LSE
Landing Signal Enlistedman
LSG
Landing Support Group
LSG/LSU
Landing Support Group/Logistics Support Unit
LSH/LSF
Landing Ship Helicopter/Landing Ship Fighter
Direction
LSI
Large-Scale Integration (MOS display)
LSIC
Large-Scale Integrated Circuit
LSL
Lump-Sum Leave (payment)
LSL BP
Lump-Sum Leave Payment, Basic Pay
LSL PMA
Lump-Sum Leave Payment, Personal Money
Allowance
LSL QTRS
Lump-Sum Leave Payment, Quarters
LSL SUBS
Lump-Sum Leave Payment, Subsistence
LSM
Landing Ship, Medium
Logistics Support Manager
LSMR
Landing Ship, Medium, Rocket
LSMSO
Landing Ship Material Supply Officer
LSO
Landing Signal Officer
LSP
Logistics System Proposal
Logistics Support Plan
Low Suction Pressure
Lump-Sum Payment
LSR
Logistics Support Requirement (system)
Loose Snow on Runway
Lump-Sum Payment upon Retirement

LSR-P
Loose Snow on Runway-Patchy
LSS
Life-Support System
Limited Storage Site
LS S
Lifesaving Station
LSSB
Light SEAL Support Boat
LSSC
Light SEAL Support Craft
LST
Landing Ship, Tank
Laser Spot Tracker
LST(H)
Landing Ship, Tank (Casualty Evacuation)
LSU
Logistic (or Landing) Support Unit
LT
Lieutenant
Line Telecommunications
Link Terminal
Loader-Transponder
LT, L/T, LTON
Long Ton
LT, LGT
Light
LTA, LA
Lighter-Than-Air
LTC
Letdown Terrain Clearance
LTCOM, LCDR, LT COMDR
Lieutenant Commander
LT COMDR, LCDR, LTCOM
Lieutenant Commander
LTD
Language Training Detachment (DLI)
LTD, LIM
Limited
LTD, L/TD
Lower 'tween Deck (stowage)
LTDS
Laser Target Designator System
LTDSTD
Limited Standard
LTFRD
Lot Tolerance Fraction Reliability Deviation
LTG, LTNG
Lighting
LT HO
Lighthouse
LTJG, JAYGEE
Lieutenant (Junior Grade)
LTL
Less Than Truckload
Little
LTLCG
Little Change
LTNG, LTG
Lightning

LTPD
Lot Tolerance Percent Defective
LTPHOTORON, LIGHTPHOTORON, VPF
Light Photographic Squadron
LTR
Later
Letter
LTS
Landfall Technique School
LTST
Indicator Light Test (NNSS)
LUBE
Lubricating (oils)
Lubrication
LUF
Lowest Useful High Frequency
LUL
"Language, Unseamanlike" (slang)
LV
Leave
Light Vessel
Live (AFRTS code)
LVA
Landing Vehicle, Assault
LVD
Absent on Leave from Ship's Duty
LVDT
Linear Variable Differential Transformer
LVG
Leaving
LVL
Level
LVN
Absent on Leave, Not Ship's Company
LVP
Low Voltage Protection
LVR
Line Voltage Regulator
LVRATS
Leave Rations
LVRATS SL
Leave Rations, Sick Leave
LVRATS SPEC
Leave Rations, Special Leave
LVR(CE)
Low Voltage Release (Continuous Effect)
LVT
Landing Vehicle, Tracked—also called
AMTRACK
LVTB
Low-Voltage Thermal Battery
LVTE
Landing Vehicle, Tracked, Engineer
LV&UPK
Leave and Upkeep
LW
Low Water
LWD
Low Water Datum
LWF
Lightweight Fighter

LWIR
Long Wave Length Infrared
LWL
Length at Waterline
Lightweight Laser
Load Waterline
LWLD
Lightweight Laser Designator
LWM
Low Watermark
LWP
Leave Without Pay
LWR
Lower
LWSC
Local Wage Survey Committee
LWT
Amphibious Warping Tug
Lightweight Type
LY
Lead Yard
Linear Yard (U/I)
LYFT
Low-Yield Fallout Trajectory
LYR
Layer
LZ
Landing Zone
Load(ing) Zone
LZL
Launch Zero Length

M

M
Aerology (TO code)
Machinery
Magnetic (bearing)
Manpower
Model
Monthly (report frequency)
Mud(dy)
MA
Maritime Administration
Mediterranean Area
Memory Address (NNSS)
Mental Ability
Mercury Atlas (rocket)
Mileage Allowance
Military Attaché
Missed Approach
Missile Alert
MA, MACH
Machinery
MA1
Master-at-Arms First Class

MAA
Master-at-Arms
Maximum Authorized Altitude
Medium Anti-Aircraft (weapon)
MAAG
Military Assistance Advisory Group
MAATC
Mobile Anti-Aircraft Training Center
MAG, MARPHIBRIG
Marine Amphibious Brigade
MABS
Marine Air Base Support (or Squadron)
Moored Acoustic Buoy System
MAC
Chief Master-at-Arms
Machine-Aided Cognition
Maintenance (or Management) Advisory
Committee
Management Analysis Course
Maximum Analysis Course
Maximum Allowable Concentration
Mean Aerodynamic Chord
Media Assistance Center
Mid-Atlantic Conference
Military Airlift (or Assistance) Command
MIUW Attack Craft
Months After Contract
Multiple Access Computers
MACA
Military Airlift Clearance Authority
MACCS
Marine Air Command and Control System
MACG
Marine Air Control Group
MACH
Machinist
MACH, MA
Machinery
MACHGR
Machine Group
MACM
Master Chief Master-at-Arms
MAC(O)
Management Analysis Course, Class "O"
MACRI
Mercantile Atlantic Coastal Routing
Instructions
MACS
Marine Air Control Squadron
Medium Altitude Communications Satellite
Senior Chief Master-at-Arms
MACSS
Medium Altitude Communication Satellite
System
MACTU
Mine and Countermeasures Technical Unit
MACV
Multi-Purpose Air-Transportable
Combat-Support Vehicle

MAD
Magnetic Airborne (or Anomaly) Detection
(equipment)
Maintenance, Assembly and Disassembly
(AEC)
Marine Air Detection
Marine Aviation Detachment
Mathematical Analysis of Downtime
MDCS Analysis Date
Mine Assembly Depot
Multi-Apertured Device
MADDAM
Macro-Module Digital Differential Analyzer
Machine
MADE
Minimum Airborne Digital Equipment
MADMAN
Master Activity Data Management
MAD-R
Multi-Apertured Device-Resistance
MADRE
Magnetic-Drum Receiving Equipment
MADT
Mean Administrative Delay Time
MAE
Mobile Ammunition Evaluation
MAERU
Mobile Ammunition Evaluation and
Reconditioning Unit
MAF
Maintenance Action Form
Marine Amphibious Force
MA/FH
Maintenance Action per Flight Hour
MAFIA
Microaerofluorometer (NBL)
MAFOG
Mediterranean Area Fighter Operations Grid
MAF/TDC
Maintenance Action Form/Technical
Directives Compliance
MAG
Magnetic (or Magneto)
Marine Aircraft Group
Military Assistance Group
MAG, MGZ
Magazine
MAGBRG
Magnetic Bearing
MAGIC
Master Activity General Information and
Control
MIDAD Automatic General Integrated
Computation
MAGLOC
Magnetic Logic (computer)
MAGT
Magnetic Tape (NNSS)
MAGTF
Marine Air Ground Task Force

MAHC
Maximum Allowable Housing Cost
MAI
Material Annex Index
MAID
Merger-Acquisition Improved Decision
MAIDS
Multi-Purpose Automatic Inspection and
Diagnostic System
MAINT
Maintenance
MAINTBN
Maintenance Battalion
MAINTSUPOFC
Maintenance Supply Office
MAINTSUPP
Maintenance and Support
MAIP
Maintenance Automatic Integrated Director
Memory Access and Interrupt Program
MAIR
Molecular Airborne Interceptor Radar
MAIREASTLANT
Maritime Air, Eastern Atlantic
MAIRMED
Maritime Air Forces, Mediterranean Area
MAIRU
Mobile Aircraft Instrument Repair Unit
MAKETRANS
When directed by CO make necessary
transfers in accordance with (manual
designated). Report to CO or command
specified in connection with settlement of
accounts.
MAL
Master Allowance List
MALE
Multi-Aperture Logic Element
MALI
Material Annex Line Item
MALRE
Marine Aircraft Launch and Recovery School
MALS
Minimum-Approach Light System
MALS/RAIL
Minimum-Approach Light System with
Runway Alignment Indicator Lights
MALT
Monetary Allowance in Lieu of Transportation
MAM
Maintenance Assist Module
MAMIE
Minimum Automatic Machine for Interpolation
and Extrapolation
MAMOEAST
Marine Aviation Material Office, East
MAMOWEST
Marine Aviation Material Office, West
MAMS
Management of Aviation Maintenance
Assistance Modules

MAN
Magnetic Automatic Navigation
Manual
Military Aviation Notice
MAN, MGR, MNGR
Manager
MANCAN
Man-Carried Automatic Navigator
MAND
Mandatory
MANFST
Manifest
MANIAC
Mechanical and Numerical Integrator and
Computer
MANMEDDEPT, MMD
Manual of the Medical Department
MAN/SAFE
Manual/Automatic Separation and Flotation
Equipment
MANTRAPERS
Manpower, Training and Personnel
MAO
Maximal Acid Output
MAOT
Maximum Allowable Operating Time
MAP
Manifold Absolute Pressure
Military Assistance Program
Missed Approach Point
Modular Aviation Package
MAPAD
Military Assistance Program Address
Directory
MAP/CIO
Military Assistance Program/Common Item
Order
MAPMIS
Manpower and Personnel Management
Information System
MAPMISMAN
Manpower and Personnel Management
Information System Manual
MAP/OSP
Military Assistance Program Offshore
Procurement
MAPS
Multiple Address Processing System
Multivariate Analysis and Prediction of
Schedules
MAPSAC
Machine-Aided Planning, Scheduling and
Control
MAPTIS
Manpower, Personnel and Training
Indoctrination System
MAPUC
Modified Area Production Urgency Committee
MAQ
Money Allowance for Quarters

MAR
Maintenance Analysis Report
Marine (Corps)
Memory Access Register
Multi-Function-Phased Array Radar
MAR, MR
March
MARAD
Maritime Administration
MARBKS
Marine Barracks
MARC
Machine Readable Cataloging
Material Accountability and Recoverability
Codes
MARCAD
Marine Aviation Cadet
MARCOMM
Maritime Commission
MARCOMMDET
Marine Communications Detachment
MARCORABSCOLLUNIT
Marine Corps Absentee Collection Unit
MARCORABSCOLLUNITDET
Marine Corps Absentee Collection Unit
Detachment
MARCORADMINDET
Marine Corps Administrative Detachment
MARCORFREIGHTOFF
Marine Corps Freight Office
MARCOREP
Marine Corps Representative
MARCORHISTCEN
Marine Corps Historical Center
MARDET
Marine Detachment
MARDIV
Marine Division
MARE
Months After Receipt of Equipment
MARENGRLAB, MEL
Marine Engineering Laboratory
MARENTS
Modified Advanced Research Environmental
Test Satellite
MARES
Maritime Automated Readiness Evaluation
System
MARFINCEN
Marine Corps Finance Center
MARI
Mercantile Atlantic Routing Instructions
MARINE
Management Analysis Reporting Information
on the Naval Environment (system)
MARIP
Maintenance and Repair Inspection Program
MARISAT
Maritime Satellite (communications)

MARLIS
Multi-Aspect Relevance Linkage Information
System
MARLNO
Marine Liaison Office
MARMAP
Maritime Resources Monitoring, Assessment
and Prediction (system)
MARP
Manpower Allocation/Requirement
Plan—normally appears as P-MARP or
M-MARP
Maximum Authorized for Repair Parts
Months After Receipt of Problem
MARS
Machine Retrieval System
Manned Astronautical Research Station
Military Affiliate Radio System
Mobile Atlantic Range Station
Multi-Aperture Reluctance Switch
MARSA
Military Assumes Responsibility for
Separation of Aircraft
MARSPTBN
Marine Support Battalion
MARSREPSYS
Military Affiliate Radio System Repeater
System
MARSTELSYS
Military Affiliate Radio System Teletypewriter
Relay System
MARTCOM
Marine Training Command
MARTD
Marine Air Reserve Training Detachment
MARV
Maneuverable Reentry Vehicle (improved
MIRV)
Maneuvering Anti-Radar Vehicle
MAS
Machine Accounting School
Marine Advisory Service (NOAA)
MASAQUE
Major Action Significantly Affecting the
Quality of the Human Environment
MA/SB
Motor Antisubmarine Boat
MASC
Magnetic Spin Control
MASER
Microwave Amplification by Stimulated
Emission of Radiation
MASF
Military Assistance in Service-Funding
(grants)
Mobile Aeromedical Staging Facility
MASG
Military Airlift Support Group
MASH
Manned Antisubmarine Helicopter

MASK
Maneuvering and Sea-Keeping (facility)
MASM
Military Assistance and Sales Manual
MASS
Marine Air Support Squadron
Maritime Anti-Standing Sonar System
(MARAD)
MASSDAR
Modular Analysis, Speed-Up, Sampling and
Data Reduction
MASSDET
Marine Air Support Squadron Detachment
MAST
Military Assistance for Safety in Traffic
(DOD/DOT)
Missile Automatic Supply Squadron
MASTER
Miniaturized Sink-Rate Telemetering Radar
Multiple Access Shared Time Executive
Routine
MAT
Material
MATCON
Microwave Aerospace Terminal Control
MATCONOFF
Material Control Office
MATCS
Marine Air Traffic Control Squadron
MATCSDET
Marine Air Traffic Control Squadron
Detachment
MATD
Mine and Torpedo Detector
MATEX
Material Expediting (program)
MATMU
Mobile Aircraft Torpedo Maintenance Unit
MATRED
Material Redistribution (program)
MATSG
Marine Aviation Training Support Group
MATSS
Marine Aviation Training Support Squadron
MATT
Mobile Acoustic Torpedo Target
MATTU
Multiple Airborne Target Trajectory System
MAU
Maintenance Augmenting Unit
Marine Amphibious Unit
MAW
Marine Air(craft) Wing
Medium Assault Weapon
MAWCS
Mobile Air Weapons Control System
MA/WD
Material Annex/Weapons Dictionary
MAWDET
Marine Aircraft Wing Detachment

MAWTS
Marine Aviation Weapons and Tactics
Squadron
MAX/MIN
Maximum Disclosure/Minimum Delay
MB
Main Battery
Military Band (AFRTS code)
Mooring Buoys
Motor Boat (USCG)
M/B
Medium Bomber (aircraft)
MBBA
Military Benefit Base Amounts
MBC
Magnetic Bias Control
MBFR
Mutual and Balanced Force Reductions
MBL
Master Bidders List
MBMU
Mobile Base Maintenance Unit
MBO
Management by Objectives
MBOH
Minimum Break-Off Height
MBR
Multiple Bomb Rack
MBR, MEM
Member
MBT
Main Ballast (or Battle) Tank
Mobile Boarding Team
MC
Main Coolant
Major Component
Mast Controller
Medical Care, Civilian Source
Medical Corps
Message Center
Miles on Course
Military Characteristics
MCA
Machinery Condition Analysis
Manning Control Authority
Maritime Control Area
Material Coordinating Agency
Minimum Crossing Altitude
MCAAS
Marine Corps Auxiliary Air Station
MCAC
Military Common Area Control
MCAF
Marine Corps Air Facility
MCAI
Maximum Calling Area Indicator
MCALF
Marine Corps Auxiliary Landing Field
MCAP
Maximum Calling Area Precedence

MCAS
Marine Corps Air Station
MCAT
Medical College Admission Test
MCB
Material Classification Board
Motor Cargo Boat (USCG)
MCB, MOBCONBAT
(Naval) Mobile Construction Battalion—see NMCB
MCBETH
Military Computer Basic Environment for Test Handling
MCBF
Mean Cycles Between Failures
MCBL
Motor Cargo Boat (Large) (USCG)
MCC
Machinery (or Main, or Master) Control Console
Mail Classification Center
Material Category (or Control) Code
Material Control Center
MILCOMS Concentration Center
Military Climb Corridor
Monitored Command Mode
Multiple Computer Complex
MCCDPA
Marine Corps Central Design and Programming Activity
MCCDS
Modified Central Computer Display Set
MCCES
Marine Corps Communications Electronics School
MCCRES
Marine Corps Combat Crew Readiness Evaluation System
MCCRTG
Marine Corps Combat Crew Readiness Training Group
MCD
Maintenance Control Department (PWD)
Marine Corps District
MCEB
Military Communications-Electronics Board
MCF
Master Control File
MCG
Mid-Course Guidance
Mobile Communications Group
MC&G
Mapping, Charting and Geodetic (or Geodesy)
MCGS
Microwave Command Guidance System
MCI
Marine Corps Institute
MCIC
Management Control Information Center

MCL
Master Configuration List
MCLWG
Major Caliber Lightweight Gun
MCM
Manual for Courts-Martial
Mine Countermeasures (ship)
MCMC
Military Construction, Marine Corps
MCMCC
Marine Corps Movement Coordination Center
MCMWTC
Marine Corps Mountain Warfare Training Center
MCN
Military Construction, Navy
MCNR
Military Construction, Naval Reserve
MCNRF
Military Construction, Naval Reserve Facilities
MCO
Missile Check-Out
Missile Control Officer
MCOI
Minority Centers of Influence
MCON, MILCON
Military Construction
MCOT
Missile Control Officer Trainer
MCOTEA
Marine Corps Operational Test and Evaluation Activity
MCOY
Military Citizen of the Year
MCP
Main Coolant Pump
Master Control Program
Master Construction Project
Maximum Calling Precedence (or Preference)
Military Construction Program
Mutual Change Proposal
MCPO
Master Chief Petty Officer
MCPOC
Master Chief Petty Officer of the Command
MCPOF
Master Chief Petty Officer of the Fleet (or Force)
MCPON
Master Chief Petty Officer of the Navy—also SEAN
MCR
Maintenance Requirements Cards
MCRB
Magnetic Compass Record Book
MCRF
Master Cross Reference File
MCRL
Master Component Repair List
Master Cross Reference List

MCRS
Marine Corps Recruiting Station
MCRSC
Marine Corps Reserve Support Center
MCS
Magnetic Card Selecting
Maintenance (or Missile) Control Section
Mine Countermeasures Ship
MCSF
Marine Corps Security Force
MCSL
Small Mine Countermeasures Ship
MCSTRANSU, MCSTU
Military Sealift Command Transportation Unit
MCSTU, MCSTRANSU
Military Sealift Command Transportation Unit
MCT
Magnetic Compass Table
Mechanical Comprehension Test
MCTS
Master Central Timing System
MCTSSA
Marine Corps Tactical Systems Support
Activity
MCU
Microprogrammed Control Unit (NBL)
MCW
Modulated Continuous Wave
MCXSERV
Marine Corps Exchange Service Branch
MD
Medical Department
Memory Data Register (NNSS)
Mine Disposal
M/D
Man/Days
MDA
Material Data Administrator
Minimum Descent Altitude
Multiple Docking Adaptor
MDAP
Mutual Defense Assistance Program
MDAS
Manpower Data Automated System
M-DAY
Mobilization Day
MDB
Material Distribution Board
MDC
Machineability Data Center
Maintenance Data Collection
Materials Distribution Center
Medium-Frequency Direction Finder
MDCS
Maintenance (and Material) Data Collection
(Sub-)System
MDD
Maintenance Due Date
Marijuana Detection Dog
MDDS
Medical or Dental Corps Special Pay

MDEU
Material Delivery Expeditor Unit
MDF
Maintenance Data Form
Master Data File
Mild Detonating Fuze
MDFMR
Mobilization Day Force Material Requirement
MDG
Machinery Defective, Government-Furnished
MDI
Miss Distance Indicator
Mobilization Day Increment
MDL
Management Data List
Master Drawing List
MDL, MINEDEFLAB
Mine Defense Laboratory
MDM
Manpower Determination Model
MDMAA
Mess Deck Master-at-Arms
MDMS
Miss Distance Measuring System
MDOA
Material Date of Arrival
MDR
Maintenance Data Report(ing)
Matter Document Reader
MDRS
Maintenance Data Reporting System
MDS
Malfunction Detection System
Minimum Discernable Signal
MDS-MPOLL
Mail Distribution Scheme/Military Post Office
Location List
MDT
Mean Diagnostic Time
MDT, MOD
Moderate
MDTA
Manpower Development and Training Act
MDU
Mobile Development Unit
ME
Magnetoelectric
Meal
Methods Engineering
MEA
Maintenance Engineering Analysis
Minimum Enroute Altitude
MEACONING
Measuring and Confusing
MEAD
Maintenance Engineering Analysis Division
(or Data)
MEAL
Mobile Equipment Allowance List
MEAR
Maintenance Engineering Analysis Record

MEAS
Measure
MEASURE
Meteorology Automated System for Uniform
Recall and Reporting
MEAWS
Maintenance Engineering Analysis Work
Sheet
MEBD
Medical Examining Board
MEC
Meteorology Engineering Center
Military Essentiality Coding (or Code)
Military Equipment Code
MECEP
Marine Corps Enlisted Commissioning
Education Program
MECH
Mechanic(al)
MECO
Main Engine Cut-Off
Manual Equipment Check-Out
MED
Medical
Mediterranean
Medium
Minimal Effective Dose
MEDAL
Micro-Mechanized Engineering Data for
Automated Logistics
MEDBN
Medical Battalion
MEDBR
Medical Branch
MEDCAP
Medical Civic Action Program
MEDDA
Mechanized Defense Decision Anticipation
MEDEVAC
Medical Evacuation
MEDIA
Missile-Era Data Integration Analysis
MEDICARE
(Dependent's) Medical Care
MEDICOS
Mediterranean Instructions to Convoys
MEDIHC
Military Experience Directed Into Health
Careers
MEDIUM
Missile-Era Data Integration-Ultimate Method
MEDMAILCOORD
Mediterranean Mail Coordinating Office
MEDOFCOMD
Medical Officer-in-Command
MEDREP
Daily Medical Status Report
MEDSARS
Maintenance Engineering Data Storage and
Retrieval System

MEDSERWRNT
Medical Service Warrant
MEDSUPDEP
Medical Supply Depot
MEDT
Military Equipment Delivery Team
MEECN
Minimum Essential Emergency
Communications Network
MEEL
Mission Essential Equipment List
MEES
Multi-Purpose Electronic Environment
Simulator
MEETAT
Maximum Improvement in Electronics
Effectiveness Advanced Techniques
MEI
Maintenance and Engineering Inspection
Manual of Engineering Instructions
MEIU
Mobile Explosives Investigative Unit
MEL
Material Engineering Laboratory
MEL, MARENGLAB
Marine Engineering Laboratory
MEL-A
Marine Engineering Laboratory-Annapolis
(MD)
MEM, MEMO
Memorandum
MEM, MBR
Member
MEMO
More Education-More Opportunities
MEMO, MEM
Memorandum
MEMQ
Married Enlisted Men's Quarters
MEMRAC
Mission-Essential Material Readiness and
Condition
MEN
Master Equipment Number
MENEX
Maintenance Engineering Exchange Program
MENS
Mission Element Need Statement
MENTRAV
Commence travel within (number of days
indicated) after completion of physical
examination
MEO
Major Engine Overhaul
Management Engineering Office
MEP
Mobile Electric Power
MEPP
Mobile Electric Power Plants
MEPS
Military Entrance and Processing Station

MEQ
Milliequivalent
MER
Maintenance Engineering Report
Multiple Ejector Rack
MERAIR
Including commercial air
MERAIRDIR
Commercial air is directed where necessary
MERCAST
Merchant Ship Broadcast
MERCO
Mercantile Communications
Merchant Ship Movement Reports
MERCOMMS
Merchant Marine Communications System
MERCOS
Merchant Codes
MERMUT
Mobile Electronic Robot Manipulator on TV
(system)
MERP
Miniature Electronic Repair Program
MERR
Minor Equipment Relocations, Replacements
MERSAIR
Merchant Ship Research and Rescue
(manual)
MERSAP
Merchant Ship Auxiliary Program
MERSIGS
Merchant Ships Signal Books
Merchant Signals
MERT
Maintenance Engineering Review Team
MERTRANSUB
Commercial transportation and subsistence
authorized
MES
Master Erection Schedule
MESA
Machinery Effectiveness System Analysis
Marine Ecosystems Analysis
MESIM
Mission Essential Sub-Systems Inoperative,
Maintenance
MESH
Medical Subject Heading (MEDLARS)
MESL
Mission Essential Sub-Systems List
MEST
Missile Electrical System Test
MET
Meteorologic(al)
Mine Warfare Exercise and Training
(material)
Mission Entry Time
METC
Military Electronics Test Center
METCAL
Meteorology and Calibration (program)

METCALANTDETEAST
Atlantic Meteorology and Calibration
Coordination Group Detachment, East
METCALANTDETWEST
Atlantic Meteorology and Calibration
Coordination Group Detachment, West
METCO
Mobile Engine Tester, Computer-Operated
METG
Middle East Task Group
METIMP
Meteorological Equipment Improvement
Program
METLO
Meteorological Equipment and Technical
Liaison Officer
METRI
Military Essentiality Through Readiness
Indices
METRL
Meteorology (requirements listing)
METT
Mission, Enemy, Terrain and Weather, and
Troops Available
METU
Mobile Electronics Training Unit
MEV
Million Electron Volts
MEW
Microwave Early Warning (radar)
MF
Main Force
Medium (or Multi-) Frequency
Millifarad
M/F
Mark(ed) For
MFAR
Modernized Fleet Accounting and Reporting
(system)
MFC
Multiple File Concept
MFCS
Missile Fire Control System
MFGEL
Master Government-Furnished Equipment
List
MFI
Major Force Issue
MFIT
Manual Fault Isolation Test
MFLT
Mean Fault Location Time
MFM
Magneto Fluidmechanic (system)
Mine Firing Mechanism
MFN
Most Favored Nation (GATT)
MFNG
Motion for a Finding of Not Guilty

MFO
Master Frequency Oscillator
Missile Firing Officer
MFP
Minimal Flight Path
MFR
Multi-Function Radar
MFS
Master Fabrication Schedule
Military Flight Service
MFSS
Missile Flight Safety System
MG
Machine Gun
Miligram (U/I)
Military Government
Motor Generator
MGB
Medium Girder Bridge
Motor Gunboat
MGC
Main Gain Control
MGCR
Marine Gas-Cooled Reactor
MGD
Million Gallons per Day
MGDA
Multiple Degaussing Cable
MGE
Maintenance Ground Equipment
MGFEL
Master Government-Furnished Equipment
List
MGGB
Modular-Guided-Glide Bomb
MGM
Mailgram
MGMT, MGT
Management
MGR, MAN, MANGR
Manager
MGRS
Military Grid Reference System
MGSE
Missile Ground Support Equipment
MGSGT
Master Gunnery Sergeant
MGT, MGMT
Management
MGU
Military Government Unit
MGZ, MAG
Magazine
MH
Magnetic Heading
Man-Hours
MHA
Man-Hour Accounting (card)
Minehunter, Auxiliary
Minimum Holding Altitude

MHAS
Man-Hour Accounting System
MHB
Master Horizontal Bomber
MHC
Minehunter, Coastal
MH-CE
Materials Handling and Construction
Equipment
MHD
Magnetohydrodynamics (power supply)
Meter Heading Differential
MHDF
Direction Finder (Medium and High
Frequency)
MHE
Material Handling Equipment
MH/FH
Man-Hours per Flying Hour
MHHFC
Machine and Hull History File Cards
MHHW
Mean Higher High Water
MHSS
Materials Handling Support System
MHVDF
Direction Finder (Medium, High and Very
High Frequency)
MHW
Mean High Water
MHWN
Mean High Water Neaps
MHWS
Mean High Water Springs
MI
Material Inspection
Medical Illustration
Methods Instruction
Military Intelligence
MIA
Missing in Action
MIAC
Material Identification and Accounting Code
MIAPL
Master Index, Allowance Parts List
MIARS
Maintenance Information Automatic Retrieval
System
Micro-film Information and Retrieval System
MIB
Marine Index Bureau
Master Instruction Book
MIBARS
Military Intelligence Battalion Aerial
Reconnaissance Report

MIC
Management Inactivation (or Information) Center
Maintenance Index Code
Marine Information Center
Material Identification and Control
Military-Industrial Complex
MICA
Macro Instruction Compiler-Assembler
MICR
Magnetic Ink Character Recognition
MICRO
Microfilm File (NARDIS)
MICRO-PAC
Micromodule Data Processor and Computer
MID
Management Information Digest (publication)
Middle
Military Intelligence Division
Missile Intelligence Directorate
MIDATL
Mid-Atlantic
MIDAS
Machine for Information Display and Simulation
Missile Defense Alarm System
MIDEASTFOR
Middle East Force
MIDIZ
Mid-Canada Identification Zone
MIDN
Midnight
Midshipman
MIDPAC
Middle Pacific
MIDS
Maintenance Index Pages
Movement Information Distribution Station
MI/DS
Management Information/Data Systems
MIG
Metal Inert Gas
MIGCAP
MIG Combat Air Patrol
MIISA
Management Information and Instructional Systems Activity
MIISADET
Management Information and Instructional Systems Activity Detachment
MIISAU
Management Information and Instructional Systems Activity Unit
MIJI
Meconing, Intrusion, Jamming and Interference
MIL
Military
Milliradian
Modular Individualized

MILCOMSAT
Military Communications Satellite
MILCOMS
Military Commands
MILCON, MCON
Military Construction
MIL CONF
Military Confinement
MILDEPT
Military Department
MILES
Multiple Integrated Laser Engagement System
MILGRP, MILGRU
Military Group
MILGRU, MILGRP
Military Group
MILJUSDOCFILE
Military Justice Docket File
MILPERS
Military Personnel
MILPERSMAN
Military Personnel Manual
MILPERSYS
Military Personnel Information Subsystem
MILPINS
Military Police Information System
MILS
Missile Impact Location System
MILSAT
Military Satellite
MILSCAP
Military Standard Contract Administration Procedure
MILSPEC
Military Specification(s)
MILSTAAD
Military Standard Activity Address Directory
MILSTAMP
Military Standard Transportation and Movement Procedure
MILSTD
Military Standard
MILSTEP
Military Standard Evaluation Procedure
Military Supply and Transportation Evaluation Procedure
MILSTICCS
Military Standard Item Characteristics Coding Structure
MILSTRAP
Military Standard Transaction Reporting and Accounting Procedures
MILSTRIP
Military Standard Requisition and Issue Procedure
MIM
Maintenance Instruction Manual
MIN
Mine(craft)
Minimum

MINAC
Miniature Navigation Airborne Computer
MINCOM
Miniaturized Communications
MIND
Magnetic Integrator Neuron Duplicator
MINDIV
Mine Division
MINECTRMEASTA
Mine Countermeasures Station
MINEDEFLAB, MDL
Mine Defense Laboratory
MINEPACSUPPGRU
Mine Force, Pacific Fleet, Support Group Unit
MINICATS
Miniaturization of the Federal Catalog
Systems Publication
MINLANT
Mine Warfare Forces, Atlantic
MINPAC
Mine Warfare Forces, Pacific
MINS
Miniature Inertial Navigation System
MINS, MINSY, MINY
Mare Island Naval Shipyard
MINSUPPU
Minecraft Support Unit
MINSY, MINS, MINY
Mare Island Naval Shipyard
MINU
Mobile Instrument Investigation Unit
MINWARTECH
Mine Warfare Technician
MINY, MINS, MINSY
Mare Island Naval Shipyard
MIO
Mobile Issuing Office
MIP
Maintenance (or Manual) Index Page
Management (or Methods) Improvement
Program
Material (or Military, or Master) Improvement
Plan
Maximum Intermittent Power
MIPE
Modular Information Processing Equipment
MIPIR
Missile Precision Instrumentation Radar
MIPR
Military Interdepartmental Purchase Request
MIPS
Military Information Processing System
MIR
Material Inspection Report
MIRACL
Mid-Infrared Advanced Chemical Laser
MIRCS
Mechanical Instrument Repair and Calibration
Shops
MIRF
Multiple Instantaneous Response File

MIRL
Medium-Intensity Runway Lights
MIRR
Material Inspection and Receiving Report
MIRRER
Microwave Identification Railroad Encoding
Reflector
MIRROS
Modulation Inducing Reactive Retrodirective
Optical System
MIRS
Micro-Interactive Retrieval System
Military Intelligence Research Station
MIRSI
Monthly Inventory Report of Special Items
MIRTRAC
Missile Infrared Tracking (system)
MIRV
Multiple Independently Targetable Reentry
Vehicle
MIS
Management Information Service (or
Sciences)
Manpower Information System
Material (or Military) Inspection Service
Metal-Insulator-Semi-conductor
Mine-Issuing Ship
Mission
MIS, MISG
Missing
MIS, MSL
Missile
MISA
Military Industrial Supply Agency
MISC
Miscellaneous
MISD
Management Information System
Development
M&ISD
Mathematical and Information Sciences
Division (ONR)
MISDO
Management Information System
Development Office
MISEG
Management Information System Executive
Group
MISG, MIS
Missing
MISIAS
Management Information Systems Inventory
and Analysis System
MIS/INAS
Management Information System for
Industrial Naval Air Stations
MISL
Manpower Information System Laboratory
MISL REWRK
Missile Rework

MISP
Management Information System Plan
MISR
Minimum Industrial Sustaining Role
MISRAN
Missile Range
MISREP
Mission Report (JTARS)
MISS
Mobile Integrated Support System
MIST
Multi-Input Standard Tape
MISTER
Mobile Integrated System Trainer, Evaluator
and Recorder
MISTRAM
Missile Trajectory Measurement
MISTRAULANT
Missile Weapons System Training Unit,
Atlantic
MISTRAUPAC
Missile Weapons System Training Unit,
Pacific
MIT
Master Instruction Tape
MITAG
Minority Affairs Task Group
MITE
Missile Integration Terminal Equipment
Multiple Input Terminal Equipment
MITMS
Military/Industry Technical Manual
Specifications
MITO
Minimum Interval Take-Off
MITRE
Authorized to omit or revisit any of the
above-mentioned places as necessary
MITREVAR
Authorized to omit or revisit any of the
above-mentioned places and to vary above
itinerary as necessary
MITS
Man in the Sea
MITVAR
Authorized to omit any of the
above-mentioned places and vary the
above itinerary as necessary
MIUW
Mobile Inshore Undersea Warfare
MIUWSU
Mobile Inshore Undersea Warfare
Surveillance Unit
MIZ
Marginal Ice Zone
MJ
Millijoule
MK
Mark (number of designation)
MKR
Marker Radio Beacon

MKSA
Meter-Kilogram-Second-Ampere
ML
Medical Technologist (ASCP)
Middle Level
Milliliter (U/I)
Military Law
Missile Launch
Money List
Motor Launch (USCG)
Small Minesweeper
ML1
Molder First Class
ML2
Molder Second Class
ML3
Molder Third Class
MLC
Chief Molder
Main (or Military) Landing Craft
Military Liaison Committee
Motor Landing Craft
Motor Launch, Cabin
Multi-Line Communications Controller
MLCM
Master Chief Molder
MLCS
Senior Chief Molder
MLD
Main Line of Defense
MLDS
Motor Launch, Double Shelter (USCG)
MLF
Multilateral Force
MLFA
Molder Fireman Apprentice
MLFN
Molder Fireman
MLG
Main Landing Gear
MLLW
Mean Lower Low Water
MLM
Multilayer Metallization (fabrication)
ML/MS
Motor Launch, Minesweeper
MLOI
Master List of Outstanding Items
MLP
Mirror Landing Practice
Multi-Level Precedence (or Procedure)
MLPP
Multi-Level Precedence Preemption
MLR
Main Line of Resistance
Mortar Locating Radar
MLS
Microwave Landing System
Missile Launching System
MLSC
Mobile Logistics Support Concept

MLSF, MOBLOGSUPPFOR
Mobile Logistics Support Force
M-L-S-R
Missing, Lost, Stolen or Recovered
(government property)
MLT
Medical Laboratory Technician (ASCP)
MLW
Mean Low Water
MLWN
Mean Low Water Neaps
MLWS
Mean Low Water Springs
MM
Memory Multiplexor
Middle Marker
Millimeter
MM1
Machinist's Mate First Class
MM2
Machinist's Mate Second Class
MM3
Machinist's Mate Third Class
MMA
Manual Metal Arc (welding)
M-MARP
Mobilization Allocation/Requirements
Plan—also see P-MARK
MMART
Mobile Medical Augmentation Readiness
Team
MMAT
Mobile Mine Assembly Team
MMC
Chief Machinist's Mate
Minelayer, Coastal
MMCC
Military Manpower Claimant Code
MMCM
Master Chief Machinist's Mate
MMCO
Maintenance Material Control Officer
MMCS
Senior Chief Machinist's Mate
MMCSA
Microwave Microminiature Communications
System for Aircraft
MMD
Minelayer, Fast
MMD, MANMEDDEPT
Manual of the Medical Department
MMES
Master Material Erection Schedule
MMF
Magnetomotive Force
Minelayer, Fleet
Mobile Maintenance Facility
MMFA
Machinist's Mate Fireman Apprentice
MMFN
Machinist's Mate Fireman

MMFO
Maintenance Management Field Office
MMG
Material Monitoring Guide
Mobile Motor Generator
MMH
Maintenance Man-Hours
Mean Man-Hours
MMH/FH
Maintenance Man-Hours per Flight Hour
MMIS
Maintenance Management Information
System
MMM
Maintenance and Material Management (3M)
Marine Multipurpose Missile
MMNIC
Main Mediterranean Naval Intelligence Center
MMNR
Merchant Marine Naval Reserve
MMO
Main Meteorological Office
MMODS
Master Material Ordering and Delivery
Schedule
MMP
Maintenance Monitor Panel
MEECN Master Plan
Merchant Marine Personnel Division
MMPC
Mobilization Material Procurement
Capabilities
MMPD
Material Movement Priority Designator
MMPNC
Medical Materiel Program for Nuclear
Casualties
MMPR
Missile Manufacturers Planning Report
MMPS
MEECN Message Processing System
MMR
Management Milestone Records
Master Material Record
Maximum Measurable Range
Merchant Marine Reserve
Military Media Review (publication)
Minelayer, River
Mobilization Material Requirements
Monthly Meteorological Records
Multimode Radar
MMRA
Mobilization Material Requirements
Adjustment
MMRBM
Mobile Medium Range Ballistic Missile
MMS
Manpower (or Munitions) Management
System
Master Manpower Schedule
Motor Minesweeper

MMSA
Manual Molded Shielded Arc
Military Medical Supply Agency
MMSRC
Mediterranean Maritime Surveillance and
Reconnaissance Center
MMU
Mobile Maintenance Unit
Modular Maneuvering Unit
MN
Manual Input (NNSS)
MN1
Mineman First Class
MM2
Mineman Second Class
MM3
Mineman Third Class
MNA
Missing-Not as a Result of Enemy Action
MNAO
Mobile Naval Airfield Organization
MNAU
Mobile Naval Airfield Unit
MNC
Chief Mineman
MNCM
Master Chief Mineman
MNCS
Senior Chief Mineman
MNFA
Mineman Fireman Apprentice
MNFN
Mineman Fireman
MNGR, MAN, MGR
Manager
MNOMU
Mobile Nuclear Ordnance Maintenance Unit
MNOS
Metal Nitrite Oxide Semiconductor
MNPO
Mobile Navy Post Office
MO
Manual Override
Master Oscillator
Medical Officer
Modification (or Monthly) Order
Month
MO, MOB
Mobile
MO, MOT, MTR
Motor
M&O
Maintenance and Operation
Management and Organization
MOA
Management Operations Audit
Matrix Output Amplifier
Minute of Angle
Month of Arrival

MOAF
Meteorological and Oceanographic
Analyst/Forecaster (course)
MOAT
Missile on Aircraft Test
MOB
Main Operating Base
Make or Buy
MOB, MO
Mobile
MOBAS
Model Basin
MOBCON
Mobilization Construction (plan)
MOBCONBAT, MCB
(Naval) Mobile Construction Battalion
MOBCTR
Mobilization Center
MOBIDIC
Mobile Digital Computer
MOBIS
Management-Oriented Budget and
Information System
MOBL
Mobile Air Pollutants
MOBOT
Mobile Robot
MOBS
Mobile Ocean Basing System
MOBSUPPBASE, MSB
Mobile Support Base
MOBSUPPGRU, MSGP, MSGR
Mobile Support Group
MOBTR
Mobile Trainer
MOC
Mechanical, Operational, Clerical
Missile Operations Center
MOCA
Minimum Obstruction (or Obstacle) Clearance
Altitude
MOCAS
Mechanization of Contract Administrative
Services
MOCEM
Meteorological and Oceanographic
Equipment Maintenance (course)
MOCOM
Mobility Command
MOD
Mate of the Deck
Military Obligation Designator
Model
Modify
Modulator
Mobile Observation Chamber—called "Norris'
Nausea Machine" or "Semisubmersible
Seasick Machine"
Month and Calendar Year of Detachment
MOD, MDT
Moderate

MOD, MODN
Modification
MODE
Mid-Ocean Dynamics Experiment
Monitoring Overseas Direct Employment
MODEM
Modulator-Demodulator
MODG
Modifying
MODN, MOD
Modification
MODS
Material Ordering and Delivery Schedule
Military Orbital Development System
Models for Organizational Design and
Staffing
MOE
MAD Operational Effectiveness
Measure of Effectiveness
MOEP
Meteorological and Oceanographic
Equipment Program
MOF
Months of Operational Flying
MOG
Material-Ordering Guide
MOGAS, MGAS
Motor Gasoline
MOH
Medal of Honor
MOIC
Medical Officer-in-Charge
MOJT
Managed On-the-Job Training
MOL
Machine-Oriented Language
MOLAB
Mobile Laboratory
MOL/ACTS
Manned Orbiting Laboratory/Altitude Control
and Transmission System
MOLECOM
Molecularized Digital Chamber
MOM
"Man on the Move" (slang)
Military Overseas Mail
MOMAGDET
Mobile Mine Assembly Group Detachment
MOMAGU
Mobile Mine Assembly Group Unit
MOMAT
Mobile Mine Assembly Team
MOMATLANT
Mobile Mine Assembly Team, Atlantic
MOMATPAC
Mobile Mine Assembly Team, Pacific
MOMAU
Mobile Mine Assembly Unit
MOMAULANT
Mobile Mine Assembly Unit, Atlantic

MOMAULANTDETKEF
Mobile Mine Assembly Unit, Atlantic, Keflavik
(IC) Detachment
MOMAUPAC
Mobile Mine Assembly Unit, Pacific
MOMCOMS
Man-on-the-Move Communications
Mobile Mine Countermeasures Command
MOMISMAINTU
Mobile Missile Maintenance Unit
MOMP
Mid-Ocean Meeting Point
MOMS
Modified Operational Missile System
MON
Monitor
Monomoy Surfboat (USCG)
MONAB
Mobile Naval Air Base
MONIL
Mobile Non-Destructive Inspection Laboratory
MONOB
Mobile Noise Barge (sound laboratory)
MOON
Meeting Our Operating Needs
MOOW
Midshipman Officer-of-the-Watch
MOP
Magnetic Orange Pipe (mine decoy)
McNeil Oblique Plotting
Message Output Processor
Mustering Out Pay
MOPAR
Master Oscillator-Power Amplifier Radar
MOPSY
Modular Self-Paced Study
MOPTAR
Multi-Object Phase Tracking and Ranging
(system)
MOQ
Married Officer's Quarters
MOR
Management Operation Ratios
Medical Officer's Report
Missile Operationally Ready
M-O-R
Middle of the Road (AFRTS code)
MORE
Minority Officer Recruitment Effort
MOREST
Mobile Arresting (gear)
MORG
Movements Reports Generator
MORS
Military Operations Research Society
MORSEAFRON, MSF
Moroccan Sea Frontier
MORT
Master Operational Recording Tape
Mortar

MOS
Management Operating System
Marine Occupational Standard
Marking of Overseas Shipments
Master Operating System
Material Ordering Schedule
Metal-Oxide-Semiconductor
Military Occupational Specialty
MOSC
Military Oil Subcommittee (NAEB)
MOS/LSI
Metal-Oxide-Semiconductor/Large-Scale
Integration
MOSP
Master Ordnance System Pattern
Medical and Osteopathic Scholarship
Program
MOST
Mobile Optical Surveillance Tracker
MOSU
Mobile Ordnance Service Unit
MOSUPPU
Mobile Support Unit
MOT
Maximum Operating Time
Military Ocean Terminal
Motion
MOT, MO, MTR
Motor
MOTARDES
Moving Target Detection System
MOTARDIV
Mobile Target Division
MOTBA
Military Ocean Terminal, Bay
Area—pronounced "Moat-bah"
MOTBY
Military Ocean Terminal, Bayonne (NJ)
MOTECS
Mobile Tactical Exercise Control System
MOTG
Marine Operational Training Course
MOTNE
Meteorological Operational
Telecommunications Network, Europe
MOTOR
Monthly Throughput Observation Report
MOTSU
Military Ocean Terminal, Sunny Point
(Southport, NC)
MOTU
Mobile Ordnance Technical Unit
MOTUDET
Mobile Ordnance Technical Unit Detachment
MOU
Memorandum of Understanding
MOV
Material Obligation Validation
Metal Oxide Varistor
Move(ment)

MOVLAS
Manually-Operated, Visual Landing Aid
System
MOVREP
Movement Reports (system)
MOVSUM
(Daily) Movement Summary
MO-YR
Month and Year
MP
Main Propulsion
Maintenance Period
Manual Proportional (altitude control system)
Marching Pack
Maritime Polar (air mass)
Material Procurement
Military Police
Multiple Punch
M&P
Management and Plans (NTS)
MPA
Main Propulsion Assistant
MPAR
Maintainability Program Analysis Report
MPB
Merit Promotion Bulletin
MPC
Manpower Priorities Committee
Material Planning and Control
Maximum Permissible Concentration (of
radiation)
Military Payment Certificate
Multi-Purpose Communications (system)
MPCO
Military Police Company
MPCRI
Mercantile Pacific Coastal Routing
Instructions
MPD
Material Property Damage
Medical Pay Date
Military Priority Date
Movement Priority Designator
Multi-Purpose Display
MPDS
Message Processing and Distribution System
MPE
Maximum Permissible Exposure (to radiation)
Monthly Project Evaluation
MP-ER
Multiple Punch, Error Release
MPG
Main Propulsion Gear
Military Products Group
MPI
Mean Point of Impact
Military Procurement Intern
MPM
Maintenance Planning Manual
Major Program Memorandums
Message Processing Modules

MPMS
Missile Propulsion Maintenance School
MPN
Manufacturer's Part Number
Military Personnel, Navy
MPO
Motion Picture (or Projector) Operator
Mustering Petty Officer
MPOS
Movie Projector Operator's School
MPP
Master Program Plan
Merit Promotion Program
Military Pay Procedures
Most Probable Position
MPPLT
Military Police Platoon
MPR
Monthly Production Report
MPRL
Master Parts Reference List
MPS
Master Program Schedule
Material Planning Study
Mathematical Programming System
Merit Promotion System
Message Processing System
Miles per Second
Mission Profile Summary (airborne ASW)
Mobile Positioning Ship
MPSA
Military Petroleum Supply Agency
MPSC
Material Planning Schedule and Control
MPT
Main Propulsion Turbine
Manpower, Personnel and Training
MPU
Message Processing Unit
Missile Power Unit
MPUL
Military Production Urgencies List
MPWS
Mobile Protected Weapon System
MPX
Multiplexer
MQT
Military Qualification Test
MR
Maintenance Review
Material Report
Memory Reference (NNSS)
Migration Ratio
Milli-Roentgen (radiation dose)
Mobilization Regulations
Modification Request
Moon Rise (time)
MR, MAR
March
MR, MRG
Medium Range

MR1
Machinery Repairman First Class
MR2
Machinery Repairman Second Class
MR3
Machinery Repairman Third Class
M/R
Map Reading
Memorandum of Receipt
Morning (or Muster) Report
M&R
Maintenance and Repair
MRA
Minimum Reception Altitude
MRASTU
Marine Reserve Aviation Supply Training Unit
MRB
Material (or Modification) Review Board
Motor Rescue Boat (USCG)
Motor Surfboat (USCG)
MRBM
Medium-Range Ballistic Missile
MRC
Chief Machinery Repairman
Maintenance Record (or Requirements) Card
Maintenance Requirements for Continued
    Unrestricted Submarine Operations to
    Design Test Depth
Material Redistribution Center
Mathematics Research Center
Movement Report Center
MRCA
Multirole Combat Aircraft
MRCC
Movement Report Control Center
MRCI
Mine Readiness Certification Inspection
MRCM
Master Chief Machinery Repairman
MRCS
Senior Chief Machinery Repairman
MR&D
Material Redistribution and Disposal
MRDAC
Manpower Research and Data Analysis
    Center
MRDR
Material Receipt Discrepancy Record
MRDS
Malfunction Rate Detection System
MRE
Mean Radial Error
MREM
Milli-Roentgen-Equivalent Man (radiation
    standard)
MREP
Maneuvering Room Equipment Panel
Medical Remedial Enlistment Program
MRES
Material Requirements Estimation System
Multiple Reentry System

MRF
Maintenance Replacement (or Requirement)
    Factor
Module Repair Facility
MRFA
Machinery Repairman Fireman Apprentice
MRFN
Machinery Repairman Fireman
MRG, MR
Medium Range
MR/HR
Milli-Roentgens per Hour
MRI
Machine Records Installation
Minimum Release Interval
MRIL
Master Repair(ables) Item List
MRIR
Medium-Resolution Infrared Radiometer
MRIS
Material Readiness Index System
MRL
Master Range (or Repair) List
MRM
Manpower Reference Model
Medium-Range Missile
Miles of Relative Movement
MRMR
Mobilization Reserve Material Requirements
MRN
Meteorological Rocket Network
MRNG
Morning
MRO
Maintenance, Repair and Operating Supplies
Management Review Officer
Material Release Order
Mid-Range Objective
Minority Recruiting Officer
Movement Report Office
MRP
Malfunction Reporting Program
Material Reliability Program
Material Review Processing
Mid-Range Plan
Military Rated Power
MR/PA
Make Ready/Put Away
MPO
Military Post Office
MRPL
Material Requirements Planning List
MRR
Material Rejection Report
Military Rights and Responsibilities
    (workshop)
Mission Review Report
MRRC
Material Requirements Review Committee

MRS
Material Routing Sheet
Medium-Range Search (USCG aircraft)
Movement Report Sheet
MRT
Maintenance Readiness Training
Mean Active Repair Time
Medium-Range Typhoon (missile)
Military Rated Thrust
MRTFB
Major Range and Test Facility Base
MRTM
Maritime
MRU
Material Recovery Unit
Minimum Replacement Unit
MRV
Multiple Reentry Vehicle
MRWS
Mobile Radar Weather System
MS
Main Steam
Management Sciences
Medical Care, Uniformed Services
Medical Survey
Medium Setting (asphault)
Medium Speed
Medium Steel
Military Standards (or Service, or
    Specification)
Milliseconds
Motor Ship
M/S
Minesweeper
Minesweeping
M&S
Maintenance and Supply
M&S, BUMED, BUM&S
(Bureau of) Medicine and Surgery
MS1
Mess Management Specialist First Class
MS2
Mess Management Specialist Second Class
MS3
Mess Management Specialist Third Class
MSA
Medical Service Account
Minesweeper, Auxiliary
MS/A
Midship Abreast (stowage)
MSAL
Medical Surveillance Action Level
MSB
Maritime Subsidy Board (MARAD)
Merchant Ship Broadcast
Minesweeping Boat
Most Significant BIT
MSB, MOBSUPPBASE
Mobile Support Base

MSC
  Chief Mess Management Specialist
  Medical Service Corps
  Military Sealift (or Sea) Command
  Minesweeper, Coastal (Non-Magnetic)
  Mobile Satellite Communications (terminal)
MSCELM
  Military Sealift Command, Eastern Atlantic
    and Mediterranean
MSCFE
  Military Sealift Command, Far East
MSCI
  Mediterranean Secret Convoy Instructions
MSCLANT
  Military Sealift Command, Atlantic
MSCLANTDET
  Military Sealift Command, Atlantic
    Detachment
MSCM
  Master Chief Mess Management Specialist
MSCO
  Military Sealift Command Office
  Minesweeper, Coastal (Old)
MSCPAC
  Military Sealift Command, Pacific
M/S/CPO
  Master/Senior/Chief Petty Officer of the
    Command
MSCREP
  Military Sealift Command Representative
MSCS
  Merchant Ship Control Office
  Senior Chief Mess Management Specialist
MSCSO
  Military Sealift Command Service Office
MSCSO-M&R
  Military Sealift Command Service
    Office-Maintenance and Repair
MSCSO-OCPO
  Military Sealift Command Service
    Office-Operations Cargo Passenger Office
MSCSO-SA
  Military Sealift Command Service
    Office-Supply Assistant
MSCU
  Military Sealift Command Unit
MSD
  Marine Sanitation Device
  Material Sciences Division (ONR)
  Metering Suction Differential
  Minesweeping Drone
MSDG
  Multi-Sensor Display Group
MSDI
  Modified Ship's Drawing Index
MSDO
  Management System Development Office
MSDV
  Marine Sanitation Device
MSER
  Management System Evaluation Force

MSF
  Minesweeper, Fleet (Steel-Hulled)
  Mobile Strike Force
MS/F
  Midship Forward (stowage)
MSG
  Message
MSGBN
  Marine Security Guard Battalion
MSGCEN
  Message Center
MSGDET
  Marine Security Guard Detachment
MSGO
  Mediterranean Secret General Orders
MSGP, MOBSUPPGRU, MSGR
  Mobile Support Group
MSGR, MOBSUPPGRU, MSGP
  Mobile Support Group
MSGR
  Messenger
MSGT
  Master Sergeant
MSH
  Mine Hunter (ship)
MSI
  Medium Scale Integration
  Minesweeper, Inshore
MSIIP
  Missile Systems Installation Interruption for
    Parts
MSIO
  Mass Storage Input/Output (system)
MSIR
  Master Stock Item Record
MSL
  Master Slave Unit
  Mean Sea Level
  Minesweeping Launch
MSL, MIS
  Missile
MSLP
  Mean Sea Level Pressure
MSM
  Medium Minesweeper (Steel-Hulled)
  Minesweeper, River
MS/MS
  Mutual Security/Military Sales
MSN
  Military Service Number
  Mission
MSNAP
  Merchant Ship Naval Auxiliary Program
MSNCDRFAIRECONRON
  Mission Commander, Fleet Air
    Reconnaissance Squadron
MSN/SSN
  Military Service Number/Social Security
    Number

MSO
Maintenance Support Office
Minesweeper, Ocean (Non-Magnetic)
MSOP
Measurement System Operating Procedure
MSP
Maintenance Support Package
Medium-Speed Printer
Minesweeper, Patrol
Multi-Purpose Semi-Submersible Platform
MSPFW
Multi-Shot Portable Flame Weapon
MSPO
Military Support Planning Officers
MSR
Main Supply Route
Management Summary Report
Master Stock Records
Material (or Monthly) Status Report
Missile Site Radar
MS/RM
Manned Storage/Retrieval Machine
MSRT
Mean Supply Response Time
MSS
Manager, System Safety
Military Supply Standard
Minesweeper, Special (Device)
Moored Surveillance System
Multiple Secondaries and Selection
MSSA
Mess Management Specialist Seaman
  Apprentice
Military Subsistence Supply Agency
MSSC
Medium SEAL Support Craft
MSSG
Management System Steering Group
Marine Amphibious Unit Service Support
  Group
MSSN
Mess Management Specialist Seaman
MST
Missile Supply Standard
Missile System Test
Mobile Service Tower
MSTP
Management Specialist Trainee Program
MSU
Material Salvage Unit
Message-Switching Unit
MSV
Multisensor Viewer
MSW
Main Sea Water
MT
Magnetic Particle Test
Manufacturing Technology
Maritime Tropical (air mass)
Military (or Motor) Transport
Mount

MT1
Missile Technician First Class
MT2
Missile Technician Second Class
MT3
Missile Technician Third Class
M/T
Measurement Ton
MTA
MAC Transportation Authorization
Military Technical Advisor
Minimum Terrain Clearance
Minor Task Authorization
MTAG
Manufacturing Technology Advisory Group
MTB
Maintenance of True Bearing
Marine Test Boat
Motor Torpedo Boat
MTBCM
Mean Time Between Corrective Maintenance
MTBER
Mean Time Between Engine Removal
MTBF
Mean Time Between Failures
MTBMA
Mean Time Between Maintenance Actions
MTBN
Motor Transport Battalion
MTBPER
Mean Time Between Permanent Engine
  Removal
MTC
Chief Missile Technician
Military Terminal Control
MTCA
Military Terminal Control Area
MTD
Maintenance Training Department
Moving (or Mobile) Target Division
MTDS
Maritime (or Marine Corps) Tactical Data
  System
MTDT
Magnetic Tape Data Terminal
MTE
Multi-System Test Equipment
MTF
Mechanized Time (or Type) Fuze
Medical Treatment Facility
MTFI
Mean Time to Fault Isolate
MTGA
Mean Time to Gain Access
MTI
Moving-Target Indicator
MTIS
Material Turned In to Store (or Stock)
MTK
Medium Tank

MTL
Maintenance Test Logic
Mean Tide Level
MTM
Methods Time Measurements
MTMAINTCO
Motor Maintenance Company
MTMTS
Military Traffic Management and Terminal
Services
MTMTS-TSP
Military Traffic Management and Terminal
Service Transportation Strike Plan
MTNS
Metal Thick Nitrite Semiconductor
MTO
Medical Transport Officer
Mission, Task, Objective
MTOAL
Mobilization Table of Allowance Listing
MTP
Master Typography Program
Multipoint
MTPCP
MANTRAPERS Plan Coordination Panel
MTPM
Mean Time to Provide Manpower
MTR
Manpower Training and Recruitment
Mean Time to Restore
Missile Tracking Radar
MTR, MO, MOT
Motor
MTRE
Missile Test and Readiness Equipment
MTS
Missile Test Set
MTST
Meter Test (NNSS)
MT/ST
Magnetic Tape/Selectric Typewriter (system)
MTT
(Steam Propulsion) Mobile Training Team
MTTF
Mean Time to Failure
MTTFF
Mean Time to First Failure
MTTR
Mean Time to Repair
MTTRM
Mean Time to Repair Module
MTU
Magnetic Tape Unit
Maintenance Training Unit
Missile Tracking Unit
Mobile Technical (or Training) Unit
MTUN
Manual Receiver Tuning Control (NNSS)
MTV
Marginal Terrain Vehicle

MTWR
Mean Waiting Time for Supply Replacement
MTX
Military Traffic Expediting
MU1
Musician First Class
MU2
Musician Second Class
MU3
Musician Third Class
MUACS
Manpower Utilization and Control System
MUC
Chief Musician
Meritorious Unit Commendation
MUCM
Master Chief Musician
MUCS
Senior Chief Musician
MUF
Maximum Usable Frequency
MUL
Master Urgency List
MULTEWS
Multiple-Target Electronic Warfare System
MULTICS
Multiple Information and Computing Service
MULTOTS
Multiple Unit Link-Test and Operational
Training System
MUNBLDG
Munitions Building
MURS
Machine Utilization Reporting System
MUS
Music(ian)
MUSA
Musician Seaman Apprentice
MUSE
Mobile Utilities Support Equipment
MUSEDET
Mobile Utilities Support Equipment
Detachment
MUSG
Machine Utilization Report Generator
MUSN
Musician Seaman
MUST
Medical Unit, Self-Contained, Transportable
Medical Unit Surgical Team
MUS&T, MUST
Manned Undersea Science and Technology
(program, NOAA)
MUTR
Makai Undersea Test Range
MUX
Multiplexing (equipment)
MUXIC
Multiplex/Multiple Voice Interior
Communications (system)

MV
  Motor Vehicle Mishap (report)
  Motor Vessel
M/V
  Merchant Vessel
MVDF
  Direction Finder (Medium and Very High
    Frequency)
MVI
  Maximum Visual Impact
  Merchant Vessel Inspection (Division)
MVO
  Money Value Only
MW
  Music of the World (AFRTS code)
MWB
  Motor Whaleboat
MWBS
  Manufacturing Work Breakdown Structure
MWCS
  Marine Wing Communications Squadron
MWDDEA
  Mutual Weapons Development Data
    Exchange Agreement
MWDDEP
  Mutual Weapons Development Data
    Exchange Program
MWE
  Mega-Watts-Electrical
MWFCS
  Multiweapons Fire Control System
MWHS
  Marine Wing Headquarters Squadron
MWHSDET
  Marine Wing Headquarters Squadron
    Detachment
MWL
  Mean Water Level
MWO
  Meteorological Watch Office
  Modified Work Order
MWP
  Management Work Package
MWR, MW&R
  Morale, Welfare and Recreation (department,
    division or funds)
MWSG
  Marine Wing Support Group
MWSGDET
  Marine Wing Support Group Detachment
MWWU
  Marine Wing Weapons Unit
MY
  May
MYDIS
  My Dispatch
MYLTR
  My Letter
MYMGM
  My Mailgram

MYMSG
  My Message
MYP
  Multi-Year Procurement
MYRAD
  My Radio
MYSER
  My Serial
MYSPDLTR
  My Speedletter
MYTEL
  My Telegram

N

N
  Naturalization
  Navigation (NAO code)
N, (N)
  Nuclear-power(ed)
N, NAV
  Navy
N, NOR
  North(ern)
NA
  National Archives
  Naval Attaché
  Naval Aviator
  Not Authorized
NA, N/A
  Not Applicable (or Available)
NA, NAC, NAVACD
  Naval Academy
NA, NAM
  North American
NA, NAVAIR
  Naval Air
NAA
  Naval Attaché for Air
NAAF
  Naval Auxiliary Air Field
NAALS
  Naval Air Traffic Control and Air Navigation
    Aids and Landing System
NAAO, NAVAREAUDOFC
  Navy Area Audit Office
NAAS
  Naval Auxiliary Air Station
NAAS, NAVAREAUDSERV
  Navy Area Audit Service
NAASW
  Non-Acoustic Antisubmarine Warfare
NAB
  Naval Advanced (or Air) Base
NAB, NAMB, NAVPHIBASE
  Naval Amphibious Base
NABA
  Naval Amphibious Base Annex

NABPARS
Navy Automatic Broadcasting Processing and
Routing System
NABS
Nuclear-Armed Bombardment Satellite
**NABTC, NABTRACOM,
NAVAIRBASICTRACOM**
Naval Air Basic Training Command
**NABTRACOM, NABTC,
NAVAIRBASICTRACOM**
Naval Air Basic Training Command
NABU
Naval Advanced Base Unit
NAC
National Agency Check
Naval Air Center
Navy Activity Control
Navy Advanced Concepts
NAC, NA, NAVACD
Naval Academy
NACAL
Navy Art Cooperation and Liaison
(committee)
NACF
New Air Combat Fighter
NACIO
Naval Air Combat Information Office(r)
NACIS
Naval Air Combat Information School
NACL
Navy (D) ARPA Chemical Laser
NACO
National Advisory Committee for Oceans
(NOAA)
Navy Cool (propellant)
NACOA
National Advisory Committee on Oceans and
Atmosphere (NOAA)
NACSB
Naval Aviation Cadet Selection Board
NACTU
Naval Attack Combat Training Unit
NAD
Naval Air Detachment (or Detail, or Depot)
NAD, NAVAMMODEP
Naval Ammunition Depot
NADC, NAVAIRDEVCEN
Naval Air Development Center
NADC/ACEL
Naval Air Development Center/Aerospace
Crew Equipment Laboratory
NADC/ACL
Naval Air Development Center/Aeronautical
Computer Laboratory
NADC/AML
Naval Air Development Center/Aeronautical
Materials Laboratory
NADC/ASL
Naval Air Development Center/Aeronautical
Structures Laboratory

NADC/ED
Naval Air Development Center/Engineering
Development Laboratory
NADEC
Navy Decision Center
NADGE
NATO Air Defense Ground Equipment
(project)
NADL
Naval Authorized Data List
NAD-LLL
Naval Ammunition Depot-Lwalualei (HI)
NADM
Naval Administration
NADO
Navy Accounts Disbursing Office
NADOP
North American Defense Operational Plan
NADPHRS
Naval Ammunition Depot Hawthorne Police
Records System
NADU
Naval Aircraft Delivery Unit
NAEB
Naval Aviation Evaluation Board
NAEC, NAVAIRENGRCEN
Naval Air Engineering Center
NAECFO, NAVAIRENGRCENFO
Naval Air Engineering Center Field Office
NAEL, NAVAIRENGLAB
Naval Air Engineering Laboratory
NAEL(SI)
Naval Air Engineering Laboratory (Ships
Installation)
NAES
Naval Air Experimental Station
NAESU, NAVAVNENGRSERVU
Naval Aviation Engineering Service Unit
NAESUDET, NAVAVENGSERVUDET
Naval Aviation Engineering Service Unit
Detachment
NAF
Naval Aircraft Factory
Non-Appropriated Funds
NAF, NAVAIRFAC
Naval Air Facility
NAFAS
Non-Appropriated Fund Accounting System
(section)
NAFC
Naval Air Ferry Command
Navy Accounting and Finance Center
NAFEC
National Aviation Facilities Experimental
Center
NAFI
Naval Air Fighting Instructions
Naval Avionics Facility, Indianapolis (IN)
Non-Appropriated Fund Instrumentalities
NAFL, NAVAIRLANT
Naval Air Force, Atlantic

NAFMC
Non-Appropriated Funds, Marine Corps
NAFP, NAVAIRPAC
Naval Air Force, Pacific
NAFS
Naval Air Fighter School
NAFSA
No American Flag Shipping Available
NAG
Naval Advisory Group
NAG, NAVASTRGRU
Navy Astronautics Group
NAGARD
NATO Advisory Group for Aeronautical
Research and Development
NAGC
Naval Armed Guard Center
NAGCO
Naval Air-Ground Center Office
NAGS
Naval Air Gunner's School
NAICOM/MIS
Navy Integrated Command Management
Information System
NAILSC
Naval Aviation Integrated Logistic Support
Center
NAIMIS
NAVAIRSYSCOM Integrated Management
Information System
NAIRU
Naval Air Reserve Intelligence Unit
NAIS
Navy Attitudinal Information System
NAIT
Naval Air Intermediate Training
NAIT(C)
Naval Air Intermediate Training (Command)
NALC
Navy Ammunition Logistic Code
NALCO
Naval Air Logistics Control Office
NALCOEASTPAC
Naval Air Logistics Control Office, Eastern
Pacific
NALCOEURREP
Naval Air Logistics Control Office, European
Representative
NALCOLANT
Naval Air Logistics Control Office, Atlantic
NALCOMIS
Naval Air Logistics Command Management
Information System
NALCOMIS-OS
Naval Air Logistics Command Management
Information System for Operating and
Support
NALCOPAC
Naval Air Logistics Control Office, Pacific

NALCOPACREP
Naval Air Logistics Control Office, Pacific
Representative
NALCOREP
Naval Air Logistics Control Office
Representative
NALCOWESTPAC
Naval Air Logistics Control Office, Western
Pacific
NALCOWESTPACREP
Naval Air Logistics Control Office, Western
Pacific Representative
NALF
Naval Auxiliary Landing Field (or Facility)
NALO
Naval Air Liaison Officer
NALO, NAVAIRLOGOFF
Naval Air Logistics Office
NALTS
National Advertising Lead Tracking System
NAM
Naval Aircraft Modification
NAM, NA
North America(n)
NAMA
Naval Aeronautical Material Area
NAMAINTRADET, NAMTD, NAMTRADET
Naval Air Maintenance Training Detachment
NAMAINTRAGRU, NAMTG, NAMTRAGRU
Naval Air Maintenance Training Group
NAMAPUS
Naval Assistant to the Military Aide to the
President of the United States
NAMARA
Navy and Marine Corps Appellate Review
Activity
NAMB, NAB, NAVPHIBASE
Naval Amphibious Base
NAMC
Naval Air and Material Center
NAMD
Naval Ammunition Depot
NAMDDU, NAVAIRMINEDEFDEVU
Navy Air Mine Defense Development Unit
NAMDI
National Marine Data Inventory
NAMDRP
Naval Aviation Maintenance Discrepancy
Reporting Program
NAMEDCEN, NAVAVMEDCEN
Naval Aviation Medical Center
NAMESAKES
Naval Aviators Must Energetically Sell
Aviation to Keep Effective Strength
NAMF
Naval Aviation Museum Foundation
NAMFI
NATO Missile Firing Installation
NAMI, NAVAERO(SP)MEDINST
Naval Aerospace Medical Institute

NAMMOS
Navy Manpower Mobilization System
NAMO
Naval Aircraft Maintenance Orders
NAMP
Naval Aviation Maintenance Program
NAMPS
Naval Manpower Planning System
NAMRI, NAVAERO(SP)MEDRSCHINST
Naval Aerospace Medical Research Institute
NAMRL, NAVAERO(SP)MEDRSCHINSTLAB
Naval Aerospace Medical Research Institute
Laboratory
NAMRU, NAVMEDRSCHU
Navy Medical Research Unit
NAMS, NAVPHIBSCOL
Naval Amphibious School
NAMSO, NAVMAINTSUPPO
Naval Maintenance Support Office
NAMT
Naval Air Maintenance Trainer
Naval Aircraft Mobile Trainer
NAMTD, NAMAINTRADET, NAMTRADET
Naval Air Maintenance Training Detachment
NAMTG, NAMAINTRAGRU, NAMTRAGRU
Naval Air Maintenance Training Group
NAMTGD, NAMAINTRAGRUDET,
NAMTRAGRUDET
Naval Air Maintenance Training Group
Detachment
NAMTRA
Naval Air Maintenance Training (or Trainer)
NAMTRADET, NAMAINTRADET, NAMTD
Naval Air Maintenance Training Detachment
NAMTRAGRU, NAMAINTRAGRU, NAMTG
Naval Air Maintenance Training Group
NAMTRAGRUDET, NAMAINTRAGRUDET,
NAMTGD
Naval Air Maintenance Training Group
Detachment
NAMTRATCLOFLT
Naval Air Maintenance Training Type
Commander Liaison Office, Fleet
NAMTRATCLOLANT
Naval Air Maintenance Training Type
Commander Liaison Officer, Atlantic
NAMTRATCLOPAC
Naval Air Maintenance Training Type
Commander Liaison Office, Pacific
NAMU
Naval Aircraft Material (Utility)
Naval Aircraft Modification Unit
NANCF
North Atlantic Naval Coastal Frontier
NAND
Inverted Output AND
NANEWS, NAVAIRNEWS
Naval Aviation News (magazine)
NANFAC
Naval Air Navigation Facility Advisory
Committee

NANFORMS
Naval Aviator/Naval Flight Officer Reporting
Management System
NANS
Naval Air Navigation School
NANWEP
Navy Numerical Weather Problems Group
NAO
Naval Aviation Observer
NSA and APA Items for Overseas Shipment
NAO, NAVAUDO
Navy Audit Office
NAOC
Naval Aviation Officer Candidate
NAOT
Naval Air Operational Training
NAOTC
Naval Air Operational Training Center
NAOTS
Naval Aviation Ordnance Test Station
NAP
Naval Academy Prepatory (student)
"Naval Airplane Pusher" (slang)
Naval Air Priorities
Naval Aviation Pilot
NAPC
Naval Air Photographic Center
Naval Air Priorities Center
NAPC, NAVAIRPROPCEN
Naval Air Propulsion Center
NAPEC, NAVAMPROENGCEN
Naval Ammunition Production Engineering
Center
NAPF
Non-Appropriated Funds
NAPI
Naval Aeronautical Publications Index
NAPOG
Naval Airborne Project PRESS Operations
Group
NAPP
Naval Aviation Preparatory Program
NAPS
National Auxiliary Publications Service
Naval Academy Preparatory School
NAPSAC
Naval Atomic Planning, Support and
Capabilities
NAPT
Naval Air Primary Training
NAPTC, NAVAIRPROPTESTCEN
Naval Air Propulsion Test Center
NAPT(C)
Naval Air Primary Training (Command)
NAPTCRO
Naval Air Primary Training Command
Regional Office
NAPUS
Nuclear Auxiliary Power Unit System

NAR
Naval Air Reserve
Notice of Ammunition Reclassification
Numerical Analysis Research
NARAD
Naval Air Research and Development
(briefing report)
NARANEXOS
Name, Rate, Social Security Number and
Expiration of Obligated Service
NARANO
Name, Rate and Social Security Number
NARASPO
Naval Regional Airspace Officer
NARB
Navy Art Review Board
NARC, NAVAIRESCEN
Naval Air Research Center
NARC, NAVALREHCEN
Naval Alcohol Rehabilitation Center
NARD, NAVALREHDRYDOCK
Navy Alcohol Rehabilitation Drydock
NARDAC
Navy Regional Data Automation Center
NARDACWASHDC
Navy Regional Data Automation Center,
Washington, District of Columbia
NARDET
Naval Air Reserve Detachment
NARDIS
Navy Automated Research and Development
Information System
NARDIV(FA)
Naval Air Reserve Division (Fleet Air)
NAREC
Naval Research Electronic Computer
NARESU, NAVAIRESU, NARU
Naval Air Reserve Unit
NARETU
Naval Air Reserve Electronics Training Unit
NARF, NAVAEROSPRECFAC
Navy Aerospace Recovery Facility
NARF, NAVAIRREWORKFAC
Naval Air Rework Facility
NARFFO, NAVAIRREWORKFACFO
Naval Air Rework Facility Field Office
NARFS, NAVAIRESFORRON
Naval Air Reserve Force Squadron
NARL
Naval Arctic Research Laboratory (ONR)
NARM
Naval Resource Model
NARMPU, NAVAIRESMOPIXU
Naval Air Reserve Mobile Photographic Unit
NARMU
Naval Air Reserve Maintenance Unit
NARS
National Archives and Records Service
Naval Air Reserve Staff
NARSTC
Naval Air Rescue Service Training Command

NARTC, NARESTRACOM
Naval Air Reserve Training Command
NARTS
Naval Air Rocket Test Station
NARTU, NAVAIRESTRAU
Naval Air Rescue Training Unit
NARU, NAVAIRESU, NARESU
Naval Air Reserve Unit
NAS
National Aeronautical Studies
National Aerospace System
Naval Aircraft Standard
NSA and APA Items for Stateside Shipment
NAS, NAVAIRSTA
Naval Air Station
NAS, NAVAUDSVC
Navy Audit Service
NASA
National Aeronautics and Space
Administration
NASANX
Naval Air Station Annex
NASAP
Navy Alcohol Safety Action Program
NASAPOFF
Navy Alcohol Safety Action Program Office
NASC
Naval Aircraft Standards Committee
NASC, NAVAIR, NAVAIRSYSCOM
Naval Air Systems Command
NASC, NAVAUDODINSCEN
Navy AUTODIN Switching Center
NASC FS
Naval Air Systems Command Fleet Support
NASCOM
NASA Communications (network)
NASCRU
Naval Air Systems Command Reserve Unit
NASD
Naval Air Supply Depot
NASDT
Naval Aviators' Speed Discrimination Test
NASEAB
Naval Air Systems Effectiveness Advisory
Board
NASIB
Naval Air Station, Imperial Beach (CA)
NASL, NASLEM
Naval Air Station, Lemoore (CA)
NASL, NAVAPSCIENLAB
Naval Applied Sciences Laboratory
NASLEM, NASL
Naval Air Station, Lemoore (CA)
NASMAGS
Naval Air Station Magazines
NASNI
Naval Air Station, North Island (CA)
NASO
National Aeronautics and Space Observatory
NASO, NAVASO
Naval Aviation Supply Office

NASP
Naval Air Survivability Program
NASRU
Naval Air Systems Command Reserve Unit
NASS
Naval Air Signal School
NASTAD
Naval Acoustic Sensor Training Aids
Department
NASTC
Naval Air Station, Twin Cities (MN)
NASU, NAVAIRSUPPU
Naval Air Support Unit
NAT
Natural
Naval Air Training
Naval Anthropomorphic Teleoperator (slave
arms)
Navigational Aids Technician
North Atlantic (regional area)
NAT, NATL
National
NAT, NAVAIRTERM
Naval Air Terminal
NATB, NATBASE
Naval Air Training Base
NATBASE, NATB
Naval Air Training Base
NATC, NATRACOM
Naval Air Training Command
NATC, NAVAIRTESTCEN
Naval Air Test Center
NATC, NAVAIRTRACEN
Naval Air Training Center
NATCO
Naval Air Traffic Coordinating Office
NATDEC, NATRADIVENGCOM
Naval Air Training Division Engineering
Command
NATDS
Navy Automated Transportation Data System
NATEC
Naval Air Training and Experimental
Command
NATECHTRA, NATT
Naval Air Technical Training
NATECHTRACEN, NATTC
Naval Air Technical Training Center
NATF(SI), NAVAIRTESTFAC(SHIPINSTAL)
Naval Air Test Facility (Ships Installation)
NATIP
Navy Technical Information Program
NATL, NAT
National
NATMILCOMSYS
National Military Commands System
NATNAVDENCEN, NNDC
National Naval Dental Center
NATNAVMEDCEN, NNMC
National Naval Medical Center

NATNAVRESMASTCONRADSTA
National Naval Reserve Master Control Radio
Station
NATO
North Atlantic Treaty Organization
NATODC, NATODEFCOL
North Atlantic Treaty Organization Defense
College
NATODEFCOL, NATODC
North Atlantic Treaty Organization Defense
College
NATOPS
Naval Air Training and Operating Procedures
Standardization
NATRA, NATRACOM, NATC
Naval Air Training Command
NATRACOM, NATC, NATRA
Naval Air Training Command
NATRADIVENGCOM, NATDEC
Naval Air Training Division Engineering
Command
NATRI
Naval Training Requirements Information
NATSF, NAVAIRTECHSERVFAC
Naval Air Technical Services Facility
NATSFQADIVLANT
Naval Air Technical Services Facility Quality
Assurance Division, Atlantic
NATSFQADIVPAC
Naval Air Technical Services Facility Quality
Assurance Division, Pacific
NATT, NATECHTRA
Naval Air Technical Training
NATTC, NATECHTRACEN
Naval Air Technical Training Center
NATTCL
Naval Air Technical Training Center,
Lakehurst (NJ)
NATTCDET, NATECHTRACENDET
Naval Air Technical Training Center
Detachment
NATTS
Naval Air Turbine Test Station
NATTS/ATL
Naval Air Turbine Test Station/Aeronautical
Turbine Laboratory
NATTU, NATECHTRAU
Naval Air Technical Training Unit
NATU, NAVAIRTU
Naval Air Training Unit
NATUS
Naturalized United States Citizen
NATW, NATWARCOL
National War College
NATWARCOL, NATWC
National War College
NAU, NAVADMINU
Naval Administration Unit
NAUT
Nautical

NAUTO
Nautophone
NAUWS, NAVADUNSEAWPNSCOL
Naval Advanced Underseas Weapons School
NAV
Naval
NAV, N
Navy
NAV, NAVIG
Navigation
NAVABSCOLLU
Navy Absentee Collection Unit
NAVACCTGFINCEN, NAFC
Navy Accounting and Finance Center
NAVACD, NA, NAC
Naval Academy
NAVACT
Naval Activities
NAVACTDET
Naval Activities Detachment
NAVADGRU
Navy Administrative Group
NAV-ADMIN
Navigation-Administration (inquiry program)
NAVADMINCOM
Naval Administrative Command
NAVADMINO
Navy Administrative Office(r)
NAVADMINU, NAU
Naval Administration Unit
NAVADMINUANX
Naval Administrative Unit Annex
NAVADS
Navy Automated Transport Documentation
System
NAVADUNSEAWPNSCOL, NAUWS
Naval Advanced Undersea Weapons School
NAVAERAUDOFC, NAAO
Navy Area Audit Office
NAVAERAUDSERV, NAAS
Navy Area Audit Service
NAVAERO(SP)RECFAC, NARF
Naval Aerospace Recovery Facility
NAVAERO(SP)MEDINST, NAMI
Naval Aerospace Medical Institute
NAVAERO(SP)MEDRSCHINST, NAMRI
Naval Aerospace Medical Research Institute
NAVAERO(SP)MEDRSCHLAB, NAMRL
Naval Aerospace Medical Research
Laboratory
NAVAERO(SP)MEDRSCHLABDET
Naval Aerospace Medical Research
Laboratory Detachment
NAVAERO(SP)REGMEDCEN, NARMC
Naval Aerospace Medical Center
NAVAIDE
Naval Aide
NAVAIDS
Navigational Aids
NAVAIDSUPPUNIT
Navigational Aids Support Unit

NAVAIR, NA
Naval Air
NAVAIR, NASC, NAVAIRSYSCOM
Naval Air Systems Command
**NAVAIRBASICTRACOM, NABTRACOM,
NABTC**
Naval Air Basic Training Command
NAVAIRDEVCEN, NADC
Naval Air Development Center
NAVAIRENGCEN, NAEC
Naval Air Engineering Center
NAVAIRENGCENFO, NAECFO
Naval Air Engineering Center Field Office
NAVAIRENGLAB, NAEL
Naval Air Engineering Laboratory
NAVAIRESCEN, NARC
Naval Air Reserve Center
NAVAIRESMOPIXU, NARMPU
Naval Air Reserve Mobile Photographic Unit
NAVAIREWORKFAC, NARF
Naval Air Rework Facility
NAVAIREWORKFACOFF, NARFO
Naval Air Rework Facility Office
NAVAIRFAC, NAF
Naval Air Facility
NAVAIRLANT, NAFL
Naval Air Forces, Atlantic
NAVAIRLOGOFF, NALO
Naval Air Logistics Office
NAVAIRLOGTASKFORREP
Naval Air Logistics Task Force
Representative
NAVAIRMAINTRADET, NAMTD
Naval Air Maintenance Training Detachment
NAVAIRMAINTRAGRU, NAMTG
Naval Air Maintenance Training Group
NAVAIRMINDEFDEVU, NAMDDU
Naval Air Mine Defense Development Unit
NAVAIRNEWS, NANEWS
Naval Aviation News (publication)
NAVAIRPAC, NAFP
Naval Air Forces, Pacific
NAVAIRPROPCEN, NAPC
Naval Air Propulsion Center
NAVAIRPROPTESTCEN, NAPTC
Naval Air Propulsion Test Center
NAVAIRESFORRON, NARFS
Naval Air Reserve Force Squadron
NAVAIRESU, NARESU, NARU
Naval Air Reserve Unit
NAVAIRSTA, NAS
Naval Air Station
NAVAIRSUPPU
Naval Air Support Unit
NAVAIRSYSCOM, NASC, NAVAIR
Naval Air Systems Command
NAVAIRSYSCOMFLEREADREP
Naval Air Systems Command Fleet
Readiness Representative

NAVAIRSYSCOMFLESUPREPCEN
Naval Air Systems Command Fleet Supply
Representative Center
NAVAIRSYSCOMHQ
Naval Air Systems Command Headquarters
NAVAIRSYSCOMMETSYSDIV
Naval Air Systems Command Meteorological
Systems Division
NAVAIRSYSCOMREP
Naval Air Systems Command Representative
NAVAIRSYSCOMREPLANT
Naval Air Systems Command Representative,
Atlantic
NAVAIRSYSCOMREPPAC
Naval Air Systems Command Representative,
Pacific
NAVAIRSYSCOMREPPNCLA
Naval Air Systems Command Representative,
Pensacola (FL)
NAVAIRSYSCOMTARANDSYSDIV
Naval Air Systems Command Target and
Range Systems Command
NAVAIRTECHREP
Naval Air Systems Command Technical
Representative
NAVAIRTECHSERVFAC, NATSF
Naval Air Technical Services Facility
NAVAIRTERM, NAT
Naval Air Terminal
NAVAIRTESTCEN, NATC
Naval Air Test Center
NAVAIRTESTFAC(SHIPINSTAL), NATF(SI)
Naval Air Test Facility (Ship Installation)
NAVAIRTRACEN, NATC
Naval Air Training Center
NAVAIRTU, NATU
Naval Air Training Unit
NAVALREHCEN, NARC
Naval Alcohol Rehabilitation Center
NAVALREHDRYDOCK, NARD
Navy Alcohol Rehabilitation Drydock
NAVALT
Navy Ship Alteration
NAVAMMODEP, NAD
Naval Ammunition Depot
NAVAMPROENGCEN, NAPEC
Naval Ammunition Production Engineering
Center
NAVAPSCIENCLAB, NASL
Naval Applied Sciences Laboratory
NAVARA
Navy Appellate Review Activity
NAVAREAUDSVC, NAAS
Naval Area Audit Service
NAVASO, NASO
Naval Aviation Supply Office
NAVASTROGRU, NAG
Naval Astronautics Group
NAVASTROGRUHQTRINJFAC
Navy Astronautics Group Headquarters,
Tracking and Injection Facility

NAVASWDATCEN
Navy Antisubmarine Warfare Data Center
NAVAUDO, NAO
Naval Audit Office
NAVAUDSVC, NAS
Naval Audit Service
NAVAUDSVCAP
Naval Audit Service, Capital Area
NAVAUDSVCHQ
Naval Audit Service Headquarters
NAVAUDSVCNE
Naval Audit Service, Northeast Area
NAVAUDSVCSE
Naval Audit Service, Southeast Area
NAVAUDSVCWEST
Naval Audit Service, Western Area
NAVAUTODINSCEN, NASC
Navy AUTODIN Switching Center
NAVAVCEN, NAVC
Naval Audio-Visual Center
NAVAVENGSERVU, NAESU
Naval Aviation Engineering Services Unit
NAVAVIONICSCEN
Naval Avionics Center
NAVAVIONICSFAC
Naval Avionics Facility
NAVAVMUSEUM
Naval Aviation Museum
NAVAVNLOGCEN
Naval Aviation Logistics Center
NAVAVNLOGCENDET
Naval Aviation Logistics Center Detachment
NAVAVNLOGCENFSO
Naval Aviation Logistics Center Field Service
Office
NAVAVNLOGCENMETALABOPS
Naval Aviation Logistics Center Meteorology
Calibration Laboratory Operations
NAVAVNMEDCEN, NAMEDCEN
Naval Aviation Medical Center
NAVAVNWPNSFAC
Naval Aviation Weapons Facility
NAVAVNWPNSFACDET
Naval Aviation Weapons Facility Detachment
NAVAVSCOLSCOM
Naval Aviation Schools Command
NAVBASE, NB
Naval Base
NAVBCHGRU, NBG
Naval Beach Group
NAVBCHPHIBREFTRAGRU
Navy Beach Amphibious Refresher Training
Group
NAVBCSTSVCDET
Navy Broadcasting Service Detachment
NAVBCSTSVCDET TASA
Navy Broadcasting Service Detachment
Television Audio Support Activity
NAVBCSTSVCWASHDC
Navy Broadcasting Service, Washington,
District of Columbia

NAVBIODYNLAB
Naval Biodynamics Laboratory
NAVBIOLAB, NABL
Navy Biological Laboratory (ONR)
NAVBIOSCILAB
Naval Biosciences Research Laboratory
NAV, NAVCAD
Naval Aviation Cadet
NAVC, NAVAVCEN
Naval Audio-Visual Center
NAVCAD, NAVC
Naval Aviation Cadet
NAVCALAB
Navy Calibration Laboratory
NAVCALABANX
Navy Calibration Laboratory Annex
NAVCALABMSG
Navy Calibration Laboratory Meteorology
Support Group
NAVCALABOPS
Navy Calibration Laboratory Operations
NAVCALS
Naval Communications Area Local Station
NAVCAMS
Naval Communication Area Master Station
NAVCAMSEASTPAC
Naval Communication Area Master Station,
Eastern Pacific
NAVCAMSLANT
Naval Communication Area Master Station,
Atlantic
NAVCAMSMED
Naval Communications Area Master Station,
Mediterranean
NAVCAMSSPECCOMMDIVEASTPAC
Naval Communication Area Master Station,
Special Communications Division, Eastern
Pacific
NAVCAMSSPECCOMMDIVLANT
Naval Communication Area Master Station,
Special Communications Division, Atlantic
NAVCAMSSPECCOMMDIVWESTPAC
Naval Communication Area Master Station,
Special Communications Division, Western
Pacific
NAVCAMSWESTPAC
Naval Communication Area Master Station,
Western Pacific
NAVCAMSWESTPACRCVRSITE
Naval Communication Area Master Station,
Western Pacific Receiver Site
NAVCAMSOAM
Naval Communication Area Master Station,
South America
NAVCARGOHANBN
Naval Cargo Handling Battalion
NAVCBCEN, NCBC
Naval Construction Battalion Center
NAVCHAPGRU
Navy Cargo Handling and Port Group

NAVCHAPGRUDET
Navy Cargo Handling and Port Group
Detachment
NAVCINTSUPPACT
Navy Counterintelligence Support Activity
NAVCINTSUPPCEN
Navy Counterintelligence Support Center
NAVCINTSUPPGRU
Navy Counterintelligence Support Unit
NAVCIVENGLAB, NCEL
Navy Civil Engineering Laboratory
NAVCLODEP
Naval Clothing Depot
NAVCLOTEXTOFC, NCTO
Navy Clothing and Textile Office
NAVCLOTEXTRSCHFAC
Navy Clothing and Textile Research Facility
NAVCM
Navigation(al) Countermeasures
NAVCOASTSYSCEN
Naval Coastal Systems Center
NAVCOMMDET
Naval Communication Station Detachment
NAVCOMMDETSPECCOMMDIV
Naval Communication Station Detachment,
Special Communications Division
NAVCOMMHQ
Naval Communications Headquarters
NAVCOMMOPNET
Naval Communications Operation Network
NAVCOMMSTA, NCS
Naval Communication Station
NAVCOMMSTASPECCOMMDIV
Naval Communication Station, Special
Communications Division
NAVCOMMSYSHQ
Naval Communications System Headquarters
NAVCOMMSYSSUPPACT
Naval Communications System Support
Activity
NAVCOMMTRACEN
Naval Communications Training Center
NAVCOMMU, NCU
Naval Communication Unit
NAVCOMPARS
Naval Communications Processing and
Receiving Station
Navy Automated Message Processing
System
NAVCOMPT
Comptroller of the Navy
NAVCOMSYSSUPPACT, NCSSA
Naval Command Systems Support Activity
NAVCOMSYSSUPPCEN, NCSSC
Naval Command Systems Support Center
NAVCOMSYSTO
Navy Commissary Store
NAVCONSTRACEN
Naval Construction Training Center
NAVCONSTRAU
Naval Construction Training Unit

NAVCONSTREGT, NCR
Naval Construction Regiment
NAVCONTDEP
Navy Contracting Department
NAVCONVHOSP
Naval Convalescent Hospital
NAVCORCOURSECEN
Naval Correspondence Course Center
NAVCORRCUSUNIT
Navy Correctional Custody Unit
**NAVCOSSACT, NAVCOMSYSSUPPACT,
NCSSA**
Naval Command Systems Support Activity
**NAVCOSSCEN, NAVCOMSYSSUPPCEN,
NCSSC**
Naval Command Systems Support Center
NAVCRUITAREA, NRA
Navy Recruiting Area
NAVCRUITBRSTA, NRBS
Navy Recruiting Branch Station
NAVCRUITCOM, NRC
Navy Recruiting Command
NAVCRUITCOMORIENTUNIT
Navy Recruiting Command Orientation Unit
NAVCRUITCOMSAT
Navy Recruiting Command Standardization
and Audit Team
NAVCRUITCOMYPFLDREP
Navy Recruiting Command Youth Programs
Field Representative
NAVCRUITDIST, NRD
Navy Recruiting District
NAVCRUITEXHIBCEN, NREC
Navy Recruiting Exhibit Center
NAVCRUITEXHIBCENCAT
Navy Recruiting Exhibit Center Catalog
NAVCRUITRACOM, NRTC
Navy Recruit Training Command
NAVCRUITSTA, NRS
Navy Recruiting Station
NAVCURRSUPPGRUPACFLT
Naval Current Support Group, Pacific Fleet
NAVCURRSUPPGRULANTFLT
Naval Current Support Group, Atlantic Fleet
NAVCURRSUPPGRUNAVEUR
Naval Current Support Group, Naval Forces,
Europe
NAVCURSERVDET
Naval Courier Service Detachment
NAVDAC
Navigation(al) Data Assimilation Computer
NAVDAF
Navy Data Automation Center
NAVDAMCONTRACEN
Navy Damage Control Training Center
NAVDATACEN
Naval Data Center
NAVDEFEASTPAC
Naval Defense Forces, Eastern Pacific
NAVDEGSTA
Navy Degaussing Station

NAVDENCEN
Naval Dental Center
NAVDENCLINIC
Naval Dental Clinic
NAVDENSCOL
Navy Dental School
NAVDENTECHSCOL
Navy Dental Technician School
NAVDEPDIRABRES
Navy Deputy Director Advanced Ballistic
Reentry Systems Division
NAVDEPNOAA
Naval Deputy National Oceanic and
Atmospheric Administration
NAVDEPT
Navy Department
NAVDET
Naval Detachment
NAVDISBAR
Navy Disciplinary Barracks
NAVDISCOM
Navy Disciplinary Command
NAVDISEASEVECTORCONCEN
Navy Disease Vector Control Center
NAVDISVECTTECOLCONCEN, NDVECC
Navy Disease Vector Ecology and Control
Center
NAVDISP, ND
Naval Dispensary
NAVDIST, ND
Naval District
NAVDIVSALVTRACEN, NDSTC
Naval Diving and Salvage Training Center
NAVDRUGREHCEN, NDRC
Naval Drug Rehabilitation Center
NAVEARB
Navy Employee Appeals Review Board
NAVEASTOCEANCEN
Naval Eastern Oceanography Center
NAVEDTRACOM, NETC
Naval Education and Training Command
NAVEDTRAPRODEVCEN, NETPDC
Naval Education and Training Program
Development Center
NAVEDTRAPRODEVCENCODIV
Naval Education and Training Program
Development Center Coordination Division
NAVEDTRAPRODEVCENDET
Naval Education and Training Program
Development Center Detachment
NAVEDTRASUPPCEN, NETSC
Naval Education and Training Support Center
NAVEDTRASUPPCENLANT, NETSCL
Naval Education and Training Support
Center, Atlantic
NAVEDTRASUPPCENPAC, NETSCP
Naval Education and Training Support
Center, Pacific

NAVEDTRASUPPCENPACNCFA
Naval Education and Training Support
Center, Pacific, Navy Campus for
Achievement
NAVELECSYSCOM, NAVELEX, NESC
Naval Electronic Systems Command
NAVELECSYSCOMHQ
Naval Electronic Systems Command
Headquarters
NAVELEM
Navy Element
NAVELEX, NAVELECSYSCOM, NESC
Naval Electronic Systems Command
NAVELEXACTS
Naval Electronic Systems Command
Activities
NAVELEXDET
Naval Electronic Systems Command
Detachment
NAVELEXENGOFF, NEEO
Naval Electronics Engineering Office
NAVELEXSITEREP
Naval Electronic Systems Command, Site
Representative
NAVELEXSYSCOMCENDET
Naval Electronic Systems Command Center
Detachment
NAVELEXSYSCOMDIV
Naval Electronic Systems Command Division
NAVELEXSYSCOMMIDWESTDIV
Naval Electronic Systems Command,
Midwest Division
NAVELEXSYSCOMSEDIV
Naval Electronic Systems Command,
Southeast Division
NAVELEXSYSCOMSOWESTDIV
Naval Electronic Systems Command,
Southwest Division
NAVELEXSYSCOMTECHLREP
Naval Electronic Systems Command
Technician Liaison Representative
NAVELEXSYSCOMENGCEN
Naval Electronic Systems Command Systems
Engineering Center
NAVELEXSYSTRAPUBMO
Naval Electronic Systems Command Training
and Publications Management Office
NAVELEXTECHREP
Naval Electronic Systems Command
Technical Representative
NAVEMSCEN, NESC
Navy Electromagnetic Spectrum Center
NAVENENVSA, NEESA
Navy Energy and Environmental Support
Activity
NAVENVPVNTMEDU, NEPMU
Navy Environmental and Preventive Medicine
Unit
NAVENVRHLTHCEN, NEHC
Navy Environmental Health Center

NAVENVPREDRSCHFAC, NEPRF
Naval Environmental Prediction Research
Facility
NAVENVSUPPCEN, NESC
Navy Environmental Support Center
NAVENVSUPPO, NESO
Navy Environmental Support Office
NAVEODFAC
Naval Explosive Ordnance Disposal Facility
NAVEODTECHCEN, NEODTC
Naval Explosive Ordnance Disposal
Technology Center
NAVETC
Navy Educational Tape Catalog
NAVEUR
Naval Forces, Europe
NAVEURWWMCCS DP
Naval Forces, Europe, Worldwide Military
Command Control System Data Processing
NAVEURWWMCCS EMSKD
Naval Forces, Europe, Worldwide Military
Command Control System Employment
Schedule
NAVEURWWMCCS MOVREP
Naval Forces, Europe, Worldwide Military
Command Control System Movement
Reports
NAVEURWWMCCS NAVFORSTA
Naval Forces, Europe, Worldwide Military
Command Control System Naval Forces
Status
NAVEX, NEX
Navy Exchange
NAVEXAM, NAVEXAMBD
Naval Examining (Board)
NAVEXAMBD, NAVEXAM
Naval Examining Board
NAVEXAMCEN
Naval Examining Center
NAVEXAMCENADVAUTHLIST
Naval Examining Center Advancement
Authorization List
NAVEXENGLANDCOM
Navy Exchange, England Complex
NAVEXHIBCEN
Naval Exhibit Center
NAVFAC
Naval Facility
NAVFAC, NAVFACENGRCOM, NFEC
Naval Facilities Engineering Command
**NAVFACCHESDIV,
   NAVFACENGRCOMCHESDIV**
Naval Facilities Engineering Command,
Chesapeake Division
NAVFACENGCOM, NAVFAC, NFEC
Naval Facilities Engineering Command
**NAVFACENGCOMCHESDIV,
   NAVFACCHESDIV**
Naval Facilities Engineering Command,
Chesapeake Division

NAVFACENGCOMCONTR
Naval Facilities Engineering Command
Contractor
NAVFACENGCOMHQ
Naval Facilities Engineering Command
Headquarters
**NAVFACENGCOMLANTDIV,
NAVFACLANTDIV**
Naval Facilities Engineering Command,
Atlantic Division
NAVFACENGCOMNORDIV, NAVFACNORDIV
Naval Facilities Engineering Command,
Northern Division
NAVFACENGCOMPACDIV, NAVFACPACDIV
Naval Facilities Engineering Command,
Pacific Division
NAVFACENGCOMSODIV, NAVFACSODIV
Naval Facilities Engineering Command,
Southern Division
NAVFACENGCOMWESDIV, NAVFACWESDIV
Naval Facilities Engineering Command,
Western Division
**NAVFACLANTDIV,
NAVFACENGCOMLANTDIV**
Naval Facilities Engineering Command,
Atlantic Division
NAVFACNORDIV, NAVFACENGCOMNORDIV
Naval Facilities Engineering Command,
Northern Division
NAVFACOC, NFOC
Naval Facility Operational Center
NAVFACSODIV, NAVFACENGCOMSODIV
Naval Facilities Engineering Command,
Southern Division
NAVFACWESDIV, NAVFACENGCOMWESDIV
Naval Facilities Engineering Command,
Western Division
NAVFAMALWACT
Navy Family Allowance Activity
NAVFINCEN, NFC
Navy Finance Center
NAVFINCEN-CLEVE, NFC-CLEVE
Navy Finance Center-Cleveland (OH)
NAVFINCEN-WASH, NFC-WASH
Navy Finance Center-Washington (DC)
NAVFINOFF, NFO
Navy Finance Office
NAVFITWEPSCOL, NFWS
Navy Fighter Weapons School
NAVFLDINTO
Navy Field Intelligence Office
NAVFLDOPINTO
Navy Field Operational Intelligence Office
NAVFLDOPSUPPGRU, NFOSG
Navy Field Operational Support Group
NAVFLITHTDEMORON
Navy Flight Demonstration Squadron
NAVFOODMGTM, NFMT
Navy Food Management Team
NAVFOR
Naval Forces

NAVFOREU
Naval Forces, Europe
NAVFORGER
Naval Forces, Germany
NAVFORJAP(AN)
Naval Forces, Japan
NAVFORKOR
Naval Forces, Korea
NAVFORSTAT
Navy Force Status (report)
NAVFRCOORD
Navy Frequency Coordinator
NAVFROF
Navy Freight Office
NAVFSSO
Navy Food Services Office
NAVFUELDEP, NFD
Navy Fuel Depot
NAVFUELSUPO, NFSO
Navy Fuel Supply Office
NAVGDENSCOL
Naval Graduate Dental School
NAVGEN
Navy General (publications)
NAVGMSCOL
Navy Guided Missile School
NAVGMU
Navy Guided Missile Unit
NAVGUN
Naval Gun (Factory)
NAVHISTCEN
Naval History Center
NAVHISTDISPLAYCEN
Navy Historical Display Center
NAVHLTHRSCHCEN, NHRC
Naval Health Research Center
NAVHOME
(U.S.) Naval Home
NAVHOMERESINFOSYS
Naval Home Resident Information System
NAVHOS, NAVHOSP, NH
Naval Hospital
NAVHOSP, NAVHOS, NH
Naval Hospital
NAVHOSPCORPSCOL
Naval Hospital Corps School
NAVHOSINGACT
Naval Housing Activity
NAVIC
Navy Information Center
NAVIG, NAV
Navigation(al)
NAVILCO, NILCO
Navy International Logistics Control Office
NAVIMAC
Naval Immediate Area Coordinator
NAVINFO
Navy Information Office (CHINFO branch)
NAVINRELACT, NIRA
Navy Internal Relations Activity

NAVINSGEN, NIG
Navy Inspector General
NAVINTCOM, NIC
Naval Intelligence Command
NAVINTSUPPCEN, NISC
Naval Intelligence Support Center
NAVINTEL, NI
Naval Intelligence
NAVINVSERV, NIS
Naval Investigative Service
NAVINVSERVO, NISSO
Naval Investigative Service Office(r)
NAVINVSERVOREP, NISOR
Naval Investigative Service Office
Representative
NAVINVSERVRA, NISRA
Naval Investigative Service Resident Agent
NAVISLO, NILO
Naval Interservice Liaison Office
NAVJNTSERVACT
Naval Joint Services Activity
NAVJUSTSCOL, NJS
Naval Justice School
NAVLEGSERVOFF
Naval Legal Service Office
NAVLEGSERVOFFDET
Naval Legal Service Office Detachment
NAVLIAGRU
Naval Liaison Group
NAVLINKSTA
Naval Link Station
NAVLIS
Navy Logistics Information System
NAVLOGENGRU
Naval Logistics Engineering Group
NAVLOGSIP
Navy Logistics Support Improvement Plan
NAVLOS
Navy Liaison Officer for Scouting
NAVMAA
Naval Mutual Aid Association
NAVMAC, NAVMMAC
Navy Manpower and Material Analysis Center
NAVMACLANT, NAVMMACLANT
Navy Manpower and Material Analysis
Center, Atlantic
NAVMACPAC, NAVMMACPAC
Navy Manpower and Material Analysis
Center, Pacific
NAVMMAG
Naval Magazine
NAVMAR
Naval Forces, Marianas
NAVMARCORESCEN, USN&USMCRC
(U.S.) Navy and (U.S.) Marine Corps Reserve
Center
NAVMAREXHIBCEN
Navy-Marine Corps Exhibit Center
NAVMARJUDACT
Navy-Marine Corps Judiciary Activity

NAVMARTRIJUDCIR
Navy-Marine Corps Trial Judiciary Court
NAVMARTRIJUDCIRBROFF
Navy-Marine Corps Trial Judiciary Court
Branch Office
NAVMARTRIJUDIC
Navy-Marine Corps Trial Judiciary
NAVMASSO, NMSSO
Navy Maintenance and Supply Systems
Office
NAVMASSODET
Navy Maintenance and Supply Systems
Office Detachment
NAVMASSODETPAC
Navy Maintenance and Supply Systems
Office Detachment, Pacific
NAVMAT, NAVMATCOM, NMC
Naval Material Command
NAVMATCOM, NAVMAT, NMC
Naval Material Command
NAVMATCOMSUPPACT, NMCSA
Naval Material Command Support Activity
NAVMAT COOPLAN
Naval Material Command
Contingency/Emergency Planning
NAVMATDATASYSGRU, NMDSG
Naval Material Data Systems Group
NAVMATDET
Naval Material Command Detachment
NAVMATEVALU, NMEU
Naval Material Evaluation Unit
NAVMATRANSOFC, NMTO
Naval Material Transportation Office
NAVMED
Naval Forces, Mediterranean
NAVMEDADMINU, NMAU
Navy Medical Administrative Unit
NAVMEDATASERVCEN, NMDSC
Naval Medical Data Services Center
NAVMEDCEN, NAMC
Navy Medical Center
NAVMEDFLDRSCHLAB
Navy Medical Field Research Laboratory
NAVMEDIS
Navy Medical Information System
NAVMEDLAB
Naval Medical Laboratory
NAVMEDLABDET
Naval Medical Laboratory Detachment
NAVMEDMATSUPPCOM, NMMSC
Naval Medical Materiel Support Command
NAVMEDNPRSCHU
Navy Medical Neuropsychiatric Research Unit
NAVMEDRSCHDEVCOM, NMRDC
Naval Medical Research and Development
Command
NAVMEDRSCHINST, NMRI
Navy Medical Research Institute
NAVMEDRSCHINSTDET
Navy Medical Research Institute Detachment

NAVMEDRSCHINST TOXDET
Navy Medical Research Institute, Toxicology
Detachment
NAVMEDRSCHLAB, NMRL
Navy Medical Research Laboratory
NAVMEDRSCHU, NMRU
Naval Medical Research Unit
NAVMEDRSCHUDET
Naval Medical Research Unit Detachment
NAVMEDSCOL
Navy School of Medicine
NAVMEDSUPPU, NMSU
Navy Medical Support Unit
NAVMGTSYSCEN, NMSC
Navy Management Systems Center
NAVMILPERSCOM, NMPC
Naval Military Personnel Command
NAVMILPERSCOM SDC
Naval Military Personnel Command Sea Duty
Component
NAVMINEDEFLAB, NMDL
Navy Mine Defense Laboratory
NAVMINEDEP, NMD
Naval Mine Depot
NAVMINENGRFAC, NMEF
Naval Mine Engineering Facility
NAVMIS
Naval Mission
NAVMISCEN, NMC
Naval Missile Center
NAVMMAC, NAVMAC
Naval Manpower and Material Analysis
Center
NAVMMACLANT, NAVMACLANT
Naval Manpower and Material Analysis
Center, Atlantic
NAVMMACPAC, NAVMACPAC
Naval Manpower and Material Analysis
Center, Pacific
NAVMOBCONSTBN, NMCB
Naval Mobile Construction Battalion
NAVMORTOFF
Naval Mortuary Office
NAVMTO
Naval Military Transportation Office
NAVMTONORVA
Naval Military Transportation Office, Norfolk,
Virginia
NAVMTOREP
Naval Military Transportation Office
Representative
NAVNETDEP
Naval Net Depot
NAVNUPWRSCOL, NNPS
Navy Nuclear Power School
NAVNUPWRTRAU, NNPTU
Naval Nuclear Power Training Unit
NAVNUPWRU, NNPU
Naval Nuclear Power Unit
NAVNZ
Naval Forces, New Zealand

NAVOBSY
Naval Observatory
NAVOBSYFLAGSTAFFSTA
Naval Observatory, Flagstaff (AZ) Station
NAVOBSYSTA
Naval Observatory Station
NAVOCEANCOMCEN
Naval Oceanography Command Center
NAVOCEANCOMDET
Naval Oceanography Command Center
Detachment
NAVOCEANCOMFAC, NOCF
Naval Oceanography Command Facility
NAVOCEANCOMMDET
Naval Oceanography Communications
Detachment
NAVOCEANO, NAVOCEANOFC, NOO
Naval Oceanographic Office
NAVOCEANOAIRSUPPGRU, VX
Naval Oceanographic Office's Aircraft
Support Squadron
NAVOCEANODET
Naval Oceanographic Office Detachment
NAVOCEANOFC, NAVOCEANO, NOO
Naval Oceanographic Office
NAVOCEANPROFAC, NOPF
Naval Ocean Processing Facility
NAVOCEANSURVINFOCEN, NOSIC
Naval Ocean Surveillance Information Center
NAVOCEANSYSCEN, NOSC
Naval Ocean Systems Center
NAVOCEANSYSCENLAB, NOSCL
Naval Oceans Systems Center Laboratory
NAVOCEANSYSCENLABDET
Naval Ocean Systems Center Laboratory
Detachment
NAVOCS
Naval Officer Candidate School
NAVOLF
Navy Outlying Landing Field
NAVOPHTHALSUPPTRACT, NOSTA
Naval Ophthalmic Support Training Activity
NAVOPSUPPGRU
Naval Operations Support Group
NAVOPSUPPGRULANT
Naval Operations Support Group, Atlantic
NAVOPSUPPGRUPAC
Naval Operations Support Group, Pacific
NAVORD
Naval Ordnance
NAVORDENGFAC, NOEF
Naval Ordnance Engineering Facility
NAVORDFAC, NOF
Naval Ordnance Facility
NAVORD ILS/MIS
Naval Ordnance Systems Command
Integrated Logistics Support/Management
Information System
NAVORDLABFIELDIV
Naval Ordnance Laboratory Field Division

NAVORDLIST
Navy Ordnance List
NAVORDMISTESTFAC, NOMTF
Naval Ordnance Missile Test Facility
NAVORDSTA, NOS
Naval Ordnance Station
NAVORDSTADET
Naval Ordnance Station Detachment
NAVORDSYSCOM
Naval Ordnance Systems Command
NAVORDSYSCOMHQ
Naval Ordnance Systems Command
Headquarters
NAVORDSYSUPPOLANT, NOSSOLANT
Naval Ordnance Systems Support Office,
Atlantic
NAVORDSYSUPPOPAC, NOSSOPAC
Naval Ordnance Systems Support Office,
Pacific
NAVORDTESTU, NOTU
Naval Ordnance Test Unit
NAVORDU
Naval Ordnance Unit
NAVORECSUPPACT, NORSA
Naval Officer Record Support Activity
NAVOSH
Navy Occupational Safety and Health
(program)
NAVOSTAT
Navigation by Visual Observation of Satellites
NAVPAC
Navigation Packages
NAVPACEN
Navy Public Affairs Center
NAVPBRO
Naval Plant Branch Representative Officer
NAVPECO
Navy Production Equipment Control Office
NAVPECOS
Navy Pentagon Computer Services Division
NAVPERSCEN
Naval Personnel Center
NAVPERSPROGSUPPACT
Naval Personnel Programs Support Activity
NAVPERSRANDCEN, NPRDC
Naval Personnel Research and Development
Center
NAVPERSRANDCENWB
Naval Personnel Research and Development
Center, Washington (DC) Branch
NAVPERSCHACT
Naval Personnel Research Activity
NAVPETOFF, NPO
Naval Petroleum Office
NAVPETRAU, NPTU
Naval Petroleum Training Unit
NAVPETRES, NPR
Naval Petroleum Reserves
NAVPETRESO, NPRO
Naval Petroleum Reserves Office

NAVPGSCOL, NAVPOSTGRADSCOL, NPGS
Navy Postgraduate School
NAVPHIBASE, NAB
Naval Amphibious Base
NAVPHIBSCOL, NAMS
Naval Amphibious School
NAVPHIL
Naval Forces, Philippines
NAVPHOTOCEN, NPC
Naval Photographic Center
NAVPLANTDEVU, NPDU
Naval Plant Development Unit
NAVPLANTREPO, NAVPRO
Naval Plant Representative Office(r)
NAVPLANTTECHREP
Naval Plant Technical Representative
NAVPOLAROCEANCEN, NPOC
Naval Polar Oceanography Center
NAVPORTCO, NPCO
Naval Port Control Office
NAVPOSTGRADSCOL, NAVPGSCOL, NPGS
Naval Postgraduate School
NAVPOWFAC, NPW
Naval Powder Factory
NAVPRIMSTDEPT
Navy Primary Standards Department
NAVPRIS
Naval Prison
NAVPRO, NAVPLANTREPO
Naval Plant Representative Office(r)
NAVPROPLT
Naval Propellant Plant
NAVPTO
Navy Passenger Transportation Office
NAVPUBFORMCEN, NPFC
Naval Publications and Forms Center
NAVPUBPRINTO, NPPO
Naval Publications and Printing Office
NAVPUBPRINTSERV, NPPS
Naval Publications and Printing Service
NAVPUBPRINTSERVO, NPPSO
Naval Publications and Printing Service Office
NAVPUBCONBD
Naval Publications Control Board
NAVPUBWKSCEN, NPWC
Navy Public Works Center
NAVPUBWKSDEPT, NPWD
Navy Public Works Department
NAVPURDEP, NPD
Navy Purchasing Department
NAVPURO, NPO
Navy Purchasing Office
NAVPVNTMEDU
Navy Preventive Medicine Unit
NAVRADCO
Naval Regional Active Duty Cryptologic
Officer
NAVRADCON, NRC
Naval Radiological Control
NAVRADLDEFLAB, NRDL
Navy Radiological Defense Laboratory

NAVRADRECFAC, NRRF
Naval Radio Receiving Facility
NAVRADSTA, NRS
Naval Radio Station
NAVRADSTA(R), NRS(R)
Naval Radio Station (Receiving)
NAVRADSTA(S), NRS(S)
Naval Radio Station (Sending)
NAVRADTRANSFAC, NRTF
Naval Radio Transmitting Facility
NAVRECCEN, NRC
Naval Recreation Center
NAVRECONTACSUPPCEN, NRTSC
Naval Reconnaissance and Tactical Support
Center
NAVRECONTACSUPPCENLANT, NRTSCL
Naval Reconnaissance and Tactical Support
Center, Atlantic
NAVRECONTECHSUPPCENPAC, NRTSCPAC
Naval Reconnaissance and Technical
Support Center, Pacific
NAVRECSTA, NRES
Naval Receiving Station
NAVREGAIRCARCONO
Navy Regional Air Cargo Control Office
NAVREGCONTO, NRCO
Navy Regional Contracting Office
NAVREGCONTODET
Navy Regional Contracting Office
Detachment
NAVREGDENCEN, NRDC
Navy Regional Dental Center
NAVREGDENCENBRFAC
Navy Regional Dental Center Branch Facility
NAVREGDENCLIN
Navy Regional Dental Clinic
NAVREGFINCEN, NRFC
Navy Regional Finance Center
NAVREGFINCENBRKLN, NRFC-B
Navy Regional Finance Center, Brooklyn
(NY)
NAVREGFINCENGLAKES, NRFC-GL
Navy Regional Finance Center, Great Lakes
(IL)
NAVREGFINCENNORVA, NRFC-N
Navy Regional Finance Center, Norfolk,
Virginia
NAVREGFINCENPEARL, NRFC-PH
Navy Regional Finance Center, Pearl Harbor
(HA)
NAVREGFINCENSDIEGO, NRFC-SD
Navy Regional Finance Center, San Diego
(CA)
NAVREGFINCENSFRAN, NRFC-SF
Navy Regional Finance Center, San
Francisco (CA)
NAVREGMEDCEN, NRMC
Naval Regional Medical Center
NAVREGMEDCENBRCLINIC
Naval Regional Medical Center Branch Clinic

NAVREGMEDCENBRHOSP
Naval Regional Medical Center Branch
Hospital
NAVREGMEDCENCLINIC
Naval Regional Medical Center Clinic
NAVREGMEDCENDET
Naval Regional Medical Center Detachment
NAVREGPEO, NRPEO
Naval Regional Plant Equipment Office(r)
NAVREGPROCO
Navy Regional Procurement Office
NAVREGS
Navy Regulations
NAVREL, NRS
Navy Relief Society
NAVREPEA
Department of the Navy Representative,
Eastern
NAVREPSO
Department of the Navy Representative,
Southern
NAVREPSW
Department of the Navy Representative,
Southwestern
NAVREPWP
Department of the Navy Representative,
Western and Pacific
NAVRES, NR
Naval Reserve
NAVRESCEN, NRC
Naval Reserve Center
NAVRESCOMICEDEFOR
Naval Reserve Commander Iceland Defense
Force
NAVRESFAC, NRF
Naval Reserve Facility
NAVRESFOR, NRF
Naval Reserve Force
NAVRESMANPWRCEN
Naval Reserve Manpower Center
NAVRESMGTSCOL, NRMS
Naval Reserve Management School
NAVRESMIDSCOL, NRMS
Naval Reserve Midshipmen's School
NAVRESO, NRSO
Navy Resale Systems Office
NAVRESOFSO
Navy Resale System Field Support Office
NAVRESOREACT
Naval Reserve Officer Recording Activity
NAVRESOREP
Navy Resale Systems Office Representative
NAVRESREDCOM, REDCOM
Naval Reserve Readiness Command
NAVRESREDCOMREG
Naval Reserve Readiness Command Region
NAVRESSECGRP, NRSG
Naval Reserve Security Group
NAVRESSO, NRSSO
Navy Resale and Services Support Office

NAVRESSOFO
Navy Resale and Services Support Office,
Field Office
NAVRESUBDET
Naval Reserve Submarine Detachment
NAVRESUPPOFC
Naval Reserve Support Office
NAVRESUPPOFCDET
Naval Reserve Support Office Detachment
NAVRESTRA, NRT
Naval Reserve Training
NAVRESTRACOM
Naval Reserve Training Command
NAVRSCHLAB, NRL
Naval Research Laboratory
NAVSAFECEN, NSC
Navy Safety Center
NAVSAT, SATNAV
Navigational Satellite
NAVSATCOMMDET
Navy Satellite Communications Detachment
NAVSATCOMMFAC
Navy Satellite Communications Facility
NAVSATCOMMNET
Navy Satellite Communications Network
NAVSCIADV
Naval Science Advisor
NAVSCITECHGRUFE
Naval Scientific and Technical Group, Far
East
NAVSCOLCEOFF
Naval Civil Engineer Corps Officers School
NAVSCOLCOM, NSC
Naval Schools Command
NAVSCOLCONST
Naval School of Construction
NAVSCOLCRYPTOREP
Naval Cryptographic Repair School
NAVSCOLCYROGENICS
Naval School of Cyrogenics
NAVSCOLDEEPSEADIVER
Navy Deep Sea Divers' School
NAVSCOLEOD
Naval Explosive Ordnance Disposal School
NAVSCOLHOSPADMIN
Naval Hospital Administration School
NAVSCOLMINWAR
Naval School of Mine War
NAVSCOLPHYDISTMGT
Naval School of Physical Distribution
Management
NAVSCOLTRANSMGT
Naval School of Transportation Management
NAVSCSCOL
Naval Supply Corps School
NAVSCSCOLDET
Naval Supply Corps School Detachment
NAVCON
Naval Schools, Construction
NAVSEA
Navy Avionics Support Equipment Appraisal

NAVSEA, NAVSEASYSCOM, NSSC
Naval Sea Systems Command
NAVSEAADSO
Naval Sea Systems Command Automated
Data Systems Office
NAVSEAADSODET
Naval Sea Systems Command Automated
Data Systems Office Detachment
NAVSEACARCOORD, NSCO
Naval Sea Cargo Coordinator
NAVSEACEN, NSSC
Naval Sea Support Center
NAVSEACENFSO
Naval Sea Support Center Fleet Support
Office
NAVSEACENHAWLAB
Naval Sea Support Center, Hawaii Laboratory
NAVSEACENREP
Naval Sea Support Center Representative
NAVSEACENLANTDET
Naval Sea Support Center, Atlantic
Detachment
NAVSEACENPACDET
Naval Sea Support Center, Pacific
Detachment
NAVSEACOHREP
Naval Sea Systems Command Complex
Overhaul Representative
NAVSEADET
Naval Sea Systems Command Detachment
NAVSEAMATREP
Naval Sea Systems Command Material
Representative
NAVSEAMQAO
Naval Sea Systems Command Material
Quality Assessment Office
NAVSEASYSCOM, NAVSEA, NSSC
Naval Sea Systems Command
NAVSEASYSCOMGTOWESTPAC
Naval Sea Systems Command Management
Office, Western Pacific
NAVSEASYSCOMHQ
Naval Sea Systems Command Headquarters
NAVSEATECHREP
Naval Sea Systems Command Technical
Representative
NAVSEC
Naval Ship Engineering Center
NAVSECENGRFAC
Navy Security Engineering Facility
NAVSECGRUACTFO
Naval Security Group Activity Field Office
NAVSECGRUACT, NSGA
Naval Security Group Activity
NAVSECGRUACTSPECOMMDIV
Naval Security Group Activity Special
Communications Division
NAVSECGRUCOM, NSGC
Naval Security Group Command
NAVSECGRUDEPT
Naval Security Group Department

NAVSECGRUDET
Naval Security Group Detachment
NAVSECGRUHQ
Naval Security Group Headquarters
NAVSECGRUMGDAT
Naval Security Group Command
Management Data
NAVSECGRU MIS
Naval Security Group Management
Information System
NAVSECMECHSDIV
Naval Ship Engineering Center,
Mechanicsburg (PA) Division
NAVSECNORDIV
Naval Ship Engineering Center, Norfolk (VA)
Division
NAVSECPHILADIV
Naval Ship Engineering Center, Philadelphia
(PA) Division
NAVSECSDIEGODIV
Naval Ship Engineering Center, San Diego
(CA) Division
NAVSECSTA, NSS
Naval Security Station
NAVSEEACT, NAVSHORELECENGACT
Naval Shore Electronics Engineering Activity
NAVSEEACTLANT,
NAVSHORELECENGACTLANT
Naval Shore Electronics Engineering Activity,
Atlantic
NAVSEEACTPAC,
NAVSHORELECENGACTPAC
Naval Shore Electronics Engineering Activity,
Pacific
NAVSERVSCOLCOM
Naval Service Schools Command
NAVSHIPENGSUPPACT
Naval Ship Engineering Support Activity
NAVSHIPLO
Naval Shipbuilding Liaison Office
NAVSHIPMISENGSYS
Naval Ships Missile Systems Engineering
System
NAVSHIPREPFAC, NSRF
Naval Ship Repair Facility
NAVSHIPREPO
Naval Ship Repair Officer
NAVSHIPRSCHDEVCEN, NSRDC
Naval Ship Research and Development
Center
NAVSHIPRSCHDEVCENANNA,
NSRDCANNADIV, NSRDC/A
Naval Ship Research and Development
Center, Annapolis (MD) Division
NAVSHIPSTO, NSSO
Navy Ships Store Office
NAVSHIPTECHSMAN
Navy Ship's Technical Manual
NAVSHIPWPNSYSENGSTA
Naval Ship Weapon Systems Engineering
Station

NAVSHIPWPNSYSENGSTADET
Naval Ship Weapon Systems Engineering
Station Detachment
NAVSHIPWPNSYSENGSTAREP
Naval Ship Weapon Systems Engineering
Station Representative
NAVSHIPYD
Naval Shipyard
NAVSHORELECENACT, NAVSEEACT
Naval Shore Electronics Engineering Activity
NAVSHORELECENACTLANT,
NAVSEEACTLANT
Naval Shore Electronics Engineering Activity,
Atlantic
NAVSHORELECENACTPAC,
NAVSEEACTPAC
Naval Shore Electronics Engineering Activity,
Pacific
NAVSHORELECENGCEN
Naval Shore Electronics Engineering Center
NAVSIT
Navy Scholarship Information Team
NAVSO
(Department of the) Navy Staff Offices
NAVSPACEPROJ
Naval Space Project
NAVSPASUR
Naval Space Surveillance (system)
NAVSPASYSAC, NSSA
Naval Space Systems Activity
NAVSPECWARGRU
Naval Special Warfare Group
NAVSPECWARGRUDET
Naval Special Warfare Group Detachment
NAVSPECWARU
Naval Special Warfare Unit
NAVSPECWARUDET
Naval Special Warfare Unit Detachment
NAVSSES
Naval Ship Systems Engineering Station
NAVSSESDET
Naval Ship Systems Engineering Station
Detachment
NAVSTA, NS
Naval Station
NAVSTAR
Navigation Satellite Tracking and Ranging
(Satellite)
NAVSTRIP
Naval Standard Requisitioning and Issue
Procedure
NAVSUBBASE, NSB
Naval Submarine Base
NAVSUBINSURV
Naval Sub-Board of Inspection and Survey
NAVSUBMEDCEN
Navy Submarine Medical Center
NAVSUBMEDRSCHLAB
Naval Submarine Medical Research
Laboratory

NAVSUBSCOL
Naval Submarine School
NAVSUBSUPPBASE, NSSB
Naval Submarine Support Base
NAVSUBSUPPBASEDET
Naval Submarine Support Base Detachment
NAVSUBSUPPFAC
Navy Submarine Support Facility
NAVSUBTRACENPAC
Naval Submarine Training Center, Pacific
NAVSUP, NAVSUPSYSCOM, NSSC
Naval Supply Systems Command
NAVSUPCEN, NSC
Naval Supply Center
NAVSUPDEP, NSD
Naval Supply Depot
NAVSUPDEPT, NSD
Naval Supply Department
NAVSUPPACT, NSA
Naval Support Activity
NAVSUPPACTDET, NSAD
Naval Support Activity Detachment
NAVSUPPFAC
Naval Support Facility
NAVSUPPFOR, NSF
Naval Support Force
NAVSUPPFORANTARCTIC
Naval Support Forces, Antarctic
NAVSUPO, NSO
Navy Supply Office
NAVSUPOANX
Navy Supply Office Annex
NAVSUPRANDDFAC
Navy Supply Research and Development
Facility
NAVSUPSYSCOM, NAVSUP, NSSC
Naval Supply Systems Command
NAVSUPSYSCOMHQ
Naval Supply Systems Command
Headquarters
NAVSURFLANT
Naval Surface Force, Atlantic
NAVSURFLANTREADSUPPGRU
Naval Surface Force, Atlantic Readiness
Support Group
NAVSURFPAC
Naval Surface Force, Pacific
NAVSURFPACDAT
Naval Surface Force, Pacific Dependents'
Assistance Team
NAVSWC, NSWC
Naval Surface Weapons Center
NAVSWCFAC
Naval Surface Weapons Center Facility
NAVSWCREP
Naval Surface Weapons Center
Representative
NAVTACDATASYSDEVSITE
Naval Tactical Data Systems Development
and Evaluation Site

NAVTACINTEROPSUPPACT
Navy Tactical Interoperability Support Activity
NAVTACINTEROPSUPPACTDET
Navy Tactical Interoperability Support Activity
Detachment
NAVTACSUPPACT, NTSA
Navy Tactical Support Activity
NAVTACDOCACT
Navy Tactical Doctrine Activity
NAVTACDOCDEVPRODACT
Navy Tactical Doctrine Development and
Production Activity
NAVTACSAT
Naval Tactical Satellite
NAVTASC
Naval Telecommunications Automation
Support Center
NAVTASCDETLANT
Naval Telecommunications Automation
Support Center, Atlantic
NAVTASCDETPAC
Naval Telecommunications Automation
Support Center, Pacific
NAVTECHMISJAP(AN)
Naval Technical Mission to Japan
NAVTECHMISEU
Naval Technical Mission in Europe
NAVTECHREP
Naval Technical Representative
NAVTECHTRACEN, NTTC
Naval Technical Training Center
NAVTECHTRACENDET
Naval Technical Training Center Detachment
NAVTELCOM
Naval Telecommunications Command
NAVTELSYSIC
Naval Telecommunications System
Integration Center
NAVTIS
Naval Training Information System
NAVTIS ADS
Naval Training Information System with
Automated Data Systems
NAVTORPSTA, NTORS, NTS
Naval Torpedo Station
NAVTRA, NT
Naval Training
NAVTRACEN, NTC
Naval Training Center
NAVTRADEVCEN, NTDC
Naval Training Devices Center
NAVTRADEVSUPCEN, NTDSC
Naval Training Devices Supply Center
NAVTRAEQUIPCEN, NTEC
Naval Training Equipment Center
NAVTRAEQUIPCENFEO
Naval Training Equipment Center Field Office
NAVTRAEQUIPCENREPCEN
Naval Training Equipment Center,
Representative for the Center

NAVTRAEQUIPCENREPLANT
Naval Training Equipment Center
Representative, Atlantic
NAVTRAEQUIPCENREPPAC
Naval Training Equipment Center
Representative, Pacific
NAVTRAIDSCEN, NTAC
Naval Training Aids Center
NAVTRAIDSFAC, NTAF
Naval Training Aids Facility
NAVTRANSCO, NTCO
Naval Transportation Coordinating Office
NAVTRAPUBCEN
Naval Training Publications Center
NAVTRASTA, NTS
Naval Training Station
NAVTRASUPPDET
Naval Training Support Detachment
NAVU
Naval Unit
NAVUARCMSCOL
Navy Unit, Army Chemical School
NAVUDET
Naval Unit Detachment
NAVUSEAMEDINSTITUTE
Naval Undersea Medical Institute
NAVUSEAWARENGSTA
Navy Undersea Warfare Engineering Station
NAVUSEAWARENGSTADET
Naval Undersea Warfare Engineering Station
Detachment
NAVUWSEC
Navy Underwater Weapons Systems
Engineering Center
NAVUWTRORDSTA, NUOS
Navy Underwater Ordnance Station
NAVUWTRSOUNDLAB
Navy Underwater Sound Laboratory
NAVUWTRSOUNDREFLAB
Navy Underwater Sound Reference
Laboratory
NAVWAG
Naval Warfare Analysis Group
NAVWARCOL, NWC
Naval War College
NAVWEPEVALFAC, NWEF
Naval Weapons Evaluation Facility
NAVWESTOCEANCEN
Naval Western Oceanographic Center
NAVWESTPAC
Naval Forces, Western Pacific
NAVWPNCEN, NWC
Naval Weapons Center
NAVWPNENGSUPPACT
Naval Weapons Engineering Support Activity
NAVWPNEVALFAC, NWEF
Naval Weapons Evaluation Facility
NAVWPNQUALASSURO
Naval Weapons Quality Assurance Office
NAVWPNSERVO, NWSO
Naval Weapons Service Office

NAVWPNSTA, NWS
Naval Weapons Station
NAVWPNSTRACEN, NWTC
Naval Weapons Training Center
NAVWPNSUPPACT
Naval Weapons Support Activity
NAVWPNSUPPCEN
Naval Weapons Support Center
NAVWUIS, NWUIS
Naval Work Unit Information System
NAVXDIVINGU
Naval Experimental Diving Unit
NAWAC
National Weather Analysis Center
NAWAS
National Warning System
NB
Narrow Band
Navy Back (type parachute)
Navy Band
NB, NAVBASE
Naval Base
NBAD
Naval Bases Air Defense
NBC
Navy Beach Commando
Nuclear, Biological and Chemical (warfare)
NBCD
Nuclear, Biological and Chemical Defense
NBCFD
Naval Base Consolidated Fire Department
NBG, NAVBEACHGRU
Naval Beach Group
NBL
No Bomb Line
NBL, NAVBIOLAB
Navy Biological Laboratory (ONR)
NBPA
Navy Board of Production Awards
NBS
National Bureau of Standards
Neutral Buoyancy Simulator
NBSS
Naval Beach Signal Station
NBT
Navigator-Bombardier Training (program)
NBTL
Naval Boiler and Turbine Laboratory
NC
National Course (screws & bolts)
Navy Chest (type parachute)
Navy Cross
New Construction
Noise Criteria
Normally Closed
Not Carried
Nurse Corps
NC1
Navy Counselor First Class
N/C, NC
Numerical Control

NCA
Naval Communications Annex
NCAB
Navy Contract Adjustment Board
NCAC
Navy Combat Art Collection
NCAP, NAVCAP
Naval Combat Air Patrol
NCAT
Navy College Aptitude Test
NCB
National Competitive Bidding
Naval Communications Board
Navy Comptroller Budget
NCB, NAVCONSTBAT
Naval Construction Battalion
NC&B
Naval Courts and Boards
NCBC, NAVCONSTBATCEN
Naval Construction Battalion Center
NCC
Chief Navy Counselor
National Climate Center (NOAA)
Naval Command College (NWC)
Naval Communications Command
Navy Cost (or Command) Center
NISTARS Central Controller
NCCCLC
Naval Command Control Communications
Laboratory Center
NCCG
Navy Central Clearance Group
NCCM
Master Chief Navy Counselor
NCCMIRS
Navy Civilian Career Management Inventory
and Referral System
NCCMP
Navy Civilian Career Management Program
NCCR
Navy Construction/Conversion Requirements
(system)
NCCS
National Command and Control System
Senior Chief Navy Counselor
NCD
Navy Cargo Documents
Navy Contracting Directive
Nuclear Commission Date
NCDC
Naval Contract Distribution Center
NCDO
Naval Central Distribution Office
NCDT&EBASE
Navy Combat Demolition Training and
Experimental Base
NCDU
Naval Combat Demolition Unit
NCEL
Navy Contractor Experience List
Nuclear Certified Equipment List

NCEL, NAVCIVENGLAB
Naval Civil Engineering Laboratory
NCF
Naval Construction Forces
NCFMS
Navy Comptroller, Financial Management
Services
NCHSSP
Navy Campus High School Studies Program
NCI
Naval Cost Inspector
NCIP
Navy Command Inspection Program
Nuclear Career Incentive Pay
NCIS
Navy Cost Information System
NCLT
Night Carrier Landing Trainer
NCM
Navy Commendation Medal
Navy Correspondence Manual
NCMP
NAVAIDS/Communications Management
Office
NCO
Net Control Officer
NCO, NONCOM
Non-Commissioned Officer
NCOA
Non-Commissioned Officer's Association
NCOIC
Non-Commissioned Officer-in-Charge
NCOLANT
Net Control Officer, Atlantic
NCOMED
Net Control Officer, Mediterranean
NCOOM
Non-Commissioned Officers' Open Mess
NCOPAC
Net Control Officer, Pacific
NCP
Navy Capabilities Plan
NCPAC
National Security Agency Central Security
Service, Pacific
NCPB
Navy Council of Personnel Boards
NCPC
Navy Civilian Personnel Command
NCPCFD
Navy Civilian Personnel Command Field
Division
NCPCFDO
Navy Civilian Personnel Command Field
Division Office
NCPD
Navy, Current Procurement Directive
NCPEG
Navy Contractor Performance Evaluation
Group

NCPI
Navy Civilian Personnel Instructions
NCR
National Capital Region
No Carbon Required (paper)
NCR, NAVCONSTREGT
Naval Construction Regiment
NCRIB
Naval Communications Improvement Review
Board
NCS
National Cryptologic School
Naval (or National) Communications System
Net Control Station
Nucleus Support Crew
NCS, NAVCOMMSTA
Naval Communication Station
NCSC
Navy Command Support Center
NCSCC
Naval Security Group Communications
Course
NCSJ
Naval Communication Station, Japan
NCSL
Naval Coastal Systems Laboratory
Naval Code and Signal Laboratory
NCSLO
Navy Control of Shipping Liaison Officer
NCSO
Naval Control of Shipping Office
NCSORG
Naval Control of Shipping Organization
NCSP
Naval Communication Station, Philippines
NCSSA, NAVCOMSYSUPPACT
Naval Command Systems Support Activity
NCSSC, NAVCOMSYSUPPCEN
Naval Command Systems Support Center
NCSU
Naval Control of Shipping Unit
NCTC, NAVCONSTRACEN
Naval Construction Training Center
NCTO, NAVCLOTHTEXOFC
Navy Clothing and Textile Office
NCTR
Naval Commercial Traffic Regulations
NCTS
Navy Civilian Technical Specialists
NCU
Navigation Computer Unit
NCU, NAVCOMMU
Naval Communication Unit
NCWTF
Naval Commander Western Sea Frontier
ND
Navy Distillate
Non-Deviation (drawing)
ND, NAVDISP
Naval Dispensary

ND, NAVDIST
Naval District
NDAAC
Navy Drug and Alcohol Advisory Council
NDAC
Nuclear Defense Affairs Committee
NDACP
Navy Drug Abuse Control Program
NDACS
Navy Drug Abuse Counselor School
NDB
Navy Department Bulletin
Non-Directional Radio Beacon (approach)
NDB, NAVDISBAR
Navy Disciplinary Barracks
NDB(ARF)
Non-Direction Radio Beacon with Airborne
Automatic Direction-Finding (equipment)
NDBDM
Navy Department Board of Decorations and
Medals
NDBS
Navy Dispatch Boat Service
NDBULCMED
Navy Department Bulletins, Cumulative
Editions
NDC
Notice of Drawing Change
NDC, NAVDENCLINIC
Naval Dental Clinic
NDCP
Navy Decision Coordinating Paper
NDDC
Navy Department Duty Chaplain
NDD&RF
Naval Drydock and Repair Facility
NDF
Navy Distillate Fuel
Night Defense Fire
NDFYP
Navy Department Five-Year Program
NDGO
Navy Department General Order
NDI
Non-Destructive Inspection
NDO
Navy Department Office
NDP
National Disclosure Policy
Navy Department Personnel
Night Defense Position
NDPC
National Disclosure Policy Committee
NDPIC
Navy Department Program Information
Center
NDRC, NAVDRUGREHCEN
Naval Drug Rehabilitation Center
NDRF
National Defense Reserve Fleet

NDRO
Non-Destructive Read-Out (memory)
NDS
Naval Dental (or Destroyer) School
Nuclear Detection Satellite
NDSL
National Defense Student Loan
NDSTC, NAVDIVSALTRACEN
Naval Diving and Salvage Training Center
NDT
Non-Destructive Test
NDTP
Nuclear Data Tape Program
NDTS/LBTS
Naval Tactical Data System/Land-Based Test
Site
NDUSTA
New duty station
NDV
No Delay of Vessel
Nuclear Delivery Vehicle
NDW
Naval District Washington (DC)
NE, NOREAST
Northeast(ern)
NEACDS
Naval Emergency Air Cargo Delivery System
NEACP
National Emergency Airborne Command Post
NEARNAVDIST
Nearest naval district
NEASP
Navy Enlisted Advanced School Program
NEAT
Navy Electronics Application Trainer
NEATICC
Northeast Asia Tactical Information
Communications Center
NEC
Navy Enlisted Classification (code)
Navy Exhibit Center
Necessary
Newspaper Editor's Course (DINFOS)
Non-Engineering Change
Not Elsewhere Classified
NEC, NAVEXAMCEN
Naval Examining Center
NECC
Navy Enlisted Classification Codes
NECOS
Navy Enlisted Occupational Classification
System
NECP
Non-Engineering Change Proposal
NEDED
Naval Explosive Development Engineering
Department
NEDEP
Navy Enlisted Dietetic Education Program

NEDN
Naval Environmental Data Network
NEDRECS
Naval Educational Development Records
NEDU, NAVXDIVINGU
Navy Experimental Diving Unit
NEEO
Naval Electronic Engineering Office
NEES
Naval Engineering Experimental Station
NEESA, NAVENENVSUPPACT
Navy Energy and Environmental Support
Center
NEF
Naval Emergency Fund
NEG
Negative
NEGDEF
Navy Enlisted Ground Defense Emergency
Force(s)
NEHC, NAVENVIRHLTHCEN
Navy Environmental Health Center
NEL
Naval Explosives (or Electronics) Laboratory
NELATS
Naval Electronics Laboratory Automatic
Tester System
NELC
Naval Electronics Laboratory Center
NELIAC
Naval Electronics Laboratory International
Algor Compilers
NEMEDRI
Northern European and Mediterranean
Routing Instructions
NEMO
Naval Experimental Manned Observatory
NEMP
Nuclear Electromagnetic Pulse
NENEP
Navy Enlisted Nursing Education Program
NEO
Navy Exchange Office(r)
NEOCS
Navy Enlisted Occupational Classification
System
NEODTC, NAVEODTECHCEN
Naval Explosive Ordnance Disposal
Technical Center
NEOP
Nuclear Emergency Operations Planning
NEP
Noise Equivalent Power
Nursing Education Program
NEPA
Nuclear Energy for Propulsion of Aircraft
(experimental program)
NEPDB
Navy-wide Environmental Protection Data
Base

NEPMU, NAVENVPVNTMEDU
Navy Environmental and Preventive Medicine
Unit
NEPRF, NAVENVPREDRSCHFAC
Naval Environmental Prediction Research
Facility
NEPSS
Naval Environmental Protection Support
Services (team)
NERRA
NALC European Repair and Rework Activity
NERRAREP
NALC European Repair and Rework Activity
Representative
NERV
Nuclear Emulsion Recovery Vehicle
NERVA
Nuclear Engines for Rocket Vehicle
Applications (experimental program)
NES
Navy Experimental Station
New Enlisted System
Not Elsewhere Specified
NESC
National Environmental Satellite Center
NESC, NAVEMSCEN
Navy Electromagnetic Spectrum Center
NESC, NAVELEX, NAVELEXSYSCOM
Naval Electronic Systems Command
NESEC, NAVELEXSYSENGCEN
Naval Electronic Systems Engineering Center
NESEP
Navy Enlisted Scientific Education Program
NESIP/POA&M
Navy Explosives Safety Improvement
Program/Plan of Action and Milestones
NESN
For NATO Use Among the English-Speaking
Nations of NATO
NESO
Navy Electronics Supply Office
NESO, NAVENVSUPPO
Navy Environmental Support Office
NESP
Navy Enlisted Scientific Program
NESTEF
Naval Electronic Systems Testing and
Evaluation Facility
NET
Noise Equivalent Temperature
Not Earlier Than
Nuclear Emergency Team
NETC, NAVEDTRACEN
Naval Education and Training Center
NETCOS
Net Control Station
NETFIPC
Naval Education and Training Financial
Information Processing Center

NETFIPCBR
Naval Education and Training Financial
Information Processing Branch
NETFMS
Naval Education and Training Financial
Management System
NETISA
Naval Education and Training Information
Systems Activity
NETOPS
Nuclear Emergency Team Operations
NETPDC, NAVEDTRAPROGDEVCEN
Naval Education and Training Program
Development Center
NETS
Naval Environmental Training System
Navy Engineering Technical Services
Network Techniques
NETSC, NAVEDTRASUPPCEN
Naval Education and Training Support Center
NETSCL, NAVEDTRASUPPCENLANT
Naval Education and Training Support
Center, Atlantic
NETSCP, NAVEDTRASUPPCENPAC
Naval Education and Training Support
Center, Pacific
NEURS
Navy Energy Usage Reporting System
NEW
Net Explosive Weight
NEWENGGRU
New England Group
NEWPOSITREP
New Position Report
NEWRADS
Nuclear Explosion Warning and Radiological
System
NEWS
Navy Electronic Warfare Simulator
NEWTS
Navy Electronic Warfare Training Simulator
NEX, NAVEX
Navy Exchange
NF
National Fine (screws & bolts)
Noise Factor (or Figure)
Nose Fuze
NF, N/F
Night Fighter (aircraft)
NF, NUC FLD
Nuclear Field
NFA
Naval Fuel Annex
NF/AEF
Nuclear Field and Advanced Electronics
Fields (program)
NFB
Naval Frontier Base
NFC
Numbered Fleet Command (ship)

NFC, NAVFINCEN
Navy Finance Center
NFC(ALLOT)
Navy Finance Center (Allotments Division)
NFC(CAD)
Navy Finance Center (Central Accounts
Division)
NFC-CLEVE, NAVFINCEN-CLEVE
Navy Finance Center-Cleveland (OH)
NFC-WASH, NAVFINCEN-WASH
Navy Finance Center-Washington (DC)
NFCU
Navy Federal Credit Union
NFD, NAVFUELDEP
Naval Fuel Depot
NFE
Not Fully Equipped
NFEC, NAVFACENGCOM
Naval Facilities Engineering Command
NFI
Net Fundable Issues
NFIS
Naval Fighting Instruction School
NFL
No Fire Line
NFMSO
Navy Fleet Material Support Office
NFMT, NAVFOODMGTM
Navy Food Management Team
NFO
Naval Flight Officer
Normal Fuel Oil
NFO, NAVFINOFF
Navy Finance Office
NFO(B)
Naval Flight Officer (Bombardier)
NFOC
Naval Flight Officer Candidate
NFOC, NAVFACOC
Naval Facility Operational Center
NFO(C)
Naval Flight Officer (Controller)
NFO(I)
Naval Flight Officer (Radar Intercept)
NFOIO
Navy Field Operational Intelligence Office
NFOIODET
Navy Field Operational Intelligence Office
Detachment
NFO(N)
Naval Flight Officer (Navigator)
NFO(S)
Naval Flight Officer (Antisubmarine Warfare)
NFOSG, NAVFLDOPSUPPGRU
Navy Field Operational Support Group
NFPS
Naval Flight Preparatory School
NFSN
For NATO Use Among the French-Speaking
Nations of NATO

NFSO, NAVFUELSUPO
Navy Fuel Supply Officer
NFSS
National Fallout Shelter Survey
NFSSO, NAVFOODSERVSYSOFC
Naval Food Service Systems Office
NFTS
Naval Flight Training School
NFWS, NAVFITWEPSCOL
Navy Fighter Weapons School
NG
Natural Gas
No Good
Not Guilty
NGCT
Navy General Classification Test
NGF
Naval Gunfire
NGF, NAVGUNFAC
Naval Gun Factory
NGFS
Naval Gunfire Support
NGLO
Naval Gunfire Liaison Officer
NGT, NITE
Night
NH, NAVHOME
Naval Home
NH, NAVHOS, NAVHOSP
Naval Hospital
NHA
Next Higher Authority (or Assembly)
NHDC, NAVHISTDISPLAYCEN
Naval Historical Display Center
NHF
Naval Historical Foundation
NHIS
Navy Hazardous Materials Information
System
NHOP
National Hurricane Operations Plan
NHRC, NAVHLTRSCHCEN
Naval Health Research Center
NI
Noise Intensity
NI, NAVINTEL
Naval Intelligence
NIA
Navy Industrial Association
NIAB
Naval Intelligence Advisory Board
NIAC
NAVSHIPS Industry Advisory Committee
NIB
Not to Interfere Basis
NIC, NAVINTCOM
Naval Intelligence Command
NICAD
Naval Cover and Deception (system)
NICE
Normal Input and Control Executive

NICO
Navy Indochina Clearing Office
Navy Inventory Control Office
NICRAD
NAVAIR/Navy Industry Cooperative Research
and Development
NICREP
Naval Intelligence Career Reserve Plan
NICRISP
Navy Integrated Comprehensive Repairable
Item Scheduling Program
NID
Naval Intelligence Division
Network Inward Dial
NID/MO
Network-In-Dial/Manout Out
NIDN
Naval Intelligence Data Network
NIDU
Navigation Instrument Developing Unit
NIEHC
Navy Industrial Environmental Health Center
NIF
Navy Industrial Fund
NIFTE
Neon Indicator Flashing Test Equipment
NIG, NAVINSGEN
Navy Inspector General
NIHOE
Nitrogen, Helium and Oxygen Experiment
NIIN
National Item Identification Number
NILCO, NAVILCO
Navy International Logistics Control Office
NILO, NAVISLO
Naval Interservice Liaison Officer
NIM
Naval Inspector of Machinery
NIMIS
Naval Intelligence Management Information
System
NIMR
Navy Industrial Management Review
NINC
Not Incorporated
NIO
Naval Inspector of Ordnance
Navigational Information Office
NIOD
Network Inward and Outward Dial
NIOSH
National Institute for Occupational Safety and
Health
NIOTC, NAVINSHOROPTRACEN
Naval Inshore Operations Training Center
NIP
Navy Interceptor Program
NIPR
Naval Intelligence Products Register

NIPS
Naval Intelligence Processing System
NMC Information Processing System
NIPSSA
Naval Intelligence Processing System
Support Activity
NIPSTF, NIPSTRAFAC
Naval Intelligence Processing System
Training Facility
NIPSTRAFAC, NIPSTF
Naval Intelligence Processing System
Training Facility
NIPTS
Noise-Induced Permanent Threshold Shift
NIR
NIS Information Reports
NIRA
Navy Industrial Relations Activity
NIRA, NAVINTRELACT
Navy Internal Relations Activity
NIRPL
Navy Industrial Readiness Planning List
NIS
National Information System
National Intelligence Survey
Naval Inspection Service
Non-Interference Basis
Not in Stock (or Store)
Not Issued
NIS, NAVINVSERV
Navy Investigative Service
NISC, NAVINTSUPPCEN
Naval Intelligence Support Center
NISMF
Naval Inactive Ship Maintenance Facility
NISO
NAVSEA Industrial Support Office
NISO, NAVINVSERVO
Naval Investigative Service Office
NISOR, NAVINVSERVOREP
Naval Investigative Service Office
Representative
NISP
Navy Integrated Space Program
NISR
Navy Initial Support Requirements
NISRA, NAVINVSERVRA
Navy Investigative Service Resident Agent
NISREGFORENSICLAB
Naval Investigative Service Regional Forensic
Laboratory
NISSU
Naval Investigative Service Satellite Unit
NISTARS
Naval Integrated Storage, Tracking and
Retrieval System
NISW, NIW
Naval Inshore Warfare
NITE, NGT
Night

NITRAS
Navy Integrated Training Resources and Administration Subsystem
NIW, NISW
Naval Inshore Warfare
NJC
Navy Job Classification (manual)
NJP
Non-Judicial Punishment
NJPMB
Navy Jet-Propelled Missile Boat
NJROTC
Navy Junior Officer Training Corps
NJS, NAVJUSTSCOL
Naval Justice School
NL
Natural Log(arithm)
Navy League
Navy Lighter
Night Letter
NLC
Navy Law Center
NLCEA
Naval Laboratory Centers' Employee Association
NLCP
Navy Logistics Capabilities Plan
NLCP-FY
Navy Logistics Capabilities Plan-Fiscal Year _____
NLD
Navy Lighter (Pontoon) Dock
NLDF
Naval Local Defense Force
NLFED
Naval Landing Force Equipment Depot
NLFM
Noise Level Frequency Monitor
NLFS
Nucleus Landing Force Staff
NLG
Nose Landing Gear
NLL
New London (CN) Laboratory
NLO
Navy Liaison Office(r)
NLRG
Navy Long-Range Guidance
NLROG
Navy Long-Range Objectives Group
NLRSS
Navy Long-Range Strategic Study
NLSS
Navy Logistics Systems School
NLT
On or before but not later than
NLU
Naval Field Liaison Unit
NM
Nautical Mile(s)
Notice to Mariners

NM, NAVMAG, NMAG
Naval Magazine
NMAA
Navy Mutual Aid Association
NMAB
National Materials Advisory Board
NMAG, NAVMAG, NM
Naval Magazine
NMAU, NAVMEDADMINU
Naval Medical Administration Unit
NMC
Navy Memorandum Corrections
NMC, NAVMATCOM
Naval Material Command
NMC, NAVMEDCEN
Naval Medical Center
NMC, NAVMISCEN
Naval Missile Center
NMC, NMCLK
Navy Mail Clerk
NMCB, NAVMOBCONSTBAT
Naval Mobile Construction Battalion
NMCC
National Military Command Center
NMCIRD
Naval Material Command Industrial Resources Detachment
NMCJS
Naval Member, Canadian Joint Staff
NMCLK, NMC
Navy Mail Clerk
N&MCM
Navy and Marine Corps Medal
NMCRB
Navy Military Construction Review Board
NMCS
National Military Command System
NMCSA, NAVMATCOMSUPPACT
Naval Material Command Support Activity
NMD
Navy Marine Diesel (fuel)
NMD, NAVMINEDEP
Naval Mine Depot
NMDF
Navy Management Data File
NMDL
Navy Management Data List(ing)
NMDL, NAVMINEDEFLAB
Navy Mine Defense Laboratory
NMDS
Naval Mine Disposal School
NMDSC, NAVMEDATASERVCEN
Naval Medical Data Services Center
NMDSG, NAVMATDATASYSGRU
Naval Material Data Systems Group
NMEF, NAVMINENGRFAC
Naval Mine Engineering Facility
NMES
Naval Marine Engineering Station
NMEU, NAVMATEVALU
Naval Material Evaluation Unit

NMFC
National Motor Freight Classification (system)
NMFRL, NAVMEDFLDRSCHLAB
Naval Medical Field Research Laboratory
NMFS
National Marine Fisheries
NMG
Navy Metrication Group
Navy Military Government
NMI
Nautical Mile(s)
No Middle Initial
NMIRO
Naval Material Industrial Resources Office
NMIS
Navy Manpower Information System
NMISMAN
Navy Manpower Information System Manual
NMLS
National Microwave Landing System
NMMFO
Navy Maintenance Management Field Office
NMMFO(W)
Navy Maintenance Management Field Office
(West)
NMMM
Navy Maintenance and Material Management
(system)
NMMMS
Navy Maintenance and Material Management
System
NMMSC, NAVMEDMATSUPPCOM
Naval Medical Materiel Support Command
NMN
No Middle Name
NMNRU, NAVMEDNPRSCHU
Naval Medical Neuropsychiatric Research
Unit
NMO
Navy Management Office
NMP
Naval Management Program
Navy Manning Plan
NMPC, NAVMILPERSCOM
Naval Military Personnel Command
NMPCRECSERDIVREGOFF
Naval Military Personnel Command
Recreational Services Division Regional
Office
NMPEX, NMPX
Naval Motion Picture Exchange
NMPNC
Naval Medical Material Program for Nuclear
Casualties
NMPS
Navy Motion Picture Service
NMPSMOPIXDISTOFF
Navy Motion Picture Service, Motion Picture
Distribution Office
NMPX, NMPEX
Navy Motion Picture Exchange

NMR
National Military Representative
Naval Management Review (magazine)
Naval Research Requirements
NMRC
Naval Material Redistribution Center
NMRDC, NAVMEDRSCHDEVCOM
Naval Medical Research and Development
Command
NMR&DO
Naval Material Redistribution and Disposal
Officer
NMRF
Navy-Marine Corps Residence Foundation
NMRG
Navy Mid-Range Guidance
NMRI, NAVMEDRSCHINST
Naval Medical Research Institute
NMRL, NAVMEDRSCHLAB
Naval Medical Research Laboratory
NMRO
Navy Mid-Range Objectives
NMRS
Navy Manpower Requirements System
Numerous
NMRU, NAVMEDRSCHU
Naval Medical Research Unit
NMS
Navy Meteorological Service
Navy Mid-Range Study
NMSB
Navy Manpower Survey Board
NMSC, NAVMGTSYSCEN
Navy Management Systems Center
NMSC, NAVMEDSUPU
Naval Medical Supply Unit
NMSSO, NAVMASSO
Navy Maintenance and Supply Systems
Office
NMTO, NAVMATRANSOFC
Naval Material Transportation Office
NMTS
Naval Mine Testing Center
NMVO
Naval Manpower Validation Office
NMVOLANT
Naval Manpower Validation Office, Atlantic
NMVOPAC
Naval Manpower Validation Office, Pacific
NMVP
Navy Manpower Validation Program
NMVT
Navy Manpower Validation Team
NMWS
Naval Mine Warfare School
NMWTS
Naval Mine Warfare Test Station
NNCC
Navy Nurse Corps Candidate
NND, NAVNETDEP
Naval Net Depot

NNDC, NATNAVDENCEN
National Naval Dental Center
NNMC, NATNAVMEDCEN
National Naval Medical Center
NNPI
Naval Nuclear Propulsion Information
NNPS, NAVNUPWRSCOL
Navy Nuclear Power School
NNPTU, NAVNUPWRTRAU
Naval Nuclear Power Training Unit
NNPU, NAVNUPWRU
Naval Nuclear Power Unit
NNSB&DDCO
Newport News Shipbuilding and Drydock
    Company
NNSS
Navy Navigation Satellite System
NNSY, NNYD
Norfolk Naval Shipyard
NNTRP
National Nuclear Test Readiness Program
NNWO
Navy Nuclear Weapons Officer
NNYD, NNSY
Norfolk Naval Shipyard
NO
Normally Open
NO, NAVOBSY, NOBSY
Naval Observatory
NO, NOV
November
NO, NU, NR
Number
NOA
New Obligation Authority
NOAA
National Oceanic and Atmospheric
    Administration
NOAA-NOS
National Oceanic and Atmospheric
    Administration-National Ocean Service
NOAA-NWS
National Oceanic and Atmospheric
    Administration-National Weather Service
NOACT
Navy Overseas Air Cargo Terminal
NODAC
Navy Occupational Development and
    Analysis Center
NOAH
National Ocean Agency Headquarters
NOAP
Naval Oil Analysis Program
NOARA
Navy Overseas Air Routing Activity
NOAS
Civilian Contract to Navy
NOB
Naval Operating Base
Naval Ordnance Bulletin
Not Observed

NOBC
Navy Officer Billet Codes
NOBS
Naval Operating Base Supplies
NOBSY, NAVOBSY, NO
Naval Observatory
NOC
Naval Officer Classification (codes)
Naval Operations Center
Not Otherwise Classified (or Coded)
NOCF, NAVOCEANCOMFAC
Naval Oceanography Command Facility
NOCONIT
No Continued Interest
NOCOST
This authorization issued with understanding
    there will not be an entitled reimbursement
    for mileage or expenses in connection
    therewith. In case the individual does not
    desire to bear this expense, consider this
    authorization cancelled.
NOCT
Naval Overseas Cargo Terminal
NOD
Network Outward Dial
Night Observation Device
NODAC
Naval Ordnance Data Automation Center
NODB
NOAA Ocean Data Buoy
NODC
National Oceanographic Data Center
Naval Operating Development Center
NODLR, NOD/LR
Night Observation Device, Long-Range
NODS
Navy Overseas Dependents' School
NOE
Notice of Execution
NOEF, NAVORDENGFAC
Naval Ordnance Engineering Facility
NO EFF
No effect(s)
NOF
(International) NOTAM Office
Naval Operating Facility
NOF, NAVORDFAC
Naval Ordnance Facility
NOFAD
Naval Ocean Floor Analysis Division
NOFORN
Not Releasable to Foreign Nationals (Special
    Handling Required)
NOFT
Naval Overseas Flight Terminal
NOI
Non-Operational Intelligence
NOIBN
Not Otherwise Indexed by Name

NOIC
National Oceanographic Instrumentation Center
Naval Officer-in-Charge

NOIO
Naval Ordnance Inspecting Officer

NOIWON
National Operations Intelligence Watch Officers Net

NOK
Next of Kin

NOL, NAVORDLAB
Naval Ordnance Laboratory

NOLC
Naval Ordnance Laboratory, Coronado (CA)

NOLO
No Line Operators
No Live Operators (on board)

NOLTESTFAC, NOLTF
Naval Ordnance Laboratory Test Facility

NOLTF, NOLTESTFAC
Naval Ordnance Laboratory Test Facility

NOMAD
Navy Oceanographic and Meteorological Automatic Device (buoy)

NOMIS
Naval Ordnance Management Information System

NOMOP
There is no record that he has received previous payment under provisions of the Mustering-Out Payment Act of 1944, Veterans Readjustment Assistance Act of 1952, or Chapter 43 of Title 38, U.S. Code.

NOMTF, NAVORDMISTESTFAC
Naval Ordnance Missile Test Facility

NONCONST
Non-Consent

NONEG
Negative replies neither required nor desired

NON-FRAG
Non-Fragmentation (bomb)

NON-TOE
Non-Table of Organization and Equipment

NOO, NAVOCEANO, NAVOCEANOFC
Navy Oceanographic Office

NOP
Naval Oceanographic Program
Naval Ordnance Plant
Navy Objectives (or Operations) Plan
Navy Ordnance Plan
Notice of Procurement
Not Operationally Priced
Not Otherwise Provided for
Nuclear Ordnance Platoon

NOPCL
Naval Officer Personnel Circular Letters

NOFP, NAVOCEANPROFAC
Naval Ocean Processing Facility

NOPHYSRET
Not required to take new physical examination unless material change in physical condition has occurred subsequent to recent physical examination

NOPROCAN
If not already processed, orders (identified by date or DTG) cancelled

NOPS
National Ocean Policy Study
Navigation Operating Procedures

NOR
Inverted Output OR
Notice of Revision
Not Operationally Ready

NOR, N
North(ern)

NORA
Naval Operations Recreation Association

NORAD
North American Air Defense Command

NORAIM
Not Operationally Ready, Aircraft Intermediate Maintenance

NORATS
Navy Operational Radio and Telephone Switchboard

NORBS
Northern Base Section

NORC
Naval Ordnance Research Center (or Computer)

NORDA
Naval Research and Development Activity

NORDM
Not Operationally Ready, Depot Maintenance

NORDO
No Radio

NOREAST, NE
Northeast(ern)

NOREIMB
This authorization is issued with the understanding that the individual will not be entitled to reimbursement for transportation, per diem or miscellaneous expenses in connection therewith. In case the individual does not desire to bear this expense, consider this authorization cancelled.

NOREX
Nuclear Operational Readiness Exchange

NORLANT
North(ern) Atlantic

NORM
Normal(ized)
Not Operationally Ready, Maintenance

NORMSHOR
Normal Tour of Shore Duty

NORPAC
North(ern) Pacific

NORPACREGREPCEN
Northern Pacific Regional Reporting Center

NORRS
  Naval Operational Readiness Reporting
    System
NORS
  Not Operationally Ready, Supply
NORSA, NAVORECSUPPACT
  Naval Officer Record Support Activity
NORSAIR
  Not Operationally Ready, Supply/Aviation
    Item Reports
NORSG
  Not Operationally Ready, Supply/Grounded
NORTHNAVFACENGCOM
  Northern Naval Facilities Engineering
    Command
NORU
  Navy Recruiting Orientation Unit
NORVA
  Norfolk, Virginia
NORVAGRP
  Norfolk, Virginia Group
NORVATEVDET
  Norfolk, Virginia Test and Evaluation
    Detachment
NORWES, NW
  Northwest(ern)
NORWESSEAFRON, NWSF
  Northwestern Sea Frontier
NORWESSECWESSEAFRON
  Northwestern Sector, Western Sea Frontier
NOS
  National Ocean Service
  Not Otherwise Specified
NOSC, NAVOCEANSYSCEN
  Naval Ocean Systems Center
NOSCL, NAVOCEANSYSCENLAB
  Naval Ocean Systems Center Laboratory
NOSIC, NAVOCEANSURVINFOCEN
  Naval Ocean Surveillance Information Center
NOSL
  Naval Ordnance Station, Louisville (KY)
NOSR
  Naval Oil Shale Reserves
NOSS
  National Orbiting Space Station
  Nimbus Operational Satellite System
NOSSO, NAVORDSYSUPPO
  Naval Ordnance Systems Support Office
NOSSOLANT, NAVORDSYSUPPOLANT
  Naval Ordnance Systems Support Office,
    Atlantic
NOSSOPAC, NAVORDSYSUPPOPAC
  Naval Ordnance Systems Support Office,
    Pacific
NOSSOREP, NAVORDSYSUPPOREP
  Naval Ordnance Systems Support Office
    Representative
NOSTA, NAVOPHTHALSUPPTRACT
  Naval Ophthalmic Support Training Activity
NOTAL
  Not to all

NOTAMS
  Notices to Airmen
NOTAP
  Navy Occupational Task Analysis Program
NOTC
  Naval Officer Training Center
NOTE, NTC
  Notice
NT FLT CK
  Not Flight Checked
NOTIP
  Northern-Tier Integration Project
NOTS
  Naval Ordnance Test Station
NOTU
  Naval Operational Training Unit
NOTUN
  Notice of Unreliability
NOU, NAVORDU
  Naval Ordnance Unit
NOV
  NSA Items Only for Overseas Shipment
NOV, NO
  November
NP
  Neap (tide)
  Nuclear Power(ed)
  Small Patrol Craft
NP, NAVPRIS
  Naval Prison
NP, PN
  North Pole
NPA
  Navy Purchasing Activity
  Network Planning and Analysis
  Non-Propulsion Attachment
  Numbering Plan Area
NPAB
  Naval Price Adjustment Board
NPAM
  Navy Priorities and Allocations Manual
NPANX
  Naval Potomac Annex
NPAP
  Navy Public Affairs Plan
NPBS
  Navy Personnel Billeting System
NPC
  Naval Publications and Forms Center
  Nucleus Port Crew
NPC, NAVPHOTOCEN
  Naval Photographic Center
NPCO, NAVPORTCO
  Naval Port Control Office
NPD
  Navy Procurement Directives
NPD, NAVPURDEP
  Navy Purchasing Department
NPDES
  National Pollutant Discharge Elimination
    System

NPDI
Non-Performance of Duty Because of
Imprisonment
NPDI(CIVIL)
Non-Performance of Duty Because of Civil
Arrest
NPDU, NAVPLANTDEVU
Naval Plant Development Unit
NPE
Navy Preliminary Evaluation
NPF
Naval Procurement Fund
NPF, NAVPOWFAC
Naval Powder Factory
NPFC, NAVPUBFORMCEN
Naval Publications and Forms Center
NPG
Naval Proving Ground
Nuclear Planning Group
NPGS, NAVPGSOL, NAVPOSTGRADSCOL
Navy Postgraduate School
NPIC
Navy Photographic Interpretation Center
NPM
Navy Programming Manual
NPMA
Navy Personnel Management Academy
NPN
Negative-Positive-Negative (transistor)
NPO
Naval Port Office
Navy Post Office
Navy Program Objectives
NPO, NAVPETOFF
Naval Petroleum Office
NPO, NAVPURO
Navy Purchasing Office
NPOC, NAVPOLAROCEANCEN
Navy Polar Oceanographic Center
NPP
Navy Propellant Plant
NPPC
Navy Program Planning Council (CNO)
NPPE
Nuclear Power Propulsion Evaluation (or
Examination)
NPPO
Navy Program and Planning Office
NPPO, NAVPUBPRINTO
Navy Publications and Printing Office
NPPS, NAVPUBPRINTSERV
Navy Publications and Printing Service
NPPSBO
Navy Publications and Printing Service
Branch Office
NPPSDET, NAVPUBPRINTSERVDET
Navy Publications and Printing Service
Detachment
NPPSNORDIV
Navy Publications and Printing Service,
Northern Division

NPPSO, NAVPUBPRINTSERVO
Navy Publications and Printing Service Office
NPPSSOEASTDIV
Navy Publications and Printing Service,
Southeastern Division
NPPSWESTDIV
Navy Publications and Printing Service,
Western Division
NPR
Naval Plant Representative
Navy Payroll
Navy Preliminary Revision
Nuclear Power Reactor
NPR, NAVPETRES
Naval Petroleum Reserves
NPRDC, NAVPERSRSCHDEVCEN
Navy Personnel Research and Development
Center
NPRO, NAVPETRESO
Naval Petroleum Reserves Office
NPRO, NAVPRO
Naval Plant Representative Officer
NPS
Navy Personnel Survey
NPS, NAVPGSCOL, NAVPOSTGRADSCOL
Navy Postgraduate School
NPSC
Naval Personnel Separation Center
NPSCE
Naval Postgraduate School Continuing
Education
NPSD
Naval Photographic Services Depot
NPSE
Navy Periodontal Screening Examination
NPSH
Net Positive Suction Head (pump)
NPT
Navy Pointer Tracker
Neuropsychiatry
Nonproliferation Treaty
NPT/E
Navy Parachute Team/East Coast
NPTF
Nuclear Power Task Force
NPTG
Nuclear Power Task Group
NPTR
National Parachute Test Range
NPTRL
Naval Personnel and Training Research
Laboratory
NPTU, NAVPETRAU
Naval Petroleum Training Unit
NPT/W
Navy Parachute Team/West Coast
NPW
Nuclear-Powered Warship
NPWC, NAVPUBWKSCEN
Navy Public Works Center

NPWD, NAVPUBWKSDEPT
Navy Public Works Department
NPWTC
NAVFAC Public Works Training Center
NQA
Nuclear Quality Assurance
NQC
Nuclear Quality Control
NQE
Nuclear Quality Engineering
NQR
Nuclear Quadropole Resonator
NR
Natural Rubber
Noise Reduction (or Review)
Non-Reproducible (copy)
Not Required (or Ready)
Nuclear Reactor
Submersible Research Vehicle
  (Nuclear-Propulsion) (concept)
NR, NAVREGS
Navy Regulations
NR, NAVRES
Naval Reserve
NR, NO, NU
Number
NRA
Naval Radio Activity
Naval Reserve Association
NRA, NAVCRUITAREA
Navy Recruiting Area
NRAB
Naval Reserve Aviation Base
NRAC
Naval Reserve Advisory Committee
NRACCO
Navy Regional Air Cargo Control Office
NRAF
Naval Reserve Auxiliary Field
Navy Recruiting Aids Facility
NRAO
Navy Regional Accounts Office
NRAS
Navy Readiness Analysis System
NRB
Naval Repair Base
Navy Reservation Bureau
NRBS, NAVCRUITBRSTA
Navy Recruiting Branch Station
NRC
Naval Research Company
Navy Recreation Center
Noise Reduction Coefficient
NRC, NAVCRUITCOM
Navy Recruiting Command
NRC, NAVRADCON
Naval Radiological Control
NRC, NAVRESCEN
Naval Recreation Center
NRC, NAVRESCEN
Naval Reserve Center

NRCC
Non-Resident Career Course
NRCO, NAVREGCONTO
Navy Regional Contracting Office
NRD
Naval Research Development
NRD, NAVCRUITDIST
Navy Recruiting District
NRDC
Naval Drug Rehabilitation Center
Naval Research and Development Center
NRDFS
Naval Radio Direction Finder Service
NRDL, NAVRADEFLAB
Naval Radiological Defense Laboratory
NRDS
Nuclear Rocket Development Station
NREB
Naval Reserve Evaluation Board
NREC, NAVCRUITEXHIBCEN
Navy Recruiting Exhibit Center
NRES, NAVRECSTA
Naval Receiving Station
NRF
Naval Repair Facility
NRF, NAVRESFAC
Naval Reserve Facility
NRF, NAVRESFOR
Naval Reserve Force
NRFC, NAVREGFINCEN
Navy Regional Finance Center
NRFC-B, NAVREGFINCENBKLN
Navy Regional Finance Center, Brooklyn
  (NY)
NRFC-GL, NAVREGFINCENGLAKES
Navy Regional Finance Center-Great Lakes
  (IL)
NRFC-N, NAVREGFINCENNORVA
Navy Regional Finance Center, Norfolk,
  Virginia
NRFC-PH, NAVREGFINCENPEARL
Navy Regional Finance Center, Pearl Harbor
  (HA)
NRFC-SD, NAVREGFINCENSDIEGO
Navy Regional Finance Center, San Diego
  (CA)
NRFC-SF, NAVREGFINCENSFRAN
Navy Regional Finance Center, San
  Francisco (CA)
NRFI
Not Ready for Issue
NRFMAU
Naval Reserve Fleet Management Assistance
  Unit
NRFO, NAVREGFINOFC
Navy Regional Finance Office
NRFS
Naval Reserve Force Study Group
NRIUW
Naval Reserve Inshore Undersea Warfare

NRL, NAVRSCHLAB
Naval Research Laboratory (ONR)
NRLREP, NAVRSCHLABREP
Naval Research Laboratory Representative
NRLUWSREFDET
Naval Research Laboratory Underwater
Sound Reference Detachment
NRLCHESBAYDET
Naval Research Laboratory Chesapeake Bay
Detachment
NRLFLTSUPPDET
Naval Research Laboratory Flight Support
Detachment
NRLSITEDET
Naval Research Laboratory Field Site
Detachment
NRLSPECPROJDET
Naval Research Laboratory Special Projects
Detachment
NRM
Noise Reduction Manual
NRMC
Naval Records Management Center
NRMC, NAVREGMEDCEN
Naval Regional Medical Center
NRMC, NAVRESMANPWRCEN
Naval Reserve Manpower Center
NRMIUW
Naval Reserve Mobile Inshore Undersea
Warfare
NRMOMAGU
Naval Reserve Mobile Mine Assembly Group
NRMS, NAVRESMGTSCOL
Naval Reserve Management School
NRMS, NAVRESMIDSCOL
Naval Reserve Midshipmen's School
NRO
Navy Retail Office
NROS
Naval Reserve Officers School
N-ROSS
Navy-Remote Ocean Sensing System
NROTC
Naval Reserve Officers Training Corps
NROTCU
Naval Reserve Officers Training Corps Unit
NROTCUNAVADMINU
Naval Reserve Officers Training Corps Unit
and Administrative Unit
NRP
Noise Review Program
Notice of Research Projects
NRPAC
Naval Reserve Public Affairs Company
NRPB
Naval Research Planning Board
Naval Reserve Policy Board
NRPC, NAVRESPERSCEN
Naval Reserve Personnel Center
NRPEO, NAVREGPEO
Naval Regional Plant Equipment Office(r)

NRPIO
Naval Registered Publications Issuing Officer
NRPM
Non-Registered Publications Memoranda
NRR
Naval Research (or Reserve) Requirement
NRRC
Naval Reserve Readiness Center
Naval Reserve Research Company
NRRF
Naval Reserve Readiness Facility
NRRF, NAVRADRECFAC
Naval Radio Receiving Facility
NRR/O
Naval Reactor Representative/Office
NRS
Naval Reserve Security Division
Navy Relief Society
Navy Resale System
NRS, NAVCRUITSTA
Navy Recruiting Station
NRS, NAVRADSTA
Naval Radio Station
NRS, NAVREL
Navy Relief Society
NRSC
Naval Reserve Supply Company
NRSG, NAVRESSECGRU
Naval Reserve Security Group
NRSO
Navy Resale System Office
NRS(R), NAVRADSTA(R)
Naval Radio Station (Receiving)
NRS(S), NAVRADSTA(S)
Naval Radio Station (Sending)
NRSSO, NAVRESSO
Navy Resale and Services Support Office
NRT, NAVRESTRA
Naval Reserve Training
NRTC, NAVCRUITRACOM
Navy Recruit Training Command
NRTF, NAVRADTRANSFAC
Naval Radio Transmitting Facility
NRTS
National Reactor Testing Station
Not Repairable This Ship
NRTSC, NAVRECONTECHSUPPCEN
Naval Reconnaissance and Technical
Support Center
**NRTSCLANT,
NAVRECONTECHSUPPCENLANT**
Naval Reconnaissance and Technical
Support Center, Atlantic
NRTSCPAC, NAVRECONTECHSUPPCENPAC
Naval Reconnaissance and Technical
Support Center, Pacific
NRX/EST
Nuclear Reactor, Experimental/Engine
System Test
NRZ
Non-Return-to-Zero

NRZI
  Non-Return-to-Zero-IBM
NS
  Navy Standard (seat type parachute)
  Nimbostratus (cloud formation)
  Non-Structural
  Normally Shut
  Nuclear Ship
NS, NAVSTA
  Naval Station
N/S
  North/South
N/S, NSF
  Not Sufficient Funds
NSA
  Navy Stock Account
  Nuclear Science Abstracts
NSA, NAVSUPANX
  Navy Supply Annex
NSA, NAVSUPPACT
  Naval Support Activity
NSACSS
  National Security Agency Central Security
    Service
NSAD, NAVSUPPACTDET
  Naval Support Activity Detachment
NSAM
  National Security Action Memorandum
  Naval School of Aviation Medicine
NSAP
  Navy Science Assistance Program
NSAT
  NAVMAT Special Assistance Team
NSATS
  NAVMAT Selected Acquisitions Tracking
    System
NSB, NAVSUBBASE
  Naval Submarine Base
NSC
  Naval Sea Cadets
  Numeric Sequence Code
NSC, NAVSAFECEN
  Navy Safety Center
NSC, NAVSCOLCOM
  Naval Schools Command
NSC, NAVSUPCEN
  Naval Supply Center
NSCC
  Naval Sea Cadet Corps
NSCC, NAVSEACARCO
  Navy Sea Cargo Coordinator
NSCCLO
  Naval Sea Cadet Corps Liaison Officer
NSCD
  Nuclear Service Control Date
NSCDET
  Naval Supply Center Detachment
NSCF
  Naval Small-Craft Facilities
NSCO
  Naval Supply Center, Oakland (CA)

NSCO, NAVSEACARCOORD
  Naval Sea Cargo Coordinator
NSCPS
  Naval Supply Center, Puget Sound
    (Bremerton, WA)
NSD
  Navy Support Date
NSD, NAVSUPDEP
  Naval Supply Depot
NSD, NAVSUPDEPT
  Naval Supply Department
NSDA
  Naval Supply Depot Annex
NSDAT
  Naval School of Dental Assisting and
    Technology
NSDAVNDEPT
  Naval Supply Depot Aviation Department
NSDDET
  Naval Supply Depot Detachment
NSE
  Naval Shore Establishment
  Noise Control
NSEC
  Naval Ship Engineering Center
NSF
  Navy Stock Fund
NSF, NAVSUPPFOR
  Naval Support Force
NSF, N/S
  Not Sufficient Funds
NSFA, NAVSUPPFORANTARCTICA
  Naval Support Force, Antarctica
NSFO
  Navy Special Fuel Oil
NSG
  National Security Group
NSGA, NAVSECGRUACT
  Naval Security Group Activity
NSGC, NAVSECGRUCOM
  Naval Security Group Command
NSGOC
  Naval Security Group Orientation Course
NSGTP
  Naval Security Group Training Publication
NSHO
  Naval Service Headquarters, Ottawa
NSHS
  Naval School of Health Sciences
NSHSDET
  Naval School of Health Sciences Detachment
NSI
  Naval Science Instructor
  Non-Standard Item
  Non-Stock(ed) Item
  Nuclear Status Indicator
NSIC
  Next Senior in Command
NSL
  Navy Standards Laboratory
  Navy Stock List

NSLI
National Service Life Insurance
NSM
Naval School of Music
NS MCM
Navy Supplement to the Manual for
Courts-Martial
NSMG
Naval School of Military Government
NSMG&A
Naval School of Military Government and
Administration
NSMP
Navy Support and Mobilization Plan
NSMRL
Naval Submarine Medical Research
Laboratory
NSMSES
Naval Ship Missile System Engineering
Station
NSN
National Stock Number
NSO, NAVSUBSOFC
Navy Subsistence Office
NSO, NAVSUPO
Navy Supply Office
NSOC
Navy Satellite Operations Center
NSP
Navy Safety Program
Navy Support Plan
NSPCC
Navy Ships Parts Control Center
NSPD
Naval Shore Patrol Detachment
NSPF
Not Specifically Provided for
NSPO
Navy Special Projects Office
NSR
Naval Supply Requirements
NSRDC, NAVSHIPRSCHDEVCEN
Naval Ship Research and Development
Center
**NSRDC/A, NAVSHIPRSCHDEVCENANNA,
NSRDCANNADIV**
Naval Ship Research and Development
Center, Annapolis (MD) Division
**NSRDCANNADIV,
NAVSHIPRSCHDEVCENANNA, NSRDC/A**
Naval Ship Research and Development
Center, Annapolis (MD) Division
NSRF, NAVSHIPREPFAC
Naval Ship Repair Facility
NSRS
Navy Supply Radio Station
NSS
Navy Standard Score
Navy Strategic Study
Navy Supply Systems

NSSA, NAVSPASYSACT
Naval Space Systems Activity
NSSB, NAVSUBSUPPBASE
Naval Submarine Support Base
NSSC, NAVSEA, NAVSEASYSCOM
Naval Sea Systems Command
NSSC, NAVSEACEN
Naval Sea Support Center
NSSCR, NAVSEASYSCOMREP
Naval Sea Systems Command
Representative
NSSI
Navy System Stock Inventories
NSSMS
NATO Seasparrow Missile System
NSSNF
Naval Strategic Systems Navigation Facility
NSSO, NAVSHIPSTO
Navy Ships Store Office
NSSS
Naval Space Surveillance System
NST
Normal Shore Tour
NSA Items for Stateside Shipment
NS&T
Naval Science and Tactics
NSTEP
Naval Scientist Training and Exchange
Program
NSTIC, NAVSCIENTECHINTELCEN
Navy Scientific and Technical Intelligence
Center
**NSTICLANT,
NAVSCIENTECHINTELCENLANT**
Navy Scientific and Technical Intelligence
Center, Atlantic
NSTICPAC, NAVSCIENTECHINTELCENPAC
Navy Scientific and Technical Intelligence
Center, Pacific
NSTM
NAVSHIPS Technical Manual
NSWC, NAVSWC
Naval Surface Weapons Center
NSWSES
Naval Ship Weapon Systems Engineering
Station
NSY, NSYD
Naval Shipyard
NSYD, NSY
Naval Shipyard
NT
Net Ton (U/I)
Nighttime
Non-Tight
Normalized and Tempered
NT, NAVTRA
Naval Training
NTAC, NAVTRAIDSCEN
Naval Training Aids Center
NTAF, NAVTRAIDSFAC
Naval Training Aids Facility

NTAFT
  Navy Technical Assistance Field Team
NTBI
  Not to be Incorporated
NTC
  Navy Test Controller
NTC, NAVTRACEN
  Naval Training Center
NTC, NOTE
  Notice
NTCC
  Naval Telecommunications Center
NTCCDET
  Naval Telecommunications Center
    Detachment
NTCO, NAVTRANSCO
  Navy Transportation Coordinating Office
NTDC, NAVTRADEVICESCEN
  Naval Training Devices Center
NT&DC
  Naval Training and Distribution Center
NTDDPA
  Naval Tactical Doctrine Development and
    Production Activity
NTDI
  Non-Destructive Testing and Inspection
NTDO
  Navy Technical Data Office
NTDS
  Navy Tactical Data System
NTDSC, NAVTRADEVSUPCEN
  Navy Training Devices Supply Center
NTE
  Navy Technical Evaluation
NTEC, NAVTRAEQUIPCEN
  Navy Training Equipment Center
NTI
  Naval Travel Instructions
NTIS
  National Technical Information Service
NTMT
  Navigation Tender Maintenance Training
NTOC
  Naval Telecommunications Operations Center
NTOCDET
  Naval Telecommunications Operations Center
    Detachment
NTORS, NAVTORPSTA
  Naval Torpedo Station
NTP
  Naval Technological Projections
  Naval Telecommunications Publication
  Navy Training Plan
NTPC
  Navy Training Plan Conference
  Navy Training Publications Center
NTPI
  Naval Technical Proficiency Inspection
NTP/IDCSP
  Navy Test Plan for Initial Defense
    Communications Satellite Program

NTPS
  Near-Term Pre-Positioning Ships
NTS
  Naval Target Subdivision
  Naval Telecommunications System
  Naval Training School
  Naval Transportation Service
NTS, NAVTRASTA
  Naval Training Station
NTS, NAVTORPSTA, NTORS
  Naval Torpedo Station
NTSA
  Naval Telecommunications System Architect
NTSA, NAVTACSUPPACT
  Navy Tactical Support Activity
NTSB
  National Transportation Safety Board
NTTC, NAVTECHTRACEN
  Naval Technical Training Center
NTU
  New Threat Upgrade (for Terrier missiles)
NTU, NAVTRAU
  Naval Training Unit
NTX
  Navy Teletypewriter Exchange
NU, NO, NR
  Number
NUB
  Navy Uniform Board
NUC
  Naval Undersea Center
  Navy Unit Commendation
NUC FLD, NF
  Nuclear Field
NUDETS
  Nuclear Detection System
NUHELI
  Nuclear Helicopter (concept)
NUKE
  Nuclear (system or personnel)
NULACE
  Nuclear Liquid Air Cycle Engine
NUMEC
  Nuclear Materials and Equipment Corporation
NUMIS
  Navy Uniform Management Information
    System
NUOS, NAVUWTRORDSTA
  Naval Underwater Ordnance Station
NUPOC
  Nuclear Propulsion Officer Candidate
    (submarine program)
NUPOC-S
  Nuclear Propulsion Officer
    Candidate-Submarine
NUPWR
  Nuclear Power(ed)
NUPWRU
  Nuclear Power Unit
NURIG
  Navy Utility Regulatory Intervention Group

NUSC, NAVUWSYSCEN
Naval Underwater Systems Center
NUSCDET
Naval Underwater Systems Center
Detachment
NUSL, NAVUWTRSOUNDLAB
Navy Underwater Sound Laboratory
NUVEP
NAVSEA Unified Vendor Evaluation Program
NUWATI
Nuclear Work Authorization Technical
Instruction
NUWEPSA, NUWPNSUPANX, NWSA
Nuclear Weapons Supply Annex
NUWPNSUPANX, NUWEPSA, NWSA
Nuclear Weapons Supply Annex
NUWPNSTRACEN, NWTC
Nuclear Weapons Training Center
NUWPNSTRACENLANT, NWTCL
Nuclear Weapons Training Center, Atlantic
NUWPNSTRACENPAC, NWTCP
Nuclear Weapons Training Center, Pacific
NUWRES
Naval Underwater Weapons Research and
Engineering Station
NV
Non-Vital
NVASS
Night-Vision Aerial Surveillance System
NVCT
Non-Verbal Classification Test
NVII
Navy Vocational Interest Inventory
NVL
Night-Vision Laboratory
NVR
Naval Vessel Register
NW
No Wind
Nuclear Warfare
NW, NORWEST
Northwest(ern)
NWA
Navy Wifeline Association
NWAC
National Weather Analysis Center
NWC, NAVWARCOL
Naval War College
NWC, NAVWPNCEN
Naval Weapons Center
NWCA
Navy Wives Club(s) of America
NWC/CS
Naval War College/Command and Staff
(course)
NWC/NW
Naval War College/Naval Warfare (course)
NWCP
Navy Weight-Control Program
NWEF, NAVWEPEVALFAC
Naval Weapons Evaluation Facility

NWF
Navy Working Fund
NWFA
Navy-Wide Finance Activities
NWIP
Naval Warfare Information Program (or
Publication)
NWISO
Naval Weapons Industrial Support Office
NWL
Naval Weapons Laboratory
NWL/D
Naval Weapons Laboratory/Dahlgren (VA)
NWP
Naval Warfare Publication
Naval Weapons Plant
NWPSC
Nationwide Postal-Strike Contingency Plan
NWPU
Numerical Weather Prediction Unit
NWRF
Navigational Weather Research Facility
NWS
National Weather Service
Naval Weapons Station
NWSA, NUWEPSA, NUWPNSUPANX
Nuclear Weapons Supply Annex
NWSC
National Weather Satellite Center
NWSF, NORWESSEAFRON
Northwestern Sea Frontier
NWSO, NAVWPNSERVO
Naval Weapons Service Office
NWSS
Navy WWMCCS Software Standardization
NWTC, NUWPNSTRACEN
Nuclear Weapons Training Center
NWTCL, NUWPNSTRACENLANT
Nuclear Weapons Training Center, Atlantic
NWTCP, NUWPNSTRACENPAC
Nuclear Weapons Training Center, Pacific
NWTG, NUWPNSTRAGRU
Nuclear Weapons Training Group
NWTGL, NUPWNSTRAGRULANT
Nuclear Weapons Training Group, Atlantic
NWTGP, NUWPNSTRAGRUPAC
Nuclear Weapons Training Group, Pacific
NWTP
Naval Warfare Tactical Publication
NWUIS, NAVWUIS
Navy Work Unit Information System
NXSR
Non-Extraction Steam Rate
NY
Navy Yard
NYOD
New York Area Office (ONR)
NYCHARL
Navy Yard, Charleston (SC)
NYK, NYNYD
New York Navy Yard

NYKGRP
New York Group
NYMI
Navy Yard, Mare Island (CA)
NYNOR
Navy Yard, Norfolk (VA)
NYNYD, NYK
New York Navy Yard
NYPE
New York, Port of Embarkation
NYPH
Navy Yard, Pearl Harbor (HA)
NYPHIL
Navy Yard, Philadelphia (PA)
NYPORT
Navy Yard, Portsmouth (NH)
NYPS
Navy Yard, Puget Sound (WA)
NYWASH
Navy Yard, Washington (DC)
NZLO
New Zealand Liaison Officer
NZSEAFRON
New Zealand Sea Frontier

O

O
Airborne Intercept (TO code)
Main Oxygen (system)
Obsolescent (-ence)
Original (copy)
O, OF, OFC
Office
O/A
Operations Analysis
OAASN
Office of the Administrative Assistant to the
Secretary of the Navy
OAC
Operation of Aircraft Costs
OACC
Oceanic Area Control Center
OAD
Officers' Accounts Division
Operational Active Data
Operational Availability Date
O&A DATE
Oath and Acceptance Date
OA-DG
Occupational Area Defense Grouping
OA DIV
Operations/Weather Service Division
OADR
Originating Agency's Determination Required
OAL
Order Action List
OAM
Orthopedic Appliance Mechanic

OANFE
Operational Aircraft Not Fully Equipped
OAO
Orbiting Astronomical Observatory
OAP
Offset Aimpoint
Overall Average Percentage
OAR
ORDALT Accomplishment Requirement (list)
OARS
Ocean Area Reconnaissance Satellite
OAS
Office of the Assistant Secretary
Other Active Military Service
OASD
Office of the Assistant Secretary of Defense
OASD(HA)
Office of the Assistant Secretary of Defense
(Health Affairs)
OASD(MRA&L)
Office of the Assistant Secretary of Defense
(Manpower, Reserve Affairs and Logistics)
OASDI
Old Age Survivors and Disability Insurance
OASIS
Ocean All-Sources Information System
OASN, OFCOFASSTSECNAV
Office of the Assistant Secretary of the Navy
OASN(FM), OFCOFASSTSECNAV(FINMGMT)
Office of the Assistant Secretary of the Navy
(Financial Management)
OASN(I&L),
   OFCOFASSTSECNAV(INSTALLOG)
Office of the Assistant Secretary of the Navy
(Installation and Logistics)
OASN(P&RF),
   OFCOFASSTSECNAV(PERSRESFOR)
Office of the Assistant Secretary of the Navy
(Personnel and Reserve Force)
OASN(R&D),
   OFCOFASSTSECNAV(RSCHDEV)
Office of the Assistant Secretary of the Navy
(Research and Development)
OAT
Outside Air Temperature
OATC
Oceanic Air Traffic Center
Overseas Air Traffic Control
OATS
Optimum Aerial Targeting Sensor
OB
Operating (or Operational) Base
Operating Budget
Ordnance Battalion (or Board)
O/B
On Berth
OBA
Oxygen Breathing Apparatus
OB/CP
Observation/Command Post

OBDB
On Board Data Bank
OBL
Operational Base Launch
OBLISERV
Obligated service of (number of months indicated) required, or execute Form NAVPERS 604
OBLISERVNATRA
Obligated to serve 3½ years following date of completion of training within the Naval Air Training Command
OBLISERVONEASIX
Execution of these orders obligates him to serve on active duty 1 year for each 6 months of schooling or fraction thereof (SECNAVINST 1920.3 series). Obligation to commence upon termination or completion of schooling and is in addition to the remaining time required by any prior ACDU obligation.
OBLISERVTHREETIME
Execution of these orders obligates him to serve on active duty a period of three times the length of the period of education (SECNAVINST 1500.4 series). Obligation to commence upon termination or completion of schooling and is in addition to the remaining time required by any prior ACDU obligation.
OBLISERVTWOYR
Execution of these orders obligates him to serve on active duty a period of 2 years. Obligation to commence upon termination or completion of schooling and is in addition to the remaining time required by any prior ACDU obligation.
OBO
Ore/Bunk/Oil (vessel)
OBRP
On Board Repair Parts
OBS
Observe
Obsolete
Obstacle
OBS, OBSN
Observation
OBS, OBSY
Observatory
OBSC
Obscure
OBSHT
Obstacle Height
OBSN, OBS
Observation
OBSR
Observer
OBSRON, VO
Observation Squadron
OBSS
Ocean Bottom Scanning Sonar

OBS SPOT
Observation Spot
OBST, OBSTN
Obstruction
OBSTN, OBST
Obstruction
OBSY, OBS
Observatory
OBTAINFUNDIS
Authorized to obtain funds in accordance with NAVCOMPMAN par. 042352-8, to make cash disbursements to cover actual expenses incurred on account of recruiting
OBTAINDORSETRANS
If he avails himself of leave, obtain endorsement from each TEMADD point as to transportation which would have been available in reporting to next TEMADD point or in returning to duty station via shortest, usually traveled route, giving dates and hours of departure and arrival. Authorized to visit countries specified in leave status. Comply with Encl. (2) current NAVPERSCOMINST 1050.1.
OC
Operations Control
OC, OCT
October
OCA
Oceanic Control Area
Operational Control Authority
OCAN
Officer Candidate Airman (program)
OCAS
Officer-in-Charge of Armament Supply
Ordnance Configuration Accounting System
OCC
Occulting (light)
Officer Correspondence Course
OCC, OPC, OPCONCEN
Operational Control Center
OCCAS
Occasional (light)
OCCSPEC
Occupational Specialties (handbook)
OCD
Office of Civilian Defense
Ordnance Classification of Defects
OC DIV
Operations/Aircraft Control Division
OCDM
Office of Civilian and Defense Mobilization
OCE
Office of Chief of Engineers
Officer Conducting the Exercise
OCEANDEVRON, VNX
Oceanographic Development Squadron
OCEI
Ocean Construction Equipment Inventory
OCFNT
Occluded Front

OCHAMPUS
Office of the Civilian Health and Medical
Program of the Uniformed Services
OCHAMPUSEUR
Office of the Civilian Health and Medical
Program of the Uniformed Services in
Europe
OCIR
Operational Capability Improvement Request
Out of Commission, In Reserve (vessel
status)
OCL
Obstacle Clearance Limits
Occlude
Ordnance Circular Letters
OCLN
Occlusion
OCMM
Office of Civilian Manpower Management
OCNLY
Occasionally
OCPR
Operation and Conversion of Naval
Petroleum Reserves
OCONUS, OUTCONUS, OUTUS
Outside Continental Limits of the United
States
OCPO
Operations Cargo Passenger Office
OCPS
Officer Candidate Preparatory School
OCR
Occur
Optical Character Recognition (or Reader)
Overhaul Condition Report
OCRD
Office of the Chief of Research and
Development
OCS
Officer Candidate School
Operations Control System
Optimum Coordinated Shipboard Allowance
List
Outer Continental Shelf
Outpatient Clinic Substation
OCSP
Out of Commission, Special (vessel status)
OCT
Octane
Office of the Chief of Transportation
OCT, OC
October
OCT/RR
Off-Course Target/Remote Reference
(display)
OCU
Operations Conversion Unit

OD
Observed Drift
Oil Distribution
Optical Density
Ordnance Data (or Detachment)
Outside Diameter
OD, O/D
On Deck
ODA
Operational Data Analysis
ODAR
Optical Detection and Ranging
ODB
Ocean Data Buoy
ODC
Office of Defense Cooperation
Officer Data Card
Other Direct Costs
Outer Dead Center
Overseas Diplomacy Coordinator
ODCR
Officer Distribution and Control Report
ODDR&D
Office of the Director, Defense Research and
Development
ODM
Office of Defense Mobilization
Operational Direction Message
ODME
Overseas Diplomacy Mission Element
ODO
Operations Duty Officer
ODP
Officer Distribution Plan
Organized Reservists in Drill Pay Status
Original Departure Point
Overseas Diplomacy Program
ODR
Omnidirection(al) Range
ODS
Ocean Data Station (USN-USCG)
Ordnance Delivery Schedule
ODSP
Overseas Duty Support Program
ODT
Omnidirectional Transmission
Overseas Diplomacy Training
ODUSD(C³I)
Office of the Deputy Under Secretary of
Defense (Communications, Command,
Control and Intelligence)
OEC
Output Exception Code
OE DIV
Operations Electronics/Material Division
OEDO
Ordnance Engineering Duty Officer
OEG
Operations Evaluation Group

OEGCMJ
Officer Exercising General Court-Martial Jurisdiction
OEL
Ordnance Equipment List
OEM
Original Equipment Manufacture
OER
Officer's Efficiency Report
OESPCMJ
Officer Exercising Special Court-Martial Jursidiction
OF
Occupational Fields
Operating Forces
Optional Form
Outfitting and Furnishing
OF, O, OFC
Office
OFC, O, OF
Office
OFCC
Office of Contract Compliance
OFCOFASSTSECNAV, OASN
Office of the Assistant Secretary of the Navy
OFCOFASSTSECNAV(FINMGMT), OASN(FM)
Office of the Assistant Secretary of the Navy (Financial Management)
OFCOFASSTSECNAV(INSTLLOG), OASN(I&L)
Office of the Assistant Secretary of the Navy (Installation and Logistics)
OFCOFASSTSECNAV(PERSRESFOR), OASN(P&RF)
Office of the Assistant Secretary of the Navy (Personnel and Reserve Force)
OFCOFASSTSECNAV(RSCHDEV), OASN(R&D)
Office of the Assistant Secretary of the Navy (Research and Development)
OFCOFINFO, OI
Office of Information
OFEA
Office of Foreign Economics Administration
OFF
Officer
OFF BUS ONLY
Official Business Only
OFFDEVDISTSYS
Naval Officer Development and Distribution Support System
OFFL
Official
OFFMAUSTSYS
Officer Master File Automated System
OFFNAVHIST, ONH
Office of Naval History
OFFPROMSYS
Officer Promotion System
OFF STA
Officer Status

OF II
Otto Fuel II
OFINDMAN
Office of Industrial Management
OFIT
Occupational Field Implementation Team(s)
OFOFLEGAFFAIRS
Office of Legal Affairs
OFP
Operational Flight Program
Operating Force Plan
OFS
Office of Field Service
OFSE
Operating Forces Support Equipment
OFSHR
Offshore
OFT
Often
Operational Flight Trainer
OF/WST
Operational Flight/Weapons System Trainer
OG
Officer-of-the-Guard
Oxygen Generator
OGC
Officer of the General Counsel
OFGBRO
Officer of the General Counsel Branch Office
OGE
Operational Group Equipment
Out-of-Ground Effect
OGOS
Outward Grade of Service
OGT
Outlet Gas Temperature
OGU
Ongoing Unit
OGW
Overload Gross Weight
OH
Off Hook
On Hand (quantity)
O/H, OVHL
Overhaul
OHDETS
Over-the-Horizon Detection System
OHF
Overhead Funds
OHH
Operation Helping Hand
OHI
Ordnance Handling Instructions
OHMSETT
Oil and Hazardous Materials Simulated Environment Test Tank
OHR
Operational Hazard Report
OI
Operating Instructions

OI, OFOFINFO
Office of Information
OIAF
Office of Information for the Armed Forces
OIC, OINC
Officer-in-Charge
OICC
Officer-in-Charge of Construction
OICCSOWESPAC
Officer-in-Charge of Construction, South
Western Pacific
OI DIV
Operations/Combat Information Center
Division
OICMATU
Officer-in-Charge, Marine Air Traffic Control
Unit
OICMILDEPT
Officer-in-Charge, Military Department
OII
Overseas Issues Identification
OIIM
Overseas Issues Identification Meeting
OIL
Ordnance Investigation Laboratory
OINC, OIC
Officer-in-Charge
OIP
Operational (or Ordnance) Improvement Plan
OIR
Office of Industrial Relations
OIRS
Operation and Inspection Route Sheet
OIST
Operator Integration Shakedown Test
OJCS
Organization of the Joint Chiefs of Staff
OJT
On-the-Job Training
OL
Operating Location
Overload
OLA
Office of Legislative Affairs
OL DIV
Operations/Lookout and Recognition Division
OLDS
On-Line Display System
OLF
Outlying Field
OL-IC
Operating Location-Iceland
OLQ
Officer-Like Quality
OLS
Optical Landing System
OLSOR
Object Location and Small Object Recovery
OLSP
Operational Logistics Support Plan

OLSS
Overseas Limited Storage Site
OLTEP
On-Line Text Executive Program
OM
Office Messenger
Operator (or Organizational) Maintenance
Outer Marker
Outfitting Material
OM1
Opticalman First Class
OM2
Opticalman Second Class
OM3
Opticalman Third Class
O&M
Operations and Maintenance (funds)
OMA
Organizational Maintenance Activity
OMB
Office of Management and Budget
OMC
Chief Opticalman
One-Man Control
OMCR
Organized Marine Corps Reserve
OMCS
Senior Chief Opticalman
OMD
Operations Maintenance Division
OMI
Ordnance Modification Instructions
OML
Overhaul Material List
OMM
Officer Messenger Mail
O&MMC
Operations and Maintenance, Marine Corps
OMM(S)C
Officer Messenger Mail (Sub) Center
O&MN
Operations and Maintenance, Navy
OMP
Overflow Maintenance Program
OMR(E)
Organic Modified Reactor (Experimental)
OMS
Operational Management System
Organizational Maintenance Squadron
OMSA
Opticalman Seaman Apprentice
OMSI
Operating and Maintenance Support
Information
OMSN
Opticalman Seaman
OMSTA
Omega Station
OMT
Operational Maintenance Trainer

OMTD
Operator/Maintenance Task Descriptions
ON
Octane Number
ONBOSUB
Onboard a Submarine
ONBOWCOM
Duty on board that vessel when placed in commission
ONBOWSERV
Duty on board that vessel when placed in service
ONC
Operational Navigation Chart
ONDE
Office of Naval Disability Evaluation
ONH, OFFNAVHIST
Office of Naval History
ON/H
On the Hatch Cover (stowage)
ONI
Office of Naval Intelligence
ONM
Office of Naval Material
ONO
Office of Naval Operations
ONOP
Office of Naval Procurement
Officer-in-Charge, Branch Office of Naval Officer Procurement
ONR
Office of Naval Research
ONRARO
Office of Naval Research Area Research Office
ONRBRO
Office of Naval Research Branch Research Office
ONRDET
Office of Naval Research Detachment
ONREAST
Office of Naval Research, East Coast Regional Office
ONRFE
Office of Naval Research, Far East Regional Office
ONRL
Office of Naval Research, London
ONRREP
Office of Naval Research Representative
ONRRR
Office of Naval Research Resident Representative
ONRWEST
Office of Naval Research, West Coast Regional Office
OOC
Out of Commission (vessel status)
OOD
Officer-of-the-Day (or -Deck)

OODF
Officer-of-the-Deck (Fleet Task Force Operations)
OODI
Officer-of-the-Deck (Independent)
OOL
Operator-Oriented Language
OOM
Officers' Open Mess
OOO
Out of Order
OOR
Office of Ordnance Research
O&OS
Ordnance and Ordnance Stores
OOSS
Overseas Operational Storage Sites
OOW
Officer-of-the-Watch
OP
Observation Post
Office of Preparedness
Officer Programs
Operation(al)
Operational Priority
Ordnance Pamphlet (or Publication)
Ordnance Personnel
Original Pack
OP, OPER, OPR
Operator
OP, OPR, OPRG
Operating
OPA
Office of Program Appraisal
Overall Probability of Attack
OPAGREE
Operational Agreement
OPAL
Optical Platform Alignment Linkage
OP-AMP
Operational Amplifier
OPANAL
Operations Analysis
OPBY
Operating Authority
OPC
Ownership Purpose and Condition (code)
OPC, OPT
Optician
OPC, OCC, OPCONCEN
Operational Control Center
OP&C
Operations Planning and Control
OPCOM
Operations Communications
OPCONCEN, OCC, OPC
Operations Control Center
OPCTR
Operations Center

OPD
Operations Division
Outpatient Department
OPDAC
Optical Data Conversion (system)
OPDAR
Optical Detection and Ranging
OPDATS
Operational Performance Data System
OPDEVFOR
Operational Development Force
OP DIV
Operations/Air Intelligence Photography
Division
OPER, OP, OPR
Operator
OPERG
Operating
O-PERS
Officer Personnel Office
OPEVAL
Operational Evaluation
OPEX
Operational Extension
Operative Extension of Enlistment
OP/GSA
Office of Preparedness/General Services
Administration
OPHOLDS
Operational Holds
OPLAN, OPPLAN
Operation(s) Plan
OPLE
Omega Position/Location Equipment
OPM
Operating Plane Month
Operations per Minute
Overhaul Planning Manual
OP&M
Office of Procurement and Material
OPME
Office of Personnel Management Evaluation
OPN
Other Procurement, Navy
OPNAV
Office of the Chief of Naval Operations
OPNAVCOMMO
Office of the Chief of Naval Operations
Communications Office
OPNAVSUPPACT
Office of the Chief of Naval Operations
Support Activity
OPNAVSUPPACTDET
Office of the Chief of Naval Operations
Support Activity Detachment
OPNAVSUPPACT FIG
Office of the Chief of Naval Operations
Support Activity Flight Information Group

OPNAVSUPPACT TCC
Office of the Chief of Naval Operations
Support Activity Telecommunications
Center
OPNAVSUPPACT WWMCCS DP
Office of the Chief of Naval Operations
Support Activity Worldwide Military
Command Control System, Data
Processing
OPNAVSUPPACT WWMCCS EMPSKED
Office of the Chief of Naval Operations
Support Activity Worldwide Military
Command Control System, Employment
Schedule
OPNAVSUPPACT WWMCCS FORSTAT
Office of the Chief of Naval Operations
Support Activity Worldwide Military
Command Control System, Force Status
OPNAVSUPPACT WWMCCS MOVREP
Office of the Chief of Naval Operations
Support Activity Worldwide Military
Command Control System, Movement
Reports
OPNAVTCC
Office of the Chief of Naval Operations
Telecommunications Center
NPNS, OPS
Operations
OPO
Officer Programs Office(r)
OPORD
Operations Order
OPPE
Operational Propulsion Plant Examination
OPPLAN, OPLAN
Operation(s) Plan
OPQ
Occupying Public Quarters
Other Public Quarters
OPR
Office (or Official) of Primary Responsibility
Operate(d)
OPR, OP, OPER
Operator
OPRED
Operational Readiness (plan)
OPREP
Operation(al) Report
OPRG, OP, OPR
Operating
OPS
Overhaul Plan Schedule
OPS, OPNS
Operations
OPSEC
Operations Security
OPSIG
Operating Signal
OPSTAT
Operational Statistics

OPSUB
Operational SUBPAY
OPSUM
Operational Submarine Duty Incentive Pay
OPT, OPC
Optician
OPTAG
Optical Aimpoint Guidance
OPTAR
Operations (or Operating) Target (funding)
OPTEVFOR
Operational Test and Evaluation Force
OPTEVFORDET
Operational Test and Evaluation Force
Detachment
OPTRA
Operational Training
OPTRARON, OTS
Operational Training Squadron
OPTRAU, OPU
Operational Training Unit
OPU
Overseas Plexiglass Unit
OPU, OPTRAU
Operational Training Unit
OQ
Order Quantity
OQE
Objective Quality Evidence
OR
Operational Requirements
Operationally Ready
Operations Research
Operations (or Operating) Room
O/R
On Request
O&R
Overhaul and Repair
ORA
Orbiting Radio Astronomical Observatory
ORC
Officers' Reserve Corps
Outstanding Performance Rating (Cash)
ORCALMIS
Ordnance Calibration Management
Information System
ORCON
Operation Report Conversion
ORD
Order(ly)
Orders (status, NAPMIS)
Ordnance
ORDALT
Ordnance Alteration
ORDC
Ordnance Research and Development Center
ORDCAN
Orders (identified by date or message
reference numbers following) are cancelled
ORDCONTECH
Ordnance Control Technician

ORDCOR
Orders (identified by date or message
reference numbers following) are corrected
ORDENG
Ordnance Engineering
ORDER
Outstanding Requisitions Defeat Endurance
Readiness
ORDFAC
Ordnance Facility
ORDIS
Ordnance Discharge
OR DIV
Operations/Radio Communications Division
ORDLIS
Ordnance Logistics Information System
ORDMAINTCO
Ordnance Maintenance Company
ORDMOD, ORMOD
Orders (identified by date or message
reference numbers following) are modified
ORDSTA
Ordnance Station
ORDU
Ordnance Unit
ORDVAC
Ordnance Variable Automatic Computer
ORE
Operational Readiness Exercise
ORG
Ordnance Research Group
Organization
ORI
Operational Readiness Inspection
ORIG
Origin(al), (-ator)
OR/MC
Operational Requirements/Military
Characteristics
ORMOD, ORDMOD
Orders (identified by date or message
reference numbers following) are modified
ORP
Officer Requirements Plan
ORQ
Outstanding Performance Rating with Quality
Step Increase
ORS
Operational Reactor Safeguards
Outstanding Requisition System
ORSE
Operational Reactor Safeguards Examination
ORT
Operating Room Technician
Operational Readiness Test
Overland Radar Technology
ORTS
Operational Readiness Test System
ORU
Other than Ship or Squadron Reinforcement
Unit (USNR)

OS
Ordnance Specifications
Ornamental Stitching
Oxygen Service
OS, O/S
Operating Systems
OS1
Operations Specialist First Class
OS2
Operations Specialist Second Class
OS3
Operations Specialist Third Class
O/S
Out of Service
Outstanding
OSA
Office of Systems Analysis
On-Site Assistance
Operational Sequence Analysis
Outfitting Stock Activity
OSAP
Ocean Surveillance Air Patrol
OSB
Officer Selection Battery
Operational Stations Book
OSBT
Officer Selection Battery Test
OSC
Chief Operations Specialist
On-Scene Commander (or Coordinator)
Oscillator
Own Ship's Course
OSCM
Master Chief Operations Specialist
OSCR
Ordnance Systems Component Rework
OSCS
Senior Chief Operations Specialist
OSD
Office of the Secretary of Defense
Officer Service Date
Own Ship's Distance
OS&D, OS/D, OSOD
Over, Short and Damaged (report)
OSDC, OSDOC
Offshore Discharge of Container Ships
OSDOC, OSDC
Offshore Discharge of Container Ships
OSD/OMB
Office of the Secretary of Defense/Office of
Management and Budget
OSF
Ocean Simulation Facility (NCSL)
OSFCO
Office of Solid Fuels Coordinator
OSH
Own Ship's Heading (SINS)
OSHA
Occupational Health and Safety
Administration

OSI
Office of Special Investigations
Operating Space Items
Operational Support Inventory
OPSIG
Operating Signal
OSILM
On-Site Integrated Logistic Management
(team)
OSIP
Operational Suitability Improvement Program
Operation and Safety Improvement Program
OSIR
Out of Service, In Reserve (vessel status)
OSIS
Ocean Surveillance Information System
OSM
Owner-Supplied Material
OSN
Ocean Sciences News (newsletter)
Office of the Secretary of the Navy
OSO
Officer Selection Office
Ordnance Supply Officer
Other Supply Officers
OSOD, OS&D, OS/D
Over, Short and Damaged (report)
OSP
Ocean Survey Program
Offshore Procurement
Outfitting Stock Point
Own Ship's Pitch (SINS)
Own Ship's Position
OSPRO
Ocean Shipping Procedures
OSQ
Officer Separation Questionnaire
Officer Student Quarters
OSR
Office of Scientific Research
Office of Security Review
On-Site Review
Operational Status Release
Operational Support Requirement
Ordnance Status Report
Own Ship's Roll (SINS)
OS&RP
Onboard Spares and Repair Parts
OSS
Ocean Surveillance Satellite
Ocean Survey Ship
Old Submarine
"One-Stop Service" (FMS)
Operational Sequencing System
Operational Storage Site
OST
Office of Science and Technology
Operational Suitability Test
Overseas Tour
Own Ship's Track

OSTD
Ordnance Standards
OS&TD
Ocean Science and Technology Division (ONR)
OSU
Optical Scanning Unit
Own Ship's Use
OSV
Ocean Station Vessel (USCG)
On Station Vehicle
OSVEY
Overseas Service Rotation Survey
OT
Occupational Therapy Technician
Oil Tight
Outfit (U/I)
OTA
Office of Technology Assessment
OT1
Ocean Systems Technician First Class
OT2
Ocean Systems Technician Second Class
OT3
Ocean Systems Technician Third Class
OTA
Office of Technical Assistance
Office of Technology Assessment
Other Than Air (USNR)
OTAC
Ordnance Tank and Automotive Command
OTC
Chief Ocean Systems Technician
Officer-in-Tactical Command
Officer Training School
Operational Training Command
OTCLANT
Operational Training Command, Atlantic
OTCM
Master Chief Ocean Systems Technician
OTCPAC
Operational Training Command, Pacific
OTCS
Senior Chief Ocean Systems Technician
OTD
Official Tables of Distances
OTDA
Office of Tracking and Data Acquisition
OT&E
Operational Test and Evaluation
OTH
Over-the-Horizon (radar)
OTH-B
Over-the-Horizon Back-scatter (radar)
OTI
Ordnance Technical Instructions
OTIS
Overseas Transfer Information Service
OTL
Operational Time Log

OTLK
Outlook
OTMS
Operational-Technical-Managerial System
OTNP
Other Than New Procurement
OTO NAVSUPPACT
Overseas Transportation Office, Naval Support Activity
OTP
One-Time Pad
OTPI
On Top Position Indicator
OTR
Other
OTRO
Overhaul Test Requirements Outline
OTS
Optical Target Simulator
OTS, OPTRARON
Optical Training Squadron
OTSA
Ocean Systems Technician Seaman Apprentice
OTS-AES
Optical Technology Satellite-Apollo Extension System
OTSN
Ocean Systems Technician Seaman
OTSR
Optimum Track Ship Routing
OTT
Ocean Tactical Targeting
Oral Trade Test
OTU, OPTRAU
Operational Training Unit
OUO
Official Use Only
OUSN
Office of the Under Secretary of the Navy
OUTBD
Outbound
OUTCONUS, OCONUS, OUTUS
Outside Continental Limits of the United States
OUTRAN
Output Translator
OUTUS, OCONUS, OUTCONUS
Outside Continental Limits of the United States
OV
Observation (aircraft)
OVC
Overcast
OVCKD
Overchecked
OVCKD FLD RATS
Overchecked Field Rations
OVHD
Overhead

OVHD PWR CAB
Overhead Power Cable
OVHL, O/H
Overhaul
OVPD
Overpaid
OVR
Over
OVRN
Overrun
OVS
Overhaul Specification
OW
Orderwire
OWA
Overhaul Work Authorization
OWC
Ordnance Weapons Command
OWD
Overhaul Work Description
OWP
Overhaul Work Package
OWS
Observation Weather Support (circuits)
Overhaul Work Scope
OX, OXY
Oxygen
OXRB
Oxygen Replacement Bottles
OXY, OX
Oxygen
OY
Overhaul Yard
OYF
Overhaul Yard-Furnished (equipment or
materials)

P

P
Patchy (runway condition)
Photo/Navigator (NAO code)
Pillar (buoy)
Planning
Polar (airmass)
Popular (AFRTS code)
Priority (message traffic)
PA
Paper (U/I)
Pattern Analysis (test)
Pending Availability
Permanent Appointment
Pilotless Aircraft
Port Agency (or Authority)
Power Amplifier
Precision Approach
Precomputed Altitude
Procurement Authorization
Program Account
Project Analysis

P A
Position Approximate
P&A
Price and Availability (information)
Procedures and Analysis
Procurement and Assignment
PAA
Pay Adjustment Authorization
PAAC
Program Analysis Adaptable Control
PAACS
Prior Active Army Commissioned Service
PAAES
Prior Active Army Enlisted Service
PAAFCS
Prior Active Air Force Commissioned Service
PAAFES
Prior Active Air Force Enlisted Service
PAAT
Personnel and Administration Assistance
Team
PAATLANT
Personnel and Administration Assistance
Team, Atlantic
PAATPAC
Personnel and Administration Assistance
Team, Pacific
PAB
Policies Allotment Board
Precision Aneroid Barometer
Price Adjustment Bulletin (NRS)
Price Assignment Board
P/AB
Port Side Abreast (stowage)
PABX
Private Automatic Branch Exchange
PAC
Pacific
Planned Availability Concept
Privacy Act Coordinator
Program Adjustment Committee
Program Application Code
Project Analysis and Control (system)
Public Affairs Company (USNR)
PACADIV
Pacific Advanced Headquarters Division
PACC
Propulsion and Auxiliary Control Console
PACCOM
Pacific Command
PACCOMOPCONCEN
Pacific Fleet Command Operational Control
Center
PACCS
Post Attack Command and Control System
PACDIV
Pacific Division

PACE
Pacific Atoll Cratering Experiment
Performance and Cost Evaluation (program)
Phased Array Control Electronics
Program for Afloat College Education
Project to Advance Creativity in Education

PACED
Program for Advanced Concepts in Electronic Design

PACEE
Propulsion and Auxiliary Control Electronic Enclosure

PACEN
Public Affairs Center

PACENLANT
Public Affairs Center, Atlantic

PACENPAC
Public Affairs Center, Pacific

PACEX
Pacific Exchange (system)

PACFAST
Pacific Forward Area Support Team

PACFASTDET
Pacific Forward Area Support Team Detachment

PACFASTREP
Pacific Forward Area Support Team Representative

PACFLT
Pacific Fleet

PACFLTCOM
Pacific Fleet Command

PACFLTPROPEXAMBD
Pacific Fleet Propulsion Examining Board

PACGCS
Prior Active Coast Guard Commissioned Service

PACGES
Prior Active Coast Guard Enlisted Service

PACHEDPEARL
Pacific Fleet Headquarters, Pearl Harbor (HA)

PACINTCEN, PIC
Pacific Intelligence Center

PACM
Pulse Amplitude Code Modulation

PACMISCEN, PMC
Pacific Missile Center

PACMISRAN, PMR
Pacific Missile Range

PACMISRANFAC
Pacific Missile Range Facility

PACMISRANFACDET
Pacific Missile Range Facility Detachment

PACMISRANFACREP
Pacific Missile Range Facility Representative

PACMISTESTCEN
Pacific Missile Test Center

PACMISTESTCEN LO
Pacific Missile Test Center Liaison Office

PACNAVCONSTFOR, PACNCF
Pacific Naval Construction Force

PACNAVFACENGCOM
Pacific Naval Facilities Engineering Command

PACNCF, PACNAVCONSTFOR
Pacific Naval Construction Force

PACOM
Pacific Command

PACOMBPO
Pacific Command Blood Program Office

PACOMDET
Pacific Command Detachment

PACOMJRO
Pacific Command Joint Medical Regulating Office

PACORNALOG
Pacific Coast Coordinator of Naval Logistics

PACREP
Pacific Representative

PACREPNAVRES
Pacific Representative of the Chief of Naval Reserve

PACREPCOMNAVSURFRES
Pacific Representative for Commander Naval Surface Reserve Force

PACRESFLT
Pacific Reserve Fleet

PACS
Pacific Area Communications System

PACSUBDSEC
Pacific Submarine Direct Support Element Coordinator

PACT
Portable Automatic Calibration Tracker
Poseidon Automatic Cable Tester
Production Analysis Control Technique

PAD
Petroleum Administration for Defense
Pilotless Aircraft Division
Pontoon Assembly Detachment
Port, Aft, Down (GQ routing)
Preferred Arrival Date
Preventing Addictive Drugs
Primary Aeronautical Designation
Projects Approval Document
Propellant-Actuated Device
Public Affairs Division

PADAR
Passive Detection and Ranging (radar)

PADD
Planned Active-Duty Date

PADIE
Prevention and Detection of Illegal Entry

PADLOC
Passive-Active Detection and Location
Passive Detection and Location of Countermeasures

PA-DRS
Performance Analysis Data Recording System

PADS
  Passive-Active Data Simulation
  Personnel (Civilian) Automated Data System
PAFCS
  Prior Active Foreign Commissioned Service
PAFES
  Prior Active Foreign Enlisted Service
PAFSO
  Plans and Fleet Support Office
PAGE
  Page Generator
PAHEL
  Pay and Health Records
PAI
  Personnel Accident Insurance
PAINT
  Post-Attack Intelligence
PAL
  Permissive Action Link
  Positive Arming Link
  Preliminary Allowance List
  Prisoner-at-Large
PALCR
  Propulsion Auxiliaries Local Control Rack
PALCRU
  Pay and Allowances Accrue from (source
    listed)
PALS
  Permissive Action Link System
PAM
  Pressure-Acoustic-Magnetic (minesweeping
    system)
  Priorities and Allocation Manual
  Pulse Amplitude Modulation
PAMCCS
  Prior Active Marine Corps Commissioned
    Service
PAMCES
  Prior Active Marine Corps Enlisted Service
PAMDS
  Price and Management Data Section
PAMIS
  Personnel Accounting Machine Installation
    System
PAMN
  Procurement of Aircraft and Missiles, Navy
PAMPA
  Pacific Area Movement Priority Agency
PAN
  Pilot-Assumed Navigation
PANDL
  Pay and Allowances
PANDLCHAR
  Pay and allowances chargeable
    (appropriation and identifying numbers
    designated)
PANES
  Prior Active Navy Enlisted Service
PANGCS
  Prior Active National Guard Commissioned
    Service

PANGES
  Prior Active National Guard Enlisted Service
PANS
  Procedures for Air Navigation Services
PANSEAFRON, PSF
  Panama Sea Frontier
PAO
  Pilot-Augmented Oscillation
  Primary Action Office(r)
  Public Affairs Office(r)
PAP
  Patrol Amphibian Plane
  Pilotless Aircraft Program
PAPP
  Productivity and Pay Plan
PAR
  Parachute
  Parachutist
  Perimeter Acquisition (or Array) Radar
  Personnel Advancement Requirement
  Precision Approach Radar
  Problem Analysis Report
  Program Adjustment Request
  Program Appraisal and Review
  Progressive Aircraft Rework
  Public Affairs Regulations
  Pulse Acquisition Radar
P/AR
  Problem/Action Report
PARC
  Periodic Aircraft Reconditioning Cycle
PARD
  Pilot Airborne Recovery Device
  Pilotless Aircraft Research Division
PAREC
  Pay Record
PARESEV
  Paraglider Research Vehicle
PARM
  Participating Managers
PARR
  Performance Analysis Reliability Reporting
PARSEC
  Parallax Second
PARSECS
  Program for Astronomical Research and
    Scientific Experiments Concerning Space
PARSYS
  Parametric Synthesis
PAR-TEM
  Partially Opened-Temporary Pay Record
PARTNER
  Proof of Analog Results Through a Numerical
    Equivalent Routine
PAS
  Personnel Accounting System
  Physically Onboard as a Prisoner
  Public Advertising System
PAS, PAX, PSGR
  Passenger

PASCALS
Projected Antisubmarine Classification and Location System
PASEP
Being Passed Separately
PASO
Port Antisubmarine Officer
PASS
Passage
Pay/Personnel Administrative Support System
PASSMAN
Pay/Personnel Administrative Support System Manual
PASTRAM
Passenger Traffic Management (system)
PASU, PATSU
Patrol Aircraft Service Unit
PAT
Passive Acoustic Torpedo
Personalized Array Translator
Physically Onboard for Treatment
Political Action Team
Preliminary Acceptance Trials
Proficiency Analytical Testing
Proof and Transit (system)
PAT, PATN, PTN
Pattern
PAT, PTL
Patrol
PATAO
Personnel and Training Analysis Office (NAVSHIPS)
PAT-C
Position, Altitude, Trajectory Control (system)
PATCO
Professional, Administrative, Technical, Clerical and Other
PAT&E
Production Acceptance Test and Evaluation
PATFOR
Patrol Force
PATN, PAT, PTN
Pattern
PATRIC
Pattern Recognition, Interpretation and Correlation
PATRON, VP
Patrol Squadron
PATRONDET
Patron Squadron Detachment
PARTONSPECPROJDET
Patrol Squadron Special Projects Detachment
PATS
Programmable Automatic Test Set
PATSU, PASU
Patrol Aircraft Service Unit
PATWING
Patrol Wing
PATWINGDET
Patrol Wing Detachment

PAU
Pilotless Aircraft Unit
PAV
Pay Adjustment Voucher
Pressure Altitude Variable
PAV
Principles and Applications of Value Engineering
Programmed Analysis for Value Engineering
PAW
Powered-all-the-Way
PAWS
Polar Automatic Weather Station
PAX, PBX
Private Branch Exchange
PAX, PAS, PSGR
Passenger
PAY
Payment
PB
All-Weather Patrol Boat
Patrol Boat
Practice Bomb
PBC
Packed by Carrier (household goods)
Practice Bomb Contained
P/BD, PBD
Program/Budget Decision
PBOS
Planning Board for Ocean Shipping
PBR
Patrol Boat, River
PBRA
Practical Bomb-Rack Adapter
PBS
Peninsular Base Section
PBV
Post-Boost Vehicle
PBX, PAX
Private Branch Exchange
PC
Paper Copy
Piece (U/I)
Pitch Cycle
Plane Commander
Positive Control
Power Control (hydraulic system)
Pressure Chamber
Prime Contractor
Program Counter (NNSS)
Propulsion Council
PC, PCLK
Pay Clerk
P/C
Plane Captain
P/C, PC
Printed Circuit
PC1
Postal Clerk First Class
PC2
Postal Clerk Second Class

PC3
Postal Clerk Third Class
PCA
Personal Cash Allowance
Physical Configuration Audit
Polar Cap Absorption—also called PCD
Position Control Area
Positive Controlled Airspace
Potentially Contaminated Area
Precision Clearing Agent (freon)
PCAM
Punch Card Accounting Machine
PCAMP
Protective Coatings and Metalizing Process
PCAN
Program Change Action Notice
PCB
Parts Control Board
Printed Circuit Board
PCC
Chief Postal Clerk
Power Control Circuit
Production Compression Capability
PCCL
Pre-Contract Cost Letter
PCCM
Master Chief Postal Clerk
PCCNL
Pacific Coast Coordinator of Naval Logistics
PCCS
Program Change Control System
Senior Chief Postal Clerk
PCD
Polar Cap Disturbance—also called PCA
Program Change Decision
PC&D
Planning and Comptroller Department
Planning and Computer Department (NSC)
PCDESIG
Plane Captain Designated (or Designation)
PCE
Patrol Escort
Power Conversion Equipment
Program Cost Estimate
Punch Card Equipment
PCEC
Patrol Vessel, Escort, Control
PCER
Patrol Rescue, Escort
PCF
Patrol Craft, Fast
PCFO
Position Classification Office
PCGOV
Port charges are being paid by foreign
government
PCH
Packing, Crating and Handling
Patrol Craft, Hydrofoil
PCI
Program Configuration Indentification

PCL
Pocket Check List
Power Control Lever
Project Control Ledgers
PCLK, PC
Pay Clerk
PCLO
Passenger Control Liaison Officer
PCM
PASS Consolidation Manual
Penalty Cost Model
Phase-Change Material
Photo-Chemical Machining
Program Change Management
Program Control and Monitor
Pulse Code Modulation
Punch Code Machine
PCMI
Photochromic Microimage
PCN
Parts Change Notice
Production Control Number
PCO
Plastic Chrome Core
Power Change Over
Procurement Contracting Officer
Prospective Commanding Officer
PCOD
Permanent Change of Duty
PCOP
Port Charges Operator
Port charges are being paid by commercial
operator
PCP
Passenger Control Point
Platoon Command Post
Preliminary Definition Plan
Program Change Proposal
Projected Definition Phase
PCPN, PRECIP
Precipitation
PCP
Pollution Control Report
Process Control Record
Program Change Record (or Request)
Publications Contract Requirements
PCS
Patrol Craft, Submarine
Permanent Change of Station (orders)
Primary Control Ship
Propulsion Control System (or Subsystem)
PC&S
Post, Camp and Station (contracts)
PCSA
Postal Clerk Seaman Apprentice
PCSC
Control Submarine Chaser
PCSN
Postal Clerk Seaman
PCSP
Program Communications Support Program

PCT
Pharmacy and Chemistry Technician
PCUS
Port charges are being paid by U.S. Army,
Navy or Air Force
PCV
Positive Crankshaft Ventilation
Primary Control Vessel
PCZ
Positive Control Zone
PD
Pad (U/I)
Paid
Per Diem
Pipe Details
Planning (or Priority, or Program) Directive
Point-Detonating
Port Director
Position Description
Position Doubtful
Preference for Duty (card)
Procedures Development
Pulse Doppler (or Duration)
PDA
Predicted Drift Angle
Principal Development Activity
Proposed Development Approach
"Public Display of Affection" (slang)
PDAAP
Program Design and Assurance Plan
PDBA
Personnel Data Base Application
PDBA/SIPM
Personnel Data Base Application/Student
Instructor Performance Module
PDC
Personnel Data Card
Personally Developed Contract
Practice Depth Charge
Program Document Control
PDD
Physical Damage Division
Priority Delivery Date
Program Design Data
PDDA
Power Driven Decontamination Apparatus
PDE
Product Design Effort
PDF
Point Detonating Fuze
PDFD
Pulse Doppler Frequency Diversity
PDI
Pre-Deployment Inspection
Product Design Information (or Integration)
Product Drawing Index
PDIR
Priority Disassembly and Inspection Report

PDL
Parts Difference List
Pass Down Log
Pass Down the Line (log)
PDLM
Periodic Depot Level Maintenance
PDM
Program Decision Memorandum
Pulse Duration Modulation
PDN
Production
P DN
Petition Denied
PDO
Property Disposal Officer
Publications Distribution Officer
PDP
Programmed Data Processor
Project Development (or Definition) Plan
Project (or Program) Definition Phase
PDQ
"Pretty Darn Quick" (slang)
PDR
Periscope Depth Range
Precision Depth Recorder
Preliminary Design Review
PDRC
Professional Recruitment and Career
Development
PDRL
Permanent Disability Retirement List
PDS
Plotter Display System
Production Design Support
PDSMS
Point Defense Surface Missile System—also
called "Seasparrow" system
PDT
Processed Directional Transmission
PE
Patrol Vessel, Eagle
Peck (U/I)
Pilot (or Probable) Error
Pistol Expert
Port Engineer
Practical Exercise
Procedure (or Preliminary) Evaluation
Production Engineering
Professional Engineer
PE, PEREF
Personal Effects
P&E
Planner and Estimator
Planning and Estimating (division)
Procurement and Expedition
PEAC
Photoelectric Auto Controller
Program Establishment and Control
PEAT
Priority Equipment Action Tabulation

PEB
Physical Evaluation Board
Pre-Expanded Bin
Propulsion Examining Board
PEBCO
Physical Evaluation Board Counseling Officer
PEBD
Pay Entry Base Date—also PBED
PEC
Personal Education Counseling
Production Equipment Code
Production Executive Committee
PECE
Proposed Engineering Change Estimates
PECI
Preliminary Equipment/Component Index
PECM
Passive Electronic Countermeasures
PECO
Production Equipment Control Office
PECP
Preliminary Engineering Change Proposal
PED
Personnel Equipment Data
Project Engineering Documentation
PEDC
Personal Effects Distribution Center
PEDIN
Peapod Dingy (USMC)
PEDRO
Pride, Efficiency, Dedication, Reliability and
Order
PEGE
Program for Evaluation of Ground
Environment
PEIF
Productivity Enhancing Incentive Fund
PEL
Physiological (or Permissible) Exposure Limit
PELSS
Precision Emitter Location Strike System
PEN
Predecessor Event Number
PENAIDS
Penetration Aids (for missiles)
PENO, PEO
Prospective Engineering Officer
PEOPLE
Program Enhancing Opportunities for
Personal Leadership Effectiveness
PEP
Peak Envelope Power
Performance Effectiveness Program
Personnel Exchange Program
PEPPARD
Propellant, Explosive, Pyrotechnic Pollution
Abatement Research and Development
PEPSS
Programmable Equipment for Personnel
Subsystem Simulation

PERA
Planning and Engineering for Repairs and
Alterations
PERA-CV
Planning and Engineering for Repairs and
Alterations-Carrier
PEREF, PE
Personal Effects
PERFMIS
During service as naval attaché perform
under the supervision of the Chief of the
Mission such duties as may be assigned by
the Navy Department
PERFONSTA
Per diem while on foreign station is payable
from locally contributed currency if
available, otherwise it is chargeable to
(appropriation and identifying numbers
designated)
PERGRA
Permission granted
PERI
Production Equipment Reserve Inventory
PERINTREP, PIR
Periodic Intelligence Report
PERISH
Perishable
PERM
Permanent
PERSMAR
Personnel Manning Assistance Report
PERMIC
Personnel Management Information Center
PERMS
Permission
PERNOGRA
Permission not granted
PERS
Personnel
PERSCEN
Personnel Center
PERSEPCOMD
Personnel and Separation Command
PERSERVDEPSERVS
Personal Services and Dependents' Services
Support System
PERSO, PERSOFF
Personnel Officer
PERSOFF, PERSO
Personnel Officer
PERSRECSYS
Navy Personnel Records System
PERSREHSUPPSYS
Navy Personnel Rehabilitation Support
System
PERSRSCHSYSTM
Personnel Management and Training
Research Statistical Data System
PERSTRANS
Personal Transportation

PERSTRANSYS
Personal Transportation System
PERT
Pertain
Pertinent
Program Evaluation Review Technique
PERTO
Pertaining to
PERT-CS
Program Evaluation Review Technique-Cost
System (expanded PERT)
PES
Production Engineering Specifications
PESD
Program Element Summary Data
PESDS
Program Element Summary Data Sheet
PET
Periodic Evaluation Test
Petition
Petroleum
PETE
Portable Electronics Test Equipment
PETRES
Petroleum Reserves
PETRESO
Petroleum Reserves Office(r)
PETSEC
Petroleum Section
PF
Patrol Escort
Performance Factor
Performance Figure (NNSS)
Power (or Protection) Factor
Pre-Fabricated
P/F
Practical Factors
PFA
Participating Field Activity
P/FACS
Program/Funds Allocation and Control
System
PFAVC, PACFLTAVCOM
Pacific Fleet Audio-Visual Command
PFB
Pre-Formed Beams (sonar)
PFC
Private First Class
PFCCG
Pacific Fleet Combat Camera Group
PFCO
Position Field Classification Officer
PFD
Pulse Frequency Diversity
PFE
Performance Fitness Examination
PFF
Permanent Family File
PFI
Power Fail Interrupt (NNSS)

PFM
Plan for Maintenance
Pulse Frequency Modulation
P&FM
Program and Financial Management
PFMPG
Pacific Fleet Mobile Photographic Group
PFN
Pulse-Forming Network
PFP
Primary Failed Part
PFRT
Preliminary Flight Rating Test
PFSV
Pilot to Forecaster Service
PFT
Physical Fitness Test
PFU
Plan for Use
PG
Patrol Combatant
Pay Grade (or Group)
Photogrammetry
Postgraduate
Pressure Gradient
Prospective Gain
PGC
Per Gyro Compass
PGH
Patrol Gunboat, Hydrofoil
PGM
Precision-Guided Munitions
PGMG
Guided Missile Motor Gunboat
PG NO DSG
Pay Grade Number Designation
P GR
Petition Granted
PGS
Postgraduate School
Predicted Ground Speed
PGSE
Peculiar Ground Support Equipment
PH
Half Pound (U/I)
Phase
Plane Handler
Purple Heart
Probability of a Hit
PH1
Photographer's Mate First Class
PH2
Photographer's Mate Second Class
PH3
Photographer's Mate Third Class
PHA
Preliminary Hazards Analysis
PHAA
Photographer's Mate Airman Apprentice
Positive High Angle of Attack

PHAN
Photographer's Mate Airman
PHARM
Pharmacist
PHC
Chief Photographer's Mate
P-HCC
Piston-Hand Control Clutch
PHCM
Master Chief Photographer's Mate
PHCS
Senior Chief Photographer's Mate
PHD
Pilots' Horizontal Display
Positioning-Head Drum
PHDAN
Physically Dangerous (materials)
PHE
Periodic Health Examination
PHER
Photographic Mechanical Equipment Repair
(course)
Plate Heat Exchanger
PHGM
Patrol Hydrofoil Guided Missile
PHIB
Amphibious
PHIBCB, ACB
Amphibious Construction Battalion
PHIBCORPS
Amphibious Corps
PHIBDET
Amphibious Detachment
PHIBEX, AMPHIBEX
Amphibious Exercise
PHIBFOR
Amphibious Force(s)
PHIBGRU
Amphibious Group
PHIBLANT
Amphibious Forces, Altantic
PHIBMAINTSUPPU, AMSU
Amphibious Maintenance Support Unit
PHIBMAINTSUPPULANT, AMSULANT
Amphibious Maintenance Support Unit,
Atlantic
PHIBMAINTSUPPUPAC, AMSUPAC
Amphibious Maintenance Support Unit,
Pacific
PHIBOPS
Amphibious Operations
PHIBOPTRAU, AOTU
Amphibious Operations Training Unit
PHIBPAC
Amphibious Forces, Pacific
PHIBRIGLEX
Amphibious Brigade Landing Excerise
PHIBRON, PR
Amphibious Squadron
PHIBTRA
Amphibious Training

PHIBTRABASE
Amphibious Training Base
PHIBTRALANT
Amphibious Training Command, Atlantic
PHIBTRANS
Amphibious Transport
PHIBTRAPAC
Amphibious Training Command, Pacific
PHIBWARTRACEN
Amphibious Warfare Training Center
PHILAGRP
Philadelphia Group
PHILSEAFRON, PSF
Philippine Sea Frontier
PH/JO, PJ
Photojournalist (-ism)
PHK
Probability of a Kill Given a Hit
PHLAGS
Phillips Load-and-Go System
PHM
Patrol Combatant Missile Hydrofoil
PHMRON
Patrol Combatant Missile Hydrofoil Squadron
PHMRON MLSG
Patrol Combatant Missile Hydrofoil Squadron
Mobile Logistics Support Group
PHNY
Pearl Harbor Navy Yard
PHONCON, TELCON
Telephone Conversation
PHONE, FONE, TEL, TP
Telephone
PHOT, PHOTO
Photograph(er)
PHOTO, PHOT
Photograph(er)
PHOTOTRIGULANT
Photographic Triangulation Group, Atlantic
PHOTOTRIGUPAC
Photographic Triangulation Group, Pacific
PHST
Packaging, Handling, Storage, Transportation
PHYS
Physical
PHYSEXAM
Physical Examination
PHYSQUAL
Request report of physical examination and
of any physical defects which disqualify
from performing military service of the
following individual(s). (Name, grade, social
security number).
PI
Preliminary Inquiry
Process Interrupts
Programmed Instruction
Proportional Integral (controller)
PI, PUBINFO
Public Information

P&I
Protection and Indemnity
PIA
Primary Insurance Amount
PIACCS
Pacific Integrated Automatic Command and Control System
PIB
Photo Interpretation Brief
PIBALS
Pilot Balloon Reports
PIC
Parent Indicator Code
Payload Integration Center
Photographic Interpretation Center
Procurement Information for Contracts
Programmed Information Center
Purpose Identification Code
Pursuant to instructions contained in _____
PIC, PACINTCEN
Pacific Intelligence Center
PIC, PICT, PIX
Picture
PICA
Procedure for Inventory Control Afloat
PICCOE
Programmed Initiations, Commitments, Obligations and Expenditures
PICM
Master Chief Precision Instrumentman
PIC-MOD
Purpose Identification Code-Month and Calendar Year of Detachment (code)
PICP
Prime Inventory Control Point
PICS
Photographic Information Condensing System
PICT, PIC, PIX
Picture
PID
Personnel Inquiry/Death/Occupational Illness (report)
Political Intelligence Division
Proportional Integral Derivative (controller)
PIDC
Procurement Intern Development Center
PIDS
Parameter Inventory Display System
PIES
Packaged Interchangeable Electronic System
Procurement and Inventory of Equipment System
PIF
Perpetual Inventory File
PIGA
Pendulous Integrating Gyro Accelerometers
PIID
Prediction Interval Initiation Date
PIIN
Procurement Instrument Identification Number

PIIU
Photo/Imagery Interpretation Unit
PILOT
Piloted-Low Speed Test
PIL STA
Pilot Station
PIM
Point and Intended Movement
Position in Miles
Pulse Interval Modulation
PIMV
Post-Inspection Material Verification
PINS
Persons in Need of Supervision
PINT
Power Intelligence
PIO
Preliminary Inquiry Officer
PIP
Pilot Integrating Pendulum
Problem (or Production) Improvement Program
Progressive Inspection Plan
PIPA
Pulse-Integrating Pendulous Accelerometer
PIPCST
Piping Cost and Weight Analysis Program
PIPMLQ
Pipe Sizing Program for Liquids-Multi-Flow
PIPS
Pneumatically-Induced Pitching System (IBDS)
Pulsed Integrating Pendulums
PIPSAR
Pipe Sizing Program for Air
PIPSLQ
Pipe Sizing Program for Liquids-Single-Flow
PIPSPK
Pipe Sizing Program-Sprinkling
PIPSST
Pipe Sizing Program-Steam
PIR
Problem Identification Report
Procurement Information Reporting
Production Improvement Reports
PIR, PERINTREP
Periodic Intelligence Reports
PIRAZ
Positive Identification Radar Advisory Zone
PIREP
Pilot Report
PIRU
Photographic Interpretation Unit
PIT
Pre-Inspection (or Pre-Installation) Testing
PITI
Precise Time and Time Interval
PIX, PIC, PICT
Picture

PJ
Procurement Justification
Pulsejet
PJ, PH/JO
Photojournalist (-lism)
(PJ)
Qualified as a Parachute Jumper
PJA
Permanent Job Assignment
PJR
Pipe Joint Record
PJSS
PACAF Jungle Survival School
PK
Position-Keeping
PK, PG, PKG
Package
PKG, PG, PK
Package
PKP
Purple-K-Powder—also called "Light Water"
PKT
Packet
PL
Pail (U/I)
Patrol Land (pilot code)
Plate
Plumbing (system)
Prospective Loss
P/L
Packing List
Plain Language
PLA
Power Level Angle
Practice Landing Approach
PLAA
Positive Low Angle of Attack
PLACE
Position Location and Aircraft Communication
Equipment
PLAD
Plain Language Address Directory
PLADS
Parachute Low-Altitude Delivery System
PLANNET
Planning Network
PLANS
Planning Analysis System
PLAT
Pilot Landing Aid Television (system)
PLATF, PLATFS
Plain Language Terminal Forecasts
PLATFS, PLATF
Plain Language Terminal Forecasts
PLATO
Programmed Logic for Automated Teaching
Operation
PLATS
Pilot Landing and Take-Off System

PLAT/VLA
Pilot Landing Aid Television/Visual Landing
Aid (system)
PLC
Platoon Leaders Class
PLCC
Propulsion Local Control Console
PLCY
Policy
PLI
Pre-Load Indicator
PLICK
Pride, Loyalty, Integrity, Capability,
Knowledge
P-LINES
Pole/Power Lines
PLL
Phase-Locked Loop
PLM
Plimsoll Mark
Production Line Maintenance
PLN, PLT
Plant
PLNSTD
Planned Standard
PLOP
Pressure Line of Position
PLR
PASS Liaison Representative
Program Life Requirement
PLRS
Position Location Reporting System
PLS
Please
PLSS
Portable Life-Support System
PLT
Pilot
Pilot Training
Post-Loading Test
Procurement Lead Time
PLT, PLN
Plant
PLUS
PERT Life-Cycle Unified System
Programmed Learning Under Supervision
PLYINST
Command delivering orders to command
specified comply current
NAVMILPERSCOMINST _____
PLYMAN
Command delivering orders to command
specified comply
NAVMILSPERSMAN _____
PLYPASSPORT
Application for passport for self (and/or
dependents) must be in accordance with
NAVMILPERSCOMINST 4650.14 series

PM
  Payload Multiplication (factor)
  Permanent Magnet
  Phase Modulation
  Planned (or Preventive) Maintenance
    (program)
  Porous (or Powered) Metal
  Position Management
  Procurement and Material
  Program Memo(randa)
  Project Manager (or Management)
  Provost Marshal
  Pulse Modulation
PM1
  Patternmaker First Class
PM2
  Patternmaker Second Class
PM3
  Patternmaker Third Class
PMA
  Permanent Mailing Address
  Personal Money Allowance
  Political-Military Affairs (unit, USNR)
  Principal Management Agreement
  Project Manager, Naval Air Systems
    Command
P-MARP
  Peacetime Manpower Allocation/Requirement
    Plan—see also M-MARP
PMB
  Program Management Branch
PMBR
  Practice Multiple Bomb Rack
PMC
  Chief Patternmaker
  Pacific Marine Center (NOAA)
  Passenger, Mail and Cargo
  Procurement, Marine Corps
  Procurement Method Coding
  Program (or Project) Management Course
    (DSMS)
PMCS
  Project Management and Control System
PMDO
  Planned Maintenance During Overhaul
    (program)
PMDS
  Point Missile Defense System
  Project(ed) Map Display System
PMDU
  Projected Map Display Unit
PME
  Precision Measuring Equipment
  Project Manager, Naval Electronic Systems
    Command
PMEL
  Precision Measuring Equipment Laboratory
PMFA
  Patternmaker Fireman Apprentice
PMFC
  Post-Maintenance Check-Flight

PMFN
  Patternmaker Fireman
PMG
  Permanent Magnet(ic) Generator
  Political-Military Group
PMI
  Program Management Instruction
  Proposed Military Improvements
PMI/MO
  Precedence Manual In/Manual Out
PMIP
  Post-Maintenance Inspection Pilot
PMK
  Performance Mark
PML
  Proposed Military Improvements
PMLFS
  Permanent Nucleus Landing Force Staff
PMLO
  Philippine Military Liaison Officer
PMM
  Planned Maintenance Manual
  Pulse Mode Multiplex
PMMP
  Preventive Maintenance Management Plan
PMO
  Polaris Material (or Missile) Office
  Program Management Office
  Project Manager, Naval Ordnance Systems
    Command
  Provost Marshal's Office
PMOLANT
  Polaris Material Office, Atlantic
PMOPAC
  Polaris Material Office, Pacific
P-MOS
  Positive-Metal Oxide Semiconductor
PMP
  Program (or Project) Management Plan
  Project Master Plan
PMPS
  Program Management Planning and
    Scheduling
PMR
  Planned Maintenance Requirement
  Procurement Management Review
  Project Manager Representative
PMR, PACMISRAN
  Pacific Missile Range
PMRA
  Projected Manpower Requirements Account
PMRM
  Periodic Maintenance Requirements Manual
  Projected Manpower Requirements Model
PMRP
  Precious Metals Recovery Program

PMS
Performance Measurements System
Planned Maintenance System (SNMMMS)
Power Management System
Project Manager, Naval Sea Systems
Command
PM&ST
Professor of Military Science and Tactics
PMSV
Pilot to Metro Service
PMT
Medical Photography Technician
PMV
Private Motor Vehicle
PN
Panel (U/I)
Part Number
Performance Number (fuels)
PN, NP
North Pole
PN1
Personnelman First Class
PN2
Personnelman Second Class
PN3
Personnelman Third Class
P/N
Part Number
PNA
Passed, but Not Advanced
Price Not Available
PNC
Chief Personnelman
PNCM
Master Chief Personnelman
PNCS
Senior Chief Personnelman
PNEC
Primary Navy Enlisted Classification (code)
PNID
Priority Network In-Dial
PNID/NOD
Priority Network In-Dial/Network Out-Dial
PNNCF
Pacific Northern Naval Coastal Frontier
PNOK
Primary Next of Kin
PNP
Positive-Negative-Positive (transistor)
PNSA
Personnelman Seaman Apprentice
PNSN
Personnelman Seaman
PNS&T
Professor of Naval Science and Tactics
PNUB
Permanent Naval Uniform Board

PO
Permanent Overflow
Petty (or Part, or Press, or Project) Officer
Planning (or Program) Objective
Project (or Purchase, or Previous) Order(s)
P&P
Plans and Operations
PO1
Petty Officer First Class
PO2
Petty Officer Second Class
PO3
Petty Officer Third Class
POA
Pacific Ocean Area
Post Overhaul Availability
POACS
Prior Other Active Commissioned Service
POAES
Prior Other Active Enlisted Service
POA&M
Plan of Action and Milestones
POAN
Procurement of Ordnance and Ammunition,
Navy
POAR
Project Order Action Request
POATSC
Pacific Overseas Air Terminal Service
Command
POB
Persons (or Projected) Onboard
POC
Point of Contact
Privately-Owned Conveyance (or
Convenience)
Production Operational Capability
POCG
Program Operations Coordinating Group
POCL
Power on Clear (NNSS)
POCM, MCPO
Master Chief Petty Officer
POCP
Program Objective Change Proposal
POCS, SCPO
Senior Chief Petty Officer
POD
Permissible Operating Distance
Plan of the Day
Port of Discharge (or Debarkation)
Price, Operation, Decision
Proof of Delivery
POE
Port of Embarkation
Projected Operational Environment
POFA
Programmed Operational and Functional
Appraisal
PO-FY
Program Objectives for Fiscal Year ____

POG
Petty Officer's Guide (publication)
Plant Operating Guide
Propulsion Operating Guide
POIC
Petty Officer-in-Charge
POINTER
Partial Orientation Interferometer
POINTERM
Appointment will be regarded as having
terminated upon this date
POINTMAIL
Letter appointment in mail
POL
Petroleum-Oil-Lubricants
Port of Loading
POLCAP
Petroleum Capabilities Report
POLIT
Political
POM
Preparation for Overseas Movement
Program Objectives Memorandum
POMA
Petty Officer's Military Academy
POMAR
Positive Operational Meteorological Aircraft
Report
POMF
Polaris Missile Facility
POMFLANT
Polaris Missile Facility, Atlantic
POMFPAC
Polaris Missile Facility, Pacific
POMS
Panel on Operational Meteorological
Satellites
POMSEE
Performance, Operating and Maintenance
Standards for Electronic Equipment
PONSE
Personnel of the Naval Shore Establishment
(report)
PONY
Pride of the Navy Yard
POO
Post Office Order
POOD
Permanent Officer-of-the-Day
POP
Position Operating Procedures
POPR
Pilot Overhaul Provisioning Review
POR
Pay on Return
Proof of Receipt
PORCO
Port Control Office(r)
PORICH
Port in which (activity designated may be)

PORSE
Post Overhaul Reactor Safeguards
Examination
POS
Peacetime Operating Status (or Stocks)
Point of Sale
Preferred Overseas Shore (duty)
POS, POSIT, POSN
Position
POSDCORB
Planning, Organizing, Staffing, Directing,
Coordinating, Reporting, and Budgeting
POSN, POS, POSIT
Position
POSS
Passive Optical Satellite Surveillance
POSTER
Post-Strike Emergency Reporting
POT
Potential
POTANN
Potomac Annex
POTS
Pre-Overhaul Tests
POTW
Publically-Owned Treatment Works
POV
Privately-Owned Vehicle
POW
Petty Officer-of-the-Watch
Powder
Prisoner of War
POWP
Preliminary Overhaul Work Package
PP
Page Printer
Plant Procedures
Power Plants (division)
Preliminary Planning
Pressure Pattern (or Plug, or Proof)
Procurement Package
P&P
Packing and Preservation
Payments and Progress
Plans and Policies
Plans and Programs
Process and Print (or Proof)
Procurement and Production
PPA
Personal Property Activity
Polypropylene Asbestos (seals)
PPAR
Priority Problem Analysis Report
PPB
Provisioning Parts Breakdown
PP&B, PPB
Planning, Programming and Budgeting
PPBS
Planning, Programming and Budgeting
System

PPC
Partial Pay Card
Patrol Plane Commander
Power Plants Change
PP&C
Production Planning and Control
Program Planning and Control
PPD
Program Planning Department
Progress Plan Decision
Project Planning Directive
PPDB
Point Positioning Data Base
PP&D
Post Processor and Display
PPE
Pre-Production Evaluation
PPEA
Plant Performance Evaluation Activity
PPF
Primary Part Failure
PPGBL
Personal Property Government Bill of Lading
PPH
Pounds per Hour
PPI
Personnel Planning Information
Plan Position Indicator
Policy Proof of Interest
PPL
Preferential Planning List
PPLA
Practice Precautionary Landing Approach
PPM
Parts per Million
Pulse Position Modulation
P&PM
Preservation and Preventive Maintenance
PPN
Patrol Plane Navigator
PP&NA
Private Plants and Naval Activities
PPNC
Patrol Plane Navigator/Communicator
P PNDG
Petition Pending
PPO
Police Petty Officer
Prior Permission Only
Projected Program Objective
Publications and Printing Office
PPOD
Production Plan of the Day
PROM
Programmable ROM
PPP
Priority Placement Program
Processing and Printing Facility
PP2P
Patrol Plane Second Pilot

PP3P
Patrol Plane Third Pilot
PPPC
Petroleum Pool Pacific Coast
PPPI
Precision (or Projection) Plan Position
  Indicator
PPR
Permanent Pay Record
Prior Permission Required
Production per Recruiter
Proprietary Procurement Request
PPS
Pre-Position Stocks
Pulse per Second
Pupil Personnel Services (team)
PPSMEC
Procurement, Precedence of Supplies,
  Material and Equipment Committees
PPSO
Personal Property Shipping Office
PPT
Parts per Thousand
Periodic (or Pre-) Production Test
PPTC
Patrol Plane Tactical Coordinator
PPTMR
Personal Property Traffic Management
  Regulations
PP&W
Publicity and Psychological Warfare
PPWO
Propulsion Plant Watch Officer
PQ
Physically Qualified
Previous Question
PQAA
Procurement Quality Assurance Action
PQAP
Planned Quality Assurance Program
PQMR
Proposed Qualitative Material Requirement
PQ&MR DIV
Physical Qualifications for Medical Records
  Division
PQS
Personnel (or Performance) Qualification
  Standards
PR
Precedence Reviewed
Prepare Reply
Press Release
Priority Regulations
Processing and Reporting (course)
Procurement Report (or Request)
Purchase Request (or Requisition)
PR, PHIBRON
Amphibious Squadron
PR, PUBREL
Public Relations

P/R
Planned Requirements
PR1
Aircrew Survival Equipmentman First Class
PR2
Aircrew Survival Equipmentman Second
Class
PR3
Aircrew Survival Equipmentman Third Class
PR I
Processing and Reporting, Phase I (course)
PR II
Processing and Reporting, Phase II (course)
PRA
Pay Record Access
Personnel Research Activity
PRAA
Aircrew Survival Equipmentman Airman
Apprentice
PRAC
Practice
PRAM
Propelled-Ascent Mine
PRAN
Aircrew Survival Equipmentman Airman
PRARS
Pitch, Roll, Azimuth Reference System
PRASD
Personnel Research Activity, San Diego (CA)
PRATE
Present Rate
PRAW
Naval Reserve Research Activity
PRB
Planned Requirements Bureau
Program Review Board
PRBC
Pressure Ratio Bleed Control
PRC
Chief Aircrew Survival Equipmentman
Package Requirements Code
Planned Requirements Conversion
PRCHT, PARA
Parachute
PRCM
Master Chief Aircrew Survival Equipmentman
PR/COM
Vessel Delivered in Partially-Completed
Status
PRCP
Personnel Readiness Capability Program
PRCS
Senior Chief Aircrew Survival Equipmentman
PRD
Period
Projected (or Planned) Rotation Date
Public Relations Division
PRDR
Preproduction Reliability Design Review
PRE
Progressive Resistive Exercise

PREC
Precedence
PRECIP, PCPN
Precipitation
PRECOM
Precommissioning
PRECOMDET
Precommissioning Detail
PRECOMSCOL
Precommissioning School
PRECOMUNIT
Precommissioning Unit
PREF
Preference
Preferred
PREFLT
Pre-Flight
PREFLTSCOL
Pre-Flight School
PREINSURV
President, Board of Inspection and Survey
PRELIM
Preliminary
PRELIMPERSACCT
In accordance with NAVPERSMAN 3860360,
activity performing preliminary procedures
for separation will carry your separation
papers and pay accounts and continue to
report you in personnel accounting system
until action is taken on proceedings and
recommended findings of physical
evaluation board.
PRELIMSEPRET
Period between date of completion of
preliminary procedures incident to
separation and date of retirement,
discharge, release from active duty or
restoration to duty status, less allowed
travel time used in arriving (place
designated) will be charged against earned
leave.
PREMEDU
Preventive Medicine Unit
PREP
Pre-Discharge Education Program
Preparatory
Prepare
PREPSCOL
Preparatory School
PRES
Present
President
Pressure
PRESAIR
Pressurized Air Compressors
PRESINSURV
President, Board of Inspection and Survey
PRESPROC
Presidential Proclamation

PRESS
Pacific Range Electromagnetic Signature
Studies
PRESTO
Program Reporting and Evaluation System
for Total Operation
PREV
Pre-Reenlistment Evaluation
Previous
PREVMEDDIV
Preventive Medicine Division
PREVMEDU
Preventive Medicine Unit
PRF
Pulse Repetition Frequency
PRI
Priority
Prison
Pulse Repetition Interval
PRIBAG
Priority Baggage
PRI BIL
Primary Billet
PRIDE
Personalized Recruiting for Immediate or
Delayed Enlistment
Personal Responsibility in Daily Effort
PRIM
Primary
Primary Radar Identification Methods
PRIMAN
Enlisted Primary Manning (codes)
PRIME
Primary (or Priority) Management Efforts
PRIN
Principal
PRINCE
Parts Reliability Information Center
PRINOBC/NEC
Primary Navy Officer Billet Classification
(code) and Navy Enlisted Classification
(code)
PRINT
Pre-edited Interpretive (system)
PRIOR
Program for In-Orbit Rendezvous
PRISE
Program for Integrated Shipboard Electronics
PRISIC
Photographic Reconnaissance Interpretation
Section Intelligence Center
PRISM
Program Reliability Information System for
Management
Program(med) Integrated System
Maintenance
PRITRA
Primary Training
PRIV
Private(ly)

PRIVAUTH
Travel authorized via privately-owned vehicle
with understanding that no additional cost
to the government is involved
PRIV MAINTD
Privately-Maintained
PRIV PROP
Private Property
PRL
Penetration Records List
Publications Requirements List
PRM GR
Permanent Grade
PRMIS
Printing Resources Management Information
System
PRO
Personnel (or Public) Relations Officer
Planned Requirements Outfitting
Price Reduces Overhead
Probation
Procedure
Proceed
Professional
PRO, PROF
Proficiency
PROB
Problem
PROBCOST
Probabilistic Budgeting and Forward Costing
PROBOUT
Proceed on or about
PROC
Photographic Reconnaissance Officers'
Course
Procurement
PROCOMP
Process Compiler
PROCON
Request diagnosis, prognosis, present
condition, probable date and mode of
disposition of following patient(s) reported
in your hospital (name, grade, social
security number)
PRODAC
Programmed Digital Automatic Control
PROF, PRO
Proficiency
PROFASTRANS
Proceed by first available government
transportation
PROF-E
Programmed Review of Operator
Functions-Elementary
PROG
Prognosis
Progress
PROGMAINT
Progressive Maintenance
PROH
Prohibit

PROIMREP
Proceed immediately and report
PROJ
Project(ile)
PROJECT IIID
(See ADLPS)
PROJMGR
Project Manager
PROJMGRASWS
Project Manager, Antisubmarine Warfare
Systems
PROJMGRSMS
Project Manager, Surface Missile Systems
PROL
Priority Reconnaissance Objectives List
PROM
Prominent
Promote(d)
PROMIS
Program Management Information System
PROML
Promulgate
PROMPT
Project Reporting, Organizing and
Management Planning Technique
PROMSS
Procedures and Relationships for the
Operation of Manual Stations and Spaces
PROM STAT
Promotion Status
PROP
Planetary Rocket Ocean Platform
Propeller
Property
PROPA BAS
Pro-Rated Basic Allowance for Subsistence
PRO ACCT REC
Property Accountability Records
PRO-PAY
Proficiency-Pay
PROPORICH
Proceed to port in which (unit located)
PROS
Prosecution
Prospective
PROSIG
Procedures Signal
PROSIGN
Procedure Sign
PROTIMEREP
Proceed in time to report (activity or station
designated by group(s) immediately
following) not later than (hour and/or date
indicated)
PROUS
Proceed to a port in the Continental Limits of
the United States
PROV
Provide
Provision(al)

PROVGR
Proving Grounds
PROVIB
Propulsion System Decision and Vibration
Analysis
PROVMAIN
Other provisions to basic orders remain in
effect
PROVMAINTCO
Provisional Maintenance Company
PROVMUSTCO
Provisional Medical Unit Self-Contained
Company
PROWDELREP
Proceed without delay and report
PRP
Personnel Reliability Program
Physical Readiness Program
Pneumatically-Released Pilot
Production Requirements Plan
Progressive Rework Plan
Public Relations Plan (or Personnel)
PRR
Passenger Reservation Request
Production Readiness Reviews
Pulse-Repetition Rate
PRSEC
Payroll Section
PRST
Persist
Probability Ratio Sequential Test
PRT
Power Recovery Turbine
Program Review Team
Pulse-Repetition Time
PRTC
Professional Rate Training Course
PRTL
Portable
PS
Patrol Sea (pilot code)
Pistol Sharpshooter
(Coolant) Pressuring System
Program Summary
PS, SP
South Pole
P/S
Power Section
PSA
Post-Shakedown Availability
Project Sensor Abilities
Public Service Announcement
PSA, PERSUPPACT
Personnel Support Activity
P/S/A
Port Side Aft (stowage)
PSANDT, PS&T
Pay, Subsistence and Transportation
PSAT
Propulsion Subsystem Availability Test

PSBL
Possible
PSC
Per Standard Compass
PSD
Physical Sciences Division (ONR)
Preferred Sea Duty
Professional Services Dates
Pseudo Stow Document
PSD, PERSUPPDET
Personnel Support Detachment
PSDA
Partial Source Data Automation
PSE
Personnel Support Equipment
Power-Supply Electronics (assembly)
PS&E
Plans, Specifications and Estimates
PSEA
Pacific and Southeast Asia
PSF
Private Source Funds
PSF, PANSEAFRON
Panama Sea Frontier
PSF, PHILSEAFRON
Philippine Sea Frontier
P/S/F
Port Side Forward (stowage)
PSG
Passage
Passing
PSGR, PAS, PAX
Passenger
PSH
Pre-Select Heading
PSI
Periodic Step Increase
Personnel Security Investigations
Pounds per Square Inch
Pressurized Sphere Injection
Programmed Student Input
PSIA
Per-Square-Inch Absolute
PSIB
Preliminary Ship Information Book
PSICP
Program Support Inventory Control Point
PSID
Patrol Seismic Intrusion Detector
PSIG
Per-Square-Inch Gauge
PSK
Phase-Shift Keying
PSK-PCM
Phase-Shift Keying/Pulse-Code Modulation
PSL
Pycnocline Scattering Layer
PS&M
Personnel Supervision and Management
(SECP)

PSN
Position
PSNCF
Pacific Southern Naval Coastal Frontier
PSNS, PSNSY
Puget Sound Naval Shipyard
PSNSY, PSNS
Puget Sound Naval Shipyard
PSO
Political Survey Officers
Port Services Office(r)
Prospective Supply Officer
Publicity Security Officer
PSP
Patrol Seaplane
Perforated Steel Plating
Performance Standards Program
Project Standard Practice
PS&QS
Planning and Quotas
PSR
Packed Snow on Runway
Performance Summary Report
Photo Scale Reciprocal
PSR-P
Packed Snow on Runway-Patchy
PSS
Propulsion Sub-System
PST
Past
Projected Sea Tour
PS&T, PSANDT
Pay, Subsistence and Transportation
PSTCO
Per Steering Compass
PSTN
Pay, Subsistence and Transportation, Navy
PSU
Power Switching Unit
PSW
Primary Shield Water
PSY-OPS
Psychological Warfare Operations
PSY-S DIV
Psychological Sciences Division (ONR)
PSYWAR
Psychological Warfare
PT
Paper Tape
Particle (or Penetration) Test
Patient (MAPMIC)
Pint (U/I)
Primary Target
Proceed (or Prothrobin) Time
PTBL
Portable
PTC
Motorboat, Submarine Chaser
Personnel Transfer Capsule
PTCA
Provisioning Technical Coding Activity

PTCAD
Provision Troop Carrier Airborne Division
PTCCS
Polar Target Card Computer System
PTD
Pilot to Dispatcher
Provisioning Technical Demonstration
PTDP
Preliminary Technical Development Plan
PTF
Fast Patrol Craft
Patch and Test Facility
PTFG
Large Guided Missile Motorboat
PTFMR
Peacetime Force Material Request
PTG
Small Guided Missile Motorboat
PTI
Pre-Trial Investigation
PTL
Petroleum Testing Laboratory
Pre-Test Laboratory
PTL, PAT
Patrol
PTM
Pulse Time Modulation (or Multiplex)
PTN, PAT, PATN
Pattern
PTO
Please Turn Over
Power Take-Off
Project Technical Office
PTR
Painter
Pilot Training Rates
PTS
Permanent Threshold Shift
Pre-Flight Test Set
Pressure Test Station
PTT
Part Task Trainers
PTTI
Precise Time and Time Interval (standards)
PTY
Party
PU
Pick Up
Propellant Utilization (system)
PUB
Public(ation), (-ity)
Publish(ed)
PUBAFF, PA
Public Affairs
PUBAFF RRU
Public Affairs Ready Reserve Unit
PUBINFO, PI
Public Information
PUBREL, PR
Public Relations

PUBWKSCEN, PWC
Public Works Center
PUBWKSDEPT, PWD
Public Works Department
PUC
Permanent Unit Code
Port Utilization Committee
Presidential Unit Citation
PUFFS
Passive Underwater Fire Control Feasibility
Study
PUI
Pilot Under Instruction
PULHES
Physical Capacity or Stamina, Upper
Extremities, Lower Extremities, Hearing
and Ears, Vision and Eyes, and Psychiatric
System
PUM
Per Unit Monthly
PUMP
Production Upgrade Management Program
PUP
Pull-Up Point
PUR
Pursuant
PUR, PURCH
Purchase
PURA
PACOM Utilization and Redistribution Agency
PURCH, PUR
Purchase
PURIF
Purification
PURS
Program-Usage Replenishment System
PUS
Propellant-Utilization System
PV
Prevailing Visibility
Public Voucher (or Volunteer)
PVC
Poly-Vinyl-Chloride (plastic pipe)
PVG
Providing Group
Proving Ground
PVL
Prevail
PVNT
Prevent
PVT
Private
PW
Potable Water
Pulse Width
PW, PUBWKS
Public Works
PWA
Public Works Administration

PWB
Psychological Warfare Branch
Pulling Whaleboat
PWBS
Product Work Breakdown Structure
PWC, PUBWKSCEN
Public Works Center
PWCACE
Public Works Center Activity Civil Engineer
PWCDET
Public Works Center Detachment
PWCMIS
Public Works Center Management
Information System
PWCMS
Public Works Center Management System
PWD
Post-Write-Disturb (pulse)
Psychological Warfare Division
PWD, PUBWKSDEPT
Public Works Department
P/WG
Port Wing (stowage)
PWI
Proximity Warning Indicator
PWLA
Public Works Lead Activity
PWM
Public Works Maintenance
PWO
Principal Warfare Officer
PWO, PWOF
Public Works Office(r)
PWOF, PWO
Public Works Office(r)
PWR
Power
Pressurized Water Reactor
PWRR
Preposition War Reserve Requirements
PWRS
Preposition War Reserve Stocks
PWS
Performance Work Statement
PWT
Public Works Transportation
PWTC
Public Works Transportation Center
PWU
Public Works Utilities
PXO
Prospective Executive Officer
PY
Planning Year
Program Year
Pyramid (U/I)
PYPER
Promote Yard Performance Efficiency and
Reliability
PYZ
Pickup Zone

Q

Q
Quarterly (report frequency)
Q, QUES
Question
QA
Quality Assurance
Quick-Acting
Q&A
Questions and Answers
QAB
Quick-Acting Buttons
QAD
Quality Assurance Division
QAD, QA/DEPT
Quality Assurance Department
QA/DEPT, QAD
Quality Assurance Department
QAET
Quality Assurance Evaluation Test
QAIP
Quality Assurance Inspection Procedure
QAL
Q Allowance List (for aviation)
QAO
Quality Assurance Office
QAP
Quality Assurance Procedures (or Program,
or Provisions)
QAR
Quality Assurance Representative
QA&R
Quality Assurance and Revalidation
QARI
Quality Assurance Receipt Inspection
QAST
Quality Assurance Service Test (nuclear)
QATS
Quarterly Advanced Training Schedule
QAVP
Quality Assurance Verification Procedures
QAWT
Quick-Acting Water-Tight
QC
Quality Control
Quarter Credit
Q CARD
Qualification Card
QCID
Quality Control and Inspection Department
QCR
Quality Control/Reliability (or Representative)
QDR
Quality Deficiency Record (or Report)
QE
Quality Evaluation
QEAD
Quality Engineering and Assurance Division

QEC
Quick Engine Change
QECA
Quick Engine Change Assembly
QECK
Quick Engine Change Kit
QECS
Quick Engine Change Stand
QEEL
Quality Evaluation and Engineering
Laboratory
QEL
Quality Evaluation Laboratory (NTS)
QEST
Quality Evaluation System Test
QF
Quality Factor (radiation dose)
QFA
Qualification Firings Alignment
QFB
Quiet Fast Boat
QFR
Quarterly Force Revision
QFS
Quick-Fit Sea
QI
Quart Imperial (U/I)
QIB
Quarterly Information Bulletin
QK FL
Quick Flashing (light)
QL
Quintal
QM1
Quartermaster First Class
QM2
Quartermaster Second Class
QM3
Quartermaster Third Class
QMA
Qualified Military Available(s)
QMAO
Qualified for Mobilization Ashore Only
QMB
Quarterly Management Bulletin (publication)
QMC
Chief Quartermaster
Quartermaster Corps
QMCM
Master Chief Quartermaster
QMCS
Quality Monitoring Control System
Senior Chief Quartermaster
QMOW
Quartermaster of the Watch
QMS
Quarterly Meteorological Summary
QMSA
Quartermaster Seaman Apprentice
QMSN
Quartermaster Seaman

QM-T
Quartermaster-Trainee
QOH
Quantity on Hand
QOL
Quality of Life
QOMAC
Quarter-Orbit Magnetic Altitude Control
QPL
Qualified Products List
QPR
Quarterly Program Review
Quarterly Progress Report
QPRS
Quarterly Project Reliability Summary
QR
Qualified Representative
Quantity Requested
Quire (U/I)
QRA
Quick-Reaction Alert
Quick Replaceable Assembly
Q&RA
Quality and Reliability Assurance
(department)
QRC
Quick-Reaction Capability (or Contract)
Q/R/M
Quality/Reliability/Maintainability
QRT
Quiet Radio Transmission (sent before SOS)
QS
Quality Surveillance
QSI
Quality Step Increase
QSSI
Quarterly Surprise Security Inspection
QSTOL
Quiet Short Take-off and Landing (aircraft)
QT
Quart (U/I)
Quenched and Tempered (steel)
QTC
Quick Transmission Change
QTR
Quarter
QTR, QTY
Quarterly
QTY
Quantity
QTY, QTR
Quarterly
QUAD
Quadrant
Quadruplicate
QUAL
Qualification
Qualify

QUALREPFLYINS
Upon qualification and completion of academic training and when directed, report as DIFOTINSCREW

QUAR
Quarantine

QUARK
Question and Response Kits

QUES, Q
Question

QUOT
Quotation

QWR
Quarterly Weight Report

QZ
Quartz

R

R
Rain
Relay
Religious (AFRTS code)
Repair
Reproducible (copy)
Resistance
Resistor

R, RD
Read

(R)
Receiver

RA
Radar
Radio Altimeter Setting Height
Ration (U/I)
Reconnaissance Aircraft
Rental Agreement
Reviewing Authority
Rotary Actuator

R/A
Radius of Action

R&A
Research and Analysis

RAADC
Regional Accounting and Disbursing Center

RAAN
Repair Activity Accounting Number

RABAL
Radiosonde Balloon (observation)

RAC
Radar Azimuth Converter
Rapid-Action Change
Reactor Accident Calculation
Refrigerant-Air Condition (system)
Request for Authority to Contract
Responsibility Analysis Chart

RACE
Radiation Adaptive Compression Equipment
Random-Access Computer Equipment

RACEP
Random Access and Correlation for Extended Performance

RACON
Radar Responder Beacon

RA (CONSPIC)
Radar Conspicuous (object)

RACS
Recruiting Allocation Control System

RAD
Radial
Radical
Radius
Rapid Access Disc
Ratio Analysis Diagram
Recruiting Advertising (or Aids) Division
Required Availability Date
Resources Allocation Display

RAD, RDO
Radio

RAD, REFRAD
Released from Active Duty

RADA
Random-Access Discrete Address System

RADBN
Radio Battalion

RADCOM
Radar Countermeasures

RADCON
Radar (or Radiological) Control

RADEX
Radar Extractor

RADFAC
Radiating Facility

RADFAL
Radiological Prediction Fallout (plot)

RADFO
Radiological Fallout

RADHAZ
Hazards from Electromagnetic Radiation

RADINDEF
Notify COMNAVMILPERSCOM not less than six months prior to (date) if member does not desire further ACDU orders. Failure to do so constitutes agreement to accept another tour of duty.

RADINJCLRDS
Radiation Injury Claims Records (NAVSEA)

RADIST
Radar Distance (indicator)

RADLDEFLAB
Radiological Defense Laboratory

RADM
Rear Admiral

RADMIS
Research and Development Information Summary

RADMON
Radiological Monitor

RADOP
Radio Operator

RADPLANBD
Radio Planning Board
RADSAFE
Radiological Safety
R/ADT
Registration/Admission, Disposition and
Transfer (TRIMIS)
RADU
Ram Air-Driven Unit
RAE
Radio Astronomy Explorer
RAETU
Reserve Airborne Electronics Training Unit
RAF
Racial Awareness Facilitator (school)
RAFLO
Radio Frequency Liaison Office
RAFT
Racial Awareness Facilitators Team
Resource Allocation for Transportation
RAG
Replacement Air Group
River Assault Group
RAI
Random-Access Inquiry
RAID
Radar and Interdiction Device
River Assault Interdiction Division
RAIL
Revised Individual Allowance List
Runway Alignment Indicator Lights—see
MALS/RAIL
RAILS
Remote Area Instrument Landing Sensor
RAIP
Recruiting Advertising Improvement Program
RAL
Rubber, Air, Lead (sound dampening
materials)
RALACS
Radar Altimeter Low-Altitude Control System
RAM
Radio Attenuation Measurement
Random-Access Memory
Readiness and Money
Redeye Air-Launched Missile
Reentry Anti-Missile
RAMAC
Random-Access Methods of Accounting and
Control
RAMEC
Rapid-Action Minor Engineering Change
RAMIS
Receive, Accept, Maintain, Issue and Store
(Regulus missiles)
RAMP
Repairable-Asset Management Office
RAMPART
Radar Advanced Measurements Program for
Analysis of Reentry Techniques

RAMPS
Resources Allocation and Multi-Project
Scheduling
RAMS
Recruiting Advertising Management System
RAMSIM
Reliability, Availability, Maintenance,
Simulation
RAMTRA
Reserve Air Maintenance Training
RAMUS
Remote Access Multi-User System
RAMVAN
Reconnaissance Aircraft Maintenance Van
RAN
Radar Navigation
Random
Reconnaissance Attack Navigator
Regional Air Navigation
Reporting Accounting Number
Request for Authority to Negotiate
RANCID
Real and Not Corrected Input Data
RANCIN
Retrieval and Analysis of Navy Classified
Information
RANCOM
Random Communications (satellite)
RANGECO
Range Company
RAO
Record Purposes Only
RAOB
Radar Observation
RAP
Recognize All Potential
Recruiter Assistance (or Assistant) Program
Rocket-Assisted Projectile
RAPCON
Radar Approach Control
RAPEC
Rocket-Assisted Personnel Ejection Catapult
RAPIDS
Real-Time Automated Personnel Identification
System
RAPLOC
Rapid Acoustic Passive Localization
RAPPI
Random-Access Plan Position Indicator
RAP-TAP
Releasable Assets Program-Transferrable
Assets Program
RAPTS
Resource Accounting Project Tracking
System
RAR
Radio-Acoustic Range (finding equipment)
Record and Report
RARC
Revoked Appointment and Returned to
Civilian Status

RA REF
Radar Reflector
RARF
Radome, Antenna and Radio Frequency
(circuitry)
RARI
Reporting and Routing Instructions
RAS
Radar Assembly Spares
Radar Automatic System
Replenishment at Sea
Requirements Audit System
RASAU
Reserve Antisubmarine Warfare Systems
Analysis Mobilization Unit
RASC
Radiological Affairs Safety Committee
RASCAL
Random-Access Secure Communications
Anti-Jam Link
RASER
Radio Frequency Amplification by Stimulated
Emission of Radiation
RASO
Radiological Affairs Support Office
RASOR
Rear Area Stand-Off Repeater
RASP
Radiological Affairs Support Program
Refined Aeronautical Support Program
Reserve Analytical Studies Project
RASTAS
Radiating Site Target Acquisition Study
RAT
Ram Air Turbine
Rocket-Assisted Torpedo
RATAN
Radar and Television Aid to Navigation
RATCC
Radar Air Traffic Control Center
RATE
Remote Automatic Telemetering Equipment
RATIO
Radio Telescope in Orbit
RATO
Rocket-Assisted Take-Off
RATOG
Rocket-Assisted Take-Off Gear
RATPAC
Radar Acquisition Tracking Probe for Active
Calibration
RATS
Radar Altimeter Target Simulator
Rations
Recruiting Attrition Tracking System
RATSCAT
Radar Target Scatter
RATT, RTT
Radio-Teletype
RAU
Retransmission Application Unit

RAV
Restricted Availability
RAVE
Research Aircraft for Visual Environment
RAVIR
Radar Video Recorder
RAW
Request for Additional Work
REWARC
Radar Warning Circuit
RAWIN
Radar Wind (sounding)
RAWINSONDE
Radar Wind Sounding and Radiosonde
(combined)
RB
Relative Bearing
Renegotiation Board
Rescue Boat
Rubber Block
R/B, R BN
Radio Beacon
RBA
Rescue Breathing Apparatus
RBDE
Radar Bright Display Equipment (FAA)
RBE
Relative Biological Effectiveness
RBFC
Retract Before Firing Contractor
RBHB
Red and Black Horizontal Bands (buoy
markings)
R BN, R/B
Radio Beacon
RBOC
Rapid-Bloom(ing) Off-Board Chaff (missile
decoy system)
RBS
Radar Bombing Score
Recoverable Booster System
Regional Briefing Station
RBC
Return Beam Vidicon
RC
Rapid Curing (asphalt)
Reactor Compartment
Reactor Cooling (system)
Reception Center
Reduced Capability
Relay Center
Resistance Capacitance (time)
R/C
Request for Checkage
RCA
Rating Change Authority (or Authorization)
Reach Cruising Altitude
Repair Cycle Asset
Riot Control Agent

RCC
  Recovery Control Center
  Resistance-Capacitance Coupling
  Rescue Coordination Center (or Control)
RCCA
  Recovery Control Center, Atlantic
RCCP
  Recovery Control Center, Pacific
RCD
  Rocket Cushioning Device
RCDR
  Radiological Control Deficiency Report
RCE
  Radiological Control Engineering
RCH
  Reach
RCL
  Ramped Cargo Lighter
RCLM
  Reclaim
RCLS
  Runway Centerline Light System
RCM
  Radar (or Radio) Countermeasures
RCMA
  Reservist Clothing Maintenance Allowance
RCMP
  Recompute Last Fix (NNSS)
RCN, RECCE, RECON, RECONN
  Reconnaissance
RCO
  Range (or Remote) Control Officer
RCP
  Radar Chart Protector
  Request for Contractual Procurement
RCPP
  Refrigeration, Compressor and Electrical
    Power, Airborne Pod Enclosure
RCPT
  Reception
  Refrigeration, Compressor and Electrical
    Power, Trailer-Mounted
RCR
  Runway Condition Reading
RCRA
  Radiologically-Controlled Radiation Area
RCRC
  Revoked Commission, Returned to Civilian
    Status
RCRS
  Reserve Combat Replacement Squadron
RCS
  Radar Control Ship
  Radar Cross Section
  Reentry Control System
  Report Control Symbol
  Rip-Out Control Sheet
RCSS
  Random Communications Satellite System
  Recruiting Command Support System

RCT
  Received Copy of Temporary
  Regimental (or Regional) Combat Team
  Repair Cycle Time
RCTL
  Resistor-Capacitor-Transistor Logic (circuitry)
RCU
  Remote Radio Control Unit
  Requisition Control Unit
RCV, REC
  Receive
RCVG
  Replacement Carrier Air Group
RCVR
  Receiver
RCVW, REDATKCARAIRWING
  Readiness Attack Carrier Air Wing
RD
  Radar
  Reference Datum
  Replenishment Demand
  Restricted Data
  Revolutionary Development (team)
RD, RND
  Round
RD1
  Radarman First Class
RD2
  Radarman Second Class
RD3
  Radarman Third Class
R&D, RSCH&DEV
  Research and Development
RDAC
  Recruiting District Assistance Council
RDB
  Research and Development Board
RDB, RDM
  Ramped Dump Barge
RDC
  Chief Radarman
  Rapid Development Capability
  Research and Development Center
RDCM
  Master Chief Radarman
RDCS
  Senior Chief Radarman
RDD
  Range Development Department (PMR)
  Required Delivery Date
RDEP
  Recruit Depot
RDF
  Radio Direction Finder
  Rapid Deployment Force
  Restoration of Damaged Facilities
RDFSTA
  Radio Direction Finder Station
RDG
  Ridge

RDI
Reliability Design Index
RDJTF
Rapid Deployment Joint Task Force
RDL
Rapid Draft Letter
RDM, RDB
Ramped Dump Barge
RDO
Regional Defense Organization
Research and Development Objective
Runway Duty Officer
RDO, RAD
Radio
RDP
Range Data Processor
RDPM
Revised Draft, Presidential Memorandum
RDS
Rounds
RDSA
Radarman Seaman Apprentice
RDSN
Radarman Seaman
RDSS
Rapidly Deployable Surveillance System
RDT
Reliability Determination Test
RDT&E
Research, Deployment, Test and Evaluation
RDT&EN
Research, Development, Test and Evaluation,
Navy
RDU
Receipt and Dispatch Unit
Refrigeration Detection Unit
RDVU
Rendezvous
RDY
Ready
RE
Radio, Electronic (system)
Reenlistment (code)
REA
Reactor Enclosure Assembly
Request for Equitable Adjustment
REACDU
Recalled to Active Duty
REACOT
Remove Errors and Complete on Time
READ
Radar Echo Augmentation Device
Real-Time Electronic Access and Display
READE
Reduce Errors and Decrease Expense
READI
Rocket-Engine Analyzer and Decision
Instrument
READJ
Readjusted

READJPAY
Readjusted Pay
READSUPPGRUDET
Readiness Support Group Detachment
READTRAFAC
Readiness Training Facility
REAF
Responsibility for discharge costs rests with
U.S. Air Force or its agent
REALCOM
Real-Time and Communications
REARM
Responsibility for discharge costs rests with
U.S. Army or its agent
REB
Radar Evaluation Branch
REC
Record
Recreation
REC, RCV
Receive
RECA
Residual Capacity Assessment
RECBKS
Receiving Barracks
RECCE, RCN, RECON, RECONN
Reconnaissance
RECCFO
Received in Connection with Fitting Out
RECCO
Reconnaissance Reporting Code
RECD
Received
RECDUINS
Received for duty under instruction
RECDUT
Received for duty
RECIP, RECIPRO
Reciprocating
RECIPRO, RECIP
Reciprocating
RECL
Reclamation
RECLUMPSUM
Entitled to receive lump sum payment equal
to two months' basic pay multiplied by
number of years total commissioned
service computed IAW 10 USC 6387 for
line officers or 10 USC 6388 for staff corps
officers. Payment may not be more than
two years' basic pay or $15,000, whichever
is lesser. Upon separation he will be
entitled to ___ months' basic pay or
$15,000, whichever is lesser.
RECM, RECOM
Recommendation

RECMOP
NAVMILPERSCOM records indicate that he has previously received payment in the amount of _____ under provisions of the Mustering Out Payment Act of 1944 and/or the Veterans Readjustment Assistance Act of 1952 and/or Chapter 43 of Title 38, U.S. Code.

RECNO
This Office has No Record of

RECO
Remote Command
Remotely Controlled (detonating device)

RECOG
Recognition
Recognize

RECOM, RECM
Recommendation

RECOMMTRANSO
Upon receipt of these orders communicate with _____ transportation officer for priority designator via government air transportation if available to (location desired)

RECOMP
Recommended Completion (date)

RECON
Reconsideration
Resources Conservation

RECON, RCN, RECCE, RECONN
Reconnaissance

RECONATKRON, RVAH
Reconnaissance Attack Squadron

RECONATKWING
Reconnaissance Attack Wing

RECONBN
Reconnaissance Battalion

RECONN, RCN, RECCE, RECON
Reconnaissance

RECOVER
Replace Engine Components Vice Engine Return

RECSATSUM
Reconnaissance Satellite Summary

RECSHIP
Receiving Ship

RECSTA
Receiving Station

RECTAD
Received for temporary additional duty

RECTADINS
Received for temporary additional duty under instruction

RECTREAT
Received for treatment

RED
Record of Emergency Data
Reduction

REDAP
Reentrant Data Processing

REDCOM, NAVRESREDCOM
Naval Reserve Readiness Command

REDOPS
Operational(ly) Readiness Report

REDS
Revised Engine-Delivery Schedule

REEL
Radiation Exposure Evaluation Laboratory

REEN, REENL
Reenlistment

REENL ALLOW
Reenlistment Allowance

REENL, REEN
Reenlistment

REF
Refer(ence)
Reflector

REFG, REFRIG
Refrigerator

REFRAD, RAD
Released from Active Duty

REFRIG, REFG
Refrigeration

REFT
Released for Experimental Flight Test

REFTRA
Refresher Training

REFURDIS
Reference Your Dispatch

REFURLTR
Reference Your Letter

REG
Registered
Regular
Regulate
Regulation

REG, RGN
Region

REGAL
Range and Elevation Guidance for Approach and Landing

REGIS
Register

REGOV
Responsibility for discharge costs rests with foreign government

REGT
Regiment

REH
Rehearing

REHAB
Rehabilitation

REI
Request for Engineering Information

REIL
Runway End Identifier Light (system)

REIMB
Reimburse

REIMBJTR
Reimbursement will be in accordance with JTR, Vol. 1, Chap. 4, Parts E and F, as applicable

REIN, REINF
Reinforced

REINCC
Resident Engineer-in-Charge of Construction

REINF, REIN
Reinforced

REINFS
Reinforcements

REINS
Radar-Equipped Inertial Navigation System

REL
Related
Reliable
Relief

RELACDU
Released from Active Duty

RELBY
When relieved by

RELDET
When relieved, detached (to duty indicated). (Date on or about which these orders become effective may be indicated.)

RELDIRDET
When relieved and when directed, detached (to duty indicated). (Date on or about which detachment is to be effective may be indicated.)

REM
Registered Equipment Management
Remitted
Roentgen Equivalent Man (or Mammal)

REMAD
Remote Magnetic Anomaly Detection

REMD
Remanded

REMG
Remanding

REMS
Responsibility for discharge costs rests with U.S. Navy or its agent

REOP
Responsibility for discharge costs rests with commercial operator or its agent

REORG
Reorganize

REP
Range Error Probability (or Probable)
Repair
Representative
Rework Excellence Program
Roentgen Equivalent Physical

REP, REPPT
Reporting Point

REP, REPT, RPT
Report

REPCAT
Report Corrective Action Taken

REPERMSG
Report in person or by message

REPFORMAINT
Representative for Maintenance Force

REPISIC
Report to the immediate superior in command, if present, otherwise by message

REPITINERARY
Report by message, in person, or by other means, to NAVATT or such command specified, giving address and itinerary while in his/their duty area. Indicate on original orders date and method of reporting.

REPL
Replace(ment)

REPLTR
Report(ing) by letter

REPMIS
Reserve Personnel Management Information System

REPMSG
Report by message to (command(s) or person(s) indicated)

REPNAVRESCEN
Upon release you are urged to contact the nearest Naval Reserve Center for information relative to Naval Reserve Training. Participants in Naval Reserve Training may earn retirement points and drill pay if a billet is available.

REPO, REPTOF
Reporting Officer

REPPAC
Repetitively-Pulsed Plasma Accelerator

REPPT, REP
Reporting Point

REPRO
Reproduce
Reproduction

REPSNO
Report(ing) through senior naval officer _____, if applicable

REPT, RPT
Repeat

REPTOF, REPO
Reporting Officer

RETRANS
Report for transportation

REQ
Request

REQ, RQR
Requirement

REQFOLINFO
Request the following information to be forwarded to this office

REQN/OPTAR
Requisition/Operating Target (log)

REQN, RQN
Requisition

REQNOM
Request Nomination
REQREC
Request Recommendation
REQSI
Request Shipping Instructions
REQUAL
Requalified
Requalify
RER
Rubberized Equipment Repair
RES
Radiation Equivalent Source
Reentry System
Reserve
RESANTISUBCARAIRGRU, CVSGR, RESASWCARAIRGRU
Reserve Antisubmarine Warfare Carrier Air Group
RESASWCARAIRGRU, CVSGR, RESANTISUBCARAIRGRU
Reserve Antisubmarine Warfare Carrier Air Group
RESASWTRACEN
Naval Air Reserve Antisubmarine Warfare Training Center
RESCAP
Rescue Combat Air Patrol
RESCEN
Reserve Center
RESCOMMIS
Reserve Command Management Information System
RESDESDIV
Reserve Destroyer Division
RESDESRON
Reserve Destroyer Squadron
RESDIST
Reserve District
RESER
Reentry System Evaluation Radar
RESFAC
Reserve Facility
RESFORONS
Reserve Force Squadrons
RESGD
Resigned
RESIG
Resignation
RES/IC
Reserve-In Commission (vessel status)
RES/IS
Reserve-In Service (vessel status)
RESMILCON
Reserve Military Construction
RESO
Regional Environmental Support Office
RESP
Responder (beacon)
Responsible

RESREP
Resident Representative
RESS
Recruiting Enlisted Selection System
REST
Radar Electronic Scan Technique
Range, Endurance, Speed and Time (computer)
REST, RSTD
Restricted
RESTOURSERV
If dependent travel is involved overseas, submit copy of agreement to remain on active duty, if required, to command having cognizance of transportation
RESTRACEN
Reserve Training Center
RESTRAFAC
Reserve Training Facility
RESUPSHIP
Resident Supervisor of Shipbuilding Conversion and Repair
RET
Retired
RET, RETAN
Retained
RET, RETD
Returned
RET-ABSTEE
Returned Absentee
RETAN, RET
Retained
RETAT
It is requested that
RETD, RET
Returned
RETDSG
Effective upon being transferred to retired list designator is changed to _____
RETNDU
Returned to duty
RETORC
Research Torpedo Configuration
RETRANS
For return transportation to
RETRO
Retroactive
RETRO FA
Retroactive Family Allowance (checkage)
RETSER
Retained in Service
RETULSIGN
Retain on board until assignment received
REU
Requesting Expeditor Unit
REURAD
Refer Your Radio Message

REV
Reverse
Review
Revolution
Revolve
REV, R/V
Reentry Vehicle
REVAR
Authorized to revisit any of the
above-mentioned places and vary itinerary
as necessary
REVD
Reversed
REVG
Reversing
REVO
Revoke
REV STAT
Revised Statutes
REWS
Reconnaissance and Electronic Warfare
Systems
REWSON
Reconnaissance, Electronic Warfare, Special
Operations and Naval Intelligence
Processing System
RF
Radio Frequency
Representative Function
RFA
Radio Frequency Amplifier
Royal Fleet Auxiliary (tankers)
RFB
Reliability Function Blocks
RFBS
Rapid Feedback Message System
RFC
Required Functional Capabilities
RFCS
Radio Frequency Carrier Shift
RFD
Ready for Delivery
RFDC
Reporting Field Designation Code
RFDC C/D
Reporting Field Designation Code
Correction/Discrepancy
RFE
Request for Evaluation
Reserve Female Enlistment
RFEP
Reserve Female Enlistment Program
RFER
Reefer (stowage)
RFI
Radio Frequency Interference
Ready for Issue (stock)
Request for Information
RFL
Refuel

RFM
Release for Manufacture
RFNA
Radio Frequency Noise Analyzer
RFO
Radio Frequency Oscillator
Reason for Outage
RFP
Request for Pricing (or Proposal)
RFPP
Radio Frequency Propagation Program
RFPS
Requests for Proposal Supplements
RFQ
Request for Quotation (or Quote)
RFS
Ready for Sea (or Service)
RFT
Readiness for Training
RFT, REFTRA
Refresher Training
RFU
Ready for Use
RG
Reduction Gearbox
Right Gun
RGA
Reduction Gearbox Assembly
RGE, RNG
Range
RGN, REG
Region
RGO
Radio Guidance Operation
RGR
Receipt of Goods Received
RGZ
Recommended Ground Zero
RH
Relative Humidity
Rhumbline (route)
RHAS
Radiant Heat-Absorbing Surface
RHAW
Radar-Homing and Warning
RHAWS
Radar-Homing and Warning System
RHC
Right-Hand Console
RHI
Range-Height Indicator
RHIO
Rank Has Its Obligations
RHIP
Rank Has Its Privileges
RHIR
Rank Has Its Responsibilities
RHOGI
Radar Homing Guidance Investigation
RHR
Roughness Height Rating

R/HR
  Roentgens per Hour
RHU
  Requisition Held Up
RI
  Radio Inertial (guiding)
  Receiving Inspection
  Recruit Induction
  Reliability Index
  Routing Identification (code)
RIAL
  Revised Individual Allowance List
RIB
  Receiver Interface Board (NNSS)
RIC
  Repairable (or Replaceable) Item Code
  Representative-in-Charge
  Resistance, Inductance, Capacitance
    (circuitry)
RICL
  Receipt Inspection Check List
RICMO
  Radar Input Countermeasures Officer
RID
  Released to Inactive Duty
RIF
  Receipt Inspection Form
  Reduction in Force
RIFT
  Reactor In-Flight Test
RIIXS
  Remote Interrogation Information Exchange
    System
RIL
  Red Indicator Lights
RILOP
  Reclamation in Lieu of Procurement
RILSD
  Resident Integrated Logistics Support
    Detachment
RIK
  Replacement-in-Kind
RIM
  Receipt Inspection Memorandum
RINA
  Resident Inspector of Naval Aircraft
RINC
  Recruiter-in-Charge
RINM, RINSMAT
  Resident Inspector of Naval Material
RINO, RINSORD
  Resident Inspector of Naval Ordnance
RINS
  Resident Inspector
RINSMAT, RINM
  Resident Inspector of Naval Material
RINSORD, RINO
  Resident Inspector of Naval Ordnance
RIO
  Radar Intercept Officer (or Operator)
  Retail Issue Outlets

RIOT
  Real-Time Input/Output Transducer
RIOTEX
  Riot Exercise
RIP
  Rapid Installation Procedures
  Reduction Implementation Panel
  Reenlistment Incentive Program
  Reliability Improvement Program
RIPOM
  Report in person if present, otherwise by
    message (command indicated)
RIPS
  Radio-Isotope Power Supply
  Range Instrumentation Planning Study
RIS
  Reading Improvement Specialist
  Retail Inventory System
RISE
  Reaching Industry with SOS Education
  Research in Supersonic Environment
RISIC
  Rubber-Insert Sound Isolation Coupling
RISS
  Range Instrumentation and Support Systems
RITE
  Rapid Information Technique for Evaluation
RIV, RVR
  River
RIVFLOT
  River Flotilla
RIVPATFLOT
  River Patrol Flotilla
RIVPATFOR
  River Patrol Force
RIVRON
  River Assault Squadron
RIVSEC
  River Section
RIVSUPPRON
  River Support Squadron
RIW
  Reliability Improvement Warranty
RJ
  Ramjet (engine)
RKO
  Range-Keeper Operator
RKT
  Rocket
RL
  Radiological Lectures
  Reel (U/I)
  Report Leaving
  Restricted Line (officer)
  Roll (U/I)
RLAD
  Radar Low-Angle Drogue
RLCD
  Relocated
RLD
  Radar Laydown Delivery

RLF
Relevant Labor Force
RLM
Rearward Launched Missile
RLMS
Radar Landmass Simulator
RLO
Repairs Liaison Officer
Restricted Line Officer
RLOS
Retention Level of Supply
RLPA
Rotating-Log Periodic Antenna
RLT
Regimental Landing Team
Recorder Lead Time
RLU
Reserve Liaison Unit
RM
Ream (U/I)
Rocket Motors
RM1
Radioman First Class
RM2
Radioman Second Class
RM3
Radioman Third Class
R-M
Ready Mariner (program)
R&M, R/M
Reliability and Maintainability
RMA
Request for Manufacturers of Articles
Reserve Maintenance Allowance
RMA, R/M/A
Reliability, Maintainability, Availability
RMAL
Revised Master Allowance List
R MAST
Radio Mast
R/MAX
Maximum Range
RMC
Chief Radioman
Reduced Material Condition
Regular Military Compensation
Rod Memory Computer
RMCB
Reserve Mobile Construction Battalion
RMCM
Master Chief Radioman
Return Material Credit Memorandum
RMCS
Senior Chief Radioman
RMI
Radio Magnetic Indicator
Recurring Maintenance Items
Reliability Maturity Index
Routine Manual In
RMI/MO
Routine Manual In/Manual Out

R/MIN
Minimum Range
RMIS
Resource Management Information System
RML
Rescue Motor-Launch
RMN
Remain
Reserve Material Account, Navy
RMO
Radar (or Radio) Material Office
RMP
Reentry Measurements Program
Regional Medical Program
RMS
Radar Maintenance Spares
Radar Manual System
Resource Management System
Root Mean Square
RMSA
Radioman Seaman Apprentice
RMSN
Radioman Seaman
RMSP
Refractory Metal Sheet Program
RMS VALUE
Root Mean Square Value
RMU
Remote Maneuvering Unit
RN
Residual Number
Ribbon (U/I)
RNCBC
Reserve Naval Construction Battalion Center
RNCBCDET
Reserve Naval Construction Battalion Center
Detachment
RNCBMU
Reserve Naval Construction Battalion
Maintenance Unit
RNCR
Reserve Naval Construction Regiment
RND, RD
Round
RNF
Receiver-Noise Figure
RNG
Radio Range
Range
RNID
Routine Network-In-Dial
RNID/NOD
Routine Network-In-Dial/Network-Out-Dial
RNMCB
Reserve Naval Mobile Construction Battalion
RNMCBDET
Reserve Naval Mobile Construction Battalion
RNO
Results Not Observed
RNS
Race, National Origin, and Sex

RNSG
Reserve Naval Security Group
RNSGC
Reserve Naval Security Group Course
RNVC
Reference Number Variation Code
RNYPO
Regional Navy Youth Programs Officer
RO
Radar Officer
Reactor Operator
Receiving Only
Recruiting Officer
Redistribution (or Retrofit, or Referral) Order
Regular Overhaul
Reproducible Ozalid (drawing)
Rip Out
Rust and Oxidation (oils)
ROA
Recorder Announcement
ROB
Report (or Reserve) on Board
ROC
Record of Changes
Reduced Operating Costs
Required Obstacle Clearance (height)
Required Operating (or Operational)
Capability
Research and Oral Communications
(DINFOS)
Reserve Officer Candidate
ROCMN
Regional Office of Civilian Manpower
Management
ROCP
Radar Out-of-Commission for Parts
ROD
Range Operations Department (PMR)
ROE
Reflector Orbital Equipment
ROF
Reporting Organization File (system)
ROFOR
Route Forecast
ROG
Receipt of Goods
ROH
Regular Overhaul
ROI
Reports of Investigation
ROICC
Resident Officer-in-Charge of Construction
ROICM
Resident Officer-in Charge of Material
ROID
Report of Item Discrepancy
ROINC
Resident Officer-in-Charge
ROJ
Range-on Jam

ROM
Read Only Memory
Receive Only-Multipoint
Recruiter of the Month
Rough Order of Magnitude
ROMACC
Range Operational Mounting and Control
Center
ROMP
Radiotelephone Operator Maintenance
Proficiency
RON
Receiving Only
RON, ROVNITE
Remain Overnight
RON, SQ, SQN
Squadron
RONLY
Receiver Only
RONS
Reserve Officers of the Naval Service
ROOST
Reusable One-Stage Orbital Space Truck
ROP
Remote Operating Panel
Reorder Point
Run of the Press
ROPEVAL
Readiness Operational Evaluation
ROPS
Roll Over Protection Structure
ROQ
Recruiter of the Quarter
RORET
Rotational Retention
RO/RO
Roll-On/Roll-Off (transport or trailer)
ROS
Ready Operating Status
Remote Optical Sighting (system)
ROSE
Remote Optical Sensing of the Environment
Rising Observational Sounding Equipment
ROSIE
Reconnaissance by Orbital Ship Identification
Equipment
ROT
Rotary
Rotate
Rotating (light)
"Rule of Thumb" (slang)
ROTAD
Required Overseas Terminal Arrival Date
ROTAS
Rotate and Slide
ROTC
Reserve Officer's Training Corps
ROTI
Recording Optical Tracking Instrument
ROTLT/BCN
Rotating Light or Beacon

ROT PROJ
Rotation Project
ROTS
Rotary Out-Trunk Switching (AUTOVON)
ROV
Repair of Vessel
ROVNITE, RON
Remain Overnight
ROWP
Reference Overhaul Work Package
RP
Awaiting separation, release or retirement
Raid Plotter
Reactor Plant
Reorder Point
Replacement Pilot
Report Passing
Reserve Personnel
Revision Proposal
Rocket Propellant (or Projectile)
RP1
Religious Program Specialist First Class
RP2
Religious Program Specialist Second Class
RP3
Religious Program Specialist Third Class
RPA
Radium Plaque Adaptometer
RPAO
Radium Plaque Adaptometer Operator
RPAODS
Remotely-Piloted Aerial Observer Designation
System
RPB
Radio Production Branch (AFRTS)
RPC
Chief Religious Program Specialist
Regional-Preparedness Committee
Registered Publications Clerk (or Custodian)
Repairable Processing Center
River Patrol Craft
RPCM
Master Chief Religious Program Specialist
RPCP
Reactor Plant Control Panel
RPCS
Senior Chief Religious Program Specialist
RPD
Radar Planning Device
Rapid
RPE
Reactor Plant Engineering
RPEP
Register of Planning Emergency Procedures
RPF
Reactor Plant Fueling
RPFI
Reactor Plant Fueling Inspection
RPFW
Reactor Plant Fresh Water

RPG
Radioisotope Power Generator
Report Program Generator
Rocket-Propelled Grenade
RPI
Radar Precipitation Integrator
Real Property Inventory
RPIE
Real Property, Installed Equipment
RPIO
Registered Publication Issuing Office
RPM
Reactor Plant Manual
Registered Publications Manual (or
Memorandum)
Reliability Performance Measure
RPMA
Real Property Maintenance Activities
(program)
RPMC
Registered Publication Memorandum
Corrections
RPN
Reserve Personnel, Navy
RPO
Registered Publications Officer
RPP
Reactor Plant Planning
RPPI
Remote Plan Position Indicator
RPPS
Retired Pay/Personnel System
RPPY
Reactor Plant Planning Year
RPS
Registered Publications Section (or System)
Revolutions per Second
RPSA
Religious Program Specialist Seaman
Apprentice
RPSN
Religious Program Specialist Seaman
RPS-PL
Registered Publications Section-Personnel
Library
RPSTL
Repair Parts and Special Tools List
RPT
Reactor Plant Test
Repeat
RPT, REP, REPT
Report
R&PT
Rifle and Pistol Team
RPTPT, REP
Reporting Point
RPTS
Reactor Plant Test Section
RPTSO
Reactor Plant Test Support Organization

RPU
Radio Phone (or Priority) Unit
Registered Publications Unit
Rotatable Pool Unit
RPV
Remotely-Piloted Vehicle
RQN, REQN
Requisition
RQR, REQ
Require
RQRD
Required
RR
Recruit Roll
Requisition Restriction (code)
Rifle Range
R&R
Range and Range-Rate
Rest and Recuperation (or Rehabilitation, or
Relaxation)
RRB
Regular Reenlistment Bonus
RRC
Readiness Reportable Code
Recognized Rescue Center
Reporting Requirements Code
Requirements Review Committee
RRE
Race-Relations Education (program)
RREB
Race-Relations Education Board
RRF
Regional Relay Facility
RRIS
Remote Radar Integration Station
RRL
Runway Remaining Lights
RRLTU
Recruit Remedial Literacy Training Unit
RRR
Readiness Removal Rate
Repairable Return Rate
RRS
Readiness Reportable Status
Ready Reserve Status
RRT
Regional Response Team
Remote Reading Thermometer
RR/T
Rendezvous Radar/Transponder
RRTS
Range-Rate Tracking System
RRVFPA
Red River Valley Fighter Pilots Association
RRU
General Ready Reserve Unit (USNR)

RS
Rapid-Setting (asphalt)
Readiness Squadron
Reconnaissance Strike
Repair Services
Revised Statutes
RS, CRUITSTA
Recruiting Station
RS, RECSTA
Receiving Station
R/S
Report of Survey
RSA
Radar Signature Analysis
RSAND
Reserve Systems Analysis Division
RSB
Radiation Safety Booklet
Reduced Size Blueprint
RSC
Rescue Sub-Center
Reserve Service Control
Rework Support Conference
Runway Surface Condition
RSCH
Research
RSCH&DEV, R&D
Research and Development
RSCHOPSDET
Research Operations Detachment
RSCS
Rate Stabilization Control System
RSDC
Remote Secure Data Change
RSDU
Radar Storm Detection Unit
RSE
Reference Sensing Elements
Remote Sensing of Environment
RSF
Render Safe Procedure
Requisition Status File
RSFPP
Retired Servicemen's Family Protection Plan
RSG
Rising
RSGN
Reassign
Resign
RSHI
Rough Service, High Impact
RSI
Rationalization, Standardization and
Interoperability
R-SI
Restricted-Security Information
RS&I
Receipt, Storage and Issue
RSL
Remote Spring Missile Launching

RSM
Ready Service Magazine
RSN
Random Sequence Number
RSO
Radiological Safety Officer
Range Safety Officer
RSOS
Resident Supervisor of Shipping
RSP
Render Safe Procedure
Reserve Stock Point
RSPE
Radar Signal Processing Equipment (course)
RSPL
Recommended Spare-Parts List
RSR
Ready Service Ring
Route Surveillance Radar
RSS
Refrigerant, Ship's Stores
RSSK
Rigid Seal Survival Kit
RSSP
Reporting Secondary Stock Point
R&SSQ
Repair and Salvage Squadron
RST
Readability, Strength and Tone (radio
    transmission)
RSTD, REST
Restricted
RSV
Research Safety Vehicle
RSVP
Restartable Solid Variable Pulse
RT
Radiographic Test
Receiving Test
Register Reference (NNSS)
Resistance Thermometer
Right Turn
RT, RTE
Route
R/T
Radiotelephone
Radio Terminology
Regular Time
R&T
Research and Technology
RTAG
Range Technical Advisory Group
RTB
Regurn to Base
RTC
Recruit Training Command (or Center)
Replacement Training Center
RTCC
Real-Time Computer Complex
RTC(W)
Recruit Training Command (Women)

RTD
Resistance Temperature Detector
RTDP
Real-Time Data Processor (system)
RTDS
Remote Target Designator System
RTE
Resistance Temperature Element
RTE, RT
Route
RTG
Radioisotope Thermoelectric Generator
Rating
Routing
RTI
Radar Target Identification
RTIRS
Real-Time Information Retrieval System
RTL
Resistor-Transistor Logic (circuitry)
RTM
Rapid Turning Magnetron
Receiver-Transistor-Modulator
RTN, RTRN
Return
RTNEE
Returnee
RTP
Request for Technical Proposal
Requirement and Test Procedures
RTQC
Real-Time Quality Control
RTRD
Retard
RTRN, RTN
Return
RTS
Radio Tape Service
Replacement Training Squadron
RTSO
Remote Terminal Security Officer
RTSS
Real-Time Scientific System
RTST
Receiver Self Test (NNSS)
RTT, RATT
Radio-Teletype
RTU
Replacement Training Unit
RTV
Responsive Television
Rocket Test Vehicle
Room Temperature Vulcanizing (silicon
    rubber)
Route Traffic Via
R&TV
Radio and Television (DINFOS)
RTZ
Real-Time Executive
RU
Radio (or Release) Unit

RUC
Reporting Unit Code
Riverine Utility Craft
RUDAOE
Report of Unsatisfactory or Defective Aviation
Ordnance Equipment
RUDM
Report of Unsatisfactory or Defective Material
RUDMIN
Report of Unsatisfactory or Defective Mine
RUDMINDE
Report of Unsatisfactory or Defective Mine,
Depth Charge or Associated Equipment
RUDTORPE
Report of Unsatisfactory or Defective Torpedo
Equipment
RUF
Rough
RUM
Remote Underwater Manipulator
RUNCIBLE
Revised Unified New Compiler with Internal
Translator, Basic Language Extended
RUPPERT
Reserve Unit Personnel Performance Report
RUSNO
Resident United States Naval Officer
RUUWS
Research Underwater-Unmanned Weapons
Sensor
RV
Recreational Vehicle
Rescue (or Research) Vessel
Runway Visibility
R/V, REV
Reentry Vehicle
RVAH, RECONATKRON
Reconnaissance Attack Squadron
RVAW
Carrier Airborne Early Warning Training
Squadron
RVP
Replacement ASW Patrol Squadron
RVR
Reverse Velocity Rotor
Runway Visual Range
RVR, RIV
River
RVV
Runway Visibility Value
RW
Radiological Warfare
Recreation and Welfare
RW BN
Red and White Beacon
RWH
Radar Warning and Homing
RWO
Reimbursable Work Order

RWR
Radar Warning Receiver
Remain Well Right of _____
RWRAT
Replacement Weather Reconnaissance
Aircraft
RWY, RNWY
Runway
RX
Report Crossing
RZ
Reconnaissance Zone
Return-to-Zero (recording)

S

S
ASW Tactical Evaluator (NAO code)
Secret
Situational (report frequency)
Snow
Spar (buoy)
Starboard
Straight-In
S, SO
South(ern)
SA
Sack (U/I)
Seaman Apprentice
Semi-Annually (report frequency)
Service Applicability
Servo Amplifier
Ship Alteration
Shipping (or Supplemental) Agreement
Shop Accessory (drawing)
Sight Angle
Special Agent (or Assignment, or
Authorization)
Superior Achievement (award)
Supervisory Authority
Systems Analysis
S&A
Safety and Arming (device)
S/A
Sub Assembly
SAA
Small-Arms Ammunition
SAAM
Special Assignment Airlift Mission
SAAP
South Atlantic Anomaly Probe
SAB
Scientific Advisory Board
S/AB
Starboard Side Abreast (stowage)
SABAR
Service Craft and Boat Accounting Report

SABER
SECNAV's Advisory Board on Educational
Requirements
SABET
SECNAV's Advisory Board on Education and
Training
SABMAR
Service Craft and Boats Machine Accounting
Report
SABMIS
Sea-Based Anti-Ballistic Missile Intercept
System
SABOSE
SECNAV's Advisory Board on Scientific
Education
SABRAC
Sabra Computer
SABRE
SAGE Battery Routing Equipment
Secure Airborne Radar Equipment
Self-Aligned Boost and Reentry (missile
system)
SAC
Security Assistance (program)
Signal Analysis Course
Special Accounting Class
Special Advisory Committee
Standard Aircraft Characteristics
Storeman's Action Copy
Substance Abuse Coordinator
Supporting Arms Coordinator
SACAM
Ship Acquisition Contract Administration
Manual (NAVSHIPS)
SACC
Supporting Arms Coordination Center
SACCS
Supreme Allied Command Automated
Command Control System
SACE
Semi-Automatic Checkout Equipment
SACEUR
Supreme Allied Commander, Europe
SACLANT
Supreme Allied Commander, Atlantic
SACMED
Supreme Allied Commander, Mediterranean
SACOM
SECNAV's Advisory Committee on Manpower
SACP
Special Assistant for Civilian Personnel
SACP/EEO
Special Assistant for Civilian Personnel/Equal
Employment Opportunity
SACR
Semi-Automatic Coordinate Reader
SACS
Sensor Accuracy Check Site

SAD
Search and Destroy
Submarine Anomaly Detector
Support Air Division
Supporting Arms Department
System Analysis Division (USNR)
Systems Automation Division
SADC
Sector Air Defense Commander
SADIE
Scanning Analog-to-Digital Input Equipment
SADL
Ship's Authorized Data List
SADS
Submarine Active Detection System
SAEC
Support Analysis of an Engineering Change
SAED
Small-Aircraft Engine Department
Submarine Antenna Engineering Division
Systems Analysis and Engineering
Department
SA(EF)
Electronics Field Seaman Apprentice
SAES
Special Assistant for Environmental Services
SAEWS
Shipboard Automated Electronic Warfare
System
SAF
Shark Attack File
Southern Attack Force
Special Action Force
Support Action Form
SAFE-BAR
Safeland Barrier
SAFECEN
Safety Center
SAFEPLAN
Submarine Air Frequency Plan
SAFEREC
Submarine Recommendations (NSC)
SAFOC
Semi-Automatic Flight Operations Center
SAFORD
Safety of Explosive Ordnance Databank
SAG
Self-Aligning Gate (circuitry)
Semi-Active Guidance
Sub-Activity Group
Superior Achievement Group
Surface Action Group
Systems Analysis Group
SAGA
System for Automatic Generation and
Analysis
SAGE
Semi-Automatic Ground Environment
(system)
SA(HS)
High School Seaman Apprentice

SAIL
Ship Active Item Listing
Ship Armament Inventory List
SAIMS
Selected Acquisition Information and
Management System
SAIP
Ship Acquisition and Improvement Panel
SAINT
Satellite Inspector (or Interceptor)
SAINTS
Single-Attack Integrated System
SAIP
Ship Acquisition and Improved Panel
Submarine Antenna Improvement Program
SAL
Service Applicability
Ship's Allowance List
SAL, SALV
Salvage
SALOA
Special Arc Light Operation Area
SALS
Short-Approach Light System
SALTE
Semi-Automatic Line Test Equipment
SALV, SAL
Salvage
SALWIS
Shipboard Air-Launched Weapons Installation
System
SAM
School of Aviation Medicine
Screen for Aeronautical Material
Seabee Anti-Pollution Movement
Special Air Mission
Surface-to-Air Missile
SAMAR
Ship Activation, Maintenance and Repair
(reserve division)
Ship Activation, Monthly Activity Report
SAMAS
Service Craft and Boats Machine Accounting
System
SAMC
Surface Ammunition Malfunction Control
(number)
SAMEM
Sustained-Attrition Minefield Evaluation Model
SAMI
Single-Action Maintenance Instruction
SAMID
Ship Anti-Missile Integrated Defense
SAMIS
Ship Alteration Management Information
System
SAMMA
Stores Account Material Management Afloat
SAMMA/SAL
Stores Account Material Management
Afloat/Ship Authorization Levels

SAMMS
Standard Automated Material Management
System
SAM-NIS
Screen for Aeronautical Material-Not in Stock
SAMOS
Satellite and Missile Observation System
SAMPS
Shore Activity Manpower Planning System
SAMS
Semi-Automatic Meteorological Station
Ship Alteration Management System
Ship Alteration Material Survey
SAMSAT
Surface-to-Air Missile Assembly and Test
SAM/SAT
South American/South Atlantic (regional area)
SAMTEC
Space and Missile Test Center
SAND
Shelter Analysis for New Designs
SANDFSO
Sea and Foreign Service Office
S AND SC
Sized and Supercalendared
SA(NSET)
Nuclear Submarine Engineering Technician
Seaman Apprentice
SAO
Special Activities Office
Support Air Observer
SAP
Security Assistance Program
Semi-Armor Piercing
SHARE Assembly Program
Ship Acquisition Project (PMS)
Ship Alteration Package
Soon as Possible
Symbolic Assembly Program
SA(PFE)
Polaris Field Electronics Seaman Apprentice
SA(PFL)
Polaris Field Launcher Seaman Apprentice
SAPIR
System of Automatic Processing and
Indexing of Reports
SAPL
System Advanced Parts List
SAPO
Sub-Area Petroleum Office
SAQAD
Submarine Antenna Quality Assurance
Directory
SAQAF
Submarine Antenna Quality Assurance
Facility
SAQR
Substance Abuse Quarterly Report

SAR
Sea-Air Rescue
Search and Rescue
Selected Acquisition Reports
Selected Air Reserve
Special Aeronautical Requirements
Standard Average and Range
Substance Abuse Report
Supply Activity Report
SARA
Search and Rescue Aid
Superior Accomplishment Recognition Award
SARBE
Search and Rescue Beacon Equipment
SARDIP
Stricken Aircraft Reclamation and Disposal
Program
SAREX
Search and Rescue Exercise
SARIE
Selective Automatic Radar Identification
Equipment
SARLANT
Search and Rescue, Atlantic
SARPAC
Search and Rescue, Pacific
SARTEL
Search and Rescue Telephone
SAS
Secure Authentication System
Selection and Appointment System
Ship Alteration Scope
Stability Augmentation System
Supply Accounting Section
Suspended Array System
SASI
Ship and Air Systems Integration
SASITS
Submarine Advanced Signal Training System
SASL
Service Approved Status List
SASM
Special Assistant for Strategic Mobility
SASN
Special Assistant to the Secretary of the
Navy
SASS
Spark Chamber Automatic Scanning System
Special Aircraft Service Group
Suspended Array Surveillance System
SASTE
Semi-Automatic Shop Test Equipment
SAT
Safe Air Travel
Scholastic Aptitude Test
Ship Assistance Team
Space Available Travel
Summer Accelerated Training
Systems Approach to Training
SAT, SATFY
Satisfactory

SATEC
Semi-Automatic Technical Control
SATELOON
Balloon Satellite
SATELLORB
Satellite Simulation Observation and
Research Balloon
SATFOR
Special Air Task Force
SAT FOR TEE
System Approach to Training for Transfer
Effectiveness Evaluation
SATFY, SAT
Satisfactory
SATIN
SAGE Air Traffic Integration
SATIRE
Semi-Automatic Technical Information
Retrieval
SATNAV
Satellite Navigation Set (NNSS)
SATP
Small-Arms Training Unit
SATS
Short Airfield for Tactical Support
SAU
Search Attack Unit
SAVAC
Simulates, Analyzes, Visualizes, Activated
Circuitry
SAVDEP
Savings Depot
SAV-DEP-SYS
Savings Deposit System
SAVE
Shortages and Valuable Excesses
SAVER
Stowable Aircrew Vehicle Escape Rotoseat
SAW
Submerged Arc Weld
SAWBET
Supply Action Will be Taken
SAWRS
Supplementary Aviation Weather Reporting
Station
SAWS
Special Airborne Weapons Subsystem
Submarine Acoustic Warfare System
SB
Secondary Battery
Shipbuilding
Slab (U/I)
Supply Bulletin
SB, SWBD
Switchboard
SB, SUBBASE
Submarine Base
S/B
Should Be

SBA
Sovereign Base Area
Standard Beam Approach
SBAE
Stabilization Bombing Approach Equipment
SBCO
Shipbuilding Company
SBCORP
Shipbuilding Corporation
SBE
Selection Board Eligible
SBI
Selection Board Ineligible
Special Background Investigation
SBL
Spaced-Based Laser
SBM
Single Buoy Marking
SBMSS
Shore-Based Message Service System
SBN
Subic Bay News (publication)
SBO
Summary Plot Board
SBP
Survivor Benefit Plan
S³BP, SSSBP
System Source Selection Board Procedures
SBPH
Submarine Base, Pearl Harbor (HI)
SBT
Shipboard Test
SBTB
Short Basic Test Battery
SBY, STBY
Standby
SC
Scattered Clouds
Section (U/I)
Security Code
Separate Contract
Sized and Calendared
Slow Curing (asphalt)
Spacecraft (pilot code)
Step Child(ren)
Stratocumulus (cloud formation)
Supply Corps
Surveillance Coordinator
S&C
Search and Clear (operation)
S-C
Secret and Confidential (files)
SCA
Service Cryptologic Agency
Stock Control Activity
Subcontractor Administrator
Superconducting Accelerator
Switching Center, AUTOVON
System Certification Authority
SCAD
Subsonic Cruise Armed Decoy

SCADAR
Scatter Detection and Ranging
SCADS
Scanning Celestial Attitude Determination
System
SCAEC
Submarine Classification and Analysis
Evaluation
SCAJAP(AN)
Shipping Control Authority, Japan
SCAMP
Scholarships for Children of American Military
Personnel
Space-Controlled Array Measurements
Program
System/Command Accounting/Monitoring of
Projects
SCAN
Switched Circuit Automatic Network
System for Collection and Analysis of
Near-Collision (reports)
SCANS
Scheduling and Control by Automated
Network System
SCAO
Senior Civil Affairs Officer
SCAP
Silent Compact Auxiliary Power
SCAR
Scientific Committee on Antarctic Research
Sub-Caliber Aircraft Rocket
SCAS
Stability Control Augmentation System
SCAT
Satellite Communications Airborne Terminal
Sequential Component Automatic Test
Service Command Air Transport
SHARE Compiler/Assembler and Translator
Speed Command Altitude/Target
Speed Control Approach/Take-Off
Submarine Classification and Tracking
Submarine Communications Applications and
Theory
SCATANA
Security Control of Air Traffic and Air
Navigation Aids
SCATER
Security Control of Air Traffic and
Electromagnetic Radiations
SCATTOR
Small Craft Assets, Training and Turnover of
Resources
SCB
Ships Characteristics Board

SCC
SAGE Control Center
Sequence Control Chart
Ship Control Console
Specification for Contract Change
Speed Control Circuits
Steering Control Console
Stress Corrosion Cracking
Surface Combat Condition

SCCF
Satellite Communications Control Facility

SCC NR
Special Cryptologic Control Number

SCD
Supply, Commissary and Disbursing
Surface Craft Division
Synchronizing Control Devices

SCDRL
Subcontractor Data Requirements List

SCE
Schedule Compliance Evaluation
Special Conditioning Equipment
Staff Civil Engineer

SCEPC
Senior Civil Emergency Planning Committee

SCEPTRON
Spectral Comparative Pattern Recognition

SCE&PWD
Staff Civil Engineer and Public Works
Department

SCERT
Systems and Computers Evaluation and
Review Technique

SCF
Support Carrier Force

SCH
Sorties Scheduled

SCH, SCOL
School

SC-HC
Scattered-to-Heavy Clouds

SCI
Sensitive Compartmented Information
Ship-Controlled Intercept
Supervisor Cost Inspector

SCIP
Shipbuilding and Conversion Improvement
Program
Ship's Capability Impaired for Lack of Parts

SCIR
Subsystem Capability and Impact Reporting
(system)

SCK
Service Change Unit

SCL
Ship Configuration Listing
Standard Components List
Symbolic Correction Loader

SCLK
Ship's Clerk

SCM
Summary Courts-Martial

SCN
Ship Construction, Navy
Shop Control Number
Southern Command Network (AFRTS)
Specification Change Notice

SCNS
Self-Contained Navigation System

SCO
Scouting

SCO, SCT
Scout

SCODA
Scan Coherent Doppler Attachment

SCOL, SCH
School

SCOMA
Shipping Control Office, Marianas

SCOPE
Scientific Cooperation Operational Research
Expedition
Subsystem for the Control of Operations and
Plan Evaluation
System to Compute Operational Probability
Equation

SCOPES
Squad Combat Operations Exercise
(Simulation)

SCOR
Special Committee on Ocean Research
(ICSU)
Subcommittee on Oceanographic Research

SCORE
Satellite Computer-Operated Readiness
Equipment
Selective Conversion and Retention
Signal Communications by Orbiting Relay
Equipment

SCORON
Scouting Squadron

SCOTRACEN
Scouting Training Center

SCP
SAGE Computer Program
Ship Control Panel
Special Career Programs
Steam-Condensing Pot

SCPO, POCS
Senior Chief Petty Officer

SCPT
SAGE Computer Programming Training

SCR
Silicon Control Rectifier
Sodium-Cooled Thermal Reactor
Sortie Completion Rate

SCRAM
Several Compilers Reworked and Modified
Short-Range Attack Missile
Signal Corps Random-Access Memory
Space Capsule Regulator and Monitor
Spares, Components, Reidentification and
Modification Program
SCRAP
Selective Curtailment of Reports and
Paperwork
SCRB
Software Change Review Board
SCRIPT
Scientific and Commercial Subroutine
Interpreter and Programs Translator
SCS
Satellite Control Satellite
Sea Control Ship
Stabilization and Control Subsystem
Supervisory Control Subsystem
SCSS
Self-Contained Starting System
SCT
Special Crew Time
Synchro Control Transformer
System Circuit Test
SCT, SCTR, SEC, SECT
Sector
SCT, SCO
Scout
SCTC
Self-Contained Training Capabilities
SCTD
Scattered (clouds)
SCTOC
Satellite Communications Test and
Operations Center
SCTR, SCT, SEC, SECT
Sector
SCTY, SEC
Security
SCU
Stock Control Unit
SCUBA
Self-Contained Breathing Apparatus
SCUP
Spectra Composite Utility
Program—pronounced "Scoop"
SCX
Subcontractor Equipment
SD
Safety Destructor
Semi-Darkness (or Diameter)
Shelter Deck (stowage)
Skid (U/I)
Special Duty
Standard Deviation
Strength Differential
Supply Department
Surface Danger (zone)
Surveillance Drone

S/D
Seadrome
S&D
Search and Destroy (operations)
Single and Double (reduction gear)
SDA
Source Data Automation
Special Duty Assignment
SDAFRS
Source Data Automated Fitness Report
System
SDAR
Submarine Departure Approval Request
SDBI
Specifications Drawing Baseline Index
SDC
Signal Data Conversion
Southern Defense Command
Submersible Decompression Chamber
SDCD
Sea Duty Commencement Date
SDCG
Special Data Converter Group
SDCP
Supply Demand Control Point
SDCU
Supply Data Communications Unit
SDD
Special Devices Division
Standard Delivery Date
System Development Department
SDF
Ship Description File
Simplified Directional Facility
SDG
Situation Display Generator
Synchro Differential Generator
SDGE
Situation Display Generator Element
SDI
Selected Dissemination of Information
Ship's Drawing Index
Situation Display Indicator
Specifications Drawing Index
SDI-KWOC
Selected Dissemination of Information-Key
Word Out of Context (system)
SDL
Systems Design Laboratory
SDLM
Standard Depot Level Maintenance
SDO
Special Duty Officer
Squadron (or Staff, or Station) Duty Officer
SDOPR
Sound Operator
SDP
Ship (or Systems) Development Plan
Statistical Data Processing
Status Display Panels
Submarine Distress Pinger

SDR
Special Drawing Rights
SDRN
Supplier Data Review Notice
SDS
Supplemental (or Source) Data Sheet
System Design Specification
SDSP
Space Defense Systems Program
SDV
Swimmer Delivery Vehicle
SE
Set (U/I)
Signal Ejector
Single-Ended
Southeast(ern)
Support Equipment
Systems Engineer(ing)
SE, SENG
Single Engine
SE, SEP, SEPT
September
S&E
Supplies and Equippage
SEA
Senior Enlisted Advisor
Sensing Element Amplifiers
Ship/Equipment/Alteration (list)
Ship's Editorial Association
Sonar Evaluation and Assistance
Southeast Asia
SEABEE, CB
Construction Battalion
SEABON
Systems Effectiveness Advisory Board
SEAC
Seacoast
Southeast Asia Command
SEACALMIS
NAVSEACOM Calibration Management
Information System
SEACO
Senior Enlisted Advisor,
Communications/Operations
SEACON
Seafloor Construction (NCEL)
SEADU
Sea Duty
SEAFRON
Sea Frontier
SEAL
Sea-Air-Land (team)
Ship Electronic Allowance List
SEAM
Sidewinder Expanded Acquisition Mode
SEAMARF
Southeast Asia Military Altitude Reservation
Facility
SEAMOD
Sea Systems Modification and Modernization
by Modularity (program)

SEAN
Senior Enlisted Advisor, Navy—also MCPON
SEAR
Systematic Effort to Analyze Results
SEARA
Stockpile Evaluation and Reliability
Assessment
SEAS
Sea School
SEATICC
Southeast Asia Tactical Information
Communications Center
SEATO
Southeast Asia Treaty Organization
SEAVEY
Sea-to-Shore Rotation Survey
SEAWEA
Sea Weather (report)
SEB
Source Evaluation Board
Support Equipment Bulletin
SEBS
Submarine Emergency Buoyancy System
SEC
Secondary Emission Cathode (or Conduction)
Second(s)
Support Equipment Change
SEC, SECT
Section
SEC, SCT, SCTR, SECT
Sector
SEC, SCTY
Security
SEC, SECY
Secretary
SECAS
Ship Equipment Configuration Accounting
System
SECBASE
Section Base
SECD
Secondary
SECDEF, SD
Secretary of Defense
SECF
Surface Effect Cruiser Escort
SECFLT
Second Fleet
SEC-FT
Second-Foot
SECGRUHQ
Security Group Headquarters
SECNAV, SN
Secretary of the Navy
SECNAVFIND
The Secretary of the Navy has found that this
permanent change of station is required by
the exigencies of the service
SECO
Sustained Engine Cutoff

SECOF
Shipboard Environmental Checkout Facility
SECR
Secret
SECS
Single-Engine Control Speed
Stem-Erected Camera System
SECT
Submarine Emergency Communications
Transmitter
SECT, SEC
Section
SECT, SCT, SCTR, SEC
Sector
SECTASKFLT
Second Task Fleet
SEC-TREAS
Secretary-Treasurer
SECY, SEC
Secretary
SED
Sequence Event Diagram
System Engineering Documentation
SEDPC
Scientific and Engineering Data Processing
Center
SEDS
System Effectiveness Data System
SEE/AN
Systems Effectiveness Evaluation Analyzer
SEEDS
Ship's Electrical and Electronic Data Systems
SEEK
System Evaluation Experiment
SEER
Submarine Explosive Echo-Ranging
SEEREP
Ship's Essential Equipment Requisition
Expediting Program
SEF
SPECAT Exclusive for
SEFF
Snakeye Free-Fall
SEFIC
Seventh Fleet Intelligence Center
SEFOR
Southwest Experiment Fax Oxide Reactor
SEG
Systems Engineering Group
SEI
Stockpile Entry Inspection
SEIE
Submarine Escape Immersion Equipment
SEIS
Submarine Emergency Identification Signal
SEL
Solar Energy Laboratory
Sound Effects Laboratory
Support Equipment List
SELCAL
Selective Calling (system)

SELD
Snakeye Low-Drag
SELS
Severe Local Storm
SELT
SAGE Evaluation Library Tape
SEM
Scanning Electron Microscope
Standard Electronic Module
SEM, SEMA
Semaphore
SEMA, SEM
Semaphore
SEMAT
Ship Electronic Module Assembly Test
SEMCA
Shipboard Electromagnetic Computability
Analysis
SEMDP
Senior Executive/Management Development
Plan
SEN
Southern European Network (AFRTS)
Successor Event Number
SEN, SR
Senior
SENAVAV
Senior Naval Aviator
SENDENTALO
Senior Dental Officer
SENG, SE
Single-Engine
SENL
Standard Equipment Nomenclature List
SENMEDO, SMO
Senior Medical Officer
SENMEM
Senior Member
SENSO
Sensor Operator
SENT
Sentence
SENT CONF
Sentence to be Confined
SENT LP
Sentence to Lose Pay
SENUSNAVOFFNAVBALTAP
Senior United States Naval Officer,
Commander Allied Naval Forces, Baltic
Approaches
SEOC
Submarine Extended Operating Cycle
SEP
Separate
Spherical Error Probable
Surface Electrical Properties
SEP, SE, SEPT
September
SEPACFOR
Southeast Pacific Force

SEPP
Safety Engineering Program Plan
SEPQUES
Prior to delivery of orders, the CO is directed to complete and return the enclosed Officer Separation Questionnaire to COMNAVMILPERSCOM (Code 402)
SEPROS
Separate (or Separation) Processing
SEPT, SE, SEP
September
SEPTAR
Seaborne Powered Target
SER
Servicing
Shore Establishment Realignment
SNAP Experimental Reactor
Space Electric Rocket (test)
Support Equipment Requirement
SER, SRL
Serial
SER, SVC
Service
SERANDA
Service record(s), health record(s), pay record(s) and personal effects
SERC
Sonar Environmental Research Card
SERE
Survival, Evasion, Resistance and Escape
SERET
Snakeye Retarded
SERGRAD
Selected and Retained Graduate
SERL
Services Electronics Research Laboratory
SERNO
Serial (or Service) Number
SERON, SERVRON
Service Squadron
SERS
Support Equipment Requirements (list)
SERV, SVC
Service
SERVDIV
Service Division
SERVFOR
Service Force
SERVGRP
Service Group
SERVHEL
Service record(s) and health record(s)
SERVLANT
Service Force, Atlantic Fleet
SERVMART, S/M
Service Mart (or Market)
SERVPA
Service record(s) and pay record(s)
SERVPAC
Service Force, Pacific Fleet

SERVPAHEL
Service record(s), pay record(s) and health record(s)
SERVREC, SR
Service record(s)
SERVRON, SERON
Service Squadron
SERVSCOLCOM
Service Schools Command
SERVSCOLCOMDET
Service Schools Command Detachment
SES
Sensor Employment Squads
Serving Sentence
Site Environmental System
Strategic Engineering Survey
Surface Effect Ship
SESAME
Service-Sort-and-Merge
SESCO
Secure Submarine Communications
SESE
Secure Echo-Sounding Equipment (sonar)
SESEC
Senior Enlisted Steam Engineering Course
SESPROJ
Surface Effect Ship Project
SESTF
Surface Effect Ship Test Facility
SET
Selective Electronic Training
Sensor Employment Teams
Smoke-Emission Test
Submarine Engineering Technician
SETAF
Southern European Task Force
SETT
Submarine Electronic Technical Training
Submarine Escape Training Tank
SEV
Severe
Surface Effects Vehicle
SEVFLT
Seventh Fleet
SEVR PAY
Severence Pay
SEWT
Simulator for Electronic Warfare Testing
SF
Ship's Force
Special Forces
Standard Form
Supervisor Furnished
Svedberg Flotation
SF, SCOFOR
Scouting Force
S&F
Sound and Flash
SFA
Single Frequency Approach

SFAO
San Francisco Area Office (ONR)
SFBNSY
San Francisco Bay Naval Shipyard
SFC
Specific Fuel Consumption
Sub-Functional Code
Surface
SFCP
Shore Fire Control Party
SFDS
Standby Fighter Director Ship
SFEC
Standard Facility Equipment Card
SFEL
Standard Facility Equipment List
SFI
Shop-Fixed Interface
SFL
Sequenced Flashing (light)
S FL
Short Flashing (light)
SFN
Ships and Facilities, Navy
SFNS, SFNSY
San Francisco Naval Shipyard
SFSNY, SFNS
San Francisco Naval Shipyard
SFO
Simulated Flameout
SFOB
Special Forces Operating Base
SFOMS
Ship's Force Overhaul Management System
SFPOE
San Francisco, Port of Embarkation
SFPPS
Shore Facilities Planning and Programming
System
SFRD
Secret: Formerly Restricted Data
SFRS
Selective File Retrieval Service
SFS
Student Flight Surgeon
SFSD
Star Field Scanning Device
S&FSD
Sea and Foreign Service Duty (pay)
S&FSD(A)
Sea and Foreign Service Duty (Aviation)
(pay)
S&FSD(S)
Sea and Foreign Service Duty (Submarine)
(pay)
SFT
Spray Flammability Temperature
SFTS
Synthetic Flight Training System
SFW
Shunt-Field Winding (wiring)

SFWI
Ship's Force Work Item
SFWL
Ship's Force Work List
SFWL(I)
Ship's Force Work List (Item)
SG
Qualified for immediate assignment to
submarines
Security Group
Snow Grains (weather symbol)
Special Grade
Steam Generator
Surgeon General
Syringe (U/I)
SGC
Simulation Generator Control
SGCP
Shipboard Gauge Calibration Program
SGD
Special Government Design
SGN
Signed
SGED
Supervisory Grade Evaluation Guide
SGF
Steam Generator Feedwater
SGLI
Serviceman's Group Life Insurance
SGM
Spark Gap Modulation
SGN
Standing Group, North Atlantic
Surgeon General, Navy
SGP
School Guarantee Program
Secondary Gun Pointer
SGSE
Standard Ground Support Equipment
1STSGT
First Sergeant
SGT
Sargeant
Satellite Ground Terminal
SGTMAJ
Sergeant Major
SGU
Sidewinder Generator Unit
SH
Sheet (U/I)
SH1
Ship's Serviceman First Class
SH2
Ship's Serviceman Second Class
SH3
Ship's Serviceman Third Class
SHA
Sideral Hour Angle
SHAC
Small Hydrofoil Aircraft Carrier (concept)

SHAPE
Supreme Headquarters, Allied Powers, Europe
SHAPM
Ship Acquisition Project Manager
SHARP
Ships Analysis and Retrieval Projects
SHARPS
Ships/Helicopter Acoustic Range Prediction System
SHAVIB
Shaft Alignment and Vibration (check)
SHC
Chief Ship's Serviceman
Superheat Control
SHCM
Master Chief Ship's Serviceman
SHCS
Senior Chief Ship's Serviceman
SHD
Special Handling Designator
SHDCD
Shore Duty Commencement Date
SHE
Special-Handling Equipment
SHEDS
Shipboard Helicopter Extended Delivery System
SHF
Super High Frequency
SHINE
Self-Help is Necessary Everywhere
SHIP
Self-Help Improvement Program
SHIPALT(S)
Ship Alteration(s)
SHIPDA
Shipping Data
SHIPDAFOL
Shipping Data Follows
SHIPDAT
Shipping Date
SHIPGO
Shipping Order
SHIPIM
Ship Immediately
SHIPMT
Shipment
SHIPOPS
Ship(board) Operations
SHIPOSI
Ship Operational Support Inventory
SHIPREPTECH
Ship Repair Technician
SHIPSEPROS
If ship or fleet command from which detached is located in CONUS at the time of detachment, report to the separation processing in accordance with NAVMILPERSMAN 3810260.2 instead of as directed above

SHIPSEPROSHI
If ship or fleet command from which detached is located in Hawaii at the time of detachment, report for separation processing in accordance with NAVMIPERSMAN 3810260.2 instead of as directed above
SHIPSTO
Ship Store Office
(SHIPYARD)MIS
Shipyard Management Information System
SHLW
Shallow
SHMD
Shore Manning Documents
SHO
Shore
SHOLS
Single-Hoist Ordnance Loading System
SHOPAT, SP
Shore Patrol
SHORAN
Short-Range Navigation (or Aid to Navigation)
SHORDU
Shore Duty
SHOROC
Shore Required Operational Capability
SHOROUTPUBINST
Shore duty beyond the seas is required by the public interest
SHORPUBINT
Shore duty is required by the public interest
SHOR(T)STAMPS
Shore Requirements, Standards and Manpower Planning System
SHORVEY
Shore-to-Sea Rotation Survey
SHOT
Senior, Headquarters OPO Team
SHP
Shaft Horsepower
SHROC
Shore Required Operational Capabilities
SHWR
Shower
SI
Selected (or Special) Intelligence
Self-Instructional (course)
Ship Installation
Showalter Index
Specific Impulse
Straight-In (approach)
SI, SPOT
Spot Inventory
SIA
Standard Instrument Approach
Station of Initial Assignment
SIAS
Submarine Integrated Antenna System

SIB
Ship Information Book
Situation Intelligence Brief
Standard Index Base
SIC
Scientific Information Center
Sonar Intelligence Center
SICB
Senior Interservice Control Board
SICCM
Supervisor Information on Civilian Career
Management
SICD
Supply Item Design Change
SICMA
Special Initial Clothing Monetary Allowance
SICMA-CIV
Special Initial Clothing Monetary
Allowance-Civilian
SICMA-NAOC
Special Initial Clothing Monetary
Allowance-Naval Aviation Officer Candidate
SICMA-NAVCAD
Special Initial Clothing Monetary
Allowance-Naval Aviation Cadet
SICR
Specific Intelligence Collection Requirements
Supply Item Change Record
SID
Standard Instrument Departure
Sudden Ionospheric Disturbance
Synchronous Identification System
SIDC
Supply Item Design Change
SIDL
System Identification Data List
SIDMS
Status, Inventory, Data Management System
SIDS
Shrike-Improved Display System
Standard Implementation Document System
SIF
Selective Identification Feature
SIFPPS
Shore Installations and Facilities Planning
and Programming System
SIG
Senior Interdepartmental Group
Ship Improvement Guide
Signal
Signature
SIG/IRG
Senior Interdepartmental
Group/Interdepartmental Regional Group
SIGMAP
Special Interest Group for Mathematical
Programming
SIGMETS
Significant Meteorological (information)
SIGMS
Signal Material Supports

SIGS
Simplified Inertial Guidance System
SIG SEL
Signal Selector
SIG STA
Signal Station
SII
SHIPALT Installation Instruction (PERA)
Statement of Intelligence Interest
SIL
Speech Interference Level (NRP)
Standard Inventory Log
SILO
Security Intelligence Liaison Office
SIM
SAM Intercept Missile (system)
Selected Item Management
SIMA
Shore Intermediate Maintenance Activity
SIMCOM
Simulator-Compiler
SIMCON
Scientific Inventory Management and Control
SIME
Security Intelligence, Middle East
SIMEX
Secondary Items Military Assistance Program
SIMFAC
Simulation Facility
SIMP
Shipboard Integrated Maintenance Program
Slow Image Motion Processor
SIMSI
Selected Inventory Management of
Secondary Items
SIMTOS
Simulated Tactical Operations System
SINEWS
Ship Integrated Electronic Warfare System
SINS
Ship's Inertial Navigation System
SIO
Specific Instructional Objectives
SIOP
Single Integrated Operational Plan
SIOP-ESI
Safeguarding the Single Integrated
Operational Plan-Extremely Sensitive
Information
SIP
System Improvement Program
SIPD
Supply Item Provisioning Document
SIPG
Service in Paygrade
SIPM
Student Instructor Performance Module
SIR
Selected Item Report
Symbolic Input Routine

SIRCS
Shipboard Intermediate Range Combat System
SIRIN
Single Readiness Information System (NORRS)
SIROS
Specialized Operating System
SIS
SAGE Interceptor Simulator
Screening/Inspection System
SISMS
Standard Integrated Support Management System
SISR
Selected Item Status Report
SISS
Submarine Integrated Sonar System
SIST
Self-Inflating Surface Target
SIT
Situation
Spontaneous Ignition Temperature
Storage Inspection Test
Storage-in-Transit
SITAP
Simulator for Transportation Analysis and Planning
SITE
Shipboard Information, Training and Entertainment (system)
SITREP
Situation Report
SITS
Secure Imagery Transmission System (TACSAT)
SIW
Self-Inflicted Wound
SIXFLT
Sixth Fleet
SIZ
Security Identification Zone
SJP
Special Job Procedure
SJUMPS
Shipboard Joint Uniform Military Pay System
SK
Skein (U/I)
Sketch
SK1
Storekeeper First Class
SK2
Storekeeper Second Class
SK3
Storekeeper Third Class
SKAMP
Station-Keeping and Mobile Platform
SKB
Skiff, Large (USCG)
SKC
Chief Storekeeper

SKCM
Master Chief Storekeeper
SKCS
Senior Chief Storekeeper
SKD, SKED
Schedule
SKE
Station-Keeping Equipment
SKED, SKD
Schedule
SKI
Skiff, Ice (USCG)
SKILL
Satellite Kill
SKIP
Skill/Knowledge Improvement Program
SKL
Skiff, Light (USCG)
SKM
Skiff, Medium
SKMC
Sickness Due to Misconduct
SKMR
Hydroskimmer
SKOR
Sperry Kalman Optical Reset (SINS)
SKSA
Storekeeper Seaman Apprentice
SKSN
Storekeeper Seaman
SKT
Skill Knowledge Test
SL
Search Light
Slide (AFRTS code)
Spool (U/I)
Support Line
S-L
Sound Locator
SLAE
Standard Lightweight Avionics Equipment
SLAM
Supersonic Low-Altitude Missile
SLAMEX
Submarine-Launched Assault Missile Exercise
SLANG
Systems Language
SLAR
Side-Looking Radar
Slant Range
SLAT
Ship-Launched Air-Targeted (missiles)
SLATE
Small Lightweight Altitude Transmission Equipment (FAA)
SLB
Side-Lobe Blanking
SLBD
Sea Lite Beam Director

SLBM
Submarine-Launched Ballistic Missile
SLC
Side-Lobe Cancellation
Simulated Linguistic Computer
SLCC
Ship Life-Cycle Coordinators
Ship Logistic Control Center (LSC)
Summary List of Component Centers
SLCM
Submarine- (or Sea-) Launched Cruise
　Missile
SLCMP
Software Life Cycle Management Plan
SLCU, STANLANCRU
Standard Landing Craft Unit
SLEP
Service Life Extension Program
State Line End Point
SLEW
Statis Load Error Washout
SLF
Special Landing Force
SLGT
Slight
SLIM
Standards Laboratory Information Manual
Submarine-Launched Intercept Missile
SLIS
Shared Laboratory Information System
SLIT
Serial/Lot Item Tracking
SLM
Ship's Logistics Manager
Sound Level Meter
Submarine-Launched Missile
SLMS
Ship-Based Long-Range Missile System
SLNC
Service Life Not Completed
SLO
Staff Legal Officer
SLOC
Sea Lines of Communication
SLOE
Special List of Equipment
SLP
Scouting Land Plane
Slope
SLPMS
Single-Level Power Management System
SLR
Side-Looking Radar
Single Lens Reflex (camera)
Slush on Runway
SLRI
Shipboard Long-Range Input
SLR-P
Slush on Runway-Patchy
SLS
Side-Lobe Suppression

SLT
Sleet
Sonobuoy Launch Tubes
SLTM
Short Lead Time Material
SLT&DL
Search Light and Sound Locator
SLV
Satellite Launching Vessel
Standard Launch Vehicle
SLW, SLO
Slow
SLWT
Side Loading Warping Tug
SM
Salvage Mechanic
Semi-Monthly (report frequency)
Sheet Metal
Shipment Memorandum
Shop Manufacture
Small
Standard Missile
Submarine, Minelaying
SM1
Signalman First Class
SM2
Signalman Second Class
SM3
Signalman Third Class
S/M, SERVMART
Service Mart (or Market)
S&M
Sequence and Monitor
SMA
Ship's Material Account
Standard Maintenance Allowance (for
　clothing)
SUBROC Missile Assembly
SHAAM
Static Multi-Attribute Assignment Model
SMACS
Serialized Missile Accounting and Control
　System
Simulated Message Analysis and Conversion
　Subsystem
SMACTRACEN
Small Craft Training Center
SMAF
Shipboard Maintenance Action Form
SMAGOL
Small Computer Algorithmic Language
SMAM
Single Mission Air Medal
SMAR
Summary of Monthly Aerological Reports
SMART
Source Management of Resources and Time
SMB
Supersonic Manned Bomber

SMC
Chief Signalman
SAGE Maintenance Control
Supply and Maintenance Command
SMCM
Master Chief Signalman
Surface Mine Countermeasures
SMCO
SAFE Maintenance Control Office
SMCS
Senior Chief Signalman
SMD
Ship Manning Document
SM&DSL
Sector Management and Direct Support
Logistics Center
SMEAC
Situation, Mission, Execution, Administrative
and Logistics, and Command and
Communications (defense tactics)
SMF
Student Master File
SMG
Submachine Gun
SMI
Saturday Morning Inspection
Statute Miles
SMIC
Special Material Identification Code
Study of Man's Impact on the Climate
Submarine Material Identification and Control
SMIPE
Small Interplanetary Probe Experiments
SMIS
(The) Society for Management Information
Systems
Supply Management Information System
SMK
Smoke
SML
Support Material List
SML, SM
Small
SMLS
Seaborne Mobile Logistic
System—pronounced "Smiles" or "Smells"
(slang)
SMMAS
Shipboard Maintenance Manpower Analysis
System
SMMR
Specific Mobilization Material Requirement
SMMS
Shipbuilding Material Management System
SMN
Spain-Morocco Network (AFRTS)
SMO
Ship's Material Office
Stabilized Master Oscillator
Supplementary Meteorological Office

SMO, SENMEDO
Senior Medical Officer
SMOLANT
Ship's Material Office, Atlantic
SMOPAC
Ship's Material Office, Pacific
SMP
Shipboard Microfilm Program
SMPR
Semi-Monthly Progress Reports
SMPT
Sound Movie Projector Technician
SMR
Special Money Requisition
SM&R
Source, Maintenance and Recoverability
(code)
SMRB
Senior Material Review Board
SM&RC
Scheduled Maintenance and Repair Code
SMRL
Station Material Readiness List
SMS
Sequence Milestone System
Shipyard Modernization System
Single Management System
Surface Missile System
SMSA
Signalman Seaman Apprentice
SMSCC
Surface Missile Systems Clearance
Committee
SMSD
Submarine Detector, Ship's Magnet
SMSN
Signalman Seaman
SMSP
Senior Medical Student Program
Surface Missile Projects Office
SMT
SUBROC Missile Technician
SMTH
Smooth
SMVLF
Shipboard Mobile Very Low Frequency
SMWHT
Somewhat
SMZ
Southern Maritime Zone
SN
Seaman
Serial (or Service) Number
Signal-to-Noise (ratio)
S/N, SN
Stock Number
SN, SECNAV
Secretary of the Navy
SNA
Student Naval Aviator

SNAB
Stock Number Action Bulletin
SNAFU
Situation Normal, All Fouled Up
SNAIAS
Ship's Navigation and Aircraft Inertial
Alignment System
SNAP
Senior Naval Aviator Present
Shipboard Non-Tactical Automatic Data
Processing Program
Student Naval Aviation Pilot
SNB
Small Navigation Buoy
SNCO
Senior Non-Commissioned Officer
SNDL
Standard Navy Distribution List
SNDS
Stock Number Data Section
SNEC
Secondary Navy Enlisted Classification
(code)
SN(EF)
Electronics Field Seaman
SNEP FIT
Saudi Naval Expansion Program Fleet
Introduction Team
SNEP PMT
Saudi Naval Expansion Program Project
Management Team
SNEP PROJMGR
Saudi Naval Expansion Program, Project
Manager
SNEP PROJMGR TAFT
Saudi Naval Expansion Program, Project
Manager, Technical Assistance Field Team
SNF
Systems Noise Figure
SNFL
Standing Naval Force, Atlantic
SNFO
Student Naval Flight Officer
SNFS
Student Naval Flight Surgeon
SNG
Synthetic Natural Gas
SN(HS)
High School Seaman
SNIT
Stock Number Identification Tables
SN(JC)
Junior College Seaman
SN(JCE)
Junior College Technical Electrician Seaman
SN(JCNE)
Junior College Nuclear Field Electronics
Seaman
SN(JCNSET)
Junior College Nuclear Submarine
Engineering Technician Seaman

SN(JCPE)
Junior College Polaris Field Electronics
Seaman
SN(JCPL)
Junior College Polaris Field Launcher
Seaman
SN(JCT)
Junior College Technical Electronics Seaman
SNL
Standard Navy (Distribution) List
SNM
Senior Naval Member
Special Nuclear Materials
Subject Named Man
SNMMMS, 3M
Standard Navy Maintenance and Material
Management System
SN(NFE)
Nuclear Field Electronics Seaman
SN(NSET)
Nuclear Submarine Electronics Technical
Seaman
SNOFORN
Secret: Not Releasable to Foreign Nationals
SNOK
Secondary Next of Kin
SNORT
Supersonic Naval Ordnance Research Track
SN(PFE)
Polaris Field Electronics Seaman
SN(PFL)
Polaris Field Launcher Seaman
SNR
Signal-to-Noise Ratio
SNS
Stabilized Night Sight
SNSL
Standard Navy Stock List
Stock-Number Sequence List
SNSL-OSI
Stock-Number Sequence List-Operating
Space Items
SNSL-SRI
Stock-Number Sequence List-Storeroom
Items
SNSN
Standard Navy Stock Number
SO
Seller's Option
Send Only
Shipment (or Signal, or Special) Order
Submarine Overhaul
Supply Officer
Surface Operating (area)
Systems Orientation
SO, S
South(ern)
SOA
Safe Operating Area
Speed of Advance (or Approach)

SOAC
Submarine Officer Advanced Course
SOAP
Spectographic Oil Analysis Program
Shaft Optimum Alignment Procedure
Submarine Overhaul Allowance Parts
Supply Operations Assistance Program
SOBDI
Ship Onboard Drawing Index
SOBLIN
Self-Organizing Binary Logical Network
SOC
Serviceman's Opportunity College
Student Origin Code
SOCALSEC
Southern California Section
SOCHINAFOR
South China Force
SOCRATES
Simulator or Creative Reasoning Applied to
Education System
SOD
Small Object Detector
Special Operations Department
Submarine Overhaul Depot
SODAR
Sound Radar
SODAS
Synoptic Oceanographic Data Assimilation
System
SODDS
Submarine Oceanographic Digital Data
System
SOEAPL
Summary of Effective Allowance Parts List
SOEASTPAC
Southeast Pacific Force
SOES
Special Operations Evaluation System
Station Operations and Engineering
Squadron
SOF
Sound on Film
Strategic Offensive Forces
Supervisor of Flying
SOFAR
Sound Fixing and Ranging
SOFCS
Self-Organizing Flight Control System
SOG
Special Operations Group
Studies and Observation Group
SOGRU
Southern Group
SOH
Safety and Occupational Health
SOI
Space Object Identification
SOIC, SOINC
Supply Officer-in-Charge

SOINC, SOIC
Supply Officer-in-Charge
SOIP
Ship Overhaul Improvement Program
SOIS
Shipping Operations Information System
SOJ
Stand-Off Jamming
SOL
"Sure Out of Luck" (slang)
Systems-Oriented Language
SOLANT, SOLANTFOR
South Atlantic Force
SOLANTFOR, SOLANT
South Atlantic Force
SOLAS
Safety of Life at Sea
SOLRAD
Solar Radiation (satellite)
SOM
Send-Only-Multipoint
Simulator Operation and Maintenance
Start of Message
SOME
Secretary's Office, Management Engineer
SOMP
Sydney Ocean Meeting Point
SOMS
Standard Operations and Maintenance
Squadron
Synchronous Operational Meteorological
Satellite
SON
Submitting Office Number
SONAR
Sound Navigation and Ranging
SOND
Secretary's Office, Navy Department
SONOAN
Sonic Noise Analyzer
SONRD
Secretary's Office, Naval Research and
Development
SONS
Statistics of Naval Shipyards
SOP
Senior Officer Present
Ship Operational Program
Standard Operating Procedure
SOPA
Senior Officer Present Afloat
SOP(A)
Senior Officer Present (Ashore)
SOPAC
South Pacific
SOPUS
Senior Officer Present, United States Navy
SOQ
Senior Officer's Quarters
Sick Officer's Quarters

SOR
Safety Ordnance Requirements
Specific Operational (or Operating)
Requirements
SORA
Secretary's Office, Records Administration
SORB
Submarine Overhaul and Refueling Building
SORG
Submarine Operations Research Group
SORR
Submarine Operations Research Report
SORT
Supply Corps Officer Refresher Training
SOS
Save Our Ship (or Souls)
Senior Officer Seminar (course)
SHARE Operating System
Ship Our Ships (program)
Silicon-on-Sapphire (components)
Source of Supply
Stamp Out Stock Errors
Supervisor of Shipbuilding
SOSCAR
Supervisor of Shipbuilding, Conversion and
Repair
SOSED
Secretary's Office, Shore Establishment
Division
SOSR
Selected Item Status Report
SOSUS
Sound Surveillance System
SOT
Ship Operational Trainer
Shortest Operational Time
Simulated Operational Training (course)
Sonar Trainer
Superintendent of Training
Systems Operability Test
SOTB
Secretary's Office, Transportation Branch
SOTD
Stabilized Optical Tracking Device
SOT I
Simulated Operational Training, Phase I
(course)
SOT II
Simulated Operational Training, Phase II
(course)
SOT III
Simulated Operational Training, Phase III
(course)
SOTIM
Sonic Observation of Trajectory and Impact
of Missiles
SOW
Stand-Off Weapon
Statement of Work
SOWES, SW
Southwest(ern)

SOWESPAC
Southwest Pacific
SOWESTPACCOM
Southwest Pacific Command
SOWESSEAFRON
Southwest Sea Frontier
SOWR
Submarine Overhaul Work Requirement
SOWRA
Submarine Overhaul Work Requirement
Authorization
SOWS
Submarine Overhaul Work Scope
SP
Qualified and screened for submarine training
Secondary Plant
Security Publication
Self-Propelled
Shore Party
Single Purpose
Smokeless Powder
Snow Pellets (weather symbol)
Special Programs (or Projects)
Speed (NNSS)
Standard Plan (or Procedure)
Steam Propulsion (or Plant)
Strip (U/I)
Sub Point
Sub-Professional
Summary Plotter
Symphonic Popular (AFRTS code)
SP, PS
South Pole
SP, SHOPAT
Shore Patrol
SP, SPEC
Specialist
SP, S/P
Seaplane
SP, SPL
Special
SPA
Sea Photographic Analysis
Shore Patrol Advance (pay)
South Pacific Area
SPAAS
Staff Personnel Accounting and Allocation
System
SPACE
Self-Programming Automatic Circuit
Evaluation
Symbolic Programming Anyone Can Enjoy
SPACP
Steam Plant Auxiliaries Control Panel
SPALT
Special Projects Alteration
SPALTS
Strategic Systems Project Alteration Kits
SPAM
Special Aeronautical Material
Support Production and Multisource

SPAMS
Ship Position and Attitude Measurements System
SPAN
Storage Planning and Allocation
SPANS
Small Passive Navigation System
SPAR
Sea-going Platform for Acoustic Research (NOL)
Symbolic Program Assembly Routine
SPARC
Shore Establishment Planning Analysis and Review Cooperation
SPARM
Solid-Propellant Augmented Rocket Motor
SPARPS
Spares and Repair Parts Support
SPARTA
Special Anti-Missile Research Test-Australia
SPASST, SPAST
Special Assistant
SPAST, SPASST
Special Assistant
SPATS
South Pacific Air Transport Service
SPC
Shop Process Card
Special Program Code
Still-Picture Camera
SPCC
Ship's Parts Control Center
Spill Prevention Control and Countermeasures
SPCM
Master Chief Steam Propulsionman
Special Courts-Martial
SPCP
Steam Propulsion Control Panel
SPD
Separation Program Designator
Ship Planning Document
Ship Project (or Program) Directive
Smokeless Powder, Diphenylamine
Speed
Speed and Heading Coordinate System (NNSS)
Student Pilot Disposition
Superheater Protection Device
SPDB
Smokeless Powder, Diphenylamine, Blend
SPDC
Spare-Parts Distributing Center
SPDF
Smokeless Powder, Diphenylamine, Flashless
SPDLTR
Speedletter
SPDN
Smokeless Powder, Diphenylamine, Nonvolatile

SPDT
Single Pole, Double Throw (switch)
SPDW
Smokeless Powder, Diphenylamine, Reworked
SPE
Signal Processing Element (NRL)
Special-Purpose Equipment
Systems Performance Effectiveness
SPEC
Specify
Specification
SPEC, SP
Specialist
SPECASTSECNAV
Special Assistant to the Secretary of the Navy
SPECAT
Special Category (messages)
SPECFORCOM
Special Forces Command
SPECK
Safety, Pride, Efficiency, Compatibility, Knowledge
SPECL
Specialize
SPECOM
Special Communications
SPECOMDIV
Special Communications Division
SPECOPS
Special Operations
SPECPROJOUK
Special Projects Liaison Offices, United Kingdom
SPEC(S)
Specification(s)
SPECTRE
Simultaneous Program Executing CATO Transcribed Reruns
SPEED
Self-Programmed Electronic Equation Delineator
Signal Processing in Evacuated Electronic Devices
Special Procedure for Expediting Development
Subsistence Prepared by Electronic Energy Diffusion
SPEEL
Shore Plant Electronics Equipment List
SPEEREBRA
Speech Research Branch
SPENAVO
Special Naval Observer
SPERT
Schedule Program Evaluation Review Technique
SPET
Solid-Propellant Electric Thruster

SPF
Studded Panel Fastener
SPGE
Steam Plant Gauge
SP GR
Specific Gravity
SPGG
Solid-Propellant Gas Generator
SPH
Statement of Personal History
SPHG
Speed and Heading (NNSS)
SPHQ
Shore Patrol Headquarters
SP HT
Specific Heat
SPI
Ship's Plan Index
Superintendent of Public Instruction
SPID
Submersible, Portable, Inflatable Dwelling
SPIE
Simulated Problem Input Evaluation
SPIL
Ships Parts Integration List
SPINS
Ship Passive Integrated Navigation System
SPINTAC
Special Interest Aircraft (program)
SPIW
Special-Purpose Individual Weapon
SPJTG
Secondary Plant Joint Test Group
SPL
Self-Propelled Launcher
Sound Pressure Level
SPL, SP
Special
SPLASH
Shipboard Platforms for Landing and
Servicing Helicopters
SPLC
Simulated Planetary Landing Capsule
SPM
Scans per Minute
Secondary Propulsion Motor
Self-Propelled Mount
Steam-Plant Manual
SPMP
Systems Project Master Plan
SPMPS
Submarine Program Management Planning
and Scheduling
SPMS
Source Program Maintenance System
SPN
Separation Program Number
SPO
Shore Patrol Officer
Special (or Systems) Projects Office(r)
Systems Program Office

SPOC
Single-Point Orbit Calculator
SPOCK
Simulated Procedure for Obtaining Common
Knowledge
SPOD
Ship's Plan of the Day
SPOOK
Supervisory Program Over Other Kinds (of
programs)
SPORT, SPT, SUPP
Support
SPOT
Speed, Positioning and Tracking
SPOT, SI
Spot Inventory
SPOTR
Special Projects Officer Technical
Representative
SPOTREPS
Significant Occurrences Reports
SPP
Sponsor Program Priorities (or Proposal)
SPP&C
Submarine Production Planning and Control
SPR
Small Purchase Request
Solid-Propellant Rocket
SPRINT
Solid-Propellant Rocket Intercept
SPRS
Single Passenger Reservation System
SPS
Ship Planning System
SPST
Single Pole, Single Throw (switch)
SPT, SPORT, SUPP
Support
SPTCO
Support Company
SPTF
Signal Processing Test Facility
S/Q
Safety Quotient
Sequential Qualification
Superquick (fuze)
SQ, SQDN, RON
Squadron
SQ, (SU)
Submarine Qualified
SQA
Submarine Quality Assurance
SQAR
Senior Quality Assurance Representative
SQAT
Ships Qualification Assistance Team
SQD
Squad
SQDN, RON, SQ
Squadron

SQ/H
    Square of the Hatch (stowage)
SQLN
    Squall Line
SQMD
    Squadron Manning Document
SQ/SD
    Special Qualification/Special Designator
    (code)
SQT
    Ship Qualification Trials
    Systems Qualification Tests
SQUID
    Superconducting Quantum Interference
    Device
SR
    Seaman Recruit
    Shaker (U/I)
    Slant Range
    Special Regulation
    Standard Range (approach)
    Study Requirement
    Sunrise
    Suppressed Range
SR, SERVREC
    Service Record
SR, S/R
    Shipment Request
SR, SRG
    Short-Range
S/R
    Storage and Repair
SRA
    Selective Restricted Availability
    Shop Replaceable Assembly
    Short-Range Attack
SRAD
    Ship's Restricted Availability Date
    Steerable Right-Angle Drive
SRAM
    Short-Range Attack Missile
SRB
    Selective Reenlistment Bonus
    Specification Review Board
    Subspecialty Requirements Board
SRBK
    Short-Range Boresight Kit
SRBM
    Short-Range Ballistic Missile
SRC
    Scheduled Removal Component (program)
    Service Record Card
    SPECAT Release Code
    Stores Reliability Card
    Submarine Rescue Chamber
SRCT
    Standard Recovery Completion Time
SRD
    Secret and Formerly Restricted Data
    Selected Record Drawing
    Service Revealed Difficulty

SRDS
    Shop Repair Data Sheets
    Systems Research and Development System
SRE
    Surveillance Radar Element
SR(EF)
    Electronics Field Seaman Recruit
SRF
    Selected Reserve Force
    Submarine Repair Facility
SRF, SHIPREPFAC
    Ship Repair Facility
SRFLANT, SHIPREPFACLANT
    Ships Repair Facility, Atlantic
SRFPAC, SHIPREPFACPAC
    Ships Repair Facility, Pacific
SRG, SR
    Short-Range
SRGS
    Survivable Radio Guidance System
SRH
    Structural Repair Handbook (publication)
SR(HS)
    High School Seaman Recruit
SRI
    Storeroom Items
SRIP
    Ship Readiness Improvement Plan
    Specification Review and Improvement
    Program
SRL, SER
    Serial
SRM
    Short-Range Missile
    Speed of Relative Motion (or Movement)
SRMBR
    Senior Member
SRN
    Satellite Radio Navigation
SR(NFE)
    Nuclear Field Electronics Seaman Recruit
SR(NSET)
    Nuclear Submarine Engineering Technician
    Seaman Recruit
SRO
    Shop Repair Order
    Superintendent of Range Operations
SRP
    Selected Records Plan
    Shark Research Panel (AIBS)
    Standard Repair Procedures
    Stern Reference Point
    Supply and Repair Parts
SR&P
    Station Resources and Planning
SR(PFE)
    Polaris Field Electronics Seaman Recruit
SR(PFL)
    Polaris Field Launcher Seaman Recruit
SRPM
    Shaft Revolutions per Minute

SR&PO
Station Resources and Planning Office
SRPS
Supply and Repair Parts Specifications
SRRT
Simultaneous Rotating and Reciprocating
Technique
SRS
Secondary Recovery Ship
Secondary Reference Standard
Simultaneous Reporting System
Substitute Route Structure
Supply Response Section
SRT
Slow-Run-Through (trials)
Space Requirement Travel
SRTU
Ship Repair Training Unit
SRU
Ship Repair Unit
Ship (or Squadron) Reinforcement Unit
SRU, SUBRU
Submarine Repair Unit
SS
Secret (or Selective, or Ship's) Service
Single-Seated (or -Stranded)
Single Shot
Slow-Setting (asphalt)
Stack (U/I)
Submarine Studies
Sub Safe (program)
Subsystem
Superimposed Seam
Sworn Statement
SS, SPECSERV
Special Services
SS, SUB
Submarine
(SS)
Qualified in Submarines
S/S
Same Size
Ship/Store
Spectrum Signature
SSA
Ship's Store Activities
Shipyard Schedule Activity
Source Selection Authority
Supply Support Agreement
SS/A
Starboard Side Aft (stowage)
SSADP
Soldier's, Sailor's and Airman's Deposit
Program
(S)SALS
Simplified Short-Approach Light System
SSAN
Social Security Account Number
SSAS
Self-Scoring Answer Sheets
Signal Assessment System

SSB
Fleet Ballistic Missile Submarine
Single Side Band (radio transceiver)
Source Selection Board
Swimmer Support Boat
SSBC
Stock Status Balance Card
SSBN
Nuclear-Powered Fleet Ballistic Missile
Submarine
SSBP, S³BP
System Source Selection Board Procedure
SSC
Service Schools Command
Shipboard Satellite Communications
(terminal)
Ship Safety Council
Ship System Command
Submarine Supply Center
Supply Support Center
Switch Scan Control (NNSS)
SSCB(B)
Submarine Safety Certification Boundary
(Book)
SSCDS
Small Ship Combat Data System
SSCM
Sub-Safe Certification Map (JIC)
SSCMA
Special Supplementary Clothing Monetary
Allowance
SS&CS
Ship's Stores and Commissary Stores
SSCT
Special Security Communications Team
SSD
Scrap Salvage Division
Specialized Support Depot
Stabilized Ship Detector
Submarine Support Division
Survival Support Device
S/SD
Ship/Store Department
SSDB
Shore Station Development Board
SSD(F)
Submarine Support Division for Fleet Support
SSD(S)
Submarine Support Division for Shore
Facilities
SSD(ST)
Submarine Support Division for Staff Support
SSE
Special Support Equipment
System Safety Engineering
SS/EAM
Shipboard System/Equipment Acquisition
Manual
SSED
Submarine Services Entry Date

SSEM
Supply Support Element Manager
SSEP
Submarine Surveillance (or Support)
Equipment Program
System Safety Engineering Plan
SSES
Ship Signal Exploitation Rate
SSF
Seconds, Saybolt Furol
Service Storage Facility
Ship's Service Force
Single-Seated Fighter
Special Service Force
SS/F
Starboard Side Forward (stowage)
SS-FORMS
Special Strike Forms (for nuclear
employment)
SSG
Guided Missile Submarine
Service School Guarantee
SSGN
Nuclear-Powered Guided-Missile Submarine
(concept)
SSGT
Staff Sergeant
SSHACS
Small Ships Accounting System
SSI
Standard System Index
SSIC
Standard Subject Identification Code
SSILS
Solid-State Instrument Landing System
SSITF
Standard Shipboard Inspection and Testing
Form
SSK
Antisubmarine Submarine
SSL
SERVMART Shopping LIst
Severe Storms Laboratory
Solid State Lamp
SSM
Sensor Simulator Materials
Ship's System Manual
Ship's Side Band Modulation
Surface-to-Surface Missile
Systems Support (or Supply) Manager
SSME
Space Shuttle Main Engine
SSMG
Ship's Service Motor Generator
SSMR
Single Senior Military Representative
SSN
Nuclear-Powered Attack Submarine
Season and Sunspot Number
Social Security Number
Supply Support Notification

SSO
Ship Safety Officer
Special Security Officer
SSORM
Standard Submarine Operations and
Regulations Manual
Standing Submarine Operations and Repair
Manual
SSP
Secondary Stock Point
Ship's Stores and Profit
Source Selection Plan
Strategic Systems Project
Sustained Superior Performance
SSPN
Ship's Stores and Profit, Navy
SSPO
Strategic Systems Project Office
SSPOTR
Strategic Systems Project Office Technical
Representative
SSPP
System Safety Program Plan
SSR
Safe Secure Rail Car
Spin-Stabilized Rockets
Stock-Status Report
Supply Support Request
SSS
Selective Service System
Service Steam System
Shift Ship Superintendent
Signature Security Service
Storage Serviceability Standard
Strike Support Ship
Supply Screening Section
Synchro Self-Shifting
SSSCP
Single Supply Support Control Point
SSSP
System Source Selection Procedure
SSSR
SAGE System Status Report
SSSS
Space-Borne Software Systems Study
SST
Safe Secure Trailer
Sea Surface Temperature
Shore Survey Team (NMVO)
Substation
Target and Training Submarine
(Self-Propelled)
SSTG
Ship's Service Turbo (or Turbine) Generator
SSTM
SAGE System Training Mission (or Missile)
SSTU
SAGE System Training Unit
SSTV
Slow-Scan Television
Submarine Shock Test Vehicle

SSU
Seconds, Saybolt Universal
Semiconductor Storage Unit
Special (or Squadron) Service Unit
Supply Screening Unit

SSURADS
Shipboard Surveillance Radar

SSV
Special Surveillance Vehicle
Submarine Support Vehicle

SSVP
Soviet Ship Vulnerability Program

SSW
Shipboard Safety Watch

ST
Oceanographic Specialist
Schmidt Trigger
Service Test (division)
Stratus (cloud formation)
Student (MAPMIS)

ST1
Sonar Technician First Class

S&T
Scientific and Technical (intelligence)

S/T
Short Ton
Sonic Telegraphy

STA
Shuttle Training Aircraft
Stationary
Straight-In Approach

STA, STN
Station

STAAS
Surveillance and Target Acquisition Aircraft
System

STAB
SEAL (or Strike) Team Assault Boat
Stabilizer

STAFS
Standard Automated Financial System

STAG
Special Task Air Group

STALO
Stable (or Stabilized) Local Oscillator

STAMIC
Set Theoretic Analysis and Measurement of
Information Characteristics

STAMINRQ
Status During Minimize Required

STAMP
Standard Amphibious Plan

STAN, STD
Standard

STANAG
Standardization NATO Agreement

STANAVFORLANT
Standing Naval Force, Atlantic

STANFLT
Standardization Flight (NATOPS)

STANLANCRU, SLCU
Standing Landing Craft Unit

STAMO
Stable Automatic Modulated Oscillator

STANO
Surveillance, Target Acquisition and Night
Observation

STAP
Standard Tactical Avionics Package

STAPL
Ship Tethered Aerial Platform

STAPLAN
Status-Time-Attrition-Planning

STAPP
Single-Threat All-Purpose Program

STAR
Selective Training and Retention (program)
Space Thermionic Auxiliary Reactor
Special Treatment and Review
Standard Terminal Arrival Route
Strikes, Transfers, Acquisitions, or Removals
(or aircraft engines)

STARAD
Starfish Radiation

STARP
Supplemental Training and Readiness
Program

STARS
Study of Tactical Airborne Radar Systems

STASS
Silent Towed Array Sonar System

STAT
Seabee Technical Assistance Team
Statistic

STATE
Simplified Tactical Approach and Terminal
Equipment

STATRAFO, STO
Standard Transfer Order

STB
Special Training Branch
Super Tropical Bleach

STBD
Starboard

STBY
Standby

STC
Chief Sonar Technician
Sensitivity Time Control
SHAPE Technical Center

STCM
Master Chief Sonar Technician

STCS
Senior Chief Sonar Technician

STD
Secondary Test Department
Shift Test Director
Standing
Submarine Test Department

STD, STAN
Standard

STDY
Steady
STE
Special (or Standard) Test Equipment
ST&E
Security Tests and Evaluations
STEDMIS
Ship's Technical Data Management
Information System
STEIN
System Test Environment Input
STEM
Seabee Tactical Equipment Management
Statistically-Tensioned Extension Mast
Stay Time Extension Module
Storage, Tubular Extendable Member
STENO
Stenographer
STEP
Ship Type Electronic Plan
Simple Transition to Electronic Processing
Special Training Enlistment Program
Standard Test Equipment Procedures
Supervisory Tape Executive Program
Supplementary Training and Education
Program
STERF
Special Test Equipment Repair Facility
STF
Staff
Stiff
STG
Strong
STG, STRAG, STRG
Straggler
STG2
Sonar Technician G (Surface) Second Class
STG3
Sonar Technician G (Surface) Third Class
STGE, STOR
Storage
STGSA
Sonar Technician G (Surface) Seaman
Apprentice
STGSN
Sonar Technician G (Surface) Seaman
STIC
Scientific and Technical Intelligence Center
STID
Ship's Test and Inspection Department
STIK
Striking
STILO
Scientific and Technical Intelligence Liaison
Officer
STINFO
Scientific and Technical Information
STINGS
Stellar Inertial Guidance System

STIR
Scientific and Technical Intelligence Register
Submarine Technical Information Record
STK
Stock
Strike
STL
Self-Test Logic (NNSS)
Stock, Time Limitation
Storage Time Limits
Studio-to-Transmitter Link
STLO
Scientific-Technical Liaison Office
STLS
Ship's Transducer Locating System
STM
Service Test Model
Steam
Storm
STMP
Ship Test Management Plan
STM-R
Short-Term Modernization Receiving
STN, STA
Station
STO
Science and Technology Objective
Ship Test Organization
Short Take-Off
STO, STATRAFO
Standard Transfer Order
STOL
Short Take-Off and Landing
STOPS
Ship's Toxicological Operational Protective
System
STOR, STGE
Storage
STO/VL
Short Take-Off, Vertical-Landing (or Land)
(aircraft)
STOW
System for Take-Off Weight
STOP
Special Troop
Standard Temperature and Pressure
Submarine Thermal Reactor
STR
Store
Strength
STRAAD
Special Techniques for Repair and Analysis
of Aircraft Damage
STRADAP
Storm Radar Data Processor
STRAG, STG, STRG
Straggler
STRAP
Star Tracking Rocket Altitude Positioning
STRATANALSUPPGRU
Strategic Analysis Support Group

STRATCOM
Strategic Communications Command
STRAW
Simultaneous Tape Read and Write
STREAM
Standard Tensioned Replenishment
Alongside Method
STRESS
Structural Engineering System Solver
STRG, STR, STRAG
Straggler
STRICOM
(United States) Strike Command
STRINGS
Stellar Inertial Guidance System
STRIP
Specification Technical Review and
Improvement Program
Standard Taped Routines for Image
Processing
Stock Turn-In and Replenishment Invoicing
Procedures
STRS
Submarine Technical Repair Standard
STRUC
Structure
STS
Ship-to-Shore
Surface Target Simulator
STS2
Sonar Technician S (Submarine) Second
Class
STS3
Sonar Technician S (Submarine) Third Class
STSC
Shipboard Tactical Satellite Communications
STSSA
Sonar Technician S (Submarine) Seaman
Apprentice
STSSN
Sonar Technician S (Submarine) Seaman
ST/STE
Special Tooling/Special Test Equipment
STTF
Service to the Fleet (newspaper)
STU
Service Trials Unit
Submersible Test Unit (NCEL)
STU, STUD
Student
STUD, STU
Student
STUTNG
Student Training
STV
Sensitivity Time Control
Steam Tank Vessel
SU
Submarine School Graduate
Sub Unit
Suit

(SU), SQ
Submarine Qualified
SUADPS
Shipboard Uniform Automatic Data
Processing System
SUB, SS
Submarine
SUBAD
Submarine Air Defense (missile system)
SUBBASE, SB
Submarine Base
SUBCAP
Rescue Submarine Combat Air Patrol
SUBCERT
Submarine Safety Certification
SUBCH
Subchapter
SUBCOM, SUBORCOM
Subordinate Command
SUBCONSENT
Assignment to active naval service subject to
consent
SUBCOR
Subject to Correction
SUBDIV
Submarine Division
SUBEASTLANT
Submarine Force, Eastern Atlantic
SUBFLOT
Submarine Flotilla
SUBGRU
Submarine Group
SUBIC
Submarine Integrated Control
SUBINSURV
Sub-Board of Inspection and Survey
SUBINSURVLANT
Sub-Board of Inspection and Survey, Atlantic
SUBINSURVPAC
Sub-Board of Inspection and Survey, Pacific
SUBJ
Subject
SUBLANT
Submarine Forces, Atlantic
SUBM
Submerged
Submitted
SUB/MBR
Subcontractor/Material Review Board

SUBNAVPERS
Within 3 days prior to detachment complete applicable items on both NAVPERS 7041/1 being forwarded with confirmation copy of this message, and submit to OIC, Navy Family Allowance Activity (PCSVAD), Cleveland, OH 44199, via CO. (Officers ordered ACDU from home submit direct to OIC, Navy Family Allowance Activity (PCSVAD), Cleveland, OH 44199.) If this order constitutes a modification, do not submit NAVPERS 7041/1 forwarded with previous orders.

SUBNEWSTA
Complete applicable items on both sides NAVPERS 7041/1 being forwarded with copy of this message to new duty station and submit to OIC, Navy Family Allowance Activity (PCSVAD), Cleveland, OH 44199, via CO.

SUBOR
Subordinate

SUBORCOM, SUBCOM
Subordinate Command

SUB-OSC
Submarine Oscillator

SUBPAC
Submarine Forces, Pacific

SUBPAR
Subparagraph

SUBPAY
Submarine Duty Incentive Pay

SUBRESUNIT
Submarine Rescue Unit

SUBROC
Submarine Rocket

SUBRON
Submarine Squadron

SUBRU, SRU
Submarine Repair Unit

SUBS
Subsistence

SUBSAFECEN
Submarine Safety Center

SUBSALVEX
Submarine Salvage Exercise

SUBSCOL
Submarine School

SUBSEC
Subsection

SUBS(GM)
Subsisted in a General Mess

SUBSLANT
Submarines, Atlantic

SUBSPAC
Submarines, Pacific

SUBSPEC
Subspecialist

SUBSTD
Substitute Standard

SUBTRAFAC
Submarine Training Facility

SUBTRAP
Submersible Training Platform

SUC
Senior Unit Commander

SUCHTRANS
Via such transportation as (command indicated) designates

SUCHTRANSVAIL
Such transportation as available

SUDAM
Sunk or Damaged (vessel report)

SUDS
Specification Updating and Simplification
Submarine Detection System

SUF
Sufficient

SUITCASE
Submarine Sail Portable Command Center

SUM
Surface-to-Underwater Missile

SUNEC
Seaborne Supply of the Northeast Command

SUP
Supply
System Utilization Procedures

SUPANX
Supply Annex

SUPBN
Supply Battalion

SUPC
Ship Unit Production Code

SUPCOM
Supreme Command

SUPCON
Superintending Contractor

SUPER
Support Program for Extraterrestrial Research

SUPG
System Utilization Procedure Guide

SUPIER
Supply Pier

SUPINSMAT
Supervising Inspector of Naval Material

SUPIR
Supplemental Photo Interpretation Report

SUPO
Supply Officer

SUPP, SPT
Support

SUPP, SUPPL
Supplement

SUPPACT
Support Activity

SUPP BAS
Supplemental Basic Allowance for Subsistence

SUPPL, SUPP
Supplemental

SUPPLOT
Supplemental Plot
SUPPLT
Supply Platoon
SUPPS
(ICAO Regional) Supplementary Procedures
SUPPT
Supply Point
SUPRAD
Supplementary Radio Requirement
SUPSALREPWCOAST
Supervisor of Salvage Representative, West
Coast
SUPSHIP
Supervisor of Shipbuilding Conversion and
Repair
SUPSYSECGRU
Supply System, Security Group
SUPT
Superintendent
SUPTNAVOBSY
Superintendent, Naval Observatory
SUPV
Supervise
Supervisor
SUR
Surrender
Surrounding
Survivor
SURANO
Surface Radar and Navigation Operator
SURCAL
Surveillance Calibration (satellite)
SURCAP
Surface Combat Air Patrol
SURF
Standard Underway Replenishment Receiving
Fixture
SURFCO
Surf Code
SURGEN
Surgeon General
SURIC
Surface Integrated Control
Surface-Ship Integrated Control (system)
SUROB
Surface Observation (report)
SURORDTECH
Surface Ordnance Technician
SURPICS
Surface Pictures (AMVER)
SURTEMS
Sea Surface Temperature Measurements
System
SURTOPS
Surface Training and Operating Procedures
Standardization (manual)
SURV
Survey
SURV, SURVL
Surveillance

SURVFOR
Surveillance Force
SURVL, SURV
Surveillance
SUS
Saybolt Universal Seconds
Signal Underwater Sound
SUSIE
Surface/Underwater Ship Intercept Equipment
SUSNO
Senior United States Naval Officer
SUSP
Suspect
Suspend
SUU
Suspension and Release Unit
SV
Selective Volunteer
Semi-Vital
Sleeve (U/I)
S/V
Surface Vessel
SVC, SERV
Service
SVFR
Special Visual Flight Rules
SVG
Servicing
SVM
Ship's Value Manual
SVR
Severe
SVRL
Several
SVTP
Sound, Velocity, Temperature and Pressure
SW
Sea Water
Security Watch
Series Winding (wiring)
Short-Wave
Switch
SW, SOUWES
Southwest(ern)
SW1
Steelworker First Class
SW2
Steelworker Second Class
SW3
Steelworker Third Class
SWA
Southwest Approaches
SWACS
Surveillance, Warning and Control System
SWAG
Standard Written Agreement
SWAL
Shallow Water Attack-Craft, Light
SWAM
Shallow Water Attack-Craft, Medium

SWAT
Sidewinder Angle Tracking
SWATH
Small Waterplane Area Twin Hull (ship concept)
SWATS
Shallow Water Acoustic Tracking System
SWB
Special Weapons Branch
SWBD, SB
Switchboard
SWBS
Ship's Work Breakdown Structure
SWC
Chief Steelworker
Ship's Weapons Coordinator
Submerged Work Center
SWCA
Steelworker Construction Apprentice
SWCL
Special Warfare Craft, Light
SWCM
Special Warfare Craft, Medium
SWCN
Steelworker Constructionman
SWCS
Senior Chief Steelworker
SWDG
Surface Warfare Development Group
SWDI
Shipyard Work Description Index
SWETTU
Special Weapons Experimental Tactical Test Unit
SWFPAC
Strategic Weapon Facility Group, Pacific
SWG
Single-Weight Glossy (photo paper)
S/WG
Starboard Wing (stowage)
SWIM
Ship Weapons Installation Manual
SWIP
Super-Weight Improvement Program
SWIR
Special Weapons Inspection Reports
SWL
Safe Working Load
Short-Wave Listeners
SWLIN
System Work List Item Number
SWM
Shipboard (or Short-) Wave Meter
SWO
Senior Watch Officer
Surface Warfare Officer
SWOB
Ship Waste Offload Barge
SWOD
Special Weapons Ordnance Division

SWOP
Special Weapons Ordnance Publication
Stop Without Pay
SWOS
Surface Warfare Officers School
SWOSCOLCOM
Surface Warfare Officers School Command
SWOSCOLCOMDET
Surface Warfare Officers School Command Detachment
SWO PQS
Surface Warfare Officer Personnel Qualification Standards
SWPA
Southwest Pacific Area
SWPF
Southwest Pacific Force
SWR
Standing Wave Ratio
SWS
Strategic Weapons System
SWTTEU
Special Weapons Test and Tactical Evaluation Unit
SWU
Special Weapons Unit
SWULANT
Special Weapons Unit, Atlantic
SWUPAC
Special Weapons Unit, Pacific
SX
Simplex
SXBT
Shipboard Expendable Bathythermograph
SY
Shipyard
SYMPAC
Symbolic Program for Automatic Control
SYNTRAIN
Synthetic Training
SYS
System
SYSARD
System for Automated Reporting (programming)
SYSCOM
Systems Command(er)
SYSIN
Systems Input
SYSOUT
Systems Output
SYSPLIN
Shipyard Special Purchase Long-Lead Material
SYSRES
Systems-Resistance
SX
Selected Depot/Immediate
SZ
Surface Zero

T

T
Tactical (NAO code)
Temporary (personnel status)
Time
Trainer (aircraft)
Transformer
True (bearing)
Tug
T, TSTM
Thunderstorm
(T)
Transmitter
TA
TACAN Approach
Technical Analysis (or Authority)
Terrain Avoidance (radar)
Transition Agreement
Transition (or True) Altitude
Travel Allowance
TAB
Tabulate
Tactical Analysis Branch
Technical Abstract Bulletin
Technological Assessment Board
Training Aids Booklet
TABCASS
Tactical Air Beacon Command and
Surveillance System
TAC
Tactic(al)
Tactical Air Command (or Control(ler))
Target Acquisition Console
Total Air Control
Training Aids Center
TRANSAC Assembler/Compiler
Transportation Account(ing) Code
TACA, TAC(A)
Tactical Air Coordinator, Airborne
TACAIR
Tactical Aircraft
TACAMO
Take Action and Move Out
TACAN
Tactical Air Navigation (system)
TACANCEN
Tactical Air Navigation Control Center
TACCAR
Time-Averaged Clutter-Coherent Airborne
Radar
TACCO, TACO
Tactical Coordinator
TACD&E
Tactical Development and Evaluation
TACDEN
Tactical Data Entry
TACDEW
Tactical Advanced Combat Direction and
Electronic Warfare

TACDIVDEN
Temporary active duty in a flying status not
involving flying
TACDIFINSDEN
Temporary active duty under instruction in a
flying status not involving flying
TACDIFINSOPS
Temporary active duty under instruction in a
flying status involving operational or
training flights
TACDIFINSPRO
Temporary active duty under instruction in a
flying status involving proficiency flying
TACDIFIPS
Temporary active duty in a flying status
involving operational or training flights
TACDIFPRO
Temporary active duty in a flying status
involving proficiency flying
TACELECWARON
Tactical Electronics Warfare Wing
TACELECRON
Tactical Electronics Warfare Squadron
TACELECRONDET
Tactical Electronics Warfare Squadron
Detachment
TACGRU
Tactical Air Control Group
TACLAND
Tactical Instrument Landing Program
TACLOG
Tactical Logistics
TACMEMO
Tactical Memorandum
TAC-NAV
Tactical Navigation (system)
TACO, TACCO
Tactical Coordinator
TACOC
Tactical Air Control Operations Center
TACOSS
Tactical Containerized Shelter System
TACOSS I
Tactical Containerized Shelter
System/Detachment Subsistence Unit
(Expandable)
TACOSS II
Tactical Containerized Shelter
System/Detachment Sanitary Unit
(Non-Expandable)
TACOSS III
Tactical Containerized Shelter
System/Detachment Medical Unit
(Expandable)
TACOSS IV
Tactical Containerized Shelter
System/Provision Storage (Dry, Frozen,
Refrigerated)

TACOSS V
Tactical Containerized Shelter System/Equipment and Shop Unit (Expandable)
TACOSS VI
Tactical Containerized Shelter System/Detachment Personnel Unit
TACOSS VII
Tactical Containerized Shelter System/Utility Unit (Expandable)
TACOSS VIII
Tactical Containerized Shelter System/Frozen Storage Unit (Non-Expandable)
TACOSS IX
Tactical Containerized Shelter System/Galley Unit, Large (Expandable), 250-man
TACOSS X
Tactical Containerized Shelter System/Sanitary Unit, Large (Expandable), 100-man
TACP
Tactical Air Control Party
TAC/R
Tactical Reconnaissance
TACREDDS
Tactical Readiness Drills
TACRON
Tactical Air Control Squadron
TACS
Tactical Air Control System
TACSAT
Tactical Satellite
TACSATCOM
Tactical Satellite Communications
TACT
Teleprinter Automatic Control Terminal
Transonic Aircraft Technology (program)
TACTAS
Tactical Towed Array Sonar
TACTASS
Tactical Towed Array Sonar System
TACTRAGRULANT
Tactical Training Group, Atlantic
TACTRAGRUPAC
Tactical Training Group, Pacific
TACV
Tracked Air Cushion Vehicle
TAD
Tactical Air Direction (nets)
Task Analysis Data
Technical Approval Demonstration
Training Aids Division
TAD, TEMADD
Temporary Additional Duty
TADC
Tactical Air Direction Center
Training Aids Distribution Center
TADIXS
Tactical Data Information Exchange Subsystem

TADL
Tactical Data Link
TADM
Tactical Atomic Demolition Munitions
TADOR
Table Data Organization and Reduction
TADSO
Tactical Digital Systems Office
TADSS
Tactical Automatic Digital Switching System
TAEG
Training Analysis and Evaluation Group
TAF
Training Aids Facility
TAF, TAFOR
Terminal Aerodome Forecast
TAFMS
Total Active Federal Military Service
TAFOT
Aerodrome Forecast in Units of English
TAFT
Technical Assistance Field Team
TAFUBAR
"Things Are Fouled Up Beyond All Recognition" (slang)
TAG
Technical Advisory Group
Training Aids Guide
Transport Air Group
TAGIS
Tracking and Ground Instrumentation System
T-AGS
Auxiliary Survey Ship
TAIU
Technical Aircraft Instrument Unit
TAK
Military Sea Transport Service AKA
TAKCAL
Tachometer Calibration
TAKD
Military Sea Transport Service LSD
TAKV
Military Sea Transport Service CVS
TAL
Training Aids Library
TALAR
Tactical Landing and Approach Radar
Talos Activity Report
TAM
Transistor-Amplifier-Multiplier
TAMET
Aerodrome Forecast in Units of Metric
TAMI
Technical Information Maintenance Instruction
TAMS
Test and Monitoring Systems
TANKOPINS
Tanker Operating Instructions
TANS
Terminal Area Navigation System

TAO
Military Sea Transport Service Tanker
Tactical Action Officer
Tactical Air Observer
Terminal Arrest Orders

TAOC
Tactical Area of Interest

TAOW
Time Allowed Off Weapon

TAP
Military Sea Transport Service APA
Target Aircraft Program
Task (or Technical) Area Plan
Technical Alteration Plan
Training Aids Platform
Tuition Assistance Program

TAPE
Tape Automatic Preparation Equipment
Tentative Annual Planning Estimate

TAPER
Temporary Appointment Pending
    Establshment of Registers (CSC)

TAPIO
Tape Input and Output

TAPIT
Tactical Photographic Image Transmission
    (subsystem)

TAPS
Time Analysis of Program Status
Trajectory Accuracy Prediction System

TAR
Tactical Aircraft Recovery
Technical Advisory Report
Temporary Active Reserve
Terrier Advanced Radar
Thrust-Augmented Rocket
Total Accomplishment Requirement
Total Assets Reporting
Training and Administration of the Naval
    Reserve

TAR, TARA
Terrain Avoidance Radar

TAR, TGT
Target

TARA, TAR
Terrain Avoidance Radar

TARCAP
Target Combat Air Patrol

TARFU
"Things Are Really Fouled Up" (slang)

TARGET
Team to Advance Research for Gas Energy
    Transformation

TARPS
Tactical Air Reconnaissance Pods

TARS
Technical and Research Staff

TARSLL
Tender and Repair Ship Load List

TARVH
Aircraft Repair Ship, Helicopter

TAS
Target Acquisition System
Technical Advisory Service
Training Aids Section
Transfer Alignment Set
True Airspeed

TASA
Task and Skill Analysis

TASC
Tactical Articulated Swimmerable Carrier
Training and Support Component (USNR)

TASES
Tactical Airborne Signal Exploitation System

TAS-I
Target Acquisition System-Integrated

TAS/IRAS
Target Acquisition System/Infrared Automatic
    System

TASKFLOT
Task Flotilla

TAS/RAS
Target Acquisition System/Radar Automatic
    System

TAS/RMS
Target Acquisition System/Radar Manual
    System

TASS
Tech Assembly System
Technical Air Armament Study

TAT
To Accompany Troops (type cargo)
Torpedo-Attack Teacher
True Air Temperature
Turn Around Time

TATC
Tactical Air Traffic Control

TATSA
Transportation Aircraft Test and Support
    Activity

TATTE
Talos Tactical Test Equipment

TAU
Twin Agent Unit

TAV
Tender Availability

TAVE
Thor-Agena Vibration Experiment

TAW
Thrust-Augmented Wing (concept)

TAWC
Tactical Air Warfare Center

TB
Technical Bulletin
Torpedo Boat
Torpedo-Bombing
True Bearing
Tub

TBA
Table of Basic Allowances
To Be Activated (or Attacked, or Announced)

TBD
 To Be Determined
 Target Bearing Designator
TBFU
 Shipboard Twin-Ball Fire Fighting Unit
TBH
 Test Bed (or Bench) Harness
TBI
 Test Bed Installation
 To Be Inactivated
TBL
 Through Bill of Lading
TBN
 To Be Nominated (or Named)
TBO
 Time Between Overhaul
TBS
 Talk Between Ships
 Training Battle Simulation
TBT
 Target Bearing Transmitter (system)
TBX
 Tactical Ballistic Experimental
TC
 Temperature and Compression (metal
   bonding)
 Time Charter (or Check)
 Total Cost
 Training Center
 Transportation (or Transceiver) Code
 Trial Counsel
 True Course
 Turret Captain
TC, TRACEN
 Training Center
T/C
 Technical Control
 Thermocouple
TCA
 Tender-Controlled Approach
 Terminal Control Area
 Track Crossing Angle
TCARC
 Tropical Cyclone Aircraft Reconnaissance
   Coordinator
TCBM
 Transcontinental Ballistic Missile
TCC
 Telecommunications Center
 Time Compression Coding
 Tracking and Control Center
 Transportation Control Committee
 Travel Classification Code
TCD
 Tentative Classification of Defects
 Tour Completion Date
TCDAF
 Tenant Command Disciplinary Action File
TCF
 Tactical Control Facility

TCG
 Transverse Center of Gravity
TCMC
 Transportation Control and Movement Center
TCMD
 Transportation Control and Movement
   Document
TCMG
 Transportable Countermeasures Group
TCN
 Transportation Control Number
TCO
 Technical (or Termination) Contracting Officer
 Telecommunications Certification Office
TCP
 Total Contract Proposal
 Trainer Change Proposal
 Training and Certification Program
TCS
 Target Control (or Cost) System
TCSP
 Tactical Communications Satellite Program
TCSS
 Tactical Control Surveillance System
TCTO
 Time Compliance Technical Order
TCU
 Tape (or Torpedo) Control Unit
 Towering Cumulus (cloud formation)
TD
 Target Discrimination (or Drone)
 Technical Directive
 Test Diagram
 Testing Device
 Touchdown (of aircraft)
 Transmitter/Distributor
 Trimming and Drainage (system)
 Tropical Depression
TD, TDY, TEMDU
 Temporary Duty
T/D
 Temperature Datum
TDA
 Today
 Transcript Deserter's Account
TDAS
 Tracking and Data Acquisition System
TDBD
 Top Down Break Down
TDC
 Taiwan Defense Command
 Technical Directive Compliance
 Through-Deck Cruiser
 Top Dead Center
 Torpedo Firing Data Computer
T&DC, T&DCEN
 Training and Distribution Center
T&DCEN, T&DC
 Training and Distribution Center
TDCF
 Technical Directive Compliance Form

TDCO
  Torpedo Data Computer Center
TDD
  Target-Detecting (or Detection) Device
  Technical Documents Department
  Test and Development Director (PERA)
TDDL
  Time-Division Data Link
TDH
  Total Discharge Head (pumps)
TDI
  Target Data Inventory
TDM
  Telemetric Data Monitor
  Test Development Manager
  Time Division Multiplex(ing)
  Torpedo Detection Modification (sonar)
TDMP
  Test Development Management Plan
TDMS
  Telegraph Distortion Measuring System
TDN
  Travel directed is necessary
TDO
  Technical Data Office
  Technical Development Objectives
  Technical Directives Ordnance
TDOC
  Technical Document
TDP
  Technical Data Package
  Technical Development Plan
  Temporary Detention of Pay
TDR
  Talos Discrepancy Report
  Torque Differential Receiver
TDRL
  Temporary Disability Retired List
TDRS
  Travelers, Defect Route Sheet
TDS
  Tactical Data System
  Target Designation System
  Total Dissolved Solids
  Training Duty Status
  Translation and Docking Simulator
TDSA
  Technical Directive Status Accounting
TDSO
  Training Device Supply Office
TDT
  Target Designation Transmitter
TDTG
  True Date-Time-Group
TDU
  Target Device Unit
  Trash Disposal Unit
  Traverse Displacement Unit
TDX
  Torque Differential Transmitter

TDY, TD, TEMDU
  Temporary Duty
TDZ
  Touchdown Zone
TDZ/CL
  Touchdown Zone/Centerline (light system)
TDZL
  Touchdown Zone Light (system)
TE
  Task Element
  Test (or Type) Equipment
  Trailing Edge
  Turbo-Electric
  Twin-Engine
T&E
  Test and Evaluation
TEA
  Task Equipment Analysis
TEAM
  Tube Earphone and Microphone
TEAMS
  Test, Evaluation and Monitoring System
TEASE
  Tracking Errors and Simulation Evaluation
TEC
  TOS Evaluation Center
  Type Equipment Code
TECG
  Test and Evaluation Coordinating Group
TECH
  Tactical Exercise Control
  Technical
  Technician
  Technology
TECHAD
  Technical Advisor
TECHAUTHIND
  Technical Paper/Author Cross-Index System
TECHEVAL
  Technical Evaluation
TECHMAN, TM
  Technical Manual
TECHNOTE
  Technical Note (or Notice)
TECHREP
  Technical Representative
TECHTRA
  Technical Training
TED
  Terminal Eligibility Date
  Thermo-Electric Drive
  Training Equipment Development
TEDS
  Turbine-Electric Drive Submarine
TEL
  Transporter-Erector-Launcher
TEL, TELEG
  Telegram
TEL, FONE, PHONE, TP
  Telephone

TELCOM
Telephone Communications
TELCON, FONECON
Telephone Conversation
TELECON
Teletype Conversation
TELEG, TG
Telegraph
TELEG, TEL
Telegram
TELEM
Telemetry
TELEM ANT
Telemetry Antenna
TELERAN
Television and Radar Navigation
TEM, TEMP, TMPRY
Temporary
TEMAC
Temporary active duty
TEMACDIFOT
Temporary active duty in a flying status
involving operational or training flights
TEMACDIFOTINS
Temporary active duty under instruction in a
flying status involving operational or
training flights
TEMACINS
Temporary active duty under instruction
TEMADD, TAD
Temporary additional duty
TEMADDCON
Temporary additional duty in connection with
TEMADDINS
Temporary additional duty under instruction
TEM-CAS
Temporary-Casualty (pay record)
TEMCON
Temporary duty connection
TEMDIFDEN
Temporary duty in a flying status not
involving flying
TEMDIFINSDEN
Temporary duty under instruction in a flying
status not involving flying
TEMDIFINSOPS
Temporary duty under instruction in a flying
status involving operational or training
flights
TEMDIFINSPRO
Temporary duty under instruction in a flying
status involving proficiency flying
TEMDIFOPS
Temporary duty in a flying status involving
operational or training flights
TEMDIFOTINS
Temporary duty under instructions in a flying
status involving operational or training
flights

TEMDIFPRO
Temporary duty in a flying status involving
proficiency flying
TEMDU, TD, TDY
Temporary duty
TEMDUCON
Temporary duty in connection with
TEMDU DIS
Temporary duty pending disciplinary action
TEMDU FFA
Temporary duty for further assignment
TEMDU FFT
Temporary duty for further transfer
TEMDU PAT
Temporary duty as a patient
TEMDU PSI
Temporary duty-programmed student input
TEMDU SEP
Temporary duty pending separation
TEMFLY
Temporary duty involving flying
TEMFLYINS
Temporary duty involving flying under
instruction
TEM-GEN
Temporary-General (pay record)
TEMINS, TEMDUINS
Temporary duty under instruction
TEMP
Tactical Electromagnetic Program
Test and Evaluation Master Plan
Transportable Electromagnetic Pulse
TEMP, TEM, TMPRY
Temporary
TEMPATT
Temporarily attached
TEMPDETD
Temporary detached duty
TEMPLINACT
Temporary duty pending disciplinary action
TEMPLINEAR
Temporary duty pending disciplinary hearing
TEMPROX
Temporary duty will cover approximately
_____ days
TEMPT
Test Equipment, Materials, Parts and Tools
TEM-RET
Temporary pay record for a retired member
called to active duty
TEMSEPRAD
Temporary duty in connection with separation
processing. Upon completion and when
directed, detached; proceed home for
release from active duty according to
instructions
TEMWAIT
Temporary duty awaiting
TENOC
Ten-Year Oceanographic Research Program

TEP
TAR Enlisted Program
Temperature Extreme Pressure (oil)
Torpedo Ejection Pump
Transportable Equation Program
TER
Terrain
Triple Ejector Rack
TER, TERR
Territory
TERCOM
Terrain Comparison
Terrain Contour-Matching (system)
TERCON
Terrain Contour
TERI
Torpedo Effective-Range Indicator
TERM
Terminate, (-ation)
TERM, TRML
Terminal
TERMINACTRAORD
If serving under orders authorizing
participation in Naval Reserve Training
Program in pay or non-pay status, directed
to request termination of inactive duty
training orders, via appropriate chain of
command, to be effective not later than day
preceding date of reporting active duty
compliance these orders
TERPACIS, TTPI
Trust Territory of the Pacific Islands
TERPS
Terminal Instrument Procedures
TERR, TER
Territory
TES
Test and Evaluation Ship (program)
TESE
Tactical Exercise Simulator and Evaluator
TESS
Tactical Environmental Support System
TEU
Technical Edit Unit
TEV
Turbo-Electric Drive
TEW
Tactical Electronic Warfare
TEWA
Threat Evacuation and Weapons Assignment
TEWDS
Tactical Electronic Warfare Decoy System
TEWS
Tactical Electronic Warfare Systems
TEXGRP
Texas Group
TEXT
Textural File (NARDIS)

TF
Task Force
Terrain-Following (radar)
Turbofan (engine)
TFBR
Technical Feedback Report
TFC
Task Force Commander
TFCC
Tactical Flag (or Force) Command Center
TFG
Tactical Fighter Group
Terminal Facilities Guides
TFO
Temporary Flight Orders
TFP
Temporary Forfeiture of Pay
TFR
Terrain-Following Radar
Trouble and Failure Report
TFS
Torpedo Firing System
TFWC
Tactical Fighter Weapons Center
TFX
Tactical Fighter Experimental
TFZ
Traffic Zone
TG
Task Group
Trunk Group
Turbo-Generator
TG, TELEG
Telegraph
TGA
Thermogravimeter Analysis
TGBL
Through Government Bill of Lading
TGL
Touch-and-Go Landing
TGM
Training Guided Missile
TGSM
Terminally-Guided Sub-Missile
TGT, TAR
Target
TGU
Technical Guidance Unit
TH
Telemetry Head
True Heading
T&H
Test and Handling (equipment)
THA
Total Hydrocarbon Analyzer
T-HA
Terminal Height Altitude
THAFE
Thousand Hours Accident Free Each
THAWS
Target Homing and Warning System

THC
True Heading Computer
THD
Thunderhead
Total Harmonic Distortion
THDR
Thunder
THERM
Thermometer
THES
Thesarus File (NARDIS)
THI
Temperature-Humidity Index
Time Handed In
THIR
Temperature/Humidity Infrared Radiometer
THK
Thick
THOU, THSD
Thousand
THP
Thrust Horsepower
THR
Turbine Heat Rate
THREE-M, 3M
(See SNMMMS)
THRFTR
Thereafter
THRU
Through
THRUT
Throughout
THS
Test History Summary
Thermal Stress
THSD, THOU
Thousand
THS-EXPER
Thermal-Stress Experiment
THTN
Threaten
THV
Threshold Limit Value
TI
Test Instrumentation (or Initiate)
Tin (U/I)
Training Instructor
TIARA
Target Identification and Recovery Aid
TIAS
Target Investigation and Acquisition Study
TIB
Technical Intelligence Brief
TIC
Target Indication Sight
Technical Information (or Intelligence) Center
Troops in Contact
TICCIT
Time-Shared Computer-Controlled
Instructional Television

TICO
Technical Information Contact Officer
TID
Tactical Information Display
TIDB
Technical Information Data Base
TIDOS
Table and Item Documentation System
TIES
Transmission and Information Exchange
System
TIF
True Involute Form (gear teeth)
TIFS
Total In-Flight Simulator (or Simulation)
TIG
Tungsten Inert Gas
TIIF
Tactical Imagery Interpretation Facility
TIL
Until
TIM
Traffic Improvement Memorandum
TIMATION
Time Navigation (satellite)
TIMI
Technical Information Maintenance
Instructions
TIMM
Thermonic Integrated Micro-Module
TINSY
Treasure Island Naval Shipyard
TIO
Target Indication Officer
TIP
Technical Information Program
Technical Improvement Plan
Total Information Package
Track Initiation and Prediction
Turn in a Pusher (program)
TIPS
Technical Information Procedures
Telemetry Impact-Prediction System
Training Improvement Proposal System
(USNR)
TIPSY
Task Input Parameter Synthesizer
TIR
Target-Indicating Room
Technical Information Release
Time in Rate
Total Indicator Reading
Transaction Item Report(ing)
TIREC
TIROS Ice Reconnaissance
TIROS
Television and Infrared Observation Satellite
TIROS-M
Television and Infrared Observation
Satellite-Meteorological (purposes)

TIRS
Tactical Intercept and Recognition System
TIR/SLIT
Transaction Item Reporting/Serial Lot Item Tracking (activities)
TIS
Target Information Section
Technical Intelligence Section
Thermal Imaging System
Time in Service
Tracking and Injection Station
TISEO
Target Identification System Electro-Optical
TIT
Turbine Inlet Temperature
TIU
Tape Identification Unit
TJS
Tactical Jamming System
TK
Tank
TKBN
Tank Battalion
TKIBU
Transmission-Keying Indicator Buffer
TKOF, TO, T/OFF, T/O
Take-Off
TKR
(Telephone) Talker
TL
Tieline
Trial
Turn Left
T/L
Training Literature
TLA
Temporary Lodging Allowance
Transition Layer
T-LA
Terminal Low Altitude (FLIP)
TLC
Thin-Layer Chromatography
TLD
Technical Logistics Data
Thermal Luminescent Dosimeter
TLDIC
Technical Logistics Data and Information Program
TLDP
Technical Logistics Data Program
TLI
Tank Level Indicator
TLL
Tender Load List
TLO
Topic Learning Objective
Training Liaison Officer
TLP
Total Loss of Pay

TLQ
Temporary Lodging Quarters
Tender Load Quantities
TLR
Tap Lower Relay
Top-Level Requirement
Trailer
Triangulation-Listening-Ranging (sonar)
TLT
Transportation Link Terminal
TLU
Threshold Logic Usage
TLV
Threshold Limit Value
Transition Level
TM
Tactical Missile
Team
Telemetering
Tone Modulation
Training (or Technical) Manual
Type Maintenance
TM1
Torpedoman's Mate First Class
TM2
Torpedoman's Mate Second Class
TM3
Torpedoman's Mate Third Class
TM, TECHMAN
Technical Manual
T/M
Torque Meter
TMA
Target Motion Analysis
Technical Manual Analysis
TMC
Chief Torpedoman's Mate
Transportation Material Command
T&MC
Test and Monitor Console
TMCM
Master Chief Torpedoman's Mate
TMCR
Technical Manual Contact Requirements
TMCS
Senior Chief Torpedoman's Mate
TMDE
Test, Measuring and Diagnostic Equipment
TMDL
Technical Manual Data List
TME
Time Entry (NNSS)
Trainee Management Element
TM&E
Test, Measuring and Equipment
TMFA
Torpedoman's Mate Fireman Apprentice
TMFN
Torpedoman's Mate Fireman
TMG
Track Made Good

TMI
Technical Manual Index
TMINS
Technical Manual Identification and
Numbering System (NAVELEX)
TML
Terminal
TMMIS
Technical Manual Management Information
System
TMO
Total Material Objective
Traffic Management Office
TMP
Total Material Package
Transitional Manpower Program
TMP, TEMP
Temperature
TMPO
Total Material Procurement Objective
TMPRLY
Temporarily
TMPRY, TEM, TEMP
Temporary
TMQAP
Technical Manual Quality Assurance Plan
TMRBM
Tactical Medium-Range Ballistic Missile
TMRP
Target Motion Resolution Processing
Technical Manual Revision Program
TMS
Time and Motion Study
TMS, TRANSMGTSCOL
Transportation Management School
T/M/S
Type/Model/Series
TMSA
Total Military Service for Advancement
TMU
Tabulating Machine Unit
Trainee Management Unit
Transit Monitoring Unit
TMW
Tomorrow
TNCL
Tail Number Configuration List
TNDCY
Tendency
TNG, TRA
Training
TNGT
Tonight
TNO
Thermonuclear
TNPO
Terminal Navy Post Office
TNPQ
Temporarily Not Physically Qualified
TNR
Trainer

TNTV
Tentative
TNW
Theater Nuclear Warfare
TO
Table of Organization
Tactical Observer
Technical Order
Transportation Officer
Troy Ounce (U/I)
TO, T/O, TKOFF, T/OFF
Take-Off
T/O
Tactical Organization
Travel Orders
TOA
Tanker Operations Assistant (MSTS)
Time of Arrival
Total Obligational Authority
TOB
Tanker Operations Branch (MSTS)
Transistor Output Buffer (or Board)
TOBEDI
(Vessel) to be Disposed of
TOBELE
(Vessel) to be Leased
TOBELN
(Vessel) to be Loaned
TOC
Tactical (or Troop) Operations Center
Tanker Operational Circulate
Total Organic Carbon
TOD
Time of Delivery
Torpedo Operations Department (NTS)
TODE
Transcript of Data Extraction
TO&E
Tables of Organization and Equipment
TOES
Trade-Off Evaluation System
TOF
Test Overflow (NNSS)
Time of File (or Fall)
TOFC
Trailer on Flat Car (shipping)
T/OFF, TKOFF, TO, T/O
Take-Off
TOGW
Take-Off Gross Weight (of missile)
TOJ
Track-On Jamming
TOO
Time or Origin
TOPLINE
Total Officer Personnel Objective Structure
for the Line Officer Force
TOPO ENGR
Topographical Engineer
TOPOPLT
Topographic Platoon

TOPS
The Operational PERT System
TOPSEC, TS
Top Secret
TOR
Technical Override
Time of Receipt
TORP
Torpedo
TORPEX
Torpedo Exercise
TOS
Tactical Operations System
TIROS Operational Satellite
TOSD
Training and Operations Support Department
TOSS
Tape-Oriented Supply System
TIROS Operational Satellite System
Total Operational Submarine Service
TOST
Technical Objectives and Selection Team
TOT
Time of Transmission (or Tape, or Target)
Total
Transportation of Things
Turbine Outlet Temperature
TOTO
Tongue of the Ocean (site of AUTEC)
TOVC
Top of Overcast
TOW
Take-Off Weight
Tube-Launched, Optically-Tracked,
Wire-Command (link guided missile)
TP
Target Practice
Technical Publication
Test Procedures
Transport Pack
Turning Point
TP, FONE, PHONE, TEL
Telephone
TPA
Test Program Analyzer
Test Project Agreement
Transfer of Pay Account
Travel via privately-owned conveyance
authorized
TPB
Technical Processes Branch (ESIC)
TPC
Tactical Pilotage Chart
Total Price Contract
Training Plans Conference
Transport Plane Commander
TPD
Test Point Data
Training Publications Division

TPDRS
Time-Phased Downgrading and
Reclassification System
TPFDL
Time Phased Force and Development List
TPFDD
Time-Phased Force Development Data
TPI
Target Position Indicator
Technical Proficiency Inspection
Tons per Inch
TPL
Technical Publications Library
TPM
Technical Performance Measurement (or
Milestone)
TPMP
Technical Performance Measurement Plan
TP&MS
Turbo Power and Marine Systems
TPO
Tentative Program Objectives
TP&O
Test Plan and Outline
TPP
Total Package Procurement
TP&P
Transients, Patients and Prisoners
TPPD
Technical Program Planning Document
TPR
Tool Performance Report
TPS
Test Pilot School
Test Program Set
Text Processing System
Threat Platform Simulator
TPT
Tail Pipe Temperature
TPTRL
Time-Phased Transportation Requirements
List
TPU
Transient Personnel Unit
TQE
Technical Quality Evaluation
TR
Timing Relay
Torque Receiver
Translation
Transpose
Travel Request
Tray (U/I)
Turn Right
TR, T/R
Transportation Request
T/R
Transmit(ter) Receive(r)
Type of Record (code)

TRA
Transfer
Tri-Annually (report frequency)
TRA, TNG
Training
TRAC
Tracer
Tractor
TRACALS
Traffic Control and Landing System
TRACE
Taxiing and Routing of Aircraft Coordinating
Equipment
Transportable Automatic Control Environment
(system)
TRACER
Turnaround Time, Repair Survival Rate and
Cost Evaluation Report
TRACOMD
Training Command
TRACOMDLANT
Training Command, Atlantic
TRACOMDPAC
Training Command, Pacific
TRACOMDSUBPAC
Training Command, Submarines, Pacific
TRACOMDWESTCOAST
Training Command, West Coast
TRACON
Terminal Approach Control
TRAD
Training Administration
TRADAR
Transaction Data Recorder
TRADEC
Training Device Computer
TRADET
Training Detachment
TRADEX
Target Resolution and Discrimination
Experiment
Tracking Radar, Experimental
TRADIX
Transistor-Digital Computer
TRAFAC
Training Facility
TRAFOLPERS
Transfer the following enlisted personnel
TRAIF
Torso Restraint Assembly with Integrated
Flotation
TRAINMAN
Training Management
TRALANT
Training Force, Atlantic
TRAM
Target Ranging and Acquisition Multisensor
Target Recognition Attack Multisensor
Test Reliability and Maintainability
TRAMP
Test Retrieval and Memory Print

TRAMPS
Temperature Regulator and Missile Power
Supply
TRAN
Transient
TRANET
Tracking Network
TRANS
Transport(ation)
TRANSAC
Transistor Automatic Computer
TRANS/DEP
Transportation of Dependents
TRANSDIV
Transportation Division
TRANSDIR
Travel via government aircraft directed
outside CONUS where available, otherwise
commercial aircraft is directed
TRANSEC
Transmission Security
TRANSFER
Transportation Simulation for Estimating
Requirements
TRANSIM
Transportation Simulator
TRANSLANT
Transports, Atlantic
TRANSMAN
Enlisted Transfer Manual
TRANSMGTSCOL, TMS
Transportation Management School
TRANSMONUNIT
Transient Monitoring Unit
TRANSITPERSU
Transient Personnel Unit
TRANSRON
Transportation Squadron
TRANSTEC
Sonar Transducer Test and Evaluation
Center (NEL)
TRAP
Terminal Radiation Program
Transit, Receive and Plot
TRAPAC
Training Force, Pacific
TRAPS
Training Requirements and Planning
Subsystem
TRARON, VT
Training Squadron
TRASTA, TS
Training Station
TRAT
Torpedo Readiness Assistance Team
TRAU, TU
Training Unit
TRAV, TVL
Travel

TRAVCHAR
Cost of travel chargeable (appropriation or department designated in following group(s). Identifying numerals may be added).

TRAVNEC
Subject travel was necessary at this time, and the length of time consumed in administrative channels prevented written orders from being issued prior to departure.

TRAWL
Tape Read and Write Library

TRB
Temperature Resistant Buff
Torpedo Retriever Boat

TRBR
Transportation Branch

TRC
Transmission Release Code

TRCCC
Tracking Radar Center Control Console

TRCVR
Transceiver

TRDTO
Tracking Radar Data Take-Off

TRE
Temperature Resistant Element
Training Readiness Evaluation

TRF
Technical Replacement Factor
Transfer
Tuned Radio Frequency

TR/FLRES
Transferred to Fleet Reserve

TRI
Test Requirement Identification

TRIA
Telemetry Range Instrumented Aircraft

TRICCSMA
Trident Command and Control Systems Maintenance Facility

TRICE
Transistorized Real-Time Incremental Computer

TRIM
Test Rules for Inventory Management
Trail Road Interdiction Mission (project)
Training Records and Information Management System
Training Requirements and Information Management

TRIMIS
Tri-Service Medical Information System

TRIP
Tartar Reliability Improvement Plan

TRIPER
Trident Planned Equipment Replacement

TRIREFFAC
Trident Refit Facility

TRIS
Transmit-Receive Image System

TRI-TAC
Joint Tactical Communications

TRITRAFAC
Trident Training Facility

TRK
Track
Truck
Trunk

TRL
Time Recovery Loop (NNSS)

TRLFSW
Tactical Range Landing Force Support Weapons

TRLP
Transport Landplane

TRM
Time Release Mechanism (ejector seat)

TRML, TERM
Terminal

TRN
Train

TRNG, TRA
Training

T&RNP
Transportation and Recruiting, Naval Personnel

TRNS
Transition

TRO
Test Requirements Outline

TRODI
Touchdown Rate of Descent Indicator

TROF
Trough

TROP
Tropical
Tropics

TRP
Troop

TRRN
Terrain

TRS
Technical Repair Standard
Transversing Rake System

TRSA
Terminal Radar Service Area

TRSP
Transport Seaplane

TRSR
Taxi and Runway Surveillance Radar

TRSSGM
Tactical Range Surface-to-Surface Guided Missile

TRSSM
Tactical Range Surface-to-Surface Missile

TRUMP
Target Radiation Unit Measurement Program
Threat Reaction Upgrade Modernization Program

TS
Tank Scope
Temperature Switch
Test Set (or Station, or Squadron)
Time Shack
"Tough Situation" (slang)
Transmitting Station
Tropical Storm
Tube Size
TS, TOPSEC
Top Secret
T-S
Temperature-Salinity (of water)
Terminal Seaplane (ELIP)
Time-Sharing
TSAF
Typical Systems Acquisition Flow
TSAM
Test Set Antenna Maintenance
Trainer, Surface-to-Air Missile
Trident Support Activities, Mechanicsburg
(PA)
TSAPG
Telecommunications Systems Architecture
Planning Group
TSC
Tactical Support Center
Tandem Switching Center
Transportable Satellite Communications
(terminal)
Transmitter Start Code
TSCC
Top-Secret Control Channel
TSCM
Technical Surveillance Countermeasures
TSCO
Top-Secret Control Officers
TSCP
Top-Secret Control Procedures
TSCS
Top-Secret Control Section
TSD
Tactical Situation Display
Technical Support Division
Toured Sea Duty
TSF
Training Summary File
TSFC
Tactical Support Functional Component
TSG
Technical Specialty Group
TSGM
Terminally-Guided Submersible
TSHWR
Thundershower
TSI
Technical Standardization Inspection
TSL
Tri-Service Laser
Troop Safety Line

TSMC
Technical Supply Management Code
TSN
Time Since New
TSO
TACAMO Systems Operator
Test-Site Office
Time Since Overhaul
TSOR
Tentative Specific Operational (or Operating)
Requirement
TSOS
Time-Sharing Operational Requirement
TSO-T
TACAMO Systems Operator in Training
TSP
Teleprocessing Services Program
Tri-Sodium Phosphate (pipe cleaner)
TSPR
Total System Performance Responsibility
TSR
Telecommunications Service Request
TSRI
Technical Skill Reenlistment Incentive
TSS
Telecommunications Switching System
Thrust-Sensitive Signal
Time-Sharing Supervisor
TSSC
Target Systems Service Change
TSTD
Total Ship Test Director
TSTM, T
Thunderstorm
TSTP
Total Ship Test Program
TSTP/AFS
Total Ship Test Program for Active Fleet
Ships
TT
Tablet (U/I)
Target Towing (aircraft)
Test and Trials
Trust Territory of the Pacific Islands—see
TTPI, TERPACIS
TT, TTY
Teletypewriter
TTA
Trials Test Assurance
TTAB
Technical Training Acceptance Board
TTAT
Torpedo Tube Acceptance Trials
TTC
Transportable Telephone Communications
TTCP
The Technical Cooperation Plan
TTE
Technical Training Equipment
TTEE
Transfer of Training Effectiveness Evaluation

TTF
Training Task Force
TTI
Time to Intercept
TTL
Transistor-Transistor Logic
TTM
Tactical Target Material
Two-Tone Modulation
TTPI
Torpedo Technical Proficiency Inspection
TTPI, TERPACIS
Trust Territory of the Pacific Islands—see also TT
TTR
Tactical Target Record
Target Track Radar
Time-Temperature Recorder
TTS
Temperature Test Station
Temporary Threshold Shift
Test and Training Satellite
Transitional Training School
TTSA
Transitional Training School, Atlantic
TTSP
Transitional Training School, Pacific
TTSU
Trunion Tile and Angle of Sight Unit
TTT
Time to Turn
Time, Transformation, Temperature (diagram)
TTTT
Tartar-Talos-Terrier-Typhon
TTY-TT
Teletypewriter
TU
Task (or Thermal) Unit
Thank You
Tube (U/I)
TU, TRAU
Training Unit
TUPC
Transfer Underwater Pressure Chamber
TURB
Turbine
TURBC
Turbulence
TURPS
Terrestrial Unattended Reactor Power System
TUSLOG
Turkish-United States Logistics Group
TUSLOGDET
Turkish-United States Logistics Group Detachment
TVC
Thrust Vector Control
TVDS
Television Distribution System

TVG
Temperature-Voltage-Gases
Time Variation of Gain
TVIG
Television Inertial Guidance
TVIS
Turbine Vibration Indicator System
TVL, TRAV
Travel
TVP
Tri-Vertiplane
TVT
Television Translator
TV TR
Television Tower
TVX
Target Vehicle, Experimental
TW
Tele-Weekly (AFRTS code)
T/W
Thrust/Weight (ratio)
TWA
Time-Weighted Average
TWAES
Tactical Warfare Analysis and Evaluation System
TWAH
This Week at Headquarters (NAVSHIPS publication)
TWD
Toward
TWEB
Transcribed Weather Broadcasts
TWIX, TWX
Teletypewriter Exchange
TWK
Total Work Content
TWLT
Twilight
TWPL
Teletypewriter, Private Lines
TWR
Torpedo Weapons Receiver
Tower
Transceiver
TWS
Track While Scanning
TWT
Telephone-Teletypewriter Exchange
Traveling Wave Tube
Two-Week Training (USNR)
TWX, TWIX
Teletypewriter Exchange
TWY
Taxiway
TX
Torque Transmitter
TYCOM
Type Commander
TYCOMSLANT
Type Commands, Atlantic

TYCOMSPAC
  Type Commands, Pacific
TYDAC
  Typical Digital Automatic Computer
TYT
  Type Training
TZ
  Time Zone

U

U
  Union (joint)
U, UN
  Unit
UA
  Unauthorized Absentee
U/A
  Units per Application
UAB
  Until Advised by
UACC
  Upper Air Control Center
UACTE
  Universal Automatic Checkout Control and
    Test Equipment
UADPS
  Uniform Automatic Data Processing System
UADPS-ICP
  Uniform Automatic Data Processing System
    for Inventory Control Point
UADPS-INAS
  Uniform Automatic Data Processing System
    for Industrial Naval Air Station
UADPS-SP
  Uniform Automatic Data Processing System
    for Stock Points
UAG
  Upper Atmosphere Geophysics
UALI
  Universal Automatic Laser Interferometer
UAM
  Underwater-to-Air Missile
UAN
  Unidentified Atmospheric Noise
UAP
  Utility Amphibious Plane
UAR
  Upper Air Route
UBFC
  Underwater Battery Fire Control
UBITRON
  Undulating Beam Interaction Electron (tube)
UB/MS
  Utility Boat, Minesweeper
UBST
  Unbonded Spool Type

UC
  UCA Summary Account Code
  Under Construction
  Unit Cost
U/C, UNCLAS
  Unclassified
UCA
  Uniform Chart of Accounts
UCCS
  Universal Camera Control System
UCL
  Upper Control Limit
UCLAR
  Rocket Launcher Control Unit
UCLS
  Underwater Crash Locator System
UCMJ
  Uniform Code of Military Justice
UCO
  Universal Weather Landing Code
UCT
  Underwater Construction Team
UD
  Undesirable Discharge
  Unit Diary
U/D
  Upper Deck
UDATS
  Underwater Damage Assessment Television
    System
UDCA
  Undesirable Discharge, Trial by Civil
    Authorities
UDDE
  Undesirable Discharge, Desertion Without
    Trial
UDFE
  Undesirable Discharge, Fraudulent Enlistment
UDL
  Urine Disposal Lock
UDM
  Unassigned Direct Material
UDMU
  Universal Decoder Memory Unit
UDOFIT
  Universal Digital Operational Flight Trainer
    Tool
UDR
  Urgent Data Request (or Requirement)
UDT
  Underwater Demolition Team
UDTPHIBSPAC
  Underwater Demolition Team, Amphibious
    Forces, Pacific
UDU
  Underwater Demolition Unit
UDUF
  Undesirable Discharge, Unfitness
UEG
  Unit Expansion Group

UEL
Upper Explosion Limit
UEPH
Unaccompanied Enlisted Personnel Housing
UER
Unsatisfactory Equipment Report
UERT
Universal Engineer Tractor, Rubber-Tired
UETA
Universal Engineer Tractor, Armored
UF
Under Frequency (controller)
UFA
Until Further Advised
UFCG
Underwater Fire Control Group
UFCS
Underwater Fire Control System
UFN
Until Further Notice
UFO
Unidentified Flying Object
UFOP
Ultra-Fast-Opening Parachute
UFSS
Unmanned Free Swimming Submersibles
UFU
Utility Flight Unit
UG
Undergoing
UHF
Ultra-High Frequency
UHS
Unit Handling System
UHT
Unit Horizontal Tail
UI
Under Instruction
U/I
Unit of Issue
U/I, UNIDENT
Unidentified
UIC
Unit Identification Code
UICP
UADPS for Inventory Control Points
Uniform Inventory Control Point (system)
UIEV
Universal Imagery Exploitation Viewer
UIR
Upper Flight Information Region
UKN
Unknown
UL
Upper Level
ULCC
Ultra-Large Crude Carrier (ship)
ULMS
Undersea Long-Range Missile Submarine
Underwater Long-Range Missile System

ULO
Unrestricted Line Officer
ULP
Utility Landplane
ULTSIGN
Ultimate Assignment
UM
Underwater Mechanic
UMA
United Maritime Authority
UMBR
Universal Multiple Bomb Rack
UMC
Unspecified Minor Construction (program)
UMIPS
Uniform Material Issue Priority System
UMM
Universal Mission Module
UMMIPS
Uniform Material Movement and Issue Priority
System
Uniform Military Material Issue Priority
System
UMMMIPS
Uniform Military Material Movement and Issue
Priority System
UMPAR
Unit Mobilization Personnel Assignment
Report
UMRS
Unsatisfactory Material Reporting
UMT
Universal Military Training
UN, U
Unit
UNA
Use No Abbreviations
UNAMACE
Universal Automatic Map Compilation
Equipment
UNASGN
Unassigned
UNAUTH, UNAUTHD
Unauthorized
UNAUTHD, UNAUTH
Unauthorized
UNB
Universal Navigation Beacon
UNCLAS, U/C
Unclassified
UND
Urgency-of-Need Designator
UNDELORDCAN
Undelivered orders (identified by date or
message reference numbers following)
cancelled
UNFAV
Unfavorable
UNFTP
Unified Navy Field
Test Program

UNIDENT, U/I
Unidentified
UNIF
Uniform(ity)
UNITAS
United International Antisubmarine Warfare (exercise)
UNITOPOS
Unit to which ordered will operate in an overseas area a contemplated continuous period of 1 year or more
UNITREPS
Unit Reports
UNIV
Universal
UNK, UNKN
Unknown
UNL, UNLTD
Unlimited
UNLGTD
Unlighted
UNLOD
Unload
UNLTD, UNL
Unlighted
UNODIR
Unless otherwise directed
UNORCAN
Unexecuted portion of orders (identified by date or message reference numbers following) cancelled
UNQUAL
Unqualified
UNREL
Unreliable
UNREP
Underway Replenishment
UNRSTD
Unrestricted
UNSAT
Unsatisfactory
UNSECNAV
Under Secretary of the Navy
UNSTBL
Unstable
UNSTDY
Unsteady
UNSVC, US, U/S
Unserviceable
UNT
Undergraduate Navigator Training
UNW
Underway
UOPH
Unaccompanied Officer Personnel Housing
U/P
Unit Price
UPA
Unauthorized Precedence Announcement

UPDATE
Universal Prefabricated Depot Automatic Test Equipment
UPH
Unaccompanied Personnel Housing
UPIR
Uniform Photo Interpretation Report
UPK
Upkeep
UPLR
Unplanned Loss Report
UPP
Upper
UPS
Uninterruptible Power System
Universal Polar Stereographic (grid)
UPSTART
Universal Parachute Support Tactical and Research Target
UPT
Undergraduate Pilot Training (program)
UPWARD
Understanding Personal Worth and Racial Dignity
UR
Unsatisfactory Report
Your
URACTY
Your Activity
URAD
Your Radio
URDIS
Your Dispatch
UREST
Universal Range, Endurance, Speed and Time
URFO
Universal Radio Frequency Oscillator
URG
Universal Radio Group
Urgent
URG, URGP
Underway Replenishment Group
URGP, URG
Underway Replenishment Group
URI
Unexpected Real Incapacitation
URL
Unrestricted Line (officer)
URLTR
Your Letter
URMGM
Your Mailgram
URMSG
Your Message
URO
Unrestricted Operation (overhaul)
Unrestricted Operations
URSER
Your Serial

URSPDLTR
Your Speedletter
URTEL
Your Telegram
URV
Undersea Research Vehicle
US
"Uncle Sam"
United States
US, UNSVC, U/S
Unserviceable
USA
United States of America
USADO
United States Defense Attaché Office
USADP
Uniform Shipboard Automatic Data
Processing
USAG
Underwater Sound Advisory Group
USARP
United States Antarctic Research Program
USB
United States Band
Upper Sideband
USBATU
United States-Brazil Aviation Training Unit
USBER
United States Mission, Berlin
USBS
Unified S-Band System
USC
United States Citizen
United States Code
USCG
United States Coast Guard
USCINCMEAFSA
United States Commander-in-Chief, Middle
East, South Asia and Africa South of the
Sahara
USCINCSO
United States Commander-in-Chief, Southern
Command
USCMA
United States Court of Military Appeals
USCOMEASTLANT
United States Commander, Eastern Atlantic
USCOMEASTLANT ERS
United States Commander, Eastern Atlantic,
Emergency Relocation Site Commander
USCOMSOLANT
United States Commander South Atlantic
Force
USCOMSUBGRUEASTLANT
United States Commander Submarine Group,
Eastern Atlantic
USDAO
United States Defense Attaché Office
USDELMC
United States Delegation to the NATO
Military Committee

USDLG
United States Defense Liaison Group
USDOCO
United States Documents Officer
USDR
United States Defense Representative
USD(R&E)
Under Secretary of Defense (Research and
Engineering)
USEES
United States Naval Engineering
Experimental Station
USELMCENTO
United States Element, Central Treaty
Organization
USER
User Interest File (NARDIS)
USF
United States Fleet
USFORAZ
United States Forces, Azores
USFR, USNFR
United States Naval Fleet Reserve
US/FRG
United States/Federal Republic of Germany
USG
United States Government
USGLI
United States Government Life Insurance
USGPO
United States Government Printing Office
USGRDR
United States Government Research and
Development Report
USGS
United States Geological Survey
United States Geographical Service
USGW
Undersea Guided Weapon
USHBP
Uniformed Services Health Benefit Program
USIC
Undersea Instrumentation Chamber
USIO
Unidentified Submerged Illuminated Object
United States Institute of Oceanography
USL
Underwater Sound Laboratory
USLO
United States Liaison Office(r)
USM
Underwater-to-Surface Missile
USMAC
United States Military Assistance Command
USMC, MC
United States Marine Corps
USMCEB
United States Military Communications
Electronics Board
USMMA
United States Merchant Marine Academy

USMS
United States Maritime Service
USMSOS
United States Maritime Service Officers
USMSTS
United States Maritime Service Training
School
USN, N
United States Navy
USNA, NA
United States Naval Academy
USNAVFORCONAD
United States Naval Forces, Continental Air
Defense Command
USNAVMILCOMUN
United States Navy Representative, Military
Staff Committee United Nations
USNAVMIS, USNM
United States Naval Mission
USNAVREGDENCEN
United States Naval Regional Dental Center
USNAVREGMEDCEN
United States Naval Regional Medical Center
USNAVSO
United States Naval Forces, Southern
Command
USNDD
United States Navy Drydock
USNFR, USFR
United States Naval Fleet Reserve
USNH
United States North of Hatteras
USNH, NH
United States Naval Hospital
USNI
United States Naval Institute
USNIP
United States Naval Institute Proceedings
(magazine)
USNLO
United States Navy Liaison Officer
United States Navy Logistics Office
USNM, USNAVMIS
United States Naval Mission
USNMPS
United States Naval Motion Picture Service
USNMRC
United States Naval Manpower Center
USNMTC
United States Naval Missile Test Center
USNOBSYSUBSTA
United States Naval Observatory, Time
Service Sub-Station
USNOO
United States Naval Oceanographic Office
USNPGS, NAVPGSCOL
United States Naval Postgraduate School
USNPO
United States Navy Project Office
USNR
United States Naval Reserve

USN-R, USN-RET
United States Navy-Retired
USN-RET, USN-R
United States Navy-Retired
USNR-R
United States Naval Reserve-Retired
USNR-S1
United States Naval Reserve-Standby 1
(Mobilization)
USNR-S2
United States Naval Reserve-Standby 2
(Mobilization)
USNRTC
United States Naval Recruit Training Center
USNS
United States Naval Ship (or Station)
USNSA
United States Naval Sailing Association
USNSPO
United States Navy Special Projects Office
USNTI
United States Navy Travel Instructions
USNTPS
United States Naval Test Pilot School
USNUSL
United States Navy Underwater Sound
Laboratory
USN&USMCRC, NAVMARCORESCEN
United States Navy and United States Marine
Corps Reserve Center
USO
United Services Organization
United States Presidential Order
USOM
United States Operations Mission
USP
United States Property
Utility Seaplane
USP&FO
United States Property and Fiscal Office(r)
USPS
Unified Shipbuilding Specifications
USRD
Underwater Sound Reference Division (ONR)
USREPO
United States Navy Reporting Officer
USRL
Underwater Sound Reference Laboratory
USRO
United States Routing Office
USS
United Seamen's Service
United States Ship
USSBS
United States Strategic Bombing Survey
USSDP
Uniformed Services Savings Deposit Program
USSOUTHCOM
United States Southern Command
USSP
United States Special Program

USSPA
Uniformed Services Special Pay Act
USSSO
United States Sending State Office
UST
Universal Subscriber Terminal
USTDC
United States Taiwan Defense Command
USUHS
Uniformed Services University of Health
   Services
USW
Undersea Warfare
USWB
United States Weather Bureau
USWDIV
Undersea Warfare Division
UT
Ultrasonic Test
Underway Trials
Utility Boat (USCG)
UT, UTIL
Utility
UT1
Utilitiesman First Class
UT2
Utilitiesman Second Class
UT3
Utilitiesman Third Class
UTA
Upper Control Area
UTC
Chief Utilitiesman
Unit-Type Code
UTCA
Utilitiesman Construction Apprentice
UTCM
Master Chief Utilitiesman
UTCN
Utilitiesman Constructionman
UTCS
Senior Chief Utilitiesman
UTD, U/TD
Upper 'tween Deck (area or stowage)
UTIL, UT
Utilities
UTL
Utility Board, Light (USCG)
UTM
Universal Test Message
Universal Transverse Mercator
UTML
Utility Motor Launch (USCG)
UTNOTREQ
Utilization of government facilities not
   required as it is considered such utilization
   would adversely affect the performance of
   assigned temporary duty
UTRANSRON, VRU
Utility Transport Squadron

UTRC
United Techniques Research Center
UTRON
Utility Squadron
UTS
Universal Time Standards
UTTAS
Utility Tactical Transport Aircraft System
UTU
Underway Training Unit
UUM
Underwater-to-Underwater Missile
UUT
Unit Under Test
UV
Ultraviolet (light)
Under Voltage (controller)
UVASER
Ultraviolet Amplification by Stimulated
   Emission of Radiation
UVHFDS
Ultraviolet Hydrogen Fire Detection System
UW
Underwater
UWAYTUNORVA
Underway Training Unit, Norfolk, Virginia
UWCS
Underwater Weapons Control System
UWORDTECH
Underwater Ordnance Technician
UWSEC
Underwater Weapons Systems Engineering
   Center
UXO
Unexploded Explosive Ordnance

V

V
Photo/Navigator (TO code)
Variable(s)
Varies (reporting frequency)
Vital
VA
Value Analysis
Veterans Administration
Visual Aids (or Approach)
VA, ATKRON
Attack Squadron
VAC
Vacant
Vacate
Vacuum
V-AC
Value-Acceleration
VADM
Vice Admiral
VAF
Voluntary Application Fill

VAH, HATRON
Heavy-Attack Squadron
VAI
Video-Assisted Instruction
VA(J)
Jet Attack Squadron
VAK
Aerial Refueling Squadron
VAL
Heavier-Than-Air, Attack, Light
Light-Attack Squadron
Vertical Assault Lift
V-AM
Valve-Amplifier
VAN, ADV
Advanced
VAND
Vacuum-Air-Nitrogen Distribution (system)
VAO
Voting Assistance Officer
VAPI
Visual-Approach Indicator
VAQ, TACELECWARON
Tactical Electronic Warfare Squadron
VAR
Variation
Visual-Aural Range
VAS
Visual Audit Sheet
VASI
Visual-Approach Slope Indicator
VAST
Versatile Avionics Shop Test
VAT
Village Assistance Team
VATE
Versatile Automatic Test Equipment
VATS
Versatile Avionics Test, Shop
VAW, CARAEWRON
Carrier Airborne Early Warning Squadron
VAX
Heavier-Than-Air, Attack, Experimental
VB
Vertical Beam
VC
Variable Contrast (photo paper)
Vector (or Voice) Control
Voyage Charter
VC, FLECOMPRON
Fleet Composite Squadron
VCA
Vacant Code Announcement
VCG
Vertical Center of Gravity
VCMR
Variable Change-to-Mass Ratio
VCNM
Vice Chief of Naval Management
VCNO
Vice Chief of Naval Operations

VCNTY, VIC
Vicinity
VCO
Voltage-Controlled Oscillator (NNSS)
V-CP
Valve-Course Pilot
VCS
Vehicle Control System
VCXO
Voltage-Controlled Crystal Oscillator (NNSS)
VD
Van Dyke (reproducible drawing)
VD, PHOTORON
Photographic Squadron
VDC
Vendor Data Control
Volts-Direct Current (NNSS)
VDF
Very-High-Frequency Direction Finder
VDG
Vertical Displacement Gyro
Vertical Display Generator
VDI
Vertical Display Indicator
VDL
Video Display Logic (NNSS)
VDP
Volunteer Reservists in Drill Pay Status
VDS
Variable-Depth Sonar
VDT
Video Display Terminal (NNSS)
VE
Air Evacuation Squadron
Value Engineering
VECO
Venier Engine Cutoff
VECP
Value Engineering Change Proposal
VEH
Vehicle
VEI
Value-Engineered Indicator
VEL
Velocity
VER
Verify
VER DUP
Verify Duplication
VERLOT
Very-Long-Range Tracking Radar
VERT
Vertical
VERT CL
Vertical Clearance
VERT-2-EXP
Vertical Double-Expansion (engine)
VERT-3-EXP
Vertical Triple-Expansion (engine)
VERT-4-EXP
Vertical Quadruple-Expansion (engine)

VERTOL, VTOL
Vertical Take-Off and Landing
VERTREP
Vertical Replenishment
VERTOL, VTOL
Vertical Take-Off and Landing
VES
Vessel
VESCA
Vessels and Cargo
VET
Veteran
VEWS
Very Early Warning Satellite
VF
Video (or Voice, or Voltage) Frequency
VF, FITRON, FIGHTRON
Fighter Squadron
VFI
VF Radar Intercept Officer (code)
VFM
Volt Frequency Monitor
VFP, LIGHTPHOTORON, LTPHOTORON
Light Photographic Squadron
V-FP
Valve-Fine Pilot
VRF
Visual Flight Rules
VFTG
Voice Frequency Terminal Group
VG
Very Good
Voice Grade
VGLI
Veterans Group Life Insurance
VH
Helicopter (pilot code)
Rescue Squadron
VHF
Very-High Frequency
VHLH
Very Heavy Lift Helicopter
VHRR
Very-High-Resolution Radiometer
VHSIC
Very-High-Speed Integrated Circuits
VI
Vial (U/I)
VIC
Variable Instrument Computer
VIC, VCNTY
Vicinity
VICI
Velocity Indicating Coherent Integrator
VID
Video
VIDA
Ventricular Impulse Detection and Alarm
VIDAR
Velocity Integration, Detection and Ranging

VIDEC
Vibration Analysis and Detection Concept
VIDS
Visual Information and Display System
VIL
Village
VIMS
Verification Information Management System
VIO
Visual Intercept Officer
VIOL
Violation
VIP
Variable Information Processing
Versatile (or Visual) Information Processor
Very Important Person
Vocational Interviewing and Placement
Volunteer Informant Program
VIPI
Very Important Person Indeed
VIPP
Variable Information Processing Package
VIPRE FIRE
Visual Precision Fire (control)
VIPS
Voice Interruption Priority System
VIR
Vendor Information Report
VIS
Visual
Visual Instrumentation Subsystem
VIS, VSBY
Visibility
VISSR
Visible Infrared Spin-Span Radiometer
VLA
Very Large Array
Very Low Altitude
Visual Landing Aids
VLBI
Very Long Baseline Interferometry
VLCC
Very Large Crude Oil Carrier (ship)
VLCN
Velocity East Coordinate System (NNSS)
VLF
Very Low Frequency
VLR
Very Long Range
VLT
Vendor Lead Time
VM
Velocity Modulation
VMA
Marine Attack Squadron
VMA(AW)
Marine All-Weather Attack Squadron
VMAQ
Marine Tactical Electronic Warfare Squadron
VMAT
Marine Attack Training Squadron

VMAT(AW)
Marine All-Weather Attack Training Squadron
VMC
Visual Meteorological Conditions
V-METER
Extinctospectopolariscopeocculogyrogravo-
adaptometer (NSAS)
VMFA
Marine Fighter Attack Squadron
VMFAT
Marine Fighter Attack Training Squadron
VMFP
Marine Tactical Reconnaissance Squadron
VMFPDET
Marine Tactical Reconnaissance Squadron
Detachment
VMGR, VMO
Marine Aerial Refueler Transport Squadron
VMO, VMGR
Marine Aerial Refueler Transport Squadron
VMR
Volunteer Military Rejectee
VMRS
Vessel Movement Reporting System
VMS
Velocity-Measuring System
VN
Velocity North-Velocity East (NNSS)
V/N
Vital/Non-Vital (code)
VO
Verbal Order
VOCAL
Vessels Ordnance Coordinating Allowance
List
VOCAL
If you desire a voluntary recall to active duty,
comply NAVMILPERSMAN 1820320.
Contact the nearest naval activity or district
for assistance.
VOCO
Verbal Order of the Commanding Officer
VOCOM
Voice Communications
VOCOM/AUTOSERVOCOM
Voice Communications/Automatic Secure
Voice Communications
VOD
Vertical Onboard Delivery
VODAT
Voice-Operated Device for Automatic
Transmission
VOG
Observation Plane Squadron
VOIS
Visual Observation Instrumentation
Subsystem
VOL
Volunteer

VOLMAIN
If you desire to remain on active duty, comply
NAVMILPERSMAN 1830150
VOLMET
Meteorological Information for Aircraft in
Flight
VOM
Volt-Ohm-Meter
VOR
VHF Omnidirectional Radio (range)
Visual Omnidirectional Range
VOR/DME
VHF Omnidirectional
Radio/Distance-Measuring Equipment
VORTAC
VHF Omnidirectional Radio and Tactical Air
Navigation
VOSA
Variable Orifice Sound Attenuator (system)
VOSL
Variable Operating and Safety Level
VOU
Voucher
VOU DED
Voucher Deduction
VOWF
Value-Operated Water Flash (nuclear reactor)
VOY
Voyage
VP
Variable-Pitch (propeller)
Vertical Planning
VP, PATRON
Patrol Squadron
VPB
Vertical Plot Board
VPM
Volts per Minute
VPR
Virtual PPI Reflectoscope (radar)
VPR-NMP
Virtual PPI Reflectoscope with Navigational
Microfilm Projector (radar)
VPT
ASW Tactical Coordinator (code)
VQ, FAIRECONRON
Fleet Air Reconnaissance Squadron
VQE
VA ESM/SIGINT Evaluator (code)
VR
Transport (pilot code)
Visual Reconnassiance
Voltage Regulator (tubes)
VR, FLETACSUPPRON
Fleet Tactical Support Squadron
VR, AIRTRANSRON, VRC
Air Transport Squadron
V/R
Very Respectfully
V&R
Vent and Replenishing

VRA
Veteran's Readjustment Appointment
VRB
Variable Reenlistment Bonus
Voice Rotating Beacon
VRBL
Variable
VRC, AIRTRANSRON, VR
Air Transport Squadron
VRE
Volume Review Exercises
VRF, AIRFERRON
Aircraft Ferry Squadron
VRS
Visual Reference System
VRU, UTRANSRON
Utility Transport Squadron
VS
Vertical Stripes (buoy)
Visual Sign (or Signal)
VS, AIRANTISUBRON
Air Antisubmarine Squadron
VSB
Visible
VSBY, VIS
Visibility
VSCF
Variable-Speed Constant-Frequency
(electrical power circuit)
VSD
Vertical Situation Display
VSF, ANTISUBFITRON
Antisubmarine Fighter Squadron
VSFI
Vertical Scale Flight Indicator
VSG
Vocational School Graduate (program)
VSI
Vertical Speed Indicator
VSM
Vestigial Sideband Modulation
VSMF
Vendor Specification Microfilm File
Visual Search Microfilm Files
VSOM
Velocity Sensor Oscillator Multiplier
VSS
Variable Stability System
V/STOL Support Ship
VST
VS-ASW Tactical Coordinator (code)
V/STOL, VTOL/STOL
Vertical Short Take-Off/Landing (aircraft)
VSTT
Variable-Speed Training Target
VSWF
Voltage Standing-Wave Frequency
VSWR
Voltage Standing-Wave Radio

VT
Variable Thrust (or Time)
Ventilation
Virbo Tool (markings)
VT, TRARON
Training Squadron
VTF
Variable Time Fuze
VTM
Voltage Turnable Magnetron
VTO
Visual (or Vocational) Training Officer
VTOHL
Vertical Take-Off and Horizontal Landing
(aircraft)
VTOL, VERTOL
Vertical Take-Off and Landing (aircraft)
VTOL/STOL, V/STOL
Vertical-Short Take-Off/Landing (aircraft)
VTR
Tracked Recovery Vehicle
Video Tape Recorder
VTS
Vessel Traffic Services (or System)
Video Tape System
VTU
Voice Terminal Unit
VTVM
Vacuum Tube Voltmeters
VU
Utility and General (pilot code)
VW
Airborne Early Warning (pilot code)
VWC
VW Airborne Intercept Controller (code)
VWS
Ventilated Wet Suit
VX, AIRDEVRON
Air Development Squadron
VXN, OCEANDEVRON
Oceanographic Development Squadron

W

W
Watts
Weapons
Weekly (report frequency)
W, WES
West(ern)
WA
Word After
WA, W/A
Weld, Attachment (JIC)
Work Authorization
WAACP
Western Atlantic Airlift Command Post

WAC
Weapon Assignment Console
World Aeronautical Chart
WAE
When Actually Employed
WAFFLE
Wide-Angle Fixed-Field Locating Equipment
WAG
Miscellaneous Auxiliary (USCG)
WAGB
Icebreaker (USCG)
WAGL
Buoy Tender (USCG)
WAGO
Oceanographic Cutter (USCG)
WAGR
Miscellaneous Auxiliary (USCG)
WAI
Wide-Angle Indicator
WAITORDERS
If, after earned leave has expired, final action
on proceedings and recommended findings
of physical evaluation board has not been
taken, continue in an awaiting orders status
with pay and allowances until final action is
taken
WALP
Weapons Assignment Linear Programming
WAML
Work Authorization Material List
WAMTMTS
Western Area, Military Traffic Management
and Terminal Service
WAO
Oiler (USCG)
WAP
Weighted Average
Work Assignment Procedures
WARES
Workload and Resources Evaluation System
WAS
Worked All States (ARRL)
WASP
War Air Service Program (CAB)
WATPL
Wartime Traffic Priority List
WATS
Wide-Area Telephone Service
WB
Weld, Butt (JIC)
Word Before
WBLC
Waterborne Logistics Craft—pronounced
"Wiblics"
WB/MC
Wide Band and Master Control
W BN
White Beacon
WBS
Work Breakdown Structure

WB SIG STA
Weather Bureau Signal Station
WC
Work Center
WCAFCO
West Coast American Flag Berth Operators
WCBSU
West Coast Base Service Unit
WCC
Weapons Control Console
Wing Command Center
Work Center Code
WCD
Weapons Classification of Defects
WCDS
West Coast Naval Publications Distribution
Center
WCN
Workload Control Number
WCP
Weapons Control Panel
WD
When Directed
WDC
Washington Document Center
WDE
Weapons Direction (or Designation)
Equipment
WDI
Weapons Data Index
Work Description Index
WDLY
Widely
WDN
Work Description Number
WDS
Weapon(s) Direction System
WEA, WX
Weather
Weather Advisory
WEARCON
Weather Observation and Forecasting Control
(system)
WEARECONRON
Weather Reconnaissance Squadron
WEAX
Route Weather Forecasts
WEC
Water Export Control
WEDGE
Weapon Development Glide Entry
WEE
Work Experience Education
WEFT
Wings, Engines, Fuselage, Tail (aircraft
recognition system)
WEIS
World Event/Interaction Survey
WEL
Weapons Equipment List

W/ENCL
With Enclosure(s)
WEP, WP, WPN
Weapon
WEPTRAEX
Weapons Training Exercise
WEPTU
Weapons Training Unit
WES
Wing Engineer Squadron
WES, W
West(ern)
WESCAR
Western Carolines
WESCOSOUNDSCOL
West Coast Sound School
WESDET
Wing Engineer Squadron Detachment
WESPAC
Western Pacific
WESTDIVNAVFACENGCOM
Western Division Naval Facilities Engineering
Command
WESTLANT
Western Atlantic
WESTOMP
Western Ocean Meeting Point
WESTPAC, WESPAC
Western Pacific
WESTPACDET
Western Pacific Detachment
WESTPACTRAMID
Western Pacific Training Program for
Midshipmen
WESTSEAFRON, WSF
Western Sea Frontier
WET
Wet Environment(al) Trainer
WF
Waffer (U/I)
Weld, Fillet (JIC)
White Falcon (publication)
WFN
Weapons and Facilities, Navy
WG
Wine Gallon (U/I)
WGBT
Wet Bulb Globe Temperature
WGM
Weighted Guideline Method
WGS
World Geodetic System (DOD)
WHAM
Work Handling and Maintenance
WHAP
Where/When Applicable
WHB
Waste Heat Boiler
WHCA
White House Communications Agency (DCA)

WHEC
High-Endurance Cutter (USCG)
WHIST
Worldwide Household Goods Information
System
WHLS
Wheels
WHP
Water Horsepower
W-HR
Watt-Hour
WHS
Warehouse
WHY DFTFT
What Have You Done for the Fleet Today?
WI
Weapons Instrumentation
WIA
Wounded in Action
WICOMATIC
Wiring and Connective Device,
Semi-Automatic
WIE
With Immediate Effect
WILCO
I Understand and Will Comply
WIN
Women in the Navy (workshop)
WWMCCS Intercomputer Network
WIP
Work in Progress
WIR
Weapons Inspection Report
WIRE
Weapons Interference Reduction Effort
(program)
WISE
Weapons Installation System Engineering
WISP
Wartime Information Security Program
WISS
Weekly Induction Schedule System
WISSA
Wholesale Interservice Supply Support
Agreement
WIT
Witness
WITHOUTACCTDATA
Issuance of this order is without accounting
data since it appears orders can be
executed without cost. If costs or
entitlements will accrue, member must
request and receive written authorization
including accounting data from
COMNAVMILPERSCOM prior to execution.
WIX
Training Cutter (USCG)
WK
Week
Work
Wreck

WKD
Weekday
WKR
Worker
WL
Water Line
Weld Seal (JIC)
WLB
Seagoing Buoy Tender (USCG)
WLC
Weapons Launching Console
WLD
West Longitude Date
WLI
Inland Buoy Tender, Large (or Small) (USCG)
Work List Item
WLIC
Construction Tender (USCG)
WLM
Coastal Buoy Tender (USCG)
WLR
River Buoy Tender, Large (or Small) (USCG)
WLV
Lightship (USCG)
WM
Weld, Bimetallic (JIC)
W/M
Weight or Measurement
WMEC
Medium-Endurance Cutter (USCG)
WN
Weld, Nozzle (JIC)
WNG
Warning
WNTF
Western Naval Task Force
WO
War Orientation
Warrant Weapons Officer
Work Order
W/O
Without
WOA
Weapons Orientation, Advanced
WOC
Without Compensation
WOCS
Women Officer Candidate School
WOD
Wind-Over-Deck
WOG
Water, Oil, Gal (valverating)
WOM
Write Only Memory
WOP
Without Pay
WOQ
Women Officer's Quarters
W OR
White and Orange (buoy)

WORP
Work Order Resource Plan
WOS
Women Officer School
WOSAC
Worldwide Synchronization of Atomic Clocks
WOSD
Weapons Operational Systems Development
WOW
War on Wastefulness
WOWAR
Work Order and Work Accomplishment
Record
WP
White Phosphorous
Will Proceed
Work Punt (USCG)
WP, WEP, WPN
Weapon
W/P
Waypoint
WPB
Patrol Craft (USCG)
WPBC
Western Pacific Base Command
WPLO
Water Port Logistics Office
WPM
Words per Minute
WPN
Weapons Procurement, Navy
WPNSCO
Weapons Company
WPNSPLT
Weapons Platoon
WPNSTRNGBN
Weapons Training Battalion
WPPG
Working Plan Preparation Guide
WPRB
Weapons Personnel Research Branch (EISO)
WPRD
Weapons Personnel Research Division
WPWOD
Will Proceed Without Delay
WR
War (or Ward) Room
War Reserve
Weapons Requirement
Weld, Rooter Boss (JIC)
Wet Runway
Women's Reserve
WR, W/R
Washroom
Work Request
W&R
Welfare and Recreation
WRA
Weapons Replaceable Assembly

WRAP
Weapons Readiness Aircraft Program
Weapons Reliability Assurance Program
WRB
Wide-Range Burner
WRC
Weapon Release Computation
Weather Relay Center
WRCS
Weapons Release Computer System
WR MESS
Wardroom Mess
WRNT
Warrant
WR-P
Wet Runway-Patchy
WRR
Water/Surface/Underwater Radio
WRT
Water Round Torpedo (tank)
WS
Weapons Specifications (or System)
Weld, Socket (JIC)
With System (SWBS)
WSAM
Weapons System Acquisition Manager (or
Management) (NPGS)
WSAT
Weapons Systems Acceptance Trials (or
Tests)
WSC
Western Sea Frontier Command
WSE
Weapons and Support Equipment
WSEF
Weapon System Effectiveness Factor
WSEG
Weapons Systems Evaluation Group
WSEIAC
Weapons Systems Effectiveness Industrial
Advisory Committee
WSESRB
Weapons System Explosives Safety Review
Board
WSET
Weapons Systems Evaluation Test
WSF, WESTSEAFRON
Western Sea Frontier
WSHFT
Wind Shift
WSIIP
Weapons Installation Interrupted for Parts
WSIM
Water Separation Index, Modified
WSMR
White Sands Missile Range
WSO
Weapons System Officer
WSP
Working Steam Pressure (valve rating)

WSPACS
Weapons Systems Programming and Control
System
WSPD
Weapons System Planning Data (or
Document)
WSPO
Weapons System Project Office
WSS
Wholesale Storage Site
WSSG
Weapons Systems Safety Guidelines
WST
Weapons System Trainer (or Test)
WSTH
Weapons Systems Tactical Handbook
WT
Water Tender
Weight
Weld, Support (JIC)
W/T
Water-Tight (integrity)
Wireless Telegraphy
WTA
Work-Task Agreement
WTCA
Water Terminal Clearance Activity
WTCON
Weight Control
WTCSS
West Coast Off-Shore Tactical Control
Surveillance System
WTF
Western Task Force
WTI
Water-Tight Integrity
WTR
Reserve Training Cutter (USCG)
Water
Western Test Range
WTS
Wing Transportation Squadron
WTSDET
Wing Transportation Squadron Detachment
WTV
Water Tank Vessel
WUC
Work Unit Code
WUT
World Utility Transporter
W/V
Wind Vector (or Velocity)
WVD
Waived
WW
Weather Wing
Wire Way
W/W
Worldwide
WWC
World Weather Center

WWMCCS, WMX
Worldwide Military Command and Control System
WWRI
Worldwide Mobile Communications Routing Index
WWSP
Worldwide Surveillance Program
WWW
World Weather Watch
WX, WEA
Weather
Weather Advisory
WXR
Weather Radar
WYTL
Harbor Tug, Small (USCG)
Harbor Tug, Small, Wood (USCG)
WYTM
Buoy Tender (USCG)
Floating Workship (USCG)
Freight Ship (USCG)
Harbor Craft (or Cutter, or Launch) (USCG)
Harbor Tug, Medium (USCG)
Inshore Patrol Cutter (USCG)
Lighthouse Tender (USCG)
Patrol Boat (USCG)
Revenue Cutter (USCG)
Revenue Steamer (USCG)
Seized Boat (USCG)
Station Ship (USCG)
Steam Derrick (USCG)

X

X
Cross (as in X-OVER)
Experimental
Index Register (NNSS)
Special Projects (TO code)
Submersible Craft (Self-Propelled)
XBT
Expendable Bathythermograph
XC
Experimental Cooling
XCOM
External Communications
XCS
Excess
X&DFLOT
Experimental and Development Flotilla (for landing craft)
XDPU
Expanded Data Processing Unit (NNSS)
XEO
Experimental Engineering Orders
XERB
Experimental Environmental Reporting Buoy

XFM
Expeditionary Force Message
XFMR
Transformer
XLR
Experimental Liquid Rocket
XMAP
Sweeper Device (vessel)
XMIT
Transmit
XMS
Experimental Development Specification
XMS, XMSN
Transmission
XMSN, XMS
Transmission
XMTL
Transmittal
XMTR
Transmitter
XO
Executive Officer
XP
Transmitter Pressure
XPC
Inshore Patrol Cutter
XPG
Converted Merchant Ship
XREP
Auxiliary Report
XRL
Extended Range Lance (missile)
XTND, EXT
Extend
XTRAN
Experimental Translation Crystal
XTRM
Extreme

Y

Y
Year
YA
Ash Lighter
YAG
Miscellaneous Auxiliary (Self-Propelled)
YAGR
Ocean Station Radar Ship
YAGT
Floating Target
YBD
Bowdock
YC
Coal Barge
Open Lighter (Non-Self-Propelled)
YCD
Fueling Barge

YCF
Car Float (Non-Self-Propelled)
YCK
Open Cargo Lighter
YCS
Years Commissioned Service
YCV
Aircraft Transportation Lighter
(Non-Self-Propelled)
YD
Floating Crane (Non-Self-Propelled)
Yard
YDG
Degaussing Vessel
YDT
Diving Tender (Non-Self-Propelled)
YE
Aircraft Homing System
Ammunition Lighter (Self-Propelled)
YEN
Ammunition Lighter (Non-Self-Propelled)
YF
Covered Lighter (Self-Propelled)
Freight Lighter
YFB
Ferryboat or Launch (Self-Propelled)
YFD
Yard Floating Drydock (Non-Self-Propelled)
YFN
Covered Lighter (Non-Self-Propelled)
YFNB
Large Covered Lighter (Non-Self-Propelled)
YFND
Drydock Companion Craft
(Non-Self-Propelled)
YFP
Floating Power Barge (Non-Self-Propelled)
YFR
Refrigerated Covered Lighter (Self-Propelled)
YFRN
Refrigerated Covered Lighter
(Non-Self-Propelled)
YFRT
Covered Lighter (Range Tender)
(Self-Propelled)
YFU
Harbor Utility Craft (Self-Propelled)
YG
Garbage Lighter (Self-Propelled)
YGN
Garbage Lighter (Non-Self-Propelled)
YH
Ambulance Boat
YHB
Houseboat
YHLC
Salvage Lift Craft, Heavy
(Non-Self-Propelled)
YHT
Heading Scow

YLA
Open Landing Lighter
YLLC
Salvage Lift Craft, Light (Self-Propelled)
YMP
Motor Mine Planter
YMS
Motor Minesweeper
YMT
Motor Tug
YN1
Yeoman First Class
YN2
Yeoman Second Class
YN3
Yeoman Third Class
YNC
Chief Yeoman
YNCM
Master Chief Yeoman
YNCS
Senior Chief Yeoman
YNG
Gate Craft (Non-Self-Propelled)
YNSA
Yeoman Seaman Apprentice
YNSN
Yeoman Seaman
YNT
Net Tender (Tug Class)
YO
Fuel Oil Barge (Self-Propelled)
YOB
Year of Birth
YOG
Gasoline Barge (Self-Propelled)
YOGN
Gasoline Barge (Non-Self-Propelled)
YOS
Oil Storage Barge (Non-Self-Propelled)
YOSS
Submersible Oil Storage Barge
YP
Patrol Craft (Self-Propelled)
Yield Point
YPD
Floating Pile Driver (Non-Self-Propelled)
YPK
Pontoon Storage Barge
YPT
Torpedo Retriever
YR
Floating Workshop (Non-Self-Propelled)
Yard Repair
YR, Y
Yearly
YR, UR
Your

YRB
Repair and Berthing Barge
(Non-Self-Propelled)
YRBM
Repair, Berthing and Messing Barge
(Non-Self-Propelled)
YRC
Submarine Rescue Chamber
YRDH
Floating Drydock Workshop (Hull)
(Non-Self-Propelled)
YRDM
Floating Drydock Workshop (Machine)
(Non-Self-Propelled)
YR, FLN
Year Flown
YRL
Covered Lighter Repair
YRR
Radiological Repair Barge
(Non-Self-Propelled)
YRST
Salvage Craft Tender (Non-Self-Propelled)
YS
Stevedoring Barge
Yankee Station
YSD
Seaplane Wrecking Derrick (Self-Propelled)
YSP
Salvage Pontoon
YSR
Sludge Removal Barge (Non-Self-Propelled)
YTB
Large Harbor Tug (Self-Propelled)
YTD
Year to Date (payroll records)
YTL
Small Harbor Tug (Self-Propelled)
YTM
Medium Harbor Tug (Self-Propelled)
YTR
Small Rescue Tug
YTRES
Yankee Tractor Rocket Escape System
YTT
Torpedo-Testing Ranging
YV
Drone Aircraft Landing Craft
YW
Water Barge (Self-Propelled)

YWN
Ammo Pontoon
Ammunition Lighter
Farm Scow
Floating Crane
Floating Pile Driver
Navy Lighterage Pontoon
Pontoon
Pontoon Barge
Prison Ship
Receiving Ship
Sand Scow
School Ship
Transfer Barge or Floating Crane
Water Barge (Non-Self-Propelled)
Yard Tug

Z

Z
Tactical (TO code)
Zenith
Zone
ZA, Z/A
Zone of Action
ZAP
Zero Anti-Aircraft Potential
ZAR
Zeus Acquisition Radar
ZBB
Zero-Based Budgeting
ZD
Zenith Distance
Zero Defects—also known as PEP and MEE
Zone Description
ZELL
Zero-Length Launch
ZEM
Zero-Error Mentality
Z/F
Zone of Fire
ZGS
Zero-Gradient Synchrotron
ZI
Zone of Interior
ZIP
Zone Inspection Program
ZMAR
Zeus Multifunction Array Radar
ZMKR, Z-MKR
Zone Marker
ZOR
Zone of Reconnaissance
ZPA
Zeus Program Analysis
ZPEN
Zeus Project Engineer Network

ZPO
  Zeus Project Office
ZR, Z/R
  Zone of Responsibility

ZSL
  Zero Sight Line
ZT
  Zone Time

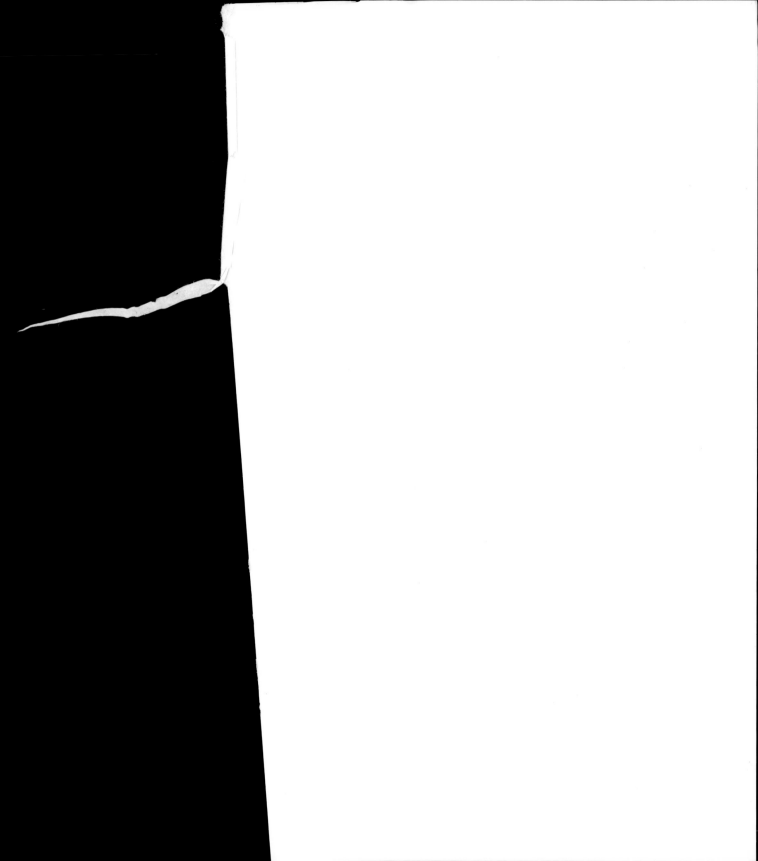

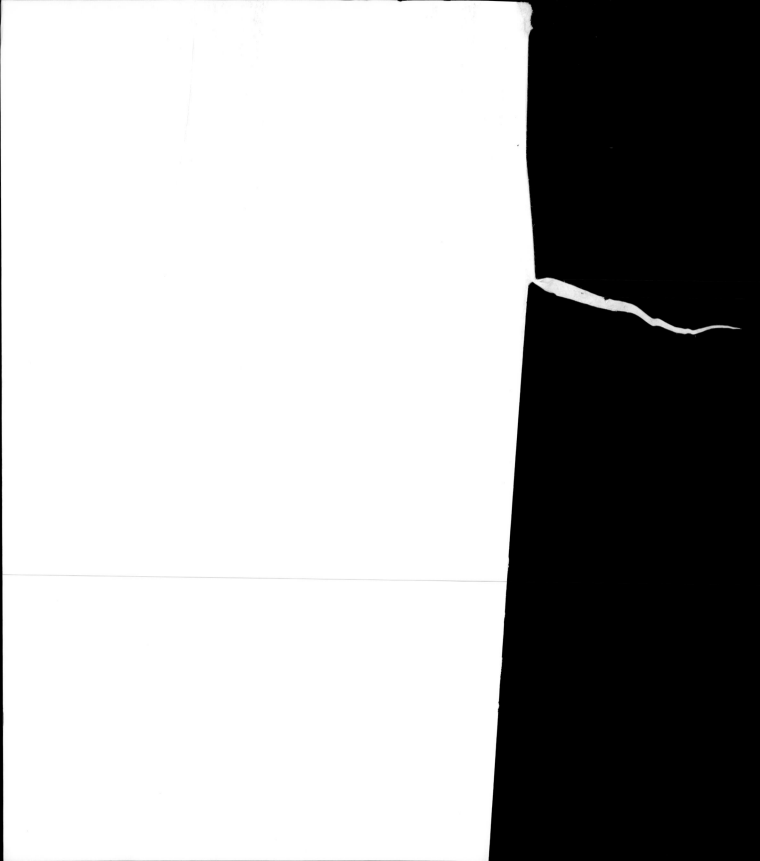